Advanced Microsoft Content Management Server Development

Working with the Publishing API, Placeholders, Search, Web Services, RSS, and SharePoint Integration

Lim Mei Ying
Stefan Goßner
Angus Logan
Andrew Connell

[PACKT]
PUBLISHING

BIRMINGHAM - MUMBAI

Advanced Microsoft Content Management Server Development

Working with the Publishing API, Placeholders, Search, Web Services, RSS, and SharePoint Integration

First edition: November 2005

Published by Packt Publishing Ltd.
32 Lincoln Road
Olton
Birmingham, B27 6PA, UK.

ISBN 1-904811-53-1

www.packtpub.com

Cover Design by www.visionwt.com

Credits

Authors
Lim Mei Ying
Stefan Goßner
Angus Logan
Andrew Connell

Technical Reviewers
Mick Badran
Spencer Harbar
David Mielcarek
Chester Ragel
Christopher Walker

Editorial Manager
Dipali Chittar

Development Editor
Douglas Paterson

Technical Editors
Richard Deeson

Indexer
Niranjan Jahagirdar

Proofreader
Chris Smith

Production Coordinator
Manjiri Nadkarni

Cover Designer
Helen Wood

About the Authors

Lim Mei Ying is a Senior Consultant with Avanade and has extensive experience in setting up MCMS systems at the enterprise level. She has spent many hours figuring out the dos and don'ts of the product, and enjoys finding new ways to solve MCMS-related problems.

She contributes actively to the newsgroup community and is a Microsoft Valuable Professional for Content Management Server. Mei Ying lives on the sunny island of Singapore and blogs at http://meiyinglim.blogspot.com. She also co-authored the earlier book, *Building Websites with Microsoft Content Management Server* (ISBN: 1-904811-16-7, Packt Publishing January 2005).

Thanks to my husband, Louis, for the much needed support throughout the many months of writing. Special thanks to my family and friends for their encouragement.

Stefan Goßner works for Microsoft as an Escalation Engineer in the Developer Support department. He provides customers with technical solutions to problems related to Microsoft Internet Server Products. Stefan has a broad and deep understanding of all areas of MCMS. His contributions to the newsgroup community have helped many people implement MCMS solutions in corporations around the globe, to the point where it has been said that if you don't know Stefan, then you're probably new to MCMS.

He maintains a huge MCMS 2002 FAQ on the Microsoft website and provides MCMS tips and tricks on his personal blog at http://blogs.technet.com/stefan_gossner.

He lives in Munich, Germany.

I would like to thank my girlfriend, Michaela, for her support throughout months of writing, reviewing, and coding for the book. Also many thanks to my colleagues in the European Developer Support Team and to my friends in the MCMS product team in the US.

Angus Logan is a Product Specialist at Data#3 Limited (http://www.data3.com.au), Australia's leading IT solutions company, and is a Microsoft Gold Certified Partner. Angus is a MCAD.NET and MCDBA, as well as a Microsoft Valuable Professional for Content Management Server. His specialities are Content Management Server, SharePoint Portal Server, .NET development, SQL Server, and Customer Relationship Management (CRM).

You can usually find Angus in the microsoft.* newsgroups or blogging (http://www.anguslogan.com).

Angus gets a real buzz from using these technologies in a presales or delivery capacity to find solutions to his customers' real-world problems.

To my friends and family, especially Michael, thank you! Working with a great team on this book made all the time and effort worthwhile.

Andrew Connell has worked with content-management solutions since obtaining his degree from the University of Florida. As one of the original developers for the most successful versions of AdmiNET, a custom web content administration product, he has consistently focused on the challenges facing businesses today as they strive to maintain an up-to-date site without having to constantly rely on technical expertise.

Andrew's background is in content-management solutions and web development using Microsoft technologies. He enjoys working with MCMS and integrating it with other products such as Microsoft SharePoint Products and Technologies.

As a Client/Server Consultant for Fidelity Information Services, Andrew has leveraged both MCMS and SharePoint Portal Server to redeploy Fidelity's intranet site as a single solution that capitalizes on the best features of both products. In 2005, he was recognized as a Microsoft Most Valuable Professional for his contributions to the MCMS community.

Andrew lives in Jacksonville, Florida in the United States, and maintains a blog at `http://www.andrewconnell.com/`.

Thank you to my wife, Meredith, and first born son, Steven, for their patience and support. Thanks to my girls Maggie and Sadie for providing me company during the many late nights it took to finish this project. Thanks also to my parents and brother for their support and the confidence they showed in me.

Shared Acknowledgements

We the authors would also like to thank the following people for supporting us and helping us along the way:

Our editors, Douglas Paterson and Richard Deeson, and the rest of the team at Packt for accepting our book proposal and for the wonderful work they have done in bringing this book to life.

Our project manager, Joel Ward, for his exceptional project management skills. Thanks for being there for us!

About the Reviewers

Mick Badran has been performing Microsoft technical classroom-based training for more than nine years, and has over 12 years commercial development experience in various languages. Mick has been consulting for Microsoft in areas of CMS, SPS, and BizTalk for over four years. Mick also specializes in customized training in these areas.

He can be reached at mickb@breezetraining.com.au and would love to hear your feedback.

Spencer Harbar is an MCSD.NET, MCSE, and MVP for MCMS, with over ten years commercial experience of architecture, design, development, deployment, and operational support of web-based applications, and hosting platforms for some of Europe's largest organizations.

Spencer maintains http://www.mcmsfaq.com—an MCMS resources portal—and is active in the public newsgroups. His experience of MCMS goes back to the days of NCompass Resolution, and he has been involved in many enterprise implementations. Selected clients include Barclays Bank plc, ScottishPower plc, Microsoft, The Royal Bank of Scotland, Scottish Enterprise, HBOS, Centrica, BASF, and The Automobile Association.

Currently working as an independent consultant, Spencer delivers enterprise content management and portal systems architecture, design, development, and deployment solutions, application security best practices, threat modeling, and the implementation of highly available Windows Server System-based hosting platforms.

Spencer resides in Edinburgh, UK, and blogs at www.harbar.net.

David Mielcarek is employed as the Internet/Domain Administrator at Lower Columbia College in Washington State. Most of the time, he utilizes one of ten programming languages to get the job done.

Starting his career as a telecommunications cryptologist in the Air Force, he merged into the corporate world. Following a term with Lockheed, he increased his abilities by taking on larger positions. In 1994, the Internet became his mainstay, and it remains so to this day.

Juggling an educational position, outside-work through his GoldBorder.com site, and raising a family of three kids, 11 cats, two dogs, and two rats allows little time for his love of drawing. You can often find him taking his short breaks at the nearest table to pencil something in his art pad.

Chester Ragel is a Computer Professional, obtaining his degree in Computer Science and Engineering from the University of Moratuwa. He is an MCSD.NET holder, and enjoys working with Microsoft technologies.

Chester contributes to the MCMS community and several IT Magazines. He lives in Sri Lanka and can be found blogging at `http://chestermr.blogspot.com`.

Christopher Walker is a Senior Consultant with Microsoft Services, providing specialist advice on integrated portal solutions (SharePoint, MCMS, BizTalk, and InfoPath). Christopher has a background in portal development and technologies with Unisys and a portal software ISV.

Christopher contributes to the community through his blog at `http://blogs.msdn.com/cjwalker/`, providing real solutions to customers using Microsoft technologies.

Christopher lives in Brisbane, Australia.

Table of Contents

Introduction

Following on from *Building Websites with Microsoft Content Management Server* (Packt Publishing, January 2005, ISBN 1-904811-16-7), this book takes MCMS development to a higher level of both power and integration. Like its predecessor, this book is packed with code examples and never-before-seen secrets of MCMS.

Microsoft Content Management Server 2002 is a dynamic web publishing system with which you can build websites quickly and cost-efficiently. MCMS provides the administration, authoring, and data-management functionality and you provide the website interface, logic, and workflow. Microsoft SharePoint Portal Server (SPS) also features in this book. SPS 2003 enables enterprises to deploy an intelligent portal that seamlessly connects users, teams, and knowledge so that people can take advantage of relevant information across business processes to help them work more efficiently.

You've mastered the basics of MCMS, and have set up your own MCMS installation. But you've only scratched the surface. This book is your gateway to squeezing every penny from your investment in MCMS and SPS, and making these two applications work together to provide an outstanding richness of content delivery and easy maintainability.

What This Book Covers

Chapter 1 demonstrates the power of the MCMS Publishing API (PAPI) by building the **CMS Explorer** administration tool to manage an MCMS website. *Chapter 2* builds on the CMS Explorer by adding the ability to manage channels and postings. *Chapter 3* looks at the creation, submission, copying, moving, and deletion of templates, template galleries, and resources through the PAPI.

In *Chapter 4*, you will learn how to prepare postings for search indexing. We look at several techniques that can improve the accuracy of search results and optimize your search engine.

SharePoint Portal Technologies complement MCMS by providing collaboration, document libraries, and searching to the robust publishing workflow of MCMS. *Chapter 5* takes you through the process of adding searching to an MCMS Site using SharePoint Portal Server, either using the MCMS Connector for SharePoint Technologies or by building your own solution.

Chapter 6 demonstrates how you can use the MCMS Connector for SharePoint to build your own components to share content between MCMS and SharePoint. *Chapter 7* shows how you can build Web Parts that integrate content from MCMS on a SharePoint portal site.

Chapter 8 discusses five custom placeholder controls that provide some frequently requested features that are not present in the default controls: a date-time picker placeholder control, a placeholder control that permits multiple attachments, an image-rotator placeholder control, a placeholder control to store all kinds of HTML tags, and a DataGrid placeholder control.

Validation of content is a key requirement in many MCMS implementations. *Chapter 9* looks at how you can apply ASP.NET validation techniques to each of the out-of-the box placeholder controls.

Static pages are often used in direct mailers, help files, and even for archiving purposes. *Chapter 10* discusses a couple of techniques that you can use to create static snapshots of postings.

The authoring experience doesn't always need to be through the browser. One author-friendly way of maintaining content is detailed in *Chapter 11*. In this chapter, we leverage the power of InfoPath to quickly create a GUI that allows authors to submit content directly from Microsoft Word, with the help of MCMS Web Services.

Since the release of MCMS in 2002, a lot of technologies have changed. Syndication of websites using RSS is the norm, and to capitalize on this, *Chapter 12* takes you through the steps involved in creating a dynamic RSS feed of your website's recent changes.

Finally, *Chapter 13* provides many invaluable insider's tips and tricks for MCMS, as well as solutions to common MCMS issues, including gems such as how to revert a posting to a previous version, change a posting's template, build a recycle bin, and export resource gallery items using the Site Deployment API.

What You Need for This Book

This book has been written for ASP.NET developers with a sound grasp of C#. To use this book, you need to have access to the following:

- Visual Studio .NET Professional or higher (2002 or 2003 version).
- Microsoft Content Management Server 2002 Developer or Enterprise edition. You can also use the Standard edition, but be aware that some features will not be available. A 120-day evaluation version of the Enterprise edition is available at http://www.microsoft.com/cmserver.

To install and run Microsoft Content Management Server 2002, you will need the following:

- The .NET Framework 1.0 or 1.1.
- One of the following operating systems: Windows Server 2003, Windows 2000 Professional, Windows 2000 Server, or Windows XP Professional.
- An installation of SQL Server 2000 Developer or Enterprise edition.

Some of the chapters utilize Microsoft SharePoint Portal Server 2003. For these chapters, you will need:

- The .NET Framework 1.1.
- Windows Server 2003.
- An installation of SQL Server 2000 Developer or Enterprise editions.
- An installation of SharePoint Portal Server 2003. A 120-day evaluation version is available at http://www.microsoft.com/sharepoint.

Conventions

In this book, you will find a number of styles of text that distinguish between different kinds of information. This section provides some examples of these styles, and an explanation of their meaning.

There are three styles for code. Code words in text are shown as follows: "Pass the path of any object as an input parameter of the `Searches.GetByPath()` method to retrieve the requested object".

If we have a block of code, it will be set as follows:

```
HierarchyItem hItem = cmsContext.Searches.GetByPath(
                "/Channels/TropicalGreen/MysteryObject");

if (hItem is Channel)
{
  // Object is a Channel
}
else if (hItem is Posting)
{
  // Object is a Posting
}
```

When we wish to draw your attention to a particular part of a code block, the relevant lines will be made bold:

```
private CmsHttpContext cmsContext;
private void Page_Load(object sender, System.EventArgs e)
{
  // Put user code to initialie the page here
  cmsContext = CmsHttpContext.Current;
  if (!Page.IsPostBack)
  {
    GetPlantFactSheets();
  }
}
```

New terms and **important words** are introduced in a bold-type font. Words that you see on the screen, in menus, on dialog boxes, and so on, appear in our text like this: "clicking the Next button takes you to the next screen".

General tips, suggestions, or important notes appear in a box like this.

Troubleshooting tips and suggestions appear in the following format:

The option for the component I want to install is grayed out and I can't select it.

That's because you do not have the prerequisites required by that component. For example, if you did not install Microsoft Visual Studio, you will not be able to install the Developer Tools. To find out what's missing, click on the component and read the description on the right-hand side of the dialog.

Any command-line input and output is written as follows:

```
sn k "c:\TropicalGreenGACKey\TropicalGreenKey.snk"
```

Reader Feedback

Feedback from our readers is always welcome. Let us know what you think about this book, what you liked or may have disliked. Reader feedback is important for us to develop titles that you really get the most out of.

To send us general feedback, simply drop an e-mail to feedback@packtpub.com , making sure to mention the book title in the subject of your message.

If there is a book that you need and would like to see us publish, then please send us a note in the SUGGEST A TITLE form on www.packtpub.com or e-mail suggest@packtpub.com .

If there is a topic that you have expertise in and you are interested in either writing or contributing to a book, then see our author guide on www.packtpub.com/authors.

Customer Support

Now that you are the proud owner of a Packt book, we want you to get the most from your purchase. Packt's Customer Support is here to try to make sure that happens, and there are a number of ways we can help you.

Downloading the Example Code for the Book

Visit http://www.packtpub.com/support, and select this book from the list of titles to view any example code or extra resources available for download for this book.

> The downloadable files contain instructions on how to use them.

Errata

Although we have taken every care to ensure the accuracy of our books' contents, mistakes do happen. If you find a mistake in one of our books—be it a mistake in text or a code error—we would be grateful if you could report this to us. By doing this you can save other readers from frustration, and also help to improve subsequent versions of this book.

To report any errata you find, visit http://www.packtpub.com/support, select your book, click on the Submit Errata link, and enter the details of your errata. Once your errata have been verified, your submission will be accepted and added to the list of existing errata. The existing errata can be viewed by selecting your title from http://www.packtpub.com/support.

Questions

You can contact us at questions@packtpub.com if you are having a problem with any aspect of the book, and we will do our best to address it.

Building CMS Explorer

The *Building Websites with Microsoft Content Management Server* book (Packt Publishing, January 2005, ISBN 1-904811-16-7) makes extensive use of MCMS's Publishing Application Programming Interface (PAPI). We show how to use it to provide custom functionality within template files, to add business processes to workflow events, to tailor the Web Author Console, and to implement forms authentication for the Tropical Green site, which the reader builds as they progress through the book.

The PAPI is in fact a huge library. You could code with it for months and still find new tricks you never knew existed! This is the first of three chapters that compliment the understanding you will have gained from the book and attempt to take your understanding of the PAPI to another level. Follow along as we demonstrate several highly useful techniques and show how they can be leveraged in a real-world scenario, as we apply them to the Tropical Green site.

Where can I download a copy of the Tropical Green website?

The code files for the Tropical Green website created over the course of the earlier book are available as a download package on this book's download page. Go to the Packt website at `http://www.packtpub.com/support/`, and choose Advanced Microsoft Content Management Server Development in the dropdown.

A Central Administrative Tool: CMS Explorer

We put some serious thought into creating an example that would not only give you a thorough grounding in the more advanced methods available in the PAPI but would also leave you with a tool that you will find handy in your day-to-day MCMS work. From our own experiences as MCMS developers working in the time-critical world of the software industry, one thing that we have found invaluable has been a custom MCMS administrative tool. In the first three chapters of this book, we walk you through the process of building such a tool, which we will name CMS Explorer.

Here's how CMS Explorer will look once completed:

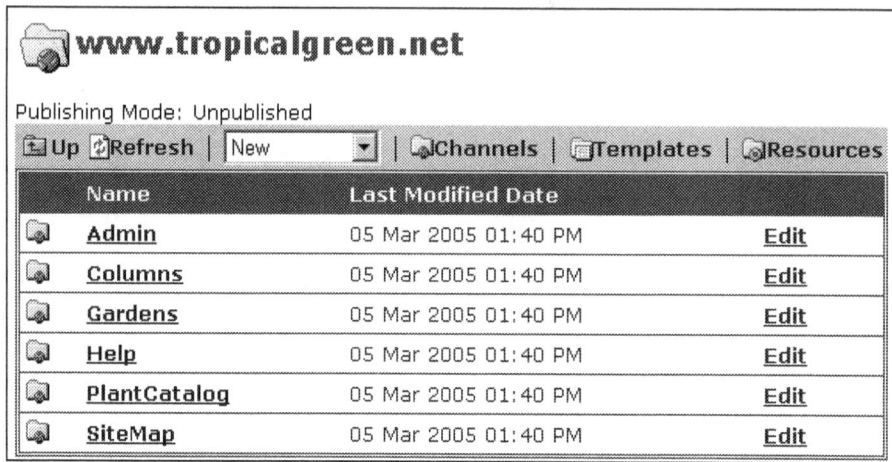

The interface is made up of two sections:

- At the top of the page (in case you hadn't guessed, we're going to create the tool as a web application), you'll see a toolbar. The toolbar provides a drop-down list with options to create new postings and channels. It also has three buttons: one to toggle to a list of channels and postings, a second to list template galleries and templates, and a third for resource galleries and resources.

- The second half of the page is a DataGrid. The grid lists the items in the current container. Each row has an Edit button, which reveals a list of actions for each object when clicked.

For navigation, you can move in two directions: click on the name of the container to see what's in it, or use the Up button on the toolbar to move up one level.

Why build a tool when the out-of-the box-solution provides not one, but three tools to manage MCMS objects? There's already a Site Manager and the Web Author as well as the Template Explorer available within Visual Studio .NET. There are several reasons why building the CMS Explorer tool is worthwhile:

- Firstly of course, you'll get first-hand experience in using many of the more advanced methods from the PAPI. After building this tool, you will not only be very comfortable with the PAPI but also well on your way to becoming an expert in it!

- Although the PAPI contains a large collection of classes, it doesn't cover everything. While it would be nice for the CMS Explorer to be able to do everything that the tools shipped with MCMS can do, it can't go beyond what's available in the PAPI. One of the secondary objectives of the next few chapters is to highlight the PAPI's limitations.

- Finally, this tool could quite likely be useful in your daily work. There are some actions that can only be done using Site Manager, some that are available only within Web Author, and others exclusive to Template Explorer. For example, you would use Site Manager to create a channel and switch over to Web Author to create postings within it. CMS Explorer attempts to fill in this gap by providing as much functionality as possible from a single location.

> You can download the entire sample from the code download section of the Packt site, at `http://www.packtpub.com/support/`.

Creating the Workspace

Let's start by creating a work area for the CMS Explorer tool. Create a new Visual C# MCMS Web Application Project in Visual Studio .NET.

1. Name the new project CMSExplorer.
2. Get the styles.css file from the book's code download. Select Project | Add Existing Item and add it to the CMSExplorer project.
3. Create a new folder and name it images. Download the image files for this tutorial from the code download section of the book's companion website and add them to the project.
4. Right-click the CMSExplorer project in the Solution Explorer and select Properties. Click Designer Defaults. Set the Page Layout field to Flow. This will set the default layout to flow instead of grid for all web forms created in the project. Click OK.
5. Right-click the Console folder and select Delete.
6. Add a new web form to the CMSExplorer project, and name it default.aspx.
7. In Design view, drag and drop the styles.css file from Solution Explorer onto the form. This applies the stylesheet to the page.
8. Switch to HTML view. Add the table below between the <form> tags to provide the basic structure of the page. We use a litCurrentContainer Literal control to display the name of the current container. The lblPublishingMode Label will be used later to display the current publishing mode.

```
<table cellSpacing="0" cellPadding="0">
<tr>
  <td>
    <table>
    <tr>
      <td valign="top">
        <asp:Image runat="server" ID="imgTitle"></asp:Image>
      </td>
      <td valign="center">
        <h1>
          <asp:Literal ID="litCurrentContainer" runat="server"/>
        </h1>
      </td>
    </tr>
    </table>
```

```
                <asp:Label ID="lblPublishingMode" runat="server"
                   CssClass="BodyText"/>
           </td>
        </tr>

        <tr>
          <td width="100%" bgcolor="#cccccc">(Space for Toolbar)</td>
        </tr>

        <tr>
          <td>(Space for DataGrid)</td>
        </tr>
        </table>
```

9. Toggle to Design view. Double-click on the form to get to its code-behind file. Above the namespace declaration, import the Microsoft.ContentManagement.Publishing namespace.

```
//MCMS PAPI
using Microsoft.ContentManagement.Publishing;

namespace CMSExplorer
{
    /// <summary>
    /// Summary description for _default.
    /// </summary>
    public class _default : System.Web.UI.Page
    {
        . . . code continues . . .
    }
}
```

The Four MCMS Publishing Modes

MCMS uses four different publishing modes:

- **Published**: Mode used for displaying a live version of the site
- **Staging**: Mode used for staging the site using Site Stager
- **Unpublished**: Mode used for displaying an unpublished version of the site (e.g. in edit site mode or in preview screens)
- **Update**: Mode used for updating the site (e.g. on the authoring screen with placeholder controls in authoring mode)

Determining the Current Publishing Mode

The current mode can be found using the CmsHttpContext.Mode property. Let's find out which mode CMS Explorer is currently using.

Above the Page_Load() event handler in the code-behind file, add the following line:

```
// the current CmsHttpContext
private CmsHttpContext cmsContext;
```

Inside the Page_Load() event, add the following code:

```
private void Page_Load(object sender, System.EventArgs e)
{
    cmsContext = CmsHttpContext.Current;
```

```
if (!Page.IsPostBack)
{
    // display the publishing mode
    lblPublishingMode.Text = "Publishing Mode: "
                             + cmsContext.Mode.ToString();
}
}
```

Save and build the solution. Navigate to http://localhost/CMSExplorer/default.aspx. Notice that the label says Publishing Mode: Published. When you first view a web page on an MCMS site, you are shown the site in its Published mode. You can ignore the broken image for now as we'll address that further along.

In Published mode, you only have access to channels and postings that have live versions and that are not marked as hidden. Channels that have expired or have their start dates set to a future date will not be available. Postings that have never been published before or are in a "Waiting For Moderator Approval", "Waiting For Editor Approval", "Submitted", "Approved" or "Expired" state will also not be accessible. Obviously, for CMS Explorer to be useable, it's got to be able to see all objects regardless of their states. In order to work with unpublished objects, we have to change the current publishing mode from Published to Unpublished, and we look at ways to accomplish this in the following sections.

Changing the MCMS Publishing Mode

There are various ways to change the MCMS publishing mode, such as by modifying the querystring parameters in the URL or by manipulating the modes via CmsHttpContext and CmsApplicationContext. Let's take a look at each of these methods.

The Ugly URL Querystring Specifies the Publishing Mode

Let's try a little experiment.

1. Open your browser and navigate to the http://localhost/tropicalgreen site.

2. Log in as an administrator. Click on the Switch to Edit Site button and observe the URL displayed in the browser's address bar. It changes from a friendly URL to an ugly long URL containing the familiar querystring parameters at its tail end:

   ```
   http://localhost/NR/exeres/71EDAD1D-9D58-4D65-8069-19DFC0114F54.htm?
   NRMODE=Unpublished
   &WBCMODE=PresentationUnpublished
   &wbc_purpose=Basic
   ```

At the same time, the Switch To Edit Site button disappears and a Switch To Live Site button appears in its place.

Now, let's make a few changes to the querystring. With the page open in Unpublished mode:

1. Change the NRMODE querystring parameter of the ugly URL from Unpublished to Published.

2. Delete the WBCMODE querystring parameter.

3. The URL at the address bar now looks something like this:
   ```
   http://localhost/NR/exeres/71EDAD1D-9D58-4D65-8069-19DFC0114F54.htm?
   NRMODE=Published&wbc_purpose=Basic
   ```

4. Click the Go button next to the address bar of the browser.

    Notice that the Switch To Live Site button changes back to the Switch To Edit Site button! You have effectively changed from Unpublished mode back to Published mode.

This test shows how publishing modes in MCMS can be controlled by playing around with the querystring of the generated ugly URL.

Toggling Modes with CmsHttpContext

When building your application, instead of messing around with the URLs, you can generate the querystrings for each mode on the fly using two properties of the ChannelItem object:

* QueryStringModeUpdate for working in Update mode
* QueryStringModeUnpublished for working in Unpublished mode

We will use this technique in CMS Explorer to switch from Published mode to Unpublished mode.

In order to get the QueryStringModeUnpublished property, we first need to get a reference to any ChannelItem. In this example, we use the root channel. If we are not in Unpublished mode, the page redirects to itself with the querystring returned by the QueryStringModeUnpublished property appended to its address. Modify the code in the Page_Load() event handler as follows:

```
private CmsHttpContext cmsContext;

private void Page_Load(object sender, System.EventArgs e)
{
    cmsContext = CmsHttpContext.Current;

    // Redirect if not in unpublished mode
    if (cmsContext.Mode != PublishingMode.Unpublished
        && cmsContext.Mode != PublishingMode.Update)
    {
        string query;
        query = cmsContext.RootChannel.QueryStringModeUnpublished;
        Response.Redirect("default.aspx?" + query);
    }

    if (!Page.IsPostBack)
    {
        //Display the publishing mode
        lblPublishingMode.Text = "Publishing Mode: "
                                + cmsContext.Mode.ToString();
    }

}
```

Save and build the solution. Navigate to http://localhost/CMSExplorer/default.aspx again. Notice that the label now says Publishing mode: Unpublished. We have successfully toggled to Unpublished mode!

The drawback of using CmsHttpContext to toggle between modes is that it requires you to first get a reference to a ChannelItem object as well as a client redirect. For this example, we used the root channel. If the user does not have rights to the root channel, the code fails.

How can I toggle to Update mode?

To toggle to Update mode, simply use the ChannelItem.QueryStringModeUpdate property instead, like so:

```
if (CmsContext.Mode != PublishingMode.Update)
{
    Response.Redirect("default.aspx?"
      + CmsHttpContext.Current.RootChannel.QueryStringModeUpdate);
}
```

Toggling Modes with CmsApplicationContext

Another popular method of toggling between modes leverages the CmsApplicationContext object. This object is typically used for stand-alone applications that run outside IIS, such as console and desktop applications. In these cases, the CmsHttpContext is meaningless and can't be used.

You can also use the CmsApplicationContext object within a web application when you require additional CmsContext objects, especially when working with different modes. You can maintain CmsHttpContext in Published mode, and have a separate CmsApplicationContext in Update mode. Another advantage to using CmsApplicationContext is that it reduces the number of client round trips required.

We won't be using CmsApplicationContext in the CMS Explorer application. Nevertheless, no lesson on mode switching is complete without introducing the class.

> The CmsApplicationContext class is covered extensively in Chapter 13, *Essential How-Tos, Tips, and Tricks*.

To use the CmsApplicationContext object, first create a new instance of it:

```
// Create a new CmsApplicationContext
CmsApplicationContext cmsContext = new CmsApplicationContext();
```

Unlike CmsHttpContext, CmsApplicationContext must be authenticated with the MCMS server using one of four authentication methods. Each authentication method accepts an input parameter of type PublishingMode specifying the mode you wish to work in.

- **AuthenticateAsCurrentUser**
  Authenticates using the credentials of the currently logged-on user. This method does not work correctly from within a web application. It is used only when running the application outside of IIS, e.g. from a console application, because it uses the process token. For web applications, using the process token means that the currently logged on user is the user configured in the machine.config file (in IIS 5) or the application pool account (in IIS 6) instead of the user that has been authenticated in CmsHttpContext (which uses the thread token).

  To authenticate as the current user:

  ```
  // authenticate as the current user
  cmsContext.AuthenticateAsCurrentUser(PublishingMode.Unpublished);
  ```

- **AuthenticateAsGuest**

  Authenticates using the guest account specified in the SCA. Works only if you have guest access turned on.

  To authenticate as the guest user:

  ```
  // authenticate as Guest user
  cmsContext.AuthenticateAsGuest(PublishingMode.Published);
  ```

- **AuthenticateAsUser**

  This method accepts at least two parameters: the user ID and the password. The user ID is always in the format WinNT://domain/UserId. The password has to be passed in as a string.

  To authenticate with a specified user ID:

  ```
  // specify the user ID, password and publishing mode
  cmsContext.AuthenticateAsUser("WinNT://domain/UserId",
                          "password",PublishingMode.Unpublished);
  ```

- **AuthenticateUsingUserHandle**

  Authenticates using a Windows token by passing in the token of the currently logged on Windows user. This method has the advantage of not requiring the developer to code a password and is often used within web applications. However, if your chosen authentication mechanism is Forms Authentication, this method will not work as Windows tokens are not issued in that case.

  To authenticate with the Windows token of the currently logged on user:

  ```
  // get a Windows token of the currently logged on user
  System.Security.Principal.WindowsIdentity ident;
  ident = HttpContext.Current.User.Identity as
      System.Security.Principal.WindowsIdentity;

  CmsApplicationContext cmsContext = new CmsApplicationContext();
  cmsContext.AuthenticateUsingUserHandle(ident.Token,
                          PublishingMode.Unpublished);
  ```

Once authenticated, you can use the Searches object to retrieve objects as you would with CmsHttpContext. The objects you access with CmsApplicationContext will be presented in the mode that you specify.

> When using the CmsApplicationContext object, make sure you dispose of it explicitly by calling the Dispose() method. Unlike the commonly used CmsHttpContext object (which is created on every web request and destroyed after the response is sent to the client), CmsApplicationContext is not automatically disposed of after use, and the object will not be destroyed until the garbage collector is called. A common result of leftover CmsApplicationContexts is server ODBC errors.

Adding Querystring Parameters to the URL with CmsHttpContext.PropagateParameter()

We are going to do lots of toggling between modes in our CMS Explorer application. To make things easier, we will write a helper function called PrepareUrl() that will use the CmsHttpContext object to generate a URL to change the publishing mode. The PrepareUrl() method will accept three input parameters:

- hItem: HierarchyItem object the user has selected to work with. It could be the start container or any of its child items.

- Mode: Publishing mode to work in. To list both published and unpublished content, we need to use Unpublished mode. To modify object property values, you need to be in Update mode.

- pageName: Name of the dialog or page to open.

The method returns the URL, which is made up of the pageName appended with the QueryStringModeUnpublished or QueryStringModeUpdate property of the root channel. The generated querystring contains the GUID of the current channel or posting somewhere in the URL but holds no information about template galleries and resource galleries. To get around this, we add more information by introducing two additional parameters:

- CMSObject: Contains a string with value "Templates" or "Resources".

- CMSObjectGuid: Stores the GUID of the template gallery or resource gallery selected by the user as the start container.

The CmsHttpContext.PropagateParameter() method inserts these two parameters into all URLs generated by MCMS within the session. Add PrepareUrl() directly below the Page_Load() event handler:

```
private string PrepareUrl(HierarchyItem hItem, PublishingMode mode,
                          string pageName)
{
  string url = "";
  if (hItem != null)
  {
    string cmsObject = "";
    if (hItem is TemplateGallery)
    {
      cmsObject = "Templates";
    }
    else if (hItem is ResourceGallery)
    {
      cmsObject = "Resources";
    }
    cmsContext.PropagateParameter("CMSObject",cmsObject);
    cmsContext.PropagateParameter("CMSObjectGuid",
                        HttpUtility.UrlEncode(hItem.Guid));

    url = pageName + "?";

    if (mode == PublishingMode.Unpublished)
    {
      url += cmsContext.RootChannel.QueryStringModeUnpublished;
    }
    else if (mode == PublishingMode.Update)
```

```
        {
            url += cmsContext.RootChannel.QueryStringModeUpdate;
        }
    }
    return url;
}
```

The next time a URL is requested from the `ChannelItem.Url` property (or any of the properties that generate URLs), the querystring includes the two additional parameters:

```
http://localhost/cmsexplorer/default.aspx?
CMSObject=Templates&

NRMODE=Unpublished&
FRAMELESS=true&
CMSObjectGuid=%7b4D1912B-9DD3-11D1-B44E-
006097071264%7d&NRNODEGUID=%7bE4D19123-9DD3-11D1-B44E-006097071264%7d
```

`PrepareUrl()` will be used to generate URLs later as we work through the CMS Explorer code.

Specifying the Parent Container

In this example we plan to use a `DataGrid` to display a list of all the objects in the selected container. However, before we can get the `DataGrid` to display a list of objects, we need to specify a parent container. The parent container will be a channel, resource gallery, or template gallery. We'll need this container to determine the objects to be displayed in the `DataGrid`. If the user hasn't specified a parent container, we use the root containers (i.e. the Channels channel, the Templates template gallery, and the Resources resource gallery).

Above and within the `Page_Load()` event handler, add the following code:

```
// the current CmsHttpContext
private CmsHttpContext cmsContext;

// the parent container whose contents we are displaying
private HierarchyItem startItem;
private void Page_Load(object sender, System.EventArgs e)
{
    cmsContext = CmsHttpContext.Current;

    // Get the URL of the current page
    string currentUrl = HttpContext.Current.Request.Url.ToString();

    // Redirect if not in unpublished mode
    if (cmsContext.Mode != PublishingMode.Unpublished
        && cmsContext.Mode != PublishingMode.Update)
    {
        string query;
        query = cmsContext.RootChannel.QueryStringModeUnpublished;
        Response.Redirect(currentUrl + "?" + query);
    }

    InitializeStartItem();

    if (!Page.IsPostBack)
    {
        // Display the publishing mode
        lblPublishingMode.Text = "Publishing Mode: "
                    + cmsContext.Mode.ToString();

        // use the start channel's display name as the
        // header for the page
```

```
        litCurrentContainer.Text = startItem.Name;
    }
}
```

Add the `InitializeStartItem()` method directly below the `Page_Load()` event handler:

```
private void InitializeStartItem()
{
    // determine the object type
    string cmsObject = "";
    if (Request.QueryString["CMSObject"] != null)
    {
        cmsObject = Request.QueryString["CMSObject"].ToString();
    }

    // determine the GUID of the working container
    string cmsObjectGuid = "";
    if (Request.QueryString["CMSObjectGuid"] != null)
    {
        cmsObjectGuid = Request.QueryString["CMSObjectGuid"].ToString();
    }

    if (cmsObjectGuid == "")
    {
        // if not specified, we start with channels
        startItem = cmsContext.Channel;
    }
    else
    {
        startItem = cmsContext.Searches.GetByGuid(cmsObjectGuid);
    }

    // no working container has been specified. Use the root containers
    if (startItem == null)
    {
        switch(cmsObject)
        {
            case "Templates":
                // using the root template gallery
                startItem = cmsContext.RootTemplateGallery;
                break;
            case "Resources":
                // using the root resource gallery
                startItem = cmsContext.RootResourceGallery;
                break;
            default:
                // using the root channel
                startItem = cmsContext.RootChannel;
                break;
        }
    }
}
```

The code first determines the type of objects you are working with: channels, template galleries, or resource galleries. It gets this information from the CMSObject querystring parameter.

For channels, the logic is straightforward. Information about the channel is available from the CmsHttpContext.Channel property. If it isn't null, the DataGrid uses that as the start channel. Otherwise, the root container is assigned to startItem.

For template galleries and resource galleries, the current gallery item can't be obtained from the current CmsHttpContext. For these objects, the PAPI gets the GUID of the working container from the CMSObjectGuid querystring parameter we inserted earlier.

Rendering Collections in a DataGrid

Our next task is to display a list of objects held by a given container in a DataGrid.

We could choose to iterate through collections of channels and postings and add them into a table. However, there's an even faster way to accomplish this: we bind the collection of items to a DataGrid. No iterations and tables are needed; simply set the collection of objects as the data source of the DataGrid and call the DataBind() method:

```
// data bind a collection to a DataGrid
DataGrid1.DataSource = myCollectionOfPostingsAndChannels;
DataGrid1.DataBind();
```

To see how this works, open default.aspx in HTML view. Drag and drop a DataGrid from the Toolbox into the cell containing the words (Space for DataGrid) and delete the text markers. Set the properties of DataGrid1 to:

Property	Value
AutoFormat	Simple 3
Width	100%
Font-size	10pt
DataKeyField	Guid
ID	DataGrid1

> The AutoFormat option is available at the bottom of the Property window in ASP.NET 1.1 with Visual Studio .NET 2003. This property allows quick formatting of our DataGrid.

Double-click on the form to get to its code-behind file. Directly below the Page_Load() event handler, add the BindData() method. The method gets a collection of all objects in the start container and sorts them by name in ascending order. The last two lines set the collection as the DataSource of DataGrid1 and call the DataGrid1.DataBind() method.

```
private void BindData()
{
    // getting a collection of all channels and
    // postings below the root channel
    if (startItem is Channel)
    {
        Channel startChannel = startItem as Channel;
        ChannelItemCollection allChildren;
        allChildren = startChannel.AllChildren;
        allChildren.SortByDisplayName(true);

        // display the collection of items retrieved in a datagrid
        DataGrid1.DataSource = allChildren;
    }
    DataGrid1.DataBind();
}
```

Lastly, in the Page_Load() event handler, add a call to the BindData() method inside the if (!Page.IsPostBack) code block:

```
if (!Page.IsPostBack)
{
  // display the publishing mode
  lblPublishingMode.Text = "Publishing Mode: "
                          + cmsContext.Mode.ToString();

  // use the start channel's display name as the
  // header for the page
  litCurrentContainer.Text = startItem.Name;
}

// bind the object collection on every page load, regardless
// of a postback
BindData();
```

Save and build the solution and navigate to `http://localhost/CmsExplorer`. The figure below shows what you will see. The image at the top is broken because we haven't assigned an image to it yet.

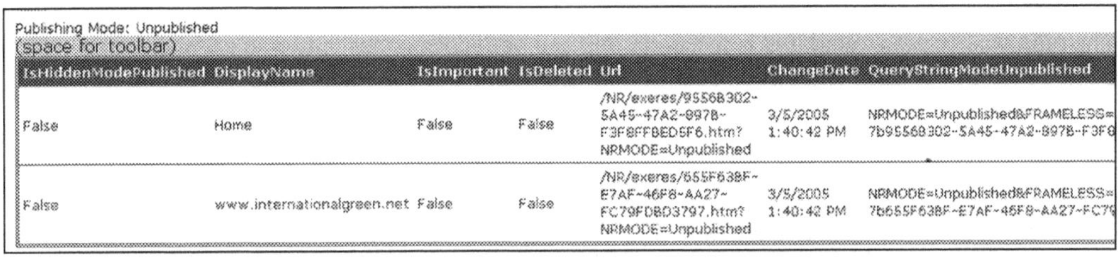

The `DataGrid` displays a list of all objects in the channel, as well their properties. It's a very useful technique for getting a bird's eye view of all the objects in a collection.

Displaying Only Selected Properties in the DataGrid

Obviously, we aren't going to display all property values in the grid. We will show only:

- Name
- Last Modified Date

First, set the `AutoGenerateColumns` property of `DataGrid1` to false. This will prevent the `DataGrid` from displaying all fields in the collection. Within the `<asp:DataGrid>` tags, add the following code:

```
<Columns>
<asp:TemplateColumn HeaderText="Name">
<ItemTemplate>
  <a id="aName" runat="server">
  <%# DataBinder.Eval(Container.DataItem, "Name") %>
  </a>
</ItemTemplate>
</asp:TemplateColumn>
<asp:BoundColumn DataField="LastModifiedDate"
                 ReadOnly="True"
                 HeaderText="Last Modified Date"
                 DataFormatString="{0:dd MMM yyyy hh:mm tt}">
</asp:BoundColumn>
</Columns>
```

Using this method, we display only the properties that we are interested in showing in the grid. You may be wondering why we didn't use a BoundColumn for the name. That's because, in this particular setup, the name field isn't static. We want to render the name field for a container (channels, template galleries, or resource galleries) as a hyperlink that reveals its contents in the grid when clicked. Since postings, templates, and resources do not contain child items, their names will remain as text.

Considerations for Template Galleries and Resource Galleries

Unlike channels, there isn't an equivalent of the AllChildren property for template galleries and resource galleries. In fact, if you study the PAPI carefully, you will find that collections of template galleries belong to the TemplateGalleryCollection class and collections of templates belong to the TemplateCollection class. Because a TemplateGalleryAndTemplateCollection class does not exist, you can't mix both into a single collection. The same applies for resource galleries and resources.

The only way to get around this is to iterate through both collections, and add each item to a DataTable. Our DataTable will consist of three columns, one for each of the properties we have chosen to display: Guid, Name, and LastModifiedDate. It is created using a PrepareDataTable() helper function added directly below the BindData() method:

```
private DataTable PrepareDataTable()
{
  DataTable dt = new DataTable();
  dt.Columns.Add(new DataColumn("Guid"));
  dt.Columns.Add(new DataColumn("Name"));
  dt.Columns.Add(new DataColumn("LastModifiedDate"));

  return dt;
}
```

Next, we iterate through the parent container and add all sub-galleries and objects as rows to our DataTable. This will give us a collection of sub-gallery names followed by a collection of objects, which we'll then bind to the DataGrid. Let's add this code to the BindData() method:

```
private void BindData()
{
  // getting a collection of all containers and
  // items below the start container

  if (startItem is Channel)
  {
    Channel startChannel = startItem as Channel;
    ChannelItemCollection allChildren;
    allChildren = startChannel.AllChildren;
    allChildren.SortByDisplayName(true);
    // display the collection of items retrieved in a datagrid
    DataGrid1.DataSource = allChildren;
  }

  else if (startItem is TemplateGallery)
  {
    TemplateGallery startTemplateGallery = startItem as TemplateGallery;
    DataTable dt = PrepareDataTable();

    // add the template galleries
    foreach(TemplateGallery tg in startTemplateGallery.TemplateGalleries)
    {
```

```
      DataRow dr = dt.NewRow();
      dr = AddItem(dr, tg);
      dt.Rows.Add(dr);
    }

    // add the templates
    foreach(Template t in startTemplateGallery.Templates)
    {
      DataRow dr = dt.NewRow();
      dr = AddItem(dr, t);
      dt.Rows.Add(dr);
    }

    DataGrid1.DataSource = dt.DefaultView;
  }

  else if (startItem is ResourceGallery)
  {
    ResourceGallery startResourceGallery = startItem as ResourceGallery;

    DataTable dt = PrepareDataTable();

    // add the resource galleries
    foreach(ResourceGallery rg in startResourceGallery.ResourceGalleries)
    {
      DataRow dr = dt.NewRow();
      dr = AddItem(dr, rg);
      dt.Rows.Add(dr);
    }

    // add the resources
    foreach(Resource r in startResourceGallery.Resources)
    {
      DataRow dr = dt.NewRow();
      dr = AddItem(dr, r);
      dt.Rows.Add(dr);
    }

    DataGrid1.DataSource = dt.DefaultView;
  }

  DataGrid1.DataBind();
}
```

Rows are added to the table using the AddItem() helper function. Add the AddItem() method directly below the PrepareDataTable() method:

```
private DataRow AddItem(DataRow dr, HierarchyItem hi)
{
  dr[0] = hi.Guid;
  dr[1] = hi.Name;
  dr[2] = hi.LastModifiedDate;

  return dr;
}
```

Adding Custom Columns to the DataGrid

Binding the entire collection to the grid and specifying only the properties you want displayed is a handy trick. But let's say you want to add an icon at the side of each object to indicate whether it's a channel, posting, template gallery, or something else. None of the existing properties in the collection gives an indication of the object's type.

At the same time, we want to supply the URLs for hyperlinks surrounding channel display names. For channels, the URLs point to default.aspx?<QueryStringModeUnpublished>, and postings won't be clickable so the Href property of their surrounding <A> tags will be left blank.

We could change our script to iterate through each object one by one and add these additional columns to a DataTable before binding it to the DataGrid. However, that would mean changing our code. The good news is that we don't have to rewrite the code. We can implement the DataGrid1_ItemDataBound event handler to populate columns with custom values depending on whether the object is a channel or a posting.

First, add a new TemplateColumn to the DataGrid:

```
<Columns>
  <asp:TemplateColumn>
   <ItemTemplate></ItemTemplate>
  </asp:TemplateColumn>
  <asp:TemplateColumn HeaderText="Name">
  <ItemTemplate>
   <a id="aName" runat="server">
   <%# DataBinder.Eval(Container.DataItem, "Name") %>
   </a>
  </ItemTemplate>
  </asp:TemplateColumn>
  <asp:BoundColumn DataField="LastModifiedDate" ReadOnly="True" HeaderText=
  "Last Modified Date" DataFormatString="{0:dd MMM yyyy hh:mm tt}"/>
</Columns>
```

The new TemplateColumn will contain an image indicating the type of the object bound to this row.

Next, we implement the DataGrid1_ItemDataBound() event handler. A quick way to register the event handler is to select the Events button 🖄 at the top of the DataGrid1 properties window (available in Design view). Double-click on the ItemDataBound field to get to the DataGrid1_ItemDataBound event handler in the code-behind file and modify it as shown below:

```
private void DataGrid1_ItemDataBound(object sender,
  System.Web.UI.WebControls.DataGridItemEventArgs e)
{
  if (e.Item.ItemType==ListItemType.EditItem
      || e.Item.ItemType==ListItemType.Item
      || e.Item.ItemType==ListItemType.AlternatingItem)
  {
    string guid = DataGrid1.DataKeys[e.Item.ItemIndex].ToString();
    HierarchyItem hItem = cmsContext.Searches.GetByGuid(guid);

    if (hItem is Channel)
    {
      // if the object is a channel, show the channel icon
      // set the Name to be a hyperlink
      // that points to default.aspx?{QueryStringModeUnpublished}
      e.Item.Cells[0].Text="<img src='images/channel.gif'>";
      HtmlAnchor aName;
      aName=e.Item.Cells[1].FindControl("aName") as HtmlAnchor;
      aName.HRef = "default.aspx?"
                  + ((Channel)hItem).QueryStringModeUnpublished;
    }
    else if (hItem is Posting)
    {
      // if the object is a posting, show the posting icon
      // leave the Name as text
      e.Item.Cells[0].Text="<img src='images/posting.gif'>";
    }
    else if (hItem is TemplateGallery)
```

```
    {
        // if the object is a template gallery, show the
        // template gallery icon
        // set the Name to be a hyperlink
        // that points to default.aspx?{QueryStringModeUnpublished}
        e.Item.Cells[0].Text="<img src='images/templategallery.gif'>";
        HtmlAnchor aName;
        aName=e.Item.Cells[1].FindControl("aName") as HtmlAnchor;
        aName.HRef = PrepareUrl(hItem, PublishingMode.Unpublished,
                                    "default.aspx");
    }
    else if (hItem is Template)
    {
        // if the object is a template, show the template icon
        // leave the Name as text
        e.Item.Cells[0].Text="<img src='images/template.gif'>";
    }
    else if (hItem is ResourceGallery)
    {
        // if the object is a resouce gallery, show the
        // resource gallery icon
        // set the Name to be a hyperlink
        // that points to default.aspx?{QueryStringModeUnpublished}

        e.Item.Cells[0].Text="<img src='images/resourcegallery.gif'>";
        HtmlAnchor aName;
        aName=e.Item.Cells[1].FindControl("aName") as HtmlAnchor;
        aName.HRef = PrepareUrl(hItem, PublishingMode.Unpublished,
                                    "default.aspx");
    }
    else if (hItem is Resource)
    {
        // if the object is a resource, show the resource icon
        // leave the name as text
        e.Item.Cells[0].Text="<img src='images/resource.gif'>";
    }
    // add actions specific to the object type
    If (e.Item.ItemType==ListItemType.EditItem)
    {
        // in the table generated by the datagrid,
        // the action column is the 4th cell
        TableCell actionCell = e.Item.Cells[4];
        AddActionItems(actionCell, hItem);
    }
    }
}
```

This method determines the type of HierarchyItem that's being bound, be it a channel, posting, resource gallery, resource, template gallery, or template. It then sets the icon in each row of the DataGrid to the URL of the image that represents that object type. If the object is a channel, template gallery, or resource gallery the object name is linked using our PrepareUrl() method to reload the page setting it as the startItem. The last section calls the AddActionItems() method, which we'll use to build an edit action menu for each row in the DataGrid. Let's take a look at this method in the following section.

Building an Edit Menu

We need to add an Edit button to each row. When the button is clicked, a list of options that can be performed on the object is displayed. The table below shows a list of options for each object type.

Object Type	Actions
Channel, Template Gallery, Template, Resource Gallery	Properties Delete
Posting	Copy Move Create Connected Posting Properties Delete
Template	Copy Move Create Connected Template Properties Delete
Resource	Replace Properties Delete

Here's how the DataGrid will appear once we're done, and we click the Edit button for the Egg Plant posting:

Name	Last Modified Date	
AloeVera	23 Apr 2005 02:59 AM	Edit
BananaTree	23 Apr 2005 02:59 AM	Edit
Bougainvillea	23 Apr 2005 02:59 AM	Edit
CoconutTree	23 Apr 2005 02:59 AM	Edit
EggPlant	23 Apr 2005 02:59 AM	Copy Move Create Connected Posting Properties Delete
Ficus	23 Apr 2005 02:59 AM	Edit
Hibiscus	23 Apr 2005 02:59 AM	Edit
Ixora	23 Apr 2005 02:59 AM	Edit
ManEatingPlant	23 Apr 2005 02:59 AM	Edit

We add two new columns to the DataGrid, one to show the Edit button and another to contain the list of possible actions.

```
<Columns>
<asp:TemplateColumn>
  <ItemTemplate></ItemTemplate>
</asp:TemplateColumn>
<asp:TemplateColumn HeaderText="DisplayName">
<ItemTemplate>
  <a id="aName" runat="server">
  <%# DataBinder.Eval(Container.DataItem, "DisplayName") %>
  </a>
</ItemTemplate>
</asp:TemplateColumn>
```

```
<asp:BoundColumn DataField="LastModifiedDate" ReadOnly="True"
  HeaderText="Last Modified Date"
  DataFormatString="{0:dd MMM yyyy hh:mm tt}"></asp:BoundColumn>

<asp:EditCommandColumn ButtonType="LinkButton" EditText="Edit">
</asp:EditCommandColumn>
<asp:TemplateColumn></asp:TemplateColumn>
</Columns>
```

When the Edit button is clicked, we set the EditItemIndex of DataGrid1 to the index of the selected row. In the events property window of DataGrid1, double-click EditCommand to register the event handler and add the following code:

```
private void DataGrid1_EditCommand(object source,
System.Web.UI.WebControls.DataGridCommandEventArgs e)
{
  DataGrid1.EditItemIndex = e.Item.ItemIndex;
  BindData();
}
```

At the same time, we want to display a list of possible actions that can be performed on the selected object. This is done by the AddActionItems() method. The method creates hyperlinks for each of the action items defined in the table above. The AddActionItems() method accepts two input parameters:

- A TableCell named actionCell. This is the cell to add action button to.

- A HierarchyItem named hItem. This is the item we are creating the action buttons for.

After determining the type of object passed to the AddActionItems() method, we add the type-specific action buttons for the current object. For example, if a posting is passed to the method Copy and Move buttons are added.

In addition to the type-specific options a Properties button is added to the menu, which applies to all objects. Finally, we will check to see if the user has permissions to delete the current object and if so, we'll add a Delete button.

Notice that we're using the URL generated by our PrepareUrl() method to assign to the NavigateUrl property of each action button. Add the AddActionItems() method below the DataGrid1_EditCommand() event handler:

```
private void AddActionItems(TableCell actionCell, HierarchyItem hItem)
{
  if (hItem is Posting)
  {
    Posting currentPosting = hItem as Posting;
    // actions for postings include:
    // Copy, Move, Create Connected Posting.

    // the copy option
    HyperLink hCopy = new HyperLink();
    hCopy.Text = "Copy<br>";
    hCopy.Target = "_blank";
    hCopy.NavigateUrl = PrepareUrl(hItem, PublishingMode.Update,
                                   "CopyPosting.aspx");
    actionCell.Controls.Add(hCopy);

    // the move option
    if (currentPosting.CanMove)
    {
```

```
                 HyperLink hMove = new HyperLink();
                 hMove.Text = "Move<br>";
                 hMove.Target = "_blank";
                 hMove.NavigateUrl = PrepareUrl(hItem, PublishingMode.Update,
                                             "MovePosting.aspx");
                 actionCell.Controls.Add(hMove);
              }

              // the create connected posting option
              HyperLink hCreateConnected = new HyperLink();
              hCreateConnected.Text = "Create Connected Posting<br>";
              hCreateConnected.Target = "_blank";
              hCreateConnected.NavigateUrl = PrepareUrl(hItem,
              PublishingMode.Update, "CreateConnectedPosting.aspx");
              actionCell.Controls.Add(hCreateConnected);
           }
           else if (hItem is Template)
           {

              Template currentTemplate = hItem as Template;
              // actions for templates include:
              // Copy, Move, Create Connected Template

              // the copy option
              HyperLink hCopy = new HyperLink();
              hCopy.Text = "Copy<br>";
              hCopy.Target = "_blank";
              hCopy.NavigateUrl = PrepareUrl(hItem, PublishingMode.Update ,
                                             "CopyTemplate.aspx");
              actionCell.Controls.Add(hCopy);

              // the move option
              if (currentTemplate.CanMove)
              {
                 HyperLink hMove = new HyperLink();
                 hMove.Text = "Move<br>";
                 hMove.Target = "_blank";
                 hMove.NavigateUrl = PrepareUrl(hItem, PublishingMode.Update,
                                             "MoveTemplate.aspx");
                 actionCell.Controls.Add(hMove);
              }

              // the create connected template option
              HyperLink hCreateConnected = new HyperLink();
              hCreateConnected.Text = "Create Connected Template<br>";
              hCreateConnected.Target = "_blank";
              hCreateConnected.NavigateUrl = PrepareUrl(hItem,
                     PublishingMode.Update, "CreateConnectedTemplate.aspx");
              actionCell.Controls.Add(hCreateConnected);
           }
           else if (hItem is Resource)
           {
              Resource currentResource = hItem as Resource;
              // Resources have an additional option
              // to Replace their contents.

              // the replace option
              if (currentResource.CanSetContent)
              {
                 HyperLink hReplace = new HyperLink();
                 hReplace.Text = "Replace<br>";
                 hReplace.Target = "_blank";
                 hReplace.NavigateUrl = PrepareUrl(hItem, PublishingMode.Update,
                                                "ReplaceResource.aspx");
                 actionCell.Controls.Add(hReplace);
              }
```

```
    }

    // add shared options include:
    // Properties and Delete.

    // the properties option
    HyperLink hProperties = new HyperLink();
    hProperties.Text = "Properties<br>";
    hProperties.Target = "_blank";
    hProperties.NavigateUrl = PrepareUrl(hItem, PublishingMode.Update,
                                    "Properties.aspx");
    actionCell.Controls.Add(hProperties);

    // the delete option
    if (hItem.CanDelete)
    {
        HyperLink hDelete = new HyperLink();
        hDelete.Text = "Delete<br>";
        hDelete.Target = "_blank";
        hDelete.NavigateUrl = PrepareUrl(hItem, PublishingMode.Update,
                                    "Delete.aspx");
        actionCell.Controls.Add(hDelete);
    }
}
```

If you receive a JavaScript error message when you test the above code, you probably need to change the ID in the opening form tag to something else, such as "CMSExplorerDefault" as the browser may not like the ID "default" that Visual Studio .NET assigned to the form.

Save and build the solution and navigate to http://localhost/CmsExplorer. At this point you can browse the channels by clicking on the channel names as well as viewing our actions menu.

The next thing we'll need is a toolbar to move up a level in the hierarchy from the currently selected parent container, to refresh the page, and to select a root path other than channels, such as templates or resources.

Building the Toolbar

The gray bar at the top of the grid is the toolbar. It will consist of six controls:

- The Up button that brings the user one level up the channel hierarchy
- The Refresh button that updates the display
- A DropDownList containing options to create a new channel, posting, template, template gallery, or resource
- The Channels button to navigate through the available channels and postings
- The Templates button to navigate through the available template galleries and templates
- The Resources button to navigate through the available resource galleries and resources

In HTML view for the default.aspx page, replace the text in the space marked (Space for Toolbar) with the code below:

```
<table cellSpacing="0" cellPadding="3">
<tr>
  <td>
    <asp:LinkButton ID="btnUp" Runat="server">
      <img src="images/parentfolder.gif" border="0" align="absmiddle">
      <span style="text-decoration:none">Up</span>
    </asp:linkbutton>
  </td>
  <td>
    <asp:LinkButton ID="btnRefresh" Runat="server">
      <img src="images/refresh.gif" border="0" align="absmiddle">
      <span style="text-decoration:none">Refresh</span>
    </asp:linkbutton>
  </td>
  <td>|</td>
  <td>
    <asp:DropDownList id="ddlNewItem" Runat="server"
           AutoPostBack="True"></asp:dropdownlist>
  </td>
  <td>|</td>
  <td>
    <asp:LinkButton ID="btnChannels" Runat="server">
      <img src="images/channel.gif" border="0" align="absmiddle">
      <span style="text-decoration:none">Channels</span>
    </asp:LinkButton>
  </td>
  <td>|</td>
  <td>
    <asp:LinkButton ID="btnTemplates" Runat="server">
      <img src="images/templategallery.gif" border="0" align="absmiddle">
      <span style="text-decoration:none">Templates</span>
    </asp:LinkButton>
  <td>|</td>
  <td>
    <asp:LinkButton ID="btnResources" Runat="server">
      <img src="images/resourcegallery.gif" border="0" align="absmiddle">
      <span style="text-decoration:none">Resources</span>
    </asp:LinkButton>
  </td>
</tr>
</table>
```

The Up Button

In Design view, double-click on the btnUp LinkButton. This button will essentially be performing the same function as the Up button in explorer, namely taking you one level back up the hierarchy.

If the current startItem is a channel and it has a parent channel we'll simply reload default.aspx, appending the information about the Unpublished mode of the parent container. If the current item is a template gallery or resource gallery, we'll try to obtain the URL using our PrepareUrl() method of the gallery's parent. If PrepareUrl() returns an empty string, the current gallery has no parent so we won't reload the page.

```
private void btnUp_Click(object sender, System.EventArgs e)
{
    // if the current item is a channel...
    if (startItem is Channel)
    {
```

```
      Channel startChannel = startItem as Channel;

      // if this channel has a parent, reload the page setting the
      // parent container to the current channel's parent
      if (startChannel.Parent!=null)
      {
        Response.Redirect("default.aspx?"
            + startChannel.Parent.QueryStringModeUnpublished);
      }
    }
    // else if the current item is a template gallery
    else if (startItem is TemplateGallery)
    {

      // if this TemplateGallery has a parent, reload the page setting
      // the parent container to the TemplateGallery's parent
      string url = PrepareUrl(((TemplateGallery)startItem).Parent,
                        PublishingMode.Unpublished, "default.aspx");
      if (url!="")
      {
        Response.Redirect(url);
      }

    }
    // else if the current item is a resouce gallery
    else if (startItem is ResourceGallery)
    {
      // if this ResourceGallery has a parent, reload the page setting
      // the parent container to the ResourceGallery's parent
      string url = PrepareUrl(((ResourceGallery)startItem).Parent,
                        PublishingMode.Unpublished, "default.aspx");
      if (url!="")
      {
        Response.Redirect(url);
      }
    }
  }
}
```

The Refresh Button

In design view, double-click on the btnRefresh button. To update the display on the DataGrid, we need to fetch the latest data from the MCMS repository. This is done in the BindData() method defined later.

```
private void btnRefresh_Click(object sender, System.EventArgs e)
{
  // refresh the content displayed in the DataGrid
  BindData();
}
```

The DropDownList

Double-click on the ddlNewItem DropDownList in the default.aspx page in Design view to get to the ddlNewItem_SelectedIndexChanged() event handler. When the user selects an item in the DropDownList, the dialog associated with the selection opens in a new browser window. The URL of the dialog is determined by the last parameter of our PrepareUrl() method. Remember the last parameter of the PrepareUrl() method allows us to specify a page other than default.aspx to add to the URL. We're going to use this to specify a specific dialog to open in a new window. Don't worry about the dialogs for now; we'll be creating them later on.

```
private void ddlNewItem_SelectedIndexChanged(object sender,
        System.EventArgs e)
```

```
{
    // get the value of the selected item in the DropDownList
    string selectedOption = ddlNewItem.SelectedItem.Value;
    string url = "";

    // depending upon the item selected...
    // construct a URL pointing to a specific dialog page
    // and append the information about the Update mode of the current
    // container
    switch(selectedOption)
    {
        case "NewChannel":
        {
            url = "CreateChannel.aspx?"
                + ((Channel)startItem).QueryStringModeUpdate;
            break;
        }
        case "NewPosting":
        {
            url = "CreatePosting.aspx?"
                + ((Channel)startItem).QueryStringModeUpdate;
            break;
        }
        case "NewTemplateGallery":
        {
            url = PrepareUrl(startItem, PublishingMode.Update,
                            "CreateTemplateGallery.aspx");
            break;
        }
        case "NewTemplate":
        {
            url = PrepareUrl(startItem, PublishingMode.Update,
                            "CreateTemplate.aspx");
            break;
        }
        case "NewResource":
        {
            url = PrepareUrl(startItem, PublishingMode.Update,
                            "CreateResource.aspx");
            break;
        }
    }

    // if a URL was generated, register a JavaScript block to open
    // a new window with the specified URL and reset the dropdownlist
    if (url != "")
    {
        // register the javascript
        string script = "";
        script += "<script language=\"javascript\">";
        script += "window.open('" + url + "');";
        script += "</script>";

        Page.RegisterClientScriptBlock("CreateNewItem",script);

        // reset the dropdownlist
        ddlNewItem.SelectedIndex = 0;
    }
}
```

Now we need to initialize the toolbar by adding the options as shown in the table below to the
ddlNewItem DropDownList. These options will be specific to the type of the startItem and our
code will ensure that these will only show up if the user has the appropriate permissions.

StartItem Type	Options Added
Channel	New Channel New Posting
TemplateGallery	New Template Gallery New Template
ResourceGallery	New Resource

For example, the options "New Channel" and "New Posting" will be added if the startItem is a channel and if the user has rights to create channels and postings within the parent channel.

Below ddlNewItem_SelectedIndexChanged() add the following PrepareToolbar() method, which inserts the options in the drop-down list:

```
private void PrepareToolbar()
{
  // remove any pre-existing options from the DropDownList
  ddlNewItem.Items.Clear();
  ddlNewItem.Items.Add(new ListItem("New",""));

  ListItem li = null;

  if (startItem is Channel)
  {
    Channel currentChannel = startItem as Channel;

    // if the user has rights to create channels, add option to create
    // a new channel
    if (currentChannel.CanCreateChannels)
    {
      li = new ListItem("New Channel","NewChannel");
      ddlNewItem.Items.Add(li);
    }

    // if the user has rights to create postings, add option to create
    // a new posting
    if (currentChannel.CanCreatePostings)
    {
      li = new ListItem("New Posting","NewPosting");
      ddlNewItem.Items.Add(li);
    }

    imgTitle.ImageUrl = "images/channelopen_big.gif";
  }

  else if (startItem is TemplateGallery)
  {
    TemplateGallery templateGallery = startItem as TemplateGallery;

    // if the user has rights to create template galleries, add option
    // to create a new template gallery
    if (templateGallery.CanCreateTemplateGalleries)
    {
      li = new ListItem("New Template Gallery",
          "NewTemplateGallery");
      ddlNewItem.Items.Add(li);
    }

    // if the user has rights to create templates, add option to create
    // a new template
    if (templateGallery.CanCreateTemplates)
```

```
        {
          li = new ListItem("New Template","NewTemplate");
          ddlNewItem.Items.Add(li);
        }

        imgTitle.ImageUrl = "images/templategalleryopen_big.gif";
    }

    else if (startItem is ResourceGallery)
    {
        ResourceGallery resourceGallery = startItem as ResourceGallery;

        // if the user has rights to create resources, add option to create
        // a new resource
        if (resourceGallery.CanCreateResources)
        {
          li = new ListItem("New Resource","NewResource");
          ddlNewItem.Items.Add(li);
        }

        imgTitle.ImageUrl = "images/resourcegalleryopen_big.gif";
    }
}
```

Next, add the following line inside the if (!Page.IsPostBack) code block at the end of the Page_Load() event handler:

```
. . . code continues . . .

if (!Page.IsPostBack)
{
    // display the publishing mode
    lblPublishingMode.Text = "Publishing Mode: "
                            + cmsContext.Mode.ToString();

    // use the start channel's display name as the
    // header for the page
    litCurrentContainer.Text = startItem.Name;

    // initialize the toolbar based on the current startItem
    PrepareToolbar();
}
```

The Channels Button

The Channels button in the CMS Explorer UI allows the user to browse through the channel structure to inspect channel and posting objects.

In Design view, double-click on the btnChannels LinkButton. When the btnChannels button is clicked, we will simply refresh the page to show the contents of the root channel. This is simply achieved by redirecting back to the default.aspx page.

```
private void btnChannels_Click(object sender, System.EventArgs e)
{
    Response.Redirect("default.aspx");
}
```

The Templates Button

The Templates button enables the user to browse the template gallery structure and view template gallery and template objects.

In Design view, double-click on the btnTemplates LinkButton. The btnTemplates button brings the user to the root Template Gallery. We use the PrepareUrl() method to get the correct URL and querystrings:

```
private void btnTemplates_Click(object sender, System.EventArgs e)
{
  string url;
  url = PrepareUrl(cmsContext.RootTemplateGallery,
                   PublishingMode.Unpublished, "default.aspx");
  Response.Redirect(url);
}
```

The Resources Button

The Resources button lets the user browse through the resource gallery structure to inspect resource gallery and resource objects.

In Design view, double-click on the btnResources LinkButton. The btnResources button brings the user to the root Resource Gallery. We use the PrepareUrl() method to get the correct URL and querystrings.

```
private void btnResources_Click(object sender, System.EventArgs e)
{
  string url;
  url = PrepareUrl(cmsContext.RootResourceGallery,
                   PublishingMode.Unpublished, "default.aspx");
  Response.Redirect(url);
}
```

The Completed User Interface

When you are done, save and build the solution. The user interface for CMS Explorer is complete! Click on the display name of Channels to drill down deeper into the hierarchy. Click the Up button to move up a level. Select the Edit button to reveal a set of actions that can be performed on each channel or posting.

Using Reflection to List Properties and their Values

In the Properties dialog, we are going to list all properties of the selected object. Usually, when you want to access a property value in code, you simply type the object name, followed by the period key and then the property name.

This is fine when you are just dealing with one or two properties, but there are over 40 properties for the channel object alone. In order to display all its property values in this way, you would have to type in at least 40 lines of code. And should there be future upgrades to the PAPI, the list may grow even longer. The good news is there's a short cut—.NET Reflection.

Reflection is a technique used to access information about a class, such as its methods, properties, events and even information about its assembly. To implement reflection, use the GetType() method of the object (inherited from System.Object), which returns an object of type System.Reflection.Type. The System.Reflection.Type class contains methods that retrieve metadata about the object's class. For example, given any object, you can get a list of its methods by calling:

```
MyObject.GetType().GetMethods();
```

and to get a list of its properties, you could call:

```
MyObject.GetType().GetProperties();
```

As you can see, reflection is a powerful feature. In this example, instead of writing 40+ lines of code to list the properties of a ChannelItem object, we will simply use reflection to iterate through each property and display its value.

Let's display the list of properties in a DataGrid. To start, add a new web form to the CMSExplorer project. Name the new web form Properties.aspx. Toggle to HTML view and add a couple of headings to the form to describe what it does:

```html
<form>
<h1>Properties of <asp:Literal Runat="server" ID="litCurrentItem"/></h1>
<h2>List of all Properties and their values</h2>
</form>
```

In the web form's code-behind file, import the Microsoft.ContentManagement.Publishing and System.Reflection namespaces and add the following code in the Page_Load() event handler:

```csharp
. . . code continues . . .
// MCMS PAPI
using Microsoft.ContentManagement.Publishing;

// for reflection
using System.Reflection;

namespace CMSExplorer
{
    /// <summary>
    /// Summary description for Properties.
    /// </summary>
    public class Properties : System.Web.UI.Page
    {
        HierarchyItem hItem; // the current item

        private void Page_Load(object sender, System.EventArgs e)
        {
            CmsHttpContext cmsContext = CmsHttpContext.Current;
            hItem = null;

            string cmsObjectGuid = "";
            if (Request.QueryString["CMSObjectGuid"]!=null)
            {
                // template gallery items and resource gallery items
                cmsObjectGuid = Request.QueryString["CMSObjectGuid"];
                hItem = cmsContext.Searches.GetByGuid(cmsObjectGuid);
            }
            else
            {
                // channels and postings
                hItem = cmsContext.ChannelItem;
            }

            // list all properties and their values in the grid
            if (hItem!=null)
            {
                litCurrentItem.Text = hItem.Path;
                ListProperties();
            }
        }
```

```
. . . code continues . . .
    }
  }
```

The code gets a reference to the `HierarchyItem` whose properties you wish to view. For template galleries, templates, resource galleries, and resources, this is obtained by getting the GUID from the `CMSObjectGuid` querystring parameter and using the `Searches.GetByGuid()` method. Channels and postings are obtained from the `CmsHttpContext.Current.ChannelItem` property.

In Design view, drag and drop the `Styles.css` file and `DataGrid` onto the `Properties.aspx` web form and give the `DataGrid` the following property values:

Property	Value
Auto Format	Simple 3
Font-Size	10pt
ID	DataGrid1

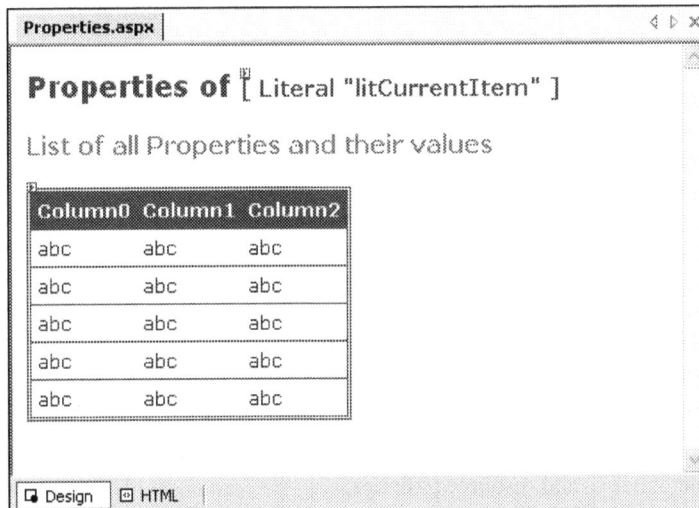

Properties.aspx ◁ ▷ ✕

Properties of [Literal "litCurrentItem"]

List of all Properties and their values

Column0	Column1	Column2
abc	abc	abc
abc	abc	abc
abc	abc	abc
abc	abc	abc
abc	abc	abc

Design | HTML

Below the `Page_Load()` event handler, add the `ListProperties()` method. The method first creates a `DataTable` containing the following columns:

- The property name
- The property value
- Whether or not the property can be written to

We use the `GetType.GetProperties()` method to retrieve a collection of all properties associated with the hierarchy item. Next, iterate through each property of the current `ChannelItem` and add each one as a row to the `DataTable`. Notice that the property value is obtained by calling `PropertyInfo.GetValue()` and passing in the hierarchy item as an input parameter. Finally, we bind the `DataTable` to the `DataGrid`.

```
private void ListProperties()
{
    // display the property names and values for the current channelitem
    DataTable dt = new DataTable();
    DataRow dr;

    // add columns for the property name, property value and
    // the boolean that indicates if the property is writable
    dt.Columns.Add(new DataColumn("PropertyName"));
    dt.Columns.Add(new DataColumn("PropertyValue"));
    dt.Columns.Add(new DataColumn("CanWrite"));

    // use reflection to iterate through a list of the object's properties
    foreach(PropertyInfo pi in hItem.GetType().GetProperties())
    {
        if (pi.PropertyType.ToString().StartsWith("System"))
        {
            dr = dt.NewRow();
            dr[0] = pi.Name;
            Object piObject = pi.GetValue(hItem, null);
            if (piObject!=null)
            {
                dr[1] = piObject.ToString();
            }
            dr[2] = pi.CanWrite.ToString();
            dt.Rows.Add(dr);
        }
    }

    // bind the datatable to the datagrid
    DataGrid1.DataSource = dt.DefaultView;
    DataGrid1.DataBind();
}
```

When you are done, save and build the solution. To see the code in action:

1. Access http://localhost/CmsExplorer.
2. Click on the Edit button on the row corresponding to the Tropical Green channel.
3. Click Properties.

The Properties page opens as shown on the facing page. Notice that all properties of the Tropical Green channel are displayed! The page also works when viewing the properties of other object types like template galleries and resource galleries.

List of all Properties and their values:

PropertyName	PropertyValue	CanWrite
ApplyOuterScriptToPostings	False	True
CanCreateChannels	False	False
CanCreatePostings	True	False
DefaultPostingName		True
IsRoot	False	False
OuterScriptFile	/TropicalGreen/Templates/HomePage.aspx	True
ChangeDate	7/1/2004 9:34:20 AM	False
DisplayName	Home	True
DisplayPath	/Channels/Home/	False
ExpiryDate	1/1/3000 12:00:00 AM	True
IsHiddenModePublished	False	True
IsImportant	False	True
IsRobotFollowable	True	True
IsRobotIndexable	True	True
QueryString	NRMODE=Unpublished&FRAMELESS=true&NRNODEGUID=%7b71EDAD1D-9D58-4D65-8069-19DFC0114F54%7d	False
QueryStringModeUnpublished	NRMODE=Unpublished&FRAMELESS=true&NRNODEGUID=%7b71EDAD1D-9D58-4D65-8069-19DFC0114F54%7d	False
QueryStringModeUpdate	NRMODE=Update&FRAMELESS=true&NRNODEGUID=%7b71EDAD1D-9D58-4D65-8069-19DFC0114F54%7d	False
SortOrdinal	0	True
StartDate	3/30/2004 7:14:34 AM	True
Url	/NR/exeres/71EDAD1D-9D58-4D65-8069-19DFC0114F54.htm?NRMODE=Unpublished	False

Updating Property Values

Look at the grid. Properties whose values we can modify using the PAPI have a `CanWrite` property value of true.

So far, we have only been reading property values and using Web Author to update them. Let's attempt to change the `Description` property value using the PAPI.

> We are going to keep it really simple and update only one property: the `Description`. You might find it a useful exercise to go ahead and add more textboxes to the page to update the other writable properties of the channel item object, like its `Name`, `DisplayName`, `StartDate`, `ExpiryDate` fields, etc.

In HTML view, add the code shown below (including the text markers) above the opening `<asp:DataGrid>` tag:

```
<p>
  <table>
  <tr>
    <td>Description:</td>
    <td>(Add the text box for the Description here)</td>
  </tr>
```

```
<tr>
  <td colspan="2" align="right">
    (Add the Update button here)
    <INPUT type="button" value="Close" onclick="javascript:window.close();">
  </td>
</tr>
</table>
(Add the Label for displaying error messages here)
</p>
```

Toggle to Design view. Drag and drop the following controls from the Web Forms section of the Toolbox and delete all text markers. We will be adding a textbox for entering the channel item's new description, a button for saving it, and a label for showing error messages (if there are any). Arrange them as shown in the diagram below and set their properties accordingly.

Control	Property	Property Value
TextBox	ID	txtDescription
	Rows	3
	TextMode	MultiLine
Button	ID	btnUpdate
	Text	Update
Label	ID	lblErrorMessage
	Text	(empty string)

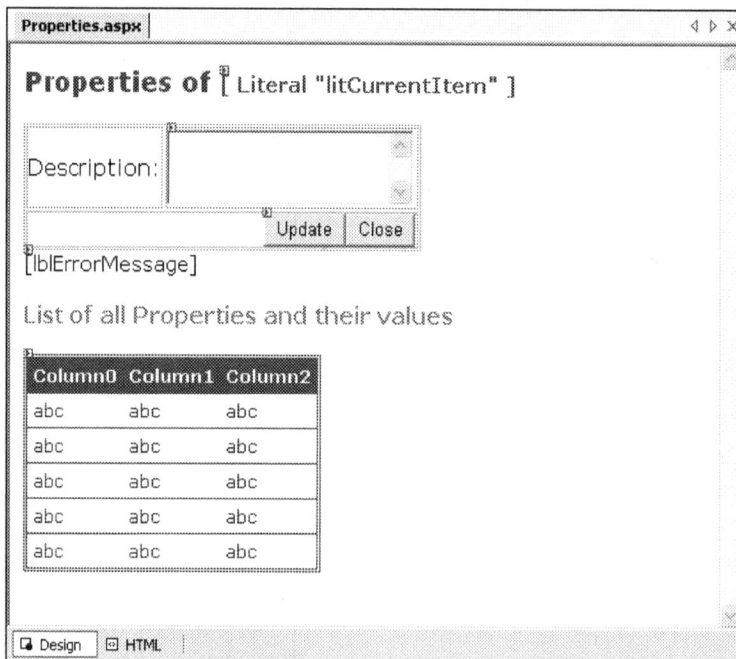

In the Page_Load() event handler, add code to read the Description of the current hierarchy item and display it on the screen.

```
private void Page_Load(object sender, System.EventArgs e)
{
    // Put user code to initialize the page here
    CmsHttpContext cmsContext = CmsHttpContext.Current;
    hItem = null;

    string cmsObjectGuid = "";
    if (Request.QueryString["CMSObjectGuid"] != null)
    {
        // template gallery items and resource gallery items
        cmsObjectGuid = Request.QueryString["CMSObjectGuid"];
        hItem = cmsContext.Searches.GetByGuid(cmsObjectGuid);
    }
    else
    {
        // channels and postings
        hItem = cmsContext.ChannelItem;
    }

    // list all properties and their values in the grid
    if (hItem != null)
    {
        litCurrentItem.Text = hItem.Path;
        if (!Page.IsPostBack)
        {
            txtDescription.Text = hItem.Description;
        }
        ListProperties();
    }
}
```

Toggle to Design mode and double-click on the btnUpdate button. In the btnUpdate_OnClick() event handler, we will write the code that updates the Description property value of the HierarchyItem based on the text entered into the textbox.

```
private void btnUpdate_Click(object sender, System.EventArgs e)
{
    try
    {
        // IMPORTANT: You must be in update mode for the code to work

        // update the description
        hItem.Description = txtDescription.Text;

        // commit the change
        CmsHttpContext.Current.CommitAll();

        // refresh the page to ensure that the change shows up in the
        // datagrid
        Response.Redirect(HttpContext.Current.Request.Url.ToString());
    }
    catch(Exception ex)
    {
        CmsHttpContext.Current.RollbackAll();

        // after a rollback the CMS context needs to be disposed.
        CmsHttpContext.Current.Dispose();

        lblErrorMessage.Text = ex.Message;
    }
}
```

Save and build the solution. Let's test it to see if it works:

1. With the properties page open, click the Refresh button.
2. Enter TropicalGreen—Live the Sunny Side of Life in the Description field.
3. Click Update.

Look at the grid again. The description property of the TropicalGreen channel has been updated!

You *must* be in Update mode for the code to work correctly. Otherwise, an error occurs with the message:

Invalid mode for update. The requested action modifies the state of an object and can only be performed when the session is in the 'Update' mode.

The Properties dialog is already in Update mode because we have generated the URL for the Properties.aspx page to be opened in Update mode using our helper function, PrepareUrl(), earlier.

Summary

We have used the MCMS Publishing API (PAPI) to create the CMS Explorer and provide a web interface with many of the features of Site Manager as well as some additional ones.

In the process of building the CMS Explorer we have learned about many of the capabilities offered by the PAPI. There are many things that we could add to the CMS Explorer to make it even more valuable to your organization. In the next chapter we will demonstrate additional PAPI features by extending our CMS Explorer project, where we will add channel and posting management functionality.

2

Managing Channels and Postings with the PAPI

In the previous chapter we used the MCMS Publishing API to create a web-based CMS management application called CMS Explorer. CMS Explorer provides a web interface for viewing the properties of channels, postings, templates, template galleries, resources, and resource galleries. In this chapter we will dig deeper into our examination of the PAPI by inserting additional functionality to manage channels and postings.

Managing Channels and Postings

Imagine a scenario where you have been asked to move contents of a legacy web portal to MCMS. The portal contains hundreds of channels and thousands of postings. One option is to hire someone to manually create the channels and postings, copying and pasting the HTML content from the old pages to the new postings and approving each and every one of them. That's definitely a viable solution but let's imagine hiring is not an option and despite the generous offer of free doughnuts and coffee, none of your co-workers are willing to take on the task. So it comes down to you, and you are understandably a little horrified at the scale of the task. Fortunately, rather than doing all the work manually, you can write a script to automate the task.

Another use of the Publishing API could be to perform complex actions such as: "When Channel A is created, postings B, C and D must be automatically created in Channel E." However complex the scenario may be, you can customize the management of channels and postings using the Publishing API.

The PAPI also contains many objects, methods, and properties that aren't exposed in the standard Web Author dialogs. For example, although you can't create channels using the standard Web Author dialogs (at least, without some customization), you can do so using the PAPI.

Creating Channels

Channel creation is available in Site Manager but not in the standard Web Author dialogs. After all, the job of creating channels is usually performed by channel managers setting up the site. Authors and editors don't have the rights to create channels. Nevertheless, you can always use the Channel.CreateChannel() method of the PAPI to implement channel creation dialogs for a given website.

In this example, we will build a Create Channel dialog for CMS Explorer.

1. To begin, add a new web form to the CMSExplorer project. Name the new form CreateChannel.aspx.

2. In Design view, drag and drop the Styles.css file from Solution Explorer onto the form to apply the stylesheet to the page.

3. Toggle to HTML view. Insert the following code between the <form> tags. The table allows us to lay out the controls that we will be adding later.

```
<table>
<tr>
  <td colspan="2">
    <h1>Create Template</h1>
    <h2>Parent Channel: (Add Literal for displaying the path here)</h2>
  </td>
</tr>
<tr>
  <td>Name:</td>
  <td>(Add the text box for the Name here)</td>
</tr>
<tr>
  <td>Display Name:</td>
  <td>(Add the text box for the Display Name here)</td>
</tr>
<tr>
  <td>Description:</td>
  <td>(Add the text box for the Description here)</td>
</tr>
<tr>
  <td colspan="2">(Add the Label for displaying error messages here)</td>
</tr>
<tr>
  <td colspan="2" align="right">
    (Add the Create Channel button here)
    <INPUT type="button" value="Close"
      onclick="javascript:window.close();">
  </td>
</tr>
</table>
```

4. Switch back to Design view, drop controls from the Web Forms section of the Toolbox onto the web form, and arrange them as shown below:

Control	Property	Property Value
Literal	ID	litParentChannel
TextBox	ID	txtName
TextBox	ID	txtDisplayName
TextBox	ID	txtDescription
	TextMode	MultiLine
	Rows	3
Button	ID	btnCreate
	Text	Create Channel

Control	Property	Property Value
Label	ID	lblErrorMessage
	Text	(empty string)

Create Channel

Parent Channel: [Literal "litParentChannel"]

Name:

Display Name:

Description:

[lblErrorMessage]

Create Channel | Close

5. While in Design view, double-click on the form to get to the code-behind file.

6. Import the Microsoft.ContentManagement.Publishing namespace:

```
. . . code continues . . .
// MCMS PAPI
using Microsoft.ContentManagement.Publishing;

namespace CMSExplorer
{
    /// <summary>
    /// Summary description for CreateChannel.
    /// </summary>
    public class CreateChannel : System.Web.UI.Page
    {
        . . . code continues . . .
    }
}
```

7. In the Page_Load() event handler, get an instance of the current channel and display its path in the litParentChannel literal:

```
private void Page_Load(object sender, System.EventArgs e)
{
    // Display the parent channel's path
    litParentChannel.Text = CmsHttpContext.Current.Channel.Path;
}
```

8. Toggle back to Design view and double-click on the btnCreate button to get to the btnCreate_OnClick() event handler. Here, we add the code that creates the channel. If an error occurs during the execution of the code, we catch it and write the error message in the lblErrorMessage label:

```
private void btnCreate_Click(object sender, System.EventArgs e)
{
    // IMPORTANT: You must be in update mode for the code to work

    CmsHttpContext cmsContext = CmsHttpContext.Current;
    try
    {
```

```
// get the parent channel
Channel parentChannel = cmsContext.Channel;

// check if we can create a channel
if (!parentChannel.CanCreateChannels)
{
  throw new Exception("Current user does not have "
                    + "permissions to create channels in channel: "
                    + parentChannel.Path);
}

// get the name of the channel
string Name = txtName.Text.Trim();

// create the new channel
Channel newChannel;
newChannel = parentChannel.CreateChannel();

// assign properties to the new channel;
newChannel.Name = Name;
newChannel.DisplayName = txtDisplayName.Text;
newChannel.Description = txtDescription.Text;

// commit the changes to the repository
cmsContext.CommitAll();

// display the success message
lblErrorMessage.Text = "Channel created successfully!";
}
catch(Exception ex)
{
  // rollback the updates
  cmsContext.RollbackAll();

  // after a rollback it is required to dispose of the CMS context
  cmsContext.Dispose();

  // display the error message
  lblErrorMessage.Text = ex.Message;
}
}
```

As you can see from the code above, creation of a channel is a fairly straightforward process. First, get an instance of the parent channel—the channel that will contain the new channel, then simply call the `Channel.CreateChannel()` method and the new channel is created.

New channels automatically inherit certain properties from their parent. Property values inherited include:

- `DefaultPostingName`
- `DefaultResourceGallery`
- `DefaultTemplateGallery`
- `StartDate` and `ExpiryDate`

Rights groups assigned to the parent channel are also automatically assigned to the new channel.

Unless otherwise specified, the new channel will be given the default name "New Channel". In the code above, we gave the new channel a name, display name, and description by setting its properties to the values entered in the textboxes.

Note that the channel will not be permanently created until a call to CommitAll() is made.

> Although we only set selected properties of the new channel, you could easily expand the interface to include all writeable properties of the channel object.

When you are done, save and build the project.

Validating Names

MCMS applies the following rules when naming an object:

- The name may only contain the characters:

  A-Z a-z 0-9 (alphanumeric only)

  _ (underscore)

  – (hyphen)

   (space)

  () (opening and closing parenthesis)

  . (period)

- The name cannot end with a period.

- The name cannot contain two consecutive periods.

To ensure that all names given to channels, postings, template galleries, templates, and resources are valid, we will define a custom method named ValidateMCMSObjectName(). The method accepts the name of the object as an input parameter and returns a Boolean. A return value of true means that the name provided by the user meets all requirements by MCMS and is valid.

Since we will be adding dialogs to CMS Explorer that create all kinds of MCMS objects, we will add the ValidateMCMSObjectName() method to a class file, Utility.cs. In this way, we can re-use the method across all web forms within the project.

1. Add a class file to the project. Name the file Utility.cs.

2. Above the namespace declaration, add System.Text.RegularExpressions.

```
using System;
using System.Text.RegularExpressions;
namespace CMSExplorer
{
    . . . code continues . . .
}
```

3. Directly below the Utility() constructor, add the ValidateMCMSObjectName() method:

```
public static bool ValidateMCMSObjectName(string name)
{
    bool isValid;

    // test for other characters as the ones in the list
    Regex regEx1 = new Regex(@"[^A-Z0-9 _\- ().]",
        RegexOptions.IgnoreCase);
```

```
        // test for "." at the end
        Regex regEx2 = new Regex(@"[\.]$", RegexOptions.None);

        // test for double "."
        Regex regEx3 = new Regex(@"\.{2}", RegexOptions.None);

        Match match1 = regEx1.Match(name);
        Match match2 = regEx2.Match(name);
        Match match3 = regEx3.Match(name);

        // valid = no invalid chars, no double dot, no dot at the end
        isValid = !match1.Success && !match2.Success && !match3.Success;

        return isValid;
    }
```

The `ValidateMCMSObjectName()` method uses three regular expressions to check the validity of the name.

The first regular expression looks like this:

```
[^A-Z0-9 _\- ().]
```

It's a pattern that finds all characters in the name that are *not* alphanumeric, spaces, underscores, opening and closing parenthesis, periods and hyphens (note that the backslash character is used as an escape character), satisfying the first condition for a valid name.

The second regular expression tests to see if the name ends with a period:

```
[\.]$
```

Again, the backslash has been used as an escape character. The period between the square brackets indicates that we are looking for periods. The dollar sign instructs the pattern to match the end of the string.

The third and last regular expressions tests for double periods in the string:

```
\.{2}
```

As before, the backslash is used as an escape character. The number 2, surrounded by curly braces, indicates that we are looking for double occurrences of the period.

Finally, we run all three regular expressions. As long as there are no invalid characters, periods at the end of the name, or consecutive periods, the name is considered to be valid.

To use the `ValidateMCMSObjectName()` method within a dialog, we will simply call it from within the code. Here's how it's done for the Create Channel dialog. Add the following code to the `btnCreate_Click()` event handler:

```
private void btnCreate_Click(object sender, System.EventArgs e)
{
    . . . code continues . . .

    try
    {
        . . . code continues . . .

        // get the name of the channel
        string Name = txtName.Text.Trim();

        // check to see if the name is valid
        if (!Utility.ValidateMCMSObjectName(Name))
```

```
    {
        throw new Exception("Specified channel name is not "
                        + "valid. Must be only alphanumeric "
                        + "characters, open or close parens, "
                        + "hyphens, underscores, periods, or "
                        + "spaces. No period at the end and no "
                        + "consecutive periods are allowed. ");
    }
    // create the new channel
    Channel newChannel;
    newChannel = parentChannel.CreateChannel();

            . . . code continues . . .
    }
    catch(Exception ex)
    {
        . . . code continues . . .
    }
}
```

Should `validateMCMSObjectName()` detect that the name is invalid, we throw an exception. Save and build the project.

Testing the Create Channel Dialog

Let's try out the Create Channel dialog:

1. Navigate to `http://localhost/CmsExplorer`.
2. Select New | New Channel from the `DropDownList`. This will open a new browser window containing the Create Channel dialog.
3. In the Create Channel dialog, enter the following values:

Property	Value
Name	MyNewChannel
DisplayName	My New Channel
Description	This channel was created using the PAPI!

4. Click Create Channel and then click Close.
5. Click Refresh in the main window.

If all goes well, the new channel is created and appears in CMS Explorer as shown below:

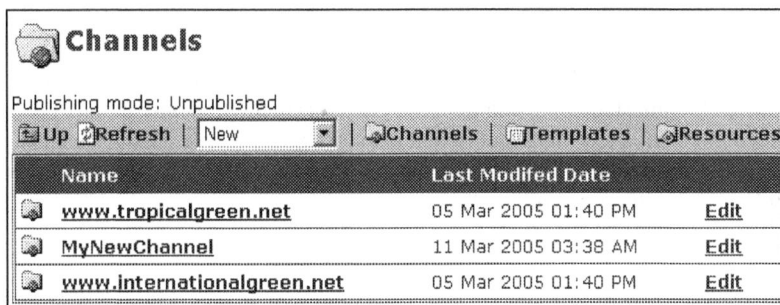

> You could also provide a **Create Channel** option in the Web Author Console by attaching this dialog using the techniques we discussed in Chapter 19, *Customizing the Web Author Console*, of the MCMS book *Building Websites using Microsoft Content Management Server* (Packt Publishing, January 2005, ISBN 1-904811-16-7).

Creating Postings

Just like channels, postings can also be created programmatically using the PAPI. To see how this is done, we will create a dialog for creating postings in CMS Explorer:

1. Add a new web form to the CMSExplorer solution, and name it `CreatePosting.aspx`.

2. In Design view, drag and drop the `styles.css` file from Solution Explorer onto the form. This applies the stylesheet to the page.

3. Toggle to HTML view and insert the following code for a table with six rows:

```
<table>
<tr>
  <td colspan="2">
    <h1>Create Posting</h1>
    <h2>Parent Channel: (Add Literal for displaying the path here)</h2>
  </td>
</tr>
<tr>
  <td>Name:</td>
  <td>(Add the text box for the Name here)</td>
</tr>
<tr>
  <td>Description:</td>
  <td>(Add the text box for the Description here)</td>
</tr>
<tr>
  <td>Template Path:</td>
  <td>(Add the text box for the Template Path here)</td>
</tr>
<tr>
  <td colspan="2">(Add the Label for displaying error messages here)</td>
</tr>
<tr>
  <td colspan="2" align="right">
    (Add the Create Posting button here)
    <INPUT type="button" value="Close"
      onclick="javascript:window.close();">
  </td>
</tr>
</table>
```

4. In Design view, add controls (from the Web Forms section of the Toolbox) to the web form and arrange them as shown in the following diagram. Note that we have simplified the interface by using a textbox to specify the template path. You could enhance this with a template picker that provides users with a friendly interface to select a template from a list of templates they have access to, similar to the Template Selection dialog used in Web Author.

Control	Property	Property Value
Literal	ID	litParentChannel
TextBox	ID	txtName
TextBox	ID	txtDescription
	TextMode	MultiLine
	Rows	3
TextBox	ID	txtTemplate
Button	ID	btnCreate
	Text	Create Posting
Label	ID	lblErrorMessage
	Text	(empty string)

Create Posting

Parent Channel: [Literal "litParentChannel"]

Name:

Description:

Template Path:

[lblErrorMessage]

Create Posting | Close

5. In Design view, double-click on the form to get to its code-behind file. Import the `Microsoft.ContentManagement.Publishing` namespace:

```
. . . code continues . . .
// MCMS PAPI
using Microsoft.ContentManagement.Publishing;

namespace CmsExplorer
{
  /// <summary>
  /// Summary description for CreatePosting.
  /// </summary>
  public class CreatePosting : System.Web.UI.Page
  {
    . . . code continues . . .
  }
}
```

6. In the `Page_Load()` event handler, get an instance of the current channel and display its path in the `litParentChannel` literal:

```
private void Page_Load(object sender, System.EventArgs e)
{
  // Display the parent channel's path
  litParentChannel.Text = CmsHttpContext.Current.Channel.Path;
}
```

7. Toggle back to Design view and double-click on the btnCreate button to get to the btnCreate_OnClick() event handler. Enter the code shown below:

```
private void btnCreate_Click(object sender, System.EventArgs e)
{
  // IMPORTANT: You must be in update mode for the code to work
  CmsHttpContext cmsContext = CmsHttpContext.Current;
  Channel parentChannel = cmsContext.Channel;

  try
  {
    // get the template the new posting would be based on
    Template template;
    template = cmsContext.Searches.GetByPath(txtTemplate.Text)
        as Template;
    if (template != null)
    {
      // check if we can create a posting
      if (!parentChannel.CanCreatePostings)
      {
        throw new Exception("Current user does not have "
                      + "permissions to create postings in channel: "
                      + "parentChannel.Path);
      }

      // get the name of the posting
      string Name = txtName.Text.Trim();

      if (!Utility.ValidateMCMSObjectName(Name))
      {
        throw new Exception("Specified posting name is not "
                      + "valid. May contain only alphanumeric "
                      + "characters, open or close parens, "
                      + "hyphens, underscores, periods, or "
                      + "spaces. No period at the end and no "
                      + "consecutive periods are allowed. ");
      }

      // create the new posting
      Posting newPosting;
      newPosting = parentChannel.CreatePosting(template);

      // set the properties of the new posting
      newPosting.Name = txtName.Text;
      newPosting.Description = txtDescription.Text;

      // commit the changes
      cmsContext.CommitAll();

      // display the success message
      lblErrorMessage.Text = "Posting created successfully!";
    }
    else
    {
      // could not access the specified template
      lblErrorMessage.Text = "Invalid Template path or you "
                      + "don't have the appropriate permissions to "
                      + "use the specified Template.";
    }
  }
  catch(Exception ex)
  {
    // rollback the changes
    cmsContext.RollbackAll();

    // after a rollback it is required to dispose of the CMS context
    cmsContext.Dispose();
```

```
        // display the error message
        lblErrorMessage.Text = ex.Message;
    }
}
```

This code first accesses the parent channel, which is the channel in which the new posting will be created. Next, based on the template path entered, we use the `Searches.GetByPath()` method to get an instance of the template object the new posting should be based on. If the template object is accessible, we pass it as an input parameter to the `Channel.CreatePosting()` method, which creates the new posting.

Once the posting has been created, we set its property values. In this example, we set the `Name` and `Description` properties to the values entered in the textboxes. You may wish to enhance this dialog to include input controls for setting all writable properties and placeholders of the posting.

The new posting isn't saved to the repository until a call to `cmsContext.CommitAll()` is made. If errors occur, a message is displayed in the `lblErrorMessage` label.

Save and build the solution. To see it in action:

1. Open `http://localhost/CMSExplorer`.
2. Click on MyNewChannel to see its contents. The channel is currently empty as we have not created any postings or channels in it.
3. From the toolbar, select New | New Posting. This will open a new browser window containing the Create Posting dialog.
4. In the Create Posting dialog, enter:

Property	Value
Name	My New Posting
Description	This posting was created using the PAPI!
Template Path	/Templates/TropicalGreen/PlantCatalog/Plant

5. Click Create Posting and then click Close.
6. Click Refresh in the main window. The new posting is created in the channel!

I'm getting the following exception: "Unable to retrieve PostingEvents. The module Microsoft.ContentManagement.Publishing.Events.PostingEventsModule must be included in the section of the web.config and must be assigned the name 'CmsPosting'." What do I do?

It's likely you didn't create an MCMS Web Application project in Chapter 1 and instead you created a regular ASP.NET Web Application. When you create an MCMS Web Application, it adds `HttpModules` to the `web.config` of the application.

To convert an ASP.NET Web Application to a MCMS Web Application, select Enable as MCMS project from the Project menu in Visual Studio .NET.

> If you have installed the Tropical Green project created in the MCMS book *Building Websites using Microsoft Content Management Server* (as mentioned in Chapter 1, *Building CMS Explorer*), note that because CMS Explorer is in a different application scope to Tropical Green, workflow event handlers added to the `global.ascx.cs` file of the Tropical Green project will not be triggered.

Connected Postings

Connected pages are two different copies of a posting object that share the same placeholder values. Because connected postings share placeholder definitions and values, any changes to the properties of one posting will be reflected in all its connected postings.

Let's create a Create Connected Posting dialog:

1. Add a web form named `CreateConnectedPosting.aspx` to the CMSExplorer project.

2. Drag and drop `Styles.css` onto the web form.

3. Toggle to HTML view and add the following table consisting of six rows between the `<form>` tags.

```
<table>
<tr>
  <td colspan="2">
    <h1>Create Connected Posting</h1>
    <h2>Original Posting: (Add Literal for displaying the path here)</h2>
  </td>
</tr>
<tr>
  <td>Display Name:</td>
  <td>(Add the text box for the Name here)</td>
</tr>
<tr>
  <td>Template Path:</td>
  <td>(Add the text box for the Template File here)</td>
</tr>
<tr>
  <td>Destination Channel:</td>
  <td>(Add the text box for the Destination Channel here)</td>
</tr>

<tr>
  <td colspan="2">(Add the Label for displaying error messages here)</td>
</tr>
<tr>
  <td colspan="2" align="right">
    (Add the Create Connected Posting button here)
    <INPUT type="button" value="Close"
      onclick="javascript:window.close();">
  </td>
</tr>
</table>
```

4. Switch back to Design view. Drag and drop the following controls from the Web Forms section of the Toolbox.

Control	Property	Property Value
Literal	ID	litOriginalPosting
TextBox	ID	txtDisplayName
TextBox	ID	txtTemplate
TextBox	ID	txtDestination
Button	ID	btnCreate
	Text	Create Connected Posting
Label	ID	lblErrorMessage
	Text	(empty string)

Create Connected Posting

Orignal Posting: [Literal "litOriginalPosting"]

Display Name:

Template Path:

Destination Channel:

[lblErrorMessage]

| Create Connected Posting | Close |

5. While in Design view, double-click on the form to open the code-behind file. Add the namespace Microsoft.ContentManagment.Publishing:

```
. . . code continues . . .
// MCMS API
using Microsoft.ContentManagement.Publishing;

namespace CmsExplorer
{
  . . . code continues . . .
}
```

6. In the Page_Load() event handler, we get an instance of the posting on which the connected posting will be based (or the original posting) and display its path in the litOriginalPosting literal. We will first retrieve the GUID of the posting from the CmsObjectGuid querystring parameter then use the Searches.GetByGuid() method to get an instance of it.

```
private void Page_Load(object sender, System.EventArgs e)
{
  // Display the path of the original posting
  Posting posting = CmsHttpContext.Current.Searches.GetByGuid(
            Request.QueryString["CMSObjectGuid"]) as Posting;
  if (posting != null)
    litOriginalPosting.Text = posting.Path;
  else
    lblErrorMessage.Text = "Requested posting does not exist.";
}
```

Connected postings are created in a very similar way to creating a new posting. To create a connected posting, call the `Channel.CreateConnectedPosting()` method. The method takes two parameters:

- The template the posting should be based on (the template needs to be identical to the template of the original posting or it needs to be a connected template of the original template).

- The original posting.

7. Switch back to Design view. Double-click on the btnCreate button to get to the btnCreate_Click() event handler. Add the code as shown:

```
private void btnCreate_Click(object sender, System.EventArgs e)
{
    CmsHttpContext cmsContext = CmsHttpContext.Current;
    Posting originalPosting;
    originalPosting = cmsContext.Searches.GetByGuid(
            Request.QueryString["CMSObjectGuid"]) as Posting;

    if ( originalPosting != null )
    {
        try
        {
            // get the destination channel
            Channel destination;
            destination = cmsContext.Searches.GetByPath(txtDestination.Text)
                    as Channel;

            if ( destination != null )
            {
                // check if the current user has permissions to
                // create postings in the target channel

                if (!destination.CanCreatePostings)
                {
                    throw new Exception("Current user does not have permissions "
                            + "to create postings in channel: "
                            + destination.Path);
                }

                // get the connected template
                Template connectedT;
                connectedT = cmsContext.Searches.GetByPath(txtTemplate.Text)
                        as Template;
                if ( connectedT != null )
                {
                    if ( connectedT.CanUseForAuthoring )
                    {
                        // create the connected posting
                        Posting newConnectedPosting;
                        newConnectedPosting = destination.CreateConnectedPosting(
                                connectedT, originalPosting);

                        // set the properties of the connected posting
                        newConnectedPosting.DisplayName = txtDisplayName.Text;

                        // commit the changes
                        cmsContext.CommitAll();

                        // display the success message
                        lblErrorMessage.Text = "Connected Posting created
successfully!";
                    }
```

```
                else
                {
                    throw new Exception("Current user does not have permissions "
                                  + "to create postings using template: "
                                  + connectedT.Path);
                }
            }
        }
        else
        {
            lblErrorMessage.Text = "Destination Channel not found";
        }
    }
    catch(Exception ex)
    {
        // rollback the changes
        cmsContext.RollbackAll();

        // after a rollback it is required to dispose of the CMS context
        cmsContext.Dispose();

        // display the error message
        lblErrorMessage.Text = ex.Message;
    }
}
else
{
    //display the error message
    lblErrorMessage.Text = "Requested posting does not exist.";
}
}
```

Save and build the solution.

The code first gets an instance of the destination channel specified in the txtDestination textbox. It then checks to see if the user has rights to create postings in the destination channel by looking at the value returned by the Channel.CanCreatePostings property value.

Once we have ascertained that the destination channel exists and that the user has the appropriate rights to create the postings within the channel, we get an instance of the connected template. The connected template's path is retrieved from the txtTemplate textbox. We proceed only if:

- The connected template exists.
- The current user has the rights to use the template to create postings. This is checked by looking at the value returned by the Template.CanUseForAuthoring property.

To create a connected posting, a call to Channel.CreateConnectedPosting() is made. We pass in both the template and the original posting as input parameters. After the connected posting has been created, we set its properties. Here, we've set its Display Name based on the value entered in the txtDisplayName text box. You can, of course, set any writable property of the posting (bear in mind that it is connected and changes to certain property definitions and values may affect other connected postings).

If all goes well, a success message is displayed on the screen. Otherwise, an error message is displayed instead and the entire operation is rolled back.

Try adding a connected posting using the dialog that we've just created.

1. Open `http://localhost/CMSExplorer`.
2. Click on MyNewChannel.
3. Click the Edit link next to the My New Posting posting we created earlier.
4. Click Create Connected Posting.
5. In the Create Connected Posting dialog, enter:

Property	Value
Display Name	MyConnectedPosting
Template Path	/Templates/TropicalGreen/PlantCatalog/Plant
Destination Channel	/Channels/TropicalGreen/

6. Click Create Connected Posting and then click Close.
7. Back at CMS Explorer, navigate to the TropicalGreen channel. You should see the new connected posting.

Copying Postings

Postings can be copied from one channel to another or even to the same channel. Unlike connected postings, postings that are created from the copy action exist as independent entities. They do not share placeholder values, and so changes to the properties of the original posting do not affect the copy in any way.

Copying can be done using the `Posting.CopyTo()` method. Let's create a Copy Posting dialog for CMS Explorer:

1. Add a new web form to the CMSExplorer project. Name the new web form `CopyPosting.aspx`.

2. In Design view, drag and drop the `Styles.css` file from Solution Explorer onto the form. This applies the stylesheet to the page.

3. Toggle to HTML view and add the code as shown below for a table with four rows, between the `<form>` tags:

```
<table>
<tr>
  <td colspan="2">
    <h1>Copy Posting</h1>
    <h2>Original Path: (Add Literal for displaying the path here)</h2>
  </td>
</tr>
<tr>
  <td>Destination Channel:</td>
  <td>(Add the text box for the Destination Channel here)</td>
<tr>
  <td colspan="2">(Add the Label for displaying error messages here)</td>
</tr>
<tr>
  <td colspan="2" align="right">
    (Add the Copy Posting button here)
    <INPUT type="button" value="Close"
```

```
            onclick="javascript:window.close();">
    </td>
  </tr>
</table>
```

4. Switch back to Design view. Drag and drop controls onto the web form and arrange them as shown in the screenshot overleaf.

Control	Property	Property Value
Literal	ID	litCurrentPosting
TextBox	ID	txtDestination
Button	ID	btnCopy
	Text	Copy Posting
Label	ID	lblErrorMessage
	Text	(empty string)

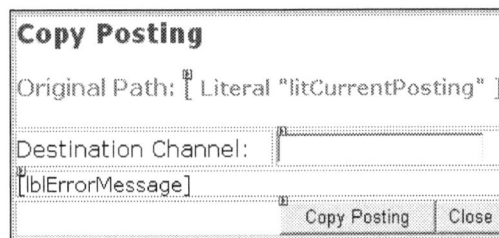

Copy Posting

Original Path: [Literal "litCurrentPosting"]

Destination Channel: [_____]

[lblErrorMessage]

[Copy Posting] [Close]

5. Double-click on the web form to get to its code-behind file. Import the `Microsoft.ContentManagement.Publishing` namespace. We will put the path of the posting we're copying into the `litCurrentPosting` label within the `Page_Load()` event handler.

```
. . . code continues . . .
// MCMS PAPI
using Microsoft.ContentManagement.Publishing;

namespace CmsExplorer
{
  /// <summary>
  /// Summary description for CopyPosting.
  /// </summary>
  public class CopyPosting : System.Web.UI.Page
  {
    protected System.Web.UI.WebControls.TextBox txtDestination;
    protected System.Web.UI.WebControls.Label lblErrorMessage;
    protected System.Web.UI.WebControls.Button btnCopy;
    protected System.Web.UI.WebControls.Literal litCurrentPosting;

    private void Page_Load(object sender, System.EventArgs e)
    {
      // display the path of the posting to be copied
      Posting posting = CmsHttpContext.Current.Searches.GetByGuid(
                    Request.QueryString["CMSObjectGuid"]) as Posting;

      if (posting != null)
        litCurrentPosting.Text = posting.Path;
```

```
      else
         lblErrorMessage.Text = "Requested posting does not exist.";
}

   . . . code continues . . .
```

6. Toggle back to Design view and double-click on the btnCopy button. In the
    btnCopy_Click() event handler, add the code as follows:

```
private void btnCopy_Click(object sender, System.EventArgs e)
{
    CmsHttpContext cmsContext = CmsHttpContext.Current;

    // get the posting to be copied
    Posting currentPosting;
    currentPosting = cmsContext.Searches.GetByGuid(
                    Request.QueryString["CMSObjectGuid"]) as Posting;

    if (currentPosting != null)
    {
       try
       {
          // get the destination channel
          Channel destination;
          destination = cmsContext.Searches.GetByPath(
                  txtDestination.Text) as Channel;

          if (destination != null)
          {
             // check if we can create postings
             if (!destination.CanCreatePostings)
             {
                throw new Exception("Current user does not have "
                        + "permissions to create postings "
                        + "in channel: " + destination.Path);
             }

             // copy the posting
             Posting copiedPosting;
             copiedPosting = currentPosting.CopyTo(destination);

             // you can proceed to set the properties of the
             // copied posting
             // e.g. copiedPosting.DisplayName =
             //            "A Copy of the posting";

             // commit the changes
             cmsContext.CommitAll();

             // display the success message
             lblErrorMessage.Text = "Posting copied successfully!";
          }
          else
          {
             // cannot access the destination channel
             lblErrorMessage.Text = "Invalid Destination channel path";
          }
       }
       catch(Exception ex)
       {
          // rollback the changes
          cmsContext.RollbackAll();

          // after a rollback it is required to dispose of the CMS context
```

```
            cmsContext.Dispose();

            // display the error message
            lblErrorMessage.Text = ex.Message;
        }
    }
}
```

The code first gets a reference to the posting to be copied followed by the destination channel specified in the `txtDestination` textbox. The `Posting.CopyTo()` method accepts the destination channel object as an input parameter. Once the copy has been created, you can proceed to set its properties. The copy operation will only be persisted after a call to `CommitAll()` is made.

In order to test the Copy Posting dialog, we first create a channel to which to copy the postings:

1. Navigate to `http://localhost/CmsExplorer`.
2. Select New | New Channel.
3. Name the new channel MyNewChannel2. Click Create Channel and then click Close.
4. Click MyNewChannel.
5. Click the Edit button on the row for My New Posting.
6. Click Copy. This will open a new browser window containing the Copy Posting dialog.
7. In the Copy Posting dialog, enter /Channels/MyNewChannel2 in the Destination Channel textbox, click Copy Posting, and then click Close.

Notice that a copy of My New Posting is created in MyNewChannel2. The copied posting has the same properties and placeholder content as the original posting with the following exceptions:

- `CreatedBy`, `LastModifiedBy`, and `OwnedBy`; which hold the server account of the person who executed the copy
- `CreatedDate` and `LastModifiedDate`; which contain the date and time that the copy operation was carried out

After copying, the copied posting's state is `Saved`. It has to be approved before it is published.

Moving Postings

You can change the parent container of a posting by moving it. Postings can be moved in both the Web Author (using the Move Posting option) and Site Manager (dragging and dropping postings from one channel to another). Once moved, postings require moderator approval if any are assigned for the destination channel.

The PAPI provides the `Posting.MoveTo()` method to move postings using code. One common application of the method is to automatically approve postings that are moved. When reorganizing large numbers of postings, it is often quicker to write a script to automate the move and to approve them immediately instead of performing these steps manually.

To see how the `Posting.MoveTo()` method is used within code, we'll create a Move Posting dialog for CMS Explorer:

1. Add a new web form to the CMSExplorer project. Name the new web form `MovePosting.aspx`.

2. In Design view, drag and drop the `styles.css` file from Solution Explorer onto the form.

3. Toggle to HTML view. Add the following code for a table with four rows between the `<form>` tags.

```
<table>
<tr>
  <td colspan="2">
    <h1>Move Posting</h1>
    <h2>Original Path: (Add Literal for displaying the path here)</h2>
  </td>
</tr>
<tr>
  <td>Destination Channel:</td>
  <td>(Add the text box for the Destination Channel here)</td>
<tr>
  <td colspan="2">(Add the Label for displaying error messages here)</td>
</tr>
<tr>
  <td colspan="2" align="right">
  (Add the Move Posting button here)
    <INPUT type="button" value="Close"
     onclick="javascript:window.close();">
  </td>
</tr>
</table>
```

4. In Design view, add controls and arrange them as shown in the diagram below:

Control	Property	Property Value
Literal	ID	litCurrentPosting
TextBox	ID	txtDestination
Button	ID	btnMove
	Text	Move Posting
Label	ID	lblErrorMessage
	Text	(empty string)

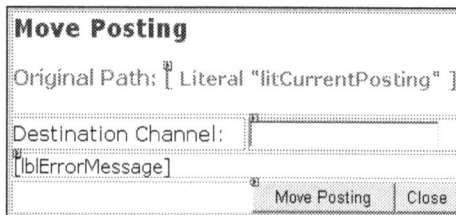

5. Double-click on the form to get to the code-behind file. As before, import the `Microsoft.ContentManagement.Publishing` namespace. In the `Page_Load()` event handler, populate the `litCurrentPosting` Literal with the path of the posting to be moved.

```
. . . code continues . . .
// MCMS PAPI
using Microsoft.ContentManagement.Publishing;

namespace CmsExplorer
{
    /// <summary>
    /// Summary description for MovePosting.
    /// </summary>
    public class MovePosting : System.Web.UI.Page
    {
        protected System.Web.UI.WebControls.TextBox txtDestination;
        protected System.Web.UI.WebControls.Label lblErrorMessage;
        protected System.Web.UI.WebControls.Button btnMove;
        protected System.Web.UI.WebControls.Literal litCurrentPosting;

        private void Page_Load(object sender, System.EventArgs e)
        {
            // display the path of the posting to be moved
            Posting currentPosting;
            currentPosting = CmsHttpContext.Current.Searches.GetByGuid(
                    Request.QueryString["CMSObjectGuid"]) as Posting;
            if (currentPosting != null)
                litCurrentPosting.Text = currentPosting.Path;
            else
                lblErrorMessage.Text = "Requested posting does not exist.";
        }

        #region Web Form Designer generated code
            . . . code continues . . .
        #endregion
    }
}
```

6. Toggle to Design view and double-click on the btnMove button. In the
    btnMove_Click() event handler, add the following code:

```
private void btnMove_Click(object sender, System.EventArgs e)
{
    CmsHttpContext cmsContext = CmsHttpContext.Current;

    // get the posting to be moved
    Posting currentPosting = cmsContext.Searches.GetByGuid(
        Request.QueryString["CMSObjectGuid"]) as Posting;

    if (currentPosting != null)
    {
        try
        {
            // get the destination channel
            Channel destination;
            destination = cmsContext.Searches.GetByPath(
                    txtDestination.Text) as Channel;

            if (destination != null)
            {
                // check if we can create postings
                if (!destination.CanCreatePostings)
                    throw new Exception("Current user does not have permissions "
                                        + " to create postings in channel: "
                                        + destination.Path);

                currentPosting.MoveTo(destination);

                // you can approve the posting
                // or set its properties here
                // e.g. currentPosting.Approve();

                cmsContext.CommitAll();
```

```
            // display the success message
            lblErrorMessage.Text = "Posting moved successfully!";
        }
        else
        {
            lblErrorMessage.Text = "Invalid Destination Channel";
        }
    }
    catch(Exception ex)
    {
        // rollback the changes
        cmsContext.RollbackAll();

        // after a rollback it is required to dispose of the CMS context
        cmsContext.Dispose();

        // display the error message
        lblErrorMessage.Text = ex.Message;
    }
    }
    else
    {
        lblErrorMessage.Text = "Requested posting does not exist.";
    }
}
```

The `Posting.MoveTo()` method accepts the destination channel as an input parameter. In the code above, we use the `Searches.GetByPath()` method to get the destination channel based on the path entered in the `txtDestination` textbox. If the channel exists, we pass it in as an input parameter to the `Posting.MoveTo()` method.

Let's see the move in action. First, if you haven't already done so, build the CMSExplorer project, then:

1. Open `http://localhost/CMSExplorer`.
2. Click on MyNewChannel.
3. Click on the Edit button of the MyPosting posting and click Move.
4. In the Move Posting dialog, enter `/Channels/MyNewChannel2/` as the destination channel. Click Move Posting.

And `MyPosting` gets moved from `MyNewChannel` to `MyNewChannel2`.

Moving postings does not modify any of their placeholder or property values. However, if there are moderators assigned to the destination channel, the posting would be in a "Waiting For Moderator Approval" state. At the same time, the `LastModifiedBy` and `LastModifiedDate` properties of the moved posting are modified to indicate the person who executed the move and the date and time that the operation was performed.

Summary

In this chapter we used the MCMS Publishing API (PAPI) to add additional functionality to our CMS Explorer management application. We demonstrated how the PAPI can be used to create new channels and postings as well as copying or moving postings from one channel to another channel. In the next chapter, we will look at the ability to manage templates, template galleries, resources, and resource galleries with the PAPI as we continue to enhance the CMS Explorer.

Managing Templates, Template Galleries, and Resources

In this chapter, we turn our attention to three main MCMS object types—templates, template galleries, and resources. We will enhance the CMS Explorer (developed in Chapter 1) to manage these objects using the MCMS Publishing API (PAPI).

Managing Template Galleries and Templates

Out of the box, you can choose to manage template galleries and templates using either Site Manager or Template Explorer, which might be OK if you are using Visual Studio .NET as your development tool (as recommended). A compelling reason to write an administrative module to manage template galleries and templates is to work with them without having to open VS.NET. We have found this particularly useful when attempting to work in an environment where VS.NET is not installed such as on a production or a staging server. Or perhaps business requirements call for certain actions to be performed when a template gallery or template is created. Whatever the occasions may be, you may need to modify template gallery and template properties, placeholder definition and custom property collections through code.

The PAPI offers a wide range of methods and properties to work with template galleries and templates. We explore the most frequently used methods in this section, beginning with the creation of template galleries.

Creating Template Galleries

Template galleries can be created from both Site Manager and Template Explorer. Now we will show you how we can create them from code. Let's add a Create Template Gallery dialog to the CMS Explorer interface.

1. Add a new web form to the project with the name `CreateTemplateGallery.aspx`.

2. In Design view, drag and drop `styles.css` from Solution Explorer onto the web form.

3. Toggle to HTML view. Insert a table with five rows. Code it in the same way as shown overleaf. A level-1 heading with the text `Create Template Gallery` forms the first row. The rest of the table consists of text labels and temporary markers indicating where the controls should go later.

```
<table>
<tr>
  <td colspan="2">
    <h1>Create Template Gallery</h1>
    <h2>
      Parent Template Gallery:
      (Add Literal for displaying the path here)
    </h2>
  </td>
</tr>
<tr>
  <td>Name:</td>
  <td>(Add the text box for the Name here)</td>
</tr>
<tr>
  <td>Description:</td>
  <td>(Add the text box for the Description here)</td>
</tr>
<tr>
  <td colspan="2">
    (Add the Label for displaying error messages here)
  </td>
</tr>
<tr>
  <td colspan="2" align="right">
    (Add the Create Gallery button here)
    <INPUT type="button" value="Close"
      onclick="javascript:window.close();">
  </td>
</tr>
</tr>
</table>
```

4. Switch back to Design view, drag the following controls from the Web Forms section of the Toolbox onto the form and delete the text markers. Arrange them as shown in the following diagram. Template galleries only have Name and Description properties to modify.

Control	Property	Value
Literal	ID	litParentGallery
TextBox	ID	txtName
TextBox	ID	txtDescription
	Rows	3
	TextMode	MultiLine
Label	ID	lblErrorMessage
	Text	(empty string)
Button	ID	btnCreate
	Text	Create Gallery

```
Create Template Gallery

Parent Template Gallery: [ Literal "litParentGallery" ]

Name:                    [                              ]

Description:             [                         ^    ]
                         [                         v    ]

[lblErrorMessage]

                              [ Create Gallery ] [ Close ]
```

5. Add the `Microsoft.ContentManagement.Publishing` namespace to the code-behind file:

```
. . . code continues . . .
// MCMS API
using Microsoft.ContentManagement.Publishing;

namespace CmsExplorer
{
    . . . code continues . . .
}
```

6. In the `Page_Load()` event handler, we get the GUID of the parent template gallery from the `CMSObjectGuid` querystring parameter, and pass it to the `Searches.GetByGuid()` method to get a reference to the gallery itself.

```
TemplateGallery parentGallery;
CmsHttpContext cmsContext;

private void Page_Load(object sender, System.EventArgs e)
{
    cmsContext = CmsHttpContext.Current;

    lblErrorMessage.Text = String.Empty;
    string cmsObjectGuid = String.Empty;
    if (Request.QueryString["CMSObjectGuid"] != null)
    {
        cmsObjectGuid = Request.QueryString["CMSObjectGuid"];

        parentGallery = cmsContext.Searches.GetByGuid(cmsObjectGuid) as
            TemplateGallery;

        if (parentGallery != null)
        {
            litParentGallery.Text = parentGallery.Path;
        }
        else
        {
            lblErrorMessage.Text = "Parent Gallery not found!";
        }
    }
}
```

7. Toggle to Design view and double-click on the `btnCreate` button. In the `btnCreate_Click()` event handler, add the following code:

```
private void btnCreate_Click(object sender, System.EventArgs e)
{
    try
    {
        if (parentGallery.CanCreateTemplateGalleries)
```

```
            {
                // get the template gallery's name
                string name = txtName.Text.Trim();

                if (!Utility.ValidateMCMSObjectName(name))
                {
                    throw new Exception("Specified template gallery name is not "
                                + "valid. Must be only alphanumeric "
                                + "characters, open or close parens, "
                                + "hyphens, underscores, periods, or "
                                + "spaces. No period at the end and no "
                                + "consecutive periods are allowed. ");
                }

                // create the template gallery
                TemplateGallery newGallery;
                newGallery = parentGallery.CreateTemplateGallery();
                newGallery.Name = name;
                newGallery.Description = txtDescription.Text;
                cmsContext.CommitAll();

                // display the success message
                lblErrorMessage.Text = "Template Gallery created successfully!";
            }
            else
            {
                lblErrorMessage.Text = "You do not have rights to create a "
                                + "template gallery.";
            }
        }
        catch (Exception ex)
        {
            // rollback all changes
            cmsContext.RollbackAll();

            // the CMS context needs to be disposed of after a rollback
            cmsContext.Dispose();

            // display error message
            lblErrorMessage.Text = ex.Message;
        }
    }
```

Before creating the template gallery, the code performs a couple of validation checks to see if:

- The user has the rights to create sub-template galleries in the parent template gallery. This is done by checking that the TemplateGallery.CanCreateTemplateGalleries property returns a Boolean true.

- The name supplied by the user is a valid template gallery name. A valid name contains only the characters, A-Z, a-z, 0-9,-, _, (space), (), and periods. It should also not end with a period or contain two or more consecutive periods. These checks are carried out by the ValidateMCMSObjectName() method defined in Utility.cs, which we created in Chapter 2.

If all validation checks pass, the code uses the TemplateGallery.CreateTemplateGallery() method to create a new template gallery object. We then set the gallery's Name and Description properties to the values entered in the textboxes. As before, we call the CmsHttpContext.CommitAll() method to save the new template gallery to the repository.

Save and build the solution. Let's create a template gallery with our new dialog:

1. From the CMS Explorer interface, click Templates.

2. Select New | New Template Gallery.

3. In the New Template Gallery dialog, enter the following values:

Property	Value
Name	MyTemplateGallery
Description	This template gallery was created from the PAPI

4. Click Create Gallery and close the dialog. Refresh CMS Explorer and check that the new template gallery is created in the root template gallery. As an exercise, you could program the dialog to close itself and refresh the parent page automatically.

Creating Templates

Another useful feature of the PAPI is its ability to generate templates through code. This is particularly useful when you need to generate many templates, consisting of placeholder and custom property definitions based on some predefined logic (for instance, a schema from a legacy application that is to be migrated to MCMS).

In this exercise, we will build a Create Template dialog for CMS Explorer:

1. Add a new web form to the CMS Explorer project. Name the new form `CreateTemplate.aspx`.

2. In Design view, drag and drop `styles.css` from Solution Explorer onto the web form.

3. Toggle to HTML view and add a table consisting of six rows as shown below:

```
<table>
<tr>
  <td colspan="2">
    <h1>Create Template</h1>
    <h2>
      Parent Template Gallery:
      (Add Literal for displaying the path here)
    </h2>
  </td>
</tr>
<tr>
  <td>Name:</td>
  <td>(Add text box for the Name here)</td>
</tr>
<tr>
  <td>Description:</td>
  <td>(Add text box for the Description here)</td>
</tr>
<tr>
  <td>Source File:</td>
  <td>(Add text box for the source file here)</td>
</tr>
<tr>
  <td colspan="2">(Add the label for displaying error messages here)</td>
</tr>
<tr>
```

```
        <td colspan="2" align="right">
          (Add the Create Template button here)
          <INPUT type="button" value="Close"
            onclick="javascript:window.close();">
        </td>
      </tr>
      </table>
```

4. In Design view, add controls from the Web Forms section of the Toolbox and
    arrange them as described below:

Control	Property	Value
Literal	ID	litParentGallery
TextBox	ID	txtName
TextBox	ID	txtDescription
	Rows	3
	TextMode	MultiLine
TextBox	ID	txtSourceFile
Label	ID	lblErrorMessage
	Text	(empty string)
Button	ID	btnCreate
	Text	Create Template

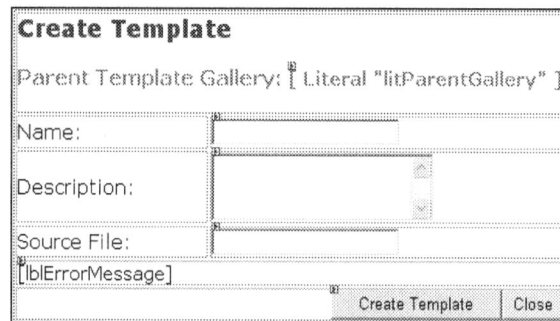

Create Template

Parent Template Gallery: [Literal "litParentGallery"]

Name:

Description:

Source File:

[lblErrorMessage]

| | Create Template | Close |

5. In the code-behind file, add the following namespaces:

    . . . code continues . . .

```
// MCMS API
using Microsoft.ContentManagement.Publishing;

// Following is required for creating placeholder definitions
using Microsoft.ContentManagement.Publishing.Extensions.Placeholders;

namespace CmsExplorer
{
  . . . code continues . . .
}
```

6. In the `Page_Load()` event handler, add code that gets a reference to the current `CmsHttpContext` object as well as a reference to the parent template gallery in which to create the new template.

```
private TemplateGallery parentGallery;
private CmsHttpContext cmsContext;

private void Page_Load(object sender, System.EventArgs e)
{
  cmsContext = CmsHttpContext.Current;

  lblErrorMessage.Text = String.Empty;

  string cmsObjectGuid = String.Empty;
  if (Request.QueryString["CMSObjectGuid"] != null)
  {
    cmsObjectGuid = Request.QueryString["CMSObjectGuid"];
    parentGallery = cmsContext.Searches.GetByGuid(cmsObjectGuid)
          as TemplateGallery;

    if (parentGallery != null)
    {
      litParentGallery.Text = parentGallery.Path;
    }
    else
    {
      lblErrorMessage.Text = "Parent Gallery not found!";
    }
  }
}
```

7. Toggle to Design view and double-click on the `btnCreate` button. In the `btnCreate_Click()` event handler, add the code shown below:

```
private void btnCreate_Click(object sender, System.EventArgs e)
{
  try
  {
    // create the new template
    Template newTemplate;

    if (parentGallery.CanCreateTemplates)
    {
      // get the template's name
      string name = txtName.Text.Trim();

      if (!Utility.ValidateMCMSObjectName(name))
      {
        throw new Exception("Specified template gallery name is not "
                + "valid. Must be only alphanumeric "
                + "characters, open or close parens, "
                + "hyphens, underscores, periods, or "
                + "spaces. No period at the end and no "
                + "consecutive periods are allowed. ");
      }

      newTemplate = parentGallery.CreateTemplate();
      newTemplate.Name = name;
      newTemplate.Description = txtDescription.Text;
      newTemplate.SourceFile = txtSourceFile.Text;

      // commit the changes
      cmsContext.CommitAll();

      // display the success message
      lblErrorMessage.Text = "Template created successfully!";
    }
```

```
      else
      {
        lblErrorMessage.Text =
              "You do not have rights to create a template.";
      }
    }
    catch(Exception ex)
    {
      // rollback all changes
      cmsContext.RollbackAll();

      // the CMS context needs to be disposed of after a rollback
      cmsContext.Dispose();

      // display error message
      lblErrorMessage.Text = ex.Message;
    }
  }
```

As before, the code performs the following validation checks before creating the template:

- Checks to see if the user has the necessary rights to create templates in the current template gallery. We do this by retrieving the value of the TemplateGallery.CanCreateTemplates property.

- Checks the name supplied in the txtName text box to see if it is a valid name. The same rules as for naming template galleries apply to templates.

The code basically uses the TemplateGallery.CreateTemplate() method to create the template. Once it has been created (and before we assign its Name, Description and SourceFile property values), the new template gets the following property values:

- The Custom Property and Placeholder Definition collections are both empty.

- CreatedBy, LastModifiedBy, and OwnedBy reflect the user that carried out the create template operation.

- CreatedDate and LastModifiedDate contain the date and time that the template was created.

- The template's state is New.

- Its name is New Template.

- SourceFile and Description are empty strings.

Once the template has been successfully created, we assign the new template the name, description, and source file values entered in the textboxes. Note that SourceFile is the PAPI equivalent of the Template File property seen in Template Explorer.

As before, in order for the changes to be made permanent, we commit them to the database. The CmsHttpContext.CommitAll() method is similar to the Save function in Template Explorer. Once committed, the state of the template changes from New to Saved. Should there be any errors, the message is displayed in the label and all changes are rolled back.

Submitting the Template

After the template has been created and committed to the repository, it will be in the Saved state. Until it is published, by checking it in with Template Explorer, other template designers are not able to modify it. The equivalent of checking in templates in the PAPI is the Template.Submit()

method. Once submitted, the template's state changes from Saved to Published. Authors and editors are then able to use it to create postings.

Modify the code in the btnCreate_Click() event handler to submit the new template as shown below:

```
private void btnCreate_Click(object sender, System.EventArgs e)
{
  try
  {
    // create the new template
    Template newTemplate;

    if (parentGallery.CanCreateTemplates)
    {
      // get the template's name
      string name = txtName.Text.Trim();

      if (!Utility.ValidateMCMSObjectName(name))
      {
        throw new Exception("Specified template gallery name is not "
                    + "valid. Must be only alphanumeric "
                    + "characters, open or close parens, "
                    + "hyphens, underscores, periods, or "
                    + "spaces. No period at the end and no "
                    + "consecutive periods are allowed. ");
      }

      newTemplate = parentGallery.CreateTemplate();
      newTemplate.Name = name;
      newTemplate.Description = txtDescription.Text;
      newTemplate.SourceFile = txtSourceFile.Text;

      // commit the changes
      cmsContext.CommitAll();

      // submit the template
      if (newTemplate.CanSubmit)
      {
        newTemplate.Submit();
        cmsContext.CommitAll();

        // display the success message
        lblErrorMessage.Text = "Template created successfully!";
      }
      else
      {
        lblErrorMessage.Text = "You do not have rights to submit"
                    + " a template.";
      }

    }
    else
    {
      lblErrorMessage.Text = "You do not have rights to create a template.";
    }

  }
  catch(Exception ex)
  {
    // rollback all changes
    cmsContext.RollbackAll();

    // the CMS context needs to be disposed of after a rollback
```

```
        cmsContext.Dispose();

        // display error message
        lblErrorMessage.Text = ex.Message;
    }
}
```

The code first checks the `Template.CanSubmit` property to see if the template can be submitted by the user. If so, it then calls the `Template.Submit()` method.

Creating Custom Property Definitions

Given a template object, you can add custom property definitions to its existing collection. In this example, we are going to take another shortcut. Instead of providing a user interface for entering the name, type, and default value of the custom property (like the one found in Template Explorer), we are going straight to coding. We will create a text custom property definition that has the following properties and values:

Property	Value
Name	LastSubmittedBy
DefaultValue	(blank string)

In the `btnCreate_Click()` event handler, add the following code within the `try` block:

```
private void btnCreate_Click(object sender, System.EventArgs e)
{
    try
    {
        // create the new template
        Template newTemplate;

        if (parentGallery.CanCreateTemplates)
        {
            . . . code continues . . .

            newTemplate = parentGallery.CreateTemplate();
            newTemplate.Name = txtName.Text;
            newTemplate.Description = txtDescription.Text;
            newTemplate.SourceFile = txtSourceFile.Text;

            // create the custom property definition
            CustomPropertyDefinition customProp;
            customProp = newTemplate.CreateCustomPropertyDefinition();
            customProp.Name = "LastSubmittedBy";
            customProp.DefaultValue = String.Empty;

            // commit the changes
            cmsContext.CommitAll();

            // submit the template
            if (newTemplate.CanSubmit)
            {
                newTemplate.Submit();
                cmsContext.CommitAll();

                // display the success message
                lblErrorMessage.Text = "Template created successfully!";
            }
            else
            {
```

```
              lblErrorMessage.Text = "You do not have rights to submit"
                                    + " a template.";
            }

        }
        else
        {
            lblErrorMessage.Text = "You do not have rights to create a template.";
        }

    }
    catch(Exception ex)
    {
        // rollback all changes
        cmsContext.RollbackAll();

        // the CMS context needs to be disposed of after a rollback
        cmsContext.Dispose();

        // display error message
        lblErrorMessage.Text = ex.Message;
    }
}
```

The code uses the `Template.CreateCustomPropertyDefinition()` method to add a custom property definition to the template. Once the custom property has been created, we assign its property values.

> When creating a template and adding custom property definitions to it with the PAPI, you must call `CommitAll()` somewhere between the `TemplateGallery.CreateTemplate()` and `Template.Submit()` calls. Otherwise, you will find that the template has an additional custom property definition named `NewCustomPropertyDefinitionX` (where X is an incremental number). This is a known bug with the PAPI.

In this example, we added a simple text custom property definition. For the more complex selection custom property definition, the technique is very similar. The code snippet below shows how to create a custom property definition named `MenuLocation` with four allowed values: `Left`, `Right`, `Top`, and `Bottom`. It specifies `Top` as the default value.

```
CustomPropertyDefinition customPropSelection;
customPropSelection = newTemplate.CreateCustomPropertyDefinition();
customPropSelection.Name = "MenuLocation";
customPropSelection.AddAllowedValue("Left");
customPropSelection.AddAllowedValue("Right");
customPropSelection.AddAllowedValue("Top");
customPropSelection.AddAllowedValue("Bottom");
customPropSelection.DefaultValue = "Top";
```

Creating Placeholder Definitions

Placeholder definitions can be created programmatically too, thanks to the PAPI's `Template.CreatePlaceholderDefinition()` method. You can add any placeholder definition to a template. Before you do so, it is a good idea to import its namespace, which is why we imported `Microsoft.ContentManagement.Publishing.Extensions.Placeholders` earlier.

In this example, we add an `HTMLPlaceholderDefinition` to the newly created template. As before, we are going to take a shortcut here and have the placeholder definition automatically created with the following property values:

Property	Value
Name	BigBoxOfContent
Description	A placeholder created from the PAPI
AllowHyperlinks	True
AllowLineBreaks	True
AllowAttachments	True
AllowImages	True
MustUseResourceGallery	False
UseGeneratedIcon	False
Formatting	FullFormatting

The `Template.CreatePlaceholderDefinition()` method accepts a single input parameter. It could be one of two objects:

- A placeholder definition type. You can create a new `HtmlPlaceholderDefinition`, `XmlPlaceholderDefinition`, `ImagePlaceholderDefinition`, `AttachmentPlaceholderDefinition`, or use one of your own creation.

- An existing placeholder definition to create copies of. Using this method, the new placeholder definition will inherit the properties of the specified placeholder definition.

Add the highlighted code to the `btnCreate_Click()` event handler. The code creates an `HtmlPlaceholderDefinition` based on the property values defined in the table above.

```
private void btnCreate_Click(object sender, System.EventArgs e)
{
  try
  {
    // create the new template
    Template newTemplate;

    if (parentGallery.CanCreateTemplates)
    {
      newTemplate = parentGallery.CreateTemplate();
      newTemplate.Name = txtName.Text;
      newTemplate.Description = txtDescription.Text;
      newTemplate.SourceFile = txtSourceFile.Text;

      // create the custom property definition
      CustomPropertyDefinition customProp;
      customProp = newTemplate.CreateCustomPropertyDefinition();
      customProp.Name = "LastSubmittedBy";
      customProp.DefaultValue = String.Empty;

      // create the placeholder definitions
      HtmlPlaceholderDefinition placeholderDef;
      placeholderDef = newTemplate.CreatePlaceholderDefinition(
          new HtmlPlaceholderDefinition()) as HtmlPlaceholderDefinition;
      placeholderDef.Name = "BigBoxOfContent";
```

```
placeholderDef.Description = "A placeholder created from the PAPI";
placeholderDef.AllowHyperlinks = true;
placeholderDef.AllowLineBreaks = true;
placeholderDef.AllowAttachments = true;
placeholderDef.AllowImages = true;
placeholderDef.MustUseResourceGallery = false;
placeholderDef.UseGeneratedIcon = false;
placeholderDef.Formatting =
    HtmlPlaceholderDefinition.SourceFormatting.FullFormatting;

// commit the changes
cmsContext.CommitAll();

. . . code continues . . .
```

The Create Template dialog is now complete. Save and build the solution. Let's test it to see if it works:

1. In CMS Explorer, click on the Templates button. Open the MyTemplateGallery template gallery created earlier.

2. Select New | New Template.

3. In the Create Template dialog, enter the following values:

Property	Value
Name	MyTemplate
Description	This template was created using the PAPI
SourceFile	/tropicalgreen/plantcatalog/plant.aspx

4. Click Create Template and close the dialog.

5. Refresh the CMS Explorer screen and verify that MyTemplate has been created in MyTemplateGallery.

Creating Connected Templates

Connected templates are created in the same way as templates, with the exception that we now call the TemplateGallery.CreateConnectedTemplate() method.

Let's try it out:

1. Add a new web form to the project with the name CreateConnectedTemplate.aspx.

2. Drag and drop Styles.css onto the web form.

3. Toggle to HTML view and enter the following code (including the text markers):

```
<table>
<tr>
  <td colspan="2">
    <h1>Create Connected Template</h1>
    <h2>
      Original Template:
      (Add literal for displaying the path of the original template here)
    <h2>
  </td>
</tr>
<tr>
  <td>Name:</td>
  <td>(Add the text box for the Name here)</td>
```

```
</tr>
<tr>
  <td>Description:</td>
  <td>(Add the text box for the Description here)</td>
</tr>
<tr>
  <td>Source File:</td>
  <td>(Add text box for the source file here)</td>
</tr>
<tr>
  <td colspan="2">(Add the Label for displaying error messages here)</td>
</tr>
<tr>
  <td colspan="2" align="right">
    (Add the Create Connected Template button here)
    <INPUT type="button" value="Close"
      onclick="javascript:window.close();">
  </td>
</tr>
</table>
```

4. Switch to Design view. Drag and drop the following controls from the Web Forms section of the Toolbox and delete the text markers.

Control	Property	Value
Literal	ID	litOriginalTemplate
TextBox	ID	txtName
TextBox	ID	txtDescription
	Rows	3
	TextMode	MultiLine
TextBox	ID	txtSourceFile
Label	ID	lblErrorMessage
	Text	(empty string)
Button	ID	btnCreate
	Text	Create Connected Template

The completed web form in Design view looks like this:

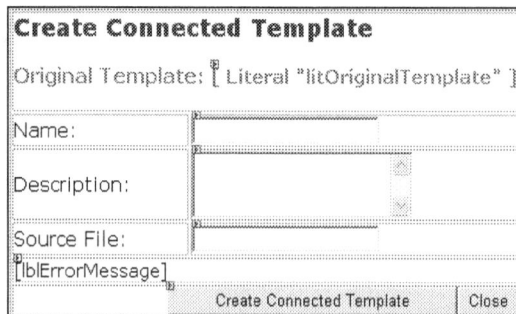

5. Now let's get an instance of the template (or the original template) on which to base the connected template. Before we do so, first consider how template designers and administrators create connected templates from CMS Explorer. They will:

- Click the Templates button.

- Navigate to the template gallery that contains the original template.

- Click the Edit link next to the original template.

- Select the Create Connected Template link.

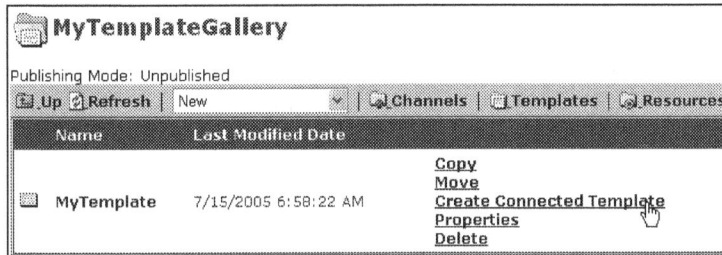

Coded within the Create Connected Template link is the path to `CreateConnectedTemplate.aspx` and a querystring parameter named `CMSObjectGuid`, which contains the GUID of the original template. Here's a sample of the generated URL, split on to several lines for readability:

```
http://localhost/cmsexplorer/CreateConnectedTemplate.aspx?
NRMODE=Update
&FRAMELESS=true
&CMSObjectGuid=%7b5010EF8C-C33C-4F68-8430-D8DFAABA2EE0%7d
&NRNODEGUID=%7bE4D19123-9DD3-11D1-B44E-006097071264%7d
```

In order to get an instance of the original template, we will extract the GUID from the `CMSObjectGuid` querystring parameter and pass it as the input parameter for the `Searches.GetByGuid()` method.

To show that we really have an instance of the original template, we will display the path of the original template on the screen. If, for some reason, we are not able to get an instance of the template, an error message will be displayed instead. We'll add the code that does the job next.

1. Double-click anywhere on the web form to get to its code-behind file. Add the `Microsoft.ContentManagement.Publishing` namespace.

```
. . . code continues . . .
// MCMS API
using Microsoft.ContentManagement.Publishing;

namespace CmsExplorer
{
 . . . code continues . . .
}
```

2. Above and within the `Page_Load()` event handler, add the highlighted code:

```
private CmsHttpContext cmsContext;
private Template originalTemplate;

private void Page_Load(object sender, System.EventArgs e)
```

```
        {
            cmsContext = CmsHttpContext.Current;

            // Clear all error messages, if any.
            lblErrorMessage.Text = String.Empty;

            // Get an instance of the original template
            string cmsObjectGuid = String.Empty;
            if (Request.QueryString["CMSObjectGuid"] != null)
            {
                cmsObjectGuid = Request.QueryString["CMSObjectGuid"];
                originalTemplate = cmsContext.Searches.GetByGuid(cmsObjectGuid)
                        as Template;

                if (originalTemplate!=null)
                {
                    // Display the template's path
                    litOriginalTemplate.Text = originalTemplate.Path;
                }
                else
                {
                    // Uh-oh we can't get an instance of the template.
                    lblErrorMessage.Text = "Original Template not found!";
                }
            }
        }
```

3. Now that we have an instance of the original template, we are ready to create a connected template. A couple of checks are first done to ensure that the user has rights to create templates in the destination template gallery as well as that the name given to the new template is valid.

    The `TemplateGallery.CreateConnectedTemplate()` method takes the original template as an input parameter and returns a reference to the new connected template. We set the name, description, and source file properties of the new connected template based on the values entered by the user in the textboxes provided. Double-click on the `btnCreate` button to get to the `btnCreate_Click()` event handler. Add the code as shown below:

```
private void btnCreate_Click(object sender, System.EventArgs e)
{
    try
    {
        // Get an instance of the template gallery
        TemplateGallery parentGallery = originalTemplate.Parent;

        // Create the new connected template
        Template newConnectedTemplate;

        if (parentGallery.CanCreateTemplates)
        {

            // get the template's name
            string name = txtName.Text.Trim();

            if (!Utility.ValidateMCMSObjectName(name))
            {
                throw new Exception("Specified template gallery name is not "
                            + "valid. Must be only alphanumeric "
                            + "characters, open or close parens, "
                            + "hyphens, underscores, periods, or "
                            + "spaces. No period at the end and no "
                            + "consecutive periods are allowed. ");
```

```
        }

        newConnectedTemplate =
            parentGallery.CreateConnectedTemplate(originalTemplate);

        //set the connected template's name
        newConnectedTemplate.Name = txtName.Text;

        //Set the connected template's description
        newConnectedTemplate.Description = txtDescription.Text;

        // Set the connected template's source file
        newConnectedTemplate.SourceFile = txtSourceFile.Text;

        // Commit the changes
        cmsContext.CommitAll();

        // Submit the connected template
        if (newConnectedTemplate.CanSubmit)
        {
          newConnectedTemplate.Submit();
          cmsContext.CommitAll();

          // display the success message
          lblErrorMessage.Text = "Connected Template created successfully!";
        }
        else
        {
          lblErrorMessage.Text = "You do not have rights to submit"
                          + " a template.";
        }
      }
      else
      {
        lblErrorMessage.Text =
                  "You do not have rights to create a template.";
      }

    }
    catch(Exception ex)
    {
      // rollback all changes
      cmsContext.RollbackAll();

      // the CMS context needs to be disposed of after a rollback
      cmsContext.Dispose();

      // display error message
      lblErrorMessage.Text = ex.Message;
    }
}
```

Try out the code!

1. On the CMS Explorer toolbar, click Templates.

2. Select the MyTemplateGallery template gallery that we created earlier.

3. Click the Edit link next for the MyTemplate template.

4. Click Create Connected Template.

5. Enter the following values in the Create Connected Template dialog:

Property	Value
Name	MyConnectedTemplate
Description	This connected template was created using the PAPI
Source File	/tropicalgreen/plantcatalog/columns.aspx

6. After you have filled in all the fields, click **Create Connected Template**.

7. Close the dialog and refresh CMS Explorer. Note that the new connected template has been created!

You can read more about creating connected templates and postings in the book *Building Websites with Microsoft Content Management Server* (Packt Publishing, January 2005, ISBN 1-904811-16-7). If you don't own this book, the relevant chapter, Chapter 6, is available to read online without charge at `http://mcmsbook.packtpub.com`.

Until the connected template is published by calling the `Template.Submit()` method, all templates connected to it will be "checked-out" by the current user and thus not available to other template designers for editing. Authors, editors, and moderators can, however, use the template for creating postings after it has been committed even though it has not been submitted.

Copying Templates

There are also methods in the PAPI for copying templates from one template gallery to another. Let's add a Copy Template dialog to CMS Explorer:

1. Add a web form named `CopyTemplate.aspx` to the project.

2. Drag and drop `Styles.css` onto the web form.

3. Toggle to HTML view and enter the following code between the `<form>` tags:

```
<table>
<tr>
  <td colspan="2">
    <h1>Copy Template</h1>
    <h2>Current Path: (Add Literal for displaying the path here)</h2>
  </td>
</tr>
<tr>
  <td>Destination Gallery:</td>
  <td>
    (Add the text box for the destination gallery here)
  </td>
</tr>
<tr>
  <td colspan="2">(Add the Label for displaying error messages here)</td>
</tr>
<tr>
  <td colspan="2" align="right">
    (Add the Copy button here)
    <INPUT type="button" value="Close"
      onclick="javascript:window.close();">
  </td>
</tr>
</table>
```

4. Switch to Design view. Drag and drop the following controls from the Web Forms section of the toolbox and set their properties as specified:

Control	Property	Value
Literal	ID	litOriginalTemplate
TextBox	ID	txtDestination
Label	ID	lblErrorMessage
	Text	(empty string)
Button	ID	btnCopy
	Text	Copy Template

Here's the completed dialog in Design view:

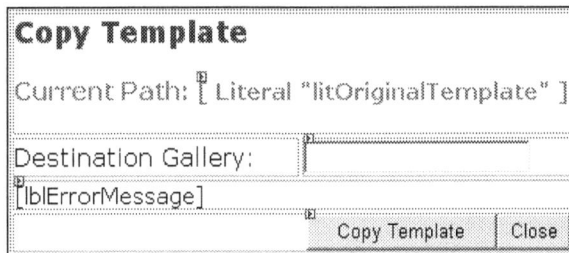

```
Copy Template

Current Path: [ Literal "litOriginalTemplate" ]

Destination Gallery: [                          ]
[lblErrorMessage]
                                    Copy Template | Close
```

To make a copy of a template, we will follow the steps below:

- o   Get an instance of the template we wish to make a copy of.
- o   Get an instance of the destination template gallery.
- o   Perform the copy operation by calling the Template.CopyTo() method.

Let's start by getting an instance of the template we wish to make a copy of.

5. Add the Microsoft.ContentManagement.Publishing namespace to the code-behind file:

```
. . . code continues . . .
// MCMS API
using Microsoft.ContentManagement.Publishing;

namespace CmsExplorer
{
   . . . code continues . . .
}
```

6. Next, we get the template's GUID from the CMSObjectGuid querystring parameter and pass it as an input parameter to the Searches.GetByGuid() method. If the method returns an instance of the template, we display its path on the screen. Otherwise, we display an error message. Add the highlighted code above and within the Page_Load() event handler.

```
private CmsHttpContext cmsContext;
private Template originalTemplate;

private void Page_Load(object sender, System.EventArgs e)
{
   cmsContext = CmsHttpContext.Current;

   // Clear all error messages, if any
   lblErrorMessage.Text = String.Empty;

   // Get an instance of the original template
   string cmsObjectGuid = String.Empty;
   if (Request.QueryString["CMSObjectGuid"] != null)
   {
      cmsObjectGuid = Request.QueryString["CMSObjectGuid"];
      originalTemplate = cmsContext.Searches.GetByGuid(cmsObjectGuid)
          as Template;

      if (originalTemplate != null)
      {
         // Display the template's path
         litOriginalTemplate.Text = originalTemplate.Path;
      }
      else
      {
         // Uh-oh we can't get an instance of the template.
         lblErrorMessage.Text = "Original Template not found!";
      }
   }
}
```

7. Now, let's get an instance of the destination template gallery. The user should have entered the path of the destination template gallery in the textbox provided. So to get an instance of the destination template gallery, we will simply use the Searches.GetByPath() method. Should the user enter an invalid path or a path of a gallery in which they do not have rights to create templates, an error message is displayed on the screen. Toggle to Design view and double-click on the btnCopy button to get to the btnCopy_Click() event handler. Add the following code:

```
private void btnCopy_Click(object sender, System.EventArgs e)
{
   try
   {
      // creating a copy of a template

      // get the destination template gallery
      TemplateGallery destinationGallery;
      string destinationGalleryPath = txtDestination.Text;
      destinationGallery = cmsContext.Searches.GetByPath(
          destinationGalleryPath) as TemplateGallery;

      if (destinationGallery != null)
      {
         if (destinationGallery.CanCreateTemplates)
         {
            // TODO:Add code to copy template here
         }
         else
         {
            // We do not have rights to create templates in the
            // specified destination template gallery
            lblErrorMessage.Text =
                      "You do not have rights to create templates "
```

80

```
                                              + "in the destination template gallery.";
            }

        }
        else
        {
            // We can't get an instance of the destination template gallery.
            lblErrorMessage.Text = "Destination Template Gallery not found!";
        }

    }
    catch(Exception ex)
    {
        // rollback all changes
        cmsContext.RollbackAll();

        // the CMS context needs to be disposed of after a rollback
        cmsContext.Dispose();

        // display error message
        lblErrorMessage.Text = ex.Message;
    }
}
```

> Go ahead and make the user interface more user-friendly by providing a Browse button for
> users to pick a destination template gallery from a tree or list instead of getting them to type
> the entire path. For the purpose of keeping the sample short, we won't go through this here.

8. With instances of both the original template and the destination template gallery, we
    are ready to start the copy operation. To do so, we will simply call the
    Template.CopyTo() method on the original template, passing the destination
    template gallery as an input parameter. The template won't be saved until we call
    CmsHttpContext.CommitAll(). We will also have to submit the template before it is
    available to other template designers. Add the code shown below:

```
private void btnCopy_Click(object sender, System.EventArgs e)
{
    . . . code continues . . .
        if (destinationGallery.CanCreateTemplates)
        {
            // copy the template
            Template copyTemplate =
                            originalTemplate.CopyTo(destinationGallery);

            // commit the copied template to the repository and its state
            // changes from "New" to "Saved"
            cmsContext.CommitAll();

            // submit it to change its state from "Saved" to "Published"
            // and to make it available to other template designers
            if (copyTemplate.CanSubmit)
            {
                copyTemplate.Submit();
                cmsContext.CommitAll();
            }

            // display the success message
            lblErrorMessage.Text = "Template copied successfully!";

        }
    . . . code continues . . .
}
```

The copied template will inherit all committed property values and custom property and placeholder definition collections from the original template.

Unlike connected templates, copied templates are not linked in any way to the original template. Updates to the original template do not change the properties, definition collection, or state of the copied template.

Let's attempt to make a copy of the Plant template:

1. In CMS Explorer, click Templates.
2. Navigate to TropicalGreen | PlantCatalog.
3. Click the Edit link for the Plant template.
4. Click Copy.
5. In the Destination Gallery field, enter /Templates/MyTemplateGallery/.
6. Click Copy Template.
7. Click Close.
8. Back at CMS Explorer, navigate to MyTemplateGallery. A copy of the Plant template now resides there.

> The only way to copy template galleries is to use Site Manager. There isn't a `TemplateGallery.CopyTo()` method in the PAPI.
>
> However, be careful when using the "Copy" function for template galleries in Site Manager. If there are connected templates within the source gallery, this relationship is not preserved in the destination gallery.

Moving Template Galleries and Templates

Template galleries and templates are moved using Template Explorer or Site Manager by dragging and dropping the object from one container into another. The PAPI offers the `TemplateGalleryItem.MoveTo()` method to move these objects programmatically.

The technique is similar to copying templates. Here's what we need to do:

- First, get a reference to the template gallery item that we wish to move.
- Next, get a reference to the destination template gallery that the template gallery item is to be moved to.
- Finally, call the `TemplateGalleryItem.MoveTo()` method.

Let's build a Move Template dialog for CMS Explorer.

Add a web form named `MoveTemplate.aspx` to the project.

1. Drag and drop `styles.css` onto the web form.
2. In HTML view, enter the following code:

```
<table>
<tr>
  <td colspan="2">
```

```
      <h1>Move Template</h1>
      (Add Literal for displaying the path here)
    </td>
  </tr>
  <tr>
    <td>Destination Gallery:</td>
    <td>
      (Add the text box for the destination gallery here)
    </td>
  </tr>
  <tr>
    <td colspan="2">(Add the Label for displaying error messages here)</td>
  </tr>
  <tr>
    <td colspan="2" align="right">
      (Add the Move Template button here)
      <INPUT type="button" value="Close"
        onclick="javascript:window.close();">
    </td>
  </tr>
</table>
```

3. Toggle to Design view. Drag and drop the following controls from the Web Forms section of the Toolbox and set their properties as shown below:

Control	Property	Value
Literal	ID	litOriginalTemplate
TextBox	ID	txtDestination
Label	ID	lblErrorMessage
	Text	(empty string)
Button	ID	btnMove
	Text	Move Template

When completed, the web form appears in Design view as shown below:

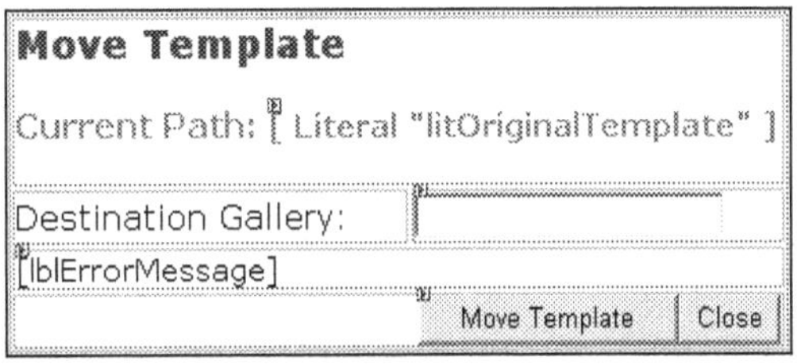

4. Double-click on the form to get to its code-behind file. Add the `Microsoft.ContentManagement.Publishing` namespace:

```
. . . code continues . . .
// MCMS PAPI
using Microsoft.ContentManagement.Publishing;

namespace CmsExplorer
{
. . . code continues . . .
}
```

5. In the Page_Load() event handler, we get an instance of the template to be moved. In previous examples, we did a check to see if the user has rights to work with an item only after the user has clicked on the button. Let's try a different approach this time. Instead of returning an error message to users who do not have the necessary permissions, we will enable or disable the button accordingly.

    We check to see if the user has rights to move the template by checking the Template.CanMove property value. If Template.CanMove returns true, it means that the user is either an administrator or assigned to a rights group that belongs to a channel manager or template designer role of the current template gallery. If the user has the rights to move the template, we keep the btnMove button enabled; otherwise, it's disabled.

    ```
    private CmsHttpContext cmsContext;
    private Template originalTemplate;

    private void Page_Load(object sender, System.EventArgs e)
    {
        cmsContext = CmsHttpContext.Current;

        // Clear all error messages, if any.
        lblErrorMessage.Text = String.Empty;

        // Get an instance of the original template
        string cmsObjectGuid = String.Empty;
        if (Request.QueryString["CMSObjectGuid"] != null)
        {
            cmsObjectGuid = Request.QueryString["CMSObjectGuid"];
            originalTemplate = cmsContext.Searches.GetByGuid(cmsObjectGuid)
                as Template;

            if (originalTemplate != null)
            {
                // Display the template's path
                litOriginalTemplate.Text = originalTemplate.Path;

                if (originalTemplate.CanMove)
                {
                    btnMove.Enabled = true;
                }
                else
                {
                    // we can't move this template.
                    lblErrorMessage.Text = "You do not have rights to "
                                        + "move this template.";
                    btnMove.Enabled = false;
                }
            }
            else
            {
                // Uh-oh we can't get an instance of the template.
                lblErrorMessage.Text = "Original Template not found!";
            }
        }
    }
    ```

6. Next, we get an instance of the destination template gallery. We perform the move operation only if the user has rights to create templates in the destination template gallery. Once we have ascertained that the destination template gallery is valid, we will call the Template.MoveTo() method, passing the instance of the destination template gallery as an input parameter. After moving a template, its state is Saved.

Until the call to `Template.Submit()` is made for the template that has been moved, other template designers are not be able to modify the moved template or any of its connected templates. Toggle to Design view and double-click on the `btnMove` button to get to the `btnMove_Click()` event handler. Add the code shown below:

```
private void btnMove_Click(object sender, System.EventArgs e)
{
  try
  {
    // Moving a template

    // get the destination template gallery
    TemplateGallery destinationGallery;
    string destinationGalleryPath = txtDestination.Text;
    destinationGallery = cmsContext.Searches.GetByPath(
        destinationGalleryPath) as TemplateGallery;
    if (destinationGallery!=null)
    {
      if (destinationGallery.CanCreateTemplates)
      {
        // move the template
        originalTemplate.MoveTo(destinationGallery);

        // commit the move to the repository and its state
        // changes to "Saved"
        cmsContext.CommitAll();

        // submit it to change its state from "Saved" to "Published"
        // and to make it available to other template designers
        if (originalTemplate.CanSubmit)
        {
          originalTemplate.Submit();
          cmsContext.CommitAll();
        }

        // display the success message
        lblErrorMessage.Text = "Template moved successfully!";
      }
      else
      {
        // We do not have rights to create templates
        // in the specified destination template gallery
        lblErrorMessage.Text = "You do not have rights to "
                              + "create templates in the "
                              + "destination template gallery.";
      }
    }
    else
    {
      // We can't get an instance of the destination template gallery.
      lblErrorMessage.Text = "Destination Template Gallery not found!";
    }

  }
  catch(Exception ex)
  {
    // rollback all changes
    cmsContext.RollbackAll();

    // the CMS context needs to be disposed of after a rollback
    cmsContext.Dispose();

    // display error message
```

```
        lblErrorMessage.Text = ex.Message;
    }
}
```

Let's move a template!

1. Navigate to the MyTemplate template that was created earlier.
2. Click Edit | Move.
3. In the Destination Gallery field, enter /templates/tropicalgreen/.
4. Click Move Template.
5. Click Close to close the dialog.
6. Back at the CMS Explorer interface, navigate to the TropicalGreen template gallery, which now contains the template, MyTemplate.

Can I use the PAPI to move template galleries?

No, template galleries can only be moved using Site Manager or Template Explorer (available in Visual Studio .NET) by dragging the template gallery and dropping it into the destination.

When template galleries are moved, all templates within it are also moved. However, unlike moving templates, moving a template gallery does not change the state of the templates it contains.

Managing Resources

The PAPI offers several methods for managing resources. In this section, we will look at how you can programmatically create and replace resources.

Creating Resources

When given the task of uploading multiple files to resource galleries, each tagged with unique names and descriptions, would you:

- Use Web Author to upload each file one at a time?
- Open Site Manager, drag all files from Windows Explorer and drop them into the resource gallery (you have to drop them actually onto the gallery icon for this to work), and toggle back to Web Author to adjust their names, display names, and descriptions?

While either of the above solutions is acceptable when the number of resources to upload is small, neither is particularly appropriate for cases where thousands of files are to be uploaded and properly tagged. It would be a tedious and time-consuming task indeed to manually handle each resource one by one.

Fortunately, using the PAPI, you can write a script to automate the job of uploading of resources. You can also set their properties how you wish as you go.

> The PAPI does not provide a method for creating resource galleries. Resource galleries can only be created by using Site Manager.

Let's build a Create Resource dialog for the CMS Explorer:

1. Add a new web form to the CMSExplorer project. Name the new web form `CreateResource.aspx`.

2. In Design view, drag and drop `styles.css` onto the web form.

3. Toggle to HTML view and add a table with six rows as shown below:

```
<table>
<tr>
  <td colspan="2">
    <h1>Create Resource</h1>
    <h2>
      Parent Resource Gallery:
      (Add Literal for displaying the path here)
    </h2>
  </td>
</tr>
<tr>
  <td>Display Name:</td>
  <td>(Add the text box for the display name here)</td>
</tr>
<tr>
  <td>Description:</td>
  <td>(Add the text box for the description here)</td>
</tr>
<tr>
  <td>File:</td>
  <td><INPUT type="file" id="File1" runat="server"></td>
</tr>
<tr>
  <td colspan="2">(Add the label for error messages here)</td>
</tr>
<tr>
  <td colspan="2" align="right">
    (Add the Create Resource button here)
    <INPUT type="button" value="Close"
      onclick="javascript:window.close();">
  </td>
</tr>
</table>
```

4. With the `CreateResource.aspx` web form open in Design view, add controls (from the Web Forms section of the Toolbox) to the form and set them up as shown below.

Control	Property	Value
Literal	ID	litParentGallery
TextBox	ID	txtDisplayName
TextBox	ID	txtDescription
	Rows	3
	TextMode	MultiLine

Control	Property	Value
Label	ID	lblErrorMessage
	Text	(empty string)
Button	ID	btnCreate
	Text	Create Resource

Create Resource

Parent Resource Gallery: [Literal "litParentGallery"]

Display Name:

Description:

File: Browse...

[lblErrorMessage]

Create Resource   Close

5. Since a file is being uploaded to the server from the form, toggle to HTML view and set the form's ENCTYPE property to multipart/form-data.

```
<body MS_POSITIONING="FlowLayout">
<form id="Form1" method="post" runat="server" enctype="multipart/form-data">
</form>
</body>
```

6. As before, in addition to the existing namespaces, add the Microsoft.ContentManagement.Publishing namespace to the code-behind file.

```
. . . code continues . . .
// MCMS PAPI
using Microsoft.ContentManagement.Publishing;

namespace CmsExplorer
{
. . . code continues . . .
}
```

7. In the Page_Load() event handler, we add code to retrieve the GUID of the parent resource gallery from the CMSObjectGuid querystring parameter. Passing it to the Searches.GetByGuid() method gets a reference to the parent resource gallery.

    Once we have gotten an instance of the parent resource gallery, we check the ResourceGallery.CanCreateResources property. If the user has the necessary rights, the property returns the Boolean true (which means that the user is an MCMS administrator, a resource manager, a template designer, or a channel manager assigned to the parent resource gallery) and the Create Resource button is enabled. Otherwise, it is disabled.

```
. . . code continues . . .

private CmsHttpContext cmsContext;
private ResourceGallery parentGallery;

private void Page_Load(object sender, System.EventArgs e)
```

```
    {
      cmsContext = CmsHttpContext.Current;
      lblErrorMessage.Text = String.Empty;
      string cmsObjectGuid = String.Empty;

      if (Request.QueryString["CMSObjectGuid"]!=null)
      {
        cmsObjectGuid = Request.QueryString["CMSObjectGuid"];
        parentGallery = cmsContext.Searches.GetByGuid(cmsObjectGuid)
            as ResourceGallery;

        if (parentGallery!=null)
        {
          litParentGallery.Text = parentGallery.Path;

          // Enable or Disable the Create Resource button
          btnCreate.Enabled = parentGallery.CanCreateResources;
        }
        else
        {
          lblErrorMessage.Text = "Parent Gallery not found!";
        }
      }
    }
```

8. Next, we will store all uploaded files in a temporary folder on the server. MCMS already provides such a folder with the necessary write permissions. Retrieve it by accessing the `CmsHttpContext.Current.TemporaryUploadFolder` property. The code first checks to see if the uploaded file has a valid name (one that adheres to the naming rules set by MCMS) then saves the uploaded file to the `Temp` folder in the MCMS Server directory. With the file uploaded, we call the `ResourceGallery.CreateResource()` method, passing in the path of the file as an input parameter. Once the resource has been created, we set its `Name` and `DisplayName` properties and commit the changes to the repository. Toggle to Design view and double-click on the `btnCreate` button. In the `btnCreate_Click()` event handler, add code shown below:

```
private void btnCreate_Click(object sender, System.EventArgs e)
{
  try
  {
    if (File1.PostedFile != null)
    {
      // the temp folder for saving the posted file to
      string filePath = CmsHttpContext.Current.TemporaryUploadFolder;

      // get the file name from the posted file
      string fileName = File1.PostedFile.FileName;
      int indexOfSlash = fileName.LastIndexOf("\\") + 1;
      fileName = fileName.Substring(indexOfSlash,fileName.Length -
          indexOfSlash);

      // append the file name to the path of the temp folder
      filePath += "\\" + fileName;

      // check to see if the file name is valid
      if (!Utility.ValidateMCMSObjectName(fileName))
      {
        throw new Exception("Specified template gallery name is not "
                    + "valid. Must be only alphanumeric "
                    + "characters, open or close parens, "
                    + "hyphens, underscores, periods, or "
```

```
                                    + "spaces. No period at the end and no "
                                    + "consecutive periods are allowed. ");
        }

        // save the file to a specified temp folder
        File1.PostedFile.SaveAs(filePath);

        // create the new resource
        Resource newResource = parentGallery.CreateResource(filePath);
        newResource.Name = fileName;
        newResource.DisplayName = txtDisplayName.Text;

        // commit the changes
        cmsContext.CommitAll();

        // delete the file that was saved to the temp folder
        System.IO.File.Delete(filePath);

        // display the success message
        lblErrorMessage.Text = "Resource created successfully!";
    }
    else
    {
        // no file was selected for uploading
        lblErrorMessage.Text = "Please select a file to upload";
    }
}
catch(Exception ex)
{
    // rollback all changes
    cmsContext.RollbackAll();

    // the CMS context needs to be disposed of after a rollback
    cmsContext.Dispose();

    // display error message
    lblErrorMessage.Text = ex.Message;
}
}
```

Files that are to be added to the resource gallery must first be uploaded to the MCMS server as physical files. The `ResourceGallery.CreateResource()` method only accepts a valid path to an existing file in the file system.

Save and build the solution. To test the new dialog:

1. Open CMS Explorer.
2. Click Resources and navigate to the PlantCatalog resource gallery.
3. Select New | New Resource from the toolbar.
4. In the Create Resource dialog, enter the following values:

Property	Value
DisplayName	MyResource
Description	This resource was created from the PAPI
File	Select any file located on your desktop

5. Click Create Resource.

Watch as the selected file is uploaded and created as a new resource in the PlantCatalog resource gallery (click the Refresh button to see the latest view).

Replacing Resources

When updating a resource, it is a good idea to replace its content instead of deleting it and uploading it again. Replacing means you preserve the GUID and URL so that hyperlinks to the resource in postings will not only be kept intact but also immediately linked to the updated content.

Using the PAPI, resources are replaced using the `Resource.SetContentFromFile()` method. In this example, we will build a new dialog for replacing resources in CMS Explorer:

1. Add a new web form to the CMSExplorer project. Name the new web form `ReplaceResource.aspx`.

2. In Design view, drag `styles.css` from Solution Explorer and drop it onto the web form.

3. Toggle to HTML view and set the form's ENCTYPE property to `multipart/form-data`:

```
<form id="Form1" method="post" runat="server"
    enctype="multipart/form-data">
</form>
```

4. Add a table with four rows:

```
<table>
<tr>
  <td colspan="2">
    <h1>Replace Resource</h1>
    <h2>Current Resource: (Add Literal for displaying the path here)</h2>
  </td>
</tr>
<tr>
  <td><INPUT type="file" id="File1" runat="server"></td>
</tr>
<tr>
  <td colspan="2">(Add the Label for error messages here)</td>
</tr>
<tr>
  <td colspan="2" align="right">
    (Add the Replace Resource button here)
    <INPUT type="button" value="Close"
    onclick="javascript:window.close();">
  </td>
</tr>
</table>
```

5. In Design view, drag and drop controls and set them up as detailed below:

Control	Property	Value
Literal	ID	litCurrentResource
Label	ID	lblErrorMessage
	Text	(empty string)
Button	ID	btnReplace
	Text	Replace Resource

Replace Resource

Current Resource: [Literal "litCurrentResource"]

| | Browse... |
| [lblErrorMessage] |

| | Replace Resource | Close |

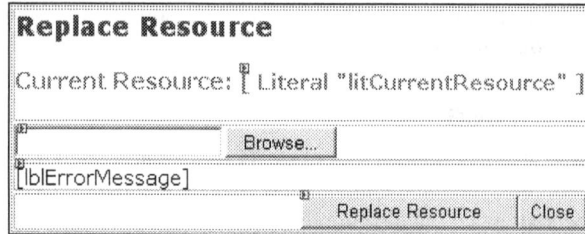

6. Add the `Microsoft.ContentManagement.Publishing` namespace to the code-behind file.

```
. . . code continues . . .
// MCMS PAPI
using Microsoft.ContentManagement.Publishing;

namespace CmsExplorer
{
  . . . code continues . . .
}
```

7. In the `Page_Load()` event handler, get the GUID of the resource to be replaced from the `CMSObjectGuid` parameter. We then pass it to the `Searches.GetByGuid()` method and display the resource's path in the `litCurrentResource` literal. Once we have an instance of the resource to be replaced, we check to see if the user has the necessary rights by checking the value returned by the `Resource.CanSetContent` property. If the `Resource.CanSetContent` property returns `true`, it means that the user is an MCMS administrator, a resource manager, a template designer, or a channel manager assigned to the parent resource gallery. The `btnReplace` button is enabled accordingly.

```
private CmsHttpContext cmsContext;
private Resource currentResource;

private void Page_Load(object sender, System.EventArgs e)
{
  cmsContext = CmsHttpContext.Current;
  lblErrorMessage.Text = string.Empty;
  string cmsObjectGuid = string.Empty;

  if (Request.QueryString["CMSObjectGuid"]!=null)
  {
    cmsObjectGuid = Request.QueryString["CMSObjectGuid"];
    currentResource = cmsContext.Searches.GetByGuid(cmsObjectGuid)
        as Resource;

    if (currentResource!=null)
    {
      litCurrentResource.Text = currentResource.Path;
      btnReplace.Enabled = currentResource.CanSetContent;
    }
    else
    {
      lblErrorMessage.Text = "Resource not found!";
    }
  }
}
```

8. Switch to Design view and double-click on the btnReplace button. In the
   btnReplace_Click() event handler, add the following code:

```
private void btnReplace_Click(object sender, System.EventArgs e)
{
  try
  {
    if (File1.PostedFile != null)
    {
      // the temp folder for saving the posted file to
      string filePath = CmsHttpContext.Current.TemporaryUploadFolder;

      // get the file name from the posted file
      string fileName = File1.PostedFile.FileName;
      int indexOfSlash = fileName.LastIndexOf("\\") + 1;
      fileName = fileName.Substring(indexOfSlash,fileName.Length -
          indexOfSlash);

      // check to see if the file name is valid
      if(!Utility.ValidateMCMSObjectName(fileName))
      {
        throw new Exception("Specified template gallery name is not "
            + "valid. Must be only alphanumeric "
            + "characters, open or close parens, "
            + "hyphens, underscores, periods, or "
            + "spaces. No period at the end and no "
            + "consecutive periods are allowed. ");
      }

      // append the file name to the path of the temp folder
      filePath += "\\" + fileName;

      // save the file to a specified temp folder
      File1.PostedFile.SaveAs(filePath);

      // replace the contents of the resource
      currentResource.SetContentFromFile(filePath);
      currentResource.Name = fileName;

      // commit the changes
      cmsContext.CommitAll();

      // display the success message
      lblErrorMessage.Text = "Resource replaced successfully!";
    }
    else
    {
      // no file was selected for uploading
      lblErrorMessage.Text = "Please select a file to upload";
    }
  }
  catch(Exception ex)
  {
    // rollback all changes
    cmsContext.RollbackAll();

    // the CMS context needs to be disposed of after a rollback
    cmsContext.Dispose();

    // display error message
    lblErrorMessage.Text = ex.Message;
  }
}
```

We first retrieve the name of the file to be uploaded and check to see if it is valid. After saving the uploaded file to the Temp folder in the MCMS Server directory, we call the Resource.SetContentFromFile() method, which accepts the path of a valid file in the file system. Just as when creating resources, this file must reside on the MCMS server. After the contents of the resource are updated, we commit the changes to the content repository.

Save and build the solution. Let's try out the Replace Resource dialog:

1. Open CMS Explorer.
2. Click Resources and navigate to the PlantCatalog resource gallery.
3. Click the Edit link next to the CoconutTree.JPG resource.
4. Click Replace.
5. In the Replace Resource dialog, browse to an existing JPG file.
6. Click Replace Resource.
7. Click Close to close the dialog.

The content of the resource is replaced with the newly uploaded file. Notice that you are only allowed to replace the resource with a file of the same MIME Type. For example, the CoconutTree.JPG resource could only be replaced with other *.JPG files. Should you have chosen, say a *.XLS file, you would have gotten the following error message:

MIME Content-Types do not match. application/vnd.ms-excel does not match image/jpg.

Deleting Objects

The PAPI has a Delete() method for each channel, posting, template, template gallery, resource gallery, and resource object. We have created quite a few test objects in the repository, so let's write a Delete dialog so that CMS Explorer can remove them:

1. Add a new web form to the CMSExplorer project and name it Delete.aspx.
2. In Design view, drag and drop styles.css from Solution Explorer onto the web form.
3. Toggle to HTML view and add a table with four rows:

```
<table>
<tr>
  <td><h1>Confirm Delete</h1></td>
</tr>
<tr>
  <td>
    Click YES to permanently delete
    (Add literal to show the path of the item to be deleted here)</td>
  </tr>
<tr>
  <td align="right">
    (Add the Yes button here)
    <INPUT type="button" value="No" onclick="javascript:window.close();"
    style="width:120px">
  </td>
</tr>
<tr>
  <td>(Add label for displaying error messages here)</td>
</tr>
</table>
```

4. Switch to Design view. Add controls (from the Web Forms section of the Toolbox) to the form and arrange them as shown in the diagram below:

Control	Property	Value
Literal	ID	litCurrentItem
	Text	(empty string)
Label	ID	lblErrorMessage
	Text	(empty string)
Button	ID	btnYes
	Text	Yes
	Width	120px

Confirm Delete

Click YES to permanently delete [Literal "litCurrentItem"]

| Yes | No |

[lblErrorMessage]

5. Open the code-behind file for the form. As before, in addition to the existing namespaces, import `Microsoft.ContentManagement.Publishing`:

    ```
    . . . code continues . . .
    ```

    ```
    // MCMS PAPI
    using Microsoft.ContentManagement.Publishing;

    namespace CmsExplorer
    {
        . . . code continues . . .
    }
    ```

6. In the `Page_Load()` event handler, we get a reference to the current `CmsHttpContext` as well as the object to be deleted as specified by the `CmsObjectGuid` querystring parameter. The path of the object to be deleted is displayed in the `litCurrentItem` literal.

    In addition, we check to see if the user has the rights to delete the object. We do so by retrieving the value of the `HierarchyItem.CanDelete` property. The `btnYes` button is enabled only if the user can delete the object.

    ```
    CmsHttpContext cmsContext;
    HierarchyItem deletedObject;

    private void Page_Load(object sender, System.EventArgs e)
    {
        cmsContext = CmsHttpContext.Current;
        lblErrorMessage.Text = String.Empty;
        string cmsObjectGuid = String.Empty;
        if (Request.QueryString["CMSObjectGuid"] != null)
        {
            cmsObjectGuid = Request.QueryString["CMSObjectGuid"];
    ```

```
        deletedObject = cmsContext.Searches.GetByGuid(cmsObjectGuid);
    }

    // display the path of the object to be deleted
    if (!Page.IsPostBack)
    {
        litCurrentItem.Text = deletedObject.Path;
    }

    btnYes.Enabled = deletedObject.CanDelete;
}
```

7. Switch back to Design view and double-click on the btnYes button. In the btnYes_Click() event handler, simply make a call to the HierarchyItem.Delete() method and commit the delete:

```
private void btnYes_Click(object sender, System.EventArgs e)
{
    try
    {
        deletedObject.Delete();
        cmsContext.CommitAll();

        // display the success message
        lblErrorMessage.Text = "Item deleted successfully!";
    }
    catch(Exception ex)
    {
        // rollback all changes
        cmsContext.RollbackAll();

        // the CMS context needs to be disposed of after a rollback
        cmsContext.Dispose();

        // display error message
        lblErrorMessage.Text = ex.Message;
    }
}
```

If any errors occur in the process, the delete operation is rolled back and an error message displayed.

You need to be aware of some key points when deleting objects using the PAPI:

- A container with objects cannot be deleted until all items within it are deleted as well.

- Objects with existing dependants cannot be deleted until all dependants are removed. For instance, if there are postings based on a template, the template cannot be deleted until those postings are also deleted.

- Postings that link to the resource will maintain a link to the resource even though the resource has been deleted. This was designed to prevent broken links. However the file will no longer be accessible by resource managers. Only administrators will be able to view them. In Chapter 13, we suggest a way handle these links in *Tip #4: How to Deal with Links to Deleted Resources*.

- Unlike the Delete option in Site Manager, where deleted objects are stored in the Deleted Items bin and can be recovered, objects deleted using the PAPI are no longer accessible once the delete has been committed. The MCMS background process will remove all resources that aren't referenced by a posting. Resources referenced by a posting can be recovered by requesting a stored procedure from Microsoft Support (reference number: SOX040517700117).

Summary

In this chapter, we learned how to use the PAPI to manage template galleries, templates, and resources. We provided several enhancements to CMS Explorer, including dialogs to create template galleries, templates, and resources. We also showed how templates can be submitted (or checked in), copied, and moved programmatically. Another feature that we explored was the replacement of existing resources, where the file contents of a resource can be replaced while preserving its GUID and URL. Finally, we looked at how objects can be deleted from the content repository using the PAPI.

As you can see the PAPI not only provides you with the basic tools to create websites managed by MCMS but also allows you to customize it to meet just about all kinds of unique business requirements.

4

Preparing Postings for Search Indexing

MCMS does not ship with a search engine. You can choose from the myriad of third-party search engines out there; or employ a ready-to-use solution that integrates with MCMS, such as Microsoft SharePoint Portal Server.

> For an offering of third-party search solutions that provide integration with MCMS, visit Microsoft's Partner website at `http://www.microsoft.com/cmserver/default.aspx?url=/CMServer/partners/`.

When evaluating a search engine for MCMS, the most critical criterion to fulfill is the ability to index pages whose content is dynamically generated. Third-party search engines that use spiders/robots to crawl web pages are well suited for MCMS-based sites. Be aware that not all search engines are able to crawl authenticated sites: if you are implementing Windows authentication or forms-based authentication, ensure that your search engine of choice supports it.

Search engines usually start at a particular page (such as the site's home page) and then the spider visits each and every link it sees. It travels throughout the site by hopping through from link to link. The content of every visited page will be added to an "index". When someone enters a given keyword in a search query, the search engine looks at the index to find pages containing that keyword.

Most search crawlers look for HTML META tags in the <head> section of a page. These tags can contain additional information about the current page, which will then also be added to the index. Typical META tags look like these:

```
<meta NAME="Location" CONTENT="Asia">
<meta NAME="Description" Content="The Hibiscus is a shrub grown in tropical
 gardens">
```

META tags are used by some search engines to implement a taxonomy. When the page is indexed, the search engine may add the contents of the Description META tag into a field called description. You could then use the search engine's API to search all pages that contain certain keywords only in this description field. Combining multiple META tags then allows complex searches. For example you could program a search for pages where the description META tag contains the word "plant" and the location META tag contains "South America" to retrieve all pages about plants in South America.

Note that not every search engine supports the use of META tags as they can be used to influence an index using information that may not be related to the content of the page. For example, engines like Google have their own internal mechanisms to generate the abstract for each page. Refer to the documentation of the search engine you are working with to find the list of META tags it recognizes.

Most search engines are capable of performing an "incremental crawls", which is the process of only indexing pages that have been modified since the last index. Performing incremental crawls, as opposed to full crawls, optimizes the indexing process. A problem with MCMS driven websites is that the page content is dynamic and content can potentially be different with every request to the site. To the search indexer, these websites either will not return last modified date information or will always appear to have been modified. As a result, MCMS sites can't be crawled incrementally. In this chapter we will develop a solution that outputs the last modified date into the HTTP response headers thus giving the search engines the ability to perform incremental crawls on MCMS sites.

In addition search accuracy can be affected by navigation controls on the page and common header and footer elements. This can lead to excess noise in search results (if, say, the "Press Release" page is listed on a shared menu control, a search for it will yield all pages with this menu). Accuracy can be improved by hiding the navigation elements when the site is being indexed. We will demonstrate how to achieve this.

Throughout this chapter, we will also explore several tips and tricks for getting the best and most accurate search engine results including the title, keywords, and description.

Influencing Search Engines with the ROBOTS META Tag

Typically, the bulk of the index contains content from pages generated by channel rendering scripts and postings. They are after all, the parts of the site that are visible to the end users. To tell search engines which pages to index and which pages to ignore and whether to follow further links from the current page you can add a special META tag to your page named ROBOTS. Most (but not all) search engines honor this META tag and evaluate its content property to see if the page should be added to the index and if links from this page should be followed.

To allow MCMS authors to benefit from this feature, channels and postings have two additional properties:

- IsRobotIndexable
- IsRobotFollowable

These two properties can be used to generate the ROBOTS META tag. As already mentioned, be aware that some search engines choose to ignore the ROBOTS META tag.

The table below summarizes the behavior of the different property settings:

IsRobotFollowable	IsRobotIndexable	META tag to render	Remarks
False	False	<meta name="ROBOTS" content="NOFOLLOW, NOINDEX">	Search engines that recognize the robot META tag will not index the page nor follow its hyperlinks.
False	True	<meta name="ROBOTS" content="NOFOLLOW, INDEX">	Search engines that recognize the robot META tag will index the page but not follow its hyperlinks.
True	False	<meta name="ROBOTS" content="FOLLOW, NOINDEX">	Search engines that recognize the robot META tag will not index the page but will follow its hyperlinks.
True	True	<meta name="ROBOTS" content="FOLLOW, INDEX">	Search engines that recognize the robot META tag will index the page and follow its hyperlinks.

For more information on the ROBOTS META tag, check out this resource:

`http://www.robotstxt.org/wc/exclusion.html#meta`

The RobotMetaTag Control and Channel Rendering Scripts

MCMS ships with a control named RobotMetaTag, which is automatically added to all template files created from the Visual Studio .NET "MCMS Template File" template. The RobotMetaTag control is used to generate the ROBOTS META tag based on the IsRobotFollowable and IsRobotIndexable properties of the page.

Unfortunately this control does not work on channel rendering scripts. If you add the control to a channel rendering script, despite setting the IsRobotFollowable and IsRobotIndexable properties of the channel, the ROBOTS META tag does not get generated. To get around this problem let's implement an enhanced version of this control that works with both channel rendering scripts and templates.

> In the WoodgroveNet sample site that comes with MCMS, the RobotMetaTag control is wrapped in a user control called HeadTags.ascx.

First, open the Tropical Green solution. Add a new class file to the TropicalGreenControlLib project with the name EnhancedRobotMetaTag.cs.

The control requires the use of methods from the namespaces highlighted below, so add them to the class file.

```
using System;
using System.ComponentModel;
using System.Web.UI;
using Microsoft.ContentManagement.Common;
using Microsoft.ContentManagement.Publishing;
using Microsoft.ContentManagement.WebControls;

namespace TropicalGreenControlLib
{
    . . . code continues . . .
}
```

Also, as we are creating a custom server control, the class will inherit from the `RobotMetaTag` class (in the `Microsoft.ContentManagement.WebControls` namespace).

```
namespace TropicalGreenControlLib
{
    /// <summary>
    /// Summary description for EnhancedRobotMetaTag.
    /// </summary>
    public class EnhancedRobotMetaTag : RobotMetaTag
    {
        public EnhancedRobotMetaTag()
        {
        }
    }
}
```

Above the `EnhancedRobotMetaTag` constructor, declare four constants, `Index`, `Follow`, `noIndex` and `noFollow`, which store the strings we will use later for generating the ROBOTS META tag. We will also remove the constructor, `EnhancedRobotMetaTag()`, as it is not required.

```
public class EnhancedRobotMetaTag : RobotMetaTag
{
    private const string Index = "INDEX";
    private const string Follow = "FOLLOW";
    private const string noIndex = "NOINDEX";
    private const string noFollow = "NOFOLLOW";
}
```

In addition to rendering the ROBOTS tag, the original `RobotMetaTag` control has a different feature: it provides an option to render a `<base>` tag, which ensures that relative links added to the template files work correctly. Here's an example of a `<base>` tag:

```
<base
href="http://localhost/TropicalGreen/Templates/GardenPublic.aspx?NRMODE=Publis
hed&NRORIGINALURL=%2fTropicalGreen%2fGardens%2fMembers%2ehtm&NRNODEGUID=%7bB95
DD11B-2954-4F84-AB60-AC0A3D39FC49%7d&NRCACHEHINT=NoModifyGuest">
```

> When using the Word Authoring Connector and documents that use internal bookmarks, the `<base>` tag can cause an entire page refresh.

As a single template file can be used by multiple postings, the URL varies from posting to posting. Links relative to the template file will not work in this situation as the browser does not know that postings and channels do not exist as complete entities on the file system. The base tag tells the browser what should be treated as the current location and allows the browser to calculate the final link based on the base tag and the information in the relative link. For example, should the template file contain a relative link, say, `<a href="MembersOnly/SomePage.htm">A Relative Link</a>`, the browser will treat the URL as if `"MembersOnly/SomePage.htm"` was pre-pended with the URL stored in the `href` attribute of the `<base>` tag.

As we are going to implement a control that extends the `RobotMetaTag` control, we need to ensure that this feature is also included in our new control.

We will write the ROBOTS META tag and `<base>` tag by overriding the `Render()` method of the control. Notice we look at the properties of a `ChannelItem` object. This ensures that the code works for both postings and channel rendering scripts.

```
protected override void Render( HtmlTextWriter writer )
{
  ChannelItem currentItem = CmsHttpContext.Current.ChannelItem;

  if( currentItem != null )
  {
    string followKey = (currentItem.IsRobotFollowable)?Follow:noFollow;
    string indexKey = (currentItem.IsRobotIndexable)?Index:noIndex;

    // write the robot META tag
    writer.Write("<meta name=\"ROBOTS\" "
               + "content=\""+followKey+","+indexKey+"\">\n");

    if( this.RenderBaseHref )
    {
      // write the Base tag
      writer.Write("<base href=\""+Page.Request.Url.AbsoluteUri+"\">\n");
    }
  }
}
```

Save and build the solution. Add the control to the toolbar as you would other custom controls and it's ready to be dropped into channel rendering scripts or template files between the <head> tags.

Outputting META Tags

As well as the ROBOTS META tag, you can emit other META tags to help indexing by the particular search engine you are working with. Common tags used by search engines include the <title> tag and the Description and Keywords META tags.

In MCMS, channels and postings have Description and DisplayName properties, which are often suitable for the Description META tag and the <title> tag respectively.

Custom properties can also be used as META tags and rendered as <meta name="CustomPropertyName" content="CustomPropertyValue">

Keywords can be entered by authors and stored as custom property values. What you will need to do then is to retrieve these values from the repository and display them as META tags in the head region of the page.

There are several ways you can go about this:

- The fastest method is to simply use <%= %> constructs or Response.Write() calls within the template HTML code.

- If content that resides in custom properties or placeholders, you can retrieve it using code-behind files.

Like regular controls, use a web user control to share code among template files in the same project. If you need to generate the same set of tags across pages stored in multiple projects, consider writing a custom control as we did for the ROBOTS tag earlier.

Using <%= %> within Template Files

Use <%= %> constructs or the Response.Write() method when you need to display single pieces of information, like display names and descriptions. Let's take a closer look by implementing the constructs in the Columns.aspx template file of the Tropical Green project.

1. Open the Tropical Green project. Open the Columns.aspx template file in HTML view.

2. At the top of the page, add a page directive to import the Microsoft.ContentManagement.Publishing namespace. This allows us to access its classes (such as CmsHttpContext) from within the template file.
   ```
   <%@ Import Namespace="Microsoft.ContentManagement.Publishing" %>
   ```

3. Look for the <title></title> tags between the <Head> tags. Replace them with:
   ```
   <title><%= CmsHttpContext.Current.Posting.DisplayName %></title>
   ```

4. Below the <title> tag, add a tag to display the description of the posting:
   ```
   <meta name="Description" content="<%=
   CmsHttpContext.Current.Posting.Description %>">
   ```

5. Save Columns.aspx.

When you next view a posting using the Columns template, you will see the DisplayName of the page in the browser's title bar.

To view the META tags, right-click on the page and select View Source. The Description META tag is nested between the <head> tags. You don't get to see it displayed in the browser, as it is used solely for search engines as they index your site. The source should look like:

```
<title>A Walk Through Jenny's Garden</title>
<meta name="Description" content="You can publish pages directly from Word to
 MCMS using Authoring Connector!">
```

Pulling META Tag Content from Custom Properties

Some META tags are more complex and can't be generated by simply retrieving property values of postings. Say you have added a custom property called Keywords to every template object created. Authors enter keywords to describe the posting when they create it, which are then used for the custom property.

In this section, we look at two alternatives for accessing that information. The first option we will explore is adding literal controls to the template files. In the second option we will create a user control to output the META tags.

Using Literal Controls

To pull content from custom properties, you could add a literal control between the <head> tags as shown below:

```
<Head>
  <asp:Literal id="litKeywords" runat="server"></asp:Literal>
  . . . code continues . . .
</Head>
```

Then, in the Page_Load() event handler of the code-behind file, you could retrieve the value of the custom property and insert it as the attribute of a <meta name="Keywords"> tag:

```
using Microsoft.ContentManagement.Publishing;
... code continues ...

private void Page_Load(object sender, System.EventArgs e)
{
    // Put user code to initialize the page here
    Posting currentPosting = CmsHttpContext.Current.Posting;

    string keywords = "";
    CustomProperty cpKeywords = currentPosting.CustomProperties["Keywords"];
    if(cpKeywords!=null)
    {
        keywords = cpKeywords.Value;
    }

    litKeywords.Text = "<meta name=\"Keywords\" content=\"" + keywords + "\">";
}
```

Overriding the Render Method of a Web User Control

Here's another approach: instead of using Literal controls within the <head> tags, you could create a web user control and override its Render() method. First get an instance of the posting, then get its custom property value, and finally create the META tag:

```
namespace TropicalGreen.UserControls
{
    using System;
    using System.Data;
    using System.Drawing;
    using System.Web;
    using System.Web.UI.WebControls;
    using System.Web.UI.HtmlControls;

    // MCMS PAPI
    using Microsoft.ContentManagement.Publishing;

    // Namespace for HtmlTextWriter
    using System.Web.UI;

    public abstract class MetaTags : System.Web.UI.UserControl
    {

        private void Page_Load(object sender, System.EventArgs e)
        {
            // Put user code to initialize the page here
        }

        protected override void Render( HtmlTextWriter writer )
        {
            CmsHttpContext cmsContext = CmsHttpContext.Current;

            Posting p = cmsContext.Posting;
            string keywords = "";
            CustomProperty cpKeywords = p.CustomProperties["Keywords"];
            if (cpKeywords != null)
            {
                keywords = cpKeywords.Value;
            }
            writer.WriteLine("<meta name=\"keywords\" Content=\""
                            + keywords +"\">");
        }

        #region Web Form Designer generated code
        . . . code continues . . .
        #endregion
    }
}
```

The MetaTags user control we have just created could also be enhanced to output the posting description and custom properties as META tags.

> You can use the same technique to add placeholder content to META tags. The MCMS Connector for SharePoint Technologies contains the customizable SearchMetaTagGenerator server control to generate META tags from properties and custom properties. This control is discussed in Chapter 5.

Configuring Templates to Allow Postings to Return Accurate Last Modified Time

Because postings are dynamically constructed, correct information about a posting's last modified date would always reflect the current date and time. Therefore, search engines can't perform incremental crawls of MCMS sites, and would always run a full crawl.

Consider the case of a website that uses the search component of SharePoint Portal Server. When SharePoint Portal Server performs an incremental index crawl, it sends HTTP GET requests for every page on the site it comes in contact with. If it finds a page that has previously been indexed, SharePoint will update its entry in the index only if the page was modified since the last index job. To decide whether or not a page has been modified, SharePoint sends a conditional HTTP GET request, which is a request that includes an If-Modified-Since HTTP header with the date and time the page was last modified. If the page has not been modified, the response will be an HTTP status code 304 (not modified) and SharePoint will not index the page. Should the response be HTTP status code 200 (OK), it means that the page has been updated and SharePoint will proceed to index it. This concept works well for static websites made up of physical files, where the last modified date reflects the actual date the page was modified.

However, because its pages are assembled on the fly, IIS will always assume that the last modified date of postings is the current date and time. Since the date stored in the If-Modified-Since HTTP header will always be an earlier date, IIS always returns a status code 200 (OK) without sending a last modified date. Therefore, the site will never be incrementally crawled by SharePoint Portal Server, and it will effectively undergo a full index every time. This behavior is seen in all search engines that make use of the If-Modified-Since HTTP Header to perform incremental crawls.

Obviously this isn't an ideal situation for the performance of a search engine's indexing process, nor is it performance-friendly for the MCMS site. In the case of our Tropical Green site, the impact is minimal because the overall number of postings is very low. However, consider a site containing 10,000 postings in which only 10% have changed since the last crawl. Instead of crawling and indexing 1,000 pages, SharePoint Portal Server indexes ten times more content than necessary.

To solve this issue, we need to modify our templates to return the actual time the posting was modified with the HTTP status code of 200; if the posting hasn't changed since the last crawl, we should return a HTTP status code of 304. Here's how we'll do this:

1. Get the last modified date of the posting was modified.
2. Get the time returned by the HTTP If-Modified-Since Header and convert it to UTC to negate any effect of time zones.

3. Compare both dates. Determine if the posting was modified since SharePoint last indexed it. If it wasn't modified, return HTTP status code 304; otherwise return HTTP status code 200.

Let's see what the code would look like. Open the code-behind file of our Columns.aspx template in the TropicalGreen project.

Add the following to the Page_Load() event handler:

```
private void Page_Load(object sender, System.EventArgs e)
{
  bool returnCode304 = false;

  // Get the If-Modified-Since HTTP header
  string myString =
    HttpContext.Current.Request.Headers.Get("If-Modified-Since");
  // If this is a conditional HTTP GET.
  if (myString != null)
  {

    // It's a conditional HTTP GET, so compare the dates
    try
    {
      DateTime incrementalIndexTime =
        Convert.ToDateTime(myString).ToUniversalTime();

      // if the conditional date sent by SharePoint is
      // the same as the last date the posting was updated,
      // return HTTP status code 304
      if (incrementalIndexTime.ToString() ==
        CmsHttpContext.Current.Posting.LastModifiedDate.ToString())
      {
        returnCode304 = true;
      }
    }
    catch{}

    // if the content didn't change,
    // return 304 and stop parsing the page
    if (returnCode304)
    {
      Response.StatusCode = 304;
      Response.End();
    }
  }
```

As a final step to get the above method working, we need to ensure that the last modified date of the posting is sent back in the Last-Modified HTTP header to the client. This can be done with the following code in Page_Load():

```
private void Page_Load(object sender, System.EventArgs e)
{
  // This is the code that causes ASP.NET to send the header.
  Response.Cache.SetLastModified(
    CmsHttpContext.Current.Posting.LastModifiedDate.ToLocalTime());

  // Put user code to initialize the page here
  . . . code continues . . .
}
```

Now let's build our Tropical Green project and make sure that it compiles correctly. When the build finishes, open a browser and navigate through the site to one of the postings in the plant catalog. If the posting is rendered as expected, we're in good shape and can proceed. Otherwise, double-check the code you added for any inconsistencies.

With our Plant template updated, you should go through the rest of the templates and add the same code above. An alternative to copying this code into every template's code-behind would be to create a helper class, which can be called in each `Page_Load()` event to determine if the 304 status code should be returned.

Dealing with Output Caching

Another thing to take into account is caching. If you are using the `@OutputCache` page directive, you'll need to remove it from your template files. You can't use standard output caching in combination with HTTP 304 handling because the `Page_Load()` event, and all the code that we have just written within it to enable incremental crawls, would not be executed if the item is already in the cache.

When cached content is delivered, you will always get back an HTTP 200 response. There are two ways to get around this: if output caching is required you would need to implement it manually as discussed in the section, *Rendering the RSS feed in Presentation Mode*, in Chapter 12, *MCMS and RSS*.

Or, you can set the cache headers in the HTTP response to ensure that the pages are cached in the browser and in downstream proxy servers. This can be achieved by adding the `Cache-Control` header to the response and also setting the cache expiry time in the `Page_Load()` event handler immediately after the code above:

```
private void Page_Load(object sender, System.EventArgs e)
{
    . . . code continues . . .

    // public header to allow caching in proxy servers and in the browser cache
    Response.Cache.SetCacheability(System.Web.HttpCacheability.Public);

    // set how long the content should be cached in a downlevel cache
    Response.Cache.SetExpires(System.DateTime.Now.AddMinutes(5));
    Response.Cache.SetValidUntilExpires(true);
}
```

As this code is likely to be used in several templates, in practice, it'd be a good idea to put it in a helper class to eliminate code duplication.

For more information on the incremental crawl issue with SharePoint Portal Server and MCMS, refer to Microsoft Knowledge Base article #832432 at
`http://support.microsoft.com/?id=832432`

Increasing Search Accuracy by Generating Search Engine Specific Pages

As our menus on our templates display not only the name of the current posting but links to other postings, we are creating additional noise for the search results. The way to overcome this is to determine when a page is requested by a crawler and then hide the listing controls. Because search engines traverse sites from links within the page, we cannot simply remove the navigational controls leaving only the main posting content: we must also create hyperlinks to the channel items (postings and channels) within the current channel.

Interrogating the User Agent

To determine if the site is being crawled, we will create a helper method that checks the `Request.Header["User-Agent"]` value and compares it to a list of known search agents stored in the `web.config` file.

Firstly, we have to set up a list of search agents in the `web.config` file. Under the `<configuration>` | `<appSettings>` element, we will insert an `<add>` element:

```
<!-- SharePoint, Google, MSN Search (Separated by | )-->
<add key="SearchUserAgents" value="MS Search|GoogleBot|msnbot" />
```

Next, we will create a helper class in the Tropical Green project. To do this, follow these steps:

1. Open the TropicalGreen solution in Visual Studio .NET.

2. In the TropicalGreen project, create a new folder called Classes.

3. Right-click on the Classes folder and choose Add | Add Class.

4. Enter the name SearchHelper.cs and click OK.

5. Import the System.Web and System.Configuration namespaces:

```
using System;
using System.Text.RegularExpressions;
using System.Web;
using System.Configuration;

namespace TropicalGreen.Classes
{
  /// <summary>
  /// Summary description for SearchHelper.
  /// </summary>
  public class SearchHelper
  {
    ... code continues ...
  }
}
```

Let's add a static method called IsCrawler(), which returns true if the Request.Header["User-Agent"] matches a value specified in the web.config:

```
public static bool IsCrawler()
{

  // Get the user agent string from the web.config
  string strUserAgents =
    ConfigurationSettings.AppSettings.Get("SearchUserAgents");

  // is it null? is it an empty string?
  if(strUserAgents != null && strUserAgents != "")
  {
    // Regular expression to identify all robots
    // robot strings need to be separated with "|" in the web.config
    Regex reAllSearch = new Regex("("+strUserAgents+")",
        RegexOptions.Compiled);

    // Get the current user agent
    string CurrentUserAgent = HttpContext.Current.Request.UserAgent;
```

```
        return reAllSearch.Match(CurrentUserAgent).Success;
    }

    // agents are not specified in the web.config
    return(false);
}
```

Hiding Navigational Elements

For each of the navigation controls in the Tropical Green solution, we will need to add a check during their loading or rendering to see if the page is being crawled.

The easiest way to do this is in the `Page_Load()` or `Render()` method of the control. We want to check if the current request is from a crawler and hide the control if it is, otherwise load it as normal:

```
if (!TropicalGreen.Classes.SearchHelper.IsCrawler())
{
    // Bind the Data
}
else
{
    // Is being crawled so hide the user control
    this.Visible = false;
}
```

Creating a Posting/Channel Listing User Control

Now we have hidden the navigational controls, we must still provide a mechanism for the crawlers to traverse the site. The simplest way is to build a user control that lists the postings and channels in the current channel but does not include their display name.

Let's now build the `CrawlingNavigationControl` user control:

1. Open the `TropicalGreen` project in Visual Studio .NET.
2. Under the user controls folder, create a new user control and give it the name `CrawlingNavigationControl`.
3. Switch to the code-behind file (`CrawlingNavigationControl.ascx.cs`).
4. Import the following namespaces:
   ```
   using System.Text;
   using Microsoft.ContentManagement.Publishing;
   ```

We will add logic to the `Page_Load()` of all templates and channel rendering scripts to create a new literal control that contains the hyperlinks. The hyperlink labels will be text that is ignored by the indexer (noise words). In this case, we use the word "and".

```
private void Page_Load(object sender, System.EventArgs e)
{
    // Is the site being crawled?
    if(TropicalGreen.Classes.SearchHelper.IsCrawler())
    {

        // declare & instantiate a string builder to hold the hyperlinks
        StringBuilder sb = new StringBuilder();

        // loop through all the channel items in the current channel
        foreach(ChannelItem item in CmsHttpContext.Current.Channel.AllChildren)
        {

            // append the hyperlink creating a unique label
```

```
        sb.Append("<a href=\"" + item.Url + "\">and</a>");
    }

    // instantiate a new literal control
    Literal litLinks = new Literal();

    // set the literal controls text
    // to be the text from the string builder
    litLinks.Text = sb.ToString();

    // add the literal control to the control collection
    this.Controls.Add(litLinks);

    }
}
```

To enable the `CrawlingNavigationControl`, you should add it to the bottom of every template file. Alternatively, if your site uses a footer user control or a header user control on every template, you could place the `CrawlingNavigationControl` in there.

Tips for Search Engine Optimization

Most search engines use proprietary algorithms for the crawling, indexing, and ranking of web pages. There is no way to guarantee a high ranking for your website but here are a few general tips that should help you.

Design and Navigation Considerations

There are several issues that may cause your website to not be indexed correctly by search engines:

Frames

If your website uses frames, the content within the frames may not be indexed. To overcome this issue, the content that needs to be indexed should be placed within the `<NOFRAMES>` tag.

Flash Content

If your homepage is primarily Flash, the content and hyperlinks may not be correctly indexed. It is recommended to reproduce the content and hyperlinks that are in Flash in HTML and either detect when the request is coming from a crawler or include it on all pages but hidden.

Image Maps and JavaScript Navigation

Image maps and navigation controls populated by JavaScript are great options for developers and users but search engines may not have the ability to parse links that are generated at run time. If your website is generating hyperlinks using image maps or JavaScript, it is recommended to reproduce the links in standard HTML.

Adding Details to the Title Tag

The `<title>` tag is one of the most important tags for search engine optimization. You should make your title describe exactly what is on the page as it will be displayed as the window title on your web browser and also as the heading for a search result. It should be unique per page and each keyword should be visible on the page as content. In addition most search engines rate words in the title tags higher than if they show up in the body, so that when the word being searched for is in the title tag, that page will show up earlier in the list of search results.

Using META Tags

META tags allow search engines to look for details about a page in a standard location. The META tags must be located within the <head> element.

Choosing your Keywords and Density

It is recommended to add the `<meta name="keywords" content="Your Keywords">` tag to your pages as some search engines use this element as they build their index. The content element contains a list of comma-separated keywords. You should use keywords that relate to the content that appears on the current page and not the entire website. An example of the keywords META tag for the Tropical Green website would be:

```
<meta name="keywords" content="Gardening information, Gardening Columns, plants
for sale Seattle, Plant reseller Seattle, Plant supplier Seattle, Garden Designers
Seattle, Online Plant Database, Garden design">
```

If you chose keywords that are too generic, such as Plant, Gardening, or Garden Design, they would have little value as they are not specific enough. By adding the location of Tropical Green (Seattle) to each keyword, people that are searching for a plant-related service in their local area (e.g. Seattle) are more likely to find Tropical Green's website.

Description

The contents of the description META tag should accurately describe the page contents for example: the description of the "A Walk in Jenny's Garden" column page would be:

```
<meta name="description" content="We take a look at Jenny's Garden and her unique
approach to garden design by combining the use of tall trees with small shrubs.">
```

The keywords META tag should not exceed approximately 1000 characters or search engines may ignore or cut it off. For the best performance, you should try to keep the description META tag as short as possible (approximately 250 characters).

Summary

Over the course of this chapter, we have looked at several ways to configure MCMS templates to get the best out of search engines. To allow MCMS postings and channel rendering scripts to be indexed and followed by search engines, the `IsRobotFollowable` and `IsRobotIndexable` properties should be set, and channel rendering scripts need to be modified to output these properties. We also explored how to enable incremental crawls for an MCMS website and how to reduce the noise in search results by rendering only relevant content and hiding navigational controls. Finally we looked at a few tips for search engine optimization by adding detail to META tags and also being cognizant of design issues that may cause the website to not be indexed correctly.

5
Searching MCMS with SharePoint

For as long as content-centric websites have been around, the need for searching the content has been there. Many of the most successful dot-com businesses have been search sites such as Yahoo! and Google. Every few months a new search site opens its doors, many of which perform aggregate searches of multiple sites simultaneously. At the other end of the spectrum, many site owners require a search capability that returns only results for their specific site.

Microsoft Content Management Server (MCMS), while a very robust content management solution, does not offer any search capabilities out of the box. However, just because you have an MCMS website doesn't mean you are stuck without search capabilities.

MCMS Search Options

There are quite a few ways to implement searching on an MCMS website, each with varying costs, implementation complexity, and limitations. As usual, each option has its advantages and disadvantages. Google (http://www.google.com) provides a Web Service API for you to submit queries against at no cost, but you are limited to 1,000 searches per day, and there are some licensing requirements regarding logo placement. Coveo (http://www.coveo.com) provides a free, no-expiration license for its Enterprise Search product, but it's limited to searching 5,000 documents (searching more than 5,000 requires a license to be purchased from Coveo). Mondosoft's (http://www.mondosoft.com) MondoSearch seamlessly integrates into MCMS and offers up a robust feature set, but it's not free.

Microsoft's enterprise portal solution, SharePoint Portal Server 2003 (SPS), contains a powerful and customizable search engine. The indexes SPS creates are accessible for searches by submitting a Microsoft SQL Full-Text query via a Web Service. If your organization has already implemented, or plans to deploy SPS, then you could leverage it as your MCMS search engine. Do be aware, however, that if your site is publicly accessible, this solution may not be as compelling, as a SharePoint External Connector license would be required. For this reason, the SharePoint search solution we look at is typically only a viable option for intranet-based MCMS sites.

In this chapter, we will leverage SPS's search to provide a robust search capability for our Tropical Green MCMS site. On the way, we'll configure SharePoint to index our Tropical Green site. We will also try out some free components you can use in your MCMS site to execute search queries against the SharePoint index.

Microsoft SharePoint Portal Server Search

To fully leverage SharePoint Portal Server Search to your advantage, you need to understand how it works and how to configure it. Before we explain how it works, there are a few key components that need to be understood:

- A **content source** contains the information that will be indexed. Content sources can be external websites, file shares, Windows SharePoint Services sites, Microsoft Exchange public folders, or other systems that provide a protocol handler for SharePoint Search such as Lotus Notes.

- **Index files** contain crawled content from one or more content sources. Aggregating and cataloging content from disparate content sources enables future search queries to be much more efficient. Index files can also be copied or propagated to SharePoint Web servers for more efficient searching. Two indexes are created by default when you create a new portal: Portal_Content and Non_Portal_Content. As expected, the former contains all content stored in the portal while the latter contains content outside of the portal.

- **Search scopes** are used to provide a logical grouping of content sources for end users to search. For example, a company may have multiple internal file shares and websites. An employee looking for a specific document doesn't care if it's in site A or file share B, they just know it's out there. An administrator can create multiple content sources and group them together in a single search scope that the user can search against. In addition, search scopes can be configured to only include specific portions of a website, providing even more granular control over what content is indexed and searchable by your users.

- The SharePoint **gatherer** is responsible for crawling all content sources, extracting content, removing noise words (such as 'and', 'a', 'the', 'or' to name only a few… noise word files are customizable so you can add your own noise words), and creating index files that will be used when search queries are executed.

The gatherer is part of the MSSearch service that performs the content crawling and creates the index files. This service runs on schedules that you can configure through the SharePoint Central Administration tool. The MSSearch service activates the gatherer, based on the specified scheduled timetable, which generates a master index for search queries.

An end user uses a search scope to select a collection of content sources to query. SharePoint looks at the catalog containing the content sources and determines the best candidates that match the search query.

Preparing the MCMS Site for Indexing

Before we can configure SharePoint to index our MCMS site, there are a few steps we need to take to make the indexing more efficient and useful. First and foremost, check if your site has the MCMS option Map Channel Names to Host Header Names set. If so, you'll need to disable it because one of the two options we have, utilizing the MCMS Connector, does not support host header names. For the rest of this chapter, we will assume our site exists in the top-level channel TropicalGreen.

> If your site uses the Map Channel Names to Host Header Names option, you may need to rename the top level channel to reflect the channel we'll use in this example (namely TropicalGreen).
>
> In addition, our example assumes you've set up MCMS and SharePoint according to Appendix A, *Setting up MCMS & SPS on the Same Virtual Server*. If your MCMS Web Entry Point and SharePoint portal are not in the same virtual server, this requirement may not affect you.

Second, we'll configure our site for guest access. The majority of our Tropical Green site is intended to be available to any anonymous visitor. While we do have one restricted section of our site, we will set up a new account that will have read access to our entire site for use by SharePoint as it crawls our site. Then we'll filter the results to ensure that the user running the search will only see items in the search results he or she has access to.

Next, we need to address how MCMS and output caching behave on requests for postings. The default page rendering behavior of MCMS is not performance-friendly to SPS searching. Because all MCMS requests return an HTTP status code of 200, SharePoint will always perform full crawls of our site and not an incremental crawl. We have already explained the details of what happens with each index crawl request and implemented a solution in Chapter 4, *Preparing Postings for Search Indexing*.

Finally, we'll add a control, supplied with the MCMS Connector for SharePoint Technologies, to our templates that makes additional metadata properties available to the index crawler, giving additional information for users searching our site.

Disabling Channel Names to Host Header Names Mapping

One of the examples we'll run through in this chapter involves using the MCMS Connector for SharePoint Technologies. The search controls shipped with MCMS Connector do not support the host header mapping feature and therefore, we cannot enable mapping the channel names to the host header names. If your site employs this option, you'll need to disable it. In addition, we should rename the top level channel www.tropicalgreen.net to TropicalGreen which is much more convenient as this will now become part of the path in the URL.

> The MCMS Connector for SharePoint Technologies requires the .NET Framework 1.1. It will not function properly on a site running version 1.0 of the .NET Framework.

This change may cause some User Controls in our site to throw errors as they reference a channel path that no longer exists. Check the following files to make sure any references to /Channels/www.tropicalgreen.net/ are changed to /Channels/TropicalGreen/:

- /Login.aspx
- /UserControls/RightMenu.aspx
- /UserControls/SiteMapTree.aspx
- /UserControls/TopMenu.aspx

You'll probably want to add an additional file in the root of our website that automatically redirects users to our site's channel. Call the file default.aspx, and it should contain the following line:

```
<% Response.Redirect("/TropicalGreen/") %>
```

Any requests for http://www.tropicalgreen.net will now be redirected to http://www.tropicalgreen.net/TropicalGreen/.

If your solution requires the Map Channel Names to Host Header Names feature, the MCMS Connector search solution will not be appropriate for your needs. You can, however, build your own custom search solution as described in detail later in this chapter.

Assigning a Search Account

Our Tropical Green site has both a public section of the site and a members-only section. If an anonymous user, or guest, executes a search, they should only see results from the public portion of the site. However, if an authenticated user executes a search query, they should see appropriate results from both the public and private portions of the site.

In order for SharePoint to index our entire site, including the members-only section, we need to create a new account that will have access to the entire site. We'll then configure SharePoint to use this account when indexing. Let's assume we have an account already created called **MCMSBOOK\SearchCrawler**. The first thing we need to do is configure SharePoint Portal Server to use this account when crawling content.

1. Start the SharePoint Central Administration by pointing to Start | All Programs | SharePoint Portal Server | SharePoint Central Administration.

2. Under the section Server Configuration, click the Configure Server Farm Account Settings link.

3. Enter the search crawler account credentials in the Default Content Access Account section and click OK.

Default Content Access Account

Specify a Windows account to use as the default account when creating an index of content sources. This account must have read access to the content being crawled. If you are installing SharePoint Portal Server with Microsoft SQL Server Desktop Engine 2000, it is recommended but not required that you specify a domain account rather than using the default setting.

☑ Specify account:

User name (DOMAIN\user name): *

MCMSBOOK\SearchCrawler

Password: *

●●●●●●●●

Confirm Password: *

●●●●●●●●

Now we need to grant our SearchCrawler account subscriber rights to the entire Tropical Green website.

We're going to assume you have already installed the MCMS Connector for SharePoint Technologies as its installer creates an MCMS Search subscriber group in Site Manager for use in searching your MCMS channel structure. Refer to Appendix B for assistance in installing the MCMS Connector.

1. Start Site Manager by pointing to Start | All Programs | Microsoft Content Management Server | Site Manager.
2. Select the User Roles button on the left panel within Site Manager.
3. Select the Subscribers user role.
4. Then right-click the MCMS Search User Subscribers role and select Properties.
5. Click the Group Rights tab to view all the channels, templates, and resources the MCMS Search User role has rights to. All channels, templates, and resources should be checked.
6. Click the Group Members tab and click the Modify button.
7. Enter the MCMSBOOK\SearchCrawler user that we added above as the SharePoint crawl account and click OK.
8. Click OK again to close the property window.

We have now configured SharePoint to crawl our site using the dedicated account and granted the account access to all content within the Tropical Green site.

Enable Guest Access for Tropical Green

Because our site will be publicly available, we need to make sure that it's not going to require visitors to log in. To configure our Tropical Green site to allow guests to view it, we need to enable guest access. If you would like full details of how this is done, full instructions are given in the first book, *Building Websites with Microsoft Content Management Server* (Packt Publishing, January 2005, ISBN 1-904811-16-7). See the section *Welcoming Guests to the Site* in Chapter 18.

If you have already configured your site for guest access, you can skip this step.

In order to allow guests into our site, we need to:

1. Create a new MCMS Guest Account in the domain or as a local user on the server.
2. Using the SCA, configure MCMS to allow guests and to use the account created in step 1 as the Guest Login Account.
3. Now that MCMS is configured to allow guests into the site, add the account created in step 1 to a subscribers' rights group and grant the rights group access to all channels, resource galleries, and template galleries that currently exist in the site, except for the Members channel located in the Gardens channel.

We've chosen to enable guest access to the site for simplicity. However, it is possible for SharePoint to index our site using Forms or Windows Authentication. For Forms Authentication, we would need to create a special home page that automatically logs the user in with a predefined account to gain access to the site so that SharePoint could start its crawl. We would have to grant the SharePoint crawler account permission to the appropriate subscriber rights group.

If you chose to create an alternate home page to automatically log SharePoint into your site, keep in mind that any user could use this page to gain access to your site. Special care should be taken if you use this method, such as adding IP restriction to this page so that only the SharePoint server can access it.

Output Caching and Last-Modified Dates of Postings

ASP.NET is not particularly sophisticated when it comes to generating HTTP status codes, simply returning an HTTP code of 200 (OK) for every request rather than sending a Last-Modified HTTP header. When SharePoint Portal Server performs an incremental index crawl, it sends HTTP GET requests for every page on the site it finds. If a page has previously been indexed and it returned a Last-Modified header, SharePoint Portal Server sends a conditional HTTP GET request that includes an If-Modified-Since HTTP header with the date previously returned in the Last-Modified HTTP header. If the response is an HTTP status code 304 (not modified), SharePoint will not index the page again. However, because ASP.NET always returns status code 200, the site will never be incrementally crawled by SPS, and will effectively undergo a full index every time the gatherer is executed. As MCMS templates files are actually a special kind of ASP.NET Web Form, this also affects postings based on these template files. Refer to Chapter 4, *Preparing Postings for Search Indexing*, for instructions on how to address this problem.

One thing to consider is channel rendering scripts and postings that contain dynamic lists of links to other postings. While these scripts and postings may not have changed since the last index, the content generated by these scripts can change between different calls to the posting. If this content is content you wish to search for, you should ensure that postings containing such controls are always indexed by not returning a Last-Modified HTTP header.

The Connector SearchMetaTagGenerator Control

The last modification we need to do is to add a control that ships with MCMS Connector for SharePoint Technologies. The `SearchMetaTagGenerator` outputs standard and/or custom page properties. In addition, we can use it to control what properties are output and even add our own custom properties. Adding the `SearchMetaTagGenerator` control to your templates is very easy. Let's add it to our `Plant.aspx` template:

1. Open the `Plant.aspx` file in **Design** view.

2. In the Toolbox, select the `Content Management Server` tab, and drag the `SearchMetaTagGenerator` to the top of our template.

If you don't see the `SearchMetaTagGenerator` in the Toolbox and you've installed the MCMS Connector for SharePoint Technologies, right-click on the Toolbox and select **Add/Remove Items**. In the **Customize ToolBox** dialog, click **Browse**, navigate to the `Microsoft Content Management Server\Server\bin\` directory, and select the `Microsoft.ContentManagement.SharePoint.WebControls.dll` assembly. Finally click OK in the **Customize ToolBox** dialog. You should now see the additional controls in your Toolbox.

If you haven't installed the MCMS Connector for SharePoint Technologies, refer to Appendix B, *MCMS Connector for SharePoint Technologies*, for download and installation information.

---

3. Click the `SearchMetaTagGenerator` control we just added, and in the property window, select one of the following `PropertyTypes`:

    *   **CustomProperties:** Generates META tags for custom page properties.

    *   **StandardProperties:** Generates META tags for standard page properties (such as `DisplayName`, `DisplayPath`).

    *   **CustomAndStandardProperties:** Generates META tags for both custom and standard page properties (default).

    *   **PropertiesFromXMLFile:** Generates META tags for the properties specified in the `SearchPropertyCollection.xml` file. More on this in just a moment.

4. For now, let's chose the `CustomAndStandardProperties` property type.

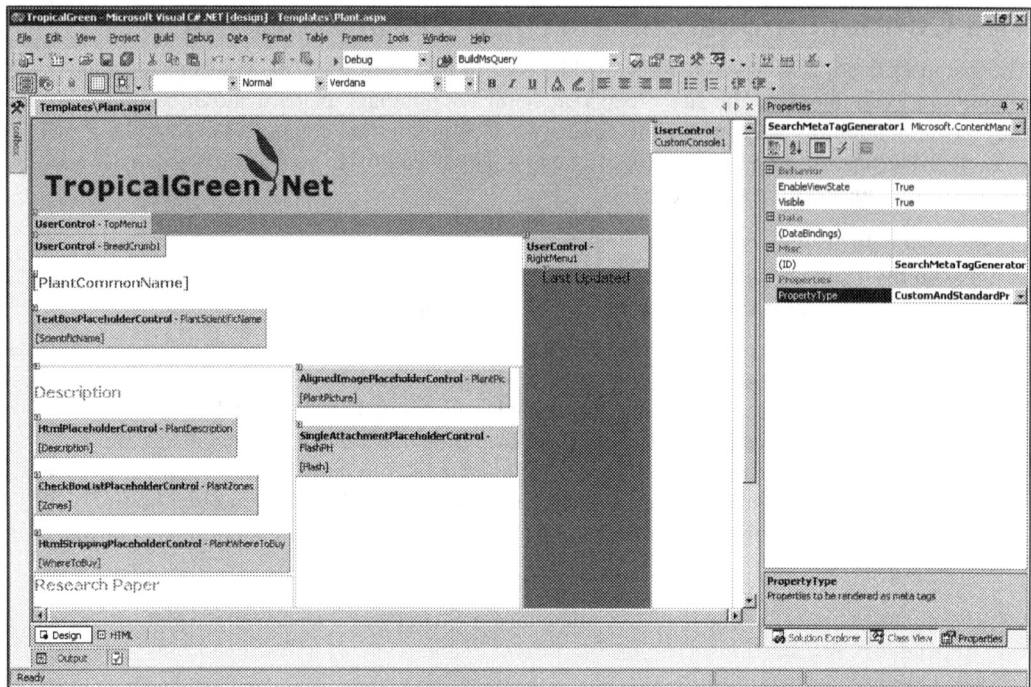

5. Because the Visual Studio .NET designer won't allow us to drop controls into the <head></head> portion of the page, we need to move the code declaration of the SearchMetaTagGenerator control from the body of the page to the heading. Switch to HTML view, find the SearchMetaTagGenerator control we just added, and move it up between the <head> and </head> tags.

6. As with any changes, we should now rebuild the Tropical Green project.

7. Open a browser, and navigate through the site to a plant posting in the plant catalog section of the site. Take a moment to view the source of the posting you navigate to. Notice all the extra META tags that have been added. Here's an example:

```
<meta name="FIRSTSAVEDBY" content="">
<meta name="CREATEDBY" content="WinNT://MCMSBook/Author1">
<meta name="CREATEDDATE" content="9/6/2004">
<meta name="DESCRIPTION" content="">
<meta name="DISPLAYNAME" content="Aloe Vera">
<meta name="DISPLAYPATH" content="/Channels/Home/Plant Catalog/Aloe Vera">
<meta name="EXPIRYDATE" content="1/1/3000">
<meta name="GUID" content="{569D1CCA-9A9D-4C43-B0C3-DB1AACD98684}">
<meta name="ISIMPORTANT" content="False">
<meta name="LASTAPPROVEDDECLINEDBY" content="WinNT://MCMSBook/Editor1">
<meta name="LASTMODIFIEDBY" content="WinNT://MCMSBook/Editor1">
<meta name="LASTMODIFIEDDATE" content="4/28/2005">
<meta name="NAME" content="AloeVera">
<meta name="PATH" content="/Channels/www.tropicalgreen.net/PlantCatalog/AloeVera">
<meta name="STARTDATE" content="9/6/2004">
<meta name="URL" content="/www.tropicalgreen.net/PlantCatalog/Aloevera.htm">
```

Notice the FIRSTSAVEDBY property listed at the top of the META tags. This is a custom property that has been added to the posting. It is added to the META tags because we selected the CustomAndStandardProperties property type in the SearchMetaTagGenerator control. The other META tags are the standard properties generated by the SearchMetaTagGenerator control.

When rendered, any posting implemented with the Plant template will contain META tags in the <HEAD> portion of the page for each of the page's custom properties and standard properties.

One of the items available to us in the PropertyType field is PropertiesFromXMLFile. This option allows us to specify exactly which properties will be exported as META tags using an XML file located at Microsoft Content Management Server\Server\IIS_CMS\WssIntegration\ SearchPropertyCollection.xml.

Once you have specified which properties you want to use, including custom properties you've added, you need to tell SharePoint to index these properties in the crawl. The console application SearchPropertiesSetup.exe included with MCMS Connector will tell SharePoint about the updated XML file. Run it using the following syntax:

```
SearchPropertiesSetup.exe –file "<path to file>\SearchPropertyCollection.xml"
```

The SearchPropertiesSetup.exe utility can be found in the following location: <install drive>:\Program Files\MCMS 2002 Connector for SharePoint Technologies\WSS\bin\.

Go ahead and execute the SearchPropertiesSetup.exe utility as above because our custom search solution will use one of the META tags it generates.

If you change the SearchPropertyCollection.xml file, you will need to re-execute the SearchPropertiesSetup.exe utility.

The MCMS Connector for SharePoint Technologies includes a help file with instructions on how to modify the XML file. Be aware that a Microsoft Support Knowledge Base article exists addressing an error in the help file instructions. The MSKB article *A problem occurs when you add the SearchMetaTagGenerator control to a template in Content Management Server 2002 Connector for SharePoint Technologies* (#872932) contains corrected instructions.

Our Tropical Green site is now configured to allow guests to visit the site, our templates have been modified to be more SPS search friendly, and we have included additional metadata in the <HEAD> section of all our rendered postings. Let's proceed to create a content source in SharePoint to index our site.

Configuring SharePoint Portal Server Search

With our MCMS site ready for indexing, we now turn to SPS. First, we will configure SharePoint to index our Tropical Green site. After creating the index, we'll create a source group that will contain the content source. Source groups are used to group content sources together in a logical collection. In our case, we'll have a single content source in our source group. The source group is what we'll reference when we create our search logic in the Tropical Green site.

> The next few steps assume you've created a portal in SPS. Refer to Appendix A, *Setting up MCMS and SPS on the Same Virtual Server*, for instructions on how to create a portal.
>
> While Appendix A details how to configure a virtual server to host an MCMS site and SharePoint portal at the same time, we do not want to do that for this chapter. We need two virtual servers, one for the www.tropicalgreen.net MCMS site and the other for the SharePoint portal.tropicalgreen.net site. Appendix A details how to create a new virtual server and a new SharePoint Portal Server portal.

Creating a New Content Source

The first step in configuring SPS search is to create a content source. One way to accomplish this is to use the SearchSetup.exe command-line tool included with the MCMS Connector. This utility can be found in the MCMS 2002 Connector for SharePoint Technologies\WSS\bin folder. The SearchSetup.exe utility creates the necessary content sources in SharePoint as well as all the site rules to include the root channel and all top-level channels in your site hierarchy in order to include and exclude the appropriate content. For more information on the SearchSetup.exe utility, refer to the help included with the MCMS Connector.

> In order to use the MCMS Connector search controls SearchInputControl and SearchResultControl, you need to use the SearchSetup.exe utility to create your content source and source group in your SharePoint portal. This is because the MCMS Connector search controls are hard-coded to look for a specific SharePoint search group named "CMSChannels". To complete the two search examples in this chapter, create two sets of content sources by following the steps in this section using the SearchSetup.exe utility and by creating the content source manually.

Creating a Content Source with the MCMS Connector Utility

Let's use the MCMS Connector SearchSetup.exe command-line utility to create a new content source and source group:

1. Open a command prompt and change the current directory to the following MCMS Connector default utility directory:

   cd "C:\Program Files\MCMS Connector for SharePoint Technologies\WSS\Bin"

2. Enter the following command to create a new content source that will index our Tropical Green website, using the MCMS guest account to crawl the content, and initiate the crawl immediately after creating the content source (replacing the user and password credentials with your MCMS guest account credentials):

```
searchsetup.exe -url "http://www.tropicalgreen.net/TropicalGreen/"
                -crawl "1"
                -user "<domain>\SearchCrawler"
                -password "<password>"
                -portalurl "http://portal.tropicalgreen.net"
```

The table below describes each of the possible switches:

Switch	Description
url	The MCMS URL that will be used by SharePoint as the start point of the crawl.
crawl	Indicates whether or not a crawl is performed immediately after SharePoint creates the content source.
	A value of "1" instructs SharePoint to perform a crawl immediately. Otherwise, set it to a value of "0" to stop SharePoint from crawling the site.
user	The user account that has access to the MCMS content to be indexed.
password	Password of the user account.
portalurl	URL of the SharePoint portal server that will contain the content source.

> You only have to run this command-line program once, not every time you update the site. If you need to perform a full crawl of the site again, you can do so by resetting the content source and executing a full crawl. Refer to the SharePoint Portal Server documentation for more information on this.

Now that we have a new content source created, let's create a new search scope to make it easier to test our search results.

Creating a New Search Scope

While SharePoint is indexing our site, we should go ahead and create a search scope.

1. Open the General Content Settings and Indexing Status page by browsing to your portal and clicking the Site Settings link in the upper right. Under the Search Settings and Indexed Content section, click the Configure search and indexing link. Then click the Manage search scopes link.

2. On the Manage Search Scopes page, click the New Search Scope button. When prompted to create a new search scope, enter the following:

Field	Value
Name:	TropicalGreen.net (SearchSetup.exe)
Topics and Areas:	Include no topic or area in this scope
Content Source Groups:	Limit the scope to the following groups of content sources: CMSChannels

Name

Type a name for this search scope.

Name *

[TropicalGreen.net (SearchSetup.exe)   ]

Topics and Areas

Select **Include all contents** if this search scope should include all areas and content source groups. Select **Include no topic or area in this scope** if this search scope should not include any area or topic contents. Select **Limit the search scope to items in the following topics or areas** and then click Change areas to select topics or areas for this search scope.

The selected area and all of its subareas will be included in this search scope.

- ○ Include all contents
- ⦿ Include no topic or area in this scope
- ○ Limit the search scope to items in the following topics or areas

  Topics and Areas

  None

  Change areas

Content Source Groups

Content sources outside the portal can be grouped into certain types, and you may want to limit your search scope to exclude or include particular content source groups.

Select **Include all content sources** if this search scope is not limited to certain content source groups.
Select **Exclude all content sources** to limit the search scope to only the default content source for this portal.

To limit the search scope to particular content source groups, select **Limit the scope to the following groups of content sources**, and then select the content source groups that apply.

- ○ Exclude all content sources
- ○ Include all content sources
- ⦿ Limit the scope to the following groups of content sources:
  - ☑ CMSChannels
  - ☐ Non-portal content
  - ☐ People
  - ☐ Sites in site directory

[OK]   [Cancel]

3. After clicking OK, SharePoint will take us back to the Manage Search Scopes page with our new scope.

4. Let's get back to the search configuration page. Click the Site Settings link in the heading of the Manage Search Scopes page. Then click the Configure search and indexing link under the Search Settings and Indexed Content section.

5. At this point, we should make sure everything is configured correctly. We've created a content source and added that source to a new site group. By now, SharePoint should have finished indexing our site (unless you added hundreds of postings to it). Look at the Non-portal content column. If you see errors, warnings, or zero documents indexed, examine the log—some errors might not be errors at all, others may indicate errors within the MCMS site itself.

Number of processed documents:	93	
Scheduled updates:	3 schedules	
Associated Portal:	Not associated	
Topic Assistant status:	The Topic Assistant has not been trained.	
Server name mappings:	None defined	
Log settings:	Do not log success; Do not log excluded URLs	
	Portal Content	**Non-Portal Content**
Documents in index:	71	22
Last update status:	Idle	Idle
Last update time:	4/30/2005 9:50 PM	4/24/2005 8:34 AM
Warnings from last update:	0	0
Errors from last update:	0	0

One common error, The address could not be found, is usually caused by links to empty channels that are not configured to use channel rendering scripts. Since we'd expect guests to receive this error when browsing the site, it's not surprising the SharePoint gatherer ran into the same problem. This is not a problem with the SharePoint index, but rather with the structure or of our site: channels that could be empty should have channel rendering scripts or be hidden from the navigation.

6. If there are no problems, we can test our index. Click the Home link in the portal navigation to get to the homepage. In the upper-right corner, select TropicalGreen.net (SearchSetup.exe) in the dropdown (the whole name may not appear due to design constraints on the width of the dropdown), enter ficus in the search box, and click the green arrow to execute the search. The search results should find the posting in the plant catalog.

http://www.tropicalgreen.net

Plant
> > Ficus Ficus Login Last Updated: 4/24/2005 8:35:43 AM
http://www.tropicalgreen.net/TropicalGreen/PlantCatalog/Ficus.htm - 8 KB
Add to My Links | Alert Me | Item details

ChannelRenderingScript
Plant Catalog • • • • • • • • • Login
http://www.tropicalgreen.net/TropicalGreen/PlantCatalog - 6 KB
Add to My Links | Alert Me | Item details

HomePage
Go Live the sunny side of life! Read articles about club members and their gardens Visit our various garden settings A-Z listing of tropical plant fact sheets Recent C...
http://www.tropicalgreen.net/TropicalGreen - 7 KB
Add to My Links | Alert Me | Item details

Your search results may not match what is indicated in the image above as your postings may have been modified recently.

We now have a SharePoint search scope created and indexing our Tropical Green site. While this search scope can be used within the portal to search our site, we will use it via the SPS Query Service Web Service from our MCMS site to provide search functionality to our users.

Creating a Content Source Manually

Another option is to manually create the content source in SharePoint rather than allowing the SearchSetup.exe utility to create it for us. We'll walk you though these steps so you will have an understanding of what's involved in creating a content source and source group in a SharePoint portal.

> Although we're explaining how to create a content source both with the `searchSetup.exe` utility and manually using the same content source names, you must choose only one method as it is not possible to create two content sources with the same name.

Let's start by creating an index of our Tropical Green website in our SharePoint portal:

> Refer to Appendix A for a walkthrough of the steps in creating a portal.

1. Start the SharePoint Central Administration by pointing to Start | All Programs | SharePoint Portal Server | SharePoint Central Administration.

2. Click List and manage portal site under the Portal Site and Virtual Server Configuration section.

3. The Manage Portal Sites page contains a list of all portals in the SharePoint farm. Drag your mouse cursor over the right-hand side of the list and click the drop-down arrow that appears when the mouse cursor is over a portal and select Manage Portal Site Properties (as seen in the image below):

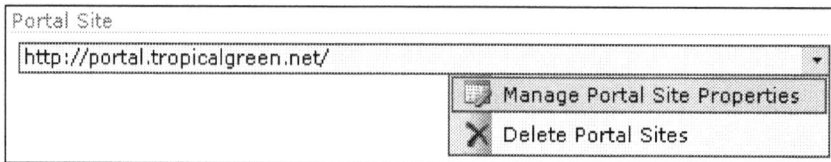

4. Under the section Search Settings and Indexed Content, click the Configure search and indexing link.

> The following instructions assume you have not enabled SharePoint's advanced search administration mode. The main difference between basic and advanced mode is advanced mode allows you to work directly with content indexes. Basic mode creates content indexes when you create a content source. In our example, basic mode is adequate for our needs.

Now we will create the content source.

1. Under the General Content Settings and Indexing Status section, click the link Add content source.

2. On the Add Content Source page, select Web page or Web site and click Next.

Content Type

Select a content type.

○ Exchange Server public folder

○ File share

⦿ Web page or Web site

Any content, from a single Web page to an entire Web site. This includes SharePoint Portal Server portal sites and Windows SharePoint Services sites.

[Next >]　[Cancel]

3. After selecting that you want to create an external website index, enter the following information on the Add Content Source: Web page or Web site page. Once you have filled out the form, click Finish.

Field	Value
Address:	http://www.tropicalgreen.net/TropicalGreen/
Description:	Tropical Green web site
Crawl Configuration	This site – follow links to all pages on this site
Participate in adaptive updates	Checked

If you intend to use the manually-created content source with the MCMS Connector controls, you need to name the content source "CMSChannels" as this name is hard-coded in the connector controls.

In this example, the virtual server acting as an MCMS Web Entry Point for our Tropical Green website handles requests for http://www.tropicalgreen.net/. The example will still work if you have set up the Tropical Green website on http://localhost/; you'll just need to make the appropriate changes in the steps to point to the correct domain.

Address and Description

Enter an address and description of the Web site to include in the content index.

Address: *

http://www.tropicalgreen.net/TropicalGreen/

Examples:
http://example.microsoft.com/my_page.htm, or
http://example.microsoft.com

Description: *

Tropical Green web site

Crawl Configuration

Page depth specifies how far to follow each series of links, starting from each link in the content source. Site hops, which occur when a link from one Web site leads to another site, can be also be limited.

Note: The crawl configuration for SharePoint Portal Server portal sites and Windows SharePoint Services sites should use the default value, **This Site - follow all links for this site.**

Including content in adaptive updates will make changes will show up more quickly in search results, but updates will use more server resources.

(•) This site - follow links to all pages on this site

( ) This page only

( ) Custom - specify page depth and site hops:

☐ Limit page depth:

Unlimited

☐ Limit site hops:

Unlimited

☑ Participate in adaptive updates

[« Back] [Finish] [Cancel]

4. Once you click Finish in the previous step, SharePoint will create the content source and present you with a confirmation page. At the bottom of the Created Web page or Web site Content Source, in the Start Update section, check the Start full update option and click OK. This will trigger the gatherer to start building an index of the Tropical Green website.

Once you have created a content source manually, follow the instructions under the section *Creating a New Search Scope* above to create a new source group using the settings in the following table:

Field	Value
Name:	TropicalGreen.net
Topics and Areas:	Include no topic or area in this scope
Content Source Groups:	Limit the scope to the following groups of content sources: Tropical Green web site

Search Rights for the MCMS Application Pool Account

SharePoint portals typically do not allow anonymous users to access the site, and users must log in. The SearchResultControl included with the MCMS Connector, which we'll use in a moment, uses the account of the application pool identity that contains the MCMS site from which a search query is triggered to access the SharePoint search service.

1. Browse to the portal we created earlier by opening Internet Explorer and navigating to http://portal.tropicalgreen.net. Then, click Site Settings in the upper right corner.

2. Under the General Settings section, select Manage security and additional settings.

3. On the Manage Site Groups page, click Add a Site Group. When prompted to enter information about the new group, enter the following values:

Property	Value
Site group name	Search Only
Description	This site group grants a user the right to query the search index
Rights	Search – Search the portal site and all related content

> When you select Search – Search the portal site and all related content, SharePoint automatically checks the View Pages – View pages in an area option. Uncheck the View Pages option after you check the Search option.

4. On the Manage Site Groups page, click Search Only, the name of our new group.
5. On the Members of "Search Only" page, click Add Members. Add the account that's configured as the identity of the application pool your MCMS site runs under. Once you've selected the account, click OK.

> To find the identity of the application pool your MCMS site runs under, open Internet Information Services. Expand the nodes for local computer | Application Pools. Look for the application pool that your MCMS site is configured to use and view its properties. The identity is listed under the Identity tab.

6. After selecting the account, on the Add User page, ensure that Search Only under the Step 2: Choose Site Groups section is checked and click OK.
7. On the last page, where SharePoint asks you to confirm the details of the account you're adding, make sure the Send the following e-mail to let these users know they have been added option is unchecked, and click Finish.

Our MCMS site now has the permissions needed to log in to our portal and execute a search.

Adding a Search Page to the MCMS Site

We have two options available to implement a search capability for our Tropical Green site:

- Leverage the ASP.NET Server Controls included in the MCMS Connector for SharePoint Technologies that allow search queries to be executed.
- Create our own solution.

The MCMS Connector includes the following three controls that assist you in implementing search functionality for an MCMS site by leveraging SharePoint search scopes:

- **SearchInputControl:** Used to create the search form input for a search to be submitted.

- **SearchResultControl:** Takes search criteria entered in the `SearchInputControl`, executes the search against the SPS search Web Service, and displays the results in list form.

- **SearchMetaTagGenerator:** Creates HTML META tags based on the `PropertyType` setting. META tags generated can include standard page properties as well as custom properties.

You can use these three controls on the same page or separate pages. This is very convenient as you may wish to include a small search keyword input box on all pages in your site that submits the search to a separate results page, but you might want to provide the search input on the search results page as well.

Once we have created a working search page using the MCMS Connector controls, we'll create a custom solution that won't include anything provided in the MCMS Connector. Our solution will include an advanced search, specific to our site, and a customized search result listing.

Both options have distinct advantages and disadvantages. Which one you'll implement on your MCMS site will depend entirely upon your requirements, customization needs, and available development time. The following table outlines a few of the more prominent advantages and disadvantages of using the MCMS Connector controls as well as rolling your own solution:

Implementing search leveraging MCMS Connector controls:

Advantages	Disadvantages
Fast install and integration into pages & templates	No customization of search input controls
Will work out of the box with minimal configuration	No customization of search result list

Implementing search with a custom solution:

Advantages	Disadvantages
Complete control over layout of search input form	Requires extra development time and testing
Complete control over search result list	
Create special advanced search based on specific site requirements	

Searching with the MCMS SharePoint Connector

The first thing we'll do for this is to create a new search page in our Tropical Green project. This page will not be a new MCMS template, but a regular ASP.NET page. You could make this a template, but there's no real advantage in doing so because there will only be a single search page on our site with no extra content.

1. In Visual Studio .NET, right-click on the Tropical Green project and select Add Web Form.

2. Name the new ASPX page `search.aspx` and click Open.

3. If the page doesn't load in Design mode, click Design in the lower left corner.

4. Change the page layout to FlowLayout.

5. Drag the /Styles/styles.css, /UserControls/TopMenu.ascx, and /UserControls/RightMenu.ascx files from Solution Explorer onto the designer.

6. Switch to HTML mode and modify the body tag as follows:
   ```
   <body topmargin="0" leftmargin="0" rightmargin="0">
   ```

7. Add the following code between the <form> and </form> tags, replacing the two user controls that were just added:

```
<form id="Form1" method="post" runat="server">
<table width="100%" border="0" cellspacing="0" cellpadding="0">
  <tr>
    <td width="100%" colspan="2" valign="top" bgcolor="#ffcc00">
      <img src="/tropicalgreen/images/Logo.gif">
    </td>
    <td vAlign="top" rowSpan="10"> </td>
  </tr>
  <tr bgColor="#66cc33">
    <td colSpan="2"><uc1:TopMenu id="TopMenu1"
          runat="server"></uc1:TopMenu></td>
  </tr>
  <tr>
    <td vAlign="top" style="PADDING-RIGHT:30px; PADDING-LEFT:30px;
                            PADDING-BOTTOM:30px;">
      <p> </p>
      <table cellspacing="0" cellpadding="10" border="1"
          bordercolor="#669900">
        <tr vAlign="top">
          <td>Tropical Green Search:</td>
        </tr>
        <tr>
          <td vAlign="top">
          </td>
        </tr>
      </table>
    </td>
    <td class="RightMenuBar" width="20%" valign="top" height="100%"
        align="center" rowspan="2" bgcolor="#669900">
      <uc1:RightMenu id="RightMenu1" runat="server"></uc1:RightMenu>
    </td>
  </tr>
</table>
</form>
```

Why did we drag the user controls onto the page and then replace the resulting HTML?

Dragging the user controls onto the page adds the <%@ Register %> lines to the ASPX for us as well as adding the user control ASP.NET tags to the HTML. We then only need to modify the HTML to make it more presentable.

You should now have a page that looks like the following when viewed in Design mode:

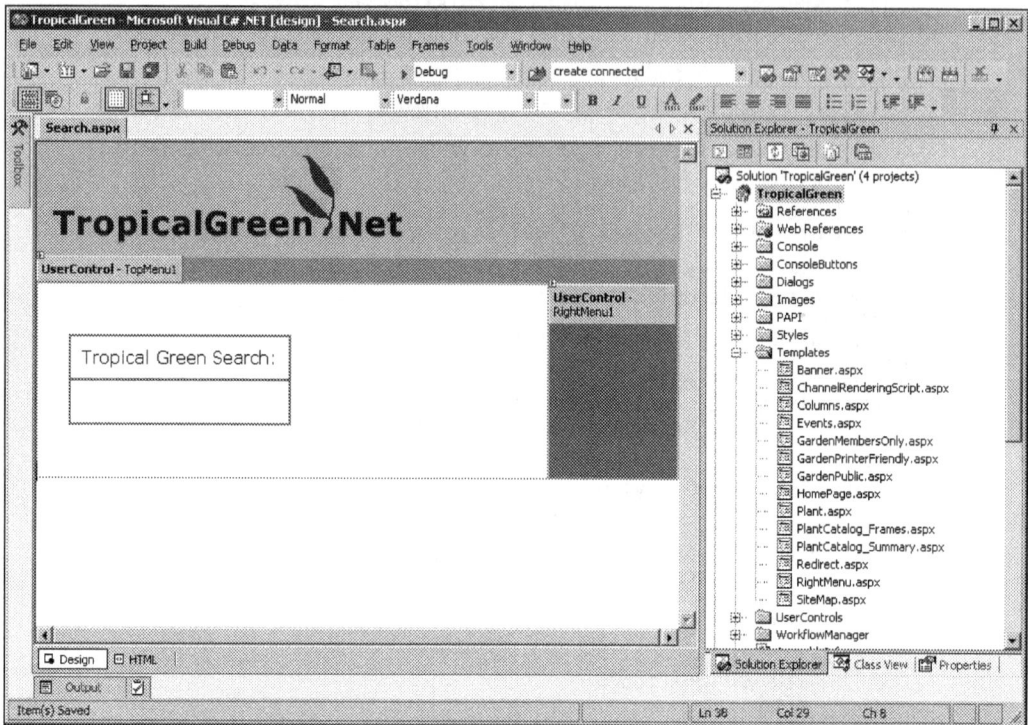

Let's save our new search page, build the Tropical Green project, and navigate to it in a browser to make sure everything is in order before we go about adding the search input and results controls.

1. Save all changes to the search.aspx page.

2. Right-click the TropicalGreen project and select Build.

3. If there are no errors in the build, open a browser and navigate to:
   http://www.tropicalgreen.net/TropicalGreen/Search.aspx.

4. If there are any issues, retrace the steps we've taken to this point, address the errors, and retry the URL.

Now that we have a working search page, we need to add some functionality to it. We'll add the two MCMS Connector server controls, make some configuration changes, build the solution, and test our search page.

1. Open the search.aspx page in Visual Studio .NET if it's not already open, and switch to Design view.

2. Open the Visual Studio .NET Toolbox and drag the SearchInputControl and SearchResultsControl into the table cell below the Tropical Green Search cell. Refer to the following image for placement:

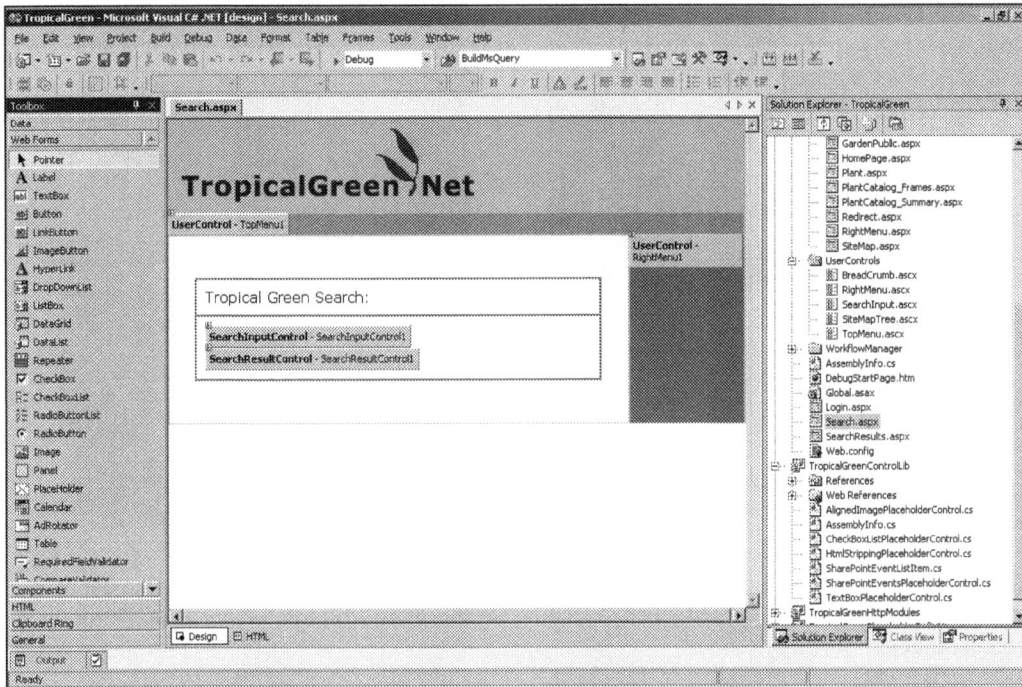

3. Select the `SearchInputControl` we added to `search.aspx` and set the following properties in the Visual Studio .NET property window:

Property	Value
SearchMode	Simple
SearchResultPage	/TropicalGreen/Search.aspx

4. Select the `SearchResultControl` we added to the `search.aspx` page and set the following properties using the Visual Studio .NET property window:

Property	Value
PortalUrl	http://portal.tropicalgreen.net/
SearchResultPageSize	10

We're using the URL of the portal created in Appendix A. Replace this URL with whatever portal you configured for the content source and search group in the steps already covered in this chapter.

Let's see if our search is working. Save all changes to `search.aspx`, build the Tropical Green project, and go to `http://www.tropicalgreen.net/TropicalGreen/Search.aspx` in a browser. You should see a page similar to the one below:

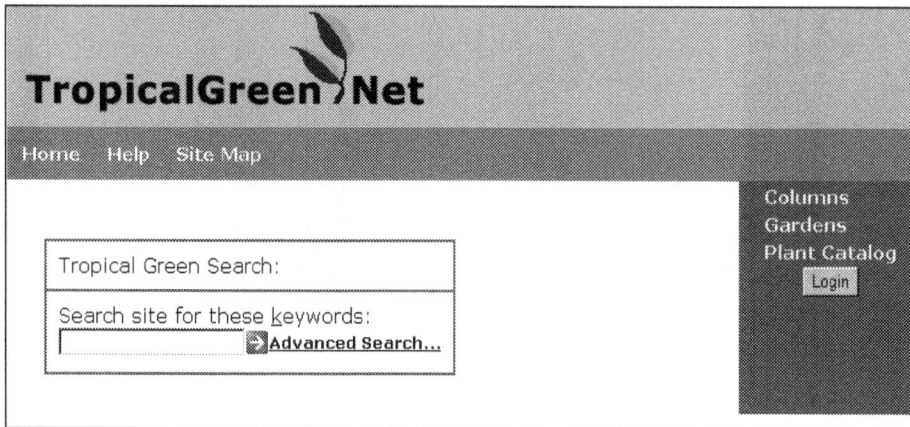

Enter a word you know will be found on the site, such as ficus. You will see the same list of search results that were returned when searching for the same string in the portal containing the content index.

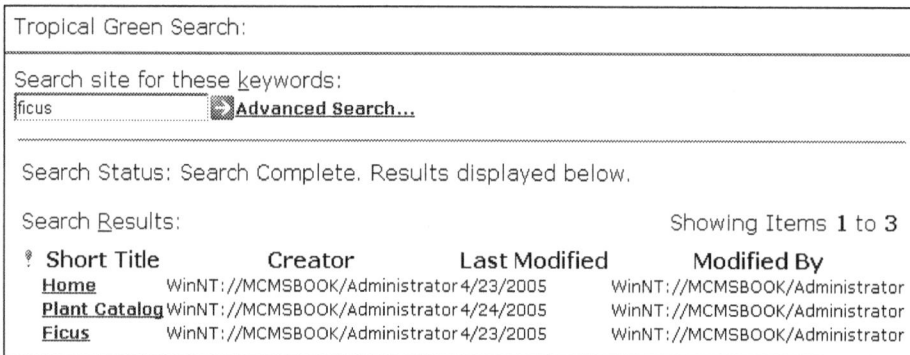

> If you receive an error message stating "There was a problem loading the input control. The error returned by the system is: Could not find part of the path c:\inetpub\wwwroot\ tropicalgreen\cms\wssintegration\searchpropertycollection.xml", double-check that you added the *CMS* virtual directory in your *TropicalGreen* web application.

At this point, we have got search capabilities on our site thanks to the MCMS Connector controls and SPS's search features. But this solution is very limited, for instance there is no way to change the look and feel of these controls and there is also no way to configure which properties are displayed in the result page, for instance to show a short description for the returned documents.

To address this, we will now build our own search controls.

Building a Custom Search Implementation

As outlined previously, there are advantages and disadvantages to the MCMS Connector search controls. The most obvious is the fact that the SearchResultControl does not allow us to configure the results returned by the SPS search We will now build our own search implementation that will leverage the SPS search Web Service, offer advanced and specialized searching to our users, and present the results in a customizable manner.

About the SharePoint Portal Server Query Service

Everything we are about to build depends upon the Query Service Web Service, included in SPS, that exposes search functionality to remote clients, such as our website. This web service accepts a request in the Microsoft.Search.Query XML format and returns a response in the Microsoft.Search.Response XML format. In order to build a robust solution, the request we submit will use the Microsoft SQL Syntax for full-text Search. One method offered by the Query Service is QueryEx, which we will use as it returns results in the form of a DataSet.

> For more information and documentation on the Microsoft SharePoint Portal Server Query Service Web Service, see the MSDN documentation at: http://msdn.microsoft.com/library/default.asp?url=/library/en-us/spptsdk/html/cSPSQueryService_SV01004360.asp.

Building a Search Input Control

The first thing we'll do is build a search input control that will submit a search query to a page for processing. This implementation will allow us to add a small search component to all of our templates quickly. Upon submitting a search query, our user control will add the query parameters to the querystring and redirect the request to the results page.

Let's first start by creating a new user control.

1. In Visual Studio .NET, right-click the User Controls folder in the Tropical Green project, and select Add | Add Web User Control.

2. Name the new control SearchInput.ascx.

3. While in Design view, drop controls from the Toolbox onto the Web Form and arrange them as shown below:

Control	Properties
TextBox	ID = txtSearchInput
Button	ID = btnExecuteSearch
	Text = Go
LinkButton	ID = lnkAdvancedSearch
	Text = advanced search options

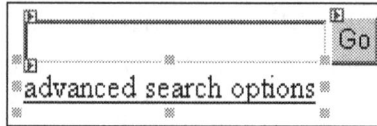

4. The `LinkButton` we created will take the user to the search results page, which we'll add some advanced searching features to later. Double-click our `LinkButton`. Visual Studio .NET will create an empty event handler for the `Click()` event. Add a single line of code to this empty event handler to redirect the user to the search results page:

```
private void lnkAdvancedSearch_Click(object sender, System.EventArgs e)
{
    Response.Redirect(Request.ApplicationPath + "/SearchResults.aspx");
}
```

5. Next, we need to create an event handler for when a user clicks our Go button. We'll take the keywords entered in the `TextBox` and send the search request to the search results page. Double-click the Go button and add the following code to the event handler:

```
private void btnExecuteSearch_Click(object sender, System.EventArgs e)
{
    string keywords = this.txtSearchInput.Text;
    keywords = HttpUtility.UrlEncode(keywords);
    Response.Redirect(Request.ApplicationPath
                + "/SearchResults.aspx?keywords="
                + keywords);
}
```

Let's see if everything is OK with our new search input control. Save your changes and build the project. If you receive any error messages, retrace your steps and ensure that there are no typos.

Before this control can be used, we need to add it to an existing template. While we'd ideally want to provide the search on all pages on our site (typically by adding it to a global heading control), we'll just add it to the homepage for now.

1. Open the `\Templates\HomePage.aspx` template and drag our new `SearchInput.ascx` into the top cell, to the right of the logo.

2. Switch to HTML view and find the control we just added. It will likely have an opening tag of `uc1:SearchInput`. Wrap this control in an HTML `DIV` and set its alignment to `right` as shown in the following code:

```
<td width="100%" colspan="2" valign="top" bgcolor="#ffcc00">
  <img src="/tropicalgreen/images/Logo.gif"> 
  <div align="right">
    <uc1:SearchInput id="SearchInput1" runat="server"></uc1:SearchInput>
  </div>
</td>
```

The `HomePage.aspx` template should now look similar to the following:

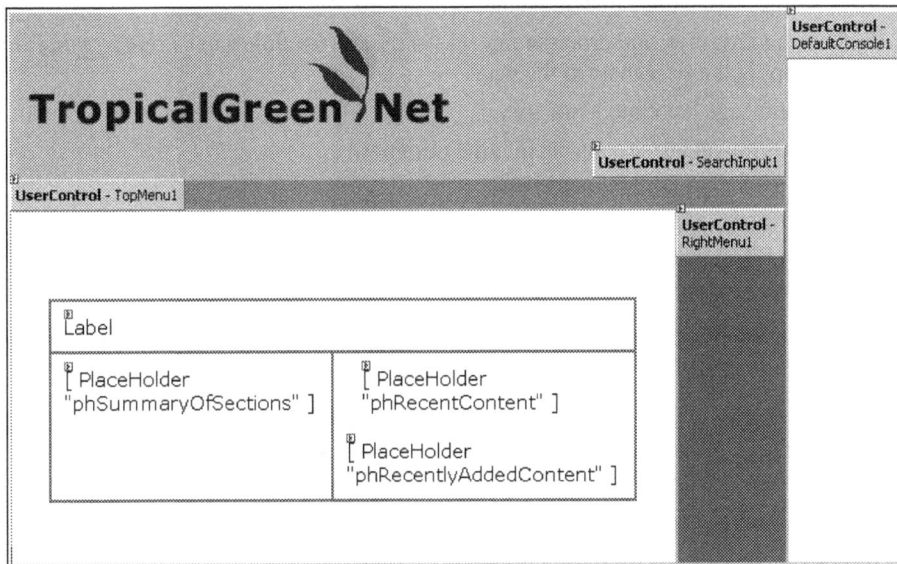

The Advanced Search and Results Page

Once we have our search input control built, we need a page that will execute the search against the SPS Query Service Web Service and display the results. In addition, like all other search result pages, we need to add advanced searching options such as limiting our search to the Tropical Green plant catalog.

Before we can start building the results page, we need to add a web reference to the SPS Query Service Web Service:

1. In Visual Studio .NET, right-click the TropicalGreen project and select Add Web Reference.

2. Enter the URL of the web service that will retrieve the search results. The URL of the Query Service is `http://[portal]/_vti_bin/search.asmx`. For this example, we'll use the portal created in Appendix A, `http://portal.tropicalgreen.net/_vti_bin/search.asmx`. Then click the Go button. You will likely be prompted for a user ID and password since this is part of the SharePoint portal virtual server, which isn't configured for anonymous access.

3. Once the web service loads and the available methods are shown in the Add Web Reference Dialog, click the Add Reference button to add the web service to our project.

For simplicity, the search results page we will create will not be a CMS template, rather it will be a standard ASP.NET Web Form in the root of the Tropical Green project.

1. Right-click the project and select Add | Add Web Form.

2. Give the new page the name `SearchResults.aspx`.

3. In Design view, drag and drop the `Styles.css` file from Solution Explorer onto the form to apply the stylesheet to the page.

4. Change the page layout to `FlowLayout`.

5. Drag the following user controls into the designer:

   • `\UserControls\TopMenu.ascx`

   • `\UserControls\RightMenu.ascx`

6. Switch to HTML view and modify the body tag as follows:
   ```
   <body topmargin="0" leftmargin="0">
   ```

7. Add the following HTML code to the page between the `<form>` tags, replacing the two controls we just added:
   ```html
   <form id="Form1" method="post" runat="server">
   <table width="100%" border="0" cellspacing="0" cellpadding="0">
     <tr>
       <td width="100%" colspan="2" valign="top" bgcolor="#ffcc00">
         <img src="/tropicalgreen/images/Logo.gif">
       </td>
       <td vAlign="top" rowSpan="10">
       </td>
     </tr>
     <tr bgColor="#66cc33">
       <td colSpan="2">
         <uc1:TopMenu id="TopMenu1" runat="server">
         </uc1:TopMenu>
       </td>
     </tr>
     <tr>
       <td vAlign="top" style="PADDING-RIGHT:30px; PADDING-LEFT:30px;
                               PADDING-BOTTOM:30px; PADDING-TOP:10px">
         <p> </p>
         <table cellspacing="0" cellpadding="10" border="1"
                                             bordercolor="#669900">
           <tr vAlign="top">
             <td>
               <b>Tropical Green Search:<b/>
             </td>
           </tr>
           <tr>
             <td vAlign="top">
               <b>Advanced Search</b>
               <p>
               <b>Search Results</b>
             </td>
           </tr>
         </table>
       </td>
       <td class="RightMenuBar" width="20%" valign="top" height="100%"
                           align="center" rowspan="2" bgcolor="#669900">
         <uc1:RightMenu id="RightMenu1" runat="server">
         </uc1:RightMenu>
       </td>
     </tr>
   </table>
   </form>
   ```

We now have the basic layout for our advanced search and search results page, which looks similar to the other templates in our site. Let's add some controls for our advanced search.

1. In Design view, drag a TextBox from the Toolbox and place it under the Advanced Search text.

2. In Design view, drag a Button from the Toolbox and place it to the right of the TextBox.

3. The next thing we need to add is a DataGrid to contain the results of the search. In Design view, drag a DataGrid control from the Toolbox to just under the Add Search Results Here text. We'll worry about formatting this control later, for now we just need something to show us our data.

4. Set the properties of the controls we just added according to the following table:

Property	Value
TextBox	ID = txtAdvancedSearch
Button	ID = btnAdvancedSearch
	Text = Go
DataGrid	ID = dgrSearchResults

Our advanced search page should now look like this:

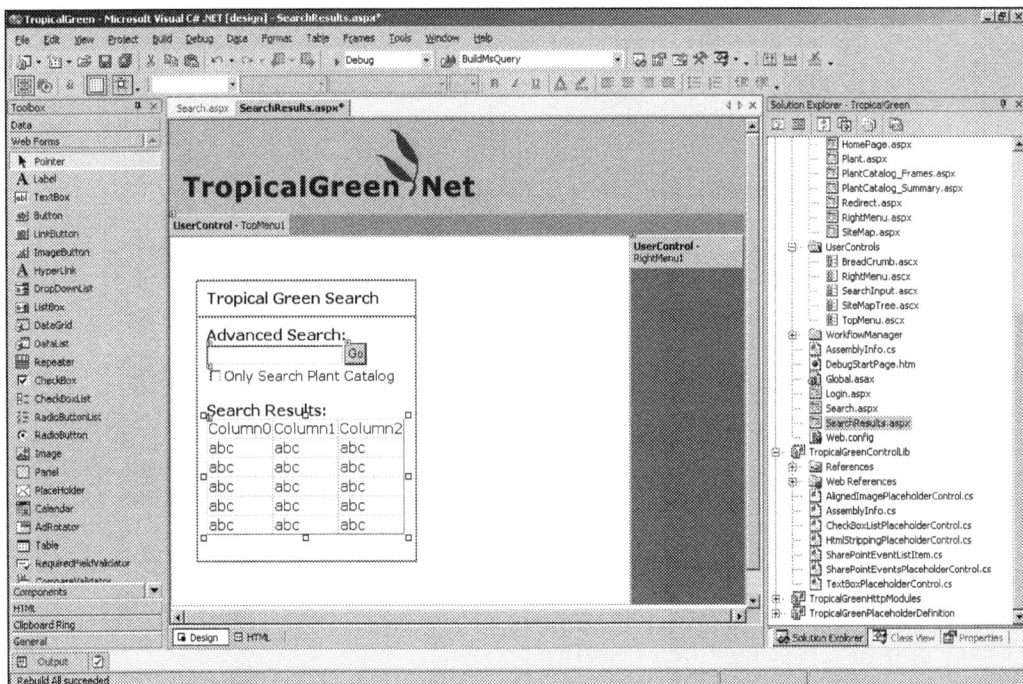

Now it's time to start coding our search logic. First, we need to add an event handler for our advanced search button.

1. In Design view, double-click the btnAdvancedSearch button to create a click event handler. Visual Studio .NET will add an event handler method to the code-behind file.

2. Add the following code to the btnAdvancedSearch_Click() event handler:

```
private void btnAdvancedSearch_Click(object sender, System.EventArgs e)
{
    string keywords = this.txtAdvancedSearch.Text;
    keywords = HttpUtility.UrlEncode(keywords);
    Response.Redirect(Request.ApplicationPath
                + "/SearchResults.aspx?keywords="
                + keywords);
}
```

Next, we need to check the querystring in the Page_Load() event handler to see if any keywords were passed from our SearchInput.ascx control or the txtAdvancedSearch TextBox.

Add the following code to check if there are any keywords supplied and execute the search if so:

```
private void Page_Load(object sender, System.EventArgs e)
{
    if (Request.QueryString["keywords"] != null
      && Request.QueryString["keywords"] != String.Empty)
    {
        string keywords = Request.QueryString["keywords"];
        DataSet ds = ExecuteSearch(keywords);
        this.dgrSearchResults.Visible = true;
        this.dgrSearchResults.DataSource = ds;
        this.dgrSearchResults.DataBind();

        // autofill the keyword input box with the search keywords
        this.txtAdvancedSearch.Text = keywords;
    }
    else
    {
        this.dgrSearchResults.Visible = false;
    }
}
```

Now we need to create the method that will execute the search against our SPS content index. This method will:

- Create an instance of the Query Service Web Service we just added to the project.

- Call a method that will build the MSQuery to submit to the Query Service.

- Execute the search.

- Bind the search results to a DataGrid.

Import the following namespaces in the SearchResults.aspx.cs file:

```
using System.Security.Principal;
using System.Runtime.InteropServices;
using System.Net;
using System.Text;
using System.Text.RegularExpressions;
using Microsoft.ContentManagement.Publishing;
```

Add the following method to the `SearchResults.aspx.cs` file after the `Page_Load()` event handler. This method will ensure the current thread is running under the original security context regardless of any impersonations that may have been invoked previously:

```
// Get reference to the RevertToSelf method
[DllImport("ADVAPI32.DLL")]
public static extern int RevertToSelf();

/// <summary>
/// Builds the appropriate MSQuery,
/// submits the query to the SPS Query Service,
/// and returns the results as a DataGrid.
/// </summary>
/// <param name="keywords">String of keywords to search for.</param>
/// <returns>DataSet of search results.</returns>
private DataSet ExecuteSearch(string keywords)
{
    // decode the list of keywords
    keywords = HttpUtility.UrlDecode(keywords);

    // create reference to the Query Service Web service
    net.tropicalgreen.portal.QueryService spsQueryService =
                        new net.tropicalgreen.portal.QueryService();

    // use the current application pool identity to login
    // to the SharePoint Query Service Web service
    WindowsIdentity CurrentUser = WindowsIdentity.GetCurrent();

    try
    {
        // use the Application Pool account to do access the
        // SharePoint Search Services
        RevertToSelf();
        spsQueryService.Credentials = CredentialCache.DefaultCredentials;
    }
    catch(System.Exception exception)
    {
        throw new System.Exception(exception.Message);
    }
    finally
    {
        // ensure that the original user is being impersonated again
        CurrentUser.Impersonate();
        CurrentUser = null;
    }

    // build MSQuery XML string to send to the Query Service
    // - change the content source to "CMSChannels" if you used SearchSetup.exe
    string msQuery = BuildMSQuery(keywords, "Tropical Green website");

    // execute the query and return the dataset
    return spsQueryService.QueryEx(msQuery);
}
```

> If you used the `SearchSetup.exe` program to create your content sources, you should use the content source group "CMSChannels" instead of "Tropical Green website" in the code above.

Our `ExecuteSearch()` method calls another method, called `BuildMSQuery()`, which constructs the MSQuery for sending to the `QueryEx()` web method. An MSQuery is composed of XML tags that provide instructions to the Query Service, such as the number of results to return in the request and a Microsoft SQL full-text (MSSQLFT) query. Building the MSSQLFT query and MSQuery is likely to be the most complicated task in implementing the SharePoint search. We'll break it into two tasks: building the actual MSSQLFT query and building the MSQuery XML string. We'll first build the full-text query that our MSQuery will use in the construction of the XML string we'll send to the Query Service.

Building the Microsoft SQL Full-Text Query

SPS's search process uses full-text indexes and queries for fast keyword lookups in order to provide timely responses to the end user. Full-text queries are very similar to regular T-SQL queries in Microsoft SQL Server, but you have additional functions, or predicates, that you can use to give your query more power. One of these predicates that is useful when searching SharePoint indexes is FREETEXT. FREETEXT takes a list of words separated by spaces, determines which words and phrases are significant, and uses that information to build an internal query to search the targeted data in an efficient manner.

First, you need to be aware of the various fields, or properties, available to you in your query. SharePoint provides a list with this information in the Site Settings administration page of your portal.

1. Open a new instance of Internet Explorer and navigate to our portal: http://portal.tropicalgreen.net.

2. Click on the Site Settings link in the upper right.

3. Under the Search Settings and Indexed Content section, click on the Manage properties from crawled documents link.

For each document crawled, the Manage Properties of Crawled Content page lists all properties that SharePoint could potentially contain indexed data on. For our purposes, we're only going to look at the two fields below, as they contain information for our search results page:

- DAV:href

- DAV:getlastmodified

Manage Properties of Crawled Content	
Use this page to view and manage properties associated with crawled documents. To hide or show properties not displayed in search, select or clear the **Hide excluded properties** check box.	
☑ Hide excluded properties	
Namespace / Property Name	Number Of Properties
⊟ DAV	12
contentclass	
creationdate	
displayname	
getcontentlength	
getcontenttype	
getlastmodified	
href	
iscollection	
isfolder	
isreadonly	
lastaccessed	
parentname	
⊞ urn:schemas.microsoft.com:fulltextqueryinfo	10
⊞ urn:schemas.microsoft.com:htmlinfo:metainfo	32
⊞ urn:schemas.microsoft.com:sharepoint:portal	1

> Notice that some of the fields listed under the `urn:schemas.microsoft.com:htmlinfo:`
> `metainfo` group are the same fields as we added to our template META tags using the
> `SearchMetaTagGenerator` user control from the MCMS Connector.

The other things we'll need are the name of the search scope we created, the name of the content
index, and our keywords. Once we have all that information, it makes most sense to construct the
MSSQLFT query in its own method for readability. We'll call this method `BuildMssqlftQuery()`
and pass it a string containing our search keywords and the search scope to query. Add the
following method at the end of the `SearchResults.aspx.cs` page:

```
/// <summary>
/// Builds the Microsoft SQL FullText query based on the parms.
/// </summary>
/// <param name="keywords">Keywords submitted for search.</param>
/// <param name="searchScope">SPS Search scope to filter.</param>
/// <returns>String of the MSSQLFT query.</returns>
private string BuildMSsqlftQuery(string keywords, string searchScope)
{
    StringBuilder mssqlftQuery = new StringBuilder();
    ArrayList whereClause = new ArrayList();

    #region FILTER: keywords
    // list of keywords to include
    if (keywords != null && keywords.Length >0)
    {
        // add the keyword filter, use a calculated weighted field
        // just as SPS does
        whereClause.Add(string.Format(" {0} {1}",
            "WITH (\"DAV:contentclass\":0,"
          + "\"urn:schemas.microsoft.com:fulltextqueryinfo:description\":0,"
          + "\"urn:schemas.microsoft.com:fulltextqueryinfo:sourcegroup\":0,"
          + "\"urn:schemas.microsoft.com:fulltextqueryinfo:cataloggroup\":0,"
          + "\"urn:schemas-microsoft-com:office:office#Keywords\":1.0,"
          + "\"urn:schemas-microsoft-com:office:office#Title\":0.9,"
          + "\"DAV:displayname\":0.9,"
          + "\"urn:schemas-microsoft-com:publishing:Category\":0.8,"
          + "\"urn:schemas-microsoft-com:office:office#Subject\":0.8,"
          + "\"urn:schemas-microsoft-com:office:office#Author\":0.7,"
          + "\"urn:schemas-microsoft-com:office:office#Description\":0.5,"
          + "\"urn:schemas-microsoft-com:sharepoint:portal:profile:"
          + "PreferredName\":0.2,contents:0.1,*:0.05) "
          + "AS #WeightedProps",
            "FREETEXT(#WeightedProps, '" +keywords.ToString().Trim() +"')")
            );
    }
    #endregion

    #region FILTER: sps source group
    // filter source group
    whereClause.Add(string.Format(" {0}",
        "(\"urn:schemas.microsoft.com:fulltextqueryinfo:Sourcegroup\" = '"
      + searchScope +"')"));
    #endregion

    //build search query
    mssqlftQuery.Append("SELECT ");
    mssqlftQuery.Append("\"DAV:href\",");
    mssqlftQuery.Append("\"DAV:getlastmodified\"");
    mssqlftQuery.Append(" FROM Non_Portal_Content..SCOPE()");
```

```
        mssqlftQuery.Append(" WHERE ");
        int i=0;
        foreach (string s in whereClause)
        {
          if (i > 0)
            mssqlftQuery.Append(" AND ");
          mssqlftQuery.Append(s);
          i++;
        }
        return mssqlftQuery.ToString();
    }
```

Notice we added a calculated field, which we used to apply certain weight to some fields. This is how SharePoint actually executes its own search. You could configure the property weighting to give more emphasis to specific properties in your query. For example, you may want to give more weight to the title of the page, or to the keywords stored in the HTML META tags, than to the contents of the page.

Now that we have this method, let's move on to creating the MSQuery string. We'll use this method in the construction of our MSQuery string.

Building the MSQuery XML String

We know that the SPS Query Service Web Service accepts a single parameter: an MSQuery string. This string is actually an XML document, but it's passed to the Query Service as a string. The XML tags in this string tell the Query Service the type of response it supports, how many records to return in the result, and the result index to start the search results at. The `<StartAt></StartAt>` element is what you can use in paging your result set. We won't be incorporating paging into our site as it is small, but you can see how easy it would be to do so.

Let's get started, by creating our `BuildMSQuery()` method that returns a complete MSQuery XML string containing all the information necessary to execute a query against a SharePoint index. Add the following method at the end of the `SearchResults.aspx.cs` page:

```
/// <summary>
/// Builds an MSQuery with an embedded MSSQLFT query embedded
/// for submission to SharePointPS Query Service.
/// </summary>
/// <param name="keywords">Keywords submitted for search.</param>
/// <param name="searchScope">SPS Search scope to filter.</param>
/// <returns>MSQuery</returns>
public string BuildMSQuery(string keywords, string searchScope)
{
    StringBuilder msQuery = new StringBuilder();

    // create the main header of the XML string
    msQuery.Append("<?xml version=\"1.0\" encoding=\"utf-8\" ?>"
            + "<QueryPacket xmlns=\"urn:Microsoft.Search.Query\" "
            + "Revision=\"1000\">"
            + "<Query domain=\"QDomain\">"
            + "<SupportedFormats>"
            + "<Format>urn:Microsoft.Search.Response.Document.Document"
            + "</Format></SupportedFormats>");

    // create the actual full-text query
    msQuery.Append("<Context>"
            + "<QueryText language=\"en-US\" type=\"MSSQLFT\">"
            + "<![CDATA[" + this.BuildMSsqlftQuery(keywords, searchScope)
            + "]]></QueryText></Context>");

    // create the range, page, and number of results
    // to return
```

```
    msQuery.Append("<Range><StartAt>1</StartAt><Count>20</Count>"
                + "</Range></Query></QueryPacket>");

    return msQuery.ToString();
}
```

> The two nodes of an MSQuery after the opening `QueryPacket` node (`Query`, and `SupportedFormats`) should not be modified. The `Context` node contains the actual search query, which you can change to suit your requirements. The last node, `Range`, contains directives used to tell the SPS Query Service Web Service how many results to return and at what index to start the result set.
>
> For example, if you displayed 20 results per page and you wanted to show the third page of results, you'd set the `StartAt` node to 41 and leave the `Count` node at 20.

We now have a complete MSQuery string with an included full-text query.

Let's see if our search will now work. Build the Tropical Green project and navigate to `http://www.tropicalgreen.net/`. Enter ficus in the search box and click Go. You should see results similar to those in the following image (we'll worry about making it more presentable in a moment):

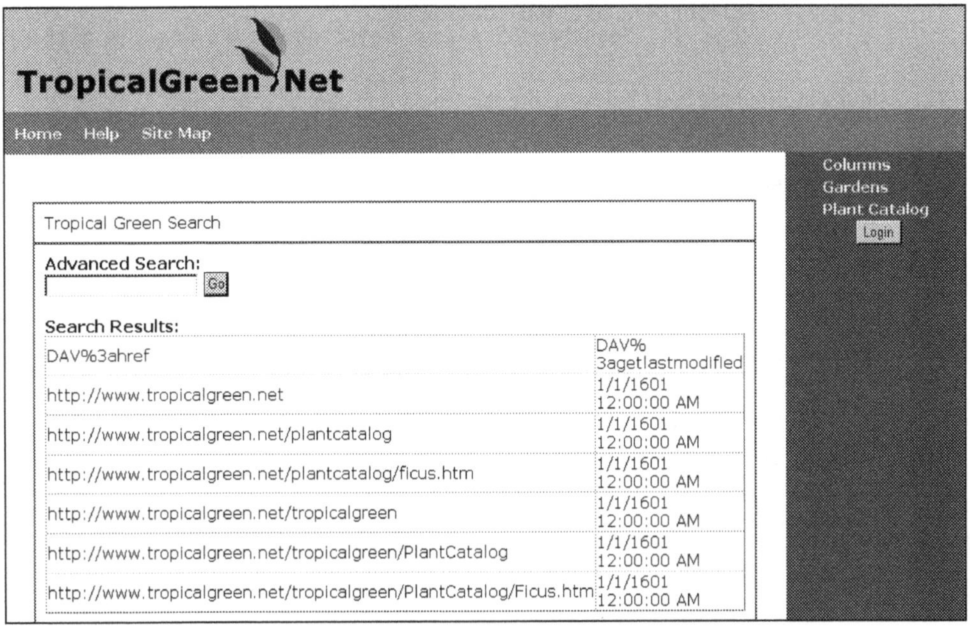

Every good search engine provides more than just keyword search. Some sites filter by topic and others by product. In our case, we could filter all our results to only the plant catalog, excluding the rest of the site. You would not be able to do this in a user-friendly manner using the controls provided by the MCMS Connector. While a knowledgeable guest could realize they could put in part of the CMS path in one of the advanced search options, it's not straightforward to the typical guest of the site. This is where you can really start to leverage your custom search components.

Let's add a filter to search just our plant catalog:

1. Open SearchResults.aspx in the Design view, and drag a CheckBox just below our advanced search textbox and assign it the following properties:

Property	Value
CheckBox	ID = chkFilterPlantCatalog Text = Only Search Plant Catalog

2. Open the code-behind file for the SearchResults.aspx page and add the following highlighted code to the btnAdvancedSearch_Click() event handler:

```
private void btnAdvancedSearch_Click(object sender, System.EventArgs e)
{
    string keywords = this.txtAdvancedSearch.Text;
    keywords = HttpUtility.UrlEncode(keywords);

    string filter = string.Empty;
    if (this.chkFilterPlantCatalog.Checked)
    {
        filter = "&filterPlantCatalog=1";
    }

    Response.Redirect(Request.ApplicationPath
                + "/SearchResults.aspx?keywords=" + keywords + filter);
}
```

3. Add the highlighted code below to the BuildMSsqlftQuery() method:

```
private string BuildMSsqlftQuery(string keywords, string searchScope)
{
    System.Text.StringBuilder mssqlftQuery =
                                new System.Text.StringBuilder();
    ArrayList whereClause = new ArrayList();

    #region FILTER: keywords
       . . . code continues . . .
    #endregion

    #region FILTER: plant catalog
    // list of keywords to include
    if ( Request.QueryString["filterPlantCatalog"] != null
        && Request.QueryString["filterPlantCatalog"].ToString() == "1" )
    {
        whereClause.Add("(\"urn:schemas.microsoft.com:htmlinfo:metainfo:PATH"
                + "\" LIKE '/channels/tropicalgreen/plantcatalog/%')");
    }
    #endregion

        . . . code continues . . .
```

Notice how we are using the urn:schemas.microsoft.com:htmlinfo:metainfo:PATH index property, which is mapped to the CMS Channel Path thanks to the SearchPropertyCollection.xml file provided with the MCMS Connector.

4. Let's see how the filter works. Save your changes and build the Tropical Green project. Once the build is complete, open your browser and navigate to `http://www.tropicalgreen.net/TropicalGreen/SearchResults.aspx`. Enter ficus in the textbox, check the Only Search Plant Catalog CheckBox, and click the Go button:

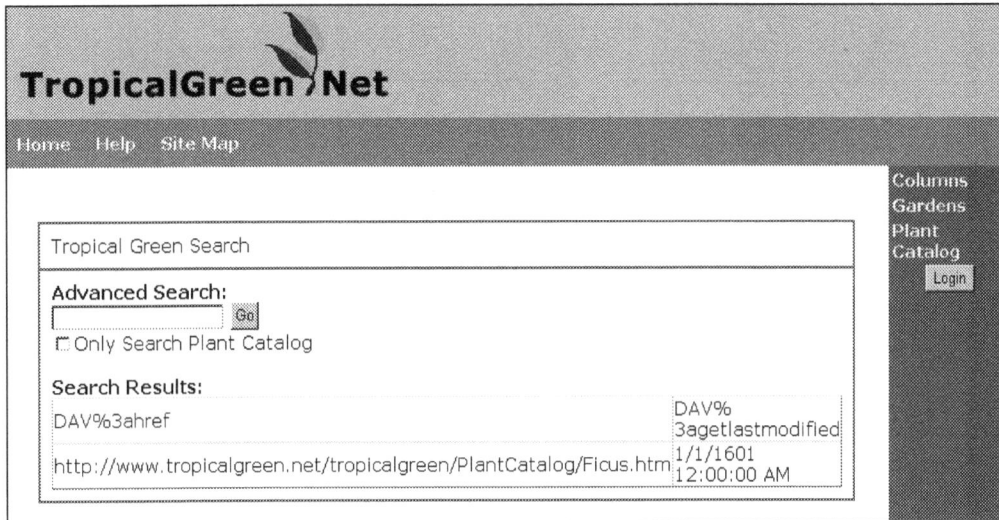

Fantastic! We now only see records inside our Tropical Green plant catalog! This gives a good idea of what filtering brings to the table. We could filter by so many things, such as displaying only postings that have been updated in the last month or week. The possibilities are almost endless.

Let's see if we can't clean up those search results by getting rid of the DataGrid and replacing it with a Repeater. At the same time, we'll add filtering of the search results so users will only see postings that they have rights to access.

Although we listed numerous SharePoint index properties in our full text query, we will only use the DAV:href property when analyzing the results in our main results page to obtain a reference to the specified MCMS channel or posting to determine if the user has rights to browse the resource and also to determine and return the actual posting's name and description.

1. Open the SearchResults.aspx page in Design view. Delete the DataGrid.

2. Drag a Repeater object onto the page where the DataGrid was. Assign the Repeater an ID of rptSearchResults.

3. While in Design view, select our new Repeater and open the Properties window. At the top of the window, click the 🔲 Events button to show all possible events we can use. Double-click the box to the right of ItemDataBound to create an empty event handler that will fire every time an item is bound to the repeater.

4. Switch back to HTML view for the SearchResults.aspx and scroll to our new Repeater.

147

5. Add the following highlighted tags into the `ItemTemplate` of our `Repeater`:

```
<asp:repeater id="rptSearchResults" runat="server">
<ItemTemplate>
  <asp:Placeholder ID="phdSearchResult" Runat="server" visible="false">
    <p>
      <b><asp:HyperLink ID="hlkResultTitle" Runat="server" /></b>
      <br>
      <asp:Literal ID="litResultDescription" Runat="server" />
    </p>
  </asp:Placeholder>
</ItemTemplate>
</asp:repeater>
```

> Notice the ASP.NET Placeholder we've added surrounding the search result. We'll use this to show and hide results that the user does or does not have permission to view.

Now that we have a `Repeater` filled with some placeholders for the content, we need to modify our data binding, which is still using a `DataGrid`.

1. Open the code-behind file for `SearchResults.aspx`, find the `Page_Load()` event handler, and modify the code to bind the only `DataTable` in the `DataSet` to the `Repeater` as shown below:

```
private void Page_Load(object sender, System.EventArgs e)
{
  if (Request.QueryString["keywords"] != null
  && Request.QueryString["keywords"].Length >0)
  {
    string keywords = Request.QueryString["keywords"];
    DataSet ds = ExecuteSearch(keywords);
    this.rptSearchResults.Visible = true;
    this.rptSearchResults.DataSource = ds.Tables[0].Rows;
    this.rptSearchResults.DataBind();
  }
  else
  {
    this.rptSearchResults.Visible = false;
  }
}
```

2. Before we implement the `ItemDataBound` event, we need to create a method that will try to obtain the MCMS `ChannelItem` reference of the URL returned in the results. Add the following method after the `Page_Load()` event handler we just modified:

```
private HierarchyItem GetResult(string url)
{
  try
  {
    // check if it's a GUID based URL
    if (url.IndexOf("RDONLYRES") >= 0)
    {
      // try to get the GUID if it's a RDONLYRES URL
      string guidRegEx = "[a-fA-F0-9]{8}-[a-fA-F0-9]{4}-[a-fA-F0-9]{4}-"
                    + "[a-fA-F0-9]{4}-[a-fA-F0-9]{12}";
      Regex regex = new Regex(guidRegEx);
      Match m = regex.Match(url);
      if (m.Success)
      {
        return CmsHttpContext.Current.Searches.GetByGuid("{"+m.Value+"}");
      }
```

```
    }
    else
    {
      // try to get the object via the URL
      return CmsHttpContext.Current.Searches.GetByUrl(url);
    }
    // if this point reached, unknown URL
    return null;
  }
  catch
  {
    return null;
  }
}
```

3. Now, find the rptSearchResults_ItemDataBound() event handler. We need to trap the event when it's binding a data item to the ItemTemplate or AlternateItemTemplate in the Repeater. Then, we'll get a reference to the data item being bound to the template, in our case a DataRow, and get references to the ASP.NET objects we added to the template. Finally, we'll use the data in the DataRow to populate the properties of our controls. Here's what our completed ItemDataBound() event handler will look like:

```
private void rptSearchResults_ItemDataBound(object sender,
System.Web.UI.WebControls.RepeaterItemEventArgs e)
{
  if ( (e.Item.ItemType == ListItemType.AlternatingItem)
    || (e.Item.ItemType == ListItemType.Item) )
  {
    // get a reference to the datarow being bound
    DataRow row = e.Item.DataItem as DataRow;
    HierarchyItem hi = GetResult(row[0].ToString());

    // get references to all the ASP.NET objects
    PlaceHolder resultContainer = e.Item.FindControl("phdSearchResult")
                                          as PlaceHolder;
    HyperLink resultTitle = e.Item.FindControl("hlkResultTitle")
                                          as HyperLink;
    Literal resultDesc = e.Item.FindControl("litResultDescription")
                                          as Literal;

    // if the URL doesn't resolve to an MCMS resource,
    // output it to the results
    if (hi != null)
    {
      // user has rights to this item so display it.
      resultContainer.Visible = true;

      // use values in DataRow to populate objects
      resultDesc.Text = hi.Description;
      if (hi is ChannelItem)
      {
        resultTitle.Text = (hi as ChannelItem).DisplayName;
        resultTitle.NavigateUrl = (hi as ChannelItem).Url;
      }
      else
      {
        if (hi is Resource)
          resultTitle.NavigateUrl = (hi as Resource).Url;
        resultTitle.Text = hi.Name;
      }
    }
  }
}
```

149

The final result looks something like this:

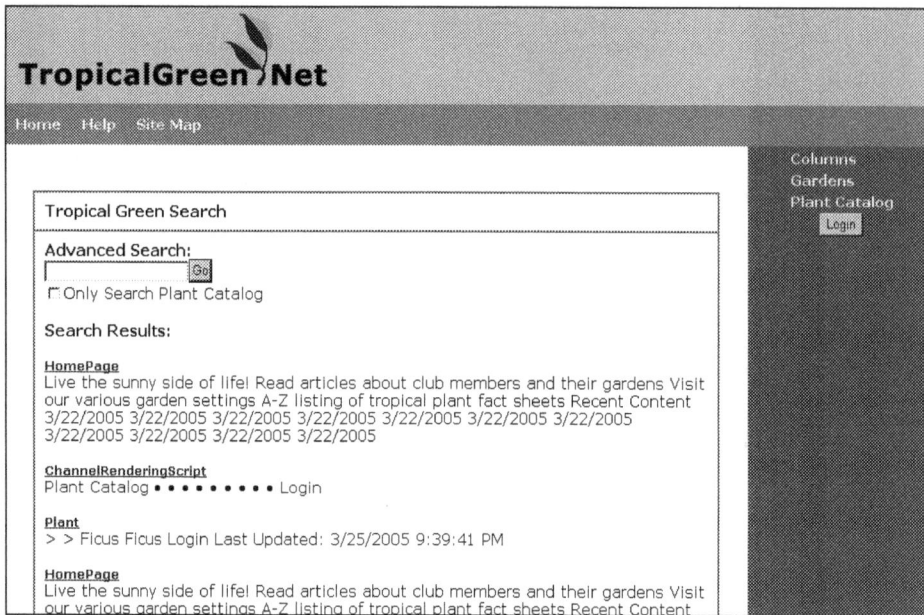

You'll see that the description field may not have exactly what we're looking for, but this technique lets us customize the search result list to our hearts' content. You could pull the description of the posting straight out of the indexed values, provided you exposed the page description using the `SearchPropertyCollection.xml` file. Or you could even have an `HtmlPlaceholder` called "Search Description" in all your templates that content owners could use to enter a description to show when the posting appears in search results.

Summary

In this chapter we discussed a few of the options available to MCMS developers for adding search functionality to their sites. We proceeded to take an in-depth look at the searching features built into SharePoint Portal Server and how they can be leveraged as a back-end search workhorse for an MCMS site. Before we could start adding the search functionality, we had to make a few changes to our site and templates, as well as build an index using SharePoint to crawl our site.

Once our site was configured for index crawls and SharePoint was configured to crawl our site and build an index, we explored in detail two options for adding search functionality to the Tropical Green site using the SharePoint crawler:

- First we implemented search using the MCMS Connector for SharePoint Technologies, an out-of-the-box solution.

- Then, we built our own solution using the SharePoint Query Service Web Service and custom full text T-SQL queries to provide search filters and customized results.

6

Publishing Content Between MCMS and SharePoint

Microsoft Content Management Server (MCMS) and SharePoint Products and Technologies (SPS and WSS) provide complementary feature sets. MCMS is a content publishing product that provides a robust publishing workflow engine. SharePoint is an online collaboration product providing users a platform to share information such as document libraries and lists. It also contains a centralized enterprise-strength search and indexing engine enabling users to search disparate content types within many smaller sites. Neither product can be seen as an alternative to each other because they have such specific and different uses. However the two products' primary features could benefit each other if leveraged correctly.

In this chapter, we'll explore publishing both MCMS and SharePoint content between the two products to demonstrate the many possibilities available for leveraging the power of each product from the other. We'll first take a look at a few different scenarios of why, how, and when you would want to publish content from one product to the other. Then, we'll look in detail at publishing content from MCMS into SharePoint and vice versa. Each analysis will examine what the MCMS Connector for SharePoint Technologies provides to accomplish these content-sharing tasks as well as discussing, and at times building, custom solutions to fill in gaps left by the Connector due to the latter's limited customization.

As you would expect, this chapter will not cover using SharePoint Portal Server as a search engine for an MCMS site, as this was covered in detail in Chapter 5, *Searching MCMS with SharePoint*.

In this chapter, we'll look at further ways in which SharePoint and MCMS can work hand in hand to provide a robust content authoring and collaboration solution.

What's the difference between SharePoint Portal Server and Windows SharePoint Services?

SharePoint, or SharePoint Products and Technologies, includes both Windows SharePoint Services (WSS) and SharePoint Portal Server (SPS). WSS is the foundation for SPS. SPS provides portal organization of WSS sites, centralized enterprise search and indexing, single sign on, and enhanced personalization and audience targeting that WSS does not provide. WSS is a prerequisite for SPS, but WSS can also be installed and run standalone.

The licensing models of the two products are different. WSS comes free with a Windows Server 2003 license, but SPS is based on a per-server and a per-user model (Client Access Licenses).

For more information on the differences in Windows SharePoint Services and SharePoint Portal Server, read the white paper *Implementing Rich Collaboration Infrastructure Using Windows SharePoint Services and SharePoint Portal Server 2003* available on Microsoft's website: http://www.microsoft.com/sharepoint/evaluationoverview.asp.

Let's first start by answering the question of why anyone would want to share content between MCMS and SharePoint in the first place.

Using MCMS and SharePoint Together

There are usually numerous ways to approach most problems when coming up with a solution. Both SharePoint and Microsoft Content Management Server have areas where they are very strong, but neither product should be seen as a replacement for the other.

Microsoft Content Management Server (MCMS) is strong in the areas of content presentation, authoring, separation of content from the presentation of the content, a robust publishing workflow, and retention of all prior versions of a document. SharePoint Products and Technologies (SPT), including both Windows SharePoint Services (WSS) and SharePoint Portal Server (SPS), are strong in the area of online collaboration, document storage and collaboration within workspaces, and rapid design and creation of custom lists.

The two products complement each other very well. They can be used in conjunction, under specific circumstances and demands, to provide a robust solution that would not only facilitate online collaboration between peers, but also offer a strong publication engine.

One of the most obvious and common implementations of a solution that combines the two products is a company intranet. Many large companies have an intranet, which contains sites whose targeted audience is company employees only. An intranet site usually serves the purpose of publishing company news, policies, procedures, and documentation to the employees, while also building a community where the employees can more effectively and efficiently accomplish their job.

In some cases, an intranet implementation built upon both SPS and MCMS would facilitate online collaboration between employees by deploying multiple portals that aggregate content from hundreds or thousands of smaller WSS sites. Small teams use these team sites for projects, development of new products, procedures, and tasks. At the same time, the human resources department is using MCMS to maintain a tight hold on company policies, standards, rules, and procedures that are more content oriented and require a publishing workflow solution. The possibilities of how the two products could be leveraged to provide a single solution are endless.

Aside from the single combined solution, SPT and MCMS can also be deployed in separate environments addressing different business challenges. For example, a company may implement its Internet site using MCMS and internal departmental sites using SPS or WSS. However, even though the two products are not combined, they can publish and pull content and data to and from each other. Consider a WSS site used by a product team to manage product-related events and documentation. The company Internet site could pull content from the events list Web Part in the WSS site to show upcoming events to non-employees. In addition, the WSS site could pull postings from the Internet site that contain product sales information for internal use. This eliminates duplication of content entry and management.

> While the solution described above outlines the use of SharePoint internally within an organization where some content is published to the Internet, it is not a common scenario. The most common case of leveraging both MCMS and SharePoint Portal Server is where both products are used internally within a company, as in the intranet example, because making SharePoint data accessible to non-employees of the company requires the purchase of an External Connector License, which is a significant cost factor.

These are just two examples of how you could use SPT and MCMS together to provide a solution to a business problem or challenge. Fortunately, Microsoft recognized the two products complement each other very well and has provided a free collection of tools and utilities for developers to get a jump start melding the two products together: the MCMS Connector for SharePoint Technologies (hereafter referred to as the Connector).

Joining MCMS and SharePoint in a Single Solution

There is no one best way for joining the two products. As we've gone over previously, each product has strong areas that can complement the other. You'll need to evaluate which best fits the needs presented in any particular business challenge. Before you make this decision, you need to understand how each product can be implemented.

MCMS can be configured to serve content from one or more IIS websites configured as MCMS Web Entry Points. Regardless of the number of MCMS Web Entry Points on a single physical server, all MCMS Web Entry Points will use the same MCMS Repository as only one database can be configured per machine.

Implementing a SharePoint portal involves extending a virtual server on a physical server. Unlike MCMS, each SharePoint portal has its own content database (a.k.a. repository). A solution that leverages both products can be contained within a single physical server or across many servers. In the case where SharePoint and MCMS reside on the same physical server, you have the option of operating them within separate virtual servers or in the same virtual server.

> A virtual server is also referred to as a website in Microsoft Internet Information Services.

As you can see, you have quite a few options as to how the two products can be implemented:

1. Hosting MCMS and SharePoint on the same physical server and the same virtual server
2. Hosting MCMS and SharePoint on the same physical server but different virtual servers
3. Hosting MCMS and SharePoint on different physical servers and thus different virtual servers

Due to the many options, one of the first things you need to decide is which of the two products will serve as the primary entry point for your solution. If SharePoint and MCMS reside on different physical servers or virtual servers, either could serve the role of primary entry point. However, if MCMS and SharePoint Portal Server are configured to operate on the same virtual server, SharePoint will be the primary entry point if users are going to the root of the site (for instance `http://www.TropicalGreen.net`).

> Operating MCMS and SPS within the same virtual directory requires some manual configuration within the SharePoint administration to exclude certain URL paths from being managed by the SharePoint ISAPI filters. This allows requests to be processed by the MCMS ISAPI filters. Unfortunately SharePoint does not allow you to exclude the root of the portal. This means any HTTP request made to the virtual server's root (such as `http://www.TropicalGreen.net/default.aspx`) will be handled by the SharePoint ISAPI filter. Only subdirectories below the root (for instance `http://www.TropicalGreen.net/TropicalGreen/default.aspx`) can be excluded from SharePoint and therefore managed by MCMS.
>
> For more information on how to set up MCMS and SharePoint on the same virtual server, refer to Appendix A, *Setting up MCMS and SPS on the Same Virtual Server*.

This chapter will address solutions that can cover both situations: MCMS and SharePoint on the same virtual server and also on different servers (virtual or physical). If you choose to operate the two products on different physical servers, you will need to implement a custom solution to publish content between the machines. The most common approach would be to use Web services.

> SharePoint ships with a long list of Web services that expose most of its content. These Web services can be found in the `_vti_bin` web application in the root of the site automatically created for each SharePoint portal and Windows SharePoint Services site. For more information on creating Web services for MCMS, refer to Chapter 11, *InfoPath with Web Services*, which covers Web services for MCMS. The Web services you create in that chapter are consumed by Microsoft Office InfoPath, but can also easily be consumed by custom code.

Once you've decided which product will take the primary role, you will need to determine the content you would like to publish or consume in your application. Will your SharePoint site present a list of postings from the MCMS site in your portal? Will your MCMS site publish the contents of a Web Part from within your SharePoint site?

This chapter will cover both options. We will show how to use and customize some of the Web Parts that are included in the Connector to view and administer your MCMS content from within SharePoint. Then we'll look at pulling documents from a SharePoint document library to an MCMS site as well as building a placeholder control that will pull the contents of a SharePoint list into a posting.

> In our examples we'll continue to use `http://portal.tropicalgreen.net/`, the SharePoint portal that we created in Appendix A, *Setting up MCMS and SPS on the Same Virtual Server* and used in the previous chapter, *Searching MCMS with SharePoint*.

Using SharePoint to Display MCMS Content

As we mentioned previously, the first thing you need to identify is which of the two products will serve the primary role as the user interface or experience. One option is to use SharePoint (either WSS or SPS) as the primary user interface and use MCMS either in a supporting role or to manage certain areas of the site. There are three very common implementations when using the two products in this scenario:

- SharePoint Portal Server is used to implement the Tropical Green intranet, which is accessible by Tropical Green employees only. Tropical Green production departments, team project collaboration sites, announcements, and important documents are stored within areas and WSS sites within the SharePoint portal. MCMS is used by the Human Resources department to maintain a very controlled publishing workflow of company policies, procedures, benefits, and employee announcements. The Human Resources documents are presented in lists and are linked to from various parts of the website.

- Similar to the previous scenario, SharePoint Portal Server is used to provide the Tropical Green intranet, which has dedicated areas for the various production departments, team project collaboration sites, and so on. Tropical Green's product groups also post tips and other helpful information to SharePoint lists. Tropical Green also uses MCMS to host its Internet site, which is the primary entry point to the company for all Tropical Green customers. The Tropical Green MCMS Internet site pulls tips from the SharePoint lists in the Tropical Green SharePoint intranet site and displays them for registered customers. In addition, the event details could be pulled from the Tropical Green SharePoint intranet and be made available on the Tropical Green MCMS Internet site. This option would require the purchase of an External Connector License, which is required when you expose SharePoint content to users outside your organization (such as the Internet).

- MCMS and SharePoint are used by Tropical Green to provide a complete intranet solution. SharePoint is primarily used to host smaller team sites and offer a centralized search engine for the entire intranet while MCMS is leveraged in content-heavy portions of the intranet.

In the scenarios above, you'll notice one common factor: the solutions pull content from one environment (such as SharePoint or MCMS) for display in another environment. Note that the content is not duplicated and is read only (with the exception of the `SharePointDocumentLibrary` placeholder, which MCMS Templates use to display content from SharePoint document libraries); it's simply pulled in thus reducing data duplication. Limiting data duplication reduces errors and the costs associated with managing and updating the information in two different products. However, the overall performance of the solution will decrease as it would perform better if it had a copy of the data rather than pulling it in real time from another product. The three scenarios above, while rather simple, should give you an idea of some of the possibilities in sharing content between SharePoint and MCMS.

The MCMS Connector for SharePoint Technologies

In February 2004, Microsoft released the Connector, which contains a collection of SharePoint Web Parts, MCMS controls, and placeholders, and a few command-line utilities developers can use to leverage the strengths of SharePoint in MCMS and vice versa. The Connector is completely free, is supported by Microsoft and fully documented, and contains a sample project (with data) demonstrating the features included in the package.

> Refer to Appendix B, *MCMS Connector for SharePoint Technologies*, for information on where to obtain the Connector, installation instructions, and details about what it includes.

The first scenario we'll look at involves the presentation of MCMS content from within SharePoint. The Connector provides three ways to view our postings within MCMS in a SharePoint site using Web Parts.

- **MCMS Page Listing Web Part**: Displays a list of postings selecting an MCMS channel. The presentation of the list can be modified using different views. We will create a custom view for this Web Part later in this chapter.

- **MCMS Pages in Production Web Part**: Displays a list of postings the current user is working on similar to the Production Manager in MCMS.

- **MCMS Pages Waiting for Approval Web Part**: Displays a list of postings that can be approved by the current user similar to the Approval Assistant in MCMS.

After installing the Connector, these three Web Parts are automatically installed on all portal sites. If you are going to create a portal after the Connector has been installed you need to install the three Web Parts, which are all contained in a single CAB file, manually. Unfortunately the documentation included with the Connector does not explain how to install the Web Parts. SharePoint requires you to use a command-line utility to install Web Parts and perform other administrative functions. This utility, `stsadm.exe`, can be found in the directory at `C:\Program Files\Common Files\Microsoft Shared\web server extensions\60\BIN\`.

Let's go ahead and install the Connector's Web Parts using STSADM.EXE, then we will look at each Web Part we have installed.

Installing the MCMS Connector Web Parts

1. Click Start | Run (or hit *Windows + R*) and enter cmd in the dialog box to bring up the command-line window.

2. Change directory to the location of the STSADM.EXE utility by entering cd `c:\Program Files\Common Files\Microsoft Shared\web server extensions\60\BIN\`.

3. Before we install, let's see what Web Parts are already installed on all portals on our site. We do this by using the enumwppacks option which will display a list of all Web Parts installed on each virtual server. Enter the following command at the prompt: `STSADM.exe -o enumwppacks`. If you haven't installed anything into your portal, you should see something like the following:

```
C:\Program Files\Common Files\Microsoft Shared\web server extensions\60\BIN>stsa
dm.exe -o enumwppacks

There are no items matching the criteria specified.

C:\Program Files\Common Files\Microsoft Shared\web server extensions\60\BIN>
```

4. Now let's go ahead and install the Connector Web Parts to all SharePoint extended virtual servers on our server. You need to find the CAB file that contains the three Web Parts included with the Connector. If you installed the Connector in the default installation directory, you'll find the CAB file at c:\Program Files\MCMS Connector for SharePoint Technologies\WSS\Bin\CmsWebParts.cab. Type the following into the command console: `STSADM.exe -o addwppack -filename "C:\Program Files\MCMS Connector for SharePoint Technologies\WSS\Bin\CmsWebParts.cab"`. You should see the following response:

```
C:\Program Files\Common Files\Microsoft Shared\web server extensions\60\BIN>STSA
DM.exe -o addwppack -filename "C:\Program Files\MCMS Connector for SharePoint Te
chnologies\WSS\Bin\CmsWebParts.cab"

cmswebparts.cab: Deploying to http://portal.tropicalgreen.net/.
Operation completed successfully.

C:\Program Files\Common Files\Microsoft Shared\web server extensions\60\BIN>
```

5. Looks like everything was installed successfully. Let's double-check and see what the enumwppacks option reports now (and also confirm the Web Parts were installed). Enter `stsadm.exe -o enumwppacks`. You should see the following:

```
C:\WINDOWS\system32\cmd.exe                                          _ □ ×

C:\Program Files\Common Files\Microsoft Shared\web server extensions\60\BIN>STSA
DM.exe -o enumwppacks

cmswebparts.cab, http://portal.tropicalgreen.net/


C:\Program Files\Common Files\Microsoft Shared\web server extensions\60\BIN>_
```

Now that we have the Connector Web Parts installed, let's take a look at each of them.

MCMS Page Listing Web Part

The MCMS Page Listing Web Part displays the postings within a specified channel. Once this Web Part is added to a SharePoint Web Part Page, you specify the MCMS site root URL and channel path that contains the postings you wish to display. Users with appropriate permissions to modify the Web Part settings can also specify the number of postings to display per page, the sorting order of the postings, and how they wish to display or view the list.

Let's add the MCMS Page Listing Web Part to a SharePoint Web Part Page and see what we get.

1. Navigate to a SharePoint portal in Internet Explorer. We'll use the portal created in Appendix A and used for our search in Chapter 5: http://portal.tropicalgreen.net.

2. Click the Edit Page link in the vertical left-hand Actions menu:

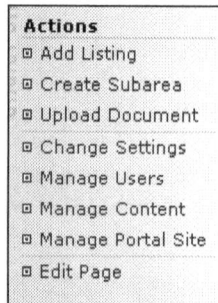

Actions
⊞ Add Listing
⊞ Create Subarea
⊞ Upload Document
⊞ Change Settings
⊞ Manage Users
⊞ Manage Content
⊞ Manage Portal Site
⊞ Edit Page

3. Now that the page is in edit mode, click the Modify Shared Page link in the upper left. Using the dynamic drop-down menu that appears, select Add Web Parts and then Browse.

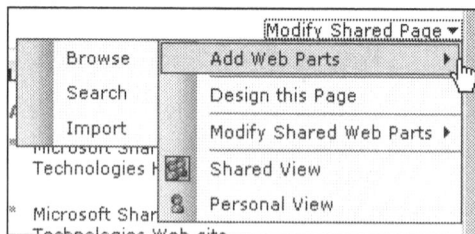

	Modify Shared Page ▼
Browse	Add Web Parts ▶
Search	Design this Page
Import	Modify Shared Web Parts ▶
Technologies	Shared View
Microsoft Shar	Personal View

4. When the SharePoint Web Part Tool Pane loads on the right-hand side of the browser, it is set to list all Web Parts in the portal's Web Part gallery (in our case, the Tropical Green Gallery). When you install Web Parts in a SharePoint site (SPS or WSS), they are added to the Virtual Server Gallery. Since we installed the Web Parts included with the Connector, we need to select the Virtual Server Gallery by clicking it.

What is the SharePoint Web Part Tool Pane?

The SharePoint Web Part Tool Pane is a task pane on a SharePoint Web Part Page used to add Web Parts from Web Part galleries, and to modify custom and common Web Part properties.

Why are the Web Parts we installed in the Virtual Server Gallery?

When you install a Web Part, you are installing it to a specific virtual server. Even when you elect to install it in all sites or in the Global Assembly Cache, the additions are made to each virtual server to tell the SharePoint portal (or site(s)) within that virtual server that it can use the Web Part.

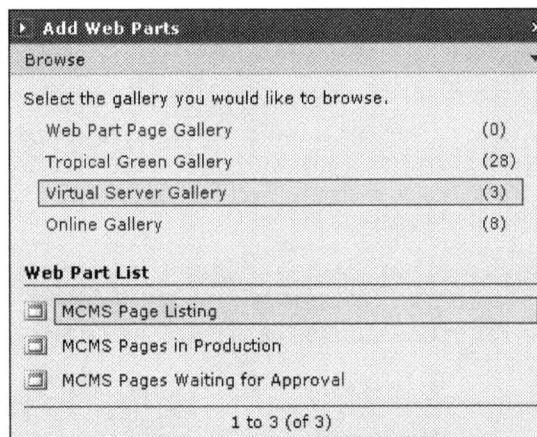

5. You should now see the three Web Parts included in the Connector listed in the Add Web Parts Tool Pane as shown in the previous image. Select the MCMS Page Listing and drag it onto the page, placing it the top zone, as shown in the following image:

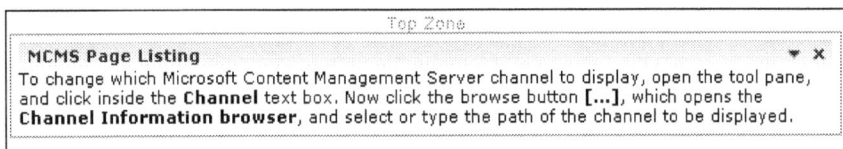

6. Now that we have our Web Part on the page, we need to configure it as it doesn't yet know what site or channel to enumerate the postings for. Click the small down arrow in the upper-right corner of the MCMS Page Listing Web Part we just added and select Modify Shared Web Part as shown:

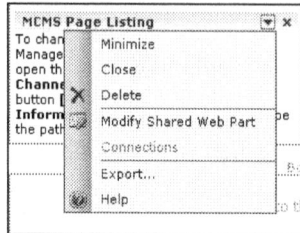

7. The Web Part properties Tool Pane now takes the place of the SharePoint Web Part Tool Pane. Expand the Custom Properties section by clicking the [+] icon to the left of the Custom Properties section heading.

8. We need to tell the Web Part the URL of our MCMS web application. Enter the following for the property MCMS Site Root URL: http://www.tropicalgreen.net/ MCMS/. Click the Apply button at the bottom of the Tool Pane.

Microsoft recommends that you use MCMS as the web application name as it's the default web application installed with every MCMS server.

9. Now we need to select a channel. Click the ellipsis (...) to the right of the Channel Path text box. A modal dialog window will open with an MCMS channel browser. Navigate to our Plant Catalog channel, select it, and click OK. Click the Apply button at the bottom of the Tool Pane.

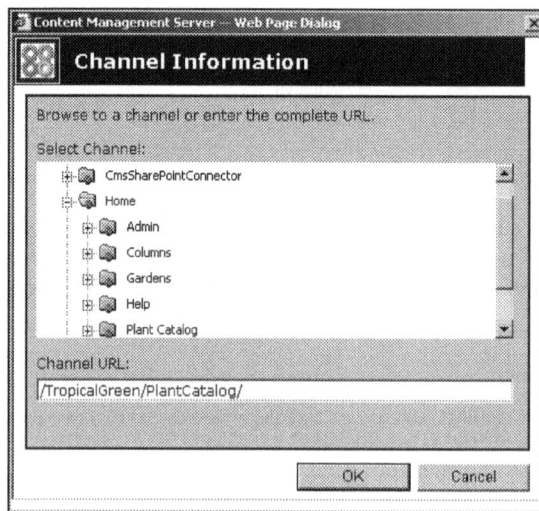

At this point you should see the Web Part display some of our postings. Use the last three custom properties (View, Items Per Page, and Sorting Order) to customize the display of the posting list. Out of the box, the Web Part provides three different predefined views to display the list of postings:

- **Basic List View**: The posting's "short title" (which is the name of a placeholder definition within the template) is displayed, hyperlinked to the actual posting, with an importance icon. The importance icon appears if the MCMS posting is marked as important. If the posting does not have a short title, the display name is used. The following image is the MCMS Page Listing Web Part configured to display the postings in the PlantCatalog channel from our Tropical Green website with the Basic List View:

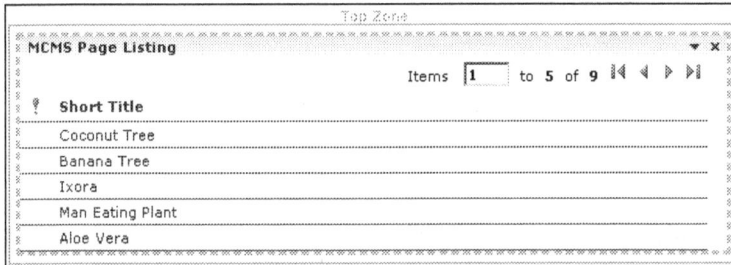

- **Page Summary List View**: This is the default view for the MCMS Page Listing Web Part. The postings contained within the specified channel are shown in a summary form including the short title (or the posting display name if the short title is not specified) hyperlinked to the posting, a summary image (if specified in a summary image placeholder within the posting), the description of the posting, and the last date the posting was modified. The following image is the MCMS Page Listing Web Part configured to display the postings in the PlantCatalog channel from our Tropical Green website with the Page Summary List View:

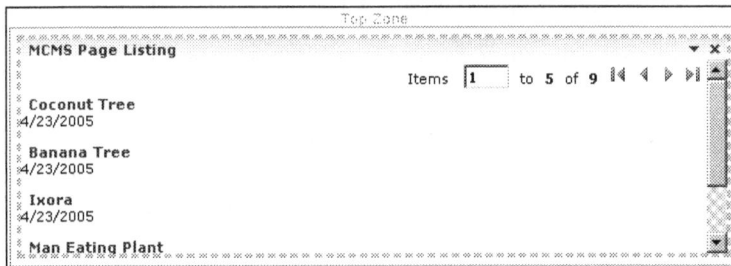

- **Detailed List View**: The last predefined view included in the MCMS Page Listing Web Part is the Detailed List View. This view contains the short title (or the posting display name if the short title is not specified) hyperlinked to the posting, the posting's owner and status (indicating the publishing state), and the person who last modified the posting as well as when it was modified. The following image is the MCMS Page Listing Web Part configured to display the postings in the PlantCatalog channel from our Tropical Green website with the Detailed List View:

If the three out-of-the-box views are not sufficient for your needs, the MCMS Page Listing Web Part is built to allow for you to create up to three additional custom views per server. If you need more than three custom views you'll need to create your own Web Part as this is a fixed limitation of the MCMS Page Listing Web Part. Custom views can be implemented by creating a strongly named assembly that contains a class that implements the `Microsoft.ContentManagement.SharePoint.Dialogs.IPageListing` interface. This interface contains a single method, `GetHtml()`, which accepts a `Microsoft.ContentManagement.SharePoint.Dialogs.PageListingsParameters` object and a `Microsoft.ContentManagement.Publishing.Posting` object and returns a single string, which should be HTML. `PageListingParameters` contains context information from the MCMS Page Listing Web Part and the `Posting` object is a reference to the current posting.

The way it works is that the MCMS Page Listing Web Part creates an HTML table with the necessary paging information, followed by another HTML table that contains a single table row and table cell for each posting in the specified channel. For each posting, it calls the `GetHtml()` method, passing in the `PageListingParameters` and current `Posting`, and places the returned string in the table cell. Unfortunately this doesn't provide complete control of the HTML inside the MCMS Page Listing Web Part, but it does allow you to control how each item in the list is being formatted and which properties should be displayed.

> If you need a more flexible Web Part, you could always build your own, as we demonstrate in Chapter 7, *Building SharePoint Web Parts*.

Once you build your strongly named assembly, you must install it into the Global Assembly Cache (GAC) and modify the `web.config` file in the MCMS web application. Let's see this in action by building our own custom view that will display the plant name, description, and the last time the posting was updated. It's nothing complex, but it will demonstrate how easy it is to create a custom view.

A Custom View for the MCMS Page Listing Web Part

We need to create a new project, then clean it up, and finally add the necessary references:

1. Open Visual Studio .NET and create a C# Class Library project. Give the new project a name of TropicalGreenPlantCatalogCustomView. Click OK to create the project.

2. Now, let's clean up the project. Delete the `class1.cs` file by right-clicking it in Solution Explorer and selecting Delete.

3. We need to add two references to the project. Right-click on the References folder in Solution Explorer and select Add Reference. Click the Browse button, navigate to the directory `C:\Program Files\Microsoft Content Management Server\Server\bin`, and add the following DLLs as references:

- `Microsoft.ContentManagement.Publishing.dll`
- `Microsoft.ContentManagement.Publishing.Extensions.Placeholders.dll`
- `Microsoft.ContentManagement.SharePoint.Dialogs.dll`

At this point we have a clean project with the necessary references. We need to add a new class to the project naming it PlantCatalogCustomView. After creating the new class, remove its constructor as we won't need it.

The `PlantCatalogCustomView` class has to implement the `IPageListing` interface. This interface contains a single method, `GetHtml()`. Let's add the necessary code:

```
using System;
using System.Text;
using Microsoft.ContentManagement.Publishing;
using Microsoft.ContentManagement.Publishing.Extensions.Placeholders;
using Microsoft.ContentManagement.SharePoint.Dialogs;

namespace TropicalGreenPlantCatalogCustomView
{
  /// <summary>
  /// Custom view implementation for MCMS
  /// Page Listing Web Part. This view presents
  /// a custom view of the TropicalGreen Plant Catalog.
  /// </summary>
  public class PlantCatalogCustomView : IPageListing
  {
    /// <summary>
    /// Method called for each posting within the specified channel.
    /// </summary>
    public string GetHtml(PageListingsParameters parameters,
                    Posting posting)
    {
    }
  }
}
```

Now we need to build the logic within `GetHtml()` that will construct an HTML string that will be used to render each posting in the specified channel. We will first build a hyperlink to the posting. Then we will display the description of the posting if a description was saved with the posting. Finally, we'll add in italics the date and time the posting was last updated.

```
public string GetHtml(PageListingsParameters parameters,
                Posting posting)
{
  StringBuilder html = new StringBuilder();

  // create link to the posting using the display name
  html.Append(string.Format(
          "&raquo; <a href=\"{0}\" target=\"_parent\">{1}</a>",
          posting.UrlModePublished, posting.DisplayName) );
  html.Append("<br>");

  // add the description to the listing
  if (posting.Description.Length >0)
  {
    html.Append(string.Format("<span style=\"margin-
```

```
left:10px;\">{0}</span><br>",
                posting.Description) );
}

// add the last date the posting was modified
html.Append(string.Format(
            "<span style=\"margin-left:10px; font-style:italic;\"
            + ">Last Modified: {0}</span>",
            posting.LastModifiedDate.ToString("F") ));

// return the built HTML string
return html.ToString();
}
```

At this point the coding is complete within our custom view. We still have to strongly name our assembly, as required for any assembly running within the SharePoint environment.

In order to strongly name an assembly, we first need a key. To create a key, we'll run the Strong Name tool from a Visual Studio .NET Command Prompt:

1. Launch a command window by selecting Start | All Programs | Visual Studio .NET 2003, Visual Studio .NET Tools | Visual Studio .NET 2003 Command Prompt.

2. We'll place the key in the root of the c: drive for simplicity. Create a key by entering the following at the command prompt:

```
sn -k c:\PlantCatalogCustomView.snk
```

   Now we need to tell the compiler to use the key we just created to strongly name our assembly when we build it. To do this, open the AssemblyInfo.cs file in our project and modify the version number and key file attributes as shown in the code below:

```
[assembly: AssemblyVersion("1.0.0.0")]
[assembly: AssemblyKeyFile("c:\\PlantCatalogCustomView.snk")]
```

3. The final steps in creating a custom view involve building our assembly in release mode and deploying it to the global assembly cache (GAC). To add our assembly to the GAC, copy the release assembly version of our project, TropicalGreenPlantCatalogCustomView.dll, and paste it in the GAC, located at c:\Windows\assembly\.

4. Let's verify our custom assembly has been successfully installed to the GAC:

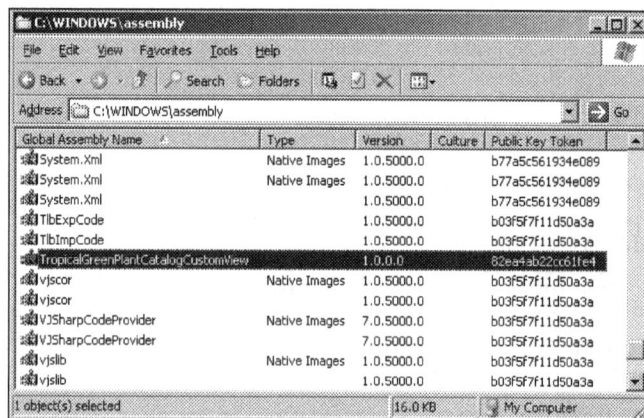

> Take note of the Public Key Token listed for our assembly. We will need this in a moment.

We have now built and deployed our first custom view for the MCMS Page Listing Web Part. However, before we can use it, we need to register it for use by modifying the web.config of our MCMS application that we specified as the Site Root URL when we added the MCMS Page Listing Web Part to the SharePoint Web Part Page. In our case it is: http://www.tropicalgreen.net/MCMS/.

> The MCMS application is created by the Server Configuration Application (SCA) when you set a virtual server as an MCMS Web Entry Point. You will find the web.config for this application in the following directory: C:\Program Files\Microsoft Content Management Server\Server\MCMS.

Open the web.config for the web application specified as the Site Root URL in the MCMS Page Listing Web Part, and add the following elements:

```
<?xml version="1.0" encoding="utf-8"?>
<configuration>
<configSections>
  <sectionGroup name="CustomPageListingViews">
    <section name="CustomView1"
type="Microsoft.ContentManagement.SharePoint.Dialogs.NameValueSectionHandler,
Microsoft.ContentManagement.SharePoint.Dialogs, Version=1.0.1000.0,
Culture=neutral, PublicKeyToken=31bf3856ad364e35" />
  </sectionGroup>
</configSections>

<CustomPageListingViews>
  <CustomView1>
    <add key="assembly" value="TropicalGreenPlantCatalogCustomView,
Version=1.0.0.0, Culture=neutral, PublicKeyToken=82ea4ab22cc61fe4" />
    <add key="pageListingType"
value="TropicalGreenPlantCatalogCustomView.PlantCatalogCustomView" />
  </CustomView1>
</CustomPageListingViews>

    . . . code continues . . .
```

> Note that the PublicKeyToken listed in the web.config above is the same as shown in the GAC.

An easy way to get the public key token is to copy it from the property window of the assembly in the GAC.

Another way to obtain the public key token is to enter the following command in a Visual Studio .NET command window: c:\sn -T [path to Web Part]mywebpart.dll.

Keep in mind that the web.config, like any XML file, is case sensitive so double-check for typos if you encounter any syntax errors.

Now everything is in place: our custom view assembly has been deployed to the GAC and has been registered as the first custom view option. Time to see if it works!

Go back to the portal, switch the page into edit mode by clicking Edit Page in the left vertical navigation, and open the SharePoint Web Part Tool Pane by selecting Modify Shared Web Part from the MCMS Page Listing Web Part's drop-down menu (activated by clicking the down arrow in the upper right). Expand the Custom Properties section for the Web Part, select Custom 1 for the View and click Apply at the bottom. Be patient as it may take a moment for your custom view to be loaded the first time. Once it loads, you should see something similar to the following screenshot:

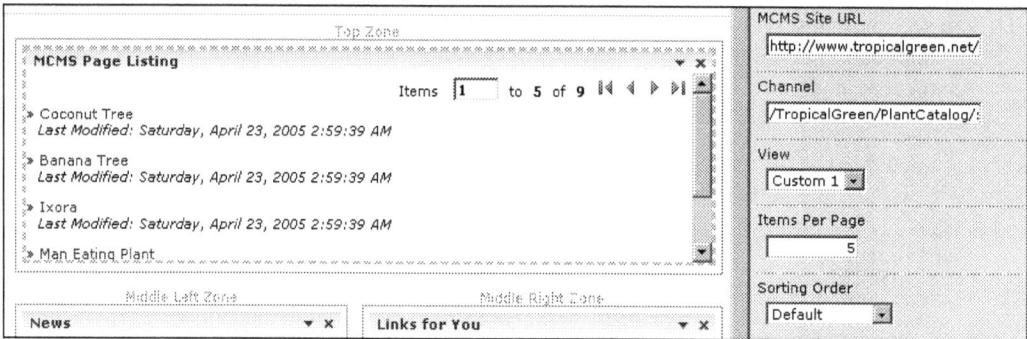

Congratulations! You've now built your first custom view for the MCMS Page Listing Web Part.

While the custom views are helpful for creating your own presentation, the MCMS Page Listing Web Part does not permit full control over the HTML output. Unfortunately you only have access to the contents of the table cell for each row, forcing a vertical list presentation. What if you wanted to show the postings in a horizontal list? What if you wanted to show only channels? What if you wanted to show subchannels and postings within a channel? The only way this is possible is by creating a custom Web Part that references the list of postings within a channel.

Let's take a look at the other two Web Parts included with the Connector.

The MCMS Pages in Production Web Part

The MCMS Pages in Production Web Part displays a list of postings in an MCMS site that the currently logged-in user has authored but that have not yet been published. The postings shown are pulled from all channels in the MCMS site, not just a specific channel. Let's take a look at this Web Part in action.

> The Connector does not support Forms Authentication because SharePoint only supports Windows Authentication. This will affect the data retrieval of the MCMS Pages in Production Web Part and the MCMS Pages Waiting for Approval Web Part.
>
> Due to this limitation, our current configuration of the Tropical Green website will not work with these two Web Parts. Regardless, we'll walk through the steps to implement and configure the Web Parts if you have an MCMS site with Windows Authentication.

The first thing we need to do is add the Web Part to the Web Part Page. We'll put it below the MCMS Page Listing Web Part we were previously working with. To add the Web Part, repeat the same steps we followed when adding the MCMS Page Listing Web Part:

1. Navigate to a SharePoint portal in Internet Explorer:
   `http://portal.tropicalgreen.net.`

2. Switch to edit mode by clicking the Edit Page link in the vertical left-hand Actions menu.

3. Click the Modify Shared Page link in the upper left. Using the drop-down menu that appears, select Add Web Parts and then Browse.

4. Switch to the Virtual Server Gallery to see our installed Web Parts for the current virtual server.

5. Now that we have our Web Part on the page, we need to set its properties. Click the small down arrow in the upper-right corner of the MCMS Pages in Production Web Part we just added to our page and select Modify Shared Web Part.

6. Expand the Custom Properties section by clicking the icon to the left of the Custom Properties section heading.

7. We need to tell the Web Part the URL of our MCMS web application. Enter http://www.tropicalgreen.net/MCMS/ for the MCMS Site Root URL property. Click the Apply button at the bottom of the tool pane.

The MCMS Pages Waiting for Approval Web Part

The MCMS Pages Waiting for Approval Web Part displays a list of postings that are pending the approval of the current user. This Web Part has exactly the same features, implementation steps, and configuration settings as the previous MCMS Pages in Production Web Part. The only difference between the two is the state of the postings. Since the two Web Parts are so similar, we won't walk through the steps in adding and configuring this Web Part on a SharePoint Web Part Page.

Why does the MCMS Page Listings Web Part work with a guest-enabled Forms Authentication MCMS site but MCMS Pages in Production Web Part and MCMS Pages Waiting for Approval Web Part not work?

When your site is configured for guest access, you have likely granted the account set as the MCMS Guest Login Account the Subscriber role in Site Manager. This is all the rights the guest account needs to enumerate through the postings within the specified channel and display them in the MCMS Page Listings Web Part. However, the MCMS Pages in Production Web Part and MCMS Pages Waiting for Approval Web Part require higher rights—such as author, editor, or moderator rights—than the Subscriber role provides, and thus, these Web Parts will display a permission error message: "The windows credentials provided could not be validated."

If our Tropical Green MCMS site wasn't set to guest access, we'd have the same problem with the MCMS Page Listings Web Part for the same reasons.

If your MCMS site was set up to use Windows Authentication and you configured the MCMS Pages in Production Web Part and MCMS Pages Waiting for Approval Web Part to use this Windows Authenticated MCMS site, the two Web Parts would look something like this:

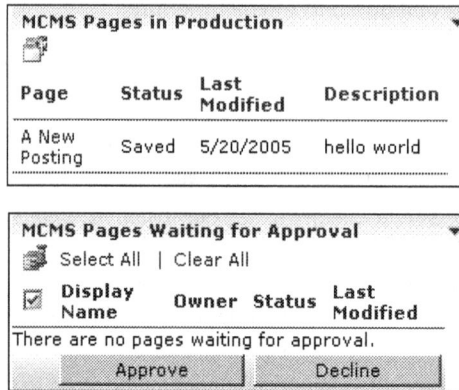

MCMS Pages in Production ▼

Page	Status	Last Modified	Description
A New Posting	Saved	5/20/2005	hello world

MCMS Pages Waiting for Approval ▼

Select All | Clear All

☑	Display Name	Owner	Status	Last Modified

There are no pages waiting for approval.

Approve	Decline

As we've demonstrated, the three Web Parts included with the Connector provide limited presentation (in the case of the MCMS Page Listing Web Part) and workflow administration (in the case of the MCMS Pages in Production and MCMS Pages Waiting for Approval Web Parts) of MCMS content. What if you need to display content from within a specific posting or a collection of channels and postings in a list?

While the MCMS Page Listing Web Part displays the postings within a channel, the presentation is somewhat restrictive. As we saw previously, each posting is listed within a one-cell-per-row HTML table. We have control over what HTML we'll put in the table cell. What if we need more control over the presentation? Or what if we wanted to show a tree-like organization of channels, sub channels, and postings?

Limitations of the MCMS Connector for SharePoint

The Connector addresses some of the most common needs and uses when publishing content from an MCMS site to SharePoint. However, as the previous questions indicate, there are many more publishing possibilities. To satisfy these requirements, we have the option of building custom Web Parts that would pull content from MCMS into SharePoint in a much more configurable manner. In order to do this, we need access to the content. This can occur in one of three ways:

1. Extend a virtual server as a SharePoint site and configure it as an MCMS Web Entry Point. This option would allow Web Parts in the SharePoint site to access the MCMS content directly via the MCMS PAPI. This is demonstrated in the Web Part we create in Chapter 7, *Building SharePoint Web Parts*.

2. Configure MCMS and SharePoint to run on two separate virtual servers. The MCMS content you wish to publish can be exposed via Web Services on the MCMS site. A SharePoint Web Part could then consume those Web Services and present the data on the SharePoint Web Part Page. Building and leveraging Web Services to expose the MCMS postings and channels is covered in Chapter 11, *InfoPath with MCMS Web Services*.

3. Use the IFRAME approach used by all Connector Web Parts, which utilizes ASP.NET Web Forms running on the MCMS server in the /CMS/WssIntegration folder.

The second option above, involving Web Services that expose content, is the most flexible solution.

> Appendix A, *Setting up MCMS and SPS on the Same Virtual Server*, will help you configure your SharePoint extended virtual server as an MCMS Web Entry Point as well.

Using MCMS to Display SharePoint Content

Up to this point we have looked at using SharePoint as the primary user interface for Tropical Green employees and leveraging the MCMS Internet site in a supporting role by pulling product information off the site. Let's flip this around and see how the Tropical Green Internet site, used primarily by our current and potential customers, can enhance the company intranet. Consider two potential scenarios that demonstrate how an MCMS site could leverage SharePoint:

- MCMS is used to implement the Tropical Green Internet site, accessible to any user with Internet access and a browser. The targeted audiences for the Tropical Green Internet site are potential new and current customers. SharePoint is used to implement the Tropical Green intranet, which contains documents with information on how to care for specific plants as well as a list of upcoming events provided by Tropical Green. Some events are only available to employees while others are available to everyone.
- As we explored in Chapter 5, *Searching MCMS with SharePoint*, you can use SharePoint as the search indexer and engine to provide powerful capabilities on the Tropical Green Internet site.

> Keep in mind that exposing SharePoint Portal Server hosted content beyond the employees in your organization requires the use of a SharePoint External Connector license.

In the first scenario, just like our previous examples of pulling MCMS content into SharePoint, content is pulled from SharePoint into MCMS. As with the previous examples, SharePoint content published within MCMS is not duplicated. We will not go into detail for the search scenario outlined above as this is covered in Chapter 5. Again, as with the previous examples, the Connector provides some assistance in demonstrating the first scenario.

The MCMS Connector for SharePoint Technologies

Previously we explored the Web Parts included with the Connector. These Web Parts were used to publish MCMS content and integrate MCMS workflow into a SharePoint site. The Connector also includes user controls and custom placeholders for use in your MCMS templates to facilitate searching with SharePoint Portal Server and publishing of documents from a SharePoint Portal Server document library.

> We have already explored all the controls and placeholders involved in implementing indexing and search capabilities in Chapter 5, Searching MCMS with SharePoint.

The SharePoint Document Placeholder enables content owners to link a document managed by SharePoint Portal Server to be presented within an MCMS posting. The content owner can also display properties of the linked document in the MCMS page. The presentation of the document and properties are controlled using XSLT stylesheets, which can be centrally controlled or individually applied to where they are needed. Once a document is linked to an MCMS posting, users can access the document either via SharePoint Portal Server or an MCMS site, which provides a seamless user experience for users viewing the document contents, regardless of the environment they access it from.

Any document stored within a SharePoint Document Library can be added to a posting via the SharePoint Document Placeholder. If the display view you choose includes an icon, the placeholder will use the icon associated with that document type on the MCMS Server. If the document type is a Microsoft Office InfoPath form or a Word Markup Language (WordML) document, you can have the contents of the document displayed in the placeholder Control. Conversely, all other document types are shown as attachments and/or the document properties. This is controlled by which XSLT options you choose to render the document library items.

> If the document is an InfoPath form, you need to ensure the user (content consumer) has rights to the SharePoint site containing the form. This is due to the fact that the SharePoint Document Library contains the template used to display the form in InfoPath.

When a document is added to an MCMS posting via the SharePoint Document Placeholder, the document is copied from the SharePoint Document Library into the MCMS repository as a local attachment. If the document is of type XML, such as an InfoPath or WordML document, the XML is saved in the MCMS placeholder as well (this content in the placeholder is set to readonly from within the MCMS site). Changes to the document in the SharePoint Document Library are not automatically reflected in MCMS. The Document Updater utility is included with the Connector to synchronize changes done in the document library into MCMS (if the "update automatically" checkbox has been checked in the SharePoint Document Placeholder control when creating the posting). The tool, WssDocumentUpdater.exe, can be found in the Connector's installation directory, C:\Program Files\MCMS Connector for SharePoint Technologies\CMS\bin\. This command-line tool can be set to run at regular intervals using the Windows Task Scheduler.

Using the SharePoint Document Placeholder

Let's see the SharePoint Document Placeholder in action. First, we need to create and upload a document to a SharePoint Document Library:

1. Create a new Microsoft Word document and enter the following text in the body of the document: This is content that is saved within a Microsoft Word file.
2. Save the document to your desktop with the filename MCMS Published Document.
3. Open Internet Explorer and browse to our SharePoint portal: http://portal.tropicalgreen.net/.

4. Under the Actions navigation on the left-hand side of the portal, click Upload Document.

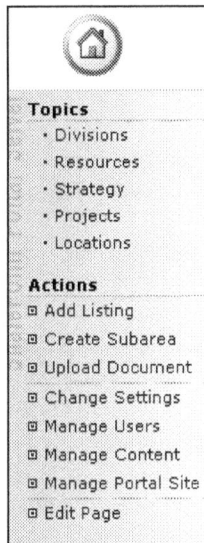

5. On the Document Library: Upload Document page, click Browse and select the document we just created. Enter your name into the Owner textbox, pick Final in the Status dropdown, make sure Add a listing for this document is checked, and click Save and Close at the top of the form.

6. On the Add Listing page, accept all the default options by simply clicking the OK button at the bottom of the page.

Upon uploading the document and creating a new listing, you will be automatically taken back to our portal homepage. If you look under the Links for You Web Part, you'll see our document listed at the top of the list:

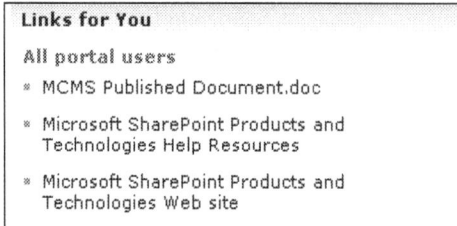

```
Links for You

All portal users
  * MCMS Published Document.doc

  * Microsoft SharePoint Products and
    Technologies Help Resources

  * Microsoft SharePoint Products and
    Technologies Web site
```

We now have a document in a SharePoint Document Library. Now we need to create a new posting in MCMS using a template that hosts a SharePoint Document Placeholder. In this situation we'll use the sample project, CmsSharePointConnector, included with the Connector to demonstrate this placeholder.

> The CmsSharePointConnector project can be found at C:\Program Files\Microsoft Content Management Server\Sample Data\CmsSharePointConnector\.
>
> Refer to Appendix B, *MCMS Connector for SharePoint Technologies*, for more information on installing the Connector, sample project, and sample data.
>
> We encourage you to do examine the CmsSharePointConnector sample code as it contains controls and styles that can be used to make your MCMS postings have the same look and feel—as well as navigation—as a SharePoint Portal Site.

Open Internet Explorer and browse to the CmsSharePointConnector project at http://portal.tropicalgreen.net/CmsSharePointConnector/.

Did you get a 404 Not Found error?

If you did, it's likely that the CmsSharePointConnector web application has not been excluded from SharePoint's managed paths. Refer to Appendix A, *Setting up MCMS and SPS on the Same Virtual Server*, to add an excluded path.

The CmsSharePointConnector homepage contains some information describing the Connector, sample data, and some useful links. We're interested in using the Internal postings and templates, so click the Internal channel link.

As you can see, the main page within the Internal channel looks just like a SharePoint portal site. We want to create a new posting using the News template as it contains a SharePoint Document Placeholder.

1. Click the **Switch To Edit Site** link and then click the **Create New Page** link after the page reloads.

2. When prompted to select a template, click the Internal Template Gallery, and then select the **News** template.

3. Once the new posting is displayed, enter the following text in the top-most HtmlPlaceholder: My first SharePoint Document Placeholder posting.

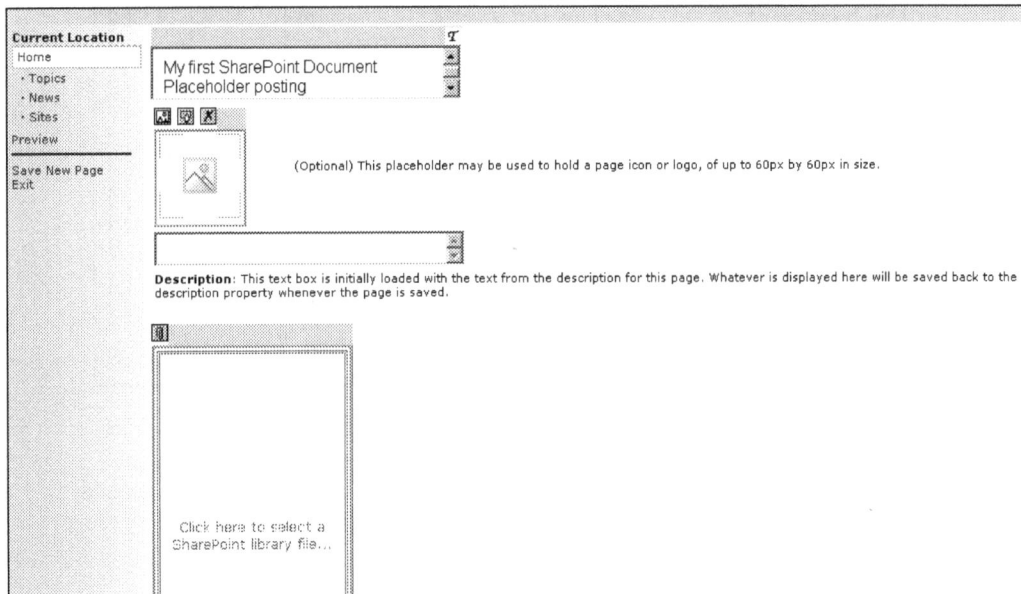

4. Now it's time to add the Microsoft Word document we just created and uploaded to the SharePoint Document Library. Activate the **Placeholder Properties** dialog by clicking on the placeholder that has the following text inside the placeholder container: Click here to select a SharePoint library file…

5. In the Placeholder Properties dialog, select the document we uploaded by clicking on the MCMS Published Document.doc link and click the Next button.

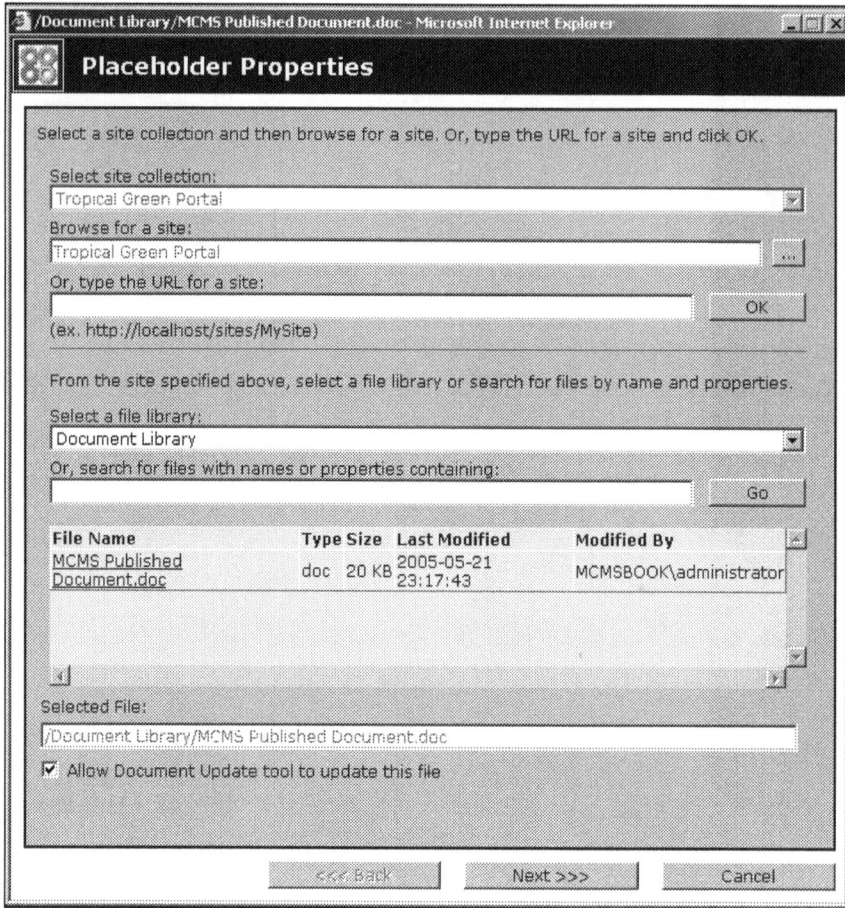

6. You will now have the option to select the layout options, which correspond to either none, an icon with file name, or an icon with file name and properties. These layout options are configurable in the catalog.xml file and what options are available depends on the file type. Select the Attachment with Icon and Properties option, followed by the Finish button.

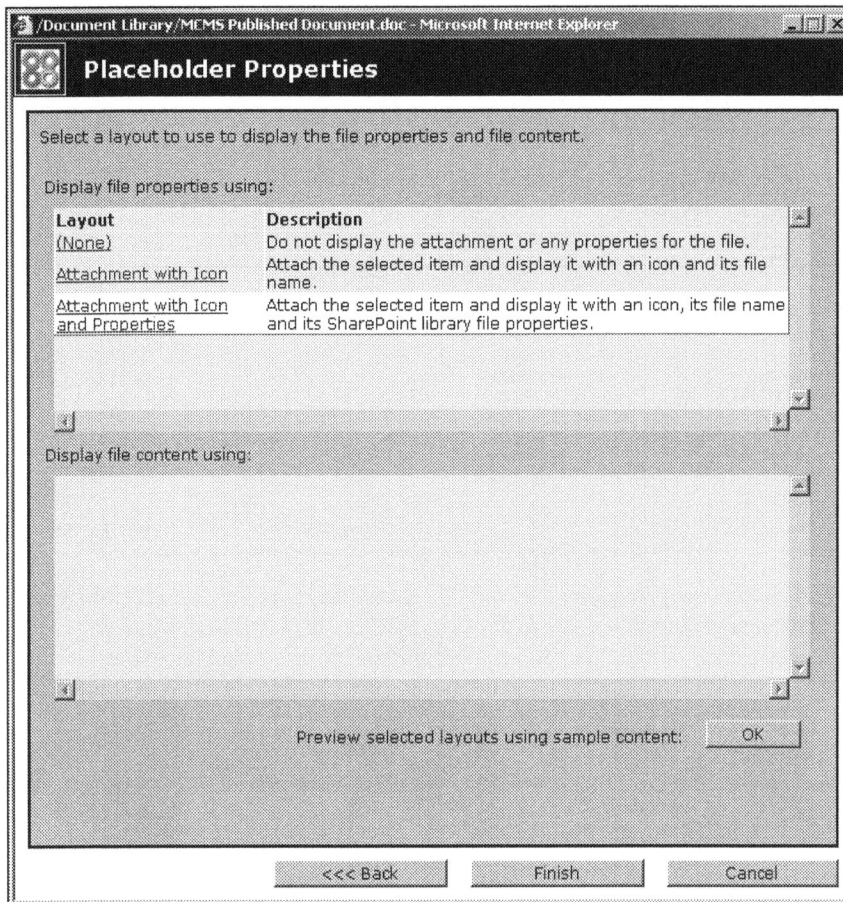

```
/Document Library/MCMS Published Document.doc - Microsoft Internet Explorer

Placeholder Properties

Select a layout to use to display the file properties and file content.

Display file properties using:

Layout              Description
(None)              Do not display the attachment or any properties for the file.
Attachment with Icon  Attach the selected item and display it with an icon and its file
                    name.
Attachment with Icon  Attach the selected item and display it with an icon, its file name
and Properties        and its SharePoint library file properties.

Display file content using:

              Preview selected layouts using sample content:    OK

          <<< Back            Finish            Cancel
```

Clicking the OK button next to the Preview selected layouts using sample content: label will open another window, giving you the option to view the various ways the document will be displayed within the posting.

Once you've selected the document and display options, the dialog will close, your posting will reload, and you will now see how the SharePoint Document Placeholder displays your document.

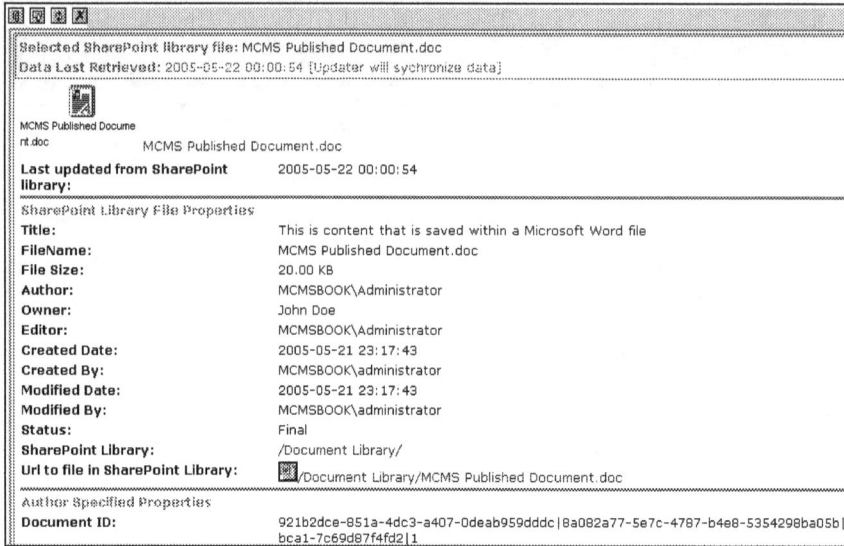

Let's save and publish the posting by clicking the **Save New Page** link in the left-hand navigation and giving it a name and display name of **My First SP Doc Placeholder Posting**. Now publish the posting by clicking the **Approve** link. After approving the posting, click the **Switch to Live Site** link to see how your posting really looks when published:

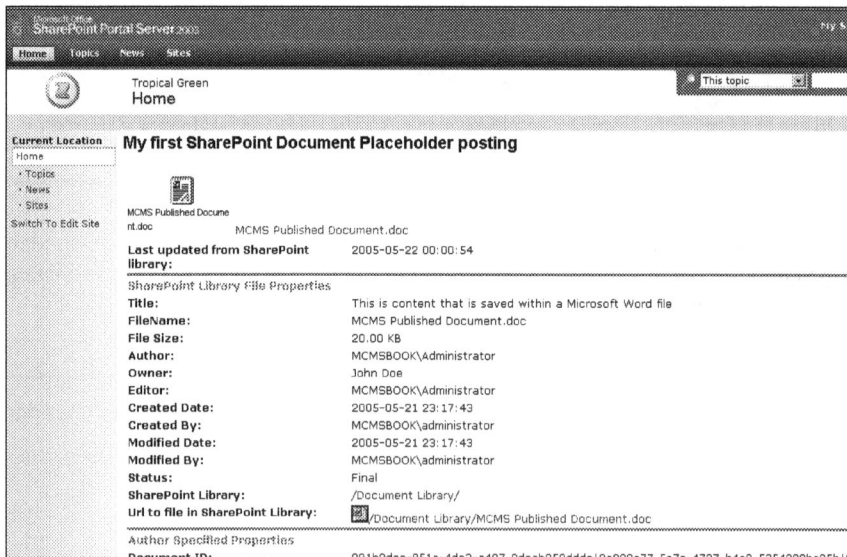

Previously we mentioned that you could use Extensible Stylesheet Language (XSL) stylesheets to transform XML from the properties and content of a document to HTML. A separate stylesheet is used for the document properties and content. All documents will have XML files for their document properties, but only InfoPath and WordML files are XML and can be transformed with a content stylesheet. You specify the stylesheet you want to use in the transformation in the Placeholder Properties dialog we just encountered when adding a document. The Connector ships with default stylesheets that we've already used. These stylesheets are found at `C:\Program Files\Microsoft Content Management Server\Server\IIS_CMS\WssIntegration\Dialogs\WssDocumentFinder\TemplateCatalog\`. The default stylesheets included with the Connector are listed in the table below:

Stylesheet Name	Description
`AttachmentIcon.xsl`	Displays the document as an icon attachment. Available only if the file attached is a document.
AttachmentIconProps.xsl	Displays the document as an icon attachment with its properties. Available only if the file attached is a document.
ImageTagOnly.xsl	Displays the image inline. Available only if the file attached is an image.
ImageAndProps.xsl	Displays the image inline with its properties. Available only if the file attached is an image.

The table above is based on documentation found in the Microsoft Content Management Server 2002 Connector for SharePoint Technologies help file, included with the Connector.

The SharePoint Document Placeholder looks at a single XML file to determine what stylesheets are available for the different types of files that can be attached to the placeholder. This file, `catalog.xml`, can be found in the same directory as the stylesheets outlined above. The `catalog.xml` file contains the following information on each of the available styles:

- Types of files the stylesheet can be applied to, such as `jpg`, `gif`, `contentxml`, or all (noted with an *)

- Descriptive name shown in the dropdown of the Placeholder Properties dialog

- Description of the stylesheet

- URL specifying the location of the XSL stylesheet used in the transformation

- A sample rendering URL, which is an XML file used to mimic the XML feed sent to the placeholder when a document is attached, giving the user a preview of the final rendering

In addition, you can also use a specific library that the stylesheet can be applied to using the `SpecificWebUrl` and `SpecificLibrary` attributes in the type node of the `catalog.xml` file. Use the `SpecificWebUrl` attribute to indicate which WSS or SPS site and the `SpecificLibrary` attribute to indicate the name of the WSS or SPS library to which the stylesheet can be applied.

You can create your own `catalog.xml` file for a specific SharePoint Document Placeholder implementation in order to restrict or provide certain rendering options for that library. Simply create a new XML file that conforms to the `catalog.xsd` schema definition file (found in the same directory as the `catalog.xml` and stylesheets) and specify this file in the HTML of your MCMS template that implements the SharePoint Document Placeholder using the

`RenderingTemplateCatalogUrl` attribute and specifying the virtual path to your catalog file. For example, if you created a new catalog called `mycatalog.xml`, the SharePoint Document Placeholder would look like this in the MCMS template file:

```
<ccl:SharePointDocumentPlaceholderControl
id="SharePointDocumentPlaceholderControl" runat="server"
KeepSynchronized="False" PlaceholderToBind="SPSDocument"
RenderingTemplateCatalogUrl="mycatalog.xml">
</ccl:SharePointDocumentPlaceholderControl>
```

Limitations of the MCMS Connector for SharePoint

Unfortunately the Connector only provides you one way to publish SharePoint content in an MCMS site: the `SharePointDocumentPlaceholder`, which we just covered. But SharePoint portals can contain much more content than just document libraries. Some of the most commonly used content elements in SharePoint are lists. SharePoint ships with many different types of configured lists such as Issues, Tasks, Links, Events, and also Custom Lists. These lists are very dynamic, powerful, and customizable as they can be built from the ground up. One of the biggest downsides of the Connector is it does not provide a method to publish SharePoint list data in an MCMS website.

It would be useful to have an MCMS placeholder control that can display data from a SharePoint list. Since this isn't included in the Connector, let's build our own!

We'll continue with our previous examples using our Tropical Green MCMS Internet site `http://www.tropicalgreen.net/TropicalGreen/` and the Tropical Green SharePoint Portal Server intranet portal `http://portal.tropicalgreen.net/`. Let's say we have an Events Web Part list in our SharePoint portal intranet that employees maintain for all Tropical Green related events:

How do I add items to my Events list?

To add, edit, or view the items in your portal's Events list, click Manage Content in the left-hand Actions menu from your portal homepage. On the Documents and Lists page, click the Events link. You may or may not have items listed in your list. To add items, click the New Item link in the list heading, enter the necessary information, and click the Save and Close link in the form heading. Repeat this process as many times as you like.

Now, what we'd like to do is display all these events on our homepage. We'll build a custom placeholder control that will retrieve these events from the SharePoint list. This custom placeholder control will be added to the existing TropicalGreenControlLib project and added to the Homepage.aspx template. The TropicalGreenControlLib project can be found in the Tropical Green download, and was created in the book *Building Websites with Microsoft Content Management Server* (Packt Publishing, January 2005, ISBN 1-904811-16-7).

A Placeholder Control to Display SharePoint List Contents

Since our placeholder control will retrieve all the items within a list, we need to determine how we'll access the actual list in the SharePoint portal. One option is to use the SharePoint API, but there is a downside to this approach: our MCMS site and SharePoint portal must reside on the same server because the SharePoint API will only access the server it's installed on, not a remote server. While this may be feasible in a test environment and some production environments, it's quite limiting. Another option is to access the SharePoint list via the Web Services included with SharePoint. The List Service Web Service contains methods that return the schema of the list, add, update, and remove items, as well as retrieve the contents of the list. Each SharePoint site has a reference to this Web Service so all lists are exposed to external applications.

Accessing the list via the Web Service is a better option than accessing it via the API. This solution can work on a server with both MCMS and SharePoint installed or if the two products are installed on separate servers.

Our placeholder control, the SharePointEventsPlaceholderControl, will leverage the SharePoint List Service Web Service to retrieve the items in the SharePoint Event list. In authoring mode, it will require the author to enter the Web Service URL of the SharePoint site and the name of the Events list.

Let's get started. The first thing we need to do is create a new class for our placeholder control and add the necessary references to the project:

1. Add a new class to the TropicalGreenControlLib project. Name the new class SharePointEventsPlaceholderControl.cs.

2. Right-click the project and select Add Web Reference...

3. Specify the List Service URL in the URL textbox and click the Go image. In our case, the address of the List Service is http://portal.tropicalgreen.net/ _vti_bin/lists.asmx. Once it loads, accept the default Web reference name by clicking the Add Reference button.

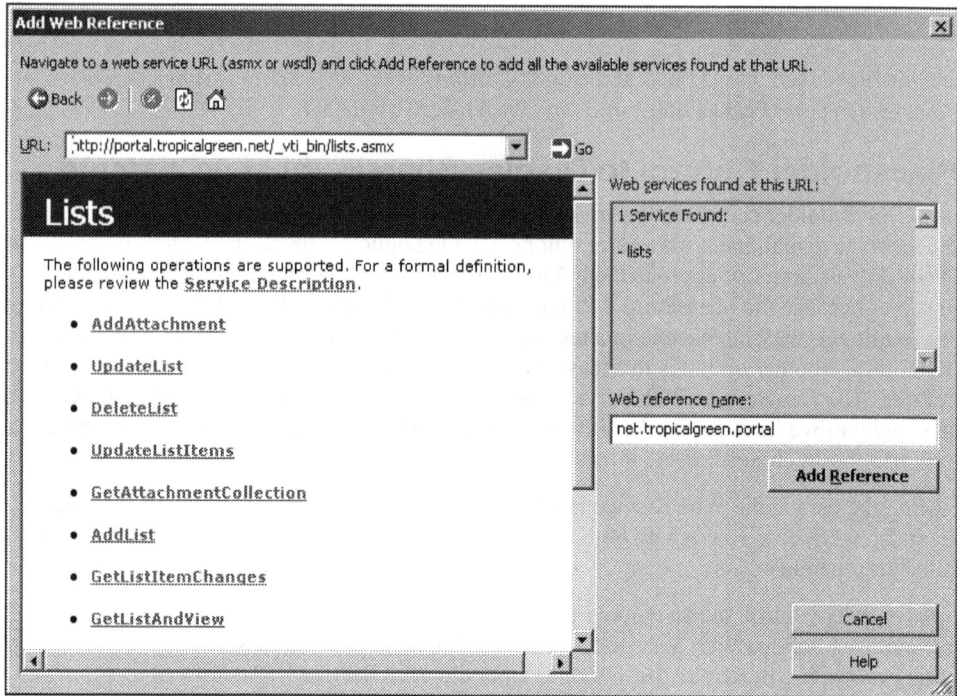

Now our project is set up with a reference to the SharePoint List Service Web Service and contains an empty code file that will contain our placeholder control.

We need to convert our new class from its empty shell to a custom placeholder control class by inheriting the base class and overriding the necessary methods. To do this, we'll add a few references to some necessary namespaces, inherit the BasePlaceholderControl class, and override five methods in the base class (we don't have to add any additional references for a custom placeholder control because we're using the TropicalGreenControlLib project, which already has all the necessary references as it contains other custom placeholder controls):

```
using System;
using Microsoft.ContentManagement.Publishing;
using Microsoft.ContentManagement.Publishing.Extensions.Placeholders;
using Microsoft.ContentManagement.WebControls;
using Microsoft.ContentManagement.WebControls.Design;

namespace TropicalGreenControlLib
{
  [SupportedPlaceholderDefinitionType( typeof(XmlPlaceholderDefinition))]
  public class SharePointEventsPlaceholderControl : BasePlaceholderControl
  {
    public SharePointEventsPlaceholderControl()
    {
    }

    protected override void CreateAuthoringChildControls
                     (BaseModeContainer authoringContainer)
    {
    }
```

```
          protected override void CreatePresentationChildControls
                       (BaseModeContainer presentationContainer)
          {
          }

          protected override void LoadPlaceholderContentForAuthoring
                       (PlaceholderControlEventArgs e)
          {
          }

          protected override void LoadPlaceholderContentForPresentation
                       (PlaceholderControlEventArgs e)
          {
          }

          protected override void SavePlaceholderContent
                       (PlaceholderControlSaveEventArgs e)
          {
          }
      }
  }
```

Our empty class now contains the skeleton of an MCMS custom placeholder control. At this point let's consider what inputs we'll need from our users when the posting is in authoring mode. The goal of this placeholder control is to retrieve the content of a SharePoint list. We already have a reference to the SharePoint List Service Web Service, which we'll use to retrieve the list contents, but we need to know the exact address of the Web Service in case this control is used to access another SharePoint site and not just our portal. The Web Service contains twelve methods, but we're only interested in GetListItems(). This method accepts a few parameters, but the only one we need to concern ourselves with is ListName (we'll accept the defaults for all the others).

We'll need to collect the following two values from the user:

- The SharePoint List Service Web Service URL of the SharePoint site or portal that contains the list we want to display
- The name of the SharePoint list

This means we'll need two TextBox controls, one for each input. We'll also add a LinkButton that will use the information provided to retrieve the items in the list and display of the events. Finally, because we want our controls to be aligned nicely, we'll use an HTML table to control the layout. To achieve this add the following highlighted code to the top of our code file:

```
using System;
using System.Collections;
using System.Net;
using System.Web.UI;
using System.Web.UI.HtmlControls;
using System.Web.UI.WebControls;
using System.Xml;
using Microsoft.ContentManagement.Publishing;
using Microsoft.ContentManagement.Publishing.Extensions.Placeholders;
using Microsoft.ContentManagement.WebControls;
using Microsoft.ContentManagement.WebControls.Design;

namespace TropicalGreenControlLib
{
    [SupportedPlaceholderDefinitionType( typeof(XmlPlaceholderDefinition))]
    public class SharePointEventsPlaceholderControl : BasePlaceholderControl
```

```
{
  // authoring controls
  TextBox txbSharePointUrl;
  TextBox txbListName;
  LiteralControl litEventItemsLiteral;
  HtmlTable tblLayout;

  public SharePointEventsPlaceholderControl()
  {
  }
  . . . code continues . . .
```

The next thing we need to do is build the user interface portion of our placeholder control. We'll do by creating an HTML table in the CreateAuthoringChildControls() method we are overriding:

```
protected override void CreateAuthoringChildControls(BaseModeContainer
authoringContainer)
{
  // create our layout table
  tblLayout = new HtmlTable();

  // build row containing the SharePoint URL input prompt
  tblLayout.Rows.Add(BuildAuthoringSharePointSiteTableRow());

  // build row containing the SharePoint Event List name input prompt
  tblLayout.Rows.Add(BuildAuthoringSharePointEventListTableRow());

  // add table to the authoring container
  authoringContainer.Controls.Add(tblLayout);
}
```

Now we need the methods that will build these HTML table rows. The first methods we'll need are the ones to create the input for the SharePoint site URL and list name:

```
private HtmlTableRow BuildAuthoringSharePointSiteTableRow()
{
  HtmlTableRow row;
  HtmlTableCell cell;

  // create sharepoint Web service label & input
  txbSharePointUrl = new TextBox();

  row = new HtmlTableRow();
  cell = new HtmlTableCell();
  cell.Controls.Add(new LiteralControl("SharePoint Portal Site URL:<br>"));
  cell.Controls.Add(txbSharePointUrl);
  row.Cells.Add(cell);

  // return the built row
  return row;
}

private HtmlTableRow BuildAuthoringSharePointEventListTableRow()
{
  HtmlTableRow row;
  HtmlTableCell cell;

  // create SharePoint event list name label & input
  txbListName = new TextBox();

  row = new HtmlTableRow();
  cell = new HtmlTableCell();
  cell.Controls.Add(new LiteralControl("SharePoint Event List Name:<br>"));
  cell.Controls.Add(txbListName);
```

```
        row.Cells.Add(cell);

        // return the built row
        return row;
    }
```

Let's see how our placeholder control looks so far. Build the TropicalGreenControlLib project. Assuming there were no errors, let's now add our placeholder control to the template. Instead of adding it to an existing template, create a new template file in the TropicalGreen project (under the `Templates` subdirectory) and name it `Events.aspx`. Use the `Homepage.aspx` template as a base for the `Events.aspx` page, but remove the content area so that your final Events template page's HTML contains the following (note the highlighted portions where we have added our new placeholder control):

```
<%@ Page language="c#" Codebehind="Events.aspx.cs" AutoEventWireup="false"
Inherits="TropicalGreen.Templates.Events" %>
<%@ Register TagPrefix="uc1" TagName="DefaultConsole"
Src="../Console/DefaultConsole.ascx" %>
<%@ Register TagPrefix="cc1" Namespace="TropicalGreenControlLib"
        Assembly="TropicalGreenControlLib" %>
<%@ Register TagPrefix="uc1" TagName="RightMenu"
Src="../UserControls/RightMenu.ascx" %>
<%@ Register TagPrefix="uc1" TagName="TopMenu"
Src="../UserControls/TopMenu.ascx" %>
<!DOCTYPE HTML PUBLIC "-//W3C//DTD HTML 4.0 Transitional//EN" >
<HTML>
  <HEAD>
    <title>Events</title>
    <meta content="Microsoft Visual Studio .NET 7.1" name="GENERATOR">
    <meta content="C#" name="CODE_LANGUAGE">
    <meta content="JavaScript" name="vs_defaultClientScript">
    <meta content="http://schemas.microsoft.com/intellisense/ie5"
      name="vs_targetSchema">
    <LINK href="/tropicalgreen/Styles/Styles.css"
      type="text/css" rel="stylesheet">
  </HEAD>
  <body leftMargin="0" topMargin="0">
    <form id="Form1" method="post" runat="server">
      <table cellSpacing="0" cellPadding="0" width="100%" border="0">
        <tr>
          <td vAlign="top" width="100%" bgColor="#ffcc00"
            colSpan="2">
            <IMG src="/tropicalgreen/images/Logo.gif">
          </td>
          <td vAlign="top" rowSpan="10">
            <uc1:DefaultConsole id="DefaultConsole1"
              runat="server"></uc1:DefaultConsole>
          </td>
        </tr>
        <tr bgColor="#66cc33">
          <td colSpan="2">
            <uc1:topmenu id="TopMenu1" runat="server"></uc1:topmenu>
          </td>
        </tr>
        <tr>
          <td style="PADDING-RIGHT: 30px; PADDING-LEFT: 30px;
            PADDING-BOTTOM: 30px; PADDING-TOP: 10px" vAlign="top">
            <p> </p>
            <b>Tropical Green Events</b>
            <cc1:SharePointEventsPlaceholderControl id="SharePointEvents"
              runat="server" PlaceholderToBind="SharePointEventsConfig" />
          </td>
          <td class="RightMenuBar" vAlign="top"
```

```
                align="center" width="20%" bgColor="#669900"
                height="100%" rowSpan="2">
                <uc1:rightmenu id="RightMenu1" runat="server"></uc1:rightmenu>
            </td>
        </tr>
    </table>
    </form>
  </body>
</HTML>
```

Once we have the template file, we need to create a template in the MCMS Template Explorer so we can create a posting using our Events template. Create a new template called Events and put it under the TropicalGreen gallery.

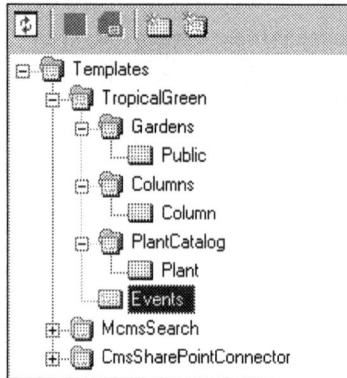

Then, create a single placeholder definition, of type XmlPlaceholder, and name it SharePointEventsConfig.

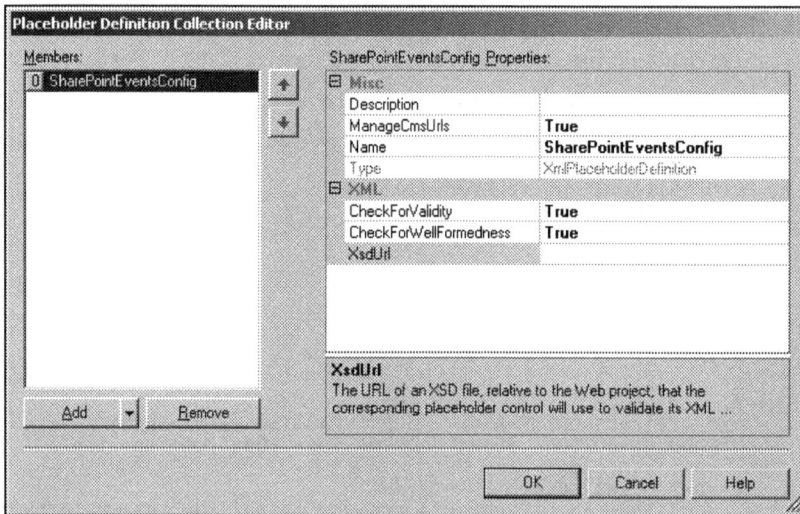

Finally, select our new Events.aspx as the template file for this new template.

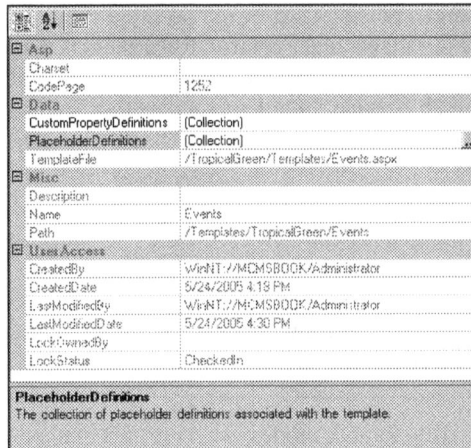

Check in the template and build the TropicalGreen project. The last thing we need to do is create a new posting using the new Events template. While it won't do much, it will help us see our control come to life as we build each piece of the placeholder control. Create the new posting by browsing to the root of the Tropical Green site, switch into edit mode, create a new posting using the Events template, and save it with the name and display name of "Events". Once the posting has been saved, go ahead and approve it.

We now have a working placeholder control (granted it doesn't do much at this point), a new template, and an events page on our Tropical Green site. While on the events page (whose URL is http://www.tropicalgreen.net/TropicalGreen/Events.htm), click the Switch To Edit Site link in the Web Author Console, and then click Edit to switch into authoring mode for the posting. You should see the input boxes and labels that we created for our placeholder:

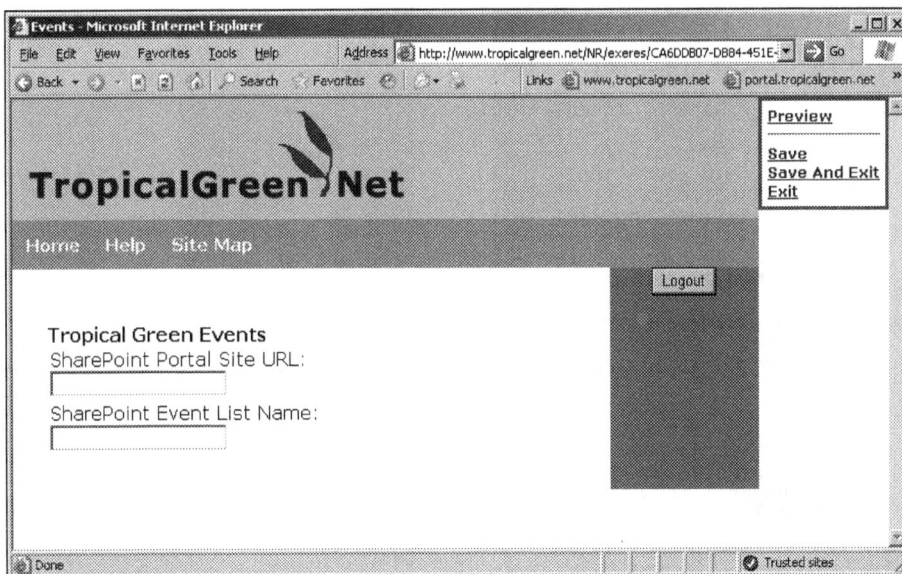

With the authoring controls and a posting to view our progress created, let's continue with adding some functionality to our placeholder control. Regardless if the posting is in authoring or presentation mode, we will need to retrieve the items from the SharePoint Events list via the SharePoint List Service Web Service. In order to access this Web Service, we need the URL of the service, the name of the list containing the items we're interested in, and valid login credentials for the site.

> For simplicity, we're going to hard-code the credentials. However, we strongly recommend you employ a more secure solution such as encrypting the username and password in the web.config of the site or allowing the content owner to enter the credentials into the placeholder control with the URL and list name. Microsoft recommends the data protection API (DPAPI) available in the .NET base class library.

Since we'll need this functionality in both modes, we'll create a method called GetSharePointListItems() that requires the Web Service URL and list name while returning an array of all items within the list. For each item returned in the array, we want to know the following information regarding the event:

- Title
- Description
- Location
- Start Date/Time
- End Date/Time

The best way to store these details is to create a new class in the TropicalGreenControlLib project. Call it SharePointEventListItem.cs and add the following code to define a business object to represent the items within a SharePoint Event list:

```
using System;

namespace TropicalGreenControlLib
{
  public class SharePointEventListItem
  {
    private string _title;
    private string _location;
    private DateTime _startDateTime;
    private DateTime _endDateTime;

    // force callers to use the Factory method below
    private SharePointEventListItem() {}

    // Factory method used to create a new SharePointEventListItem
    public static SharePointEventListItem CreateItem (string title,
        string location, DateTime start, DateTime end)
    {
      SharePointEventListItem li = new SharePointEventListItem();
      li._title = title;
      li._location = location;
      li._startDateTime = start;
      li._endDateTime = end;
      return li;
    }
```

```
      // title of the event
      public string Title
      {
        get
        {
          return _title;
        }
      }

      // location where the event will take place
      public string Location
      {
        get
        {
          return _location;
        }
      }

      // datetime when the event will begin
      public DateTime StartDateTime
      {
        get
        {
          return _startDateTime;
        }
      }

      // datetime when the event will end
      public DateTime EndDateTime
      {
        get
        {
          return _endDateTime;
        }
      }
    }
  }
```

Now that we have an object that will contain each item in the list, add the
GetSharePointEventListItems() method to the end of our placeholder control class,
SharePointEventsPlaceholderControl.cs. This method will use the specified URL to call a
SharePoint Web Service to retrieve a list of all the items within the specified list.

```
private ArrayList GetSharePointEventListItems(string sharePointUrl,
                                              string listName)
{
  ArrayList wsResultArray = new ArrayList();

  // make sure URL and list name are provided
  if ( (sharePointUrl == string.Empty) || (listName == string.Empty) )
    return null;

  // we hardcode the Web service credentials for simplicity
  //   You are strongly recommended to secure the login credentials
  //   in the same way you'd secure any other credentials such
  //   as a database connection string
  // NOTE: You'll need to change the credentials to use an account on your
  //   computer that has access to the SharePoint Web services and the
  //   specified list.
  NetworkCredential nc = new
    NetworkCredential("administrator", "password", "MCMSBOOK");

  // create a reference to the SharePoint List Service web service;
  //   assign the provided url and credentials
  net.tropicalgreen.portal.Lists spWsList =
    new TropicalGreenControlLib.net.tropicalgreen.portal.Lists();
```

```
        sharePointUrl = sharePointUrl +"/_vti_bin/Lists.asmx";
        spWsList.Url = sharePointUrl.Replace("//","/");
        spWsList.Credentials = nc;

        try
        {
            // retrieve all items returned by the Web service;
            //    we aren't interested in special queries, so pass null
            //    for all parameters except the list name
            XmlNode wsXmlResults = spWsList.GetListItems
                (listName, null, null, null, null, null);

            // if nothing was returned by the Web service,
            //    return null indicating an error
            if (wsXmlResults == null)
                return null;

            // convert XML data to business object
            wsResultArray = ExtractListData(wsXmlResults);
        }
        catch
        {
            // an error occured... return null to indicate error
            return null;
        }

        return wsResultArray;
    }
```

You may notice that the authentication method used here in creating the NetworkCredential object for the Web Service is different from the method we implemented in Chapter 5, *Searching MCMS with SharePoint*, in the section *Search Rights for the MCMS Application Pool Account*.

In the search implementation, we used the application pool identity as our credentials and granted that identity access to the SharePoint site. In this implementation, we have explicitly created a NetworkCredential under a specific user account. Either method will work in either situation. The different methods have been implemented in the two chapters to demonstrate the alternative options available to the developer.

Now we need the method that extracts the list data from the XML format returned by the Web Service and converts it to an array of our SharePointEventListItem business object. Add the following method to the placeholder control class:

```
private ArrayList ExtractListData(XmlNode wsXmlResults)
{
    ArrayList wsResultArray = new ArrayList();
    SharePointEventListItem li;

    // for each result returned, extract the necessary information
    //    creating a new item and adding it to the result ArrayList
    foreach (XmlNode resultItemNode in wsXmlResults.ChildNodes[1].ChildNodes)
    {
        // make sure the result item has attributes, because if not
        //    it's an invalid result... so skip it
        if (resultItemNode.Attributes == null)
            continue;

        li = SharePointEventListItem.CreateItem(
            resultItemNode.Attributes["ows_Title"].Value.ToString(),
```

```
            resultItemNode.Attributes["ows_Location"].Value.ToString(),
            Convert.ToDateTime(resultItemNode.Attributes["ows_EventDate"].Value
                        .ToString()),
            Convert.ToDateTime(resultItemNode.Attributes["ows_EndDate"].Value
                        .ToString())
        );
        wsResultArray.Add(li);
    }

    return wsResultArray;
}
```

We need one last method to render our SharePoint Event list items before we wire up the custom placeholder control and preview events. Add the following method to the placeholder control class. This method calls our GetSharePointEventListItems() method to obtain a list of all items within the specified SharePoint list. Once it has the contents of the SharePoint list, it renders them for presentation using HTML:

```
private void DisplaySharePointEventListItems(string spWsUrl, string
spListName)
{
    SharePointEventListItem li;

    // make sure enough information provided in the input boxes
    if ( (spWsUrl == string.Empty) || (spListName == string.Empty) )
        return;

    // get the SharePoint items
    ArrayList items = GetSharePointEventListItems(spWsUrl, spListName);

    // verify results returned
    if (items == null)
        litEventItemsLiteral.Text =
                        "<p>No events at this time. Please check back "
                    + "later.</p>";
    else
    {
        litEventItemsLiteral.Text = string.Empty;

        // loop through each item in the list
        foreach (object o in items)
        {
            // cast the object in the ArrayList as a SharePointEventListItem
            li = o as SharePointEventListItem;

            // if the cast was successful, show the event & increment the counter
            if (li != null)
            {
                litEventItemsLiteral.Text += string.Format(
                        "<p><b>{0}</b><br>{1}<br><em>{2} - {3}</em></p>",
                        li.Title, li.Location,
                        li.StartDateTime.ToString("MMM dd, yyyy h:ss tt"),
                        li.EndDateTime.ToString("MMM dd, yyyy h:ss tt"));
            }
        }
    }
}
```

At this point we have overridden the CreateAuthoringChildControls() method to create our authoring controls and created all the methods necessary to retrieve and display items from the SharePoint Event list. The last two tasks to wrap up the authoring mode of our placeholder control are to override the LoadPlaceholderContentForAuthoring() method, which retrieves previously saved configuration information from the XmlPlaceholder object bound to our placeholder

189

control, and to override the SavePlaceholderContent() method, which saves the configuration information in the underlying XmlPlaceholder object.

The LoadPlaceholderContentForAuthoring() method will get the information about the configured SharePoint Event list from the bound XmlPlaceholder object, extract the SharePoint List Service Web Service URL and the name of the Event list, and call our DisplaySharePointEventListItems() method to display the content of the list:

```
protected override void LoadPlaceholderContentForAuthoring
                                        (PlaceholderControlEventArgs e)
{
  EnsureChildControls();

  XmlDocument placeholderContents = new XmlDocument();
  string sharePointUrl = string.Empty;
  string spListName = string.Empty;

  // load the saved config from the posting
  placeholderContents.LoadXml(((XmlPlaceholder)this.BoundPlaceholder)
        .XmlAsString);

  // extract the necessary information
  sharePointUrl = placeholderContents.DocumentElement.ChildNodes[0]
        .Attributes["sharePointUrl"].Value;
  spListName = placeholderContents.DocumentElement.ChildNodes[0]
        .Attributes["listname"].Value;

  // bind the config info to the text boxes
  txbSharePointUrl.Text = sharePointUrl;
  txbListName.Text = spListName;

  // show the items
  DisplaySharePointEventListItems(sharePointUrl, spListName);
}
```

The SavePlaceholderContent() method will create a small XML string containing the Web Service URL and list name and insert it into the bound placeholder:

```
protected override void SavePlaceholderContent(PlaceholderControlSaveEventArgs e)
{
  string config = string.Empty;

  // make sure enough information is provided in the input boxes
  if ( (txbSharePointUrl.Text == string.Empty)
    || (txbListName.Text == string.Empty) )
    return;

  // save the config information
  config = string.Format("<config><sharepointlist sharePointUrl=\"{0}\""
               + "listname=\"{1}\" /></config>",
                  txbSharePointUrl.Text, txbListName.Text);

  ((XmlPlaceholder)this.BoundPlaceholder).XmlAsString = config;
}
```

Let's see how our control looks in authoring mode. Build the TropicalGreenControlLib project, open a browser, and navigate to http://www.tropicalgreen.net/TropicalGreen/Events.htm. If you hadn't logged in already, go ahead and do so. Once you're logged in, click the **Switch To Edit Site** link in the Web Author Console, and then click **Edit** to switch into authoring mode for the posting. Enter the following into the two input boxes and click **Save and Exit** in the Web Author Console:

Name	Value
SharePoint Portal Site URL	http://portal.tropicalgreen.net
SharePoint Event List Name	Events

Now all we need is to wire up the two additional methods to create and populate the presentation controls for our placeholder control using `CreatePresentationChildControls()`, get the information about the configured SharePoint Event list from the bound placeholder, and call `DisplaySharePointEventListItems()` to display the items using the method called `LoadPlaceholderContentForPresentation()`:

```
protected override void CreatePresentationChildControls
        (BaseModeContainer presentationContainer)
{
  litEventItemsLiteral = new LiteralControl();
  presentationContainer.Controls.Add(litEventItemsLiteral);
}

protected override void LoadPlaceholderContentForPresentation
        (PlaceholderControlEventArgs e)
{
  EnsureChildControls();

  XmlDocument placeholderContents = new XmlDocument();
  string sharePointUrl = string.Empty;
  string spListName = string.Empty;

  // load the saved config from the posting
  placeholderContents.LoadXml(((XmlPlaceholder)this.BoundPlaceholder)
            .XmlAsString);

  // extract the necessary information
  sharePointUrl = placeholderContents.DocumentElement.ChildNodes[0]
            .Attributes["sharePointUrl"].Value;
  spListName = placeholderContents.DocumentElement.ChildNodes[0]
            .Attributes["listname"].Value;

  // show the items
  DisplaySharePointEventListItems(sharePointUrl, spListName);
}
```

That should do it... build the TropicalGreenControlLib project one last time and navigate back to the Events page at `http://www.tropicalgreen.net/TropicalGreen/Events.htm`.

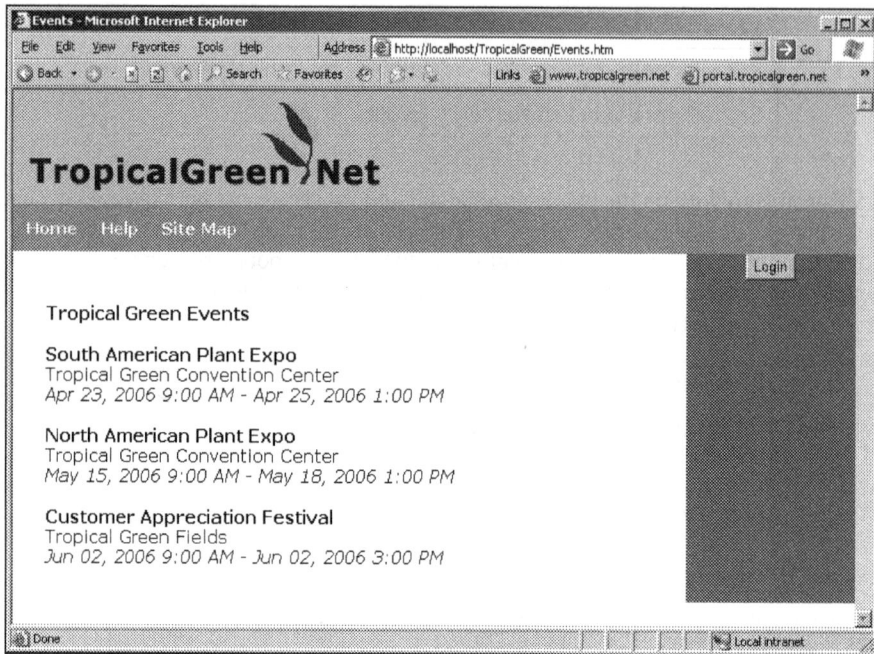

We now have a placeholder control that will extract items from a SharePoint Events list using the SharePoint List Service Web Service. Where could we go from here? This control could be taken to the next level by creating a friendlier input dialog where the content author would enter the URL of the SharePoint portal or site and the placeholder control would return a list of child sites to choose from, as well as a selection of all the SharePoint lists available in each site. Instead of being coded towards the Events list, we could modify the `GetSharePointEventListItems()` and `DisplaySharePointEventListItems()` to retrieve and display any type of SharePoint list.

But why stop there? We could adopt the MCMS Page Listing Web Part model in creating custom views by passing the entire `ArrayList` (maybe creating a more intelligent strongly typed collection) to an assembly to provide complete control over the rendering of the presentation. If your MCMS site also supports Windows Authentication, or if your SharePoint portal is configured for anonymous access, you could determine if the current user has access to the specified list and if so, create a hyperlink straight into the SharePoint item detail page. We could also take the raw XML result returned by the Web Service and run it through an XSLT for a more dynamic rendering of the content (such as implementing paging).

Your business needs and requirements may affect the design and implementation of your own placeholder that pulls information from a SharePoint list. In our example, the placeholder pulls the information from the SharePoint list every time the placeholder is displayed in both authoring and presentation mode. This may not be a performance-friendly method to render the list contents in the placeholder as Web Services incur their own overhead. In addition, if your company has strict auditing requirements where you need to produce a copy of the posting from a given time, the solution as we designed wouldn't suffice, as the content is pulled on demand from the SharePoint list and the contents of the list being displayed are not stored in the placeholder.

These are just some of the additional issues you'd need to consider when designing and developing your own implementation. The hard part of pulling content from a SharePoint List Service Web Service has been demonstrated in this brief placeholder control. You can use your imagination in customizing this placeholder control for your specific needs.

Summary

In this chapter, we have covered various ways of publishing MCMS content within a SharePoint site, as well as publishing SharePoint content within an MCMS site. In each of these two situations we explored what the MCMS Connector for SharePoint Technologies—a free download provided by Microsoft—provides to assist in publishing content between the two environments.

For publishing SharePoint content within an MCMS site, we used the SharePoint Document Placeholder on an MCMS template to display properties and/or contents of a document stored within a SharePoint document library. In addition, we built a new placeholder control, which works as an aggregator for the content of a SharePoint list.

To publish MCMS content within a SharePoint site, we used the Page Listing Web Part shipped with the Connector to display all the postings within a specified channel in an MCMS site as a list in SharePoint. We also saw the two administration Web Parts included in the Connector, MCMS Pages in Production and MCMS Pages Waiting for Approval, and how they can assist with the publishing workflow of an MCMS site.

7

Building SharePoint Web Parts

In the previous chapters, we have looked at some different ways of integrating MCMS and SharePoint by using custom code and by using the components shipped with the MCMS Connector for SharePoint Technologies. One important thing we haven't yet covered is the creation of custom Web Parts for SharePoint to integrate MCMS content into a SharePoint site or portal. In this chapter, we will create a configurable Web Part that acts as a navigation component for the postings in a specified channel. But before we get into the detail of the MCMS Navigation Web Part we are going to build, let's take a look at what Web Parts are.

Microsoft SharePoint Portal Server (SPS) and Windows SharePoint Services (WSS) display content and interactive components within pages called **Web Part Pages**. The building blocks that make up these pages are **Web Part Zones** that can consist of one or more Web Parts. These Web Parts can be arranged on the Web Part Page as desired by a business user with the required privileges.

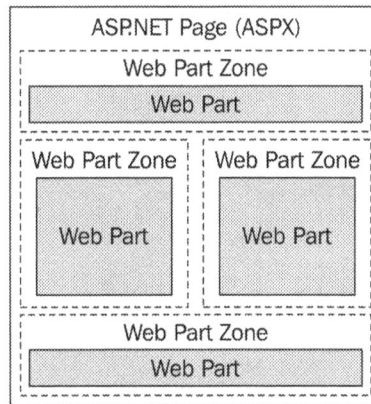

A Web Part is a single module that can be arranged on a Web Part Page to provide specific functionality such as a calendar. MCMS ships with only three placeholder controls whereas SPS and WSS ship with many Web Parts installed for handling announcements, contacts, tasks, events, data viewing, and XML. These Web Parts provide a good starting point and are easily configured to address most users' requirements without developer intervention.

For a variety of reasons, including closer integration, more specific requirements, and performance or complexity issues, you may need to create a Web Part from the ground up. There are several avenues a developer can take during the early stages in the design of a Web Part:

- Configure the out-of-the-box WSS/SPS lists and Web Parts to provide the required method of data storage, data input, and presentation

- Develop the Web Part from scratch as an ASP.NET Server Control

- Develop the business logic as a Web Service and use the XML Web Part or the DataView Web Part as the GUI

- Develop a separate web form and use an Iframe to integrate the portal and your satellite application. Browser compatibility should be considered when using this approach

- Design and develop your Web Part as a .NET User Control and leverage generic Web Parts such as 'SmartPart' (http://www.smartpart.info) to host your .NET user control

Each of these approaches has advantages and disadvantages that should be weighed up at design time such as ease of development, extensibility, scalability, interoperability, deployment, and security. The following table sums these up:

Method	Existing Web Parts	Using Web service as business layer with XML Web Part / DataView Web Part	User Control integrated with Smart Part	ASP.NET Server Control	IFrame to ASP.NET Web Form
Ease of Development	No development required	Simple	Requires knowledge of SmartPart but is simply ASP.NET User Control development	Complex	Simple
Extensibility	Depends on the functionality provided by the specific Web Part	Developer has limited control over the UI but gains FrontPage 2003 as a development tool and a separate ASP.NET business layer.	Very Extensible	Very Extensible	Very Extensible
Scalability	Scaled with the WSS/SPS server.	End point Web service must be scaled as necessary.	Scaled with the WSS/SPS server	Scaled with the WSS/SPS server	The framed ASP.NET application must be scaled as necessary.

Interoperability	Can easily interact with other parts of WSS/SPS	Interacting with WSS/SPS objects is more complex but still possible.	Can easily interact with other parts of WSS/SPS	Can easily interact with other parts of WSS/SPS	Interacting with WSS/SPS objects is more complex but still possible.
Deployment	No deployment required for out-of-the-box Web Parts and very simple deployment for downloadable Web Parts	No deployment required	Installation of the Smart Part Web Part is required.	Complex	Simple
Security	No security impact	No SPS/WSS security impact as security will be enforced by the ASP.NET Web service	No security impact	Security is enforced by SPS/WSS.	Enforced by the ASP.NET Web application
Notes	Requires the least amount of development knowledge	Great for .NET developers that need to display data external to WSS/SPS in a Web Part Page	Allows you to run .NET User Controls as Web Parts. Allows development of a rich UI within the Web Part Framework.	Provides the most flexibility during development but requires manual definition of the UI. Is executed within the Web Part Framework.	Allows a separate ASP.NET Web application to be used via SharePoint

Throughout this chapter, we will focus on the ASP.NET Server Control method.

The SharePoint MCMS Navigation Control

During the course of this chapter, we will develop a Web Part as a server control by building a Web Part that acts as an MCMS navigation component. The server control methodology has been selected as it is the most flexible method. End users with WSS/SPS Web Designer rights will be able to add the Web Part to a Web Part Page and configure the Web Part by specifying the MCMS Channel. The items in the configured MCMS Channel will be rendered in the Web Part using an **XSLT** (**Extensible Stylesheet Language Transformations**) stylesheet to produce the following display:

```
Extensible MCMS Page Listing Web Part  ▼  ✕
Channels

     • WoodgroveIntranet
     • CmsSharePointConnector
     • McmsSearch
     • WoodgroveASP
     • WoodgroveInternational
     • WoodgroveNet
     • WoodgroveNetVB
```

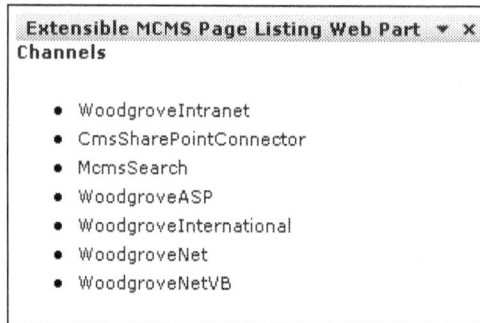

To build this Web Part, we'll perform the following steps:

- Prepare the development environment
- Create the Web Part Project
- Create the Web Part
- Define custom properties for the Web Part
- Develop custom properties for the Web Part
- Build the Data Layer
- Build the Presentation Layer
- Deploy the Web Part

> The Web Part we are building will run under both SPS and WSS as we will not be using any features specific to Microsoft SharePoint Portal Server.

Preparing the Development Environment

To most efficiently develop Web Parts as ASP.NET Server Controls, we need to install the Visual Studio .NET templates necessary for Web Parts. These templates don't ship with Visual Studio .NET 2003, but are available for download from the Microsoft website at:

`http://www.microsoft.com/downloads/details.aspx?FamilyID=CAC3E0D2-BEC1-494C-A74E-75936B88E3B5&displaylang=en`

> During installation of the Web Part templates, you will be prompted for the location of `Microsoft.SharePoint.dll`. This assembly is located in `Program Files\Common Files\Microsoft Shared\Web Server Extensions\60\ISAPI\` on your SharePoint (WSS/SPS) Server. You might need to copy `Microsoft.SharePoint.dll` to your development PC from the server with SPS or WSS installed.

Creating the Web Part Project

Web Parts should be built using the Web Part Library project. So let's go ahead and create this project.

1. In Visual Studio .NET, select Create New Project (*Shift + Ctrl + N*).

2. Select the project type as Visual C# Projects, and choose the new Web Part Library template from the right-hand pane.

3. Name the new project ExtensibleMCMSPageListingWebPart, and place the project directory under My Documents\Visual Studio Projects.

4. Click OK.

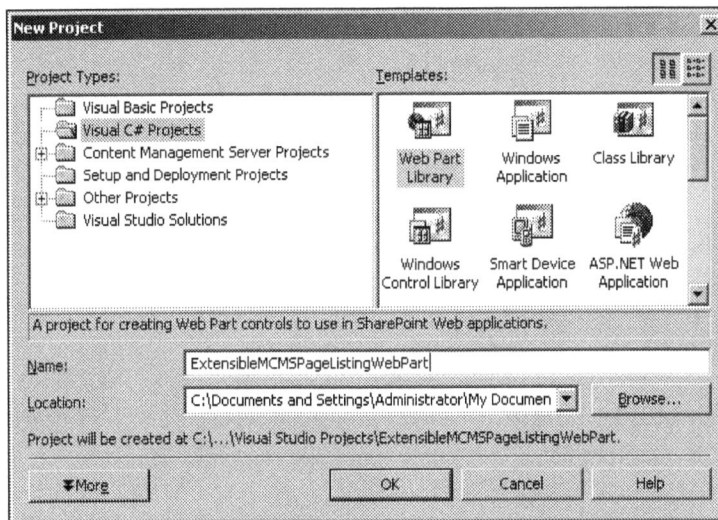

Once our new project is created, we can see a variety of files and references that have been created by the template:

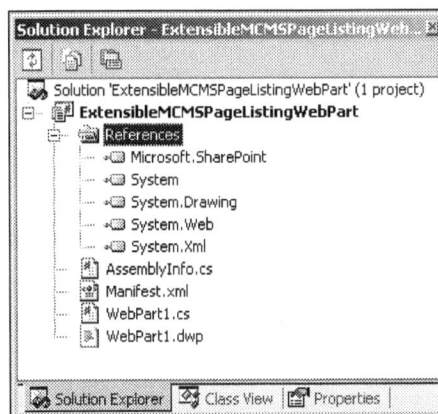

Some of the most important of these are:

- References to:
  - `Microsoft.SharePoint`—SharePoint's main API
  - `System.Web`—.NET Framework namespace holding classes for web operations
  - `System.Xml`—.NET Framework namespace holding classes for XML operations
- `AssemblyInfo.cs`—used to define the metadata of the assembly and to specify a key file to sign it.
- `Manifest.xml`—used to populate CAB files during the deployment process.
- `WebPart1.cs`—an empty Web Part template similar to the `Class1.cs` file created when using a `Class Library` template.
- `WebPart1.dwp`—an XML file used when deploying Web Parts to Windows SharePoint Services. It contains the references to the assembly name and the class name used by the Web Part.

You can delete the following files from the solution: `WebPart1.cs`, `WebPart1.dwp`, and `Manifest.xml`, as we will create our own later on.

Creating the Web Part

We now have the Web Part project set up with the necessary references, so let's create the Web Part.

1. In Solution Explorer, right-click on the project name, and select Add New Item.
2. Select the Web Part file template from the Code category, name it `NavigationWebPart.cs`, and click Open.

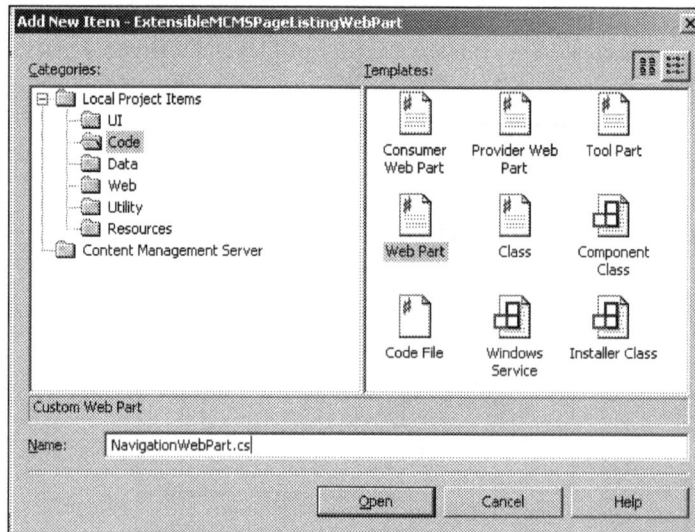

If you choose `Consumer/Provider Web Part` or `Tool Part`, several interfaces will be implemented to enable Web Part communication. For the navigation Web Part, we can use the generic `Web Part` template as it does not need to communicate with other Web Parts.

You should now see the `NavigationWebPart.cs` file in Solution Explorer and the code should be open in code view. As you will see from the generated code, a Web Part inherits from `Microsoft.SharePoint.WebPartPages.WebPart`, which in turn inherits from `System.Web.UI.Control`.

The `NavigationWebPart` class has attributes that are used by the Web Part infrastructure and Visual Studio .NET. Please remove the attribute `DefaultProperty("Text")` as the navigation Web Part will not have a default property. The class attributes should now be:

```
[ToolboxData("<{0}:NavigationWebPart runat=server></{0}:NavigationWebPart>"),
XmlRoot(Namespace="ExtensibleMCMSPageListingWebPart")]
```

The `ToolboxData` attribute defines the display name of the Web Part for use in the Visual Studio .NET Toolbox. As the properties on the class will be serialized into the Web Part Storage System, we must define the XML namespace using the `XmlRoot` attribute.

Defining Custom Properties for the Web Part

We will now define and develop the custom properties that will be used to configure this Web Part. The table below lists all the custom properties that our Web Part will expose. The details of these properties will be discussed later in the chapter.

Property	Description	Data type	Default Value	Category
Mode	The Web Part mode that is used to specify data sources and exception handling, primarily used for troubleshooting	enmMode {DebugWithTestData, DebugShowXml, DebugShowException, Production}	Production	MCMS Listing Mode
SortBy	The sort order of the ChannelItemCollection	enmSortBy {Default, ChangeDate, DisplayName, DisplayPath, ExpiryDate, Importance, Ordinal, StartDate}	Default	MCMS Listing Configuration
StartChannel	The channel to list the child items of	String	/Channels/	MCMS Listing Configuration

Property	Description	Data type	Default Value	Category
PresentationXsl	The XSL stylesheet used to control the presentation of the data	String	Load from DefaultXsl.xslt	MCMS Listing Presentation
TestXml	XML for testing the transformation without connecting to MCMS	String	Load from TestXml.xml	MCMS Listing Presentation

After the Web Part has been added to a Web Part page, its custom properties can be modified in the browser by selecting Modify Shared Web Part (or Modify Personal Web Part) from the top right corner of the Web Part.

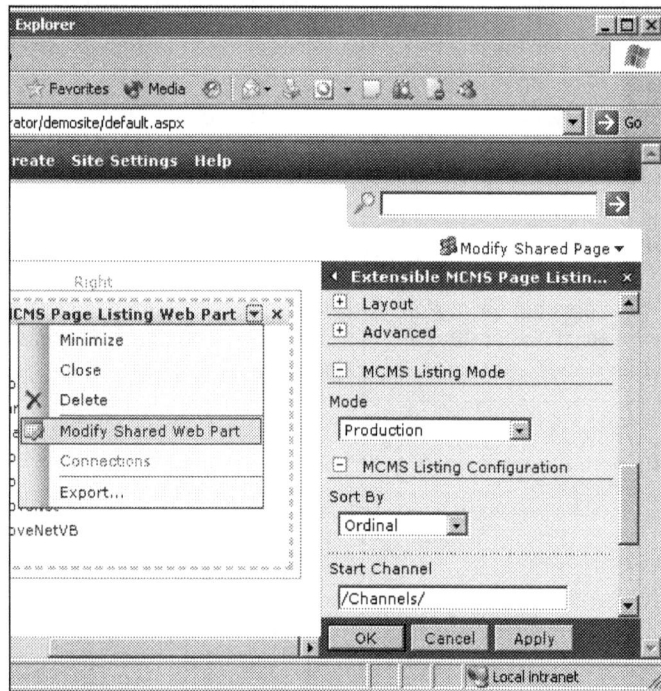

As you can see above, the controls that are used for each property will vary based on the data type. The property we specified earlier, Mode, is of type enmMode, which has four possible values so the ToolPane renders a drop-down list. The ToolPane will also render a textbox for numbers and strings. Custom properties can be grouped using the Category attribute on the property and this allows us to group multiple properties, for example MCMS Listing Configuration.

Developing Custom Properties for the Web Part

In NavigationWebPart.cs, we'll remove some additional code that has been added by the template before we create our properties. Remove all the generated comments and the following:

```
private const string defaultText = "";

private string text = defaultText;

[Browsable(true),
 Category("Miscellaneous"),
 DefaultValue(defaultText),
 WebPartStorage(Storage.Personal),
 FriendlyName("Text"),
 Description("Text Property")]
public string Text
{
  get
  {
    return text;
  }
  set
  {
    text = value;
  }
}
```

Also remove this auto-generated line from the `RenderWebPart()` method:

```
Output.Write(SPEncode.HtmlEncode(Text));
```

Then add the import for the `System.Web` namespace, and `NavigationWebPart.cs` should now look like this:

```
using System;
using System.ComponentModel;
using System.Web;
using System.Web.UI;
using System.Web.UI.WebControls;
using System.Xml.Serialization;
using Microsoft.SharePoint;
using Microsoft.SharePoint.Utilities;
using Microsoft.SharePoint.WebPartPages;

namespace ExtensibleMCMSPageListingWebPart
{
  [ToolboxData("<{0}:NavigationWebPart
   runat=server></{0}:NavigationWebPart>"),
   XmlRoot(Namespace="ExtensibleMCMSPageListingWebPart")]
  public class NavigationWebPart : Microsoft.SharePoint.WebPartPages.WebPart
  {
    /// <summary>
    /// Render this Web Part to the output parameter specified.
    /// </summary>
    /// <param name="output"> The HTML writer to write out to </param>
    protected override void RenderWebPart(HtmlTextWriter output)
    {
    }
  }
}
```

At the top of the class, we need to declare two enumerations that will be used throughout the class. The first enumeration is `enmMode`, which will facilitate troubleshooting of the new Web Part. There will be four different modes for testing different functionality:

- `DebugShowXml`—the Web Part will dump the XML data received from MCMS so the user may review it.

- `DebugWithTestData`—allows the user to test the XSLT by showing preconfigured test data together with the currently configured XSLT stylesheet.

- `DebugShowException`—used to test the actual MCMS data together with the current configured stylesheet. If exceptions occur, they will be displayed in clear text—something you would avoid on a production site.

- `Production`—similar to `DebugShowException` but hides the exception details and displays a friendly error message.

```
#region declarations - enumerations, constants and private variables

//  The mode of the Web Part used for troubleshooting and exception handling.
public enum enmMode
{
    DebugWithTestData,     // Render the Web Part using the XSLT and TestXml
    DebugShowXml,          // Output the XML
    DebugShowException,    // If an exception is thrown return the details
    Production             // Mode for running in production, suppress error
                           // messages.
}
```

The second enumeration, `enmSortBy`, specifies the sort order of the channel items returned by MCMS:

```
public enum enmSortBy
{
    Default,       // No Sort
    ChangeDate,
    DisplayName,
    DisplayPath,
    ExpiryDate,
    Importance,
    Ordinal,
    StartDate
}

#endregion
```

In the next step, we define the custom properties for the Web Part. Each public property will get and set a private variable and will also have a default value. The following table shows the Web Part Framework attributes assigned to each of the public properties:

Attribute Name	Description
Browsable	Must be set to True for the custom property to appear in the ToolPane.
Category	Defines the grouping in the ToolPane. If this value is left empty or is not defined, the category will be Custom Properties.
DefaultValue	The value of the Web Part will be stored in the Web Part storage system if it differs from this attribute.
Description	The tooltip that will be displayed over the friendly name in the ToolPane.
FriendlyName	The name that will be displayed in the ToolPane.
ReadOnly	If this is set to True, the custom property will be displayed in the ToolPane but the user will be unable to modify it.
WebPartStorageAttribute	Custom properties can be stored at a per-user level by setting this to Storage.Personal or on a global level by using Storage.Shared. If it is set to Storage.None the value will not be stored in the Web Part storage system and the property will not appear in the ToolPane.

Required properties for our Web Part are the mode it should be running in (`Mode`), the column to use for sorting (`SortBy`), the channel that should be enumerated (`StartChannel`), and a property to define the XSLT stylesheet to be used for rendering (`PresentationXsl`).

We'll also have a property (`TestXml`) that is only used in `DebugWithTestData` mode. This property will allow us to configure the test XML data to be used when debugging the XSLT stylesheet.

```
#region properties

// Declare the private variables for the Mode property
// By default we run the Web Part in Production mode (suppressing exceptions)
const NavigationWebPart.enmMode _ModeDefault =
                        NavigationWebPart.enmMode.Production;
private NavigationWebPart.enmMode _Mode = _ModeDefault;

// Set the attributes for the property
[ Browsable(true) ]
[ Category("MCMS Listing Mode") ]
[ DefaultValue(_ModeDefault) ]
[ Description("The mode of the webpart.") ]
[ FriendlyName("Mode") ]
[ WebPartStorageAttribute(Storage.Shared) ]
public NavigationWebPart.enmMode Mode
{
  get{ return _Mode; }
  set{ _Mode = value; }
}
```

The `SortBy` property sets the sort order of the channel items returned by MCMS. By default the channel items will be sorted by `ordinal`.

```
// Declare the start channel private variables
const NavigationWebPart.enmSortBy _SortByDefault =
                        NavigationWebPart.enmSortBy.Ordinal;
private NavigationWebPart.enmSortBy _SortBy = _SortByDefault;

// Set the attributes for the property
[ Browsable(true) ]
[ Category("MCMS Listing Configuration") ]
[ DefaultValue(_SortByDefault) ]
[ Description("The Sort order of the webpart.") ]
[ FriendlyName("Sort By") ]
[ WebPartStorageAttribute(Storage.Shared) ]
public NavigationWebPart.enmSortBy SortBy
{
  get{ return _SortBy; }
  set{ _SortBy = value; }
}
```

The `StartChannel` property sets the path of the channel whose child items (channels and/or postings) we will list:

```
//  Declare the start channel private variables, default is /Channels/
const string _StartChannelDefault = "/Channels/";
private string _StartChannel = _StartChannelDefault;

//  Set the attributes for the property
[ Browsable(true) ]
[ Category("MCMS Listing Configuration") ]
[ DefaultValue(_StartChannelDefault) ]
[ Description("The channel to list the child items of.") ]
[ FriendlyName("Start Channel") ]
[ WebPartStorageAttribute(Storage.Shared) ]
public string StartChannel
```

```
  {
    get{ return _StartChannel; }
    set{ _StartChannel = value; }
  }
```

The next two properties we will add are the TestXml and PresentationXsl properties. Both properties will load data from a file stored in the Web Part resources folder (wpresources) if their value is not set. This ensures that the Web Part will have a default XSLT stylesheet and XML test data present when it is first added to a page:

```
// Declare the Presentation XSLT private variables
// Default is empty because we will load from a file
const string _PresentationXslDefault = "";
private string _PresentationXsl = _PresentationXslDefault;

// Set the attributes for the property
[ Browsable(true) ]
[ Category("MCMS Listing Presentation") ]
[ DefaultValue(_PresentationXslDefault) ]
[ Description("The XSLT the MCMS listing will display.") ]
[ FriendlyName("Presentation Xslt") ]
[ WebPartStorageAttribute(Storage.Shared) ]
public string PresentationXsl
{
  get
  {
    if (_PresentationXsl == "")
    {
      // load XSLT from the wpresources folder if _PresentationXsl not set
      string XslFile = "/wpresources/ExtensibleMCMSPageListingWebPart/"
                     + "DefaultXsl.xslt";

      try
      {
        System.Xml.XmlDocument _doc = new System.Xml.XmlDocument();

        // Get the path of the DefaultXsl.xslt that is stored in
        // /wpresources/ExtensibleMCMSPageListingWebPart/
        _doc.Load(HttpContext.Current.Server.MapPath(XslFile));

        // Set the local variable to be the string representation
        // of the XSL file
        _PresentationXsl = _doc.OuterXml;
      }
      catch
      {
        _PresentationXsl = "Failed to load from "
                         + HttpContext.Current.Server.MapPath(XslFile);
      }
    }
    return _PresentationXsl;
  }
  set{ _PresentationXsl = value; }
}

// Declare the TestXsl private variables
const string _TestXmlDefault = "";
private string _TestXml = _TestXmlDefault;

//  Set the attributes for the property
[ Browsable(true) ]
[ Category("MCMS Listing Presentation") ]
[ Description("The Xml to be parsed for testing when in debug mode.") ]
[ FriendlyName("Test XML") ]
[ WebPartStorageAttribute(Storage.Shared) ]
[ DefaultValue(_TestXmlDefault) ]
```

```
public string TestXml
{
  get
  {
    if (_TestXml == "")
    {
      // load XML from the wpresources folder if _ TestXml not set
      string XmlFile = "/wpresources/ExtensibleMCMSPageListingWebPart"
                       + "/TestXml.xml";
      try
      {
        System.Xml.XmlDocument _doc = new System.Xml.XmlDocument();

        // Get the path of the TestXml.xml that is stored in
        // /wpresources/ExtensibleMCMSPageListingWebPart/
        _doc.Load(HttpContext.Current.Server.MapPath(XmlFile));

        // Set the local variable to be the string representation
        // of the XML file.
        _TestXml = _doc.OuterXml;
      }
      catch
      {
        _TestXml = "Failed to load from "
                   + HttpContext.Current.Server.MapPath(XmlFile);
      }
    }
    return _TestXml;
  }
  set{ _TestXml = value; }
}
#endregion
```

For code manageability, use #region and #endregion to effectively organize sections of your code files in Visual Studio .NET.

Building the Data Layer

The Web Part will generate XML that lists all the ChannelItems in the configured StartChannel using the configured SortOrder. The use of XML facilitates the separation of the presentation layer from the data layer. Our data layer will be another class in the Web Part project but it could have been placed in an entirely different assembly for further abstraction.

As we are using the MCMS Publishing API (PAPI), this Web Part will only run on an SPS/WSS server with MCMS installed as the PAPI cannot connect to remote MCMS servers. If SPS/WSS and MCMS live on different servers, one solution is to use Web Service calls from the Web Part to the MCMS server.

1. In Visual Studio .NET, right-click on the ExtensibleMCMSPageListingWebPart project and choose Add New Item.
2. Under the Add sub-menu, choose Add New Class.

3. Enter `NavigationWebPartMCMSIntegration` as the name and click OK.

4. Add a reference to `Microsoft.ContentManagement.Publishing.dll`. As with other library files from the `Microsoft.ContentManagement` namespace, this is found in the `<install directory>/Microsoft Content Management Server/server/bin` directory.

5. You should now have the empty `NavigationWebPartMCMSIntegration` class on screen. Add the following namespaces to the new class file:

```
using System;
using Microsoft.ContentManagement.Publishing;
using System.Security.Principal;
using System.Web;
using System.Xml;
using System.IO;
```

6. We will now add the `GetListing()` method, which connects to MCMS and generates the XML listing all the `ChannelItems`:

```
public static System.Xml.XmlDocument GetListing(string StartChannelPath,
                          NavigationWebPart.enmSortBy sortBy)
{
    // Get the channel from the searches object
    Channel startChannel = CmsHttpContext.Current.Searches.GetByPath(
                                          StartChannelPath) as Channel;

    // Was the channel found?
    if (startChannel != null)
    {
        // Get all Children from the Start Channel
        ChannelAndPostingCollection _Children = startChannel.AllChildren;

        // Sort the Items
        _Children = SortMCMSChannelItems(sortBy, _Children);

        // Declare the string writer and the XmlTextWriter
        StringWriter tw = new StringWriter();
        XmlTextWriter _Writer = new XmlTextWriter(tw);

        // Write the <Channel> element
        _Writer.WriteStartDocument();
        _Writer.WriteStartElement("Channel");
        _Writer.WriteAttributeString("path", startChannel.Path);
        _Writer.WriteAttributeString("displayname", startChannel.DisplayName);

        // Loop through all the channel items
        foreach (ChannelItem _ChannelItem in _Children)
        {
            // Write the ChannelItem element and set its attributes
            _Writer.WriteStartElement("ChannelItem");
            _Writer.WriteAttributeString("path", _ChannelItem.Path);
            _Writer.WriteAttributeString("url", _ChannelItem.Url);
            _Writer.WriteAttributeString("displayname",
                            _ChannelItem.DisplayName);

            // Check what type of Channel Item it is and set the type attribute
            if (_ChannelItem is Posting)
            {
                _Writer.WriteAttributeString("type", "Posting");
            }
            else
            {
                _Writer.WriteAttributeString("type", "Channel");
            }
            _Writer.WriteEndElement();
```

```
    }
    // Close the <Channel> element & finalize the XML document

    _Writer.WriteEndElement();
    _Writer.WriteEndDocument();
    _Writer.Flush();
    _Writer.Close();
    XmlDocument _ChannelItemsAsXml = new XmlDocument();

    // Load the text from the string writer into the XML document
    _ChannelItemsAsXml.LoadXml(tw.ToString());

    return(_ChannelItemsAsXml);
  }
  else
  {
    throw new Exception("The Channel (" + StartChannelPath
                        + ") could not be found or the user does not have "
                        + "subscriber rights on the channel.");
  }
}
```

To sort the ChannelAndPostingCollection returned by MCMS, we add the
SortMCMSChannelItems() method:

```
public static ChannelAndPostingCollection SortMCMSChannelItems(
                                NavigationWebPart.enmSortBy SortBy,
                                ChannelAndPostingCollection ChildItems)
{
  switch(SortBy)
  {
    case NavigationWebPart.enmSortBy.ChangeDate:
      ChildItems.SortByChangeDate();
      break;

    case NavigationWebPart.enmSortBy.DisplayName:
      ChildItems.SortByDisplayName();
      break;

    case NavigationWebPart.enmSortBy.DisplayPath:
      ChildItems.SortByDisplayPath();
      break;

    case NavigationWebPart.enmSortBy.ExpiryDate:
      ChildItems.SortByExpiryDate();
      break;

    case NavigationWebPart.enmSortBy.Importance:
      ChildItems.SortByImportance();
      break;

    case NavigationWebPart.enmSortBy.Ordinal:
      ChildItems.SortByOrdinal();
      break;

    case NavigationWebPart.enmSortBy.StartDate:
      ChildItems.SortByStartDate();
      break;

    default:
      break;
  }
  return(ChildItems);
}
```

> For ease of coding and efficiency, the GetListing() and SortMCMSChannelItems()
> methods are marked as static so they can be accessed without instantiating the
> NavigationWebPartMCMSIntegration class.

Now that our helper data layer class is in place, we must also create a test XML file in the solution
that will be deployed to SharePoint as a resource.

1. In Visual Studio .NET, right-click on the ExtensibleMCMSPageListingWebPart
    project and choose Add New Item.

2. From the Categories pane, select Data and then select XML File.

3. Enter TestXml.xml as the name and click Open.

XML and XSLT are case sensitive so be sure to use the correct case when adding
elements within these files.

Enter the following XML into the file. This is similar XML to that which will be generated by the
GetListing method.

```xml
<?xml version="1.0" standalone="no" ?>
<Channel path="/Channels/" displayname="Channels">
  <ChannelItem path="/Channels/Site/1" url="/Site/1.htm"
       displayname="Display 1" type="Posting" />
  <ChannelItem path="/Channels/Site/2" url="/Site/2.htm"
       displayname="Display 2" type="Posting" />
  <ChannelItem path="/Channels/Site/3" url="/Site/3.htm"
       displayname="Display 3" type="Posting" />
  <ChannelItem path="/Channels/Site/4" url="/Site/4.htm"
       displayname="Display 4" type="Posting" />
  <ChannelItem path="/Channels/Site/5" url="/Site/5.htm"
       displayname="Display 5" type="Posting" />
  <ChannelItem path="/Channels/Site/6" url="/Site/6.htm"
       displayname="Display 6" type="Posting" />
</Channel>
```

This code could be extended to mimic the ChannelItems from child channels as well, like so:

```xml
<?xml version="1.0" standalone="no" ?>
<Channel path="/Channels/" displayname="Channels">
  <ChannelItem path="/Channels/Site/5" url="/Site/5.htm"
       displayname="Display 5" type="Posting" />
  <ChannelItem path="/Channels/Site/6" url="/Site/6"
       displayname="Display 6" type="Channel">
  <ChannelItem path="/Channels/Site/6/1" url="/Site/6/1.htm"
       displayname="Display 6.1" type="Posting" />
  </ChannelItem>
</Channel>
```

But for now we will keep it simple and only list the items for the immediate channel.

Building the Presentation Layer

The Web Part needs to override methods provided by the SharePoint Framework in order to 'hook in'
to the page request. This custom code will then be executed, and will call our GetListing() method

to connect to MCMS and generate the XML file of the channel items. After that, the page and sub-channel listing will be displayed.

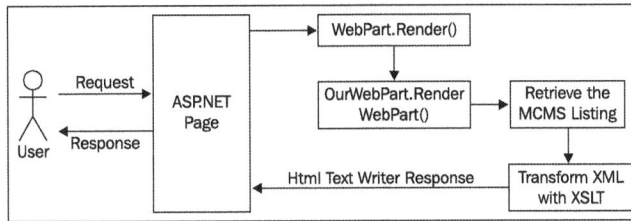

The chart below shows an overview of how our code will work:

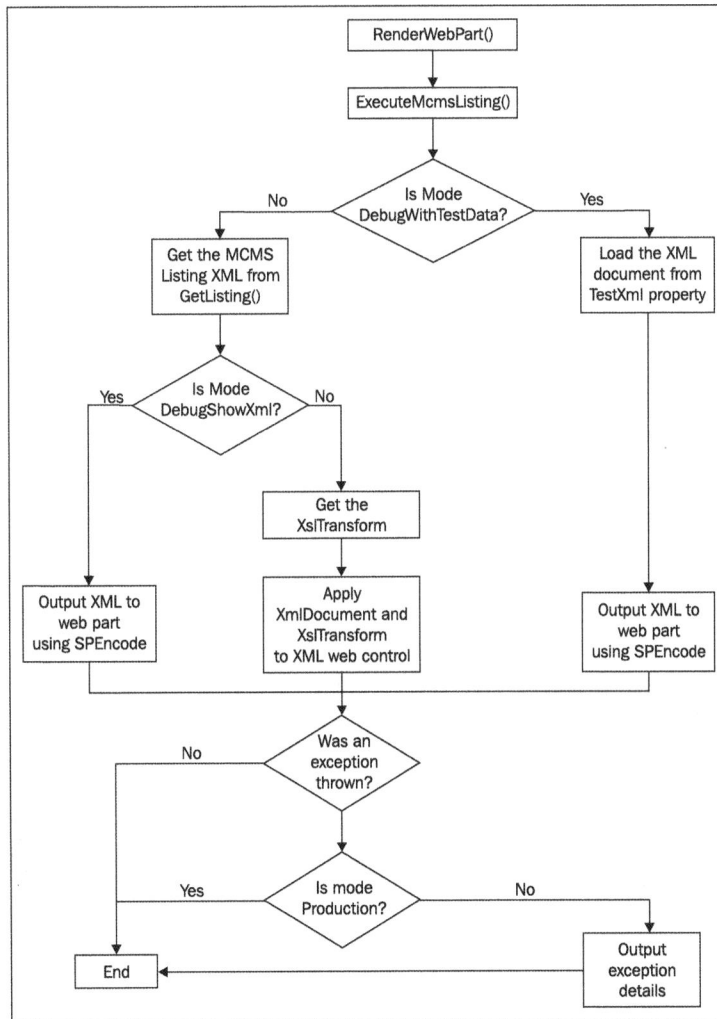

As we are building the Web Part as a server control, we must declare our controls and instantiate them by overriding the `CreateChildControls` method in `NavigationWebPart.cs`:

```
#region declarations - Web controls

protected System.Web.UI.WebControls.Xml XmlXslWebControl;

#endregion

#region Preparing the controls

protected override void CreateChildControls()
{
  XmlXslWebControl = new System.Web.UI.WebControls.Xml();
  this.Controls.Add(XmlXslWebControl);
}

#endregion
```

The `System.Web.UI.WebControls.Xml` Web Control can transform XML using specified XSLT, which is more efficient than developing the XML/XSLT by hand.

The `RenderWebPart()` method needs to be overridden to ensure that the rest of our code is being executed. Let's add the code to the `RenderWebPart()` method to generate the MCMS listing:

```
#region Methods

protected override void RenderWebPart(HtmlTextWriter output)
{
  // Check our child controls are created OK
  EnsureChildControls();

  try
  {
    // Get the Page listing from MCMS
    ExecuteMCMSListing(output);
  }
  catch(Exception ex)
  {
    // In production show only a short message with no internal exception
    // details
    if (this.Mode == enmMode.Production)
    {
      // Suppress Exceptions
      output.Write("An Error Occurred in the Navigation Web Part.");
    }
    else
    {
      // Output detailed exception message (escape characters)
      output.Write(SPEncode.HtmlEncode(ex.Message + "," + ex.Source + ","
                                     + ex.StackTrace));
    }
  }
}
```

The next method, `ExecuteMCMSListing()`, determines which mode the Web Part is running in and retrieves the channel listing data. The channel listing data can be read from MCMS or can be loaded from the test XML file on the file system.

```
/// <summary>
/// Executes the MCMS listing code
/// </summary>
private void ExecuteMCMSListing(HtmlTextWriter output)
{
  // Check the mode we are in and perform the correct action
  switch (this.Mode)
  {
    case enmMode.Production:
    case enmMode.DebugShowException:

      // Set up the Xml/Xsl Webcontrol and render its output to the
      // HtmlTextWriter
      XmlXslWebControl.Transform = GetTransform();
      XmlXslWebControl.Document = NavigationWebPartMCMSIntegration.GetListing(
                                      this.StartChannel, this.SortBy);
      XmlXslWebControl.RenderControl(output);
      break;

    case enmMode.DebugShowXml:

      System.Xml.XmlDocument _Listing =
              NavigationWebPartMCMSIntegration.GetListing(this.StartChannel,
                                                this.SortBy);

      // Output the escaped XML directly to the HtmlTextWriter
      output.Write(SPEncode.HtmlEncode(_Listing.OuterXml));

      break;

    case enmMode.DebugWithTestData:

      // Get the Test XML Data & load into an XmlDocument
      System.Xml.XmlDocument _DataDocument = new System.Xml.XmlDocument();
      _DataDocument.LoadXml(this.TestXml);

      // Setup XML/XSLT Web control and render its output to HtmlTextWriter
      XmlXslWebControl.Transform = GetTransform();
      XmlXslWebControl.Document = _DataDocument;
      XmlXslWebControl.RenderControl(output);
      break;

    default:
      throw new Exception("Invalid Mode!");   }
}
```

To retrieve the xslTransform object, we will create a helper method called GetTransform(). This method will return an xslTransform object by loading the XSLT stylesheet from the file system into an XmlDocument object. The XmlDocument object is then loaded into an xslTransform object and returned:

```
/// <summary>
/// Get the XSLT as a System.Xml.XslTransform object
/// </summary>
/// <returns>The System.Xml.XslTransform object</returns>
private System.Xml.Xsl.XslTransform GetTransform()
{
  // Get the XSLT and load it into an XML document
  System.Xml.XmlDocument _TransformDoc = new System.Xml.XmlDocument();
  _TransformDoc.LoadXml(this.PresentationXsl);

  System.Xml.Xsl.XslTransform _Transform = new System.Xml.Xsl.XslTransform();

  // Load our XSLT
  _Transform.Load(_TransformDoc.CreateNavigator(), null, null);

  return(_Transform);
}
#endregion
```

> As we are dynamically adding controls to the `Controls` collection, the first call in `RenderWebPart()` should be to `EnsureChildControls()`. The `EnsureChildControls()` method calls `CreateChildControls()` if the `ChildControlsCreated` property is false.

We must also define the XSLT stylesheet that will be used to transform our XML into HTML.

1. In Visual Studio .NET, right-click on the `ExtensibleMCMSPageListingWebPart` project and select Add New Item.

2. From the Categories pane, select Data and then select XSLT File.

3. Enter `DefaultXsl.xslt` as the name and click Open. Enter the following XSLT in the code panel:

```
<?xml version="1.0" standalone="no"?>
<xsl:stylesheet xmlns:xsl="http://www.w3.org/1999/XSL/Transform"
version="1.0">
  <xsl:template match="/">
    <b>
      <a href="{@url}">
        <xsl:value-of select="/Channel/@displayname" />
      </a>
    </b>
    <br />
    <ul>
      <xsl:apply-templates />
    </ul>
  </xsl:template>

  <xsl:template match="//ChannelItem">
    <li><a href="{@url}"><xsl:value-of select="@displayname" /></a></li>
    <ul><xsl:apply-templates /></ul>
  </xsl:template>
</xsl:stylesheet>
```

At this point let's build the entire solution to see if there are any compilation errors.

Web Part Deployment

Web Parts are compiled as .NET assemblies and can be reused many times in Windows SharePoint Services and SharePoint Portal Server. Web Parts are usually deployed using cabinet (`.CAB`) files. We will create a cabinet file project in Visual Studio .NET that will encapsulate the assemblies and metadata for our Web Part. This cabinet file must then be installed using the `stsadm.exe` utility that comes with WSS/SPS. To deploy the Web Part we will perform the following steps:

1. Prepare the Web Part Description

2. Prepare the Web Part Manifest

3. Create a CAB file deployment project

4. Execute the deployment

Another installation tool for packaging and deploying Web Parts, called WPPackager, is available at `http://www.microsoft.com/downloads/details.aspx?familyid=0fda5912-c136-4b44-911a-011adfcc66e3&displaylang=en`. WPPackager creates a Windows Installer File (`.MSI`) for your Web Part, which performs the necessary configuration of SPS/WSS during installation.

For more information on this tool, see *Using WPPackager to Package and Deploy Web Parts for Microsoft SharePoint Products and Technologies* at `http://msdn.microsoft.com/library/default.asp?url=/library/en-us/odc_SP2003_ta/html/sharepoint_deployingwebparts_msi.asp`.

Preparing the Web Part Description (.DWP) File

When deploying a Web Part to SharePoint, several files should be populated during the deployment process. One of these files is the Web Part Description (`.DWP`) file.

1. In Visual Studio .NET, right-click on the `ExtensibleMCMSPageListingWebPart` project and choose **Add New Item**.
2. In the **Categories** pane on the left, expand **Local Project Items** and select **Data**.
3. Select **Web Part DWP**.
4. Enter the name as `NavigationWebPart` and click **OK**.

The `.DWP` file describes our Web Part, giving the default values for properties and any assemblies that the Web Part requires. Let's create this file for our navigation Web Part:

```xml
<?xml version="1.0" encoding="utf-8"?>
<WebPart xmlns="http://schemas.microsoft.com/WebPart/v2" >
  <Title>Extensible MCMS Page Listing Web Part</Title>
  <Description>
    Displays MCMS Postings and Channels within a specified channel and
    transforms the display using XSLT.
  </Description>
  <Assembly>ExtensibleMCMSPageListingWebPart</Assembly>
  <TypeName>ExtensibleMCMSPageListingWebPart.NavigationWebPart</TypeName>
</WebPart>
```

The values specified in this file allow Windows SharePoint Services to generate metadata for the Web Part. The meanings of the elements are given in the table below:

Element Name	Description
Title	Title that the user will see in the Web Part Library and the default title of the Web Part once it is added in a Web Part Zone.
Description	Tooltip that will appear over the Web Part title in the Web Part library.
Assembly	Assembly name. For this sample we are only using the assembly name but it is also possible to use the complete Web Part assembly description like so: AssemblyName(without the .DLL extension), Version=VersionNumber, Culture=Culture, PublicKeyToken=PublicKeyToken
TypeName	The namespace-qualified class name.

Preparing the Web Part Manifest File

When deploying a Web Part as a CAB file, we must create a Web Part manifest file that gives the CAB file deployment project the details of our Web Part and our Web Part description files.

1. In Visual Studio. NET, right-click on the `ExtensibleMCMSPageListingWebPart` project and choose 'Add New Item'.

2. In the Categories pane on the left, expand Local Project Items and select Data.

3. Select WPManifest.

4. Enter the name as `Manifest` and click Open.

Enter the following code for this file to correspond to our Web Part:

```xml
<?xml version="1.0"?>
<WebPartManifest xmlns="http://schemas.microsoft.com/WebPart/v2/Manifest">
  <Assemblies>
    <Assembly FileName="ExtensibleMCMSPageListingWebPart.dll">
      <ClassResources>
        <ClassResource FileName="TestXml.xml"/>
        <ClassResource FileName="DefaultXsl.xslt"/>
      </ClassResources>
      <SafeControls>
        <SafeControl Namespace="ExtensibleMCMSPageListingWebPart"
                     TypeName="*" />
      </SafeControls>
    </Assembly>
  </Assemblies>
  <DwpFiles>
    <DwpFile FileName="NavigationWebPart.dwp"/>
  </DwpFiles>
</WebPartManifest>
```

`Manifest.xml` allows us to include multiple assemblies, resources, and Web Part description files in our deployment CAB file. The elements are explained below:

Element Name	Description
`Assemblies`	Allows us to include multiple assemblies in our cabinet file.
`Assembly`	Used to define an assembly by setting the `FileName` attribute to the DLL name.
`ClassResources`	Defines the resources used by our classes. The paths to the resources must be relative to the project files. Resources are supporting files such as images or data files.
`SafeControls`	Lists the safe controls that will be used by this Web Part (so they can be added to the `web.config` of the SharePoint site on deployment).
`DwpFiles`	Used to define the Web Part Description files used by this Web Part.

Creating the Deployment Project

At this point, we have a completed Web Part project with the necessary deployment configuration files. Now we need to create a deployment project to encapsulate the Web Part and other necessary files into a single cabinet file for installation.

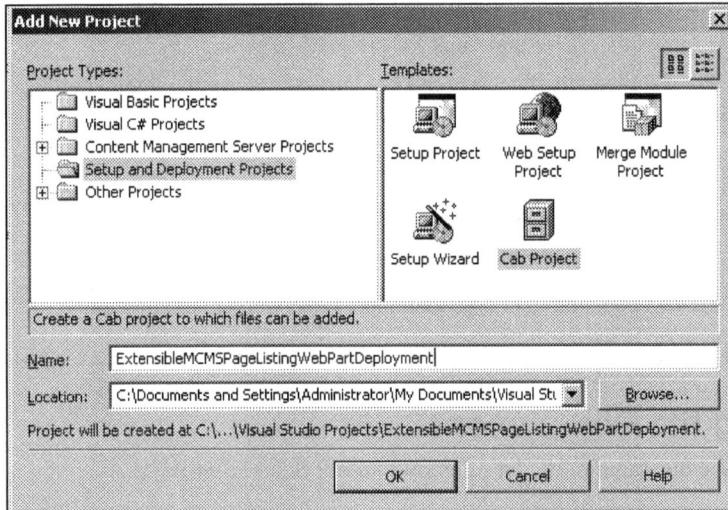

1. In Visual Studio .NET, right-click on the ExtensibleMCMSPageListingWebPart solution and choose 'Add New Project'.

2. In the Project Types pane, select Setup and Deployment Projects and in the templates pane, select Cab Project.

3. Enter the name ExtensibleMCMSPageListingWebPartDeployment and click OK.

4. Right-click on the ExtensibleMCMSPageListingWebPartDeployment project and select Add and then Project Output.

5. Select ExtensibleMCMSPageListingWebPart from the project drop-down list.

6. Holding down the *Ctrl* key, select Primary Output and Content Files and click OK.

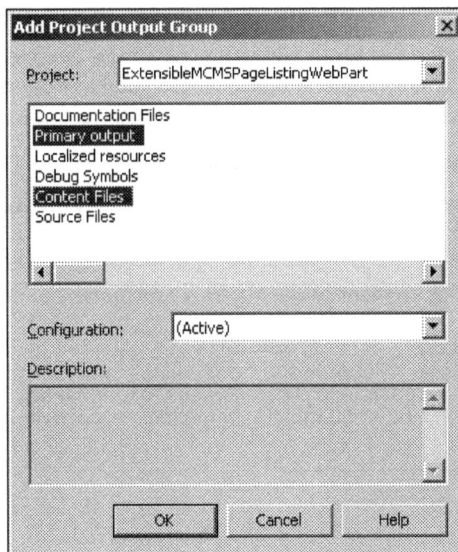

7. In the `ExtensibleMCMSPageListingWebPart` project, right-click on `NavigationWebPart.dwp` and click Properties.

8. Set the Build Action attribute to `Content`. This will allow the deployment project to add the file to the package.

Your deployment project should now look like this:

```
⊟  🔳 ExtensibleMCMSPageListingWebPartDeployment
   └ 🔁 Content Files from ExtensibleMCMSPageListingWebPart (Active)
   └ 🔁 Primary output from ExtensibleMCMSPageListingWebPart (Active)
```

Now build your deployment project by right-clicking on the project and selecting Build.

Executing the Deployment

Now that we have our cabinet file, let's deploy it to our SharePoint server.

> If you are developing on a remote workstation, copy the cabinet file to your server before following the steps below.

We will deploy it using `stsadm.exe`, which you will find under `<local_drive>\Program Files\Common Files\Microsoft Shared\Web Server Extensions\60\bin\`.

Start a DOS command prompt, and enter the following commands:

```
cd "C:\Program Files\Common Files\Microsoft Shared\web server extensions\60\BIN\"

STSADM.EXE -o addwppack -filename "C:\Documents and Settings\Administrator\
My Documents\Visual Studio Projects\ExtensibleMCMSPageListingWebPartDeployment\
Debug\ExtensibleMCMSPageListingWebPartDeployment.cab" -globalinstall -force
```

> The Path `C:\Documents and Settings\Administrator\My Documents\Visual Studio Projects\` may need to change depending on where you have created the project.

If the Web Part was successfully deployed, you should see:

```
ExtensibleMCMSPageListingWebPartDeployment.cab: Deploying to http://server/.
Operation completed successfully.
```

> When you compile the deployment project in `Release` mode, the command line will change to:
>
> ```
> STSADM.EXE -o addwppack -filename C:\Documents and Settings\Administrator
> \My Documents\Visual Studio Projects\ExtensibleMCMSPageListingWebPartDepl
> oyment\Release\ExtensibleMCMSPageListingWebPartDeployment.cab" -globalins
> tall -force
> ```

Here's what happens when this command is executed:

- A copy of our Web Part assembly is placed in the `bin` directory of the SharePoint site.
- The Web Part is added to the `safeControls` element of the SharePoint site's `web.config`.
- A copy of the CAB file is added to the SharePoint configuration database.
- Resources used by the assembly are copied into the `wpresources` directory for the site. This directory can be found at `c:\inetpub\wwwroot\wpresources\`.
- The `.dwp` files are copied into the `wpcatalog` directory of the site. This directory can be found at `c:\inetpub\wwwroot\wpresources\`.

As we are not installing our Web Part into the GAC or specifying a Code Access Security Policy, we need to increase the trust level of the SharePoint site to `Full` by following these steps:

1. Open the SharePoint site's `web.config` (typically `c:\inetpub\wwwroot\Web.config`).
2. Update the `trust` element's `level` attribute to `Full`.
3. Save `web.config`.

There are a lot of security considerations when writing Web Parts such as: Trust Levels, whether or not to put the Assembly in the GAC, and Code Access Security. For more information, see `http://msdn.microsoft.com/library/default.asp?url=/library/en-us/odc_sp2003_ta/html/sharepoint_wsscodeaccesssecurity.asp`.

Right-Click Deployment of Web Part CAB Files

If you are frequently redeploying Web Parts to your server, running `stsadm.exe` can be a laborious task. To simplify this, we can create a batch file and a type mapping that will let us right-click on the Web Part to install it.

To do this:

1. Create a batch file called `C:\Program Files\Common Files\Microsoft Shared\web server extensions\60\BIN\deploy_webparts.bat`.
2. Edit the batch file and enter the following:
   ```
   STSADM.EXE -o addwppack -filename %1 -globalinstall -force
   pause
   ```
3. Save and close the batch file
4. Now, open Windows Explorer and choose Tools | Folder Options | File Types from the menu.
5. If no entry exists for CAB files, click New and enter CAB.
6. Select the entry for CAB files and click Advanced.
7. Select New and enter an action name of Install Web Part.
8. Under Application Used to Perform action, enter C:\Program Files\Common Files\Microsoft Shared\web server extensions\60\BIN\deploy_webparts.bat.

9. Click OK, OK again, and then click **Close**.

10. Browse to `C:\Documents and Settings\Administrator\My Documents\Visual Studio Projects\ExtensibleMCMSPageListingWebPartDeployment\Debug\`, right-click on `ExtensibleMCMSPageListingWebPartDeployment.cab` and choose Install Web Part to deploy your Web Part.

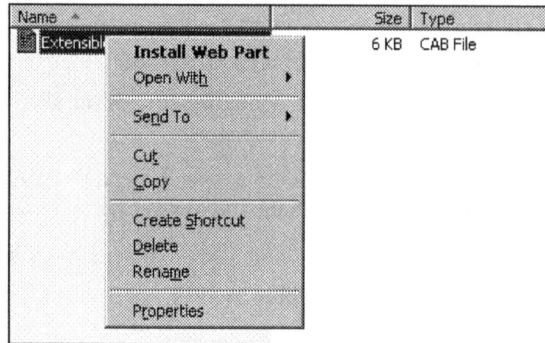

Adding Our Web Part to a Page

The Web Part has now been deployed to the server. Next it needs to be added to a Web Part Page to see all the pieces come together.

1. Start Internet Explorer and browse to your favorite WSS site (making sure you have designer permissions on the site).

2. Click the Modify Shared Page link and choose Add Web Parts | Browse:

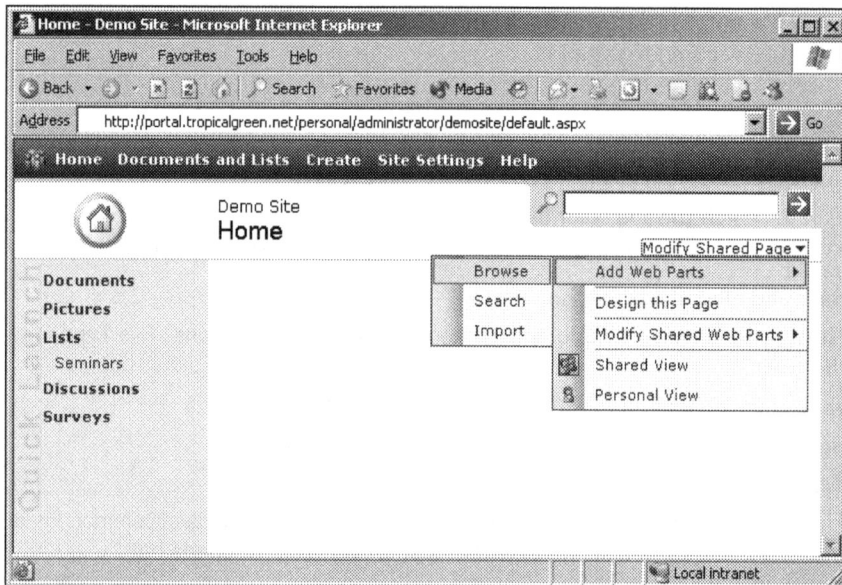

3. You will now see the Tool Pane with a list of Web Part Libraries. Select the Virtual Server Gallery:

4. Click on the Extensible MCMS Page Navigation Web Part and drag it into any Web Part Zone on the left-hand side of your screen. You should see the following:

If the Extensible MCMS Page Navigation Web Part does not appear in the Virtual Server Gallery, redeploy the Web Part to the server using the method outlined in *Executing the Deployment* verifying that no errors occur during the **stsadm.exe -o addwppack** command.

If the error message An error has occurred appears, verify the trust level settings in the web.config are sufficient.

Another error that frequently occurs is A Web Part or Web Form Control on this Web Part Page cannot be displayed or imported because it is not registered on this site as safe. If you see this, verify the contents of the Manifest.xml and NavigationWebPart.dwp files for typos.

5. To close the Tool Pane, click on the X in the top right corner.

Configuring the Web Part

We have now added our Web Part to the Web Part Page and it is working with the default settings. In the next step, we will change these settings.

1. On the top right corner of the Web Part, click the down arrow to bring up the Web Part menu and select Modify Shared Web Part

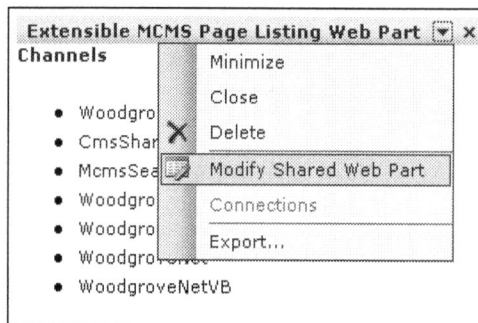

As we have set the WebPartStorage attribute on our properties to Storage.Shared we can only modify the shared view, which applies to this instance of the Web Part for all users. If we want users to store personalized Web Part custom property values, we must set the WebPartStorage attribute on our property to Storage.Personal.

2. The Tool Pane will now appear on the right-hand side of your screen.
3. Expand the MCMS Listing Presentation group.
4. Copy the contents of DefaultXsl.xslt into the Presentation XSLT textbox (a larger textbox can be opened by clicking the ellipsis [...] to the right of the textbox).

5. Copy the contents of TestXml.xml into the Test XML textbox.

6. Click Apply to see the settings on-screen or OK to apply the settings and close the Tool Pane.

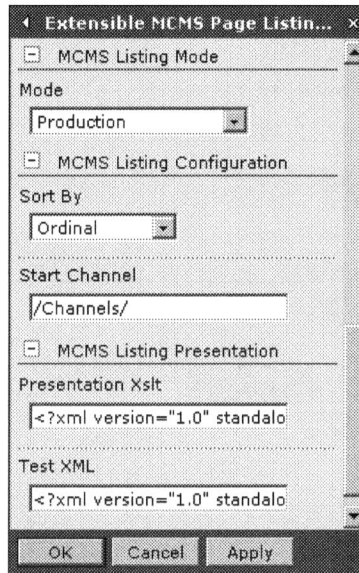

The page should refresh and the Web Part will render a list of items in the MCMS /channels/ path.

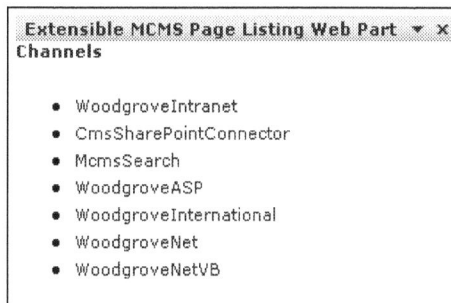

Debugging the Web Part

As our Web Part is now running via WSS/SPS, we cannot debug the Web Part directly by using the Visual Studio .NET Start Debugging option.

By default WSS/SPS has debugging turned off. To turn on debugging, edit the web.config for the IIS Virtual Server and set the debug attribute to true.

To debug our Web Part from the SPS/WSS server using Visual Studio .NET, we must add the Web Part to a Web Part Page and perform the following actions:

1. Open the `ExtensibleMCMSPageListingWebPart` project in Visual Studio .NET.

2. Set a breakpoint on the `RenderWebPart()` method in `NavigationWebPart.cs`.

3. From the Tools menu, select Debug Processes (or hit *Alt + Ctrl + P*).

4. Select the `w3wp.exe` process and click Attach.

5. Verify that the Common Language Runtime is checked and click OK:

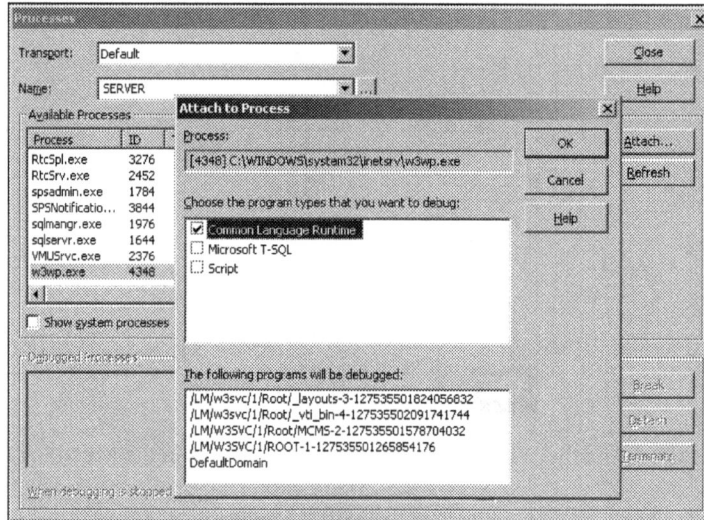

6. Click Close on the Processes dialog and refresh the Web Part Page.

7. Your breakpoint should now be selected and you should be able to step through the code.

Your Web Part must be compiled in Debug configuration to ensure that the debug symbols are deployed to the server.

Summary

In this chapter, we've explored the basics of the Web Part Framework by building an MCMS Navigation Web Part that can display MCMS channel items from within a SharePoint site. In development, we utilized the Web Part templates for Visual Studio .NET to create our Web Part. This allows us to leverage Visual Studio .NET's Server Control development architecture. Our Web Part generates an XML representation of the channel items and sub-channels that were found in a specified channel. The XML data was then transformed using a configurable XSLT stylesheet. Finally, we deployed our Web Part to the SharePoint server by creating a CAB file deployment project and running the SharePoint `STSADM.EXE` deployment tool.

8

Useful Placeholder Controls

One of the most exciting features of MCMS is the flexibility to create custom placeholder server controls. You can create placeholder controls of all shapes and sizes, providing myriad solutions tailored to the needs of authors in any organization. If something is not available out of the box—build it! And there is a good chance that you don't even have to build custom placeholder controls from scratch. MCMS developers around the world may have already built a similar control in their own work. This chapter compiles a collection of commonly requested and very useful placeholder controls.

- **Date-time picker placeholder control**
  This provides a picker for authors to select a date and time value in the format of their choice. Say goodbye to badly formed and invalid dates with this nifty control.

- **Placeholder control that accepts multiple attachments**
  This enables authors to upload as many files as they need by giving them a control that acts like multiple `SingleAttachmentPlaceholderConrols` working in concert. We will also explore the undocumented Insert Attachment dialog that ships with Web Author and show how you can reuse it within custom placeholder controls.

- **Image rotator placeholder control**
  Authors can manage web advertisements using this control that selects an image randomly from a specified resource gallery. A random image is displayed each time the control is loaded in presentation view.

- **Placeholder control to store all kinds of HTML tags**
  If you have ever wanted to allow authors to upload restricted HTML tags and JavaScript, this control is for you. We show you the modifications required to get the `HtmlPlaceholderControl` to accept all HTML tags—including IFRAME, OBJECT, and APPLET tags and form elements!

- **DataGrid placeholder control**
  This uses the familiar DataGrid to manage XML content. Authors can add, edit, and delete rows of XML content without needing to know the technical details behind it all. We also show how placeholders that demand a postback can be handled gracefully without incurring the leave warning alert.

Before We Begin

It's always a good idea to place all code related to custom placeholder controls within a project separate from your main MCMS web project. It allows cleaner deployment of controls across websites. In this chapter, we will do just that. Follow the steps outlined below to set up a project where we will build all class files for the custom placeholder controls in this chapter:

1. Create a new Visual C# Class Library named `UsefulPlaceholderControls`.
2. Add the following references to the project:
    *   `Microsoft.ContentManagement.Common`
    *   `Microsoft.ContentManagement.Publishing`
    *   `Microsoft.ContentManagement.Publishing.Extensions.Placeholders`
    *   `Microsoft.ContentManagement.WebControls`
    *   `System.Web`

The library files from the `Microsoft.ContentManagement` namespace can be found in the `Microsoft Content Management Server\Server\bin\` directory.

Delete the `Class1.cs` file that was created by the wizard. We won't need it.

A Date-Time Picker Placeholder Control

Have you ever tried getting authors to enter date and time values in a regular textbox? Even with well-placed instructions showing the proper format for the date (such as MM/DD/YYYY), you will often find that dates collected are invalid. Here are some real-life examples taken from a website that provided textboxes for entering the promotion start and end dates of a product:

Dates entered	Why it's not valid
Start Date: Immediate! End Date: 31 February 2004 07:00 AM	The word "immediate" isn't a valid date and 31 February 2004 does not exist, not even in a leap year!
Start Date: 1 January 2005 :00:00 AM End Date: 31 December 2005 (or while stocks last!)	While the start date is valid, the start time is missing the hour component. The end date appears valid, but it has extra text, *or while stocks last*, appended to it—making it invalid.
Start Date: 1 January 2005 End Date: 31/05/2005	In the start date, the word "January" is misspelled. The month and day fields in the end date are mixed up.

To ensure that date and time fields are entered correctly, authors can be provided with a date-time picker control, instead of a textbox. The date-time picker control includes a single-line, read-only textbox that displays the selected date and time. As the textbox is read-only, authors can't amend its contents—making it impossible for authors to enter invalid dates.

Dates are selected by clicking on a Pick Date button, located next to the textbox. When it is clicked, a dialog for picking a date and time opens. The dialog contains a calendar for selecting the date and two dropdowns for choosing the time values.

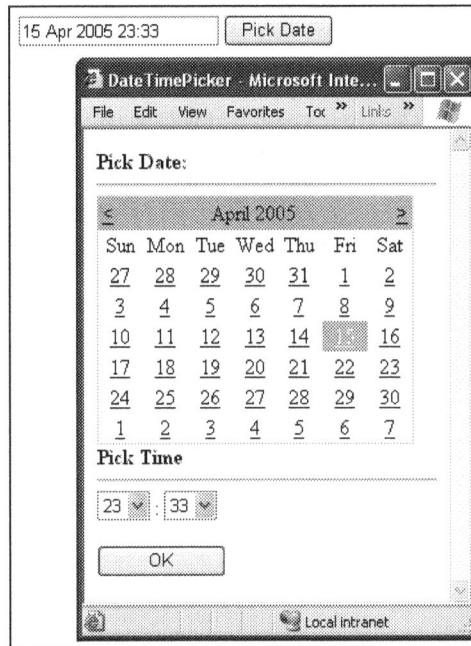

In presentation view, the selected date and time appears on screen.

To make it almost impossible for invalid dates to be saved in the database, the contents of date-time picker control are usually validated before being saved.

MCMS does not ship with a date-time picker placeholder control, so let's build one from scratch.

The DateTimePickerPlaceholderControl Class

Let's begin building the date-time picker placeholder control by adding a class file named `DateTimePickerPlaceholderControl.cs` to the `UsefulPlaceholderControls` project.

The control requires the use of methods from the namespaces highlighted below, so add them to the class file.

```
using System;

using System.Web.UI.HtmlControls;
using System.Web.UI.WebControls;
using Microsoft.ContentManagement.Publishing;
using Microsoft.ContentManagement.Publishing.Extensions.Placeholders;
using Microsoft.ContentManagement.WebControls.Design;
using Microsoft.ContentManagement.WebControls;
```

```
namespace UsefulPlaceholderControls
{
    . . . code continues . . .
}
```

As the selected date and time is a single-line value, it will be easiest to store it as text within an HtmlPlaceholder (alternatively, you could store it in an XmlPlaceholder—however, that also means that you will have to extract the information from the saved XML later, which requires a little more code). The control will therefore support HtmlPlaceholderDefinitions. In addition, as none of the placeholder controls that ship with MCMS resembles a date-time picker, we will build the control from the ground up and have it inherit from the BasePlaceholderControl class:

```
namespace UsefulPlaceholderControls
{
    [SupportedPlaceholderDefinitionType(typeof(HtmlPlaceholderDefinition))]
    public class DateTimePickerPlaceholderControl : BasePlaceholderControl
    {
        public DateTimePickerPlaceholderControl()
        {
        }
    }
}
```

Loading the Controls for Authoring

In authoring mode, the date-time picker placeholder will include:

- A textbox for displaying the selected date and time.
- A button for picking the date. When the button is clicked, a dialog appears for the author to pick the date and time.

We will use a table to arrange the TextBox and Button controls side by side. Below the table, we will add a Label for showing any exceptions that may occur during the loading process. Here's the completed control in authoring mode:

Let's start by adding the table to the authoring container. Override the CreateAuthoringChildControls() method as shown below. The table consists of a single row with two cells.

```
protected override void CreateAuthoringChildControls
                    (BaseModeContainer authoringContainer)
{
    // Add a table to help in the layout of the controls
    Table table = new Table();
    TableRow tr = new TableRow();
    table.Rows.Add(tr);

    TableCell td1 = new TableCell();
    TableCell td2 = new TableCell();
    tr.Cells.Add(td1);
    tr.Cells.Add(td2);

    // Add the table to the authoring container
    authoringContainer.Controls.Add(table);
}
```

Now, let's add the read-only TextBox control to the cell on the left-hand side. The TextBox control will be given an ID of SelectedDateTime. We define the instance of the TextBox as a class-wide variable as we will be accessing it from other methods within the class.

```
private TextBox txtAuthoring;

protected override void CreateAuthoringChildControls
                     (BaseModeContainer authoringContainer)
{
    . . . code continues . . .

    // Add a Textbox
    txtAuthoring = new TextBox();
    txtAuthoring.ID = "SelectedDateTime";
    txtAuthoring.ReadOnly = true;
    td1.Controls.Add(txtAuthoring);

}
```

Next, we will add the Pick Date button. When the button is clicked, it calls up the dialog for selecting the date and time. Attached to the dialog's URL are a couple of querystring parameters:

- **CallingControl** stores the name of the TextBox control to which the dialog will write the selected date and time. This is the client ID of the TextBox, as dynamically generated by ASP.NET when the page is displayed. If you actually run the control, you will find that its client ID is the concatenation of all the parent controls' IDs:

  ```
  DateTimePickerPlaceholderControl1_AuthoringModeControlsContainer_SelectedD
  ateTime
  ```

- **InitialValue** stores the previously selected date and time values that will be used as default values by the dialog.

The code snippet below assumes that the URL of the date-time picker dialog is /tropicalgreen/ dialogs/datetimepicker.aspx. If you plan to store the dialog somewhere else, simply adjust this value accordingly.

```
protected override void CreateAuthoringChildControls
                     (BaseModeContainer authoringContainer)
{
    . . . code continues . . .

    // Add a Button that shows a pop up when clicked
    HtmlButton b = new HtmlButton();
    b.ID = "SelectedDateTime";
    b.InnerText = "Pick Date";

    string url = "";
    url = "/tropicalgreen/dialogs/datetimepicker.aspx?"
        + "CallingControl=" + txtAuthoring.ClientID + "&"
        + "InitialValue=\' + document.all. " + txtAuthoring.ClientID
        + ".value +\'";

    b.Attributes.Add("onclick","window.open('" + url + "');");
    td2.Controls.Add(b);
}
```

Finally, we add a Label control to the authoring container. The Label will be used to display error messages that may occur along the way. Like the TextBox, we will make it a class-wide variable as we will be using it within other methods.

```
private TextBox txtAuthoring;
private Label lblMessage;

protected override void CreateAuthoringChildControls
                      (BaseModeContainer authoringContainer)
{
   . . . code continues . . .

   // Add a label for displaying messages
   lblMessage = new Label();
   authoringContainer.Controls.Add(lblMessage);
}
```

Retrieving Saved Content

When the posting is opened for editing, the textbox of the date time picker control shows the previously saved date and time value. For new postings, there won't be a previous selection; we will just use the current date and time. Override LoadPlaceholderContentForAuthoring():

```
protected override void LoadPlaceholderContentForAuthoring
                       (PlaceholderControlEventArgs e)
{
   EnsureChildControls();

   try
   {
      if (WebAuthorContext.Current.Mode == WebAuthorContextMode.AuthoringNew)
      {
         // The default value of the control is the current date and time
         txtAuthoring.Text = DateTime.Now.ToString("dd MMM yyyy HH:mm");
      }
      else
      {
         txtAuthoring.Text = ((HtmlPlaceholder)this.BoundPlaceholder).Text;
      }
   }
   catch(Exception ex)
   {
      lblMessage.Text = "Failed to load placeholder content: " + ex.Message;
   }
}
```

Saving the Date and Time

When the posting is saved, we read the value stored in the TextBox and write it to the underlying HtmlPlaceholder. Any exceptions are trapped using a try-catch block and the detailed error message appears on screen. Add the overridden SavePlaceholderContent() method to the code:

```
protected override void SavePlaceholderContent(PlaceholderControlSaveEventArgs e)
{
   EnsureChildControls();
   try
   {
      ((HtmlPlaceholder)this.BoundPlaceholder).Html = txtAuthoring.Text;
   }
   catch(Exception ex)
```

```
    {
      lblMessage.Text = ex.Message;
    }
  }
```

Validating the Date and Time

To ensure that only valid dates are saved, we will override the OnSavingContent() method. We check to see if the value to be saved is a valid date by attempting to convert the string stored in the TextBox to a DateTime object. If it is a valid date, we won't get an exception. Otherwise, we catch the exception and the save operation can be canceled.

```
protected override void OnSavingContent(PlaceholderControlSavingEventArgs e)
{
  try
  {
    DateTime.Parse(txtAuthoring.Text.Trim());
    base.OnSavingContent(e);

    // Clear any messages on the screen
    lblMessage.Text = "";
  }
  catch(Exception ex)
  {
    e.Cancel = true;
    lblMessage.Text = ex.Message;
  }
}
```

Presenting the Selected Date and Time

In presentation mode, the selected date and time are displayed on the screen in a Label control. Let's override the CreatePresentationChildControls() method and add a Label control to the presentation container.

```
private Label lblPresentation;

protected override void CreatePresentationChildControls
                        (BaseModeContainer presentationContainer)
{
  lblPresentation = new Label();
  presentationContainer.Controls.Add(lblPresentation);
}
```

The previously saved date and time value in the underlying HtmlPlaceholder is retrieved from the content repository and displayed in the Label control loaded earlier. Add the overridden LoadPlaceholderContentForPresentation() method as shown:

```
protected override void LoadPlaceholderContentForPresentation
                        (PlaceholderControlEventArgs e)
{
  EnsureChildControls();
  try
  {
    lblPresentation.Text = ((HtmlPlaceholder)this.BoundPlaceholder).Text;
  }
  catch(Exception ex)
  {
    lblPresentation.Text = ex.Message;
  }
}
```

The date-time picker placeholder control is complete. Next, let's build the dialog for selecting the date and time.

The Date and Time Picker Dialog

The Date and Time picker dialog contains:

- An ASP.NET Calendar control for choosing the date
- Two DropDownList controls, one for selecting the hour, another for the minute
- A Button control for setting the date and time value

Add a Web Form named DateTimePicker.aspx to the MCMS web project (in this example, we have added it to the Dialogs folder of the Tropical Green project). Ensure that the Page Layout property is changed to FlowLayout. Now toggle to HTML view and add the following headers to the form:

```
. . . code continues . . .

<form id="DateTimePicker" method="post" runat="server">
  <b>Pick Date:</b>
  <hr>
  <b>Pick Time</b>
  <hr>
</form>

. . . code continues . . .
```

Switch back to Design view. Drag and drop the following controls onto the Web Form and arrange them as shown opposite.

Control	Property	Property Value
Calendar	ID	Calendar1
DropDownList	ID	ddlHour
DropDownList	ID	ddlMinute
Button	ID	btnOK
	Text	OK
	Width	100px

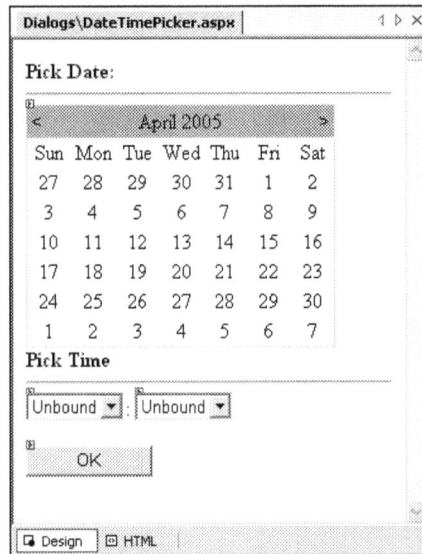

Double-click on the form to get to the code-behind file. Within the `Page_Load()` event handler, we retrieve the previously selected date and time from the `InitialValue` query string parameter. If for some reason (maybe the TextBox was empty), the parameter doesn't contain a valid date and time, we use the current date and time instead.

```
private void Page_Load(object sender, System.EventArgs e)
{
  if(!Page.IsPostBack)
  {
    // Retrieve the previously saved date and time
    DateTime initialDate;

    try
    {
      initialDate = DateTime.Parse(Request.QueryString["InitialValue"]
                  .ToString());
    }
    catch
    {
      // No previously saved date and time found.
      // Use the current date and time.
      initialDate = DateTime.Now;
    }
  }
}
```

The previously selected date and time is used to initialize the Calendar control and the two drop-down lists that make up the hour and minute of the selected time. In the `Page_Load()` event handler, we also fill in the hour and the minute dropdowns.

```
private void Page_Load(object sender, System.EventArgs e)
{
  if (!Page.IsPostBack)
  {
    . . . code continues . . .

    Calendar1.SelectedDate = initialDate;
```

```
                    Calendar1.VisibleDate = initialDate;

                    // fill up the dropdown list for hours
                    for (int i=0; i <= 23; i++)
                    {
                      ListItem li = new ListItem();
                      li.Text = i.ToString("00");

                      if (initialDate.ToString("HH") == li.Text)
                      {
                        li.Selected = true;
                      }
                      ddlHour.Items.Add(li);
                    }

                    // fill up the dropdown list for minutes
                    for (int i=0; i <= 59; i++)
                    {
                      ListItem li = new ListItem();
                      li.Text = i.ToString("00");
                      if (initialDate.ToString("mm") == li.Text)
                      {
                        li.Selected = true;
                      }
                      ddlMinute.Items.Add(li);
                    }
                }
            }
```

Toggle back to Design view and double-click on the OK button to get to the btnOK_Click() event handler. Here, we will generate the client-side script that passes the selected date and time value back to the calling control. The calling control is retrieved from the CallingControl query string parameter. Earlier, we have set this to contain the ID of the TextBox used by the date-time picker placeholder control.

To write the selected date and time, we retrieve the values of the Calendar control and of the hour and minute drop-down lists. Using a JavaScript call, we write the value to the TextBox.

```
        private void btnOK_Click(object sender, System.EventArgs e)
        {
            string callingControl = Request.QueryString["CallingControl"];
            System.Text.StringBuilder script = new System.Text.StringBuilder();
            script.Append("<script language=\"javascript\">");
            script.Append("window.opener.document.all." + callingControl + ".value='"
                        + Calendar1.SelectedDate.ToString("dd MMM yyyy") + " "
                        + ddlHour.SelectedItem.Value + ":"
                        + ddlMinute.SelectedItem.Value
                        + "';");
            script.Append("window.close();");
            script.Append("</script>");

            Page.RegisterClientScriptBlock("PickDate",script.ToString());
        }
```

And that completes the dialog. Save and build the solution.

While the dialog works fine, I need a more portable control that can be used across projects without having to recreate the Web Form each time I use the control. What are my options?

To deploy the control across multiple projects, consider one of the following options:

1. Create a folder within the /IIS_CMS/ folder and store the dialog there. As all MCMS web projects have a virtual directory named CMS mapped to the IIS_CMS folder, the path of the dialog would be /CMS/SubFolder/datetimepicker.aspx.

2. You could follow the concept used by MCMS when deploying the /nr/ folder across all websites on the same computer by adding the folder that contains the DateTimePicker control to each virtual website that uses it.

3. Alternatively, use the technique MCMS uses when deploying the /cms/ folder to new MCMS template projects. Add the folder that contains the DateTimePicker control to each template project that requires it. When getting the path of the control from within the code, use the value returned from Page.Request.ApplicationPath. To automate this for new projects, you could create a new enterprise template for Visual Studio .NET. For more information about creating and editing enterprise templates, see http://msdn.microsoft.com/library/en-us/vsent7/html/vxoriEnterpriseTemplates.asp.

4. Rewrite the date time picker control so that the calendar, hour and minute drop down menus are generated on the control itself. You can embed them within a <div> tag and use client-side script to show them when the Pick Date button is clicked.

Adding the Placeholder Control to a Template File

To add the control to an MCMS project, you will have to add the component to the Toolbox:

- Right-click on the tab you wish to add the control to.
- Select Add/Remove Items and choose to add a .NET Framework Component.
- Select Browse... and select UsefulPlaceholderControls.dll. Click Open.
- Click OK to close the dialog and add the control(s) to the Toolbox.

Once the control has been added to the Toolbox, you can drag and drop it onto a template file and set its properties as you would with regular placeholder controls.

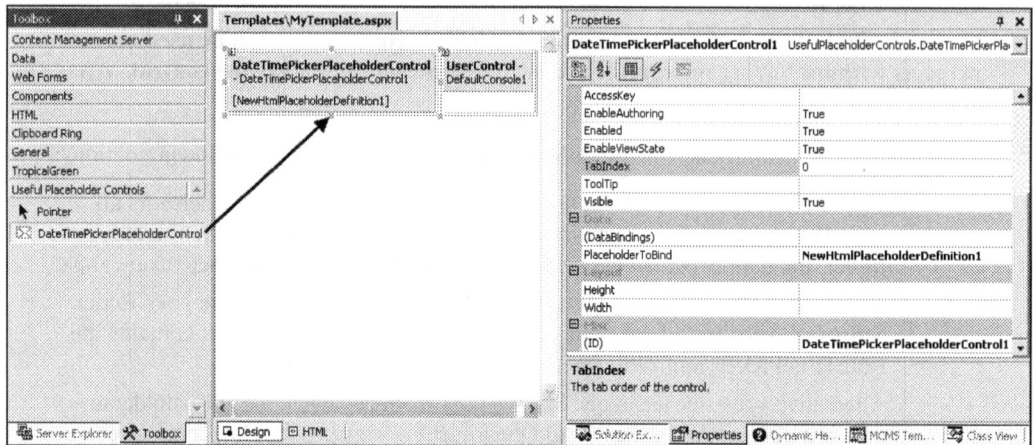

Go ahead; add the date-time picker placeholder control to an existing template file. Set the PlaceholderToBind property to an appropriate HtmlPlaceholderDefinition. Navigate to a posting that uses the template and edit it. You should see a textbox and a Pick Date button. Click on the Pick Date button and select a date. Save the posting. Notice that the TextBox and Button controls are replaced by a single Label showing the date and time that you have selected.

A Placeholder Control for Multiple Attachments

We have seen SingleImagePlaceholderControl and SingleAttachmentPlaceholderControl at work. They are nifty controls for managing single files. Authors are able to upload files directly from their local computers or pick from shared resources in the resource gallery.

However, the biggest drawback of these controls is that files must be handled one at a time. More often than not, authors will need to attach multiple images or attachments. They could have a list of documents that support an article or a series of images that accompany a story. Whatever the case may be, a single slot for attachments may not always be sufficient.

You can get around this single-file limitation in one of three ways:

- Provide authors with an HtmlPlaceholderControl.
- Increase the number of SingleAttachmentPlaceholders and SingleImagePlaceholderControls on the page. Provide as many as the author requires.
- Build a custom placeholder control that allows the upload of multiple files and images.

Let's consider the first option, which calls for the use of the HtmlPlaceholderControl. With the WYSIWYG editor, authors can upload as many images and attachments as they need to. On the other hand, they can also add unwanted text to the placeholder control. While giving authors complete freedom keeps them happy, it may cause problems when authors get carried away applying their own styles and layouts. More often than not, site owners would like more control over how the uploaded content is displayed and perhaps even to limit the number of images and attachments included—none of which can be accomplished using an HtmlPlaceholderControl.

The second option of increasing the number of `SingleAttachmentPlaceholders` and `SingleImagePlaceholderControls` on the page could be feasible if the number of attachments and images required can be accurately estimated. One major shortcoming of this approach is that for every placeholder control introduced, a corresponding placeholder definition must be created. Should the estimated number of attachments be large, so would the number of corresponding placeholder definitions. The larger the number of placeholders used by a posting, the more information needs to be retrieved by database queries, potentially compromising the overall performance of the site.

Clearly, neither of these out-of-the box solutions satisfies this requirement completely. To bridge the gap, let's explore the last option and build our own custom placeholder control that accepts multiple attachments with a friendly graphical user interface.

The maximum number of attachments will be decided by the developer. As a placeholder control, it will have different views in presentation and authoring modes. In authoring mode, the control will be displayed as a table with multiple rows, each row providing a slot for authors to upload an attachment. One interesting aspect of this control is that it will reuse the Insert Attachment dialog that ships with Web Author.

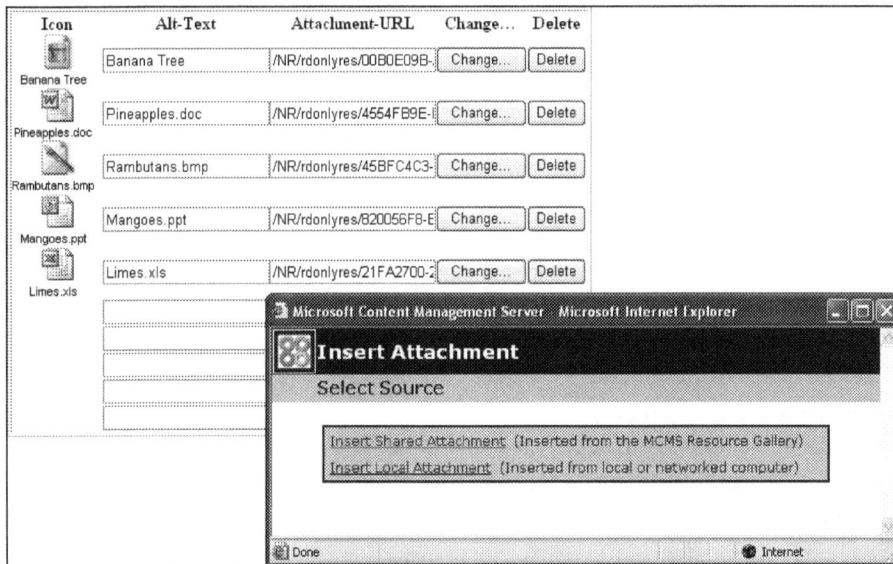

In presentation view, the attachments are displayed as a list of hyperlinks. Developers can choose to display links as icons or text. Here, we have chosen to show them as a list of icons. You can of course enhance the code to arrange them in any way you like, horizontally, vertically, or even within a table.

The MultipleAttachmentPlaceholderControl Class

To begin, we add a class named MultipleAttachmentPlaceholderControl.cs to the UsefulCustomPlaceholders project.

The class file uses the methods from the namespaces highlighted below. Add them above the namespace declaration:

```
using System;

using System.Xml;
using System.Web;
using System.Text;
using System.Web.UI;
using System.Web.UI.WebControls;
using Microsoft.ContentManagement.Publishing;
using Microsoft.ContentManagement.WebControls;
using Microsoft.ContentManagement.WebControls.Design;
using Microsoft.ContentManagement.Publishing.Extensions.Placeholders;

namespace UsefulCustomPlaceholders
{
   . . . code continues . . .
}
```

A good way to manage lists like the one we are creating here is to store them as XML. XML gives us the flexibility to present the attachments in a wide range of ways later on. The control will therefore support XmlPlaceholderDefinition and be built by inheriting from BasePlaceholder:

```
[SupportedPlaceholderDefinitionType(typeof(XmlPlaceholderDefinition))]
public class MultipleAttachmentPlaceholderControl : BasePlaceholderControl
{
   . . . code continues . . .
}
```

The control will provide three properties for developers:

- **MaxAttachments**. Specifies the maximum number of attachments supported by the control. The initial value will be set to 10. Developers can change this value at design time by adjusting the value in the control's Properties dialog.

- **DisplayAsIcon**. Specifies if the attachments are to be displayed as icons or text. Similar to the UseGeneratedIcon property in the HtmlPlaceholderDefinition class.

- **ResourceGalleryOnly**. Specifies if files from the author's computer can be uploaded as an attachment or if authors must choose from resources within resource galleries.

Add the following three properties below the class constructor:

```
private static int m_maxAttachments = 10;
public int MaxAttachments
{
  get
  {
    return m_maxAttachments;
  }

  set
  {
    m_maxAttachments = value;
  }
```

```
}
private bool m_displayAsIcon = false;
public bool DisplayAsIcon
{
  get
  {
    return m_displayAsIcon;
  }
  set
  {
    m_displayAsIcon = value;
  }
}
private bool m_resourceGalleryOnly = false;
public bool ResourceGalleryOnly
{
  get
  {
    return m_resourceGalleryOnly;
  }
  set
  {
    m_resourceGalleryOnly = value;
  }
}
```

Generating the Table of Attachments

The user interface for authors consists of the following:

- A table with multiple rows, one for each attachment.
- Each row consists of a button labeled Change... that calls Web Author's Insert Attachment dialog, a Delete button to remove the attachment from the list, and textboxes for displaying the attachment's display text and URL.
- It also shows an icon that represents the uploaded attachment.

Here's the Multiple Attachment Placeholder control in authoring view:

Icon	Alt-Text	Attachment-URL	Change...	Delete
			Change...	Delete
			Change...	Delete
			Change...	Delete
			Change...	Delete
			Change...	Delete
			Change...	Delete
			Change...	Delete
			Change...	Delete
			Change...	Delete
			Change...	Delete

Usually, when building custom placeholder controls, the logic for adding these controls is coded by overriding the `CreateAuthoringChildControls()` method. We won't do that here because we will be making heavy use of JavaScript within our control. The easiest and most fuss-free way of adding all that client-side script would be to code in the old fashion way: as regular HTML.

Therefore, in the overridden `CreateAuthoringChildControls()` method, we will simply add a single Literal web control. Later on, we will attach HTML code to the `Text` property of this Literal control. Add the following code below the `ResourceGalleryOnly` property:

```
private System.Web.UI.WebControls.Literal baseAuthoringContainer;

protected override void CreateAuthoringChildControls
                    (BaseModeContainer authoringContainer)
{
    baseAuthoringContainer = new Literal();
    authoringContainer.Controls.Add(baseAuthoringContainer);
}
```

Now, let's create the table. Because the table is dynamically generated, with placeholder content mixed with HTML, we'll code it in the overridden `LoadPlaceholderContentForAuthoring()` method.

The table consists of five columns:

Column 1	Column 2	Column 3	Column 4	Column 5
Displays the attachment as an icon. The icon shown is related to the type of the file. For example, Office Word documents will have icons that look as shown below.	Contains a TextBox control that shows the display text of the attachment. It also holds a hidden form field for storing the URL of the icon displayed in Column 1. It's hidden, so you can't see it in presentation view, but its value will be used by the client-side script that we will be coding later on.	Contains a read-only TextBox that shows the URL of the attachment.	Provides a button labeled Change… that triggers the upload process.	Contains a Delete button to remove the attachment from the list.
📄 Doc1.doc	Alt-Text [Doc1.doc]	Attachment-URL [/NR/rdonlyres/00000015/i]	Change… [Change...]	Delete [Delete]

As we are writing the code from a class file, we can't insert HTML directly as we would with regular HTML or ASPX files. Instead, we will write the code as a string variable and add it to the `Text` property of the Literal control we created earlier. We shall start with the table's header. Append the following code to the class file:

```
private string crlf = "\n";

protected override void
LoadPlaceholderContentForAuthoring(PlaceholderControlEventArgs e)
```

```
    {
        StringBuilder htmlCode = new StringBuilder();

        // table surrounding the authoring time placeholder control child controls
        htmlCode.Append("<table border=1><tr><td>" + crlf);
        htmlCode.Append("<table cellspacing=0 cellpadding=0>" + crlf);
        htmlCode.Append("<tr>" + crlf);
        htmlCode.Append("<th width=200>Icon</th>" + crlf);
        htmlCode.Append("<th width=200>Alt-Text</th>" + crlf);
        htmlCode.Append("<th>Attachment-URL</th>" + crlf);
        htmlCode.Append("<th>Change...</th>" + crlf);
        htmlCode.Append("<th>Delete</th>" + crlf);
        htmlCode.Append("</tr>"  + crlf);

        baseAuthoringContainer.Text = htmlCode.ToString();
    }
```

Next, we will generate the rows that make up the table. As a row is required for each attachment, we will construct as many rows as specified by the MaxAttachments property.

In the first column where the attachment's icon is displayed, we create an empty table cell. The cell's name is made unique by prepending MAPH_AttIcon and a number to the name of the placeholder to bind. The name of the cell will be used by the client-side script later to identify the cell for the addition of the attachment's icon. Add the highlighted code to the LoadPlaceholderContentForAuthoring() method.

```
protected override void
LoadPlaceholderContentForAuthoring(PlaceholderControlEventArgs e)
{
    . . . code continues . . .

    string sPhName = this.PlaceholderToBind;

    for (int i = 0; i < m_maxAttachments; i++)
    {
        htmlCode.Append("<tr>");

        // Add the cell for the attachment's icon
        htmlCode.Append("<td align=center id=\"MAPH_AttIcon_" + sPhName
                    + "_" + i.ToString() + "\"></td>" + crlf);
    }
    baseAuthoringContainer.Text = htmlCode.ToString();
}
```

The second cell holds two controls: a hidden control and a Text Box. The TextBox stores the attachment's display text and has a name that begins with MAPH_AttName_. It is editable, so authors can update the display text here. The hidden form field stores the icon and has a name prepended with MAPH_AttIconUrl_. Add the code that generates both controls to the LoadPlaceholderContentForAuthoring() method:

```
protected override void LoadPlaceholderContentForAuthoring
                        (PlaceholderControlEventArgs e)
{
    . . . code continues . . .

    for (int i = 0; i < m_maxAttachments; i++)
    {
        . . . . code continues . . .

        // Add the cell for the attachment's display text
```

```
        htmlCode.Append("<td align=center>");

        // Add a hidden form field to store the icon
        htmlCode.Append("<input type=\"hidden\" name=\"MAPH_AttIconUrl_" + sPhName
                + "_" + i.ToString() + "\">");

        // Add the Text box to display the attachment's display text
        htmlCode.Append("<input type=\"text\" name=\"MAPH_AttName_" + sPhName
                + "_" + i.ToString() + "\">");

        // End the cell
        htmlCode.Append("</td>" + crlf);
    }

    . . . code continues . . .
}
```

In the third cell, we generate a single read-only textbox that displays the attachment's URL. We give it a unique name by appending the placeholder's name and a number to the string MAPH_AttLink_. Later on, we will display the URL here using client-side script.

```
protected override void LoadPlaceholderContentForAuthoring
                            (PlaceholderControlEventArgs e)
{
    . . . code continues . . .

    for (int i = 0; i < m_maxAttachments; i++)
    {
        . . . code continues . . .

        // Add the cell for that attachment's URL
        htmlCode.Append("<td align=center>");

        // Add the read-only Text box to display the attachment's URL
        htmlCode.Append("<input readonly type=\"text\" name=\"MAPH_AttLink_"
                + sPhName + "_" + i.ToString() + "\">");

        // End the cell
        htmlCode.Append("</td>" + crlf);
    }

    . . . code continues . . .
}
```

Next, we add the cell with the Change... button as a fourth column. The button opens the Insert Attachment dialog.

```
protected override void LoadPlaceholderContentForAuthoring
                            (PlaceholderControlEventArgs e)
{
    . . . code continues . . .

    for (int i = 0; i < m_maxAttachments; i++)
    {
        . . . code continues . . .

        // Add the cell that contains the button
        htmlCode.Append("<td width=100 align=center>");

        // Add the Change… button to trigger the upload process
        htmlCode.Append("<INPUT type=BUTTON value=\"Change...\" onclick=\""
                + GetAttachmentDialog(i) + "\">");

        // End the cell
```

```
    htmlCode.Append("</td>" + crlf);
  }
  . . . code continues . . .
}
```

Finally, we finish off the table by adding the cell that holds the Delete button.

```
protected override void LoadPlaceholderContentForAuthoring
                      (PlaceholderControlEventArgs e)
{
  . . . code continues . . .

  for (int i = 0; i < m_maxAttachments; i++)
  {
    . . . code continues . . .

    // Add the cell for the Delete button
    htmlCode.Append("<td align=center>");

    // Add the Delete button
    htmlCode.Append("<input type=\"button\" value=\"Delete\" "
              + "onclick=\"DeleteAttachment("+i+")\">");

    // End both the cell and the row
    htmlCode.Append("</td></tr>" + crlf);
  }

  // End the first table
  htmlCode.Append("</table>" + crlf);

  // End the second table
  htmlCode.Append("</table>" + crlf);

  baseAuthoringContainer.Text = htmlCode.ToString();
}
```

Deleting Attachments

To delete attachments, we will write a client-side function that clears the contents of the textboxes, table cells, and hidden form field for the selected attachment. Add the RenderDeleteAttachmentJavascript() helper function to the code.

```
private void RenderDeleteAttachmentJavascript()
{
  StringBuilder script = new StringBuilder();

  // Get the name of the placeholder
  string sPhName = this.BoundPlaceholder.Name;

  script.Append("<SCRIPT>");
  script.Append("function DeleteAttachment(i)");
  script.Append("{" + crlf);
  script.Append("eval('document.all.MAPH_AttIcon_"+sPhName+"_'
            + i).innerHTML='';");
  script.Append("eval('document.all.MAPH_AttIconUrl_" + sPhName+"_'
            + i).value='';");
  script.Append("eval('document.all.MAPH_AttName_" + sPhName + "_'
            + i).value='';");
  script.Append("eval('document.all.MAPH_AttLink_" + sPhName + "_'
            + i).value='';");
  script.Append("}" + crlf);
  script.Append("</SCRIPT>");

  Page.RegisterClientScriptBlock("MAPH_DeleteAttachment", script.ToString());
}
```

At the end of the LoadPlaceholderContentForAuthoring() method, call the RenderDeleteAttachmentJavascript() method.

```
protected override void
LoadPlaceholderContentForAuthoring(PlaceholderControlEventArgs e)
{
    . . . code continues . . .

    RenderDeleteAttachmentJavascript();
}
```

Reusing the Insert Attachment Dialog

We need a dialog for authors to specify the file to attach and its display text. While it is possible to write one from scratch, a better idea would be to reuse the Insert Attachment dialog that ships with Web Author.

The Insert Attachment dialog provides the author with the option of either attaching a shared resource or a local attachment. Depending on the whether the developer has allowed local attachments, the author may be restricted to only selecting attachments from resource galleries. In such cases, the Insert Local Attachment link will not be available. After the author has made the selection, he or she is provided with a field for entering the display text of the attachment.

Calling the Dialog

To call the Insert Attachment dialog, we borrow the WBC_launchAttachmentGallery() method found in the AuthFormClientIE.js used by Web Author. The method accepts six arguments that affect the dialog's behavior.

Argument	What it does
strPostQueryString	A querystring containing information about the posting in unpublished mode such as its GUID or, if it's a new posting, the channel's GUID.
strPhName	The name of the placeholder.
strPhType	The value here determines how the Insert Attachment dialog passes information about the attachment back to the calling control. When dealing with attachments, Web Author recognizes the following values: • **MultiPurpose**. Applies to controls that accept HTML with full formatting. • **SingleAttachment**. Used by the SingleAttachmentPlaceholderControl for single file uploads. • **ThinEditIE**. Similar to MultiPurpose. The difference is that insertions to the placeholder use the placeholder document object model (DOM) instead. We will use this option in this example.
bAllowUpload	A Boolean to indicate if local attachments are allowed. A value of false means that only resource gallery items can be attached.
bAttachIcon	A Boolean flag to indicate if the attachment should be rendered as an icon. When it is set to true, the attachment is added to the content as an icon. Otherwise, it will be displayed as a text link.
bAllowVideo	The last Boolean indicates if video attachments are supported. This is a throwback to the previous version of MCMS where videos were supported. In MCMS 2002, this value should always be set to false.

Putting it all together, here's the script that launches the Insert Attachment dialog. Of course, the GUIDs and the placeholder name are variables that will have to be dynamically generated. The following code snippet would allow local attachments and use icons to represent attachments:

```
WBC_launchAttachmentGallery('wbc_purpose=Basic&NRMODE=Unpublished&WBCMODE=Pres
entationUnpublished&FRAMELESS=true&NRCHANNELGUID={C40686DA-83CE-452F-AF24-
3D990FA2BAC1}&NRNODEGUID={7AF93078-5FF8-4963-A9F9-B1A0977258A7}',
'NewHtmlPlaceholderDefinition1', 'ThinEditIE', true, true, false);
```

The GetAttachmentDialog() method generates the required client-side script. The script gathers information about:

• The channel's and posting's GUIDs.
• The name of the placeholder the control is bound to.
• Whether or not local attachments are allowed.
• Whether the attachments should be displayed as icons or text. For this control, we will always set this parameter to true as we want icons to be displayed in the authoring table.

Once it has collected the necessary data, it puts them together as arguments of the WBC_launchAttachmentGallery() function. Add the GetAttachmentDialog() method now:

```
private string GetAttachmentDialog(int i)
{
    // Check to see if the NRCHANNELGUID querystring contains a value
    // If it does, then it's most likely a new posting
    string channelGUID = Page.Request.QueryString["NRCHANNELGUID"];
    if (channelGUID != "")
    {
        channelGUID = "&NRCHANNELGUID="+channelGUID;
    }

    // Get the GUID from the NRNODEGUID querystring parameter
    string postingGUID = Page.Request.QueryString["NRNODEGUID"];

    // Get the name of the placeholder to bind
    string placeholderName = this.PlaceholderToBind;

    // Are local attachments allowed?
    string allowLocalAttachments = (!m_resourceGalleryOnly).ToString();

    StringBuilder script = new StringBuilder();

    // Specify the name of the placeholder that we are adding the attachment to
    script.Append("MAPH_DestPH ='" + placeholderName + "_" + i.ToString()
                                                              + "';");

    // Launch the Insert Attachment Dialog
    script.Append("WBC_launchAttachmentGallery('"
                + "wbc_purpose=Basic&"
                + "NRMODE=Unpublished&"
                + "WBCMODE=PresentationUnpublished&"
                + "FRAMELESS=true" + channelGUID + "&"
                + "NRNODEGUID=" + postingGUID + "','"
                + "'" + placeholderName + "','"
                + "'ThinEditIE',"
                + allowLocalAttachments.ToLower() + ","
                + "true,"
                + "false);");

    script.Append("return false");

    return script.ToString();
}
```

Returning Values from the Dialog

The Insert Attachment dialog allows the author to specify the attachment and its display text. It's not a modal dialog. Therefore, in order for content to be written back to the placeholder control, the dialog accesses client-side functions within the calling window.

Depending on the chosen placeholder type, Web Author prepares different client-side routines. The "ThinEditIE" placeholder type used in this example calls the WBC_setThinEditIEAttachment() method found within the AuthFormClientIE.js script (located in the <install directory>\ Microsoft Content Management Server\Server\IIS_CMS\WebAuthor\Client\ PlaceholderControlSupport\ directory).

We need to modify the WBC_setThinEditIEAttachment() routine to update the authoring table with the attachment's icon, display text, and URL. The tricky part is doing so without modifying the original code (or we will cross Microsoft support boundaries, plus not modifying the original file safeguards the code from being overwritten when future service packs are applied). As a workaround, we will create a modified version of the method and add it to the page. When the browser sees two JavaScript methods with the same name, one defined in within the page and a second in a separate *.js file, the browser will choose to run the one embedded within the page.

To begin, let's take a look at the original WBC_setThinEditIEAttachment() routine shown below. It accepts three input parameters:

- The name of the placeholder that's accepting the attachment
- The URL of the uploaded attachment
- The display name of the attachment

It uses the URL and display name of the attached file to construct an HTML anchor tag. The anchor tag is added to the placeholder by calling the insertHtml() method of the placeholder's DOM. Don't worry about typing in the code for now. We will be writing a server-side function to generate this script on the fly later.

```
function WBC_setThinEditIEAttachment(strPhName, strURL, strDispText)
{
  var strMyDispText = strDispText;
  if (strMyDispText == "")
  {
    strMyDispText = strURL;
  }

  document.all["NCPHRICH_" + strPhName].insertHtml("<a href=\"" + strURL
                            + "\">" + strMyDispText + "</a>");
}
```

While the WBC_setThinEditIEAttachment() method works perfectly for regular HtmlPlaceholderControls, in order for it to function correctly within the MutipleAttachmentPlaceholderControl, we need to make several modifications:

- The method calls an object with an ID of NCPHRICH_(PlaceholderName): our custom control has a different naming convention and executing this line of code will result in an error.
- Instead of inserting an entire anchor tag in an HtmlPlaceholderControl, we need to pass information about the attachment back to the appropriate hidden fields and cells within the table in the multiple attachment placeholder control.

Client-Side Script for All Types of Placeholder Controls

Let's tackle the first problem. By default, the WBC_setThinEditIEAttachment() method works only with the out-of-the-box placeholder controls. Placeholder controls that ship with MCMS have IDs prepended with the text NCPHRICH to differentiate them from custom controls that we build. Our control does not have the ID of NCPHRICH_(PlaceholderName). As a result, the following line of code will lead to 'document.all[...]' is null or not an object errors when the dialog is used with custom controls.

```
document.all["NCPHRICH_" + strPhName].insertHtml("<a href=\"" + strURL
                            + "\">" + strMyDispText + "</a>");
```

On the other hand, we can't remove the line of code entirely as there may be some out-of-the-box placeholder controls on the same page that require it. To get around this, we will wrap the line in a check to see if the object is undefined (which will be the case for the multiple attachment placeholder control). Again, don't worry about adding the code to the class file for now, we will show you how the JavaScript gets injected later.

```
function WBC_setThinEditIEAttachment(strPhName, strURL, strDispText)
{
  var strMyDispText = strDispText;
  if (strMyDispText == "")
  {
    strMyDispText = strURL;
  }

  if(typeof document.all["NCPHRICH_" + strPhName] != 'undefined')
  {
    document.all["NCPHRICH_" + strPhName].insertHtml("<a href=\"" + strURL
                                        + "\">" + strMyDispText + "</a>");
  }
}
```

Passing Attachment Information to the Placeholder Control

Now, on to the second problem of passing information about the attachment back to the multiple attachment placeholder control. We will populate the hidden fields and textboxes with information about the attachment's icon, display text and URL.

To get this information, let's look at two input parameters passed into the WBC_setThinEditIEAttachment() method:

Input Parameter	What it means
StrUrl	As the name suggests, this parameter contains the URL of the attachment.

strMyDispText	Stores the icon. The returned HTML is an image tag, which looks like this:
	
	`<img alt="Plants are Green!"`
	`src="/NR/rdonlyres/670B7551-5A53-4B0A-`
	`99782B7AD3EE7BC8/0/MyAttachment.doc?`
	`thumbnail=true&label=Plants%20are%20Green%21"`
	`border="0">`

So strUrl contains the URL of the attachment and strMyDispText holds the icon as shown in the script below:

```
function WBC_setThinEditIEAttachment(strPhName, strURL, strDispText)
{
  var strMyDispText = strDispText;
  if (strMyDispText == "")
  {
    strMyDispText = strURL;
  }

  if(typeof document.all["NCPHRICH_" + strPhName] != 'undefined')
  {
    document.all["NCPHRICH_" + strPhName].insertHtml("<a href=\"" + strURL
                                        + "\">" + strMyDispText + "</a>");
  }
  else
  {
    // Return the image of the icon
    if (typeof document.all["MAPH_AttIcon_" + MAPH_DestPH] !='undefined')
    {
```

```
        document.all[\"MAPH_AttIcon_\" + MAPH_DestPH].innerHTML = strMyDispText;
    }

    // Return the attachment's URL
    if (typeof document.all[\"MAPH_AttLink_\" + MAPH_DestPH] != 'undefined')
    {
        document.all[\"MAPH_AttLink_\" + MAPH_DestPH].value = strURL;
    }

    // Return the icon
    if (typeof document.all[\"MAPH_AttIconUrl_\" + MAPH_DestPH]
                                                        != 'undefined')
    {
        document.all[\"MAPH_AttIconUrl_\" + MAPH_DestPH].value = strMyDispText;
    }
  }
}
```

What about the display text? We need to extract the display text from the `alt` attribute of the icon's image tag. To do so, we will split `strMyDispText` using double-quotes (") as the separator. Let's say the original HTML is:

```
<img alt="DisplayText" src="AttachmentUrl" border="0">
```

The array formed after splitting is shown below where the second element of the resulting array contains the display text from the `alt` attribute:

```
Array Item 0:   <img alt=
Array Item 1:    DisplayText
Array Item 2:   src=
Array Item 3:   AttachmentUrl
Array Item 4:   border=
Array Item 5:   0
Array Item 6:   >
```

The extracted values are deposited into the hidden form fields and textboxes generated earlier.

```
    function WBC_setThinEditIEAttachment(strPhName, strURL, strDispText)
    {
        . . . code continues . . .

        if(typeof document.all["NCPHRICH_" + strPhName] != 'undefined')
        {
        . . . code continues . . .
        }
        else
        {
            . . . code continues . . .

            // Split strMyDispText using the double-quote character as the separator
            elements = strMyDispText.split('\"');

            // Return the Display Text
            if (typeof document.all[\"MAPH_AttName_\" + MAPH_DestPH] != 'undefined')
            {
                // The display name is the second element of the array
                document.all[\"MAPH_AttName_\" + MAPH_DestPH].value = elements[1];
            }
        }
    }
```

Generating the WBC_setThinEditIEAttachment() Method

As our custom placeholder control is constructed entirely from server-side code, we need to generate the client script above on the fly and register it with `Page.RegisterStartUpScript()`. To do so, we must add the helper function `RenderResourceGalleryRelatedJavascript()` shown below to the code:

```
private void RenderResourceGalleryRelatedJavascript()
{
StringBuilder script = new StringBuilder();

// Start the script block
script.Append("<SCRIPT language=\"javascript\">" + crlf);

// Declare the MAPH_DestPH variable
script.Append("var MAPH_DestPH = \"\";" + crlf);

// Define WBC_setThinEditIEImage function to replace one defined by MCMS
script.Append("function WBC_setThinEditIEAttachment(strPhName, strURL,"
            + "strDispText){" + crlf);

script.Append("var strMyDispText = strDispText;" + crlf
            + "if (strMyDispText == \"\") "
            + "{"
            + "strMyDispText = strURL;"
            + "}" + crlf);

script.Append("if(typeof document.all[\"NCPHRICH_\" + strPhName] !=
'undefined')"
            + "{"
            + "document.all[\"NCPHRICH_\" + strPhName].insertHtml"
            + "(\"<a href=\\\" + strURL + \\\">\" + strMyDispText
            + \"</a>\");"
            + "}" + crlf);

script.Append("else"
            + "{"
            + "elements = strMyDispText.split('\"'); " + crlf);

script.Append("if(typeof document.all[\"MAPH_AttIcon_\"
            + MAPH_DestPH]!='undefined')"
            + "{"
            + "document.all[\"MAPH_AttIcon_\"
            + MAPH_DestPH].innerHTML=strMyDispText;"
            + "}" + crlf);

script.Append("if(typeof document.all[\"MAPH_AttLink_\"
            + MAPH_DestPH]!='undefined')"
            + "{"
            + "document.all[\"MAPH_AttLink_\" + MAPH_DestPH].value = strURL; "
            + "}" + crlf);

script.Append("if(typeof "
            + "document.all[\"MAPH_AttIconUrl_\"+MAPH_DestPH]!='undefined')"
            + "{"
            + "document.all[\"MAPH_AttIconUrl_\"
            + MAPH_DestPH].value =strMyDispText;"
            + "}" + crlf);

script.Append("if (typeof "
            + "document.all[\"MAPH_AttName_\"+MAPH_DestPH]!='undefined')"
            + "{"
            + "document.all[\"MAPH_AttName_\"
```

```
                           + MAPH_DestPH].value = elements[1];"
                           + "}" + crlf);

        // Close the if-else block
        script.Append("}" + crlf);

        // Close the function
        script.Append("}" + crlf);

        // Close the script block
        script.Append("</SCRIPT>");

        // Register the script
        this.Page.RegisterStartupScript("WBC_setThinEditIEAttachment",
                                                        script.ToString());
    }
```

Finally, at the end of the `LoadPlaceholderContentForAuthoring()` method, we add a call to the `RenderResourceGalleryRelatedJavascript()` method:

```
    protected override void LoadPlaceholderContentForAuthoring(
                                            PlaceholderControlEventArgs e)
    {
        . . . code continues . . .

        RenderResourceGalleryRelatedJavascript();
    }
```

Saving the List of Attachments

When the posting is saved, the `SavePlaceholderContent()` method is called. Here, we will loop through all rows in the table to look for attachments. If an attachment is found, we create an XML node consisting of the attachment's URL, display text, and icon. At the end of the routine, the list of attachments is saved.

For example, if we have chosen to display attachments as icons, the saved XML would be:

```
<Attachments>
  <Attachment>
    <DisplayText>Aloe Vera</DisplayText>
    <Url>/NR/rdonlyres/73C94F98-1424-41EE-B4FA-D2301314A7FA/0/AloeVera.JPG
    </Url>
    <Icon><img alt="AloeVera.JPG" src="/NR/rdonlyres/73C94F98-1424-41EE-B4FA-
D2301314A7FA/0/AloeVera.JPG?thumbnail=true&label=AloeVera.JPG" border="0">
    </Icon>
  </Attachment>
</Attachments>
```

Add the overridden `SavePlaceholderContent()` method directly below the `LoadPlaceholderContentForAuthoring()` method.

```
    protected override void SavePlaceholderContent(PlaceholderControlSaveEventArgs e)
    {
        string sPhName = this.PlaceholderToBind;

        EnsureChildControls();

        // Save the list of attachments as XML
        XmlPlaceholder xph = (XmlPlaceholder) base.BoundPlaceholder;

        XmlDocument xd = new XmlDocument();
        XmlNode xnRoot = xd.CreateElement("Attachments");
```

```
        for (int i = 0; i < m_maxAttachments; i++)
        {
            if (Page.Request.Form["MAPH_AttLink_" + sPhName + "_"+i.ToString()] != "")
            {
                XmlNode xAttachment = xd.CreateElement("Attachment");

                // Store the attachment's display text
                XmlNode xDisplayName = xd.CreateElement("DisplayText");
                xDisplayName.InnerText = Page.Request.Form["MAPH_AttName_" + sPhName
                                + "_" + i.ToString()];
                xAttachment.AppendChild(xDisplayName);

                // Store the attachment's URL
                XmlNode xUrl = xd.CreateElement("Url");
                xUrl.InnerText = Page.Request.Form["MAPH_AttLink_" + sPhName + "_"
                                + i.ToString()];
                xAttachment.AppendChild(xUrl);

                // Store the icon
                XmlNode xIcon = xd.CreateElement("Icon");
                xIcon.InnerText = Page.Request.Form["MAPH_AttIconUrl_" + sPhName + "_"
                                + i.ToString()];
                xAttachment.AppendChild(xIcon);

                // Add the node to the XML Doc
                xnRoot.AppendChild(xAttachment);
            }
        }
    }
    xph.XmlAsString = xnRoot.OuterXml;
}
```

Retrieving Saved Content

To display the stored content, we first have to retrieve it. Here's the plan:

- First prepare three arrays for storing the attachment URLs, icons, and display text.

- Next, retrieve the saved XML from the underlying xmlPlaceholder.

- Once we have the XML, we extract information about the attachment from the tags and store them in the arrays that we have prepared.

- Finally, we load the content back into the table of all uploaded attachments.

Preparing Arrays for Storing Information about the Attachments

Let's prepare three string arrays for storing a list of attachment URLs, icons, and display text. Add the following code to the start of the LoadPlaceholderContentForAuthoring() method:

```
// Stores the URL of the attachment
private string[] attUrl = new string[m_maxAttachments];

// Stores the icon
private string[] attIcon = new string[m_maxAttachments];

// Stores the Display text
private string[] attName = new string[m_maxAttachments];

protected override void LoadPlaceholderContentForAuthoring
                    (PlaceholderControlEventArgs e)
{
    . . . code continues . . .
}
```

Retrieving Previously Saved XML

We retrieve the saved XML from the `XmlPlaceholder.XmlAsString` property. If the string is empty, as will be the case for a new posting, we add the root element to make it valid:

```
protected override void
LoadPlaceholderContentForAuthoring(PlaceholderControlEventArgs e)
{
    // Get saved content
    XmlPlaceholder xph = (XmlPlaceholder) base.BoundPlaceholder;
    string xmlContent = xph.XmlAsString;

    if (xmlContent == "")
    {
      xmlContent = "<Attachments />";
    }

    XmlDocument xd = new XmlDocument();
    xd.LoadXml(xmlContent);
    . . . code continues . . .
}
```

Extracting Information about the Attachments from the XML

Now that we have the saved XML, we need to extract the attachment's URL, icon, and display text from it. The attachment's display text is taken from the `<DisplayText>` element; its URL is retrieved from the `<URL>` element, and the image of the entire icon from the `<Icon>` element.

```
protected override void
LoadPlaceholderContentForAuthoring(PlaceholderControlEventArgs e)
{
    . . . code continues . . .
    xd.LoadXml(xml);

    // Extract URLs and AltText
    int index = 0;
    foreach (XmlNode xn in xd.DocumentElement.ChildNodes)
    {
      attUrl[index] = xn.SelectSingleNode("Url").InnerText;
      attIcon[index] = xn.SelectSingleNode("Icon").InnerText;
      attName[index] = xn.SelectSingleNode("DisplayText").InnerText;
      index++;
    }

    . . . code continues . . .
}
```

We are now ready to populate the table with the saved content.

Populating the Table with the Saved Attachments

There are four fields in the table that require information about the attachments:

- The cell with an ID beginning with MAPH_AttIcon for holding the attachment's icon

- The hidden form field with an ID beginning with MAPH_AttIcon for holding the attachment's icon

- The textbox with an ID beginning with MAPH_AttName for storing the display text

- The read-only textbox with an ID beginning with MAPH_AttLink for storing the URL of the attachment

Let's start with the icons. The attachment's icon is displayed in the first cell of each row. We will get the icon stored in the `attIcon[]` array and add it to the cell. Add the code highlighted below:

```
protected override void LoadPlaceholderContentForAuthoring(
                                          PlaceholderControlEventArgs e)
{
    . . . code continues . . .

    // Add the cell for the attachment's icon
    htmlCode.Append("<td align=center id=\"MAPH_AttIcon_" + sPhName
                + "_" + i.ToString() + "\">" + attIcon[i] + "</td>" + crlf;

    . . . code continues . . .
}
```

The icon is also stored in a hidden field in the second column of the table. The hidden field has a name starting with `MAPH_AttIcon` and, like the cell in the first column, will be populated with the contents of the `attIcon[]` array.

```
protected override void
LoadPlaceholderContentForAuthoring(PlaceholderControlEventArgs e)
{
    . . . code continues . . .

    // Add a hidden form field to store the icon
    htmlCode.Append("<input type=\"hidden\" name=\"MAPH_AttIconUrl_" + sPhName
                + "_"+i.ToString() + "\" value='" + attIcon[i] + "'>");

    . . . code continues . . .
}
```

The display text of the attachment is shown in a textbox with a name that starts with `MAPH_AttName`. We will set it to hold the contents of the `attName[]` array.

```
protected override void
LoadPlaceholderContentForAuthoring(PlaceholderControlEventArgs e)
{
    . . . code continues . . .

    // Add the Text box to display the attachment's display text
    htmlCode.Append("<input type=\"text\" name=\"MAPH_AttName_" + sPhName
                + "_" + i.ToString() + "\" value='" + attName[i] + "'>");

    . . . code continues . . .
}
```

The last item to fill in is the URL of the attachment. These are displayed in the textboxes that begin with `MAPH_AttLink`. The contents of the `attUrl[]` array will be used to fill in their values.

```
protected override void LoadPlaceholderContentForAuthoring(
                                          PlaceholderControlEventArgs e)
{
    . . . code continues . . .

    // Add the read-only Text box to display the attachment's URL
    htmlCode.Append("<input readonly type=\"text\" name=\"MAPH_AttLink_"
                + sPhName + "_" + i.ToString()+"\" value='"+attUrl[i]+"'>");

    . . . code continues . . .
}
```

Displaying the Attachments

In presentation view, we'll display the attachments in HTML. Let's use the same trick as we did earlier for the authoring control and use a Literal control to store the generated HTML code.

```
private Literal basePresentationContainer;
protected override void CreatePresentationChildControls(
                                BaseModeContainer presentationContainer)
{
  basePresentationContainer = new Literal();
  presentationContainer.Controls.Add(basePresentationContainer);
}
```

With the underlying data in XML, you can format the layout of the attachments any way you like. For example, you could display them vertically, horizontally, or even within a table. The LoadPlaceholderContentForPresentation() method below displays the attachments side by side. Basically, for each attachment in the list, an anchor tag is created. At the end of the routine, we get a series of anchor tags, with single spaces between them.

```
protected override void LoadPlaceholderContentForPresentation(
                                PlaceholderControlEventArgs e)
{
  // The output HTML
  StringBuilder html = new StringBuilder();

  // Retrieve previously saved content
  string xml = ((XmlPlaceholder)this.BoundPlaceholder).XmlAsString;

  // Load the XML into an XmlDocument
  XmlDocument xd = new XmlDocument();
  xd.LoadXml(xml);

  // Display the list of attachments
  foreach(XmlNode xn in xd.DocumentElement.ChildNodes)
  {
    // Get the Display Text
    string displayText = xn.SelectSingleNode("DisplayText").InnerText;

    // Get the URL
    string url = xn.SelectSingleNode("Url").InnerText;

    // Get the icon
    string icon = xn.SelectSingleNode("Icon").InnerText;

    // Create the opening anchor tag
    html.Append("<a href=\"" + url + "\">");

    if (m_displayAsIcon)
    {
      // Display attachments as icons
      html.Append(icon);
    }
    else
    {
      // Display attachments as text
      html.Append(displayText);
    }

    // Create the closing anchor tag
    html.Append("</a>");

    // Add a space
    html.Append(" ");
```

```
    }
    basePresentationContainer.Text = html.ToString();
}
```

Here, we used the XML DOM to format the content. You could also consider using an Extensible Stylesheet (XSL) to perform the transformation. Using XSL is probably a more flexible solution, as it makes changing the format a lot easier if you need to do so.

The Multiple Attachment placeholder control is complete. Save and compile the solution.

Using the MultipleAttachmentPlaceholderControl

Follow the steps outlined in the *Adding the Placeholder Control to a Template File* section to add the MultipleAttachmentPlaceholderControl to a template file of your choice. Set the DisplayAsIcon property to true or false depending on whether you would like to display the attachments as icons or text. Add an XmlPlaceholderDefinition to the template. Set the PlaceholderToBind property of the control to the XmlPlaceholderDefinition that you have just created, and you are ready to roll!

An Image Rotator Placeholder Control

We have all seen advertisements on websites. There are banners arranged horizontally at the top of the page, medium-sized square boxes located at a corner, long vertical banners on either side of the page—advertisements are everywhere. Generally, advertisements are just images designed to draw attention and entice visitors to click on them. A popular form of advertising these days is Shockwave Flash, which offers greater interactivity with low file size.

As advertisements are so popular on the Web, authors often have the responsibility of maintaining the list of advertisements on display. The image rotator placeholder control that we will build in this section provides the basic function of swapping pictures with each page load. All you will need to do to transform the images to actual advertisements is to make them clickable.

In authoring view, a textbox will be presented to authors. Here, they will specify a resource gallery that contains the images that will be displayed.

Please enter a resource gallery path:

In presentation view, the placeholder control randomly selects and displays an image from the resource gallery. The images are randomly selected each time the page loads, so the visitor generally gets to see a different advertisement on each visit.

To up the cool factor of this control a notch, let's give it the capability of rendering both image files and Flash files.

The ImageRotatorPlaceholderControl Class

To create the image rotator placeholder control, add a class file named ImageRotatorPlaceholderControl.cs to the UsefulPlaceholderControls project. The class requires the use of the methods from the following namespaces, so add them in.

```
using System;

using System.ComponentModel;
using System.Xml;
using System.Web.UI.HtmlControls;
using System.Web.UI.WebControls;
using Microsoft.ContentManagement.Publishing;
using Microsoft.ContentManagement.Publishing.Extensions.Placeholders;
using Microsoft.ContentManagement.WebControls.Design;
using Microsoft.ContentManagement.WebControls;

namespace UsefulPlaceholderControls
{
}
```

Let's store information about the images that will be displayed by the control as XML. As such, the control will only support placeholders defined from the XmlPlaceholderDefinition. In addition, since MCMS does not ship with a placeholder control that resembles an image rotator; we will build it from scratch, inheriting from the BasePlaceholderControl class.

```
. . . code continues . . .

[SupportedPlaceholderDefinitionType(typeof(XmlPlaceholderDefinition))]
public class ImageRotatorPlaceholderControl : BasePlaceholderControl
{
    . . . code continues . . .
}
```

The ResourceGalleryPath property will contain the path of the resource gallery that holds the images that will be displayed. Add it directly below the ImageRotatorPlaceholderControl() constructor.

```
private string m_resourceGalleryPath;
[
Bindable(false),
Browsable(false),
DesignerSerializationVisibility(DesignerSerializationVisibility.Hidden),
]
public string ResourceGalleryPath
{
  get
  {
    return m_resourceGalleryPath;
  }
  set
  {
    m_resourceGalleryPath = value;
  }
}
```

Specifying the Resource Gallery

Here's how the list of images is maintained: first, resource managers will upload all the images to a target resource gallery. In authoring view, the control appears as a single-line textbox. Authors will enter the path of the target resource gallery into the textbox.

To keep the example simple, we will make the following assumptions:

- All files in the specified resource gallery will be added to the list of images to be displayed (even if they are really Word documents!).

- All files in the list are equally important. There is an equal chance of each file being chosen to be displayed in the control when presented.

- The visitor viewing the page must have at least subscriber access to the resource gallery. Otherwise, the placeholder control won't be able to read the files in the gallery and no matter how many times the page is refreshed, nothing gets displayed.

Loading the TextBox

As mentioned earlier, we'll provide authors with a single-line textbox to specify the path of the resource gallery containing the images. Next to the textbox are simple instructions requesting the author to enter the path. We will use a table to organize the layout of the instructions and the textbox. Add the overridden `CreateAuthoringChildControls()` method to the code.

```
TextBox txtResourceGalleryPath;
protected override void CreateAuthoringChildControls(
                                 BaseModeContainer authoringContainer)
{
  Table table = new Table();
  TableRow tr = new TableRow();
  table.Rows.Add(tr);

  TableCell td1 = new TableCell();
  td1.Text = "Please enter a resource gallery path:";
  tr.Cells.Add(td1);

  TableCell td2 = new TableCell();
  txtResourceGalleryPath = new TextBox();
  td2.Controls.Add(txtResourceGalleryPath);
  tr.Cells.Add(td2);

  authoringContainer.Controls.Add(table);
}
```

We could have created an interface for authors to select a resource gallery from a tree or a list, and have the author choose from the resource galleries that he or she has access to, but let's keep the sample simple for now and stick to a single textbox.

Saving the Selected Resource Gallery Path

When the posting is saved, the path of the resource gallery is stored as XML back to the underlying `XmlPlaceholder` in the following format:

```
<ResourceGallery>
  <Path>/resources/myimages/</Path>
</ResourceGallery>
```

You may be wondering why we choose to store the information as XML instead of HTML, since we are only interested in a single value, namely the path of the resource gallery containing the images. The reason is because, later on, should you decide to include more information such as a specific list of images instead of using all images in the gallery, they will be easier to store and extract if they are saved as XML. Add the overridden `SavePlaceholderContent()` method directly below the `CreateAuthoringChildControls()` method.

```
protected override void SavePlaceholderContent(PlaceholderControlSaveEventArgs e)
{
  EnsureChildControls();
  ((XmlPlaceholder)this.BoundPlaceholder).XmlAsString =
      "<ResourceGallery><Path>"
      + txtResourceGalleryPath.Text + "</Path></ResourceGallery>";
}
```

Loading Previously Saved Values

The control retrieves the previously saved resource gallery path and displays it in the textbox. As what we have saved to the content repository is XML, we will use the helper function `GetResourceGalleryPath()` (defined later) to extract it.

```
protected override void LoadPlaceholderContentForAuthoring(
                                        PlaceholderControlEventArgs e)
{
  EnsureChildControls();

  string xml = ((XmlPlaceholder)this.BoundPlaceholder).XmlAsString;
  m_resourceGalleryPath = GetResourceGalleryPath(xml);

  txtResourceGalleryPath.Text = m_resourceGalleryPath;
}
```

The `GetResourceGalleryPath()` helper function accepts the entire XML string that has been saved in the underling `XmlPlaceholder` as an input parameter. It loads it into an `XmlDocument` object and retrieves the path of the resource gallery from the `<Path>` child element.

```
private string GetResourceGalleryPath(string xml)
{
  string rgPath = "";
  try
  {
    XmlDocument xd = new XmlDocument();
    xd.LoadXml(xml);
    rgPath = xd.DocumentElement.SelectSingleNode("Path").InnerText;
  }
  catch
  {}
  return rgPath;
}
```

Rotating Images Randomly

In presentation view, a file is randomly picked from the resource gallery. As the resource gallery accepts files of all types, we won't know if the selected file is an image, a Flash file, an Office document or a PDF. Therefore the control that we load in the presentation container has to be generic, like the ASP.NET `PlaceHolder` control from the `System.Web.UI.WebControls` namespace (don't confuse this with the MCMS placeholder controls!). We will use the `CreatePresentationChildControls()` method to add the `PlaceHolder` control to the presentation container.

```
PlaceHolder ph;
protected override void CreatePresentationChildControls(
                                    BaseModeContainer presentationContainer)
{
  ph = new PlaceHolder();
  presentationContainer.Controls.Add(ph);
}
```

When loading content, the placeholder control first ensures that all child controls, in this case the single `PlaceHolder` control we added earlier, have been created at run time before proceeding. Once it has done so, it retrieves the path of the resource gallery from the underlying `XmlPlaceholder`. To extract the information from the XML, we will use the `GetResourceGalleryPath()` method defined earlier.

```
protected override void LoadPlaceholderContentForPresentation(
                                        PlaceholderControlEventArgs e)
{
  EnsureChildControls();

  // Get the current CmsHttpContext
  CmsHttpContext cmsContext = CmsHttpContext.Current;

  // Get an instance of the selected resource gallery
  string xml = ((XmlPlaceholder)this.BoundPlaceholder).XmlAsString;
  m_resourceGalleryPath = GetResourceGalleryPath(xml);

  ResourceGallery rg = cmsContext.Searches.GetByPath(m_resourceGalleryPath)
                  as ResourceGallery;
}
```

Once we have an instance of the resource gallery, a random number is generated. Again, we will write a helper function, `RandomNumberGenerator()`, to pick a number from zero to one less than the number of resources in the gallery:

```
private int RandomNumberGenerator(int max)
{
  // generate a random number
  int seed;
  int index = 0;
  seed = (int)System.DateTime.Now.Ticks % System.Int32.MaxValue;
  System.Random rand = new System.Random(seed);
  index = rand.Next(0,max);

  return index;
}
```

Next, we get the resource that corresponds to the randomly chosen index. Modify the `LoadPlaceholderContentForPresentation()` method as shown below:

```
protected override void LoadPlaceholderContentForPresentation(
                                        PlaceholderControlEventArgs e)
{
  . . . code continues . . .

  if (rg != null)
  {
    // Randomly select a resource from the gallery
    int indexOfResource = RandomNumberGenerator(rg.Resources.Count);
    Resource r = rg.Resources[indexOfResource];
  }
}
```

To determine the file's type, we check its MIME type (Multipurpose Internet Mail Extensions type). MIME types are used by the browser to determine how content should be displayed. For example, a file with the MIME type `applications/x-shockwave-flash` will be played within a Flash player instead of being displayed as an image or text. The exact value returned by the `Resource.MimeType` property depends on the server's registry.

Why don't we check the file extension instead? Don't all images have a file extension like GIF, JPEG, or even BMP?

We could check the file extension. However, doing so would mean having a collection of all possible file extensions. For example, to decide whether the file is actually an image, we would have to check if the file extension is *.bmp, *.gif, *.jpg, *.jpeg—the list goes on. While it's a workable way of getting the job done, it is by no means exhaustive. What if someone uploads a *.png file? Our list will have to be updated with the latest file extension.

Checking the MIME type is a more efficient way of detecting the file type. Regardless of its extension, all images will have the word "image" as the main content type. The sub-type (for example, gif, jpeg, or png for images) follows after a forward slash.

Main Content Type	Sub Type	Mime Type
Image	GIF	image/gif
Image	JPEG	image/jpeg
Image	PNG	image/png
Applications	x-shockwave-flash	applications/x-shockwave-flash

Once we have determined if the resource is an image, a Flash file, or something else altogether, we decide how to display it. For images, the answer is pretty straightforward; we create an Image control and set its ImageUrl property to point to the image.

```
protected override void LoadPlaceholderContentForPresentation(
                                      PlaceholderControlEventArgs e)
{
  . . . code continues . . .

  if (rg != null)
  {
    // Randomly select a resource from the gallery
    int indexOfResource = RandomNumberGenerator(rg.Resources.Count);
    Resource r = rg.Resources[indexOfResource];

    if (r.MimeType.StartsWith("image"))
    {
      // If it is an image, display it
      Image img = new Image();
      img.ImageUrl = r.Url;
      ph.Controls.Add(img);
    }
  }
}
```

Flash files are played using a Flash plug-in. Visitors should already have the plug-in installed, otherwise the browser will prompt them to install it from download.macromedia.com. In Internet Explorer, the Flash plug-in is really an ActiveX control, which we can invoke using the HTML <object> tag as shown overleaf. The <EMBED></EMBED> element is included overleaf to support non-Microsoft browsers that don't use ActiveX technology. Because it is surrounded by the <OBJECT></OBJECT> tag, it will be ignored by Internet Explorer.

The highlighted code below indicate places where we have to replace `MyMovie.swf` with the actual URL of the resource:

```
<OBJECT classid="clsid:D27CDB6E-AE6D-11cf-96B8-444553540000"
codebase="http://download.macromedia.com/pub/shockwave/cabs/flash/swflash.cab#
version=7,0,0,0" id="MyMovie">
<PARAM NAME=movie VALUE="MyMovie.swf">
<PARAM NAME=quality VALUE=high>
<PARAM NAME=bgcolor VALUE=#FFFFFF>
<EMBED src="MyMovie.swf" quality=high bgcolor=#FFFFFF
    NAME="MyMovie" TYPE=\"application/x-shockwave-flash"
    PLUGINSPAGE="http://www.macromedia.com/go/getflashplayer">
</EMBED></OBJECT>
```

A Literal control is used to display the entire HTML string. Add the highlighted portion as shown to the `LoadPlaceholderContentForPresentation()` method:

```
protected override void LoadPlaceholderContentForPresentation(
                                        PlaceholderControlEventArgs e)
{
    . . . code continues . . .

    if (r.MimeType.StartsWith("image"))
    {
        // If it is an image, display it
        Image img = new Image();
        img.ImageUrl = r.Url;
        ph.Controls.Add(img);
    }
    else if (r.MimeType.EndsWith("x-shockwave-flash"))
    {
        // If it is a shockwave flash file, display it
        Literal swf = new Literal();
        string html = "<OBJECT classid=\"clsid:D27CDB6E-AE6D-11cf-96B8-"
                + "444553540000\" "
                + "codebase=\"http://download.macromedia.com/pub"
                + "/shockwave/cabs/flash/swflash.cab#version=7,0,0,0\""
                + "id=\"" + r.Name + "\">"
                + "<PARAM NAME=movie VALUE=\"" + r.Url + "\">"
                + "<PARAM NAME=quality VALUE=high>"
                + "<PARAM NAME=bgcolor VALUE=#FFFFFF>"
                + "<EMBED src=\"" + r.Url + "\" quality=high "
                + "bgcolor=#FFFFFF NAME=\"" + r.Name + "\" "
                + "TYPE=\"application/x-shockwave-flash\" "
                + "PLUGINSPAGE=\"http://www.macromedia.com/go/"
                + "getflashplayer\"></EMBED></OBJECT>";
        swf.Text = html;
        ph.Controls.Add(swf);
    }
}
```

For all other file types, we will simply display their thumbnails within an `Image` control. You could choose not to display them at all and get the random-file generator to pick only images and Flash files. Or perhaps you may have some other creative way of tackling such files. For example, you could read the contents of a text file to make a quote-of-the-day control. If you do, just add the logic to deal with them here.

```
protected override void LoadPlaceholderContentForPresentation(
                                        PlaceholderControlEventArgs e)
{
    . . . code continues . . .

    if (r.MimeType.StartsWith("image"))
```

```
{
    . . . code continues . . .
}
else if (r.MimeType.EndsWith("x-shockwave-flash"))
{
    . . . code continues . . .
}
else
{
    // For all other types, show the thumbnail
    Image img = new Image();
    img.ImageUrl = r.UrlThumbnail;
    ph.Controls.Add(img);
}
}
```

The control is complete. Save and build the solution.

The selected resource gallery contains many file types. But I only wish to display images in the control. Is there a quick way to filter the unwanted files without deleting them from the gallery?

You could use the `ResourceCollection.FilterByMimeType()` or `ResourceCollection.FilterByExtension()` methods of the PAPI to retrieve resources of specific MIME types or extensions. For example, the following code selects only images from the gallery.

```
// Get an instance of the resource gallery
ResourceGallery rg = cmsContext.Searches.GetByPath(m_resourceGalleryPath)
                     as ResourceGallery;
// Select only images from the resource
ResourceCollection rc = rg.FilterByMimeType("image", true);
```

Using the Image Rotator Placeholder Control

To use the image rotator placeholder control, add it to a template file and bind it to an `XmlPlaceholderDefinition`. Within a posting, supply the control with the path of a resource gallery that contains some resources. Load the posting in presentation view and watch the images rotate on each load.

With a few modifications, the control can be enhanced to accommodate advertisements:

- Store the URL of the site that the visitor will be redirected to in the resource's description field.
- Wrap the images, Flash movies, and icons of attachments within an anchor tag. Set the `href` attribute to point to the target website.

A Placeholder Control to Store All HTML Tags

Have you tried storing JavaScript or form elements, like a textbox or button control, in an `HtmlPlaceholder` object? If you have, you will have found that all `<script>`, `<input>`, and some other tags are stripped away when the page is saved.

263

Consider a posting that contains a single HtmlPlaceholderControl that allows authors to edit the HTML source code (the AllowHtmlSourceEditing property has been set to true).

FullFormatting and line breaks have been permitted on the underlying HtmlPlaceholder object, so this particular placeholder accepts the full spectrum of tags. If we enter code into the control that contains among other things a textbox, a button, and some JavaScript:

```
<table border="1">
<tr>
  <td>
    Greet the world:
  </td>
  <td>
    <input type="textbox" name="MyTextBox">
    <input type="button" value="Show it!" onclick="Greet();">
  </td>
</tr>
</table>
<script language="javascript">
function Greet()
{
  alert(document.all.MyTextBox.value);
}
</script>
```

On a regular web page, you would expect the resulting HTML page to look as shown below. When users click on the Show it! button, a pop-up message displays the contents of the textbox.

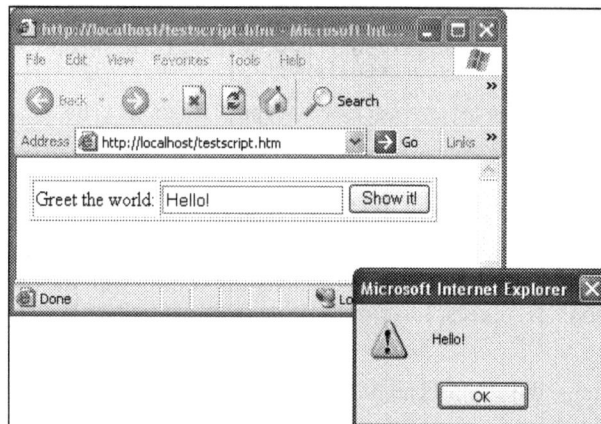

However, that is not what we see when the posting is saved. Instead what we get is a stripped down version of what we just entered. Only the words Greet the world and the table structure remain.

And if you look at the HTML source, only the following code snippet is left. The <input> type controls are gone and so are the <script> tags and everything that was between.

```
<TABLE border=1>
  <TBODY>
  <TR>
```

```
        <TD>Greet the world: </TD>
        <TD></TD>
    </TR>
    </TBODY>
</TABLE>
```

What happened? The `HtmlPlaceholder` object was designed to store only specific tags such as the `<table>`, `<tr>`, and `<td>` tags (note that these table tags are only accepted when full formatting is allowed). The full list can be obtained from the documentation.

Where can I find a full list of tags accepted by the HtmlPlaceholder?

The full list of allowed tags is documented in the MCMS manual, in the chapter *Mapping HTML Placeholder Definition Properties to Content Authoring Behavior*. The online version can be found at `http://msdn.microsoft.com/library/en-us/sitedevl/htm/cms_sd_dev_vsnetintegration_1cua.asp`.

Such restrictions are placed to prevent potentially dangerous tags from being entered and saved in placeholders. Such code could potentially cause infinite loops that open new browser windows, steal cookies, and even launch malicious applets or other controls.

Nevertheless, there may be times when your authors need to contribute content that contains these prohibited tags. Authors may need to embed client-side script, IFRAMEs, applets, or ActiveX controls within placeholder content. Usually, these objects are defined within the template file, but doing so requires the developer to insert the code. Tech-savvy authors may wish to manage such content themselves, bypassing potential workflow bottlenecks caused by busy developers.

The default `HtmlPlaceholder` placeholder object does not allow all tags. To get around this, we will build a custom placeholder control. Let's call it the `AllTagsHtmlPlaceholderControl`. The control will have the same look and feel as the `HtmlPlaceholderControl` but it will modify the content so that the underlying `HtmlPlaceholder` no longer detects the disallowed tags when the posting is saved.

Here's the completed `AllTagsHtmlPlaceholderControl` in authoring view. It looks exactly like the `HtmlPlaceholderControl`. Authors won't even know the difference.

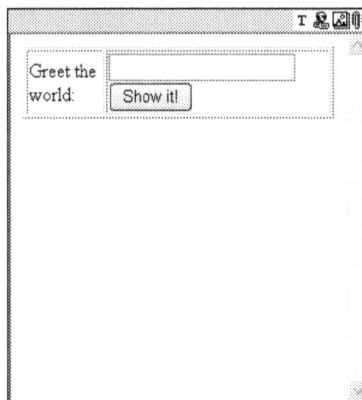

The magic about it is that after the posting is saved, the previously "illegal" elements and JavaScript remain! The screenshot below shows the HTML code within the placeholder control after it has been saved:

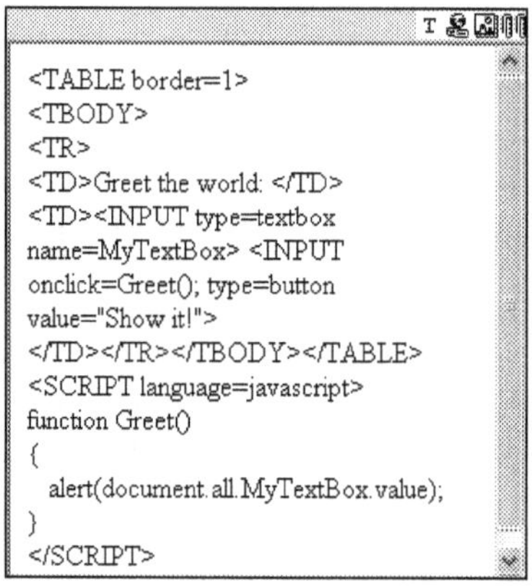

The AllTagsHtmlPlaceholderControl Class

Begin by adding a class file named AllTagsHtmlPlaceholderControl.cs to the UsefulPlaceholderControls project. Add the required namespaces above the namespace declaration:

```
using System;
using Microsoft.ContentManagement.Publishing;
using Microsoft.ContentManagement.Publishing.Extensions.Placeholders;
using Microsoft.ContentManagement.WebControls.Design;
using Microsoft.ContentManagement.WebControls;

namespace UsefulPlaceholderControls
{
    . . . code continues . . .
}
```

As we are simply modifying the way the HtmlPlaceholderControl behaves, the control will inherit from the HtmlPlaceholderControl class and support only HtmlPlaceholderDefinitions:

```
[SupportedPlaceholderDefinitionType(typeof(HtmlPlaceholderDefinition))]
public class AllTagsHtmlPlaceholderControl : HtmlPlaceholderControl
{
    public AllTagsHtmlPlaceholderControl()
    {
    }
}
```

We don't need to do anything in the constructor, so leave it empty.

Saving All Kinds of Tags

The trick behind getting the placeholder to accept all kinds of tags is to not save them as tags in the first place.

Tags are defined by an opening less-than sign (<), the element's name, followed by a closing greater-than sign (>). For example, the tag that describes the start of a script block is <script>.

To fool the placeholder into accepting every tag, regardless of whether it's a simple bold tag <b> or a script tag <script>, we will replace all less-than (<) and greater-than (>) characters with the strings "~LT~" and "~GT~" respectively. As a result, what gets saved to the placeholder is just funny looking text like this:

```
~LT~script~GT~
function Greet()
{
   alert(document.all.MyTextBox.value);
}
~LT~/script~GT~
```

The converted text does not contain any restricted tags. It is saved to the placeholder without any problems. Interestingly, the popular Telerik r.a.d. editor uses the same technique to allow special tags.

Since the conversion process is done when the posting is saved, we will modify the SavePlaceholderContent() method. Add the overridden SavePlaceholderContent() method directly below the constructor. Within the save, we will call a method named Escape() (defined right after this) that converts all tags to text.

```
protected override void SavePlaceholderContent(PlaceholderControlSaveEventArgs e)
{
   EnsureChildControls();
   ((HtmlPlaceholder)(this.BoundPlaceholder)).Html = Escape(this.Html);
}
```

Escaping Tags

The Escape() method simply replaces all less-than (<) characters with ~LT~ and all greater-than characters (>) with ~GT~.

It is probably worth noting that only HTML markup tags will contain the < and > characters. If an author enters these characters as part of the main text within the placeholder, MCMS encodes the less-than character to < and the greater-than character to >. Therefore we don't have to worry about the Escape() routine messing up content entered by the author.

```
private string Escape(string input)
{
   return input.Replace("<","~LT~").Replace(">","~GT~");
}
```

UnEscaping Tags

The act of reverting the ~LT~ and ~GT~ characters back to the < and > characters is done by the UnEscape() method. Add it directly below the Escape() method.

```
private string UnEscape(string input)
{
   return input.Replace("~LT~","<").Replace("~GT~",">");
}
```

Loading Content for Authoring and Presentation

To display the content, all we need to do is unescape the ~LT~ and ~GT~ strings back to the < and > characters respectively.

The first place where content is displayed is in authoring view when authors update the placeholder's content. We only need to convert the text when the placeholder is being edited, or when the Web Author is in the `AuthoringReedit` mode. The `UnEscape()` method defined earlier does the conversion. Add the overridden `LoadPlaceholderContentForAuthoring()` method shown below:

```
protected override void LoadPlaceholderContentForAuthoring(
                                    PlaceholderControlEventArgs e)
{
  EnsureChildControls();
  if (WebAuthorContext.Current.Mode == WebAuthorContextMode.AuthoringReedit)
  {
    base.Html = UnEscape(((HtmlPlaceholder)(base.BoundPlaceholder)).Html);
  }
  else
  {
    base.LoadPlaceholderContentForAuthoring(e);
  }
}
```

Uploaded content is, needless to say, also shown in presentation view. Regardless of whether or not the content is displayed when viewing the posting for preview or published modes, the ~LT~ and ~GT~ strings must be converted back to < and > characters respectively. We will do the conversion in the overridden `LoadPlaceholderContentForPresentation()` method. Append the method to the code:

```
protected override void LoadPlaceholderContentForPresentation(
                                    PlaceholderControlEventArgs e)
{
  EnsureChildControls();
  base.Html = UnEscape(((HtmlPlaceholder)(base.BoundPlaceholder)).Html);
}
```

The control is complete. Save and build the solution.

Using the AllTagsHtmlPlaceholderControl

To use the `AllTagsHtmlPlaceholderControl`, copy the `UsefulPlaceholderControl.dll` library file to the `bin` directory or add it as a reference to the project. After adding the control to the Toolbox, drag and drop it onto template files as you would with regular placeholder controls. Set the `PlaceholderToBind` property of the control to an existing `HtmlPlaceholderDefinition`.

In addition, if authors are planning to save restricted tags like <script> blocks and <input> elements, you will need to set the `AllowHtmlSourceEditing` property of the control to true. The WYSIWYG editor does not allow authors to copy and paste the restricted tags in Design view. They will have to click on the HTML button on the authoring toolbar before pasting the HTML code into the control.

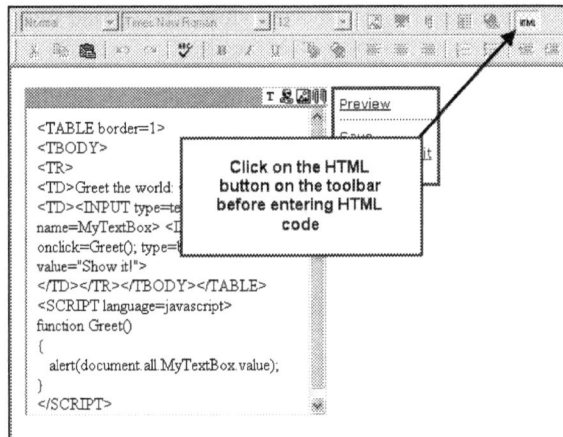

A DataGrid Placeholder Control

One of the most versatile controls in ASP.NET is the DataGrid control. Its basic function is to display content in the form of a table. What makes it really powerful are the additional properties, methods, and events packed into it that help developers perform a myriad of complex tasks such as sorting, paging, and style formatting with minimal code.

In MCMS applications, DataGrids are often used to manage XML content. DataGrids hide complex details from authors who don't even need to know that they are working with XML. Users select the row they wish to update by clicking on an Edit button. The row transforms into a series of editable textboxes. When the Save button is clicked, the content is written back to the content repository.

The DataGrid placeholder control that we will build in this section will perform these basic functions:

- **Automatically display XML content as a table.** You don't have to write oodles of code to message the XML into a readable format. We will simply bind it to a DataGrid and voilà! It appears as a nicely formatted table.

- **Allow authors to edit XML by clicking on an Edit button.** Each editable cell transforms into a textbox where authors enter values. The best part is that they won't have to worry about how the XML data is structured nor how the backend schema looks. The DataGrid placeholder control will take care of the details.

- **Allow authors to add rows.** With the DataGrid placeholder control, authors can add as many table rows (or, as many XML nodes) as they need to. There is complete flexibility in the number of items the control can carry.

- **Allow authors to delete rows.** A delete button will be provided on each row for authors to remove any row of content that is no longer required.

- **Save the XML back to the underlying XmlPlaceholder when the Save button is clicked.** Each row will be automatically fashioned into XML based on the schema that you have defined, guaranteeing that only valid XML is saved back into the placeholder, leaving no chance for authors to mess up.

Here's the DataGrid placeholder control in authoring view. The second row is currently being edited. See how easy it is for authors to modify XML content.

		CommonName	Description
Edit	Delete	Aloe Vera	The health benefits of eating the inner leaves of the Aloe Vera have made it popular. Also used to make gels and cream known to have rejuvenating properties.
Update	Delete	Hibiscus	Woody shrub with flowers
Add			

In publishing view, it appears as a regular table. The look and feel of the table can be easily adjusted with CSS stylesheets.

CommonName	Description
Aloe Vera	The health benefits of eating the inner leaves of the Aloe Vera have made it popular. Also used to make gels and cream known to have rejuvenating properties.
Hibiscus	Woody shrub with flowers available in many colors.

The DataGridPlaceholderControl Class

Let's build the DataGrid placeholder control. Start by adding a class named DataGridPlaceholderControl.cs to the UsefulPlaceholderControls project.

Add the following namespaces:

```
using System;

// Add references to the Microsoft.ContentManagement Namespace
using Microsoft.ContentManagement.Publishing;
using Microsoft.ContentManagement.Publishing.Extensions.Placeholders;
using Microsoft.ContentManagement.WebControls;
using Microsoft.ContentManagement.WebControls.Design;

// Add additional namespaces
using System.Web.UI.WebControls;
using System.ComponentModel;
using System.Data;
using System.Text.RegularExpressions;
using System.IO;
using System.Xml;

namespace UsefulPlaceholderControls
{
}
```

Since it manages XML content, the control will support the XmlPlaceholderDefinition. In addition, since MCMS does not ship with any placeholder control that supports the XmlPlaceholderDefinition, we will build the control entirely from scratch and inherit from the BasePlaceholderControl class.

```
[SupportedPlaceholderDefinitionType( typeof(XmlPlaceholderDefinition) )]
public class DataGridPlaceholderControl : BasePlaceholderControl
{
    . . . code continues . . .
}
```

The control contains a single public property named XmlAsString for retrieving and setting the XML content. Add the property below the class constructor.

```
private string xmlAsString = "";
[
Bindable(false),
Browsable(false),
DesignerSerializationVisibility(DesignerSerializationVisibility.Hidden),
]
public string XmlAsString
{
  get
  {
    return xmlAsString;
  }
  set
  {
    xmlAsString = value;
  }
}
```

Loading the DataGrid for Authoring

In authoring view, the placeholder control contains a single DataGrid. Typically, when using the DataGrid within a Web Form, you would drag and drop it from the Toolbox, toggle to HTML view, and add columns as shown here:

```
<asp:DataGrid id="DataGrid1" runat="server">
<Columns>
  <asp:EditCommandColumn EditText="Edit" UpdateText="Update">
  </asp:EditCommandColumn>
  <asp:ButtonColumn CommandName="Delete" Text="Delete"></asp:ButtonColumn>
</Columns>
</asp:DataGrid>
```

The DataGrid also contains a special Properties window (to see it, click on the ellipsis in the Columns field of the property window) that allows you to define columns, paging, and other properties with a friendly graphical user interface.

Unfortunately, since we are creating a custom placeholder control and working with class files, we can't leverage these conveniences. We've got to do it the hard way and configure the DataGrid control using code.

First, let's load the DataGrid to the authoring container of the placeholder control. We will do this in the CreateAuthoringChildControls() method. The DataGrid object is defined as a class-wide variable as we will need to reference it in other methods throughout the class, like the one for loading content into the control.

```
private DataGrid dg;
protected override void CreateAuthoringChildControls(
                                    BaseModeContainer authoringContainer)
{
  // Add a DataGrid control to the authoring container
  dg = new DataGrid();
  authoringContainer.Controls.Add(dg);
}
```

With the DataGrid created, we are ready to insert columns. The first column that we will add is the Edit/Update column. In DataGrid speak, that is the EditCommandColumn. It contains an Edit link for authors to select a row in the grid that they wish to modify. When it is clicked, the row transforms into a series of textboxes. After authors have modified the contents of the row, they click the Update link to save their work back to the grid.

Of course, the Edit and Update links won't perform the work of editing and updating without our programming the necessary logic. We will do so by writing the OnEditCommand() method for editing and the OnUpdateCommand() method for updating, later on. Meanwhile, we register these methods to the DataGrid's EditCommand and UpdateCommand events respectively.

```
. . . code continues . . .
protected override void CreateAuthoringChildControls(
                              BaseModeContainer authoringContainer)
{
    // Add a DataGrid control to the authoring container
    dg = new DataGrid();

    // Add an Edit/Update column to the DataGrid
    EditCommandColumn c0 = new EditCommandColumn();
    c0.EditText = "Edit";
    c0.UpdateText = "Update";
    dg.Columns.Add(c0);
    dg.EditCommand += new DataGridCommandEventHandler(this.OnEditCommand);
    dg.UpdateCommand += new DataGridCommandEventHandler(this.OnUpdateCommand);

    authoringContainer.Controls.Add(dg);
}
```

We will also provide a Delete button for authors to remove rows from the DataGrid. The column type that automatically creates a button in a DataGrid is the ButtonColumn. Like the edit and update links added earlier, we need to program the logic for deleting the items. We do so in the OnDeleteCommand() event handler, which we will work on later. For now, we will register the method to the DataGrid's DeleteCommand event as another DataGridCommandEventHandler.

```
. . . code continues . . .
protected override void CreateAuthoringChildControls(
                              BaseModeContainer authoringContainer)
{
    . . . code continues . . .

    // Add a Delete button to the DataGrid
    ButtonColumn c1 = new ButtonColumn();
    c1.CommandName = "Delete";
    c1.Text = "Delete";
    dg.Columns.Add(c1);
    dg.DeleteCommand += new DataGridCommandEventHandler(this.OnDeleteCommand);

    authoringContainer.Controls.Add(dg);
}
```

Next, we add a Label for error messages (if any) when loading and saving content from the DataGrid. Remember to define the Label as a class-wide variable so that it can be accessed by other methods within the class.

```
. . . code continues . . .
private Label lblMessage;
protected override void CreateAuthoringChildControls(
                              BaseModeContainer authoringContainer)
```

```
{
    . . . code continues . . .

    // Add a Label Control for displaying messages
    lblMessage = new Label();
    authoringContainer.Controls.Add(lblMessage);
}
```

Finally, we include an Add button for authors to insert new rows to the DataGrid. For simplicity, we will just add the button below the DataGrid control. The logic for adding rows to the grid will be handled by the `OnAddCommand()` method that we will define later. In the meantime, we will register the method to the `Click()` event of the Add button.

```
. . . code continues . . .
protected override void CreateAuthoringChildControls(
                                    BaseModeContainer authoringContainer)
{
    . . . code continues . . .

    // Add an "Add" button to the DataGrid
    Button add = new Button();
    add.Text = "Add";
    add.Click += new EventHandler(this.OnAddCommand);
    authoringContainer.Controls.Add(add);
}
```

The DataGrid now contains the essential buttons for managing content. Authors can edit, update, add, and delete rows from the DataGrid. If you could see it now, it would look like this:

Now, let's move on and load content from the underlying `XmlPlaceholder` to the DataGrid.

Retrieving Placeholder Content

We will retrieve content from the `XmlPlaceholder` and load it to the DataGrid within the `LoadPlaceholderContentForAuthoring()` method as shown below. The first step in the process is to call the base placeholder control's `EnsureChildControls()` method, which checks that all child controls (including the DataGrid control) have been completely loaded before we work with them.

```
protected override void LoadPlaceholderContentForAuthoring(
                                    PlaceholderControlEventArgs e)
{
    EnsureChildControls();

    lblMessage.Text = "";
}
```

The DataGrid will retrieve saved XML content from the underlying `XmlPlaceholder` and display it as rows and columns. Consider a case where the placeholder contains an XML listing of two plants with common names and short descriptions as shown below:

```
<TropicalPlants>
<Plant>
  <CommonName>Aloe Vera </CommonName>
  <Description>
```

273

```
The health benefits of eating the inner leaves of the Aloe Vera have made it
popular. Also used to make gels and cream known to have rejuvenating
properties.
   </Description>
</Plant>
<Plant>
   <CommonName>Hibiscus</CommonName>
   <Description>
Woody shrub with flowers available in many colors.
   </Description>
</Plant>
</TropicalPlants>
```

When loaded into the DataGrid, each plant is displayed as a row and the plant's common name and description are shown as columns as arranged in the following table.

Common Name	Description
Aloe Vera	The health benefits of eating the inner leaves of the Aloe Vera have made it popular. Also used to make gels and cream known to have rejuvenating properties.
Hibiscus	Woody shrub with flowers available in many colors.

As you can see, the layout of the DataGrid is inferred from the XML content. This works well if the placeholder actually holds some previously saved XML content. However, new pages have empty placeholders. Or perhaps, the author could have left the grid empty. How would the DataGrid know what data columns to add?

To get around this, we will store the XML schema in the placeholder's description. Following the example above, the template designer needs to create an XmlPlaceholderDefinition and set its Description property to:

```
<TropicalPlants><Plant><CommonName></CommonName><Description></Description>
</Plant></TropicalPlants>
```

When the page loads for the first time, or if the saved XML doesn't contain any child nodes, we will get the default XML content from the placeholder's description. This will provide the information required by the DataGrid to add the required data columns.

Here's the code that retrieves the XML and decides whether or not there is sufficient information to create the table structure:

```
protected override void LoadPlaceholderContentForAuthoring(
                                         PlaceholderControlEventArgs e)
{
   . . . code continues . . .

   // Retrieved previously saved XML
   xmlAsString = ((XmlPlaceholder)this.BoundPlaceholder).XmlAsString;

   bool isEmpty = false;
   if (xmlAsString.Trim() == "")
   {
      // Default Content is read off from the Description
      // property of the bound placeholder
      xmlAsString = base.BoundPlaceholder.Definition.Description;
      isEmpty = true;
   }
   else
```

```
  {
    XmlDocument xd = new XmlDocument();
    xd.LoadXml(xmlAsString);
    if (xd.DocumentElement.ChildNodes.Count == 0)
    {
      xmlAsString = base.BoundPlaceholder.Definition.Description;
      isEmpty = true;
    }
  }
}
```

Instead of letting the XML define the columns in the grid, why not add the CommonName and Description fields as columns to the DataGrid in the CreateAuthoringChildControls() method?

We could have added the data fields as bound columns in the CreateAuthoringChildControls() method as follows:

```
BoundColumn c2 = new BoundColumn();
c2.HeaderText = "Common Name";
c2.DataField = "CommonName";
```

However, that also means that the DataGrid can only be used when the content consists of a Common Name field and a Description, which defeats the purpose of building a control that is usable across projects.

Alternatively, consider providing a property to the template designer that holds a collection of column names and their corresponding data fields. The DataGrid could be generated based on the contents of this property.

Now that we have retrieved the stored XML, we need to convert it to a DataSet and bind it to the DataGrid. Fortunately, the DataSet has a ReadXml() method that transforms XML strings directly into a DataSet object. We will first convert the raw XML string to a StringReader object, before passing it as an input parameter of the DataSet.ReadXml() method.

Each time authors click on the Add, Edit, Update, or Delete buttons, a postback is made. As you probably already know, the Web is stateless, which means that between postbacks, the Web Form does not remember the contents of the DataGrid. In order to get the grid to retain content across postbacks, we will save the DataSet to the page's **viewstate**.

Any errors that may occur during the process are trapped with a try-catch block. The detailed error message is displayed in the Label.

```
private DataSet ds;
protected override void LoadPlaceholderContentForAuthoring(
                                        PlaceholderControlEventArgs e)
{
  . . . code continues . . .
  try
  {
    // Convert the loaded XML to a DataSet
    System.IO.StringReader sr = new System.IO.StringReader(xmlAsString);
    ds = new DataSet();
    ds.ReadXml(sr);

    // Store is as part of the Viewstate
```

```
        ViewState["ds"] = ds;

        // Make the first item editable if the list is empty
        if (isEmpty)
        {
          dg.EditItemIndex = 0;
        }

        // Bind the Data to the DataGrid
        if (ds.Tables.Count>0)
        {
          dg.DataSource = ds;
          dg.DataBind();
        }
      }
      catch(Exception ex)
      {
        // Uh-oh. We have an error. Write the error details to the Label
        lblMessage.Text = "Failed to load placeholder content for authoring"
                          + ex.Message;
      }
    }
}
```

Saving the Modified XML

Each time the XML content is retrieved from the XMLAsString property, we need to convert the
content stored in the DataSet back to XML. To do so, we need to modify the XmlAsString
property as follows:

```
public string XmlAsString
{
  get
  {
    ds = (DataSet)ViewState["ds"];
    if (ds != null)
    {
      // Check that there are no empty rows
      foreach (DataRow row in ds.Tables[0].Rows)
      {
        bool isEmpty = true;
        for (int i = 0; i < ds.Tables[0].Columns.Count; i++)
        {
          if (row[i].ToString().Trim() != string.Empty)
          {
            isEmpty = false;
          }
        }
        // The row is empty. Remove it from the table
        if (isEmpty)
        {
          ds.Tables[0].Rows.Remove(row);
        }
      }
      return ds.GetXml();
    }
    else
    {
      return xmlAsString;
    }
  }
  set
  {
    xmlAsString = value;
  }
}
```

We will get the converted XML contents from the modified `XmlAsString` property and save it to the placeholder. Append the `SavePlaceholderContent()` method to the code.

```
protected override void SavePlaceholderContent(PlaceholderControlSaveEventArgs e)
{
    EnsureChildControls();
    try
    {
        ((XmlPlaceholder)this.BoundPlaceholder).XmlAsString = this.XmlAsString;
    }
    catch(Exception ex)
    {
        lblMessage.Text = "Save Placeholder Failed: " + ex.Message;
    }
}
```

Adding a Row

The addition of a row to the DataGrid is a five-step process:

- First, we retrieve the `DataSet` from the viewstate.
- From the `DataSet`, we get the `DataTable` that contains our XML content in the form of rows and columns.
- We add a row to the `DataTable`.
- The `DataSet` that contains the modified `DataTable` with the new row is saved to the viewstate and bound to the DataGrid.
- The new row, appended to the bottom of the table, is made editable.

Here's the code that adds a row to the table:

```
protected void OnAddCommand(object source, EventArgs e)
{
    // Retrieve the DataSet from the ViewState
    ds = (DataSet)ViewState["ds"];

    // Add a new row to the table
    DataTable dt = ds.Tables[0];
    DataRow r = dt.NewRow();
    dt.Rows.Add(r);

    // Save the modified DataSet
    ViewState["ds"] = ds;

    // Bind data to the DataGrid
    dg.DataSource = ds;
    dg.DataBind();

    // Make the newly added item editable
    dg.EditItemIndex = dt.Rows.Count -1;
}
```

Deleting a Row

Deleting rows in the DataGrid is the opposite of adding rows:

- First get the copy of the DataSet saved in the viewstate.
- Remove the row that has been marked for deletion. We can retrieve the index of the selected row from the DataGridCommandEventArgs argument.
- Set all rows to be uneditable.
- Save the modified DataSet back to the viewstate.
- Refresh the DataGrid by rebinding it with the latest content.

This is the completed OnDeleteCommand() event handler. Append it to the code.

```
protected void OnDeleteCommand(object source, DataGridCommandEventArgs e)
{
    // Retrieve the DataSet from the ViewState
    ds = (DataSet)ViewState["ds"];

    // Remove the selected row
    ds.Tables[0].Rows.RemoveAt(e.Item.ItemIndex);
    dg.EditItemIndex = -1;

    // Save the modified DataSet
    ViewState["ds"] = ds;

    // Bind data to the DataGrid
    dg.DataSource = ds;
    dg.DataBind();
}
```

Editing a Row

When the Edit button is clicked, we set the corresponding row to be editable. Simply retrieve the index of the selected row from the DataGridCommandEventArgs and assign it to the EditItemIndex of the grid. To refresh the display on the screen, we retrieve the DataSet from the viewstate and rebind it to the DataGrid.

Add the OnEditCommand() event handler to the code.

```
protected void OnEditCommand(object source, DataGridCommandEventArgs e)
{
    // Set the selected row to be editable
    dg.EditItemIndex = e.Item.ItemIndex;

    // Retrieve the DataSet from the ViewState
    ds = (DataSet)ViewState["ds"];

    // Bind data to the DataGrid
    dg.DataSource = ds;
    dg.DataBind();
}
```

Updating a Row

Let's examine what happens when a row is updated. In update mode, the DataGrid automatically transforms the row into a series of textboxes. What we need to do is to retrieve each textbox and write its values back to the corresponding cell in the DataSet.

In order to do this, let's examine the layout of the DataGrid when a row is being edited.

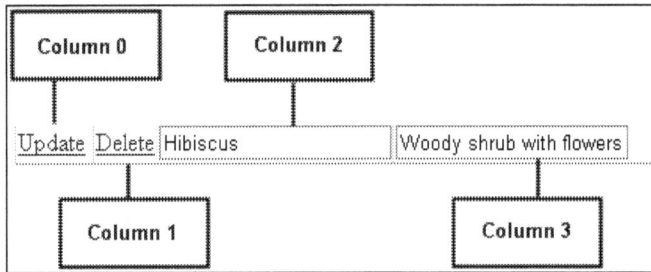

Notice that the textbox that holds the plant's common name is in the third column and that for the description is in the fourth column. Therefore, to retrieve the plant's common name and description, we look at the textboxes in the third and fourth cells of the row that is being edited.

Once we have retrieved the updated values, we modify the corresponding row in the DataSet and save it back to the viewstate. We refresh the DataGrid by binding it with the latest content and setting all rows to be uneditable. Add the OnUpdateCommand() event handler to the code.

```
protected void OnUpdateCommand(object source, DataGridCommandEventArgs e)
{
  // Retrieve the DataSet from the ViewState
  ds = (DataSet)ViewState["ds"];

  // Update the row that has been modified by the author
  DataRow row = ds.Tables[0].Rows[e.Item.ItemIndex];

  // Retrieve the value of each TextBox
  for (int i = 2; i < e.Item.Cells.Count; i++)
  {
    TextBox t = e.Item.Cells[i].Controls[0] as TextBox;
    row[i-2] = t.Text.Trim();
  }

  // Save the modified DataSet
  ViewState["ds"] = ds;

  // Bind data to the DataGrid
  dg.DataSource = ds;
  dg.DataBind();

  // Set all rows to be uneditable
  dg.EditItemIndex = -1;
}
```

Displaying the XML in Presentation Mode

In presentation mode, we can choose to display the XML in a variety of ways. We could use the XML Document Object Model (DOM) to iterate through each node and present it in a list (for instance as a table). Or, you could choose to write an XSL stylesheet to transform the XML into any format you wish. A faster way to go about presenting the XML would be to bind it to one of the many ASP.NET controls that support data binding, like the Repeater or DataGrid controls.

Since we have been working with the DataGrid control in this example, let's continue to use it. In presentation mode, we load a DataGrid control as well as a Label for displaying error messages to the container.

```
protected override void CreatePresentationChildControls(
                                 BaseModeContainer presentationContainer)
{
    // Add the DataGrid
    dg = new DataGrid();
    presentationContainer.Controls.Add(dg);

    // Add the Label for error messages
    lblMessage = new Label();
    presentationContainer.Controls.Add(lblMessage);
}
```

We retrieve the previously saved XML content from the placeholder, convert it to a DataSet object using the same technique we used earlier and bind it to the DataGrid. Any exceptions are caught and a message is displayed. Note that it may not be a good idea to show the detailed error message in an actual implementation. We wouldn't want to show ugly messages to visitors viewing the page! Instead, you may want to consider hiding the DataGrid altogether and logging the error elsewhere, like a log file.

```
protected override void LoadPlaceholderContentForPresentation(
                                 PlaceholderControlEventArgs e)
{
    EnsureChildControls();

    lblMessage.Text = "";

    try
    {
        xmlAsString = ((XmlPlaceholder)this.BoundPlaceholder).XmlAsString;

        if (xmlAsString != String.Empty)
        {
            // Convert the loaded XML to a DataSet
            System.IO.StringReader sr = new System.IO.StringReader(xmlAsString);
            ds = new DataSet();
            ds.ReadXml(sr);

            // Bind the Data to the DataGrid
            if (ds.Tables.Count > 0)
            {
                dg.DataSource = ds;
                dg.DataBind();
            }
        }
    }
    catch(Exception ex)
    {
        // Oops! We have an error. Write the error details to the Label
        // In an actual implementation, you may want to hide the DataGrid
        // altogether and not display an error message.
        lblMessage.Text = "Failed to load placeholder content for presentation: "
                          + ex.Message;
    }
}
```

Using the DataGrid Placeholder Control

We now have a working DataGrid placeholder control. It isn't complete yet, but we have done enough to give it a spin.

1. Follow the steps outlined in the *Adding the Placeholder Control to a Template File* section, and add the DataGrid placeholder control to a template file of your choice.

2. Add an `XmlPlaceholderDefinition` to the template. Give it the following `Description` and save the template:

   ```
   <TropicalPlants><Plant><CommonName></CommonName><Description></Description>
   </Plant></TropicalPlants>
   ```

3. Create a new posting based on the selected template. The DataGrid appears with the first row added, but it is empty. Click on the Edit button to set the plant's common name and description.

You will probably get a warning alert with the message:

Are you sure you want to navigate from this page? Refreshing or leaving this page will lose all unsaved changes. Please OK to continues, or Cancel to stay on the current page.

That doesn't sound friendly. We will show you how to remove this alert in the next section. Meanwhile, ignore it and click OK. Set the plant's common name to Hibiscus and the description to A beautiful plant.

Click Update. If the leave warning alert pops up again, just ignore it. Notice that the row now contains the modified content. Save the new page and approve it. Now, switch back to live mode and the contents of the DataGrid are presented as a table.

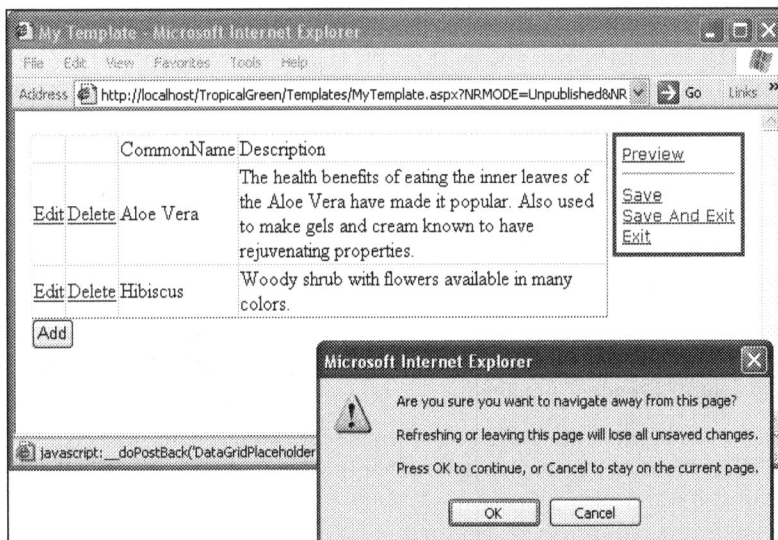

Turning Off the Leave Warning Alert

When trying out the DataGrid placeholder control, we saw that each time any of the buttons trigger a postback to the server, the leave warning alert pops up. We aren't actually leaving the page, we are merely refreshing it after a postback, so the alert really isn't necessary. Why does the alert keep popping up?

The reason lies in both the way the leave warning alert has been programmed and the how the DataGrid renders each button.

The leave warning alert was designed to appear when the browser's OnBeforeUnload() event is fired. Usually, this happens when the browser window closes or when the page navigates to a different location. If you look at the source code, you will find that the Edit, Update, and Delete buttons are generated as anchor tags:

```
<a href="javascript:__doPostBack('DataGridPlaceholderControl1$AuthoringModeCon
trolsContainer$_ctl0$_ctl2$_ctl0','')">Edit</a>
```

This means that when clicking on the Edit, Update, or Delete links, we have instructed the browser to unload the current page and refresh itself after the postback. Therefore, the OnBeforeUnload() event fires and the warning appears.

To prevent it from appearing, we could do one of three things:

- Suppress the alert entirely by setting the EnableLeaveAuthoringWarning attribute to false on the Web Author Console. While it's a possible solution, this isn't desirable as authors will still appreciate the warning to safeguard them from closing the browser before saving unfinished work.

- Change all links to HTML submit buttons that transmit the contents of the Web Form using an HTTP Post request so that the OnBeforeUnload() event does not get fired. Note for instance that you don't get the alert when you click on the Add button. Nevertheless, not everyone agrees that buttons are aesthetically pleasing, so this may not be always be the best solution.

- Modify the anchors to perform the postback from the onclick() event handler instead of from within the href attribute. The anchor's onclick() event behaves like the submit button. The page's URL does not change when it fires, therefore the OnBeforeUnload() event isn't triggered and we won't get the alert. Let's look at this solution in detail.

What we need to do is to cut the JavaScript that was originally generated within the anchor's href attribute and paste it into its onclick() event handler. An appropriate place to do so would be from within the control's Render() method.

We are only interested in performing this task when the DataGrid is being updated, so our code will only take effect in the AuthoringNew and AuthoringReedit modes. For all other modes, we'll leave the control as it is.

This is the regular expression that we will use to grab the href attribute and its value. The (?<PostBackScript>.*?) part of the statement stores the value of the href attribute in a variable named PostBackScript.

```
href=\"javascript(?<PostBackScript>.*?)\"
```

Once we locate the `href` attribute, we replace it with the following string. What used to be the value of the `href` attribute is now within the anchor's `onclick()` event handler.

```
href="#" onclick="${PostBackScript}$; return false;"
```

Add the overridden `Render()` method to the class:

```
protected override void Render(System.Web.UI.HtmlTextWriter output)
{
    // only do a change if in Authoring mode
    if (WebAuthorContext.Current.Mode == WebAuthorContextMode.AuthoringReedit
    || WebAuthorContext.Current.Mode == WebAuthorContextMode.AuthoringNew)
    {
        TextWriter tempWriter = new StringWriter();
        base.Render(new System.Web.UI.HtmlTextWriter(tempWriter));

        string orightml= tempWriter.ToString();

        // This regular expression grabs everything within the href attribute
        // including the href attribute itself
        Regex hrefRegex = new Regex("href=\"javascript(?<PostBackScript>.*?)\"",
                            RegexOptions.Singleline);

        // Replace the href to point to the page itself without changing its URL
        // Get the onclick() event to perform the postback instead
        string newhtml = hrefRegex.Replace(orightml, "href=\"#\""
                            + "onclick=\"${PostBackScript};return false;\"");

        output.Write(newhtml);
    }
    else
    {
        base.Render(output);
    }
}
```

Now try clicking on the Edit, Update, or Delete buttons. Notice that the leave warning alert does not appear anymore! However, if you try to close the browser, the alert pops up as it should.

> There is another problem when using postbacks: the page doesn't return to the point where you originally were after it refreshes. This can be annoying to authors. Imagine clicking on the Edit button and being brought back to the top of the page. You will have to scroll down to the exact location you were before the postback (which could be a long way down if the page is lengthy) to continue editing the row.
>
> To solve this problem, we need to find a way for the browser to "remember" where it was before the button was clicked. Several tools are available in the market that do this. Most rely on hidden form fields to store the position of the cursor as well as client-side routines to record the co-ordinates of the cursor.
>
> Here is the URL for one such example written by Steve Stchur for the website 4GuysFromRolla: http://aspnet.4guysfromrolla.com/articles/111704-1.aspx.

> ASP.NET provides a property called SmartNavigation that attempts to solve this problem. Unfortunately, SmartNavigation does not work with MCMS template files. If you turn it on, you will find that it has no effect on the form's behavior whatsoever, and the page still jumps on each postback.

Summary

The PAPI support for creating custom placeholder controls gives developers some powerful tools for tailoring websites to meet the demanding requirements of today's users. In this chapter, we covered five commonly requested placeholder controls:

- **The date-time picker placeholder control.** This provides authors with a calendar control, preventing invalid dates from being saved.

- **A placeholder control that accepts multiple attachments.** This allows template designers to specify the maximum number of attachments allowed in a control.

- **The Image rotator placeholder control.** This swaps images on each load and even displays Macromedia Flash files. It can be extended to show content from other file types.

- **A placeholder control to store all kinds of HTML tags.** This empowers authors to manage content that contains otherwise illegal HTML tags such as buttons with JavaScript.

- **A DataGrid placeholder control.** This eases the management and editing of structured XML content.

Over the course of this chapter, we have covered several tips and tricks that you should find useful when creating other types of custom controls. We showed how the MCMS Web Author dialogs can be reused from within a custom placeholder control, how a control can be programmed to work with existing structures such as the resource manager, and how the leave warning alert can be disabled when working with complex controls like the DataGrid.

9

Validating Placeholder Controls

Before content is saved, it is often necessary to validate it to ensure some level of data integrity. It's often necessary to look for empty fields, check for invalid date formats, or even compare values between two or more controls.

Typically web forms can't be submitted until such validation checks have been passed. For example, when an author attempts to submit a form without filling in a mandatory field, a friendly error message appears on the screen. He or she will have to enter content into the field before the form can be submitted successfully.

Such validation techniques are common in regular web applications. However, for MCMS websites, validation, if done at all, is often secondary. Part of the reason lies in the fact that ASP.NET validation controls, which work great with controls in regular web forms, do not work with MCMS placeholder controls.

To get around this problem, we need to build our own controls to validate MCMS placeholder controls. In this chapter, we show you how to build custom validation controls that check the contents of the following controls:

- `HtmlPlaceholderControl`
- `SingleImagePlaceholderControl`
- `SingleAttachmentPlaceholderControl`

Our validation controls will be able to ensure that each control has a value provided—something not possible using the regular ASP.NET validation controls. You can, of course, extend the examples in this chapter to perform more complex validation.

Limitations of the ASP.NET Validation Controls

ASP.NET provides several time-saving techniques for performing client-side and server-side validation in the form of a set of validation controls. There is the `RequiredFieldValidator` for ensuring that mandatory fields are never left empty, the `RangeValidator`, which checks that the entered value lies within acceptable limits, the `CompareValidator` for comparing values entered in two different controls, and the `RegularExpressionValidator`, which checks if the value matches the pattern defined by a given regular expression.

With minimal effort, developers can make use of these controls to provide validation within web forms. For example, to check that a required field has not been left empty, simply drag and drop the `RequiredFieldValidator` from the toolbox onto the web form, set the name of the control to be validated and a friendly error message to display. With the validation control in place, the form may only be submitted when the field is filled in. Otherwise, an error message appears on the screen.

Unfortunately, validating MCMS placeholder controls isn't as straightforward. Say, you have an `HtmlPlaceholderControl` that shouldn't be left blank. You drag and drop a `RequiredFieldValidator` onto the template file and set its `ControlToValidate` property to that of the placeholder control. The template looks complete.

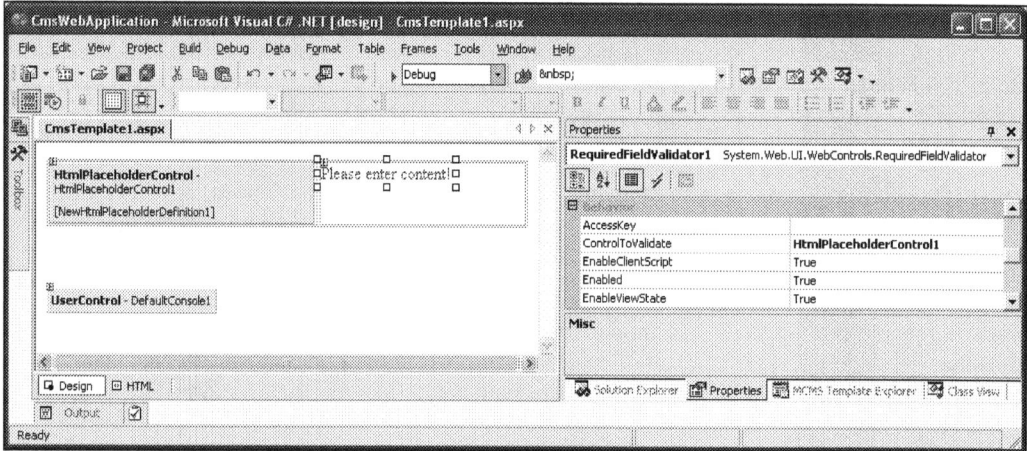

However, when you attempt to create a posting based on the template (or view an existing posting based on it), you get the following error message:

Control 'HtmlPlaceholderControl1' referenced by the ControlToValidate property of 'RequiredFieldValidator1' cannot be validated.

This technique does not work because the `RequiredFieldValidator` was designed for a limited subset of controls, including standard controls such as the `TextBox`, `ListBox`, `DropDownList`, and `RadioButtonList`, but not the `HtmlPlaceholderControl`, or any of the other MCMS placeholder controls for that matter.

So let's get started on this chapter's mission: building our own validation controls that will be suitable for MCMS placeholder controls.

The MCMSValidators Project

Before we begin writing the code samples in this chapter, let's create a project file to store our code:

1. In Visual Studio .NET, create a new Class Library project.
2. Name the new project MCMSValidators.

3. Add the following references to the project:
   - `System.Web`
   - `Microsoft.ContentManagement.Publishing.dll`
   - `Microsoft.ContentManagement.Publishing.Extensions.Placeholders.dll`
   - `Microsoft.ContentManagement.WebControls.dll`

   The library files from the `Microsoft.ContentManagement` namespace can be found in the `<install directory>/Microsoft Content Management Server/server/bin` directory.

4. Delete `Class1.cs`, the file that was generated by the wizard. We won't need it.

Validating the HtmlPlaceholderControl

The first control that we will build is a custom validation control that works with the `HtmlPlaceholderControl`. Our validator will ensure that some text has been entered into the control before the page can be saved. If the author forgets to fill in content, the page will not save and an error message appears on the screen.

The figure below shows how the control works when completed. The author has left `HtmlPlaceholderControl1` empty. When he or she tries to save the page, an error message, This is a required field, appears next to the placeholder, instructing him or her to fill it out before proceeding.

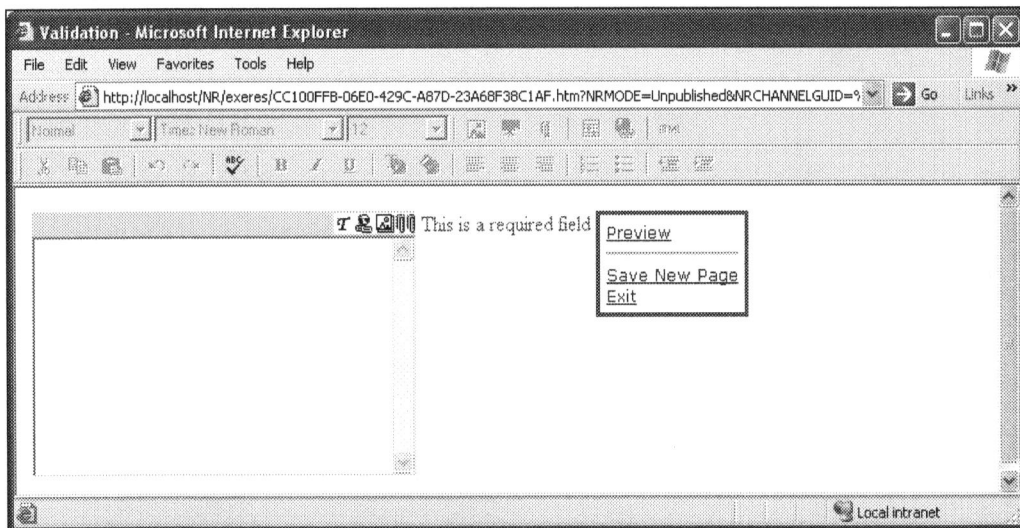

Retrieving the Current Value of the HtmlPlaceholderControl

In order to validate the `HtmlPlaceholderControl`, we need to first read off its contents. There are two ways to get its stored value—we could use server-side or client-side scripts.

We could choose to use server-side scripts and get the value stored in the `Html` property of the `HtmlPlaceholderControl` when the page does a postback. However, performing server-side validation introduces several levels of complexity to the design. After each postback, a check has to be done to see if the page is valid. Should one placeholder control contain invalid content, you need to cancel all attempts to save the page and ensure that all placeholders remember their unsaved values. That's a lot of work, which we will discuss in the section *Implementing Server-Side Validation*.

It's much simpler to perform the validation using client-side JavaScript. The trick is to retrieve the value of the `HTMLPlaceholderControl` from the client-side ActiveX control. To do so, we will have to dig a little deeper into the HTML code sent to the browser in Authoring mode.

Here's a snippet of the code sent to the browser in Authoring mode for an `HtmlPlaceholderControl` with the ID `HtmlPlaceholderControl1`. The key parts have been highlighted.

```
<span id="HtmlPlaceholderControl1" name="HtmlPlaceholderControl1">
. . . code continues . . .
<OBJECT
CODEBASE="/TropicalGreen/CMS/WebAuthor/Client/PlaceholderControlSupport/
NRDHtml.cab#Version=5,0,4484,0" ID="NCPHRICH_HtmlPlaceholderDefinition1"
CLASSID="CLSID:B33422AC-C567-4F7D-BB28-6583371EC4EE" width="300" height="300">
    <PARAM NAME="PostUrl" VALUE="/TropicalGreen/CMS/WebAuthor/Controls/
ActiveXHtmlEditControl/ActiveXUpload.aspx?NRMODE=Update&NRNODEGUID={1B5ED208-
75A5-4C86-A9FD-8A8B764FC805}&ph=About">
    <PARAM NAME="HTML" VALUE="">
    <PARAM NAME="CodePage" VALUE="65001">
    <PARAM NAME="Charset" VALUE="utf-8">
</OBJECT>
. . . code continues . . .
</span>
```

The generated ID of the ActiveX control is the name of the underlying `HtmlPlaceholder` object pre-pended with `NCPHRICH_`. We will use this ID to access the ActiveX control object from client-side script. The value to be retrieved is stored in the second `<PARAM>` tag named `HTML`. To retrieve the current content of the control, we simply use the `HTML` property as shown in the following code (don't worry about typing this in: we will show you how it's injected to the code file later). The JavaScript here copies the content of an `HtmlPlaceholderControl` to a variable named `content`.

```
<script language="javascript">
  var content = document.all.NCPHRICH_HtmlPlaceholderDefinition1.HTML
</script>
```

As MCMS Web Author supports only Internet Explorer 5.x and above, the client-side scripts used in this chapter have been written specifically for Internet Explorer browsers.

I'm working with the Telerik MCMS placeholder control. How can I use client-side scripts to access its content?

The technique for using client-side scripts to access content in the Telerik MCMS placeholder control is similar. First, we need to get the ID of the object that contains the HTML. To do so, enter some text into the Telerik MCMS placeholder control and save the page. Go back to authoring mode and view the HTML source of the page using Notepad. Press *Ctrl+F* and search for the text that you have just entered. Take note of the ID of the <div> tag that holds the content, which in v2.12 of the control resembles this:

```
radEditorContainer(ID of control)_AuthoringModeControlsContainer_Editor(ID
of Control)_AuthoringModeControlsContainer
```

For a placeholder control with the ID RadEditorPlaceholderControl1, the JavaScript that retrieves its content is as follows:

```
<script language="javascript">

var content =
document.all.radEditorContainerRadEditorPlaceholderControl1_AuthoringModeC
ontrolsContainer_EditorRadEditorPlaceholderControl1_AuthoringModeControlsC
ontainer.innerHTML;

</script>
```

Note that in different versions of the control, the ID given to the <div> tag surrounding the content varies. You will have to check the generated source code to get the ID of <div> tag for the particular version you are working with.

Checking for an Empty HtmlPlaceholderControl

Now that we know how to retrieve the current content of an HtmlPlaceholderControl, we can proceed to validate it. An HtmlPlaceholderControl is considered to be empty when one of the following conditions is met:

- It contains an empty string.
- It contains only invisible tags and spaces, like <p> </p>, or <p><div> </div></p> for example.

Depending on your requirements, you may also need to check to see if the placeholder content contains default text.

The JavaScript used to check for these conditions is covered in this section. The name of the control to be validated will be added to the name of the routine to ensure that if multiple validation controls have been placed on the same template file; they will each have their own client-side routines. The code makes use of the client-side isEmpty() method to check to see if the placeholder is empty.

There is a tiny glitch with the `HtmlPlaceholderControl`. When authors select all text and delete it (by pressing *Ctrl + A* followed by the *Delete* key), only visible content is removed. Instead of an empty placeholder control, what we may get is a control that has values such as: `<P> </P>`, `<div><font face=arial> </font></div>`—and other combinations of tags without text. When HTML source editing is not allowed, these tags are not seen by authors. To weed out empty tags, we will implement the `isEmpty()` routine. This routine may look complex at first but it's really quite simple.

The HTML stored in the placeholder could consist of tags that resemble one of the following:

Tags	Remarks	Valid?
`<img src="URLofMyPicture.gif"><hr>`	A single image or a horizontal rule	Yes
`<p><div> </div></p>`	Not an empty string but it also does not contain meaningful content	No
`<p><div>I love plants!</div></p>`	A mixture of text and tags	Yes

To detect empty placeholders, let's consider the first type of content—images and horizontal rules, which are defined by a single `<img>` or `<hr>` tag and do not require a closing tag. Placeholders storing such single-tagged elements are *not* empty placeholders. Our first task is to look for any of these tags within the content. As long as one of these tags exists, it's not empty. For example, if the stored HTML is `<p><img src="URLofMyPicture.gif"></p>`, it's not empty.

Once we have considered all visible tag elements, we look at all other tags. The only way to decide if the content is a mixture of text and tags or just a combination of meaningless tags is to remove all the tags and see what we have left. Here's how we will do it: a regular expression matches the opening and closing angle brackets of an HTML tag and everything between and is used to effectively delete all remaining tags. Say the placeholder contains the following HTML:

```
<div><font face=arial> This Placeholder has Content </font></div>
```

The regular expression removes all tags, so the `<div></div>` and `<font></font>` tags will be stripped away. After it has done its job, we are left with only:

```
 This Placeholder has Content 
```

Finally, we remove spaces and non-breaking spaces (` `), which leaves us with the following string of text:

```
ThisPlaceholderhasContent
```

At the end of the process, if the placeholder still contains text, it means that it isn't empty.

The complete JavaScript routine is shown below. Again, don't worry about coding it. We will show you how it can be used in a custom validation control right after this.

```
<script language="javascript">
function validateHtmlPlaceholderControl1
{
  var content = document.all.NCPHRICH_HtmlPlaceholderDefinition1.HTML
  if (isEmpty(content))
  {
    // content is invalid
    return false;
  }
```

```
      else
      {
        // content is valid
        return true;
      }
    }
    function isEmpty(content)
    {
      // Add more tags to ignore in this list if you need to.
      // Here, we ignore <hr> and <img> tags
      // Additional tags should be added and separated with a "|" character.
      var tagsToKeep = "img|hr";

      // This regular expression matches all <img> and <hr> tags
      var regExpTagsToKeep = "<\\s*(" + tagsToKeep + ")\\b[^>]*>";
      var reTagsToKeep = new RegExp(regExpTagsToKeep, "gim");

      // exit if one of the tags to keep is included.
      if (content.match(reTagsToKeep))
      {
        // Placeholder is not empty.
        return false;
      }

      // This regular expression gets all tags in the content
      var regExpForAllTags = "<[^>]*>";
      var reAllTags = new RegExp(regExpForAllTags,"gim");

      // Remove all tags by replacing with an empty string
      content = content.replace(reAllTags, "");

      // Remove all spaces and non-breaking spaces ( )
      content = content.replace(" ","");
      content = content.replace(" ","");

      if (content == "")
      {
        // if after removing all tags, we are left with an empty string
        // Placeholder is empty.
        return true;
      }
      else
      {
        // if after removing all tags, we still have content.
        // Placeholder is not empty.
        return false;
      }
    }
  </script>
```

Matching Tags with Regular Expressions

The isEmpty() JavaScript function we've just seen makes use of two regular expressions. The first checks the HTML for instances of <img> and <hr> tags. Recall that as long as the HTML contains these single tagged items, it's not empty. Let's take a closer look at the expression:

```
<[\s|/]*(img|hr)\b[^>]*>
```

The first and last characters, < and >, match the opening and closing angle brackets of all HTML tags.

After the opening angled bracket comes the escape sequence for a space or a forward slash, followed by an asterisk (the Kleene star), \s*. This ensures that tags with spaces after the opening angle bracket (such as < img>) and closing tags are included in the match.

The next part of the expression is a parenthesized list of the tags we're looking for, (img|hr). We follow it with the boundary symbol, \b, which ensures tags that include "img" and "hr" in their names, like <funnyhrtag> or <strangeimgtag>, will not be included in the match.

Finally, the character class [^>]* matches all characters except the closing angle bracket. This means that it doesn't matter what lies between <img (or <hr) and the closing angle bracket, >, so the tag can have any number of attributes, for instance <img border="0" name="img1"> or <hr width="100%">, and the expression will still match it.

The second regular expression, that matches all tags regardless of what lies between the angled brackets, is simpler, and you might be able to deduce how it does its work:

```
<[^>]*>
```

We have the opening and closing angle brackets, and between them the character class, [^>]*, which as before matches all characters except for the closing angle bracket.

Building the Required HTML Placeholder Validator

We are ready to build the RequiredHtmlPHValidator—a validator that ensures that authors do not leave an HtmlPlaceholderControl empty before the page is saved. To begin, add a class file named RequiredHtmlPHValidator.cs to the MCMSValidators project. Add the following namespaces above the namespace declaration.

```
using System;
using System.Text;
using System.Text.RegularExpressions;
using System.Web.UI;
using System.Web.UI.WebControls;
using Microsoft.ContentManagement.WebControls;
using Microsoft.ContentManagement.Publishing;
using Microsoft.ContentManagement.Publishing.Extensions.Placeholders;
namespace MCMSValidators
{
    . . . code continues . . .
}
```

Instead of starting from scratch, our control will inherit the BaseValidator class of the System.Web.UI.WebControls library. BaseValidator already has the basic elements for web control validation such as the ControlToValidate and ErrorMessage properties. This will allow us to implement our control with less code.

```
. . . code continues . . .
public class RequiredHTMLPHValidator: BaseValidator
{
}
. . . code continues . . .
```

We don't have to do anything within the RequiredHTMLPHValidator() constructor, so we will leave that empty.

To implement the RequiredHTMLPHValidator control, we will override the following methods of the BaseValidator class.

Method Name	What we will program it to do
`ControlPropertiesValid()`	Check to see if the control specified in the `ControlToValidate` property is an `HtmlPlaceholderControl`. If it isn't, the validation control will not be generated when the page loads.
`OnPreRender()`	Inject the client-side JavaScript that checks for empty placeholder controls.
`AddAttributesToRender()`	Pass the name of the client-side JavaScript to be called to the built-in `evaluationfunction()` method used by all ASP.NET validation controls. Without this step, the script injected in the `OnPreRender()` method will not be fired when the page is validated.
`EvaluateIsValid()`	We will write logic for performing server-side validation here.

Overriding the ControlPropertiesValid() Method

Let's start by overriding the `ControlPropertiesValid()` method of the base class, `BaseValidator`. The `ControlPropertiesValid()` method returns a Boolean that indicates whether or not the control to be validated exists and is of the correct object type. In this case, we want it to return true only when the control specified can be found. If the object exists, we proceed to check to see if it is indeed an `HtmlPlaceholderControl`.

When the control specified does not exist or isn't a `HtmlPlaceholderControl`, the `ControlPropertiesValid()` property returns false and the validation control will not be generated when the page loads.

Add the `ControlPropertiesValid()` method directly below the `RequiredHTMLPHValidator()` constructor:

```
protected override bool ControlPropertiesValid()
{
  Control ctrl = FindControl(ControlToValidate);

  if (ctrl != null)
  {
    return (ctrl is HtmlPlaceholderControl);
  }
  else
  {
    return false;
  }
}
```

Overriding the OnPreRender() Method

Next, we will make use of the client-side JavaScript that we wrote in the previous section. Being a server-side control, we can't enter the script as it is. We need to inject it into the page by calling the `Page.RegisterClientScript()` method. An appropriate place to do so would be in the overridden `OnPreRender()` method of our custom validator.

Is it possible to put the entire JavaScript in an external *.js file rather than injecting it into the page?

You could put the entire JavaScript into an external *.js file. However, the script is dynamically generated based on the name of the control to validate. For it to work from a static file, you will have to fix the name of the validate() function and modify it to accept the name of the control to validate as an input parameter.

Another compelling reason to inject the script instead of maintaining it in a separate *.js file is to facilitate deployment. By injecting the code, we only need to install the single library file (in our case that's MCMSValidators.dll) and not worry about the path or the existence of the *.js file as well. In addition, we can put aside any concerns about old cached versions of the file should the script be updated.

Add the OnPreRender() method directly below the ControlPropertiesValid() method:

```
// register the client-side validation script
protected override void OnPreRender(System.EventArgs e)
{
  base.OnPreRender(e);
  // Add the script only in authoring mode.
  if (WebAuthorContext.Current.Mode == WebAuthorContextMode.AuthoringNew
   || WebAuthorContext.Current.Mode == WebAuthorContextMode.AuthoringReedit)
  {
    string phName = "NCPHRICH_";
    if ((FindControl(this.ControlToValidate)) == null
     || !(FindControl(this.ControlToValidate) is HtmlPlaceholderControl))
      return;
    phName += ((HtmlPlaceholderControl)FindControl(this.ControlToValidate) )
            .BoundPlaceholder.Name;
    StringBuilder sb = new StringBuilder();
    sb.Append("<script language=\"javascript\">");
    sb.Append("function validate" + this.ControlToValidate + "()      \n");
    sb.Append("{                                                       \n");
    sb.Append("   var content = document.all." + phName + ".HTML;      \n");
    sb.Append("   if (ReqHtmlPhValid_isEmpty(content))                 \n");
    sb.Append("   {                                                    \n");
    sb.Append("     return false;                                      \n");
    sb.Append("   }                                                    \n");
    sb.Append("   else                                                 \n");
    sb.Append("   {                                                    \n");
    sb.Append("     return true;                                       \n");
    sb.Append("   }                                                    \n");
    sb.Append("}                                                       \n");
    sb.Append("</script>");

    StringBuilder sb2 = new StringBuilder();
    sb2.Append("\n<script language=\"javascript\">               \n");
    sb2.Append("function ReqHtmlPhValid_isEmpty(content)              \n");
    sb2.Append("{                                                     \n");
    sb2.Append("   // Add more tags to ignore if you need to          \n");
    sb2.Append("   // Here, we ignore <hr> and <img> tags             \n");
    sb2.Append("   // additional tags need to be added and separated  \n");
    sb2.Append("   // with a '|' character.                           \n");
    sb2.Append("   var tagsToKeep = \"img|hr\";                       \n");
    sb2.Append("   // This reg ex matches all <img> and <hr> tags     \n");
    sb2.Append("   var regExpTagsToKeep =                             \n");
    sb2.Append("     \"<[\\\\s|/]*(\" + tagsToKeep + \")\\\\b[^>]*>\"; \n");
```

```
sb2.Append("var reTagsToKeep=new RegExp(regExpTagsToKeep,\"gim\");  \n");
sb2.Append("   // Check if a tag to keep is included & exit         \n");
sb2.Append("   if (content.match(reTagsToKeep))                      \n");
sb2.Append("   {                                                     \n");
sb2.Append("      // Placeholder is not empty.                       \n");
sb2.Append("       return false;                                     \n");
sb2.Append("   }                                                     \n");
sb2.Append("   // This reg ex gets all tags in the content           \n");
sb2.Append("   var regExpForAllTags = \"<[^>]*>\";                   \n");
sb2.Append("   var reAllTags = new RegExp(regExpForAllTags,\"gim\"); \n");
sb2.Append("   // Remove all Tags by replacing with an empty string  \n");
sb2.Append("   content = content.replace(reAllTags, \"\");           \n");
sb2.Append("   // Remove all spaces and non-breaking spaces ( ) \n");
sb2.Append("   content = content.replace(\" \",\"\");                \n");
sb2.Append("   content = content.replace(\" \",\"\");           \n");
sb2.Append("   if (content == \"\")                                  \n");
sb2.Append("   {                                                     \n");
sb2.Append("      // All tags removed, leaving an empty string       \n");
sb2.Append("      // Placeholder is empty.                           \n");
sb2.Append("      return true;                                       \n");
sb2.Append("   }                                                     \n");
sb2.Append("   else                                                  \n");
sb2.Append("   {                                                     \n");
sb2.Append("      // After removing all tags, we still have content  \n");
sb2.Append("      // Placeholder is not empty.                       \n");
sb2.Append("      return false;                                      \n");
sb2.Append("   }                                                     \n");
sb2.Append("}                                                        \n");
sb2.Append("</script>");

if (this.RenderUplevel && this.EnableClientScript)
{
  if (!Page.IsClientScriptBlockRegistered("ReqHtmlPhValid_" + phName
                                 + "_ClientScript"))
  {
    Page.RegisterClientScriptBlock("ReqHtmlPhValid_" + phName +
                                 "_ClientScript", sb.ToString());
  }

  if (!Page.IsClientScriptBlockRegistered("ReqHtmlPhValid_IsEmpty"))
  {
    Page.RegisterClientScriptBlock("ReqHtmlPhValid_IsEmpty ",
                                 sb2.ToString());
  }
}
}
}
```

Notice that we registered the validate*NameOfControlToValidate*() and
ReqHtmlPhValid_isEmpty() methods within two separate client script blocks. By registering the
first client script block with a unique key, ReqHtmlPhValid_*NameOfPlaceholder*_ClientScript,
each validation control will have its own version of the validate*NameOfControlToValidate*()
method. The second client script block is registered with a fixed key named
ReqHtmlPhValid_IsEmpty. By fixing the key, only one copy of the ReqHtmlPhValid_isEmpty()
method will be generated even if there are multiple validation controls on the same page.

Overriding the AddAttributesToRender() Method

Now that we have defined the client-side validate*NameOfControlToValidate*() method that
performs the validation, we need figure out how to trigger it when the page is validated. To do so
we will borrow some functionality found in the ASP.NET WebUIValidation.js script. The

`WebUIValidation.js` script file contains methods that support client-side validation, so we can use it to save us re-writing all that functionality from scratch. Before we do so, let's take a look at how client-side validation works with regular ASP.NET validation controls.

Consider the case of a simple web form that contains several fields, including an ASP.NET button. When the button is clicked, the fields are validated. How does the action of clicking the button trigger validation? For the answer, take a look at the generated HTML code for the button; here's what you will see:

```
<input type="submit"
       name="Button1"
       value="Button"
     onclick="if (typeof(Page_ClientValidate)=='function')
Page_ClientValidate();"
       language="javascript"
            id="Button1" />
```

Notice that embedded within the `onclick` event of the button, is a call to a method named `Page_ClientValidate()`. The `Page_ClientValidate()` function is defined within the `WebUIValidation.js` file and looks like this:

```
function Page_ClientValidate()
{
  var i;
  for (i = 0; i < Page_Validators.length; i++) {
    ValidatorValidate(Page_Validators[i]);
  }
  . . . code continues . . .
}
```

The `Page_ClientValidate()` method in turn calls the `ValidatorValidate()` method (also found within the `WebUIValidation.js` file) for each validation control found on the page. The `ValidatorValidate()` method performs the crucial step of retrieving the name of the client-side validation routine from an attribute named `evaluationfunction` (highlighted below) and executes it.

```
function ValidatorValidate(val)
{
  . . . code continues . . .
  if (typeof(val.evaluationfunction) == "function")
  {
    val.isvalid = val.evaluationfunction(val);
  }
  . . . code continues . . .
}
```

Therefore, in order to trigger our client-side routine when the page validates, we will have to add an attribute named `evaluationfunction` to the validation control and assign the name of our function, `validateNameOfControlToValidate`, as its value.

The good new is that the `BaseValidator` class has just the method for adding attributes. It's called `AddAttributestoRender()`. We will override this method in the base class to insert the `evaluationfunction` attribute to the control. Add the following code directly below the `OnPreRender()` method:

```
// Wiring the client-side javascript to the WebUIValidation.js script file
protected override void AddAttributesToRender(System.Web.UI.HtmlTextWriter
writer)
{
  base.AddAttributesToRender(writer);
```

```
if (this.RenderUplevel && this.EnableClientScript)
{
    // Perform validation only in authoring mode.
    if (WebAuthorContext.Current.Mode == WebAuthorContextMode.AuthoringNew
     || WebAuthorContext.Current.Mode == WebAuthorContextMode.AuthoringReedit)
    {
        writer.AddAttribute("evaluationfunction", "validate"
                            + this.ControlToValidate);
    }
}
}
```

Overriding the EvaluateIsValid() Method

To complete the code, we need to implement the `EvaluateIsValid()` method of the base class or the project will not compile. This is where we implement server-side checks. For now, we will leave the `EvaluateIsValid()` empty and program it to always return `true`. While this isn't something you should do in a production environment, don't worry. We'll be filling this method out later to provide server-side validation in the section *Implementing Server-Side Validation*. Add the `EvaluateIsvalid()` method directly below the `AddAttributesToRender()` method.

```
protected override bool EvaluateIsValid()
{
    bool valid = true;
    return valid;
}
```

The custom validation control is now complete. Save and compile the solution.

Adding the Custom Validator to the Template File

Before using our custom control, we first need to copy it to the `bin` directory of our project file or add it as a reference to the MCMS web application project. After you have done that, add the control to the Visual Studio .NET Toolbox by choosing the **Add/Remove Items** option (or **Customize Toolbox** option for VS.NET 2002). You can then drag and drop it onto template files. For the control to work properly, you will have to set the `ControlToValidate` property to contain the value of the ID of the `HtmlPlaceholderControl` that you are validating and the `ErrorMessage` property to contain a friendly error message for the author.

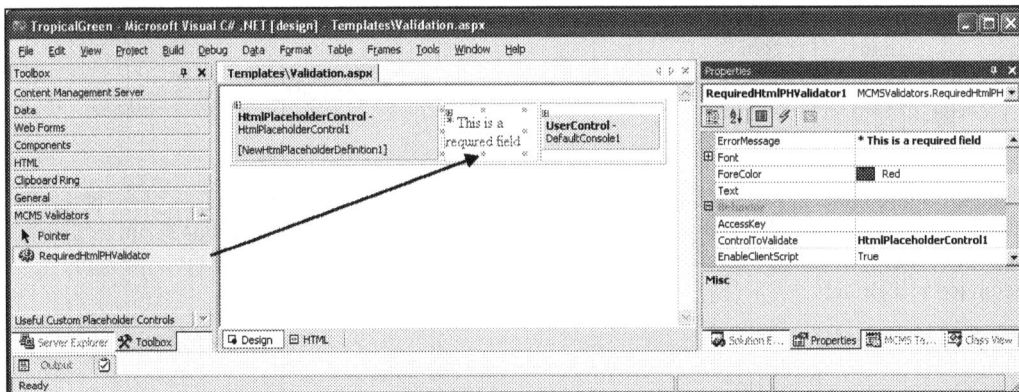

The ID of the HtmlPlaceholderControl does not appear in the ControlToValidate dropdown list. Shouldn't the dropdown list be populated with placeholder IDs that match the type of control being validated?

In order for the ID of the control to be included in the dropdown, we have to make the `HtmlPlaceholderControl` compatible with the ASP.NET validation control architecture. We will do just this in the section, *The HtmlPlaceholderControl with Validation*.

Preventing Pages with Invalid Content from Being Saved

There's still a problem to be tackled. Although the custom validation control has all the necessary code, it won't work unless someone clicks on an ASP.NET control, such as a Button, that has its `Control.CausesValidation` property set to true. Otherwise, the page will still be saved even if required placeholders are not filled in.

If you looked at the way the controls on the Default Console are coded (in the `Defaultconsole.ascx` file), you will find that they are simply HTML anchor tags. HTML anchor tags are not buttons and therefore do not trigger page validations. As a result, clicking on any of the action links on the console will not fire our custom validation control.

We need the validator to fire when the user clicks one of the following three action buttons:

- Save New Page
- Save
- Save and Exit

We will modify the behavior of each of the three buttons to cancel the save action when the page is not valid.

To find out how to force each of these controls to validate the page when clicked, we will once again get clues from ASP.NET. Earlier, we saw how ASP.NET generates a Button control:

```
<input type="submit"
       name="Button1"
      value="Button"
    onclick="if (typeof(Page_ClientValidate)=='function')
Page_ClientValidate();"
     language="javascript"
           id="Button1" />
```

The highlighted line shows the code used to ensure that client-side validation takes place before the form is submitted. It basically calls the `Page_ClientValidation()` client-side script of the `WebUIValidation.js` file. This line of code ensures our HTML anchors will exhibit the same behavior as a Button.

We need to insert it before calling the client-side save methods, which means we should modify each of the three Console Action buttons, starting with the Save New Page control.

Save New Page with Validation

Add a class file named ValidatedSaveNewAction.cs to the MCMSValidators project. Above the namespace declaration, add the following required namespaces:

```
using System;
using Microsoft.ContentManagement.Publishing;
using Microsoft.ContentManagement.WebControls;
using Microsoft.ContentManagement.WebControls.ConsoleControls;
namespace MCMSValidators
{
}
```

Instead of re-writing the Save New Page action control from scratch, we will create it by inheriting from the AuthoringSaveNewAction class:

```
public class ValidatedSaveNewAction : AuthoringSaveNewAction
{
}
```

The only modification we need to make is to override the ActionJavascript property. We first check to see if the control is available to the user. If it is, we look for the presence of validation controls using the Page.Validators.Count property. Once we have ascertained that there are validation controls present, we inject the JavaScript statement to call the Page_ClientValidate() method.

Below the ValidatedSaveNewAction() constructor, add the overridden ActionJavascript property:

```
public override string ActionJavascript
{
  get
  {
    string strReturn = null;
    if (this.Available)
    {
      // Check to see if we have any validation controls on this page
      if (this.Page.Validators.Count > 0)
      {
        strReturn += "if (typeof(Page_ClientValidate) == 'function') ";
        strReturn += "{";
        strReturn += "    if (!Page_ClientValidate()) return false;";
        strReturn += "}";
      }
      strReturn += base.ActionJavascript;
    }
    return strReturn;
  }
}
```

Save and Exit with Validation

The next button that we will modify is the Save and Exit button. Add a class file named ValidatedReeditSaveAndExitAction.cs to the MCMSValidators project. Insert the required namespaces as shown below:

```
using System;
using Microsoft.ContentManagement.Publishing;
using Microsoft.ContentManagement.WebControls;
using Microsoft.ContentManagement.WebControls.ConsoleControls;
namespace MCMSValidators
{
}
```

Like the Save New Page action control, we will modify the Save and Exit control by inheriting directly from the AuthoringReeditSaveAndExitAction class.

```
public class ValidatedReeditSaveAndExitAction :
AuthoringReeditSaveAndExitAction
{
}
```

We will override the ActionJavascript method in exactly the same way as for the Save New Page action control. Add the ActionJavascript method directly below the ValidatedReeditSaveAndExitAction() constructor:

```
public override string ActionJavascript
{
  get
  {
    string strReturn = null;
    if (this.Available)
    {
      // Check to see if we have any validation controls on this page
      if (this.Page.Validators.Count > 0)
      {
        strReturn += "if (typeof(Page_ClientValidate) == 'function') ";
        strReturn += "{";
        strReturn += "   if (!Page_ClientValidate()) return false;";
        strReturn += "}";
      }
      strReturn += base.ActionJavascript;
    }
    return strReturn;
  }
}
```

Save with Validation

Finally, we will modify the Save button. Add another class to the MCMSValidators project. Name the new class file ValidatedReeditSaveAction.cs. The implementation of this class file is exactly the same as the earlier two except that it inherits from the AuthoringReeditSaveAction class. The code below shows the complete code file:

```
using System;
using Microsoft.ContentManagement.Publishing;
using Microsoft.ContentManagement.WebControls;
using Microsoft.ContentManagement.WebControls.ConsoleControls;
namespace MCMSValidators
{
  public class ValidatedReeditSaveAction : AuthoringReeditSaveAction
  {
    public ValidatedReeditSaveAction()
    {}
    public override string ActionJavascript
    {
      get
      {
        string strReturn = null;
        if (this.Available)
        {
          // Check to see if we have any validation controls on this page
          if (this.Page.Validators.Count > 0)
          {
            strReturn += "if (typeof(Page_ClientValidate) == 'function') ";
            strReturn += "{";
```

```
                    strReturn += "        if (!Page_ClientValidate()) return false;";
                    strReturn += "}";
                }
                strReturn += base.ActionJavascript;
            }
            return strReturn;
        }
    }
  }
}
```

The three modified console action buttons are complete. Save and compile the solution.

Adding the Modified Buttons to the Authoring Console

Now that we have modified the three buttons that trigger a save, we can use them to replace the ones on the Default Console by updating the `DefaultConsole.ascx` file. Before we do, it is a good idea to make a backup of it so we can always revert to a working version.

Open the `DefaultConsole.ascx` file in HTML view (you can find it in the `Console` folder of your MCMS web application project). At the top of the file, right after the `<% Control %>` directive, add the following statement:

```
<%@ Register TagPrefix="ValidatedControls"
    Namespace="MCMSValidators" Assembly="MCMSValidators" %>
```

Locate each of the save buttons to be replaced, starting with the **Save New Page** button. Look for the following block of code:

```
<CmsConsole:AuthoringSaveNewAction id="AuthoringSaveNewAction1"
    runat="server">
<A id="AuthoringSaveNewAnchor" href="#" target=_self
    onclick="<%# Container.ActionJavascript %>;return false" >
<%# Container.Text %>
</A>
<BR>
</CmsConsole:AuthoringSaveNewAction>
```

Replace it with this code that uses our modified Save New Page action control:

```
<ValidatedControls:ValidatedSaveNewAction id="ValidatedSaveNewAction1"
    runat="server">
<A id="ValidatedSaveNewAnchor" href="#" target=_self
    onclick="<%# Container.ActionJavascript %>;return false" >
<%# Container.Text %>
</A>
<BR>
</ValidatedControls:ValidatedSaveNewAction>
```

Next, replace the Save and Save and Exit buttons. Locate the following block of code (hint: search for the string `AuthoringReeditSaveAction`):

```
<CmsConsole:AuthoringReeditSaveAction id="AuthoringReeditSaveAction1"
    runat="server">
<A id="AuthoringReeditSaveAnchor" href="#" target=_self
    onclick="<%# Container.ActionJavascript %>;return false" >
<%# Container.Text %>
</A>
<BR />
</CmsConsole:AuthoringReeditSaveAction>
<CmsConsole:AuthoringReeditSaveAndExitAction
            id="AuthoringReeditSaveAndExitAction1" runat="server">
```

```
<A id="AuthoringReeditSaveAndExitAnchor" href="#" target=_self
   onclick="<%# Container.ActionJavascript %>;return false" >
<%# Container.Text %>
</A>
<BR />
</CmsConsole:AuthoringReeditSaveAndExitAction>
```

Replace it with the following that uses the modified buttons for Save and Save and Exit:

```
<ValidatedControls:ValidatedReeditSaveAction id="ValidatedReeditSaveAction1"
   runat="server">
<A id="ValidatedReeditSaveAnchor" href="#" target=_self
   onclick="<%# Container.ActionJavascript %>;return false" >
<%# Container.Text %>
</A>
<BR />
</ValidatedControls:ValidatedReeditSaveAction>
<ValidatedControls:ValidatedReeditSaveAndExitAction
   id="ValidatedReeditSaveAndExitAction1" runat="server">
<A id="ValidatedReeditSaveAndExitAnchor" href="#" target=_self
   onclick="<%# Container.ActionJavascript %>;return false" >
<%# Container.Text %>
</A>
<BR />
</ValidatedControls:ValidatedReeditSaveAndExitAction>
```

The new console actions are now active.

The next time you attempt to save the page without first entering something into the HtmlPlaceholderControl that is validated, the page will not be saved, and an error message will be produced on the client without a round trip to the server.

Implementing Server-Side Validation

We have seen how validation can be performed against the HtmlPlaceholderControl using client-side scripts. Client-side validation essentially reduces round-trips to the server just to find out if they have left out any fields. However, client-side validation does have its limitations. For instance, we can't exactly be 100% sure that the validation did take place on the client. The user could have made a copy of the page, fired up his or her favorite HTML editing tool and modified the page to remove any form of validation. If that happens, invalid content may still find its way into the system.

In addition, not all types of validation can be done on the client. For example, you may need to match the contents of a placeholder control against an existing store of information in an online database. Or perhaps requirements dictate performing routines that can only be executed on the server.

In this example, we will extend our simple check for an empty placeholder control. Instead of the JavaScript validation on the client, we will do it server-side.

To be absolutely sure that validation is being performed on the server, let's throw in an extra check. We will check to see if the user has entered a minimum of 50 characters of text—a common requirement for articles that require say, a summary of at least a certain length. You can of course, extend the code to perform more complex validation routines.

The trouble with server-side validation is that the default placeholder controls are not designed to deal with it without some customization. Here is what we have to do to get it to work. We will need to:

- Build the RequiredHtmlPHValidator described earlier.

- Modify the HtmlPlaceholderControl to cancel the save in the event the server-side validation fails. We do this by creating our own custom placeholder control.

- Replace all HtmlPlaceholderControls that require server-side validation with the custom placeholder control.

- And finally, modify all save action controls to cancel the entire save operation when one or more placeholders contain invalid content.

The HtmlPlaceholderControl with Validation

We've already built the RequiredHtmlPHValidator control so let's dive straight in and build a custom HtmlPlaceholderControl that understands validation. Add a class file to the MCMSValidators project and name it HtmlPHWithValidation.cs. Add the required namespaces above the namespace declaration as shown below:

```
using System;
using System.Web.UI;
using Microsoft.ContentManagement.WebControls;
using Microsoft.ContentManagement.Publishing;
namespace MCMSValidators
{
}
```

As our custom control will have all the features of HtmlPlaceholderControl, let's inherit directly from it.

```
public class HtmlPHWithValidation : HtmlPlaceholderControl
{
}
```

Next, we will add the ValidationProperty attribute, which instantly makes the HtmlPlaceholderControl compatible with the ASP.NET validation architecture:

- When setting the ControlToValidate property of matching validation controls, the HtmlPlaceholderControl's ID will appear in the dropdown (recall that previously, we had to type in the ID manually).

- You will be able to use the control with all ASP.NET validation controls. If you were to add, say, the RequiredFieldValidator and set its ControlToValidate property to that of our custom placeholder control, validation will now take place without any errors.

Add the ValidationProperty attribute above the class declaration and specify Html as the property to be validated.

```
[ValidationProperty("Html")]
public class HtmlPHWithValidation : HtmlPlaceholderControl
{
}
```

If adding the ValidationProperty attribute makes the control compatible with all ASP.NET validation controls, why didn't we use this approach to validate placeholder content?

Technically, we could have simply added the ValidationProperty attribute to all placeholder controls and used this approach to address the problems raised in the earlier section.

However, there are several reasons why we did not do so. Firstly, HTML isn't exactly plain text. You would still need to find ways to run the regular expressions to check to see if the placeholder control was really empty.

In addition, if you used this approach to validate MCMS placeholder controls, you would find that validation occured in all publishing modes. This means that when the placeholder control contains invalid content, the error message appears even in published mode! To hide the error message, you would have to customize the validation control to perform validation only in the AuthoringNew and AuthoringReedit modes as we did in the example above.

Adding the ValidationProperty attribute isn't a magic bullet; a fair amount of customization is still required.

When validation of the page fails, we need to cancel the save event. To do so, we will modify the behavior of the placeholder control's OnSavingContent() event handler. The OnSaving() event handler is called just before the contents are written to the content repository, so it gives us a chance to cancel the event should the content not be valid.

First, we will trigger validation by calling the Page.Validate() method. The code that gets triggered is the EvaluateIsValid() function of the RequiredHtmlPHValidator we built earlier. We did not really require the results of this method then as we depended on client-side JavaScript to perform the validation. However, during server-side validation, the result returned by this function is crucial. It decides whether or not the content is valid and if the page should be saved.

We check the results of the Page.Validate() method by looking at the Page.IsValid flag. If validation is successful, we save the page. Otherwise, the save is canceled by setting e.Cancel to be true. It is probably worthwhile to note that when canceling the save, the contents of the placeholder control are not erased or modified. The control still holds the invalid data. It is therefore important to give meaningful error messages that are displayed on the screen so that the author knows that the save has failed.

Add the overridden OnSavingContent() method directly below the HtmlPHWithValidation() constructor.

```
protected override void OnSavingContent(PlaceholderControlSavingEventArgs e)
{
  Page.Validate();
  if (!Page.IsValid)
  {
    e.Cancel = true;
  }
```

```
        else
        {
            base.OnSavingContent(e);
        }
    }
```

And the control is complete!

The RequiredHTMLPHValidator with Server-Side Validation

Earlier, when building the `RequiredHtmlPHValidator` control, we took a quick look at how server-side validation could be accomplished, but didn't actually write the code that does the work. Let's revisit the control and finish up the code by repeating the logic for checking to see if the control contains content on the server-side.

First, we will modify the `EvaluateIsValid()` method to perform validation only when in update mode. We look for the `HtmlPlaceholderControl` to validate and use the Boolean `IsEmpty()` method (defined next), which returns true when the placeholder is empty and false otherwise.

```
protected override bool EvaluateIsValid()
{
    bool valid = true;
    // perform validation only in update mode
    if (CmsHttpContext.Current.Mode == PublishingMode.Update)
    {
        HtmlPlaceholderControl ctrl;
        ctrl = FindControl(ControlToValidate) as HtmlPlaceholderControl;
        if (IsEmpty(ctrl.Html))
        {
            valid = false;
        }
    }
    return valid;
}
```

Next, we add the `IsEmpty()` method directly below the `EvaluateIsValid()` method. It's the server-side version of the JavaScript routine that we coded earlier.

```
private bool IsEmpty(string content)
{
    // Add more tags to ignore in this list if you need to.
    // Here, we ignore <hr> and <img> tags
    // additional tags need to be added and separated
    // with a '|' character.
    string tagsToKeep = "img|hr";

    // This regular expression matches all <img> and <hr> tags
    string regExpTagsToKeep = "<\\s*(" + tagsToKeep + ")\\b[^>]*>";
    Regex reTagsToKeep = new Regex(regExpTagsToKeep,
                RegexOptions.IgnoreCase | RegexOptions.Compiled);

    // Check if one of the tags to keep is included and exit.
    if (reTagsToKeep.IsMatch(content))
    {
        // Placeholder is not empty.
        return false;
    }

    // This regular expression gets all tags in the content
    string regExpForAllTags = "<[^>]*>";
    Regex reAllTags = new Regex(regExpForAllTags,
            RegexOptions.IgnoreCase | RegexOptions.Compiled);
```

```
    // Remove all Tags by replacing with an empty string
    content = reAllTags.Replace(content, "");

    // Remove all spaces and non-breaking spaces ( )
    content = content.Replace(" ","");
    content = content.Replace(" ","");

    if (content == "")
    {
       // All tags removed, we are left with an empty string
       // Placeholder is empty.
       return true;
    }
    else
    {
       // After removing all tags, we still have content.
       // Placeholder is not empty.
       return false;
    }
  }
}
```

You may be wondering why we performed the same type of validation twice. After all, if the client-side routine checks to see if the placeholder is empty, why repeat the same inspection on the server? This is just an added precaution to be double-sure that validation does occur. Most of the time, the client-side validation routine executes without a hitch. However, it's always a good idea to repeat the validation on the server as well to address what-if scenarios where the client-side routine fails. For instance, there could be a bug that prevented the client script from running, or perhaps authors could have disabled client-scripts on their browsers. Without checking the content again on the server, there is a possibility, no matter how small, of saving invalid content.

Checking the Length of Text Entered

We mentioned earlier that we plan to do more than check for empty placeholders. In this example, we will add an extra check to see if the author has entered at least 50 characters of text.

Let's go back to the `EvaluateIsValid()` method of the `RequiredHTMLPHValidator.cs` class. We will add a call to `IsLessThanMin()` to decide whether or not the content has met the minimum length requirement.

The limit is stored in the `MinLength` property value. Developers can set its value using get and set accessors. The default value of 0 implies that there is no limit to the amount of text entered. So in our case, the developer will have to set the `MinLength` property to 50.

As we are only interested in actual text, not tags, we will filter out all tags from the content using the `RemoveAllTags()` method. The method uses a regular expression to match all tags in the content and replace them with empty strings. All non-breaking spaces are removed as well. At the end of the routine, only text is left. For example, if the placeholder contained the following HTML content:

`<table><tr><td> <p>  I love tropical plants! </p></td></tr></table>`

After running `RemoveAllTags()`, we are left with just the text:

`I love tropical plants!`

The `IsLessThanMin()` method accepts the text-only string as an input. We check the length of the string, and anything less than the number specified in the `MinLength` property is considered invalid.

Add the highlighted code to the `RequiredHTMLPHValidator.cs` class.

```
protected override bool EvaluateIsValid()
{
  bool valid = true;
  //  perform validation only in update mode
  if (CmsHttpContext.Current.Mode == PublishingMode.Update)
  {
    HtmlPlaceholderControl ctrl;
    ctrl = FindControl(ControlToValidate) as HtmlPlaceholderControl;
    if (IsEmpty(ctrl.Html) || IsLessThanMin(RemoveAllTags(ctrl.Html)))
    {
      valid = false;
    }
  }
  return valid;
}
// Property for storing the maximum length of the content
private int minLength = 0;
public int MinLength
{
  get
  {
    return minLength;
  }
  set
  {
    minLength = value;
  }
}
// Remove all tags
private string RemoveAllTags(string content)
{
  // This regular expression gets all tags in the content
  string regExpForAllTags = "<[^>]*>";
  Regex reAllTags = new Regex(regExpForAllTags,
  RegexOptions.IgnoreCase | RegexOptions.Compiled);

  content = reAllTags.Replace(content, "");

  // Remove non-breaking spaces ( )
  content = content.Replace(" ", "");
  return content;
}
// Determine if the content is below the specified minimum length
private bool IsLessThanMin(string content)
{
  bool lessThanMin = false;
  if (minLength > 0)
  {
    if (content.Length < minLength)
    {
      lessThanMin = true;
    }
  }
  return lessThanMin;
}
```

Save and build the solution. To use the custom control, follow the steps outlined in the earlier section *Adding the Custom Validator to the Template File*. In a nutshell, you will need to:

- Add a reference to MCMSValidators in the MCMS web project.
- Add the control to the Toolbox.

- Replace any HtmlPlaceholderControl that requires validation with this control and bind it to an HtmlPlaceholderDefinition.

- Add the RequiredHTMLPHValidator control and set its ControlToValidate property to the HtmlPHWithValidation control you wish to validate. Give it an appropriate error message (such as Please enter more than 50 characters). In addition, set the MinLength property to 50.

On the next save, notice that the placeholder content can't be saved unless you have entered more than 50 characters of text (not inclusive of tags and non-breaking spaces).

Canceling the Save Operation

In the example above, we validated an HtmlPlaceholderControl and saved its contents only if it contained more than 50 characters of text. However, did you notice that content from regular placeholder controls continued to be saved? We have only prevented the HtmlPHWithValidation's content from being saved. The rest of the page went on to be saved back to the repository.

What if you had chosen the Save and Exit option? Instead of canceling the save of the entire page, the page toggles back to the AuthoringUnpublished mode without informing the author that placeholder content has not been saved. Clearly, authors won't be too pleased to find out that all their hard work has disappeared simply because they left one placeholder blank.

To get around these issues, we will modify all buttons that perform saves in the Web Author Console to:

- Check to see if there are validation controls on the page. If there are, call for the page to be validated.

- Raise an error should the page contain invalid content, canceling the entire save operation.

- Display an error message on screen, informing authors that the save operation has failed.

Let's start by modifying the Save and Exit button. We will alter the original behavior of the button by overriding the PerformActionBehavior() method to check to see if the page contains invalid content. If it does, we will cancel the save and display an error message in the Error Console. Otherwise, we proceed with the save.

In the ValidatedReeditSaveAndExitAction.cs class file, add the following overridden PerformActionBehavior() method directly below the ActionJavascript property:

```
protected override void PerformActionBehavior()
{
    // Get the current CmsHttpContext
    CmsHttpContext cmsContext = CmsHttpContext.Current;
    // Get the current Web Author Context
    WebAuthorContext wac = WebAuthorContext.Current;
    // Check to see if there are validation controls on the page
    if (Page.Validators.Count > 0)
    {
        // Validation Controls exist. Validate the page.
        Page.Validate();
        // Check to see if the page is valid.
        if (Page.IsValid)
```

```
    {
        // Yes, the page is valid. Continue with the save.
        base.PerformActionBehavior();
    }
    }
    else
    {
        base.PerformActionBehavior();
    }
}
```

Save and build the MCMSValidators project.

In edit mode, enter less than 50 characters to the HtmlPHWithValidation placeholder control to see what happens when validation fails, and attempt to save the page. This time, an error message appears on the Error console as shown below:

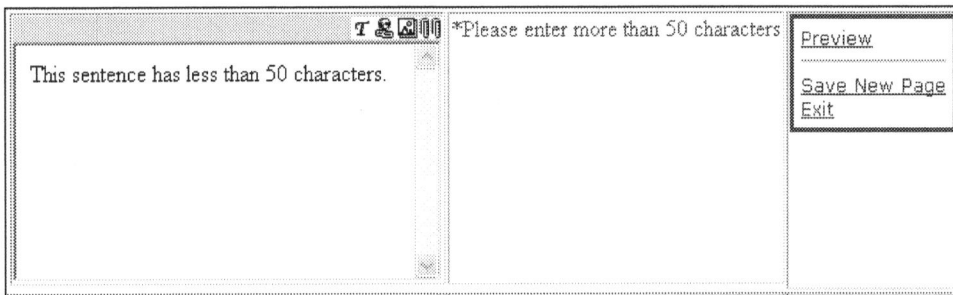

Nothing on the page was saved! All placeholder controls retain their original content. To complete the solution, repeat the steps above and add the overridden PerformActionBehavior() method to the following action controls:

- AuthoringReeditSaveAction
- AuthoringSaveNewAction

Validating the SingleImagePlaceholderControl

The technique for validating a SingleImagePlaceholderControl is similar to that of the HtmlPlaceholderControl. We first need to find a way to read its contents using client-side script. Once we have the content, we can proceed to check to see if it is valid. If it isn't, we cancel the save.

Let's build a required SingleImagePlaceholderControl validator. In this example, we will program the validator to verify that the author has uploaded a picture to the control.

Retrieving the Value of the SingleImagePlaceholderControl

The SingleImagePlaceholderControl is rendered on the browser as a series of hidden form fields and images organized neatly within tables.

Here's a snippet of the generated code:

```
. . . code continues . . .
<input type="hidden" value="" name="NCPH_ImagePlaceholderDefinitionName"
    placeholderType="singleImage" />
```

```
<input type="hidden" value="" name="NCPHHRef_
ImagePlaceholderDefinitionName"/>
<input type="hidden" value="" name="NCPHAltText_
ImagePlaceholderDefinitionName"/>
<input type="hidden" value="" name="SingleImagePlaceholderControl1:
AuthoringModeControlsContainer:ImageEditControl" />
. . . code continues . . .
```

The highlighted line shows the hidden form field that is used to store the name of the image that has been uploaded. To get its value, we simply use the following JavaScript:

```
<script language="javascript">
var fileName = document.all.NCPH_ImagePlaceholderDefinitionName.value;
</script>
```

> The other hidden form fields contain the alternate text and the hyperlink that the image points to when clicked. The alternate text is held in the NCPHAltText_NameOfPlaceholderDefinition hidden field. The NCPHHRef_NameOfPlaceholderDefinition hidden field corresponds to the hyperlink. Replace the text NameOfPlaceholderDefinition with the name of the placeholder as defined in Template Explorer.

Checking for an Empty SingleImagePlaceholderControl

The NCPH_NameOfPlaceholderDefinition field contains the path and filename of the uploaded image. It stores an empty string when an image has not been uploaded to the placeholder control. To determine whether or not the author has left it blank, we will use the following JavaScript:

```
<script language="javascript">
function validateIDOfPlaceholder()
{
  var fileName = document.all.NCPH_ImagePlaceholderDefinitionName.value;
  if (filename == '')
  {
    return false;
  }
  else
  {
    return true;
  }
}
</script>
```

The string IDOfPlaceholder will be replaced with the actual ID of the placeholder control. In this way, each placeholder control will have its own client-side validation function.

The RequiredImagePHValidator

Let's build the RequiredImagePHValidator. First, add a class file named RequiredImagePHValidator.cs to the MCMSValidator project.

Add the required namespaces above the namespace declaration.

```
using System;
using System.Web.UI;
using System.Web.UI.WebControls;
using System.Text;
```

310

```
using Microsoft.ContentManagement.WebControls;
using Microsoft.ContentManagement.Publishing;
namespace MCMSValidation
{
}
```

As before, inherit from the `BaseValidator` class:

```
public class RequiredImagePHValidator: BaseValidator
{
}
```

Next, we inject the JavaScript function used for performing the client-side validation using the `Page.RegisterClientScriptBlock()` function within the overridden `OnPreRender()` method. The `AddAttributesToRender()` method wires the JavaScript to the evaluationfunction attribute. Add the following code directly below the `RequiredImagePHValidator()` constructor:

```
// register the client-side validation script
protected override void OnPreRender(System.EventArgs e)
{
   base.OnPreRender(e);
   // Add the script only in authoring mode.
   if (WebAuthorContext.Current.Mode == WebAuthorContextMode.AuthoringNew
    || WebAuthorContext.Current.Mode == WebAuthorContextMode.AuthoringReedit)
   {
   string phName = "NCPH_";
   if ((FindControl(this.ControlToValidate) == null)
    || !(FindControl(this.ControlToValidate) is SingleImagePlaceholderControl))
     return;
   phName +=
((SingleImagePlaceholderControl)FindControl(this.ControlToValidate) )
           .BoundPlaceholder.Name;
   StringBuilder sb = new StringBuilder();
   sb.Append("<script language=\"javascript\">");
   sb.Append("function validate" + this.ControlToValidate + "()      \n");
   sb.Append("{                                                       \n");
   sb.Append("   var fileName = document.all." + phName + ".value;    \n");
   sb.Append("   if (fileName == '')                                  \n");
   sb.Append("   {                                                    \n");
   sb.Append("      return false;                                     \n");
   sb.Append("   }                                                    \n");
   sb.Append("   else                                                 \n");
   sb.Append("   {                                                    \n");
   sb.Append("      return true;                                      \n");
   sb.Append("   }                                                    \n");
   sb.Append("}                                                       \n");
   sb.Append("</script>");
   if (this.RenderUplevel && this.EnableClientScript)
   {
     if (!Page.IsClientScriptBlockRegistered("ReqImgPhValid_" + phName
                              + "_ClientScript"))
     {
       Page.RegisterClientScriptBlock("ReqImgPhValid_"+phName+"ClientScript",
                              sb.ToString());
     }
   }
   }
}
// wiring the client-side javascript to the Template File
protected override void AddAttributesToRender(
                              System.Web.UI.HtmlTextWriter writer)
{
   base.AddAttributesToRender(writer);
   if (this.RenderUplevel && this.EnableClientScript)
   {
```

```
        // perform validation only in authoring mode.
        if (WebAuthorContext.Current.Mode == WebAuthorContextMode.AuthoringNew
         || WebAuthorContext.Current.Mode == WebAuthorContextMode.AuthoringReedit)
        {
          writer.AddAttribute("evaluationfunction", "validate"
                              + this.ControlToValidate);
        }
      }
    }
```

We want the `ControlPropertiesValid()` method to return true when the control to validate is a `SingleImagePlaceholderControl`. Add the following code below the `AddAttributesToRender()` method:

```
    // get the validator to work with the SingleImagePlaceholderControl
    protected override bool ControlPropertiesValid()
    {
      Control ctrl = FindControl(ControlToValidate);

      if (ctrl != null)
      {
        return (ctrl is SingleImagePlaceholderControl);
      }
      else
      {
        return false;
      }
    }
```

Finally, we implement the `EvaluateIsValid()` method. Although we have implemented exactly the same check using client-side scripts, it's always a good idea to repeat the check on the server. Here, we check the `ImageUrl` property of the `SingleImagePlaceholderControl`. Validation passes only if an image has been uploaded to the placeholder control.

```
    protected override bool EvaluateIsValid()
    {
      bool valid = true;
      if (CmsHttpContext.Current.Mode == PublishingMode.Update)
      {
        SingleImagePlaceholderControl ctrl;
        ctrl = FindControl(ControlToValidate) as SingleImagePlaceholderControl;
        if (ctrl.ImageUrl == "")
        {
          valid = false;
        }
      }
      return valid;
    }
```

The control is complete. Save and build the project.

Validating the SingleAttachmentPlaceholderControl

The `SingleAttachmentPlaceholderControl`, like the other placeholder controls, can't be validated with the default ASP.NET server-side validation controls. In this section, we will build a custom validation control, named `RequiredAttachmentPhValidator`, that checks to see if a file has been uploaded to the control. If no attachments have been uploaded, the page will not be saved.

As before, we will first find out how to read off the content of the
`SingleAttachmentPlaceholderControl`. We will then write the client-side JavaScript that will
perform the checking to be used within our validator.

Stored Values of the SingleAttachmentPlaceholderControl

Let's take a look at the generated code for the `SingleAttachmentPlaceholderControl`. Among
the various elements that make up the code, the `SingleAttachmentPlaceholderControl` contains
several key hidden form fields as highlighted below:

```
. . . code continues . . .
<table border="1" cellpadding="0" cellspacing="0">
<tr>
<td>
<input type="hidden" value="" name="NCPH_AttachmentPlaceholderDefinitionName"
 placeholderType="singleAttachment" />
<input type="hidden" value=""
 name="NCPHDispText_AttachmentPlaceholderDefinitionName"/>
<input type="hidden" value=""
 name="SingleAttachmentPlaceholderControl1:AuthoringModeControlsContainer:
AttachmentEditControl" />
<input id="SingleAttachmentPlaceholderControl1_AuthoringModeControlsContainer
_AttachmentEditControl" name="NCPHAttach_AttachmentPlaceholderDefinition1"
size="25" value="No Attachment Set" readOnly="true" tabindex="-1" />
</td>
</tr>
</table>
. . . code continues . . .
```

The field named `NCPH_AttachmentPlaceholderDefinitionName` contains the path of the file that
has been uploaded to the control. The next field,
`NCPHDispText_AttachmentPlaceholderDefinitionName`, holds the display text.

To retrieve these values, we will use the following JavaScript:

```
<script language="javascript">
// get the file name
var fileName = document.all.NCPH_AttachmentPlaceholderDefinitionName.value;
// get the display text
var displayText =
        document.all.NCPHDispText_AttachmentPlaceholderDefinitionName.value;
</script>
```

Checking for an Empty SingleAttachmentPlaceholderControl

Armed with the script that retrieves the value, we can now check to see if a file has been uploaded
to the control by checking to see if the `NCPH_AttachmentPlaceholderDefinitionName` contains
an empty string. If it does, no file has been uploaded and the validation fails. We will use the
script below in our validator:

```
<script language="javascript">
function validateIDOfPlaceholder()
{
  // get the file name
  var fileName = document.all.NCPH_AttachmentPlaceholderDefinitionName.value;

  if (filename == '')
  {
    return false;
  }
}
```

```
      else
      {
        return true;
      }
    }
</script>
```

The RequiredAttachmentPHValidator

We've already built two custom validators, and this third one follows the familiar pattern. We'll dive straight into the code and just highlight the interesting points.

Add a class file named `RequiredAttachmentPHValidator.cs` to the `MCMSValidators` project. Code it as shown below:

```
using System;
using System.Web.UI;
using System.Web.UI.WebControls;
using System.ComponentModel;
using System.Text;
using Microsoft.ContentManagement.WebControls;
using Microsoft.ContentManagement.Publishing;
namespace MCMSValidators
{
  public class RequiredAttachmentPHValidator : BaseValidator
  {
    public RequiredAttachmentPHValidator()
    {
      // nothing to do
    }
    // register the client-side validation script
    protected override void OnPreRender(System.EventArgs e)
    {
      base.OnPreRender(e);
      // Add the script only in authoring mode.
      if (WebAuthorContext.Current.Mode == WebAuthorContextMode.AuthoringNew
      || WebAuthorContext.Current.Mode ==
                                  WebAuthorContextMode.AuthoringReedit)
      {
        string phName = "NCPH_";
        if ((FindControl(this.ControlToValidate) == null)
        || !(FindControl(this.ControlToValidate)
            is SingleAttachmentPlaceholderControl))
          return;
        phName +=

        ((SingleAttachmentPlaceholderControl)
            FindControl(this.ControlToValidate)).BoundPlaceholder.Name;
        StringBuilder sb = new StringBuilder();
        sb.Append("<script language=\"javascript\">");
        sb.Append("function validate" + this.ControlToValidate + "()      \n");
        sb.Append("{                                                       \n");
        sb.Append("  var fileName = document.all." + phName + ".value;    \n");
        sb.Append("  if (fileName == '')                                   \n");
        sb.Append("  {                                                     \n");
        sb.Append("    return false;                                       \n");
        sb.Append("  }                                                     \n");
        sb.Append("  else                                                  \n");
        sb.Append("  {                                                     \n");
        sb.Append("    return true;                                        \n");
        sb.Append("  }                                                     \n");
        sb.Append("}                                                       \n");
        sb.Append("</script>");
        if (this.RenderUplevel && this.EnableClientScript)
```

```
        {
          if (!Page.IsClientScriptBlockRegistered("ReqAttPhValid_" + phName
            + "_ClientScript"))
          {
            Page.RegisterClientScriptBlock("ReqAttPhValid_" + phName
                                    + "ClientScript", sb.ToString());
          }
        }
      }
    }
  }
  // wiring the client-side javascript to the Template File
  protected override void AddAttributesToRender(
                                System.Web.UI.HtmlTextWriter writer)
  {
    base.AddAttributesToRender(writer);
    if (this.RenderUplevel && this.EnableClientScript)
    {
      // perform validation only in authoring mode.
      if (WebAuthorContext.Current.Mode == WebAuthorContextMode.AuthoringNew
      || WebAuthorContext.Current.Mode ==
                                WebAuthorContextMode.AuthoringReedit)
      {
        writer.AddAttribute("evaluationfunction", "validate"
                        + this.ControlToValidate);
      }
    }
  }
  // get the validator to work with the SingleAttachmentPlaceholderControl
  protected override bool ControlPropertiesValid()
  {
    Control ctrl = FindControl(ControlToValidate);

    if (ctrl != null)
    {
      return (ctrl is SingleAttachmentPlaceholderControl);
    }
    else
    {
      return false;
    }
  }
  protected override bool EvaluateIsValid()
  {
    bool valid = true;
    if (CmsHttpContext.Current.Mode == PublishingMode.Update)
    {
      // Check the AttachmentUrl property to see if the control is empty.
      SingleAttachmentPlaceholderControl ctrl;
      ctrl = FindControl(ControlToValidate) as
        SingleAttachmentPlaceholderControl;
      if (ctrl.AttachmentUrl == "")
      {
        valid = false;
      }
    }
    return valid;
  }
  }
  }
}
```

Examine the code and you will find that it is very similar to the previous two custom validation controls.

- The JavaScript that checks to see if a file has been uploaded to the SingleAttachmentPlaceholderControl is injected into the template file within the OnPreRender() method.

- The ControlPropertiesValid() method verifies that a control to be validated is indeed a SingleAttachmentPlaceholderControl.

- Finally, the EvaluateIsValid() method performs a server-side check to see if the SingleAttachmentPlaceholderControl.AttachmentUrl property contains a path to a file. If it doesn't, the method returns false. As in the previous examples, this method would probably not be triggered as we are relying on client-side checks for validation. If you need to perform server-side validation, you will have to create a custom placeholder control as described in the section *Implementing Server-Side Validation*.

Summary

In this chapter, we explored how MCMS placeholder controls can be validated. We started by showing that the validation web controls shipped with ASP.NET can't be used with MCMS placeholder controls. To get around this limitation, we built three validation controls, one for the HTMLPlaceholderControl, a second for the SingleImagePlaceholderControl, and a third for the SingleAttachmentPlaceholderControl. We demonstrated how simple checks for empty placeholders can be performed using client-side scripting techniques. We also illustrated that server-side validation is possible by building custom placeholder controls. The methods discussed in this chapter can be extended to cover more complex and rigorous validation requirements from checking to see if telephone numbers, zip codes or email addresses are in a valid format to validating against content stored in an external database.

10
Staging Static Pages

Websites today are dynamic and versatile. Dynamic sites offer many advantages over static sites. Using MCMS, you get to personalize and work with the PAPI to create a truly interactive and personalized user experience. For example, we have seen how navigation structures can be hidden or shown based on an individual's access rights. In fact, content gets updated so frequently and the demand for interactivity is so high that content management systems, like MCMS, assemble pages on the fly. At the very most, snapshots of pages are cached in memory or on the server's hard disk to speed up the process of delivering pages. The cache is invalidated after a certain time period has elapsed or when the content changes. Nothing is ever frozen: only fresh content is served.

In a book about creating dynamic sites, you may find it strange that this entire chapter is devoted to staging static pages. The truth is, despite the fast-paced demands of technology, there is a need to slow things down a little. Static copies of an entire website can be useful on occasions such as:

- Creating pages to be packaged on offline media like CD ROMs. User guides and help files are often included with shrink-wrapped software in the form of electronic documents on CDs. Even Microsoft help files (or CHM files) are themselves built from static HTML files.

- Taking a snapshot of the site for archival or back-up purposes.

- Creating static files for indexing by Index Server or other search engines that require the presence of physical files.

- Sharing content across multiple servers. Yes, you could install MCMS on the other servers, or even syndicate content using web services. However, sometimes, the best solution is the simplest—just make static copies of shared content and use a good file copy technique like FTP to transport them (and sidestep the need to acquire more production MCMS licenses).

If you need to generate static versions of MCMS websites, there are two options available:

- Use the Site Stager utility that ships with MCMS 2002.
- Write a custom staging tool that generates a static snapshot of each page.

> Important Note: Site Stager only stages static pages from postings based on ASP templates. It does *not* work for postings based on ASP.NET templates.

In this chapter, we will look at each of these options in turn and discuss the pros and cons of each in the process. We will take a brief look at Site Stager to get an idea of how it works and borrow some of its techniques to create our own version that works with ASP.NET-based websites.

Site Stager in Brief

First generation websites were made up of collections of HTML files. To create a page, a webmaster would open an HTML editor (for the die-hard developer, the tool would most probably be a text-editing tool like Notepad) and hand-code lines and lines of tags and code; a very time consuming task indeed.

With the introduction of scripting languages like ASP, static websites evolved to second-generation sites that included dynamic components. Web developers wrote much less code to generate much more HTML using scripting languages like ASP and Cold Fusion. For example, a single do-while loop could generate hundreds of table rows with only a few lines of code. Nevertheless, content was often mixed with code and webmasters were still tasked to update the site when fresh content came in.

As with all trends, the migration of static sites to dynamic ones was not an overnight phenomenon. The earlier version of MCMS, MCMS 2001, provided a utility known as Site Stager that generated static pages of a website. Site Stager was designed to bridge the gap between yet-to-be-upgraded static websites and the second-generation dynamic website. With Site Stager, site owners could continue to create collections of static HTML or ASP pages, while gradually moving towards the more fluid ASP-database designs.

Power websites of today are managed by enterprise content management systems like MCMS. A content management system delegates the task of authoring to business users. Information gets delivered as soon as it becomes available, bypassing old bottlenecks. Webmasters now concentrate their efforts on coding templates. Code in a single template can be used to serve up unlimited numbers of pages!

In the Enterprise version of MCMS 2002, Site Stager still exists but works only for postings created from ASP-based templates. If you are using ASP.NET-based templates, Site Stager will not churn out valid static snapshots of the site. Pages will be created but they probably won't contain content from placeholders and will appear to be empty. Microsoft's stand is that websites today are too dynamic in nature and that most sites will probably not need to support static pages. Future versions of MCMS may not include Site Stager.

> Site Stager is not available in the standard edition of MCMS 2002.

Let's try out first-hand how Site Stager works. For the purpose of the example that follows, get access to a site that uses ASP-based template files if you can. Otherwise, if your site uses ASP.NET-based templates, such as the TropicalGreen site, you can follow the example below, but the generated static pages will not contain placeholder content and will appear to be empty files.

Installing Site Stager

The first step to using Site Stager is to install it. To find out if Site Stager has already been installed on your machine, select Start | Programs | Microsoft Content Management Server. See if an entry for Site Stager is listed.

Otherwise, follow the steps below to install Site Stager:

1. From the Control Panel, choose to Add/Remove Programs.
2. Select Microsoft Content Management Server from the list of currently installed programs. Click Change.
3. In the Program Maintenance dialog, choose to Modify the program features.
4. In the Custom Setup dialog, select the Site Stager component.

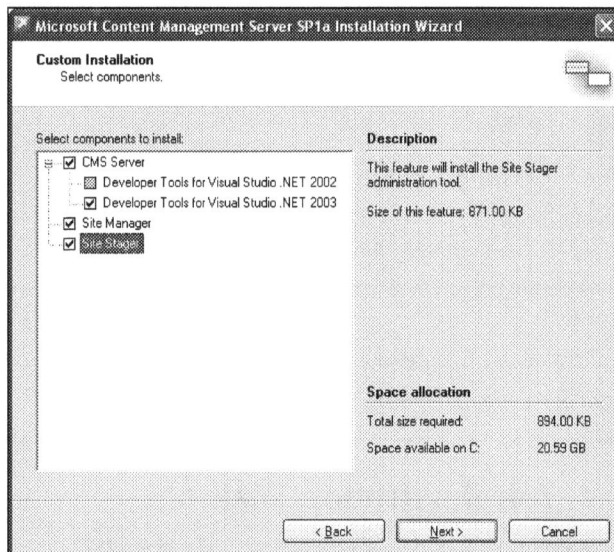

5. Click Next to confirm your selection.
6. Click Install to begin the installation process.
7. When the installation completes, click Finish to close the dialog.

An entry for Site Stager is now available in the Start menu. Click on it to start it.

Defining the Destination User

When you first start Site Stager, you will be asked to specify the destination user, that is, the user whose credentials will be used to create folders and files on the target server. The user should have the following rights on the machine running Site Stager:

- Member of the local computer's administrators group.
- "Log on locally" rights.
- "Log on as a batch job" rights.

In addition, the user needs to have write access to all directories where the generated HTML files are to be stored.

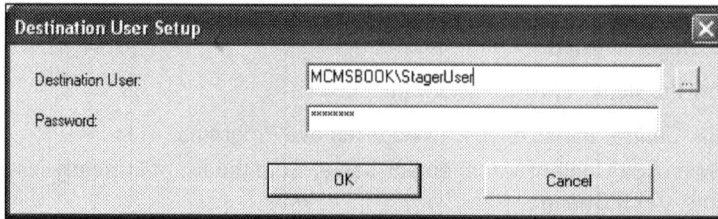

I have entered the credentials of the destination user. Each time I click on the OK button, I get an error message that says "Destination User Invalid – Destination User does not have 'log on as a batch job' access. Please choose another user". What can I do?

To give a user "log on as a batch job" access, follow these steps:

- Select Administrative Tools | Local Security Policy.
- In the Local Security Settings dialog, navigate to the Security Settings | Local Policies | User Rights Assignment folder.
- Right-click on the Log on as a batch job entry and select Properties from the context menu.
- To add a user to the list, in the Properties dialog, click Add User or Group....
- When you have added the user, click OK to close the dialog.

The Site Stager Administration Dialog

The Site Stager Administration dialog lists all staging profiles. It displays the profile's name, activity (whether or not it is active and/or running), destination directory, and description as entered by the developer.

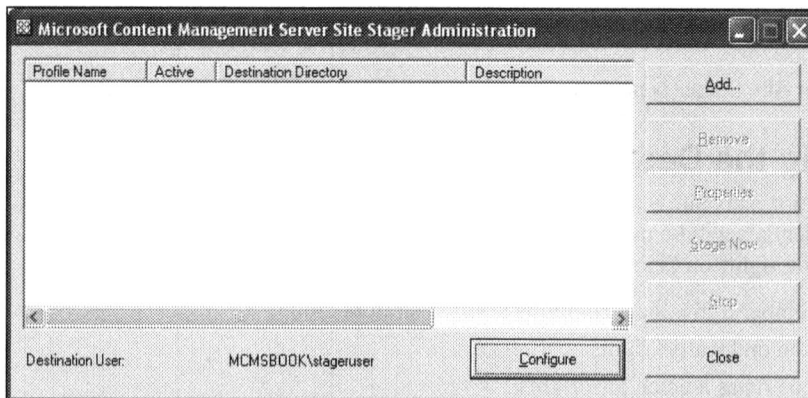

Creating a Staging Profile

To create a new profile click Add.... The following dialog appears:

The dialog is divided into four sections:

- **General area**: Specify a name for the profile, a URL to a site map page that contains links to all pages that will be staged, a description for the profile, and check the Active checkbox to indicate whether or not this profile is enabled. You can also specify a shell application that will be launched after the files have been staged.

- **Source Setup**: Specify the MCMS user account and password that will be used to retrieve the channels and postings.

- **Destination Setup**: Provide the path where all files and folders will be generated as well as the name of the index files.

- **Staging Options**: Provides several options used to configure whether or not staging is done incrementally as well as the file names and location of resources.

The table below describes each field. Enter the test values as indicated. Click OK when you are done.

Field	Description	Test Value
Profile Name	Enter the name of the profile. Give it a meaningful name. This value will be used by administrators to differentiate various profiles on the same server.	My Staging Profile
Active	Check this box to activate the profile. Or, uncheck it to prevent scheduled jobs from running at the specified times.	Checked
Site Map URL	Contains the default setting of: `http://ContentServer/nr/system/staging/sitemap.asp` The `sitemap.asp` file provides the stager with an XML list of all channels and postings to be staged. You can make copies of `sitemap.asp` and customize it. For example, instead of staging the entire site, you can generate selected portions of it.	`http://localhost/nr/system/staging/sitemap.asp`
Description	Enter a description of the profile. Again, this is displayed on the Site Stager Administration dialog, so it is a good idea to provide meaningful descriptions. Consider adding background information such as what the profile does and who created it.	Created by [Your Name] to see how Site Stager works
Shell After Staging	Specify an application to run right after the stager completes here. A common practice is for administrators to attach scripts that double-check that all files have been successfully generated.	Leave blank

Source Setup

Stage As User	Enter the name of the MCMS user that will be used to stage files. This user should be given the following access rights: Subscriber access to all channels that will be staged. To prevent certain portions of the site from being staged, simply deny the user access to these areas of the site. Member of at least one resource manager or template designer rights group. The rights group need not be assigned to any container.	Enter the ID of a user with at least subscriber rights to the channels and template designer rights to the templates in the following format: DOMAIN\UserName
User Password	Enter the password of the 'Stage As' user.	Enter password

Destination Setup

Default Filename	Indicate the file name of all channel rendering scripts. Site Stager suggests the name `index.htm`. Feel free to change this value accordingly. You could rename the files to `default.asp`, `default.htm`, or even `default.abc`.	Default.htm

Field	Description	Test Value
Destination Directory	Specify the destination directory. This could be a local directory on the host server or a mapped path to a remote server. Be sure that the destination user defined earlier has write access to this path.	Let's try staging to a folder in the c:\ drive. C:\test

Staging Options

Field	Description	Test Value
Staged Channel/ Posting names	Choose one of two options: • **Use Source**. Follows the names of channels and postings on the source. As an example, for a posting named About, the generated file will be named About.htm. • **Generate New**. Instructs Site Stager to generate a new name for each folder and file. All folders generated start with the letters ch followed by a number (such as ch1, ch2). Files start with the letter p followed by a number (such as p1, p2).	Choose Use Source
Incremental Staging	Choose one of two options: • **Synchronized**. Deletes all files on the destination folder and creates new files and folders to replace them. This ensures that all postings deleted on the source server are also removed on the destination. • **Passive**. Does not delete any files on the destination folder. Postings that have been deleted on the source will continue to remain on the destination.	Choose synchronized staging
Default extension for HTML files	By default, all staged files are generated as HTML files. To stage other file types, specify the file extension here.	htm
Store Resources Separately	All resources will be generated in a folder named /Resources/. To specify a separate directory, check this box.	Leave this box unchecked
Virtual Path	Enter the virtual path of the directory where resources will be staged. All URLs pointing to resources will be amended to use this path.	Leave blank
Destination Subdirectory	Specify the name of the subdirectory where the resources will be staged.	Leave blank

Running a Job

Back at the Site Stager Administration dialog, highlight the profile that we have just created and click Stage Now to start the staging process. You will receive a message letting you know that the staging process may take a while, depending on the number of pages staged and that all details will be logged to Site Stager's log file. Click OK.

Notice that the text in the Active column changes from Yes to Yes (Currently Staging). The process will run for as long as is required for all pages to be staged. If you open Windows Explorer and navigate to the c:\test folder, you will see several new folders and HTML files being added.

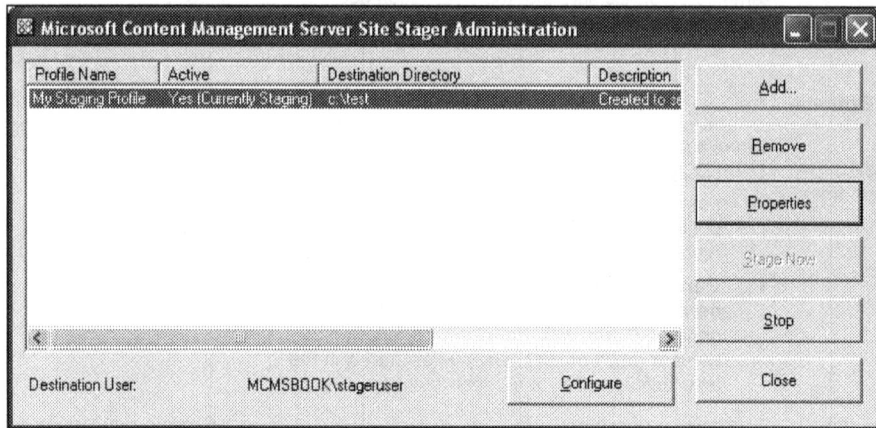

Scheduling a Profile

You could also schedule the job to run at specific times.

1. To edit an existing profile, select it in the Site Stager Administration dialog and click Properties.

A quick way to edit a profile is to double-click on it.

---

2. Click on the Schedule tab.
3. Click New to add a schedule.
4. Set the time and the frequency with which the job will be repeated. You can choose to schedule the job daily, weekly, monthly, once, at system startup, or at logon. For more complex schedules, click on the Advanced... button.
5. To delete an existing schedule, click Delete.
6. When you are ready, click OK to close the Properties dialog.

To save processing power on both destination and source servers and to minimize network traffic, try to schedule jobs as far apart as possible. It's also a good idea to ensure that jobs do not overlap. In addition, schedule the jobs at the low usage times of your website, such as the early hours of the morning.

Deleting a Profile

To delete a profile, simply select it from the Site Stager Administration dialog and click Delete.

The ASP.NET Stager Application

In the previous section, we have seen how Site Stager works. It is a good tool for creating static snapshots of ASP-based sites. Obviously, we don't want to take a huge step back and convert all our templates from ASP.NET to ASP. How, then, shall we stage sites that make use of the newer and improved ASP.NET? To get around this limitation of Site Stager, we will build our very own version of the staging tool. The good news is that we won't start entirely from scratch: we will borrow some of the concepts and ideas behind Site Stager.

Let's build a console application that mimics what Site Stager does for MCMS 2001 or ASP-based templates in MCMS 2002. Note that the application uses the MCMS PAPI and will need to be executed on a server that has MCMS installed.

Here's what the application will do:

- Walk through the entire channel structure, starting from a specified start channel. For each posting and channel cover page found, a static HTML file is generated.

- Scan through each channel cover page and posting for attachments and stage them.

- Provide settings for administrators to change the behavior of the stager. For example, administrators can specify the start channel, whether or not hidden postings will be staged, and so on.

We will make the assumption that the staged pages will be placed in the same folder structure as found in Site Manager. For relative links within pages to remain unbroken, the pages should not be nested within sub folders. For example, `http://tropicalgreen1` can be staged to `http://tropicalgreen2` but not to `http://servername/tropicalgreen3/`.

The DotNetSiteStager Project

Let's start by creating a Visual C# Console Application project named `DotNetSiteStager`. Rename `Class1.cs` to `Stager.cs`.

Add the following references to the project:

- `Microsoft.ContentManagement.Publishing.dll` (located in the `<install directory>/Microsoft Content Management Server/Server/bin/` directory)

- `System.Web`

The following namespaces are also required by the solution. Add them above the namespace declaration:

```
using System;
using System.IO;
using System.Net;
using System.Web;
using System.Text;
using System.Collections;
using System.Text.RegularExpressions;
using Microsoft.ContentManagement.Publishing;
```

```
namespace DotNetSiteStager
{
    . . . code continues . . .
}
```

Configuring Stager Settings

The .NET stager will provide several configurable settings as shown in the following table. Notice that some settings are equivalent to fields available in Site Stager. We did say that we were going to borrow some of Site Stager's ideas!

Setting	Description	Value for Example
m_DestinationDirectory	Specifies the folder where we will create all staged folders and files. This could be a location on the source server itself, or a directory on a remote server in the network. Equivalent to the Destination Directory field of Site Stager.	C:\StagedSite\
m_StartChannel	The channel that the stager will begin staging from. You can change the start channel to point to any channel within the hierarchy, allowing you to increase or reduce the scope of the stager accordingly.	/Channels/www.tropicalgreen.net/
m_LogFile	The path of the file that the stager will use to write all warnings and error messages to.	C:\StagedSite\logs\
m_SourceHost	The name of the host server. As the stager must be executed on the source MCMS server, the value is typically http://localhost. But for sites with map channel names to host header turned on, you can specify the host name instead (e.g. http://www.tropicalgreen.net).	http://www.tropicalgreen.net
m_UserAgent	Allows you to specify the value of the UserAgent HTTP header, which identifies the browser version and platform of the client. This accommodates sites that are rendered differently for different client platforms or browsers.	Mozilla/4.0 (compatible MSIE 6.0 Windows NT 5.1)
m_StageAsUser	The account that will be used to retrieve all MCMS objects from the repository. Restricting the access rights of the 'Stage As' user will limit the stager's scope. Equivalent to the Stage As User field of Site Stager, minus the domain name, which is defined separately here.	StagerUser
m_StageAsPwd	The password of the 'Stage As' user account. Equivalent to the User Password field of Site Stager.	StagerPassword

Setting	Description	Value for Example
m_StageAsDomain	The domain of the 'Stage As' user account.	localmachine
m_DoNotExportHiddenItems	A flag to indicate whether or not hidden files and channels will be staged as well. A value of false stages hidden files.	True
m_DefaultFileName	The name of the file generated for channel rendering scripts and default postings. Equivalent to the Default Filename field in Site Stager.	default
m_DefaultFileExtension	The file extension of all generated postings. Equivalent to the Default Extension for HTML files field in Site Stager.	htm
m_HttpHeader	This is an additional header that will be added to the request to allow the application to behave differently if the site is hit by the stager or by a browser. For example, you could replace active scripts that work only on dynamic pages with content that will work on a static copy.	DotNetSiteStager
m_CodePage	The default encoding used to download a static version of each page. If your site uses different character sets (for instance, if it is a multilingual site), you may define a different code page.	UTF-8
m_BaseUrl	The RobotMetaTag inserted in all template files injects a <base> tag into all postings. If you are planning to stage the files to a different host from the source, such as when generating files from http://www.tropicalgreen.net to http://tropicalgreen, you could set this value to http://tropicalgreen.	http://tropicalgreen

As the behavior of the methods within the class depends on the values of these settings, let's declare all of them as class variables. We will also declare an ArrayList object for storing attachment URLs, a CmsApplicationContext variable for working with the MCMS PAPI and a NetworkCredential object for downloading pages later. Add the following code above the Main() method:

```
private static string m_LogFile;
private static string m_StageAsUser;
private static string m_StageAsPwd;
private static string m_StageAsDomain;
private static bool m_DoNotExportHiddenItems;
private static string m_StartChannel;
private static string m_SourceHost;
private static string m_UserAgent;
private static string m_HttpHeader;
```

```
private static string m_DefaultFileName;
private static string m_DestinationDirectory;
private static string m_DefaultFileExtension;
private static string m_CodePage;
private static string m_BaseUrl;
private static string m_LocalBaseUrl;

// ArrayLists for handling attachments
private static ArrayList m_AttachmentUrls;

// CmsApplicationContext for working with the MCMS PAPI
private static CmsApplicationContext cmsContext;

// Network credentials for downloading pages
private static NetworkCredential m_credentials;
[STAThread]
static void Main(string[] args)
{
   . . . code continues . . .
}
```

Our application will handle two types of files:

- **ContentPage**: Postings and channel rendering scripts
- **ContentBinary**: Images, Office documents, and other attachments

We will declare an enumeration named EnumBinary to identify each of these file types. Add the following code above the Main() routine.

```
// Have enum values for each file type handled
enum EnumBinary
{
  ContentBinary,
  ContentPage
}
```

Within the Main() routine, we will initialize each of the variables declared above. Go ahead and change their values. You will at the very least have to set the 'Stage As' user, domain, and password as well as the start channel and the destination directory to match the environment of your computer.

```
[STAThread]
static void Main(string[] args)
{
  // Set parameter values
  m_LogFile = @"c:\StagedSite\logs\";
  m_StageAsDomain = "localmachine";
  m_StageAsUser = "StagerUser";
  m_StageAsPwd = "StagerPassword";
  m_DoNotExportHiddenItems = true;
  m_StartChannel = "/Channels/www.tropicalgreen.net/";
  m_SourceHost = "http://www.tropicalgreen.net";
  m_UserAgent = "Mozilla/4.0 (compatible MSIE 6.0 Windows NT 5.1)";
  m_HttpHeader = "DotNetSiteStager";
  m_DefaultFileName = "default.htm";
  m_DestinationDirectory = @"c:\StagedSite\";
  m_DefaultFileExtension = "htm";
  m_CodePage = "UTF-8";
  m_BaseUrl = "http://tropicalgreen";
  m_LocalBaseUrl = m_BaseUrl;
  m_AttachmentUrls = new ArrayList();
}
```

A better idea would be to store the settings within an Application configuration file (app.config). In this way, you don't have to re-compile the code each time any of the settings changes. For simplicity, we will leave them as class variables in this example.

Recording Messages to a Log File

As the stager progresses through its job, it may encounter exceptions when staging certain URLs. Instead of terminating the entire process, we will trap all exceptions and write all error messages to a log file. The location of the log file is set in the m_LogFile variable defined earlier.

The helper function that writes messages to the log file is shown below. Add it directly below the Main() method.

```
private static void WriteToLog(string message)
{
  Console.WriteLine(message);
  FileStream fsLog = new FileStream(m_LogFile, FileMode.Append,
                                    FileAccess.Write);
  StreamWriter wLog = new StreamWriter(fsLog);
  wLog.WriteLine(message);
  wLog.Flush();
  wLog.Close();
  fsLog.Close();
}
```

For audit purposes, we will record the current date and time as well as the settings that we defined earlier in the log file. Within the Main() routine, add the following code:

```
[STAThread]
static void Main(string[] args)
{
  . . . code continues . . .
  // Ensure that the logfile directory is created
  Directory.CreateDirectory(m_LogFile);
  // Generate the name of the log file (in the format log_yyyyMMdd_HHmm.txt)
  if(!m_LogFile.EndsWith("\\"))
  {
    m_LogFile = m_LogFile + "\\";
  }
  m_LogFile = m_LogFile + "log_" + DateTime.Now.ToString("yyyyMMdd_HHmm")
              + ".txt";

  System.Text.StringBuilder sb = new System.Text.StringBuilder();
  string newLine = System.Environment.NewLine;

  // Write the timestamp to the log file
  sb.Append(DateTime.Now.ToString("dd MMM yyyy HH:mm") + newLine);
  sb.Append("----------" + newLine);

  // Write the settings to the log file
  sb.Append("Log File = " + m_LogFile + newLine);
  sb.Append("Stage As Domain = " + m_StageAsDomain + newLine);
  sb.Append("Stage As User = " + m_StageAsUser + newLine);
  sb.Append("Do No Export Hidden Items = " + m_DoNotExportHiddenItems
            + newLine);
  sb.Append("Start Channel = " + m_StartChannel + newLine);
  sb.Append("HTTP Host = " + m_SourceHost + newLine);
  sb.Append("User Agent = " + m_UserAgent + newLine);
  sb.Append("HTTP Header = " + m_HttpHeader + newLine);
  sb.Append("Default File Name = " + m_DefaultFileName + newLine);
```

```
        sb.Append("Destination Directory = " + m_DestinationDirectory + newLine);
        sb.Append("Default File Extension = " + m_DefaultFileExtension + newLine);
        sb.Append("Base Url = " + m_BaseUrl + newLine);
        sb.Append("Code Page = " + m_CodePage + newLine);
        WriteToLog(sb.ToString());
    }
```

Logging in as the 'Stage As' User

The staging process will run using the credentials of the 'Stage As' user. The user ID of the 'Stage As' user is pieced together by appending WinNT:// with the user's domain and ID. Since we are running the code as a console application, we won't have a current CmsHttpContext. Therefore, we will use the CmsApplicationContext object to carry out the process and use the CmsApplicationContext.AuthenticateAsUser() method to log in. The default publishing mode is Published, so only live channels and postings will be staged.

You may be wondering why we didn't set the publishing mode to Staging instead of Published. This is because URLs are generated differently when running the application in Staging mode. In Staging mode, the MCMS PAPI generates URLs for channels and postings in the following format:

```
<NCOMPASSSTAGINGSERVER>/NR/exeres/9556B302-5A45-47A2-897B-F3F8FFBED5F6.htm?NRMODE=
Staging&CMSAUTHTOKEN=77px32pfk5zz2nofimsv5tphe3wuxhqp6s7vx3avlhegvgutvpymze672w6ww
wi5vxje2bfntpzgp</NCOMPASSSTAGINGSERVER>
```

This unique URL was used by Site Stager to identify which links it needs to make a static copy of and to follow when staging the site. Site Stager would also modify these links in the generated page with the names of the new host server and destination directories.

If you plan to run the application in Staging mode, you will have to handle these links in the same way. However, to keep this example short, we won't attempt to do so.

We will also impersonate the user that runs the staging process to create a set of network credentials for downloading each channel item and attachment later.

The choice of the 'Stage As' user is important because the application only stages pages the user has access to (recall that as part of the identity management feature of MCMS, a user can only view pages that he or she has been granted rights to). You can limit the scope of the stager to stage only selected sections of the site by limiting the user's rights. For example, to stage the PlantCatalog channel, give the 'Stage As' user rights to that channel. This gives you flexibility in planning the size of each deployment. The more pages staged, the longer it takes to complete each task.

If you have left the m_StageAsUser variable as an empty string, an attempt will be made to log in as the guest user.

Add the following highlighted code to the Main() method:

```
[STAThread]
static void Main(string[] args)
{
    . . . code continues . . .
    try
    {
        // Login to MCMS as the 'Stage As' user
        cmsContext = new CmsApplicationContext();
        if (m_StageAsUser != "")
        {
            cmsContext.AuthenticateAsUser("WinNT://" + m_StageAsDomain + "/"
```

```
                                          + m_StageAsUser, m_StageAsPwd);
        m_credentials = new NetworkCredential(m_StageAsUser,
        m_StageAsPwd, m_StageAsDomain);
      }
      else
      {
        cmsContext.AuthenticateAsGuest();
        m_credentials = null;
      }
    }
    catch
    {
      WriteToLog("Error: Unable to authenticate with MCMS server.");
    }
}
```

Revealing Hidden Postings

Next, the application picks up the setting stored in the m_DoNotExportHiddenItems variable and uses it to set the CmsApplicationContext.SessionSettings.AutoFilterHidden property. When this is set to false, the CmsApplicationContext will reveal items set to be hidden when published (or channel items with the ChannelItem.IsHiddenModePublished property set to true). As a result, channel items that are hidden will be staged.

```
[STAThread]
static void Main(string[] args)
{
  . . . code continues . . .
  // Reveal all hidden postings?
  cmsContext.SessionSettings.AutoFilterHidden = m_DoNotExportHiddenItems;
}
```

Staging Channels and Postings

The next step of the process is to generate static pages for each channel and posting that the 'Stage As' user can see. Here's a quick synopsis of what we will be doing:

- Get an instance of the start channel defined in the m_StartChannel variable.
- Iterate through all channels and postings, beginning from the start channel.
- For each channel and posting, issue an HTTP request.
- Get the response and save it to a file.

Getting the Start Channel

Before walking through the list of channels and postings, we first need to get the start channel specified in the m_StartChannel variable. The iteration process begins from this channel.

Once we have an instance of the start channel, we are ready to begin the iteration process, triggered by the CollectChannel() method defined next.

Append the code highlighted below to the Main() routine:

```
[STAThread]
static void Main(string[] args)
{
    . . . code continues . . .
    // Start the iteration process
    Channel rootChannel = cmsContext.Searches.GetByPath(m_StartChannel)
                as Channel;
    if (rootChannel != null)
    {
        CollectChannel(rootChannel);
    }
    else
    {
        WriteToLog("Error: Start Channel '" + m_StartChannel + "' cannot be "
                + "found or user does not have sufficient rights!");
    }
}
```

Iterating Through the Channel Tree

From the start channel, the CollectChannel() method walks through the rest of the tree, looking for channels and postings.

When it sees a channel, it will create a static version of the channel rendering script or default posting and all postings in its collection. The method calls itself recursively until all channels in the tree have been staged.

The Download() helper method will perform the task of downloading the content and generating static pages as we will see later. Add the CollectChannel() method to the code:

```
static void CollectChannel(Channel channel)
{
    // Download the channel rendering script or the default posting
    Download(GetUrlWithHost(channel.Url), channel.Path.Replace(
            m_StartChannel,"/"), m_DefaultFileName, EnumBinary.ContentPage);
    // Download all the postings within the channel
    foreach (Posting p in channel.Postings)
    {
        WriteToLog("Info: Downloading Posting: " + p.Path);
        Download(GetUrlWithHost(p.Url), channel.Path.Replace(m_StartChannel,"/"),
                p.Name, EnumBinary.ContentPage);
    }
    foreach (Channel c in channel.Channels)
    {
        CollectChannel(c);
    }
}
```

The CollectChannel() method uses a helper function, GetUrlWithHost(), which replaces any host names found within the URL with the value stored in the m_SourceHost variable. The reason we do this is to handle links that do not have the host name as part of the URL, particularly for sites that do not have host header mapping turned on. For such sites, Channel.Url will return a value without the host header, like this: /plantcatalog/ficus.htm. To successfully issue the HTTP request that gets the page, the host value (which in our case will be http://www.tropicalgreen.net) has to be pre-pended to the URL.

```
private static string GetUrlWithHost(string url)
{
  // Remove the host name e.g. http://www.tropicalgreen.net
  // from the URL
  if (url.StartsWith("http://"))
  {
    // Remove http://
    url = url.Remove(0,7);
    // Remove the host name e.g. www.tropicalgreen.net
    url = url.Remove(0,(url + "/").IndexOf("/"));
  }
  // add the source host to the URL
  url = m_SourceHost + url;
  return url;
}
```

Issuing an HTTP Request

The helper function that issues HTTP requests for all URLs to be staged is the `Download()` method. It accepts four input parameters:

- **url**: The URL of the channel, posting and, later on, attachment.

- **path**: The path of the directory the static file will be created in.

- **fileName**: The name of the static file that will be created.

- **flag**: The type of content that is being downloaded. We recognize two content types: content pages (channels and postings) and binaries.

To issue an HTTP request, we will utilize the `HttpWebRequest` object from the `System.Net` namespace. We will first create a request based on the URL of the channel or posting, then we will set the request to use the credentials of the 'Stage As' user (if one has been defined). It is here that we will make use of the user agent and header information defined earlier.

Notice that we have not allowed the request to be redirected automatically. That's because in this example, we won't attempt to handle pages that perform redirections. For example, if a page has `Response.Redirect()` statements coded within it, they will be ignored. You can, of course, enhance the tool to handle server-side page redirects (for an example of how to do so, see `http://www.gotdotnet.com/Community/UserSamples/Details.aspx?SampleGuid=153B8D20-EE51-4105-AAEF-519A7B841FCC`).

```
static void Download(string url, string path, string fileName,
                     EnumBinary flag)
{
  try
  {
    string filePath = m_DestinationDirectory + path.Replace("/","\\");
    // Download the file only if it has not been downloaded before
    if (!File.Exists(filePath))
    {
      // Create a new request based on the URL
      HttpWebRequest request = (HttpWebRequest)WebRequest.Create(url);

      // Make a request based on the specified 'Stage As' user
      if (m_credentials != null)
      {
        request.Credentials = m_credentials;
      }

      request.UserAgent = m_UserAgent;
```

```
      request.Headers.Add(m_HttpHeader, "true");
      request.AllowAutoRedirect = false;
  }
}
catch(Exception ex)
{
  StringBuilder sb =  new StringBuilder();
  string newLine = System.Environment.NewLine;
  sb.Append("----------" + newLine);
  sb.Append("Exception of type [" + ex.GetType() + "] has been thrown!"
          + newLine);
  sb.Append("Error Processing URL:" + url + newLine);
  sb.Append("Message: " + ex.Message + newLine);
  sb.Append("Source: " + ex.Source + newLine);
  sb.Append("Stack Trace: " + ex.StackTrace + newLine);
  sb.Append("----------" + newLine);
  WriteToLog(sb.ToString());
  }
}
```

Use our custom DotNetSiteStager HTTP header to program your pages to behave differently when they are requested by our staging tool. For example, to include selected content on a generated static page, you would do something like this:

```
if (Request.Header("DotNetSiteStager" != null)
{
  // The following line of code will only execute when the page
  // is requested by the stager
  Response.Write("Page generated by DotNetSiteStager.");
}
```

Getting Responses and Creating Files

After issuing an HTTP request, we call the HttpWebResponse.GetResponse() method to get the response. If all goes well, we will get an HTTP 200 (OK) status code, which means that the page was downloaded successfully.

The resulting byte-array is then converted to a static file using a FileStream object.

```
static void Download(string url, string path, string fileName,
                     EnumBinary flag)
{
  // Stage only postings
  if (flag == EnumBinary.ContentPage)
  {
    try
    {
      . . . code continues . . .
      // Get the response;
      HttpWebResponse response = request.GetResponse() as HttpWebResponse;

      // If all goes well, we will retrieve a status code of 200 (OK)
      if (response.StatusCode == HttpStatusCode.OK)
      {
        BinaryReader br = new BinaryReader(response.GetResponseStream());
        int contentLength = (int)response.ContentLength;
        byte[] buffer = br.ReadBytes(contentLength);

        // Process page and download attachments
        ProcessPageAndGetAttachments(response.ContentEncoding, ref buffer);

        Directory.CreateDirectory(filePath);
        if (fileName.IndexOf(".") < 0)
        {
          fileName = fileName + "." + m_DefaultFileExtension;
```

```
        }
        FileStream fs = new FileStream(filePath + fileName,
            FileMode.Create);
        fs.Write(buffer, 0, buffer.Length);
        fs.Close();
      }
    }
    . . . code continues . . .
  }
  . . . code continues . . .
}
```

Notice that before generating the file, we make a call to a helper function, namely ProcessPageAndGetAttachments(), which attempts to do two things:

- Correct the <base> tag to point it to the URL of the destination site. For example, when generating files from http://tropicalgreen to http://www.tropicalgreen.net, the host name stored in the href attribute of the <base> tag is changed accordingly.

- Set the code page based on the encoding type identified in the response from the MCMS server. Should the encoding type be undetermined, it uses the default value stored in the m_CodePage variable.

Add the ProcessPageAndGetAttachments() method directly below the Download() method.

```
private static void ProcessPageAndGetAttachments(string encodingName,
                                                 ref byte[] buffer)
{
  // Check to see if encoding information is available
  if (encodingName.ToLower().IndexOf("charset=") >= 0)
  {
    // Encoding information is available. Use it!
    encodingName = encodingName.Substring(encodingName.IndexOf("charset=")
        + 8);
  }
  else
  {
    // No encoding information found. Use the default setting.
    encodingName = m_CodePage;
  }
  // Convert the buffer to a string so that we work with it.
  Encoding enc = Encoding.GetEncoding(encodingName);
  string content = enc.GetString(buffer);
  // Process the page
  // Correct the <base> tag
  if (m_BaseUrl != "")
  {
    content = content.Replace("<base href=\"" + m_SourceHost, "<base href=\""
        + m_BaseUrl);
  }
  // Set the code page
  if (m_CodePage != "")
  {
    content = content.Replace("<HEAD>","<HEAD>\n<meta http-equiv=\""
        + "Content-Type\"content=\"text/html; charset=" + enc.WebName
        + "\">");
  }
  // Update the buffer with the modified content
  buffer = enc.GetBytes(content);
}
```

You may be wondering why we named the method ProcessPageAndGetAttachments() when it doesn't deal with attachments. That's because later on, we will enhance this method to handle attachments as well.

Staging Attachments

Up to this point, we have programmed the stager to generate files for channel cover pages and postings. Let's proceed to stage links to resources, images, and other attachments within these pages. Here's the game plan:

1. We will first scan through each channel cover page and posting for a list of all attachments.
2. We will add the URL of any attachments found to an ArrayList.
3. Once we have collected a list of attachments for each channel cover page or posting, we will proceed to download and stage them using the same technique for downloading and generating static files that we used earlier.

Collecting a List of Attachments to Download

The first step in the process is to scan all channel cover pages and postings for attachments. Earlier, we declared an ArrayList class variable, m_AttachmentUrls, which contains a list of attachment URLs to be downloaded and staged.

```
[STAThread]
static void Main(string[] args)
{
  m_AttachmentUrls = new ArrayList();
  . . . code continues . . .
}
```

Scanning Pages for Attachments

Since we are already scanning postings in the ProcessPageAndGetAttachments() method, let's enhance it to look for attachments.

Information about attachments is embedded within HTML tags. It can be found in:

- The href attribute of the <base>, <a>, and <link> tags.
- The src attribute of the <script>, <xml>, <img>, <embed>, <frame>, and <iframe> tags.
- The background attribute of the <body>, <td>, <th>, <table>, and <layer> tags.

For each tag, we will look for the attribute that contains the attachment and extract its URL. For example, if the content contains an image tag:

```
<img border=0 src="/nr/rdonlyres/0/tree.gif">
```

We will grab the entire <img> tag and extract the value of the src attribute, which contains the URL of the attachment. The helper function that searches for attachments is called FindAttachment() (defined later). Add calls to FindAttachment() to the ProcessPageAndGetAttachments() method as shown below.

```
private static void ProcessPageAndGetAttachments(string encodingName,
                                                  ref byte[] buffer)
{
    . . . code continues . . .
    // Replace special characters to make it easier to find
    content = content.Replace("\t"," ").Replace("\n"," ").Replace("\r", " ");
    // Get attachments

    // Start searching for attachments!
    FindAttachment(ref content, "base", "href");
    FindAttachment(ref content, "a", "href");
    FindAttachment(ref content, "link", "href");
    FindAttachment(ref content, "script", "src");
    FindAttachment(ref content, "xml", "src");
    FindAttachment(ref content, "img", "src");
    FindAttachment(ref content, "frame", "src");
    FindAttachment(ref content, "iframe", "src");
    FindAttachment(ref content, "embed", "src");
    FindAttachment(ref content, "body", "background");
    FindAttachment(ref content, "td", "background");
    FindAttachment(ref content, "th", "background");
    FindAttachment(ref content, "table", "background");
    FindAttachment(ref content, "layer", "background");
}
```

Of course, depending on the tags used by authors, the list above may not be exhaustive. Feel free to add more tags and attributes to the list.

The FindAttachment() method accepts three input parameters:

- **input**: The HTML of the page being scanned
- **tagName**: The tag to look for (e.g. <img>)
- **attribute**: The attribute that stores the attachment's URL (e.g. src)

It looks for all instances of the tag in the content. For example, when it finds an <img> tag, it extracts the URL from its src attribute using the ExtractUrlFromTag() method (defined later).

If a URL has been successfully extracted, it is added to the list of URLs using the AddToUrlList() helper function (also defined later).

<base> tags are handled separately. Earlier, we discussed how <base> tags are injected into all postings by the RobotMetaTag. The browser interprets all relative links by pre-pending the value in its href attribute to them. If FindAttachment() sees a <base> tag, it calls the SetBaseUrl() routine, which stores the extracted URL in the m_LocalBaseUrl variable for use later when downloading relative links.

Add the FindAttachment() method to the class:

```
private static void FindAttachment(ref string input, string tagName,
                                    string attribute)
{
    // Pattern that extracts all tags with the specified tagName
    string pattern = @"<\s*" + tagName + @"\b[^>]*>";

    // The regular expression that finds all the tags
    Regex findTags = new Regex(pattern, RegexOptions.IgnoreCase);

    foreach (Match tag in findTags.Matches(input))
    {
        // Extract the URL from each tag based on the specified attribute
        string url = ExtractUrlFromTag(tag.Value, attribute);
        // We have successfully extracted a URL
```

```
        if (url != "")
        {
            // Handle <base> tags
            if (tagName == "base")
            {
                // Set the base path for pages that have it defined.
                SetBaseUrl(url);
            }
            else
            {
                // Add the URL to the array list
                AddToUrlList(url);
            }
        }
    }
}
```

The regular expression used to pick up all tags of the specified type is exactly the same as the one used in Chapter 9, *Validating Placeholder Controls*.

When the `FindAttachment()` method encounters a tag it's looking for, it calls the `ExtractUrlFromTag()` method to pull out the attachment's URL. Once it finds the attribute within the tag, it checks to see if the URL is stored between double quotes or single quotes and extracts it. Should the method be unable to find the attribute (perhaps the attribute can't be found), it returns an empty string.

```
// Get the URLs from a specific property of the current html tag
static string ExtractUrlFromTag(string tagValue, string attribute)
{
    // e.g. of input: <img src="http://www.tropicalgreen.net/myimage.jpg">
    string url = "";

    // Pattern to match the attribute
    string pattern = attribute + @"\s*=\s*(\""|')*[^(\""|')>]*";

    // After extraction, the input string will be:
    //   src = "http://www.tropicalgreen.net/myimage.jpg"
    Regex findAttribute = new Regex(pattern, RegexOptions.IgnoreCase);
    Match att = findAttribute.Match(tagValue);

    if (att.Success)
    {
        url = att.Value;

        // Get the position of the "=" character
        int equal = url.IndexOf("=");

        // Get only the URL
        url = url.Substring(equal + 1);

        // Trim spaces
        url = url.Trim();

        // Remove the opening double quotes or single quote
        if (url.StartsWith("\"") || url.StartsWith("'"))
        {
            url = url.Substring(1);
        }
        // Remove the closing double quotes or single quote
        if (url.EndsWith("\"") || url.EndsWith("'"))
        {
            url = url.Substring(0, url.Length-1);
        }
    }
    return url;
}
```

The SetBaseUrl() routine handles <base> tags. <base> tags are typically embedded between <head> tags. Here's an example of a <base> tag:

```
<base href="http://tropicalgreen/TropicalGreen/Templates/Plant.aspx?
NRMODE=Published&NRORIGINALURL=%2fPlantCatalog%2fAloeVera%2ehtm&NRNODEGUID=%7b
569D1CCA-9A9D-4C43-B0C3-DB1AACD98684%7d&NRCACHEHINT=NoModifyGuest">
```

Notice that the URL of the template file is stored in its href attribute. Browsers add this href value to all relative links found within the page. In the SetBaseUrl() method, we will extract the value of the href attribute of the <base> tag and store it in the m_LocalBaseUrl variable. Later on, we will use this value to construct the actual URLs of relative attachments found on the page.

```
private static void SetBaseUrl(string url)
{
  if (url.IndexOf("?") > -1)
  {
    url = url.Substring(0,url.IndexOf("?"));
  }
  if (!url.EndsWith("/"))
  {
    object o = CmsContext.Searches.GetByUrl(url);
    if (o != null)
    {
      if (o is Channel)
      {
        url += "/";
      }
    }
  }
  url = url.Substring(0,url.LastIndexOf("/")+1);
  if (url.StartsWith("http://"))
  {
    url = url.Remove(0,7);   // remove "http://"
    url = url.Remove(0,(url+"/").IndexOf("/"));
  }
  m_LocalBaseUrl = url;
}
```

Storing Information about the Attachments to a List

Once an attachment is found, we record its URL and format type to an ArrayList. Before we do so, we prepare the URL and run several checks to see if it's valid. We will do all that in the AddToUrlList() method.

First, bookmarks are removed. Examples of bookmarks include "Back To Top"-type hyperlinks that typically look like this: <a href="somepage.htm#Top">. Since bookmarks are place markers that point to locations within the page itself, we can shave them off the URL and still be able to download the page. Add the AddToUrlList() method to the class:

```
private static void AddToUrlList(string url)
{
  // Remove internal bookmarks from the URL
  string origUrl = url;
  if (url.IndexOf("#") >= 0)
  {
    url = url.Substring(0, url.IndexOf("#"));
  }
}
```

All relative URLs have to be converted to absolute URLs so that they can be downloaded and staged. We use the value stored in the <base> tag, if one has been found.

```
private static void AddToUrlList(string url)
{
  . . . code continues . . .
  // Convert Relative URLs to Absolute URLs
  if (!url.StartsWith("/"))
  {
    url = m_LocalBaseUrl + url;
  }
}
```

Next, we remove host information from the URL. This makes it easier for us to process the rest of the URL later, especially when attempting to check to see if the attachment is a channel item.

```
private static void AddToUrlList(string url)
{
  . . . code continues . . .
  // Remove host information from the URL
  if (url.StartsWith(m_SourceHost))
  {
    url = url.Remove(0, m_SourceHost.Length);
  }
}
```

We will only add URLs that are valid. Valid URLs:

- Will not contain single or double quotes.

- Will not link to other ports (such as http://localhost:81/somepage.htm) or other domains. Since we have removed host information earlier on (which leaves us with URLs such as :80/ or :80/somepage.htm), we simply look for the presence of a colon to check for URLs that have a port number.

- Will not contain querystring parameters. We will enforce that by ensuring that the URL does not contain a question mark. The reason for not processing pages with querystrings is because they are likely to be dynamic pages (*.aspx or *.asp) and static snapshots of these pages aren't able to process querystring parameters.

```
private static void AddToUrlList(string url)
{
  . . . code continues . . .
  // Check URLs to see if they are valid
  bool isValidUrl = true;
  string reason = "";
  if ((url.IndexOf("'") >= 0 || url.IndexOf("\"") >= 0)
      || url.IndexOf(":") >= 0 || url.IndexOf("?") >= 0)
  {
    // URL is invalid
    isValidUrl = false;
    reason = "Ignoring invalid url or url from external domain";
  }
}
```

We will also check to see if the URL belongs to a posting or channel cover page that will be staged by the CollectChannel() method defined earlier. We could leave out this check and have the stager generate these pages as many times as they appear, but remember that the smaller the number of files staged, the faster the process!

Notice that we used a helper function, EnhancedGetByUrl(). It basically does the same job as the Searches.GetByUrl() method, but includes several improvements as we shall see later.

```
private static void AddToUrlList(string url)
{
  . . . code continues . . .
  // Check to see if the URL refers to a channel item that
  // will be staged
  if (isValidUrl)
  {
    ChannelItem ci = EnhancedGetByUrl(url) as ChannelItem;
    if (ci != null)
    {
      if (ci.Path.ToLower().StartsWith(m_StartChannel.ToLower()))
      {
        isValidUrl = false;
        reason = "";
      }
    }
  }
}
```

As part of keeping the number of attachments in the list as small as possible, before adding the attachment's URL to our list, we will check if the URL has been recorded before. If it has, we won't add it again.

Finally, the URL has been adjusted, verified, and is ready to be added to the list. This is the easy part. Simply add the URL and the format of the attachment to the ArrayList. If the URL has been rejected, we will record it in the log file together with the reason for not staging it.

```
private static void AddToUrlList(string url)
{
  . . . code continues . . .
  if (isValidUrl)
  {
    url = url.Replace("&amp;","&");
    if (!m_AttachmentUrls.Contains(url))
    {
      m_AttachmentUrls.Add(url);
    }
  }
  else
  {
    if (reason != "")
    {
      WriteToLog(reason + " : " + origUrl);
    }
  }
}
```

Enhancing the Searches.GetByUrl() Method

When the "Map Channel Names to Host Headers" option is turned on, the top-level channel name becomes a host header. For example, if the channel directly beneath the root channel is named tropicalgreen, the URL of the channel becomes http://tropicalgreen, instead of http://localhost/tropicalgreen. This feature allows a single MCMS server to host multiple websites, each with a different host header name.

> To check whether the "Map Channel Names to Host Headers" option is set to "Yes" or "No", open the MCMS Server Configuration Application and check the value of this option in the General tab.

> Note that the "Map Channel Names to Host Headers" feature is not available in MCMS Standard Edition.

However, the `Searches.GetByUrl()` method does not work reliably for sites where channel names are mapped to host header names. When the `Searches.GetByUrl()` method is fed the URL of, say, the top-level channel, `http://tropicalgreen`, we would expect it to return an instance of the `tropicalgreen` channel. The trouble is it returns a null object instead. This is because an issue with the `Searches.GetByUrl()` method causes it to expect the input URL to be `http://localhost/tropicalgreen` regardless of whether the "Map Channel Names to Host Headers" option is set to "Yes" or "No". We will create the `EnhancedGetByUrl()` method to get around this problem.

The `EnhancedGetByUrl()` method first checks to see if the "Map Channel Names to Host Headers" option is set to "Yes" or "No". It does so by looking at the published URL of the root channel. When "Map Channel Names to Host Headers" has been set to "Yes", the root channel's URL will be `http://Channels`. Otherwise, it will simply be `/Channels/`.

If the "Map Channel Names to Host Headers" option is set to "Yes", we will convert the input URL to a path and use the `Searches.GetByPath()` method to retrieve an instance of the channel item. For example, if the URL is `http://tropicalgreen/plantcatalog`, the routine converts it to the channel's path: `/Channels/tropicalgreen/plantcatalog`. Add the following code to the class:

```
static ChannelItem EnhancedGetByUrl(string url)
{
  if (IsMapChannelToHostHeaderEnabled())
  {
    // Remove "http://" from the URL and remove any trailing forward slashes
    string hostName = m_SourceHost.ToLower().Replace("http://","").Trim(new
                      Char[] {'/'});
    // Convert the URL to a path
    string Path = HttpUtility.UrlDecode(url);
    Path = Path.Replace("http://","/Channels/");
    if (!Path.StartsWith("/Channels/"))
    {
      Path = "/Channels/"+hostName+Path;
    }

    if (Path.EndsWith(".htm"))
    {
      Path = Path.Substring(0,Path.Length - 4);
    }
    if (Path.EndsWith("/"))
    {
      Path = Path.Substring(0,Path.Length - 1);
    }
    return (ChannelItem)(cmsContext.Searches.GetByPath(Path));
  }
  else
  {
    return cmsContext.Searches.GetByUrl(url);
  }
}
static bool IsMapChannelToHostHeaderEnabled()
{
  return (cmsContext.RootChannel.UrlModePublished == "http://Channels/");
}
```

Downloading the Attachments

Once we have collected a list of attachments for each channel cover page or posting, we are ready to generate static copies of them. To do so, we will call a helper function `DownloadAttachments()` at two points in the `CollectChannel()` method:

- After the channel's cover page has been staged
- After each posting has been staged

Add the calls to the `DownloadAttachments()` method as shown in the highlighted portions of the code below:

```
static void CollectChannel(Channel channel)
{
    // Download the channel itself
    WriteToLog("Info: Downloading Channel: " + channel.Path);
    Download(GetUrlWithHost(channel.Url), channel.Path.Replace(
        m_StartChannel,"/"),
        m_DefaultFileName, EnumBinary.ContentPage);

    // Download all attachments in the cover page or channel rendering script
    DownloadAttachments();

    // Download all the postings within the channel
    foreach (Posting p in channel.Postings)
    {
        WriteToLog("Info: Downloading Posting: " + p.Path);
        Download(GetUrlWithHost(p.Url), channel.Path.Replace(m_StartChannel,"/"),
            p.Name, EnumBinary.ContentPage);

        // Download all attachments in the posting
        DownloadAttachments();
    }
    foreach (Channel c in channel.Channels)
    {
        CollectChannel(c);
    }
}
```

The `DownloadAttachments()` method loops through each element of the `m_AttachmentUrls` array and extracts the attachment's path and file name from its URL. The `Download()` method that we defined earlier is called to stage each attachment as a static file.

```
private static void DownloadAttachments()
{
    for (int i = 0; i < m_AttachmentUrls.Count; i++)
    {
        string path = m_AttachmentUrls[i].ToString();
        string[] arrPath = path.Split('/');
        string fileName = arrPath[arrPath.Length - 1];
        path = "";
        for (int j = 0; j < arrPath.Length - 1; j++)
        {
            path += arrPath[j] + "/";
        }
        Download(GetUrlWithHost(m_AttachmentUrls[i].ToString()), path, fileName,
            EnumBinary.ContentBinary);
    }
    m_AttachmentUrls.Clear();
}
```

The paths of all attachments and images will follow that of the original page. As long as you do maintain the hierarchy of the staged folders, for instance staging from `http://SourceServer/ tropicalgreen/` to `http://DestinationServer/tropicagreen/`, the URLs within each page will not need to be updated.

Running the DotNetSiteStager

The DotNetSiteStager application is complete! Run the application to stage static versions of your site. We ran the stager on the Tropical Green website and here's a snapshot of the folders and files that were staged:

Name ▲	Size	Type
Admin		File Folder
Columns		File Folder
Gardens		File Folder
logs		File Folder
NR		File Folder
PlantCatalog		File Folder
SiteMap		File Folder
TropicalGreen		File Folder
webctrl_client		File Folder
default.htm	6 KB	HTML Document

Within each folder are static versions of postings and attachments. For example, the `PlantCatalog` folder contains HTML snapshots of each plant posting:

Name ▲	Size	Type
AloeVera.htm	9 KB	HTML Document
BananaTree.htm	10 KB	HTML Document
Bougainvillea.htm	9 KB	HTML Document
CoconutTree.htm	9 KB	HTML Document
default.htm	7 KB	HTML Document
EggPlant.htm	8 KB	HTML Document
Ficus.htm	8 KB	HTML Document
Hibiscus.htm	11 KB	HTML Document
Ixora.htm	8 KB	HTML Document
ManEatingPlant.htm	9 KB	HTML Document

The static pages generated by DotNetSiteStager include the Web Author Console. How can I remove it?

DotNetSiteStager takes a snapshot of each page as seen by the 'Stage As' user. If the Web Author Console is included in each generated page, this most probably means that the 'Stage As' user has been given authoring rights. To prevent the Web Author Console from being included in the staged files, use an account that has only subscriber rights to the channels staged. In addition, staging pages with the Console may result in HTTP 500 errors as additional HTTP header information is required to download and generate them correctly.

Suggested Improvements

There are various enhancements that could be made to the DotNetSiteStager application. Here are a few suggestions:

- Staging links found within attachments. For example, if an HTML attachment contains links to cascading stylesheets or linked script files, the stager could be intelligent enough to pick these up and stage them too.

- Handle client-side redirection. This is required to ensure that links to elements that do a server-side redirect (such as channel rendering scripts, HTTP modules, controls, and template code) are simulated with client-side HTTP redirection using meta tags.

- Remove ViewState information in the staged pages, if there is any. ViewState information preserves the state of a page across postbacks. As static pages do not perform postbacks, we can safely remove it. To do so, you could use a regular expression to remove the `<input name="__viewstate">` tag from each generated page.

- The entire .NET stager tool could be coded to work via a web service. In this way, you could invoke the staging of static pages from a remote computer.

A more sophisticated and complete version of DotNetSiteStager that, among other things, handles client-side redirection and the staging of attachments linked from resources (not channel items) can be found on GotDotNet, The Microsoft .NET Framework Community, at the following address:

```
http://www.gotdotnet.com/Community/UserSamples/Details.aspx?SampleGuid=153B8D20-
EE51-4105-AAEF-519A7B841FCC
```

Summary

While staging static pages appears to be taking a step back from modern web technologies that rely on dynamic websites, business processes sometimes dictate the necessity to deliver snapshots of pages. Be it in order to send out content in mailers, on CDs, in help files, or to create a collection of files to be indexed by a file-based search engine, developers may need to generate static versions of channels and postings.

In this chapter, we first looked at Site Stager, a utility that ships with MCMS 2002, and how it can be used to stage static pages of ASP-based postings. However, Site Stager does not work for postings based on the newer ASP.NET template files.

To stage snapshots of dynamic postings based on ASP.NET templates, we wrote our own version of Site Stager, DotNetSiteStager. The custom stager walks through all channels and postings in the hierarchy, downloading and generating static versions of each page that it sees. The tool also stages static versions of attachments linked from postings and channel rendering scripts.

11
InfoPath with MCMS Web Services

The usual way to maintain content in MCMS is by using the Web Author (in the browser) or the Authoring Connector for Microsoft Word. But often customers would like to use MCMS with other editing components to make integration into their business workflow easier. With Microsoft Office System 2003, the Office product has matured since the release of MCMS 2002 and now contains an information-gathering and management program named InfoPath. InfoPath is a powerful tool for designing electronic forms using a combination of XML and XSL. By combining InfoPath with MCMS 2002 via Web services, we can allow content authors to focus only on content and not worry about presentation. We can reduce the training time required for authors, as using InfoPath can be a lot simpler than learning how to operate the Web Author (for instance, switching between modes, selecting templates, and submitting postings) and also reduce the need to create extensive customizations to the Web Author interface.

This combination provides users with an electronic forms solution that has a rich GUI and which allows data to be easily shared between applications, making it perfect for customers who require an integrated business workflow solution. In this chapter, we will demonstrate how to combine InfoPath and the power of ASP.NET Web services with MCMS's robust content repository. Similar methods can also be used by software developers to build interfaces that provide distributed authoring capabilities from a variety of applications, including BizTalk, SharePoint Products and Technologies, and Commerce Server.

Project Overview

Throughout this chapter, we will develop a solution that will enable MCMS Authors to maintain content stored in the MCMS repository using InfoPath 2003 via ASP.NET Web services.

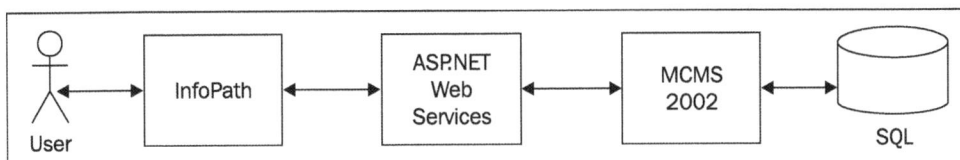

The user will be able to launch a single InfoPath form and select the posting they wish to modify, which can be based on any MCMS template. A Web service call will then be made that loads the posting, placeholders, and custom properties from the MCMS repository, using the MCMS Publishing API (PAPI). The InfoPath form will then be populated with this data so the user can make their modifications to the content. Once the changes are complete they can then be sent back to the ASP.NET Web service and saved to MCMS.

For simplicity the solution outlined in this chapter will only permit editing of HtmlPlaceholders and Text custom properties of existing postings, but it could be extended to create new postings, use different types of placeholders, and to set selection custom properties. For further enhancement ideas, see the *Possible Enhancements to this Solution* section at the end of the chapter.

The form we will create retrieves and displays the posting and template details, and allows modifications to the custom properties and placeholders. The placeholders will use InfoPath's rich text control that allows formatting of the content. A bonus of this solution is that all placeholder content will be transformed into XHTML (Extensible HyperText Markup Language, which at its most basic level is HTML that conforms to XML standards) as InfoPath's data is stored in XML.

MCMS Authoring InfoPath Form

This InfoPath form can retrieve and update existing MCMS postings.

Posting To Load (e.g. /channels/www.tropicalgreen.net/PlantCatalog/AloeVera):
/channels/www.tropicalgreen.net/plantcatalog/aloevera

[Run Query]

Name	AloeVera
Display Name	Aloe Vera
Posting Path	/Channels/www.tropicalgreen.net/Pl...
Posting ID	569d1cca-9a9d-4c43-b0c3-db1aac...
Template Name	Plant
Template Path	/Templates/TropicalGreen/PlantCatal...
Template ID	b78e84d6-5905-4f9e-a7bb-97ea2d2...

Custom Properties

FirstSavedBy

Placeholders

Description

Microsoft.ContentManagement.Publishing.Extensions.Placeholders.HtmlPlaceho

This is some test content for the description placeholder.

ScientificName

Microsoft.ContentManagement.Publishing.Extensions.Placeholders.HtmlPlaceho

This is the scientific name.

What are ASP.NET Web Services?

ASP.NET Web services allow software developers to create an interface for their application that supports integration across application domains. ASP.NET Web services consist of one or more Web methods. Web methods are like methods of regular .NET objects, but are invoked over a network and executed on the server that hosts the Web service. This is similar to Remote Procedure Calls (RPC) and DCOM object invocation.

When calling a Web method, parameters may be passed and any return value can be retrieved. As the method call is sent to the machine hosting the Web service using HTTP, the objects being passed as parameters are transformed into a format suitable for transmission. In this case, XML serialization is employed, which is the process of converting an object from its binary form in memory to HTTP-safe XML format.

We have chosen to use ASP.NET Web services to integrate InfoPath with MCMS as it allows us to use the robustness of .NET while maintaining a flexible GUI built in InfoPath. Web services are platform independent and are also the preferred integration method for InfoPath. Another possible solution would be to develop the code within InfoPath by scripting the queries to MCMS and handcrafting the InfoPath form, but we would then lose the benefits of having one centralized store for business logic and processing thus reducing our ability to scale and support the solution.

Creating the MCMS Web Service Project

The MCMS Authoring Web service will access MCMS via the Publishing API. A series of Web methods will allow developers to retrieve template details, and update postings. The MCMS Authoring Web service project will be created from the MCMS Web Service project template in Visual Studio .NET 2003. The MCMS Web Service project template automatically includes the correct references and web.config entries to talk to MCMS.

Let's go ahead and create this ASP.NET Web service application:

1. Launch Visual Studio .NET and from the File menu, select New | Project.
2. From the Project Types panel, select Visual C# Projects under Content Management Server Projects.
3. From the Templates panel, select MCMS Web Service.
4. Enter the location as http://localhost/McmsAuthoringWebService and click OK.

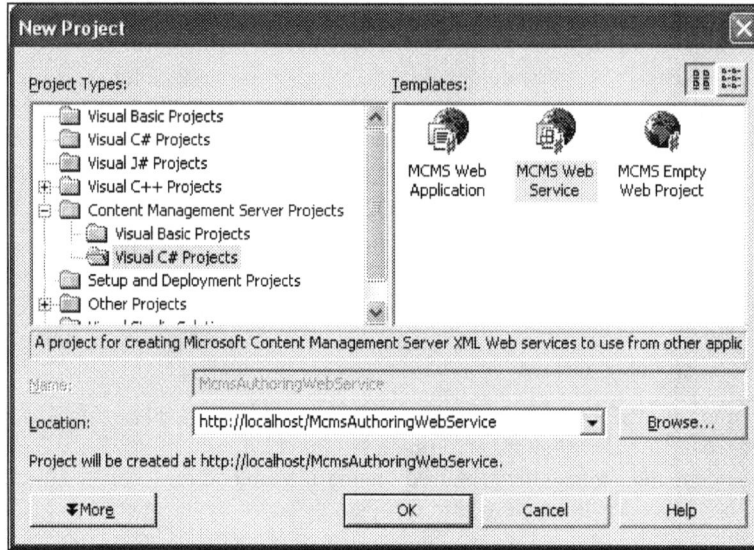

A project should now be created and you will notice all the required MCMS references are already created. You can delete the Console folder from the project as we do not need it.

Creating the Business Layer

Now we have created our project let's look at the business layer. The classes in the business layer will encapsulate the key properties of MCMS objects such as Name, Path, Value, and ID (equating to MCMS's Guid property). All the objects in our object model must be serializable, that is, it must be possible to convert them into XML so they can be transferred via Web services. We cannot transfer the standard PAPI objects directly via ASP.NET Web services as there is no immediate way to serialize them to XML. Therefore, we will be recreating portions of the MCMS object model in our own classes that do support serialization so they can be sent and received by ASP.NET Web services.

The PAPI classes do not contain default constructors, hence cannot be serialized into XML. For more on XML Serialization see http://msdn.microsoft.com/library/default.asp?url= /library/en-us/cpguide/html/cpconintroducingxmlserialization.asp.

We will develop the following classes:

- LightweightPosting
  - LightweightTemplate
  - LightweightPlaceholderCollection
    - LightweightPlaceholder
  - LightweightCustomPropertyCollection
    - LightweightCustomProperty

The classes are prefixed with Lightweight so they will not be confused with the classes in the Microsoft.ContentManagement.Publishing namespace. These classes will be used by our Web service layer and will be transferred as XML via the ASP.NET Web service we are going to build.

For development of these classes, we will start with the least dependent classes and work our way up the hierarchy.

Maintaining Custom Properties

The ASP.NET Web service will load and maintain the custom properties of postings. To facilitate this, we will create two objects, namely LightweightCustomProperty and LightweightCustomPropertyCollection.

The LightWeightCustomProperty object is essentially like the CustomProperty object found in the MCMS PAPI—with one major difference: it is serializable; all its properties and methods can be re-packaged as XML, ready to be consumed by a Web service and understood by InfoPath. The LightWeightCustomPropertyCollection object will basically store a collection of LightWeightCustomProperty objects, very much like the CustomProperties object from the PAPI.

We'll start by creating the LightWeightCustomProperty class:

1. In Visual Studio .NET, right-click on the McmsAuthoringWebService project and add a class called LightweightCustomProperty.

2. Add the Microsoft.ContentManagement.Publishing namespace to the file:

    ```
    using System;
    using Microsoft.ContentManagement.Publishing;
    namespace McmsAuthoringWebService
    {
        /// <summary>
        /// Summary description for LightweightCustomProperty.
        /// </summary>
        public class LightweightCustomProperty
        {
        . . . code continues . . .
    }
    ```

3. Add the following public variables to the class:

    ```
    /// <summary>
    /// The name of the custom property name in MCMS
    /// </summary>
    public string Name;

    /// <summary>
    /// The Current value of the custom property in MCMS
    /// </summary>
    public string Value;
    ```

Name and Value should more properly be defined as properties but in this example, they have been defined as public variables for brevity.

---

4. For an object to be serialized, it must have a constructor that takes no arguments. This default constructor is needed by the .NET Framework during serialization, and is added by VS .NET when we create a class. However, we also need to add the following constructor that accepts values for the public variables as its arguments:

```
/// <summary>
/// Instantiate the custom property setting the Name and Current value.
/// </summary>
/// <param name="_Name">The name of the custom property</param>
/// <param name="_Value">The current value of the custom property</param>
public LightweightCustomProperty(string _Name, string _Value)
{
  this.Name = _Name;
  this.Value = _Value;
}
```

5. The custom property values will be saved back to the relevant MCMS posting. So let's create the Save() method, which sets the custom property's value for the posting passed in as a parameter.

```
/// <summary>
/// Save the custom property value
/// </summary>
/// <param name="_Posting">The posting to be updated</param>
public void Save(Posting _Posting)
{
  // Get the custom property of the posting and set the value
  _Posting.CustomProperties[this.Name].Value = this.Value;
}
```

A posting may use a template with multiple custom properties defined. To store this collection of custom properties, we will define a strongly typed collection of LightweightCustomProperty objects called LightweightCustomPropertyCollection.

1. Create a new class in Visual Studio .NET and give it a name of LightweightCustomPropertyCollection. Add the namespace Microsoft.ContentManagement.Publishing to it, and make it extend System.Collections.CollectionBase.

```
using System;
using Microsoft.ContentManagement.Publishing;
namespace McmsAuthoringWebService
{
  /// <summary>
  /// Summary description for LightweightCustomPropertyCollection.
  /// </summary>
  public class LightweightCustomPropertyCollection
                      : System.Collections.CollectionBase
  {
    . . . code continues . . .
  }
}
```

2. As LightweightCustomPropertyCollection is a strongly typed collection, the default property will be a LightweightCustomProperty.

```
/// <summary>
/// The indexed LightweightCustomProperty
/// </summary>
public LightweightCustomProperty this[int index]
```

```
{
  get
  {
    // Cast the list item to a LightweightCustomProperty
    return(this.InnerList[index] as LightweightCustomProperty);
  }
  set
  {
    this.InnerList[index] = value;
  }
}
```

3. We will now define the Add() method that we will need in order to add a LightweightCustomProperty to the collection.

```
/// <summary>
/// Add an item to the collection
/// </summary>
/// <param name="item">The LightweightCustomProperty to be added</param>
public void Add(LightweightCustomProperty item)
{
  this.InnerList.Add(item);
}
```

4. The LightweightCustomPropertyCollection will be populated by a Microsoft.ContentManagement.Publishing.Posting object so we will define the Load() method. The Load() method will enumerate the custom properties of the posting and for each custom property it will instantiate a LightweightCustomProperty and add it to the collection.

For the purposes of this example we are only maintaining custom properties of type Text. This code could be extended to support custom properties of type Selection.

```
/// <summary>
/// Load the lightweight custom property collection from a posting.
/// </summary>
/// <param name="_Posting">Posting to be loaded from</param>
public void Load(Posting _Posting)
{
  if (_Posting != null)
  {
    // Loop through the custom properties
    foreach (CustomProperty _CustomProperty in _Posting.CustomProperties)
    {
      // Check if the cutsom property is of type 'text'
      // (custom properties will have > 0 allowed values)
      if (_CustomProperty.AllowedValues.Count == 0)
      {
        // Instantiate a lightweight custom property and
        // add it to the collection
        this.Add(new LightweightCustomProperty(_CustomProperty.Name,
            _CustomProperty.Value));
      }
    }
  }
}
```

5. We also need to be able to save all the custom properties that are held in the collection.

```
/// <summary>
/// Save the collection of custom properties
/// </summary>
/// <param name="_Posting">
/// Posting to save the custom property value to
/// </param>
public void Save(Posting _Posting)
{
    // Loop through the custom properties in the collection
    foreach (LightweightCustomProperty _LightweightCustomProperty in this)
    {
        // Save the custom property against the posting
        _LightweightCustomProperty.Save(_Posting);
    }
}
```

Now we have defined our classes for maintaining the custom properties, the project should look like this in Class View:

Creating the Lightweight Template Class

The template's path and GUID will be included in the InfoPath form so users know what template a posting is using. To do this we will create the LightweightTemplate class, which is a serializable cut-down representation of the Microsoft.ContentManagement.Publishing.Template class.

1. In Visual Studio .NET, right-click on the McmsAuthoringWebService project and create a new class called LightweightTemplate.

2. Add the Microsoft.ContentManagement.Publishing namespace.

```
using System;
using Microsoft.ContentManagement.Publishing;
namespace McmsAuthoringWebService
{
    /// <summary>
    /// Summary description for LightweightTemplate.
    /// </summary>
    public class LightweightTemplate
    {
        . . . code continues . . .
    }
}
```

3. Define the following public variables in the class:

```
/// <summary>
/// The name of the template in MCMS
/// </summary>
public string Name;

/// <summary>
/// The path of the template in MCMS
/// </summary>
public string Path;

/// <summary>
/// The Guid of the template in MCMS
/// </summary>
public Guid ID;
```

4. As the template object will be loaded from an instance of the `Microsoft.ContentManagement.Publishing.Template` class, we will now define the `Load()` method:

```
/// <summary>
/// Load the lightweight object from the MCMS Template
/// </summary>
/// <param name="_Template">The MCMS template to load from</param>
public void Load(Template _Template)
{
    this.Name = _Template.Name;
    this.Path = _Template.Path;

    // Create a new guid object because MCMS stores Guids in string format.
    this.ID = new Guid(_Template.Guid);
}
```

Maintaining Placeholder Values

The ASP.NET Web service will be able to load and maintain placeholder values of postings. To do this we will create two objects, namely `LightweightPlaceholder` and a corresponding `LightweightPlaceholderCollection`.

1. In Visual Studio .NET, right-click on the project and a new class called `LightweightPlaceholder`.

2. Add the following namespaces to the file:

```
using System;
using System.Xml;
using System.IO;
using Microsoft.ContentManagement.Publishing;
using Microsoft.ContentManagement.Publishing.Extensions.Placeholders;
```

```
namespace McmsAuthoringWebService
{
    . . . code continues . . .
}
```

3. Now, let's add the following public variables to our class, which will contain the placeholder's name, the type of placeholder, and its value:

```
/// <summary>
/// The placeholder name in MCMS
/// </summary>
public string Name;

/// <summary>
/// The type of placeholder e.g. Microsoft.ContentManagement.Publishing.
/// Extensions.Placeholders.HtmlPlaceholder
/// </summary>
public string Type;

/// <summary>
/// The XmlNode representation of the current value of the placeholder
/// </summary>
public XmlNode Value;
```

To be able to load an XmlNode with HTML, we will convert the HTML into well-formed XHTML. We will do this by using a publicly available tool called SgmlReader, by Chris Lovett, who works for a small outfit known as the Microsoft Corporation.

SGML stands for Standard Generalized Markup Language, the precursor to XML. The SgmlReader suite of tools provides many ways to create well-formed XML, but for the purposes of this example we will only need SgmlReader.dll.

To set up and configure the SgmlReader, follow these steps:

1. Download the tool from GotDotNet, at http://www.gotdotnet.com/Community/ UserSamples/Details.aspx?SampleGuid=b90fddce-e60d-43f8-a5c4-c3bd760564bc.

2. Extract the ZIP file to c:\sgml\SgmlReader.

3. Create a directory under <local_drive>\Program Files called SgmlReader and copy the C:\SGML\SgmlReader\SgmlReaderDll\bin\release\SgmlReaderDll.dll file to the new folder.

We are now ready to create the CleanHtml() method, which will convert HTML into well-formed XHTML, for instance from <img src="theImage.jpg"> into <img src="theImage.jpg"></img>. This method will utilize the SgmlReader assembly we previously referenced. Before it is converted, the HTML must be wrapped in a single tag, in this case <html>, so the SgmlReader will recognize it as one element. Once it is returned from the SgmlReader, we will escape some characters that cannot be escaped by InfoPath and we will remove the enclosing <html> element from the content.

1. Open the McmsAuthoringWebService project in Visual Studio .NET, and add a reference to <local_drive>\Program Files\SgmlReader\SgmlReaderDll.dll.

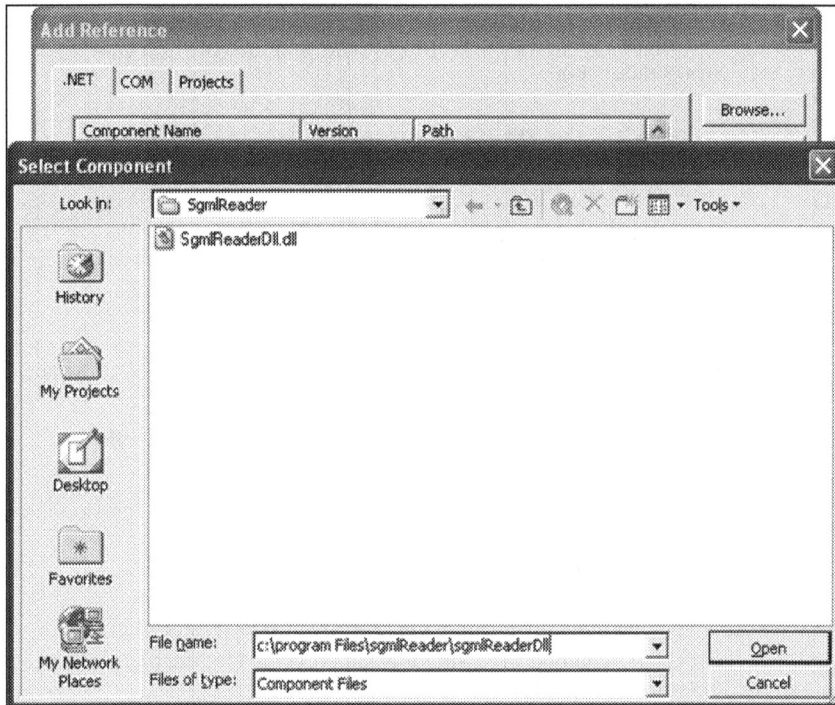

2. Create the following method in `LightweightPlaceholder.cs`:

```
/// <summary>
/// Convert 'badly formed' HTML into well formed XHTML using the
/// SgmlReader utility by Chris Lovett, Microsoft Corporation
/// </summary>
/// <param name="BadlyFormedHtml">The badly formed HTML</param>
/// <returns>Well formed XHTML representation of the HTML</returns>
public string CleanHtml(string BadlyFormedHtml)
{
    // Wrap the entire HTML string in a single tag so the
    // SGMLReader can process the data as one element
    BadlyFormedHtml = "<html>" + BadlyFormedHtml + "</html>";

    // Load the string reader with the badly formed HTML
    StringReader _stringReader = new StringReader(BadlyFormedHtml);

    // instantiate and set the badly formed HTML string reader
    // as the input stream of the SgmlReader
    Sgml.SgmlReader _sgmlReader = new Sgml.SgmlReader();
    _sgmlReader.InputStream = _stringReader;

    // Instantiate the string writer and xmltext writer
    // that will be used to hold the well formed XHTML
    StringWriter _stringWriter = new StringWriter();
    XmlTextWriter _xmlTextWriter = new XmlTextWriter(_stringWriter);

    // Read the stream
```

```
        _sgmlReader.Read();

        // loop through the SgmlReader until the end of the stream
        while(!_sgmlReader.EOF)
        {

          // add a node to the XML text writer
          _xmlTextWriter.WriteNode(_sgmlReader, true);

        }

        // cleanup the XML text writer
        _xmlTextWriter.Flush();
        _xmlTextWriter.Close();

        // Replace non-breaking spaces ( ) with spaces
        // as InfoPath escapes these in placeholders.
        string strCleanedXHTML = _stringWriter.ToString().Replace(" ",
                                                                   " ");

        // Remove the surrounding <html> tag by using an XmlDocument
        // Create a new XmlDocument and load in the clean XHTML
        XmlDocument _tempDocument = new XmlDocument();
        _tempDocument.LoadXml(strCleanedXHTML);

        // Get the html node and return the inner XML
        return _tempDocument.SelectSingleNode("/html").InnerXml;
    }
```

3. Now we are able to create well-formed XHTML from HTML stored in an HtmlPlaceholder, we can populate the XmlNode property that the placeholder content will be stored in for use by InfoPath.

```
    /// <summary>
    /// Create an XHTML XmlNode from 'badly formed' HTML
    /// </summary>
    /// <param name="BadlyFormattedHtml">The badly formed HTML string</param>
    /// <returns>XHTML XmlNode representation of input HTML</returns>
    public XmlNode LoadXHTML(string BadlyFormattedHtml)
    {
        // Create a temporary XmlDocument object to generate nodes
        System.Xml.XmlDocument tempDocument = new System.Xml.XmlDocument();

        // Create a wrapper node for the data so InfoPath will correctly detect
        // the XHTML content
        System.Xml.XmlElement theNode =
          (System.Xml.XmlElement)tempDocument.CreateNode(
            System.Xml.XmlNodeType.Element, "theNode", "");

        // Create a "RichText" element in the XHTML namespace
        System.Xml.XmlElement theRichText = (System.Xml.XmlElement)
            tempDocument.CreateNode(System.Xml.XmlNodeType.Element, "RichText",
                               "http://www.w3.org/1999/xhtml" );

        // Clean the badly formed HTML and set the inner XML of the RichText node
        theRichText.InnerXml = CleanHtml(BadlyFormattedHtml);

        // Append the RichText node to the wrapper node
        theNode.AppendChild( theRichText );

        //Return the wrapper element.
        return theNode;
    }
```

4. Next we will add a constructor to the `LightweightPlaceholder` class that accepts a `Microsoft.ContentManagement.Publishing.Placeholder` parameter. The `Name` and `Type` properties are set along with the `Value` property. To load the value we will first verify the placeholder is an `HtmlPlaceholder` and then will call the `LoadXHTML()` method passing in the placeholder's HTML. `LoadXHTML()` will convert the placeholder's HTML into an `XmlNode`.

```
/// <summary>
/// Instantiate and load a MCMS placeholder
/// </summary>
/// <param name="_Placeholder">MCMS placeholder to load</param>
public LightweightPlaceholder(Placeholder _Placeholder)
{
    // Set the name and the type of placeholder
    this.Name = _Placeholder.Name;
    this.Type = _Placeholder.GetType().ToString();

    // Is this an HtmlPlaceholder?
    if (_Placeholder is HtmlPlaceholder)
    {

        // Convert the contents of the placeholder to XHTML
        // and set the Value property
        this.Value = LoadXHTML(((HtmlPlaceholder)_Placeholder).Html);

    }
}
```

5. The placeholder values will be saved back to MCMS for the relevant posting. So let's create the `Save()` method. This solution currently only works with `HtmlPlaceholders` so we must first check to see if the placeholder is an `HtmlPlaceholder` and then we can set the `Html` property to the XML stored in the `Value` `XmlNode`.

```
/// <summary>
/// Save the placeholder contents to a posting
/// </summary>
/// <param name="_Posting">Posting to save against</param>
public void Save(Posting _Posting)
{
    // Set the placeholder value for the current placeholder
    // to the InnerXml of the Value property
    // Note: This will only work with HtmlPlaceholders. If enhanced for
    // other placeholders we would check the placeholder type before
    // casting.
    if (_Posting.Placeholders[this.Name] is HtmlPlaceholder)
    {
        ((HtmlPlaceholder)_Posting.Placeholders[this.Name]).Html =
                this.Value.InnerXml;
    }
    else
    {
        throw new Exception("The placeholder '" + this.Name
                        + "' is not an HtmlPlaceholder.");
    }
}
```

Maintaining Placeholder Collections

Let's now create a collection class to hold `LightweightPlaceholders` that we'll call `LightweightPlaceholderCollection`. The `LightweightPlaceholderCollection` will be used as postings may have more than one placeholder defined.

1. In Visual Studio .NET, create a new class, `LightweightPlaceholderCollection`, and add the MCMS `Publishing` and `Placeholders` namespaces to it. Also change the class to extend `System.Collections.CollectionBase`:

```
using System;
using Microsoft.ContentManagement.Publishing;
using Microsoft.ContentManagement.Publishing.Extensions.Placeholders;
namespace McmsAuthoringWebService
{
    /// <summary>
    /// Summary description for LightweightPlaceholderCollection.
    /// </summary>
    public class LightweightPlaceholderCollection
                    : System.Collections.CollectionBase
    {
        . . . code continues . . .
    }
}
```

2. As `LightweightPlaceholderCollection` is a strongly typed collection, the default property will be a `LightweightPlaceholder`:

```
/// <summary>
/// The indexed LightweightPlaceholder
/// </summary>
public LightweightPlaceholder this[int index]
{
    get
    {
        // Cast the list item to a LightweightPlaceholder
        return(this.InnerList[index] as LightweightPlaceholder);
    }
    set
    {
        this.InnerList[index] = value;
    }
}
```

3. We now define the `Add()` method that will add a `LightweightPlaceholder` to the collection:

```
/// <summary>
/// Add an item to the collection
/// </summary>
/// <param name="item">The LightweightPlaceholder to be added</param>
public void Add(LightweightPlaceholder item)
{
    this.InnerList.Add(item);
}
```

4. The `LightweightPlaceholderCollection` will be populated by loading a `Microsoft.ContentManagement.Publishing.Posting` object, so let's create the `Load()` method.

For the purposes of this example we are only maintaining placeholders of type `HtmlPlaceholder`. The code could be easily extended to maintain different types of placeholders.

```
/// <summary>
/// Load the lightweight Placeholder collection from a posting.
/// </summary>
/// <param name="_Posting">Posting to be loaded from</param>
public void Load(Posting _Posting)
{
    if (_Posting != null)
    {
        // Loop through the Placeholders
        foreach (Placeholder _Placeholder in _Posting.Placeholders)
        {
            // Check if the custom Placeholder is an HtmlPlaceholder
            if (_Placeholder is HtmlPlaceholder)
            {
                // Instantiate a lightweight Placeholder and
                // add it to the collection
                this.Add(new LightweightPlaceholder(_Placeholder));
            }
        }
    }
}
```

5. To save the content of all the placeholders in the collection, we will create a `Save()` method that iterates through all the placeholders and calls `Save()` for each:

```
/// <summary>
/// Save the collection of placeholders
/// </summary>
/// <param name="_Posting">Posting to save the placeholder values to</param>
public void Save(Posting _Posting)
{

    // Loop the Placeholders in the collection
    foreach (LightweightPlaceholder _LightweightPlaceholder in this)
    {

        // Save the Placeholder against the posting
        _LightweightPlaceholder.Save(_Posting);

    }

}
```

Now we have defined our classes for maintaining custom properties and placeholders, and for storing template definition data, the McmsAuthoringWebService project should look as in the figure overleaf:

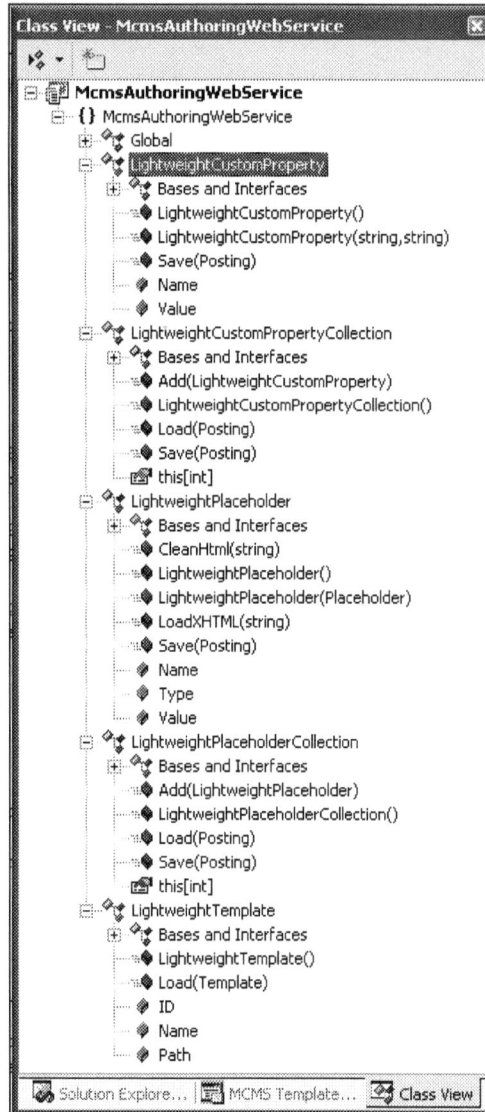

Creating an Object to Maintain Postings

The ASP.NET Web service will be able to load and maintain postings. To do this we will create a class called LightweightPosting. In Visual Studio .NET, right-click on the project McmsAuthoringWebService and add a new class called LightweightPosting. Add the namespaces highlighted below:

```
using System;
using System.IO;
using System.Security.Principal;
```

```
using System.Xml;
using System.Xml.Serialization;
using Microsoft.ContentManagement.Publishing;
namespace McmsAuthoringWebService
{
  /// <summary>
  /// Summary description for LightweightPosting.
  /// </summary>
  public class LightweightPosting
  {
    . . . code continues . . .
  }
}
```

The LightweightPosting class needs to contain several public variables:

```
#region Declarations and public variables

/// <summary>
/// The MCMS name of the posting
/// </summary>
public string Name;

/// <summary>
/// The MCMS Display name of the posting
/// </summary>
public string DisplayName;

/// <summary>
/// The MCMS Path of the posting
/// </summary>
public string Path;

/// <summary>
/// The GUID of the posting
/// </summary>
public Guid ID;

#endregion
```

To retrieve the CmsContext for the current user in Update mode, we will define a helper property on the class that returns just such a CmsContext. You'll also notice that, because we require the object to be in Update mode, we are using the CmsApplicationContext class instead of CmsHttpContext.

```
#region MCMS Current Context

/// <summary>
/// Declare the cms context as a private variable so we
/// don't need to load it every time we access the property.
/// </summary>
private CmsContext _CurrentCmsContext;

/// <summary>
/// Get the current MCMS context in update mode.
/// </summary>
private CmsContext CurrentCmsContext
{
  get
  {
  // Do we need to load the cmscontext?
  if (_CurrentCmsContext == null)
  {

    // Create the new application context
    CmsApplicationContext cmsContext = new CmsApplicationContext();
```

```
                    // We need to get the identity of the current user
                    WindowsIdentity ident = System.Web.HttpContext.Current.User.Identity
                                           as WindowsIdentity;

                    // Authenticate into update mode
                    cmsContext.AuthenticateUsingUserHandle(ident.Token,PublishingMode.Update);

                    // Set the private variable
                    _CurrentCmsContext = cmsContext;

                }

                // Return the private variable
                return(_CurrentCmsContext);
                }
            }

        #endregion
```

> This process of authenticating the CmsApplicationContext by calling the method
> AuthenticateUsingUserHandle() will only work when using Windows authentication.

Next we'll define a property to load the Microsoft.ContentManagement.Publishing.Posting
object, which corresponds to the current LightweightPosting object. This property will use the
Microsoft.ContentManagement.Publishing.Searches class to load the posting, and it will
throw an exception if the posting is not found:

```
    #region Related MCMS Posting

    /// <summary>
    /// The MCMS Posting object private variable
    /// (so we don't need to reload it when accessing the property)
    /// </summary>
    private Posting _Posting;

    /// <summary>
    /// The MCMS Posting object that corresponds to this Lightweight posting.
    /// It loaded from the Path property
    /// </summary>
    private Posting CmsPosting
    {
      get
      {
        // Is the posting object set?
        if (_Posting == null)
        {
          // Make sure the Guid for the posting is set
          if (this.Path != null)
          {
            // Perform a search to get the posting object by path
            _Posting = (Posting)CurrentCmsContext.Searches.GetByPath(this.Path);

            // Verify the posting object was found
            if (_Posting == null)
            {
              throw new Exception("The posting could not be found at path '"
                                  + this.Path + "'");
            }
          }
        }
      }
```

```
        // Return the posting object
        return(_Posting);
    }
    set
    {
        _Posting = value;
    }
}

#endregion
```

To access the custom properties for the current posting, we will add the `CustomProperties` property to the `LightweightPosting` class, which will, if necessary, load a `LightweightCustomPropertyCollection`:

```
#region Property - Custom Properties

/// <summary>
/// The lightweight custom properties private variable
/// </summary>
private LightweightCustomPropertyCollection _CustomProperties;

/// <summary>
/// Get/Set the lightweight custom properties collection.
/// If _CustomProperties is null the custom properties will be
/// loaded by the current CmsPosting
/// </summary>
public LightweightCustomPropertyCollection CustomProperties
{
    get
    {
        // Have the custom properties been loaded?
        if (_CustomProperties == null)
        {

            // Instantiate the new lightweight custom properties
            _CustomProperties = new LightweightCustomPropertyCollection();

            // Load by current MCMS Posting
            _CustomProperties.Load(this.CmsPosting);

        }

        // return the collection
        return(_CustomProperties);

    }
    set
    {
        // set the local variable
        _CustomProperties = value;
    }
}

#endregion
```

Similarly to how we loaded the custom properties for the posting, we will now add the `Placeholders` property, which instantiates a `LightweightPlaceholderCollection` and loads it for the current MCMS posting:

```
#region Property - Placeholders

/// <summary>
/// The lightweight Placeholders private variable
/// </summary>
```

```
private LightweightPlaceholderCollection _Placeholders;

/// <summary>
/// Get/Set the lightweight Placeholders collection.
/// If _Placeholders is null the Placeholders will be
/// loaded by the current CmsPosting
/// </summary>
public LightweightPlaceholderCollection Placeholders
{
  get
  {

    // Have the Placeholders been loaded?
    if (_Placeholders == null)
    {

      // Instantiate the new lightweight Placeholders
      _Placeholders = new LightweightPlaceholderCollection();

      // Load by current MCMS Posting
      _Placeholders.Load(this.CmsPosting);

    }

    // return the collection
    return(_Placeholders);

  }
  set
  {
    // set the local variable
    _Placeholders = value;
  }
}

#endregion
```

The LightweightPosting class will also contain the Template property, which will hold the LightweightTemplate that the posting is using. We instantiate a LightweightTemplate and populate it from the current MCMS posting's template:

```
#region Property - Templates

/// <summary>
/// The lightweight Template private variable
/// so the object is not loaded every time
/// the property is requested
/// </summary>
private LightweightTemplate _Template;

public LightweightTemplate Template
{
  get
  {

    // check if the template is already loaded
    if(_Template == null)
    {

      // Instantiate the new lightweight posting class
      _Template = new LightweightTemplate();

      // Load the lightweight template
      // by the current MCMS postings template
      _Template.Load(this.CmsPosting.Template);
```

```
        }
        // return the private variable
        return(_Template);
    }
    set
    {
        // Set the private variable
        _Template = value;
    }
}
```

    #endregion

Now add in the constructor logic to populate the Name, DisplayName, Path, and ID of LightweightPosting from an MCMS posting object. We will initialize the CustomProperties, Placeholders, and Template properties by calling the ToString() method, which implicitly instantiates the objects by calling the default constructor. Once the objects are initialized, they will be populated. After that, we can dispose of the CurrentCmsContext object as we won't need it any more.

```
#region Constructor - Instantiate by MCMS Posting Object

/// <summary>
/// Instantiate and load the LightweightPosting
/// object from an MCMS MCMS Posting object.
/// </summary>
/// <param name="_Posting">MCMS Posting object</param>
public LightweightPosting(Posting _Posting)
{
    this.Name = _Posting.Name;
    this.DisplayName = _Posting.DisplayName;
    this.Path = _Posting.Path;
    this.ID = new Guid(_Posting.Guid);

    // Initialize the properties
    this.CustomProperties.ToString();
    this.Placeholders.ToString();
    this.Template.ToString();

    // Dispose the context
    this.CurrentCmsContext.Dispose();
}
```

    #endregion

Now we have defined the properties to load MCMS objects such as the template, placeholders, and custom properties, we will add the Save() method to save any changes to the property values or collections to MCMS. The Save() method checks to see if DisplayName or Name have been changed and if they have it will overwrite the values of the Posting object. It then calls the Save() method on the Placeholders property to save the value of each placeholder. The posting is then submitted and the transaction is committed.

```
#region Save

/// <summary>
/// Save the Lightweight posting object's properties
/// and collections to the MCMS database.
/// </summary>
public void Save()
{

    // Check if the display name has changed
    if (this.DisplayName != this.CmsPosting.DisplayName)
    {
        // it has changed - apply the change to the posting object
        this.CmsPosting.DisplayName = this.DisplayName;
    }

    // Check if the posting name has changed
    if (this.Name != this.CmsPosting.Name)
    {
        // it has changed - apply the change to the posting object
        this.CmsPosting.Name = this.Name ;
    }

    // Save the placeholders collection passing in the current posting
    this.Placeholders.Save(this.CmsPosting);

    // Can we submit the posting?
    if (this.CmsPosting.CanSubmit)
    {
        // Yes, submit it
        this.CmsPosting.Submit();

        // Commit the transaction
        this.CurrentCmsContext.CommitAll();

    }

    // Dispose of the current CMS Context
    this.CurrentCmsContext.Dispose();
}

#endregion
```

The LightweightPosting object should now look like this:

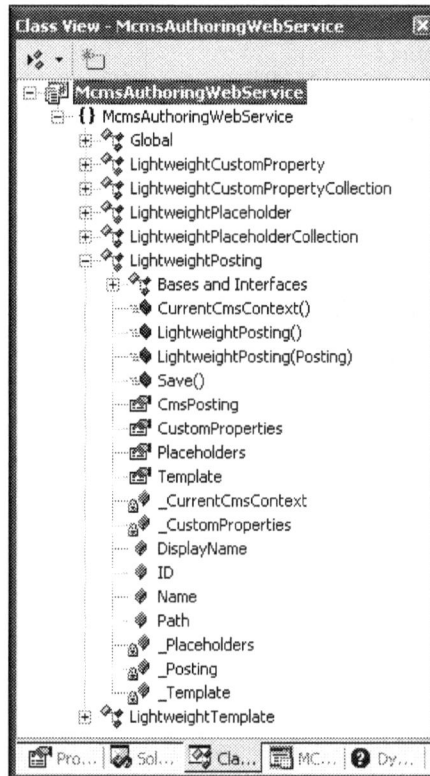

After finishing the previous steps, we have successfully created the business layer. Now build the entire solution and verify that there are no compilation errors.

Creating the ASP.NET Web Service

We will now create an ASP.NET Web service (.asmx) to encapsulate our Web methods. The first Web method, GetPosting(), will return a serialized LightweightPosting object and during serialization the properties and public fields will be serialized and nested in the XML. The second Web method, SavePosting(), will accept a LightweightPosting and call the Save() method to update MCMS.

To create the ASP.NET Web service, perform the following steps:

1. In Visual Studio .NET, right-click on the McmsAuthoringWebService project and select Add | Add Web Service.

2. Name this Web service Authoring.asmx and click OK.

3. Click on the Click Here link to switch to code view.

4. Add the following namespaces to the file:

    ```
    using System.Security.Principal;
    using Microsoft.ContentManagement.Publishing;
    ```

5. Delete the following code as we will not be needing it:

```
// WEB SERVICE EXAMPLE
// The HelloWorld() example service returns the string Hello World
// To build, uncomment the following lines then save and build the project
// To test this web service, press F5

//     [WebMethod]
//     public string HelloWorld()
//     {
//         return "Hello World";
//     }
```

The GetPosting() Web Method

Now let's define our GetPosting() Web method that will populate one of our custom
LightweightPosting objects from MCMS. For GetPosting() to be accessible via a Web service
it must have the [WebMethod] attribute. If the strPath parameter is an empty string we will
initialize an empty LightweightPosting object so the complete object model is serialized.

```
/// <summary>
/// Gets a Lightweight posting and all the properties by path
/// </summary>
/// <param name="strPath">Path of the posting</param>
/// <returns>LightweightPosting</returns>
[WebMethod]
public LightweightPosting GetPosting(string strPath)
{
    // Did we pass in a path?
    if (strPath == "")
    {
        // Define a lightweight posting object
        LightweightPosting _LightweightPosting = new LightweightPosting();

        // Initialize the Custom Properties, Placeholders and Template
        _LightweightPosting.CustomProperties =
                new LightweightCustomPropertyCollection();
        _LightweightPosting.Placeholders =
                new LightweightPlaceholderCollection();
        _LightweightPosting.Template = new LightweightTemplate();

        // Create an empty placeholder
        LightweightPlaceholder _placeHolder = new LightweightPlaceholder();

        // Load an empty string into the Value property
        _placeHolder.Value = _placeHolder.LoadXHTML("");

        // Add the placeholder to the collection
        _LightweightPosting.Placeholders.Add(_placeHolder);

        // Return the posting object
        return(_LightweightPosting);
    }
    else
    {
        // Declare a Posting object
        Posting _Posting = null;

        // Create the new application context
        CmsApplicationContext cmsContext = new CmsApplicationContext();

        // We need to get the identity of the current user
        WindowsIdentity ident = System.Web.HttpContext.Current.User.Identity
```

```
                              as WindowsIdentity;

        try
        {
          // Authenticate into update mode
          cmsContext.AuthenticateUsingUserHandle(ident.Token,
              PublishingMode.Update);
        }
        catch(Exception ex)
        {
          // Dispose of the CMS Context
          cmsContext.Dispose();

          throw new Exception("Failed to Authenticate user by handle. "
                           + "The user may not have author permissions.", ex);
        }

        // Get the MCMS Posting object by path
        _Posting = (Posting)cmsContext.Searches.GetByPath(strPath);

        // Verify the posting was found
        if (_Posting == null)
        {
          // Dispose the CMS Context
          cmsContext.Dispose();

          throw new Exception("The posting was not found at path '"
                           + strPath + "'");

        }

        // Instantiate the lightweight posting passing
        // in the MCMS posting to the constructor.
        LightweightPosting _LightweightPosting = new LightweightPosting(_Posting);

        // Dispose the CMS Context
        cmsContext.Dispose();

        // Return the lightweight posting
        return(_LightweightPosting);
      }
    }
```

Configuring IIS Security

As we are using the current user's Windows identity to authenticate the CmsApplicationContext, we should verify anonymous access to this Web service is disabled.

1. In the web.config file, verify the authentication element is set to:
   <authentication mode="Windows" />

2. In the Internet Information Services (IIS) management console, right-click on the McmsAuthoringWebService virtual directory and select Properties.

3. Select the Directory Security tab.

4. Under Anonymous access and authentication control, select Edit.

5. Uncheck Anonymous access and check Integrated Windows authentication.

6. Click OK and close all opened dialogs.

7. Close the IIS management console.

Testing the Web Service

To test it out, we can set the Web service as the start page for the project by right-clicking on authoring.asmx in Solution Explorer, and selecting Set As Start Page. Then start without debugging by pressing *Control-F5* or selecting Start Without Debugging from the Debug menu.

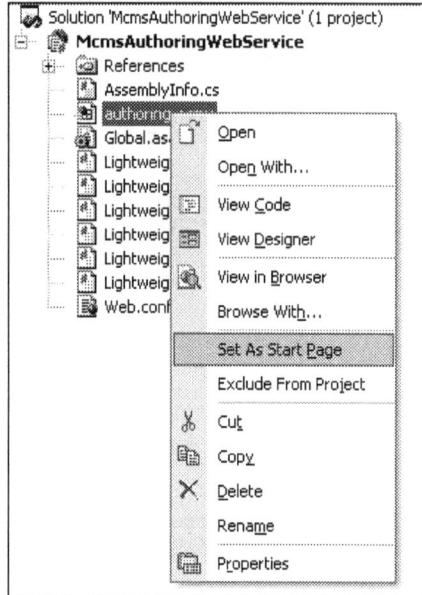

We should now see the ASP.NET Web service test page, listing GetPosting as the single available Web method:

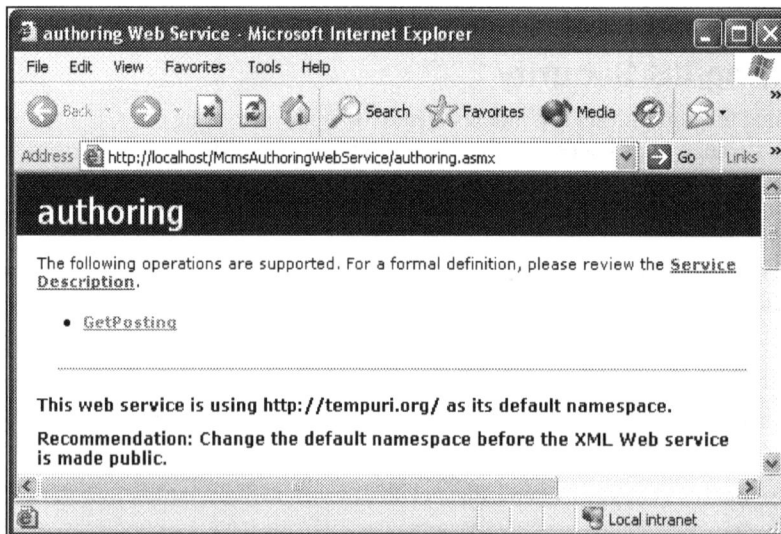

The sample site we are using is the Tropical Green site, available from the code download section for this book on the Packt website.

If you now click on GetPosting, you will see a textbox for the parameter strPath. Enter /channels/ www.tropicalgreen.net/PlantCatalog/AloeVera into the box and click Invoke.

You will now see the serialized view of the `LightweightPosting` object and all its serializable properties:

The SavePosting() Web Method

Let's create another Web method, SavePosting(), which will accept a LightweightPosting object as a parameter and save its contents to MCMS. Add the following code to the authoring.asmx.cs file and rebuild the solution:

```
/// <summary>
/// Save a lightweight posting object to MCMS
/// </summary>
/// <param name="_Posting">LightweightPosting object to save</param>
[WebMethod]
public void SavePosting(LightweightPosting _Posting)
{
  // Save the posting
  _Posting.Save();
}
```

The SavePosting() Web method cannot be tested from the browser as we did for GetPosting() as it requires a complex datatype (LightweightPosting) as a parameter. We will test SavePosting() via the InfoPath form we will create shortly.

Preparing the InfoPath Environment

At this point you need to have Microsoft InfoPath 2003 and Office 2003 Service Pack 1 (SP1) installed on your computer. If your Office 2003 installation does not have SP1 currently applied, you will be able to download it from:

```
http://www.microsoft.com/downloads/details.aspx?FamilyID=9c51d3a6-7cb1-4f61-837e-
5f938254fc47
```

You should also download the InfoPath 2003 SDK for further reference from:

```
http://www.microsoft.com/downloads/details.aspx?FamilyId=351F0616-93AA-4FE8-9238-
D702F1BFBAB4
```

To verify Service Pack 1 has been installed, start InfoPath and click Help | About Microsoft Office InfoPath. The name of the latest service pack is printed next to the product's version number.

Creating the InfoPath Document

InfoPath documents require an InfoPath template (.xsn), designed in InfoPath, before they can create an InfoPath form template and connect it to a Web service for data retrieval and submission. Follow these steps to create an InfoPath template that will connect to the Web service we just created:

1. Launch Microsoft InfoPath 2003.
2. On the left-hand side of the Fill Out a Form window, select Design a Form. If the Fill Out a Form window is not open, select File | Design a Form.
3. From the Task Pane on the right-hand side, select New from Data Connection.
4. In the Data Connection Wizard, select Web Service and click Next.
5. Select Receive and submit data and click Next.

6. Enter the Web service URL as http://localhost/McmsAuthoringWebService/
authoring.asmx and click Next.

7. For the Retrieve operation we must select the GetPosting operation and click Next.

8. Click Next again. We use the same Web service address for the submit functionality,
so again, click Next.

9. Select the SavePosting operation and click Next.

10. There are several ways to submit data to a Web service. The entire XML document
can be submitted or a specific node can be selected. For this form, we will submit
only the `GetPostingResult` node that represents the result of the previous Web
service call. Under Parameter options, click the ⬚ Modify button to open the Select
a Field or Group dialog.

11. Expand the dataFields node and the s0:GetPostingResponse node, then select the
GetPostingResult node and click OK.

Depending on whether or not you have .NET 1.1 Service Pack 1 installed, the XML
document namespace may be s0 or tns, because once the service pack is installed, VS
.NET generates the Web service description (WSDL) file differently. Either s0 or tns will
work in this solution.

12. The submit data Field or group textbox will now be populated with an XPath
query representing the path to the `GetPostingResult` node in InfoPath's internal
data structure.

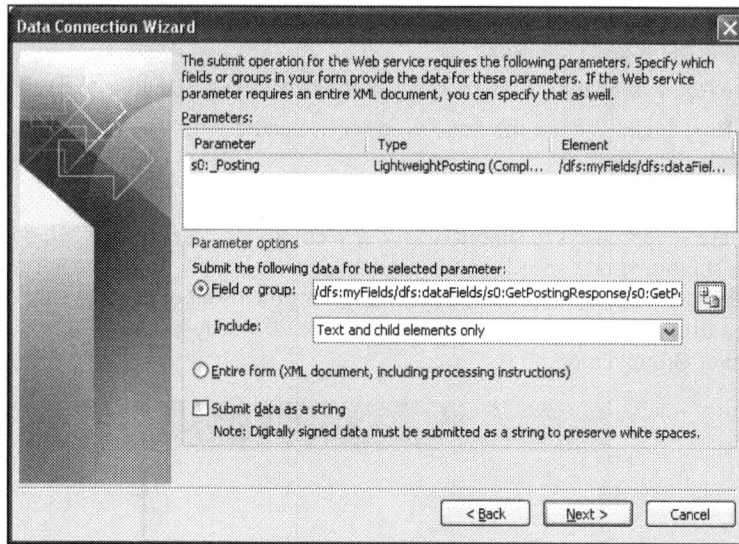

13. Click Next. Leave the data connection name as Main submit and click Finish.

The InfoPath template should now be created and the Data source window should now reflect the structure of the Web service.

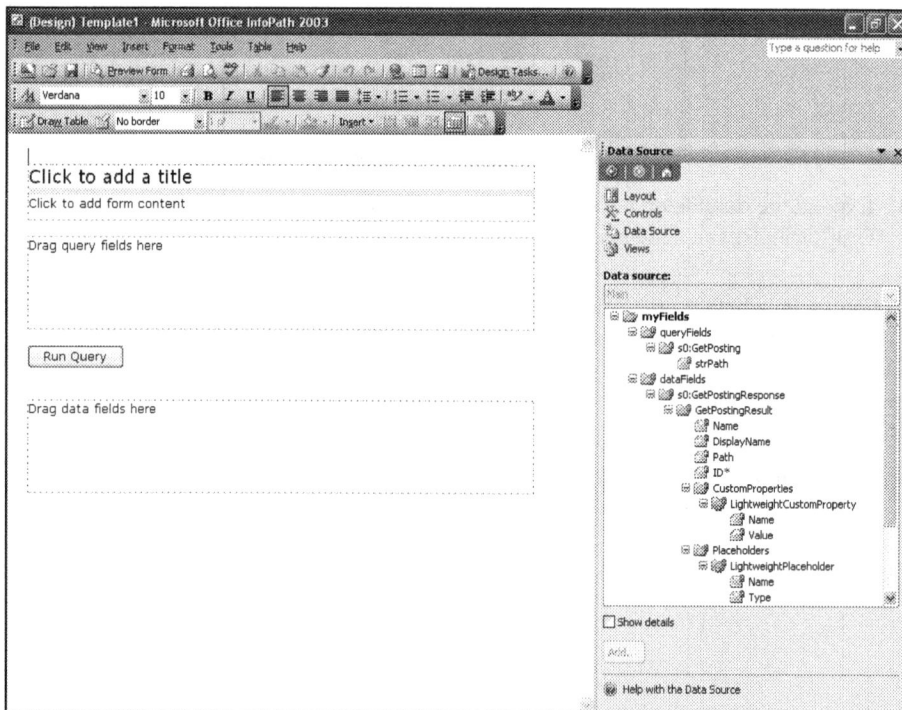

Finally, we'll enter some brief instructions below the title. Click anywhere on the Click to add form content label. In the space provided, enter This InfoPath form can retrieve and update existing MCMS postings.

Creating the Controls in InfoPath

By generating the document from an XML Web service, InfoPath allows us to create a functional user interface in a matter of minutes as opposed to hours or days in other environments. To allow the user to enter the path of a posting and query the Web service, follow these steps:

1. In the task pane, select the Data Source category.
2. Expand myFields, queryFields, and s0:GetPosting.
3. Drag the strPath element into the area on the form labeled Drag query fields here.
4. Change the label strPath to Posting To Load (e.g. /Channels/www.TropicalGreen.net/ PlantCatalog/AloeVera).
5. Drag the Run Query button into the space below the strPath textbox, and remove the extra line breaks where the Run Query button previously was.
6. Select the bottom border of the layout table and drag it up to reduce the height of the table.

Our form now allows a user to enter the path of a posting, which is passed to the ASP.NET Web service, which returns a serialized LightweightPosting object.

Let's create the user interface that displays the posting's properties and allows them to be edited.

1. In the Data Source pane, expand dataFields and s0:GetPostingResponse.
2. Drag the GetPostingResult node on top of the Drag data fields here label.
3. A context menu will appear listing actions that can be performed. For this node, we will create the section with controls, so click Section with Controls.

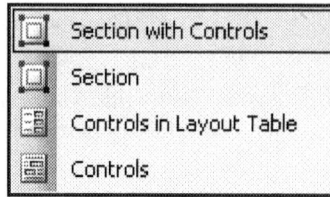

4. The following form has now been generated. Don't worry about the layout for now, we'll make it friendlier to use in the next section.

Cleaning up the Generated Form

The interface that InfoPath generates when we chose Section with Controls is fully functional but not very aesthetically pleasing nor does it contain all the correct control configurations. We can rearrange the controls on the form by simply dragging and dropping them into different areas.

Firstly, let's get all the common posting and template properties laid out a little better.

1. Place the cursor to the left of the topmost Name: label (the label directly below the title) and from the Table menu, select Insert | Layout Table.

2. Set the number of columns to 2, the number of rows to 7, and click OK.

3. A layout table has now been generated. Add the following text into separate cells in the first column:

   Name

   Display Name

   Posting Path

   Posting ID

   Template Name

   Template Path

   Template ID

4. Select the cells and set the text to be bold.

5. We must now move the text fields that were generated next to their corresponding label. Drag the four text fields next to the Name, Display Name, Posting Path, and ID labels below the table up into the right-hand column of the first four rows. Then delete the superfluous labels.

6. The textboxes relating to template properties have been generated in the section right at the bottom of the form as they are represented by another XML element. Drag these textboxes up into the column next to their corresponding label. You can easily verify to which object the properties are related by selecting them and having a look in the Data Source pane on the right-hand side. The top table should now look like this:

Name	
Display Name	
Posting Path	
Posting ID	
Template Name	
Template Path	
Template ID	

7. To remove the now-redundant template optional section at the bottom of the form, simply click on the Optional Section label and press the *Del* key.

```
Name:
Path:
ID:
○ Optional Section
```

The following properties in the table we just created are read-only:

- Posting Path
- Posting ID
- Template Name
- Template Path
- Template ID

To set a textbox to be read-only, right-click on the textbox and select Text Box Properties. Select the Display tab, check the Read-only box, and click OK. Do this for all of the above textboxes.

The next thing we must do is clean up the custom properties section of the form.

```
Name                    Value


■ Repeating Table



○ Optional Section
```

Follow this procedure to improve this section's look and feel:

1. Click the Repeating Table label and then press *Ctrl-Home* to go to the beginning of the box. Enter the title Custom Properties in bold text.

2. Inside the repeating table, click on the textbox underneath Name, press the right arrow, then *Enter* to insert a line break.

3. Drag the Value textbox (the textbox, not the label) under the Name textbox, and right-click on the second column and select Delete | Columns. Then right-click on the Name label and select Delete | Rows.

4. Set the Name textbox to be read-only following the steps discussed before, as users cannot modify this field. With the Name textbox selected, select Format | Font from the menu and check the Bold box.

5. Next, drag the repeating table's right-hand side to fit the width of the optional section.

6. Right-click on the LightweightCustomProperty repeating table and select Borders and Shading. Choose a border for the bottom and the top of the table and click OK.

Next we must to stop users from being able to insert or delete the custom property sections as the number of custom properties will not vary and is determined by the response of the ASP.NET Web service.

1. Right-click on the Repeating Table label and select Repeating Table Properties.

2. In the Default settings section on the Data tab, uncheck the Allow users to insert and delete rows box and click OK.

3. Right-click on the optional section that contains the Custom Properties label, and select Section Properties.

4. Uncheck the Allow users to delete the section box and click OK.

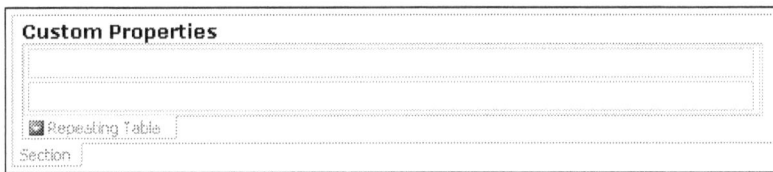

Let's now clean up the generated placeholders section below the LightweightPlaceholder Repeating Table.

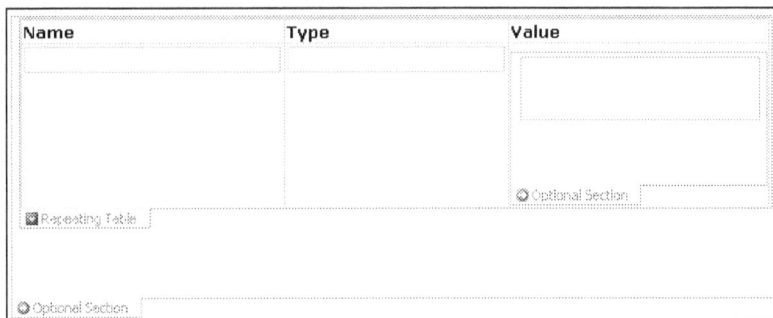

1. Place the cursor to the left of the LightweightPlaceholder Repeating Table. Enter the heading Placeholders, and set it to bold.

2. Drag the Type textbox into the first column under the Name textbox.

3. Right-click on the Name label, and select Delete | Rows. Right-click on the second column and select Delete | Columns.

4. Click on the theNode rich text box and press *Del*.

5. Right-click in the third column and select Delete | Columns.

6. Set the Name textbox to bold, and set the Type textbox to italics.

7. From the top of the Task Pane on the right-hand side of the screen, select the Data Source category (or select View | Data Source from the menu) and expand the following nodes: dataFields, s0:GetPostingResponse, GetPostingResult, Placeholders, LightweightPlaceholder, and Value and drag the theNode into the placeholders Repeating Table.

If the task pane doesn't appear on the right-hand side, select View | Task Pane to show it.

8. Drag the right-hand side of the LightweightPlaceholder table to the right so the width is consistent with the LightweightCustomProperty table.

9. Set the Name and Type textboxes to be read-only.

10. Right-click on the LightweightPlaceholder table and select Borders and Shading. Apply a border to the bottom and the top of the table and click OK.

11. Modify the placeholder table so that users cannot insert or delete rows, and set the placeholder's optional section so that users cannot delete it.

12. Delete the excess line breaks after the end of the placeholder repeating table, and your form should resemble the following figure:

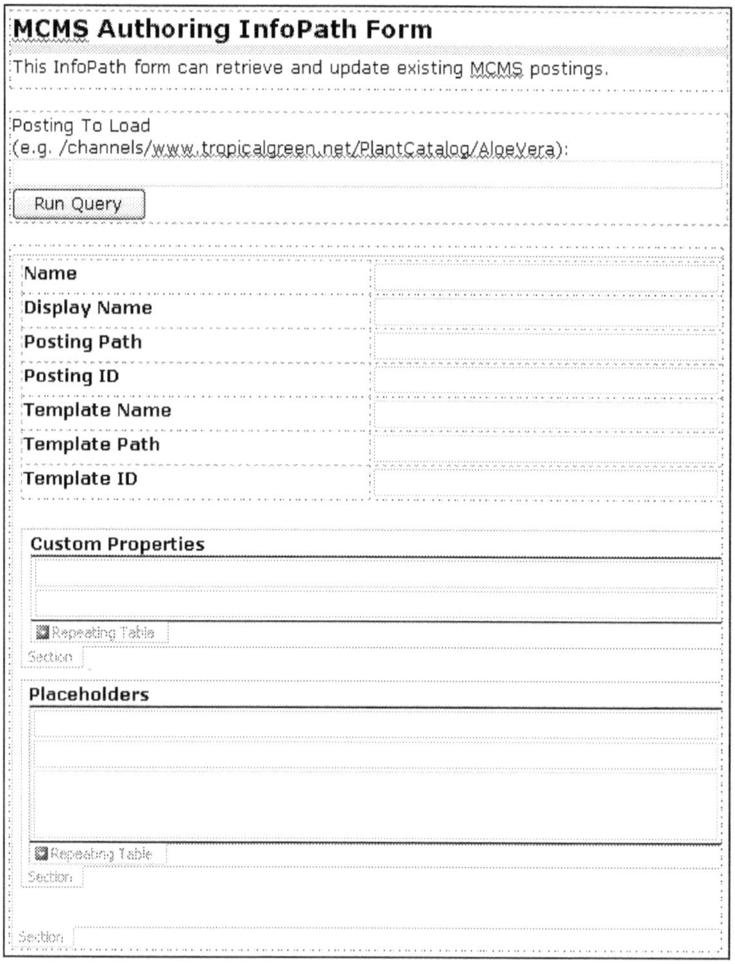

Testing the InfoPath Form

Now we have cleaned up the generated form, we can test it both from a look-and-feel point of view and for Web service integration.

To test the InfoPath form, click Preview Form ⟨ Preview Form ⟩ on the toolbar, or choose File | Preview Form | default. Enter the posting to load as /channels/www.tropicalgreen.net/plantcatalog/aloevera, and click Run Query.

MCMS Authoring InfoPath Form

This InfoPath form can retrieve and update existing MCMS postings.

Posting To Load (e.g. /channels/www.tropicalgreen.net/PlantCatalog/AloeVera):

/channels/www.tropicalgreen.net/plantcatalog/aloevera

⟨ Run Query ⟩

Name	AloeVera
Display Name	Aloe Vera
Posting Path	/Channels/www.tropicalgreen.net/Pl...
Posting ID	569d1cca-9a9d-4c43-b0c3-db1aac...
Template Name	Plant
Template Path	/Templates/TropicalGreen/PlantCatal...
Template ID	b78e84d6-5905-4f9e-a7bb-97ea2d2...

Custom Properties

FirstSavedBy

Placeholders

Description

Microsoft.ContentManagement.Publishing.Extensions.Placeholders.HtmlPlaceho

The health benefits of eating the inner leaves of the Aloe Vera have made it popular. Also used to make gels and cream known to have rejuvenating properties.

ScientificName

Microsoft.ContentManagement.Publishing.Extensions.Placeholders.HtmlPlaceho

---

Update some placeholder values and custom properties from the toolbar at the top of the screen and press Submit. If you browse to `http://www.tropicalgreen.net/PlantCatalog/AloeVera.htm`, the updates should now be visible—you may need to switch into Unpublished Mode as the changes will require editor approval before going live. When you're done, click Close Preview at the top of the screen and the form will return to design mode.

Saving the InfoPath Form

Once development of the InfoPath template is complete, it can be distributed by publishing the finished form to a shared location such as SharePoint, a Web server, or a network share. Alternatively the template can be saved to the file system for modification later.

To save the template to the local file system, select File | Save, and choose Save from the dialog. Then simply enter or browse to a suitable location and click Save.

Possible Enhancements to this Solution

Here are some possible enhancements that could easily be incorporated into this solution:

- The ability to create new postings by selecting a template.
- Support for Selection Type Custom Properties.
- Support for placeholder objects other than the HtmlPlaceholder.
- Support for pasting images into the rich text box, which must be decoded and uploaded to the resource gallery.
- An ability to save for later modification.
- Another view in the InfoPath form that allows the user to list and select postings they want to modify.

Summary

Over the course of this chapter, we've seen a lot of the power of Microsoft Office InfoPath 2003 as we quickly created a flexible content authoring solution utilizing its rich UI. At the same time, we were able to maintain a standard data representation between the tiers of the solution.

Along the way, we explored ASP.NET Web services, in particular how to create a .NET object model that is serializable as XML so that it can be sent and received via ASP.NET Web services.

We generated a form using InfoPath and bound this form to our ASP.NET Web service. The InfoPath form's layout was generated automatically from the Web services definition, and it was a simple matter to rearrange the generated interface. Testing the form is also child's play, as we saw when we retrieved a sample posting, made some modifications, and submitted the changes.

12
MCMS and RSS

The Web has been changing over the past few years. Gone are the days when you must browse to a website to see it has changed. You may browse to a website to get an overall view of the content but instead of taking time out of your busy day to check each of your favorite websites, why not aggregate all the changes automatically so you can quickly scan for relevant content? Really Simple Syndication (RSS), an XML format, has been around for several years and it provides the foundation of providing content and updates to users.

RSS already has wide adoption in the Weblog (blog) community and now corporate and community sites are catching on to this way of increasing content coverage through syndication. The effectiveness of a Content Management System can generally be gauged by the amount of time it takes to maintain content along with the time it takes users of the website to find the content changes. If users are notified of content changes without having to browse back to the website, we reduce the time it takes for users to view new information.

Looking Ahead

In this chapter, we will create and configure an RSS feed that syndicates the latest content to users of the Tropical Green website. We will also create an RSS aggregator placeholder that can be configured by authors to consume RSS feeds and display their contents.

Overleaf is a screenshot of the structure of the RSS feed we will be generating in this chapter.

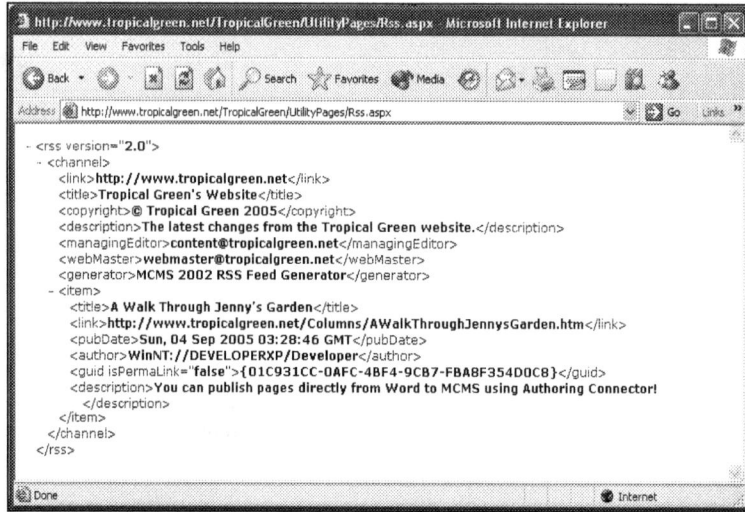

```
- <rss version="2.0">
  - <channel>
      <link>http://www.tropicalgreen.net</link>
      <title>Tropical Green's Website</title>
      <copyright>© Tropical Green 2005</copyright>
      <description>The latest changes from the Tropical Green website.</description>
      <managingEditor>content@tropicalgreen.net</managingEditor>
      <webMaster>webmaster@tropicalgreen.net</webMaster>
      <generator>MCMS 2002 RSS Feed Generator</generator>
    - <item>
        <title>A Walk Through Jenny's Garden</title>
        <link>http://www.tropicalgreen.net/Columns/AWalkThroughJennysGarden.htm</link>
        <pubDate>Sun, 04 Sep 2005 03:28:46 GMT</pubDate>
        <author>WinNT://DEVELOPERXP/Developer</author>
        <guid isPermaLink="false">{01C931CC-0AFC-4BF4-9CB7-FBA8F354D0C8}</guid>
        <description>You can publish pages directly from Word to MCMS using Authoring Connector!
        </description>
      </item>
  </channel>
</rss>
```

The screen below is the authoring interface for the RSS Aggregation control we will also be building. It allows the user to enter the URL of the RSS feed to display, and configure aspects of the presentation mode view.

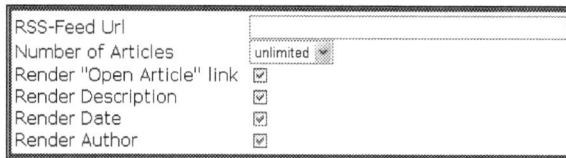

In presentation mode, our RSS Aggregation control will display each article in the RSS feed and depending on configuration the Open Article link, description, date, and author, as in the following screenshot:

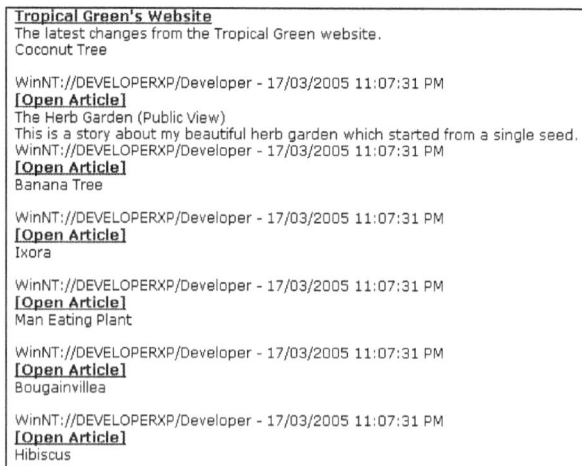

The Structure of an RSS Feed

An RSS feed is an XML document that conforms to a certain specification. We'll be using RSS version 2.0, as described at `http://blogs.law.harvard.edu/tech/rss`. The following table outlines the elements that an RSS feed contains.

Parent	Element	Description
(this is the root element)	`rss`	The top level element of the RSS feed.
`rss`	`channel`	
`channel`	`link`	The URL to the website.
`channel`	`title`	The title of the RSS Feed, such as Tropical Green.
`channel`	`copyright`	Copyright information pertaining to the RSS feed.
`channel`	`description`	The description of the RSS feed.
`channel`	`managingEditor`	The e-mail address for the person responsible for the content.
`channel`	`webMaster`	The e-mail address of the Webmaster.
`channel`	`generator`	The name of the application used to generate the feed.
`channel`	`item`	A repeating element for each article to be aggregated.
`item`	`title`	The title of the article. In this case we are using the `DisplayName` property of the posting.
`item`	`link`	The link to the HTML version of the article (or more information).
`item`	`pubDate`	The date the item was published.
`item`	`author`	The author's name or e-mail address for the item.
`item`	`guid`	A Globally Unique ID for the item. This element maps perfectly to MCMS as postings already have GUIDs.
`item`	`description`	The content that will be included for this item.

Remember that as the RSS feed is XML, all element names are case sensitive. Below is a sample feed:

```
<rss version="2.0">
  <channel>
    <link>http://localhost</link>
    <title>Tropical Green's website</title>
    <copyright>© Tropical Green 2005</copyright>
    <description>The latest changes from the Tropical Green
                 website.</description>
    <managingEditor>content@tropicalgreen.net</managingEditor>
    <webMaster>webmaster@tropicalgreen.net</webMaster>
    <generator>MCMS 2002 RSS Feed Generator</generator>
    <item>
      <title>A Walk Through Jenny's Garden</title>
      <link>http://localhost/www.tropicalgreen.net/Columns
            /AWalkThroughJennysGarden.htm</link>
      <pubDate>Thu, 17 Mar 2005 13:07:31 GMT</pubDate>
      <author>WinNT://DEVELOPERXP/Developer</author>
```

```
<guid isPermaLink="false">{01C931CC-0AFC-4BF4-9CB7-FBA8F354D0C8}</guid>
<description>You can publish pages directly from Word
            to MCMS using Authoring Connector!</description>
    </item>
  </channel>
</rss>
```

Providing Content as an RSS Feed

We will create a mechanism that will allow users to point their RSS aggregator to a page and retrieve the postings that have been updated within a set number of days. An RSS aggregator is a program that can retrieve items from one or more RSS feeds and display the items in a readable form.

Creating the RSS Feed

For the purposes of this example, we will create a new web form in the Tropical Green sample site.

Let's jump right into the code:

1. Launch the Tropical Green solution in Visual Studio .NET.
2. Create a new folder to store our RSS web form by right-clicking on the TropicalGreen project and selecting Add | New Folder. Name the new folder UtilityPages.
3. Create a new web form in the UtilityPages folder by right-clicking on UtilityPages and selecting Add | Add New Web Form.
4. Name the item rss.aspx and click Open.
5. We should now have a blank web form created and opened in Design view.

The web form we are creating will return XML and not HTML, so we need to remove the generated elements from the rss.aspx file as they will not form part of our RSS XML document.

1. At the bottom left of the screen, Click HTML to switch to HTML mode.
2. Delete everything below the Page directive:

```
<%@ Page language="c#" Codebehind="rss.aspx.cs" AutoEventWireup="false"
          Inherits="TropicalGreen.UtilityPages.rss" %>
```

3. As many different aggregators can hit your feed in an automated manner, the impact of the feed on the overall site performance could be huge. The frequency with which aggregators will poll the feed for changes cannot be controlled by us as the setting is usually configurable on the aggregator itself. To minimize this impact on site performance, we will implement output caching for the web form serving the feed. Add the following directive just below the Page directive to set output caching to 300 seconds, or five minutes:

```
<%@ OutputCache Duration="300" VaryByParam="none" %>
```

4. Switch to code view for the web form, and we'll start adding the code generates our RSS feed. Import the following namespaces:

```
using System;
using System.Collections;
```

```
using System.ComponentModel;
using System.Data;
using System.Drawing;
using System.Web;
using System.Web.SessionState;
using System.Web.UI;
using System.Web.UI.WebControls;
using System.Web.UI.HtmlControls;
using System.Configuration;
using Microsoft.ContentManagement.Publishing;
using Microsoft.ContentManagement.Publishing.Extensions.Placeholders;
using System.IO;
using System.Xml;
using System.Text;

namespace TropicalGreen.UtilityPages
{
    /// <summary>
    /// Summary description for rss.
    /// </summary>
    public class rss : System.Web.UI.Page
    {
        . . . code continues . . .
    }
}
```

Let's create the GenerateRssXml() method, which returns the latest updates from our MCMS website as a string in RSS format. First we set up the temporary memory stream and XmlTextWriter needed to create the XML stream for sending to the client:

```
/// <summary>
/// Generate the RSS feed xml
/// </summary>
/// <returns>RSS XML</returns>
private string GenerateRssXml()
{
    // Create the Memory Stream
    MemoryStream _MemoryStream = new MemoryStream();

    // Create an XmlTextWriter to write to the memory stream
    XmlTextWriter Xmlwriter = new XmlTextWriter(_MemoryStream, Encoding.UTF8);

    // Create the top element <rss>
    Xmlwriter.WriteStartElement("rss");

    // Set the version attribute of the RSS Feed
    Xmlwriter.WriteAttributeString("version","2.0");

    // Create the Channel Element
    Xmlwriter.WriteStartElement("channel");
```

The general information for the RSS feed, such as Link, title, and copyright, will be read from the web.config file, and we'll create these web.config entries later. GenerateRssXml() relies on two helper methods that we will develop shortly, GetPostingSummary(), which will retrieve the summary of a posting (either an HtmlPlaceholder or the Description property), and GetAccountFriendlyName(), which is designed to return the author's full name.

```
    // Get the general info from the web.config
    string strFeed_Title = ConfigurationSettings.AppSettings.Get("RSS_Title");
    string strWebsiteUrl =
                ConfigurationSettings.AppSettings.Get("RSS_WebsiteUrl");
    string strFeed_Copyright = ConfigurationSettings.AppSettings.Get(
                "RSS_Copyright");
```

```
            string strFeed_Description = ConfigurationSettings.AppSettings.Get(
                            "RSS_Description");
            string strFeed_ManagingEditor = ConfigurationSettings.AppSettings.Get(
                            "RSS_ManagingEditor");
            string strFeed_Webmaster = ConfigurationSettings.AppSettings.Get(
                            "RSS_WebMaster");
            string strStartChannel = ConfigurationSettings.AppSettings.Get(
                            "RSS_StartChannel");

            // Get the number of days of changes to include in the RSS Feed
            int intDaysOfChangesToInclude =
                    int.Parse(ConfigurationSettings.AppSettings.Get(
                                        "RSS_NumberOfDaysOld"));

            // Create all the elements that describe the RSS Channel
            XmlWriter.WriteElementString("link", strWebsiteUrl);
            XmlWriter.WriteElementString("title", strFeed_Title);
            XmlWriter.WriteElementString("copyright", strFeed_Copyright);
            XmlWriter.WriteElementString("description", strFeed_Description);
            XmlWriter.WriteElementString("managingEditor", strFeed_ManagingEditor);
            XmlWriter.WriteElementString("webMaster", strFeed_Webmaster);
            XmlWriter.WriteElementString("generator", "MCMS 2002 RSS Feed Generator");
```

GenerateRssXml() creates the XML string by using an XmlTextWriter and looping through the collection of postings retrieved by the Searches.NewPostings() method from the MCMS PAPI:

```
            // Get all the postings within N days
            PostingCollection _PostingCollection = CmsHttpContext.Current.Searches
                        .NewPostings(intDaysOfChangesToInclude);

            // Sort the postings
            _PostingCollection.SortByLastModifiedDate();

            // Loop through the postings found
            foreach (Posting _Posting in _PostingCollection)
            {
              // Check the posting is within a channel (for everything use "/channels")
              if (_Posting.Path.ToLower().StartsWith(strStartChannel))
              {

                // Create the item element (i.e. 1 RSS item)
                XmlWriter.WriteStartElement("item");

                // Set the title element to be the posting's display name
                XmlWriter.WriteElementString("title", _Posting.DisplayName);

                if (_Posting.Url.StartsWith("/"))
                {
                  // URL without hostname.
                  // Set the link of the posting to be the servername + URL
                  XmlWriter.WriteElementString("link", strWebsiteUrl
                                        + _Posting.Url);
                }
                else
                {
                  // Set the link of the posting to be the posting URL with hostname
                  XmlWriter.WriteElementString("link", _Posting.Url);
                }

                // Set the published date to be the last modified date
                // This could also be the CreatedDate
                // IMPORTANT: Must be formatted to type "r"
                XmlWriter.WriteElementString("pubDate",
                            _Posting.LastModifiedDate.ToString("r") );

                // Set the author element and get the friendly name
```

```
Xmlwriter.WriteElementString("author", GetAccountFriendlyName(
                _Posting.LastModifiedBy.ClientAccountName));

// Set the GUID element to the posting's guid
// Also set the isPermaLink attribute to false.
Xmlwriter.WriteStartElement("guid");
Xmlwriter.WriteAttributeString("isPermaLink","false");
Xmlwriter.WriteRaw(_Posting.Guid);
Xmlwriter.WriteEndElement();

// Output the posting's summary as the description element
Xmlwriter.WriteElementString("description",
                            GetPostingSummary(_Posting));

// Close the </item> element
Xmlwriter.WriteEndElement();
        }
    }
```

Next, we close the XML elements, flush the `Xmlwriter`, and return the XML string.

```
// Close the <channel> element
Xmlwriter.WriteEndElement();

// Close the <rss> element
Xmlwriter.WriteEndElement();

// Flush the XmlWriter
Xmlwriter.Flush();

// Reset the position of the memory stream
_MemoryStream.Position = 0;

// create a new stream reader and read the memory stream
StreamReader _StreamReader = new StreamReader(_MemoryStream);

// Return the contents of the stream reader
return (_StreamReader.ReadToEnd());
    }
```

The first helper method, `GetPostingSummary()`, must retrieve the description or content for the posting that will be described by the RSS feed.

`GetPostingSummary()` uses a configuration variable called `RSS_Summary_PlaceholderName`, which will be read from the `web.config` file. `RSS_Summary_PlaceholderName` can store the name of the placeholder that will be aggregated into the RSS feed in the description element. If the value is empty or the placeholder is not found, the posting's description property (`Posting.Description`) will be used instead.

Let's add the `GetPostingSummary()` method to the `rss` class.

```
/// <summary>
/// Get the summary for a posting
/// </summary>
/// <param name="_Posting">Posting to get the summary for</param>
/// <returns></returns>
private string GetPostingSummary(Posting _Posting)
{

    string _Summary = "";

    // Get the Summary Placeholder's name from the Web.config
    string SummaryPlaceholderName =
```

```
                    ConfigurationSettings.AppSettings.Get("RSS_Summary_PlaceholderName");

        // Verify if a valid SummaryPlaceholder exists
        if (SummaryPlaceholderName != ""
            && _Posting.Placeholders[SummaryPlaceholderName] != null
            && _Posting.Placeholders[SummaryPlaceholderName] is HtmlPlaceholder)
        {
            // Get the placeholder from the posting's placeholder
            // collection and cast it to be HtmlPlaceholder
            HtmlPlaceholder _SummaryPlaceholder =
                _Posting.Placeholders[SummaryPlaceholderName] as HtmlPlaceholder;

            // Return the placeholder's contents
            _Summary = _SummaryPlaceholder.Html;
        }
        else
        {
            // Either the summary placeholder name was not
            // defined or the placeholder was not found

            // Return the description of the posting instead.
            _Summary = _Posting.Description;
        }
        // some rss readers have problems with empty description tags
        if (_Summary.Trim() == "")
            _Summary = " ";

        return(_Summary);
    }
```

The next helper method we will define is `GetAccountFriendlyName()`, which would typically be used to retrieve the author's full name (for example, `John Citizen` as opposed to `WINNT://COMPUTERNAME/USERNAME`). The author's name is then embedded in the RSS feed for each item.

For example purposes this method is only a stub that returns the username that was passed in. This method would typically be extended to connect to your Active Directory to retrieve the user's account and then their full name but this will change depending on your environment and configuration.

Sample code on how to implement this can be found on Stefan's blog:
http://blogs.technet.com/stefan_gossner/archive/2003/12/21/44902.aspx

---

```
/// <summary>
/// Get the friendly name based on the client account name
/// </summary>
/// <param name="strClientAccountName">MCMS client account name to change.
/// </param>
/// <returns>Friendly name for the user (firstname lastname)</returns>
private string GetAccountFriendlyName(string strClientAccountName)
{
    // Connect to Active Directory and
    // get the current user's full name and return it
    return(strClientAccountName);
}
```

To invoke the `GenerateRssXml()` method, we will override the `Render()` method and write the returned XML string to the response stream. You will also notice that we are changing the page's content type to `text/xml` by setting the `Response.ContentType` property.

```
/// <summary>
/// Overridden render method that calls the
/// GenerateRssXml method and writes it to the output stream.
/// </summary>
/// <param name="writer"></param>
protected override void Render( HtmlTextWriter writer)
{
    // change the page response to XML instead of HTML
    Response.ContentType = "text/xml; charset=utf-8";

    // write the GenerateRssXml's response to the response stream.
    writer.Write(GenerateRssXml());
}
```

Defining Global Settings in the Web.config

For flexibility, we need to define several variables in the <appSettings> element of the web.config for use by the methods in rss.aspx.cs. The settings specified in the web.config will apply to the entire site.

Within the <configuration> element in the web.config, add the <appSettings> element and the following keys:

```
<configuration>
  <appSettings>
    <add key="RSS_Summary_PlaceholderName" value="Summary" />
    <add key="RSS_Title" value="Tropical Green's Website" />
    <add key="RSS_WebsiteUrl" value="http://www.tropicalgreen.net" />
    <add key="RSS_Copyright" value="© Tropical Green 2005" />
    <add key="RSS_Description"
        value="The latest changes from the Tropical Green Website." />
    <add key="RSS_ManagingEditor" value="content@tropicalgreen.net" />
    <add key="RSS_WebMaster" value="webmaster@tropicalgreen.net" />
    <add key="RSS_StartChannel" value="/channels/www.tropicalgreen.net/" />
    <add key="RSS_NumberOfDaysOld" value="20" />
  </appSettings>
. . . code continues . . .
```

For even more flexibility, this configuration data could be stored in channel properties and the RSS feed could be generated by a posting or a channel rendering script rather than a web form.

Testing the RSS Feed

To test the feed we can load the page directly in a web browser and see the response. To do this we will set rss.aspx as the start page and start without debugging.

1. Right-click on rss.aspx, and select Set as Start Page.

2. From the Debug menu, select Start Without Debugging.

3. The page should now be loaded and the RSS should appear:

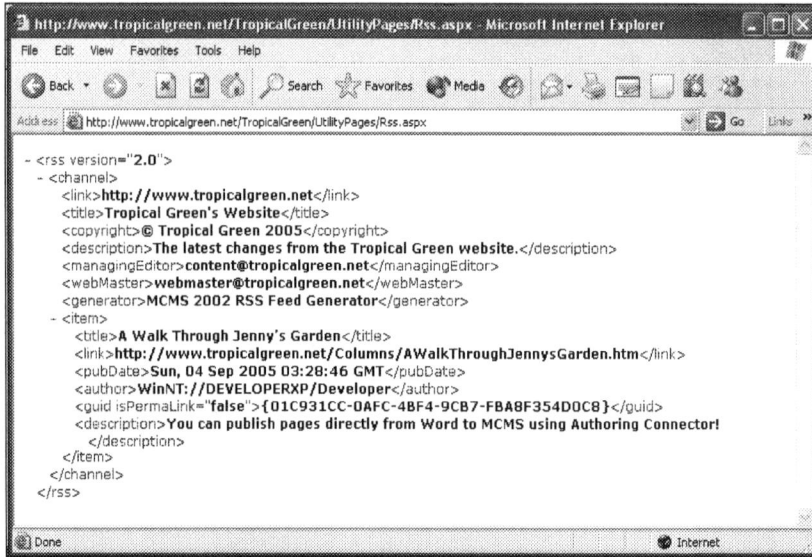

For postings to be included in the RSS feed, they must have been created or modified and published in the last 20 days, as this is the timeframe we configured in the web.config.

Testing the RSS Feed in an Aggregator

If you have an RSS aggregator on your computer, you can test the RSS feed by pointing your aggregator at http://localhost/TropicalGreen/UtilityPages/rss.aspx. Below is a screenshot of the feed being aggregated by RSS Bandit (www.rssbandit.org), which is one of the most popular of the free RSS aggregators.

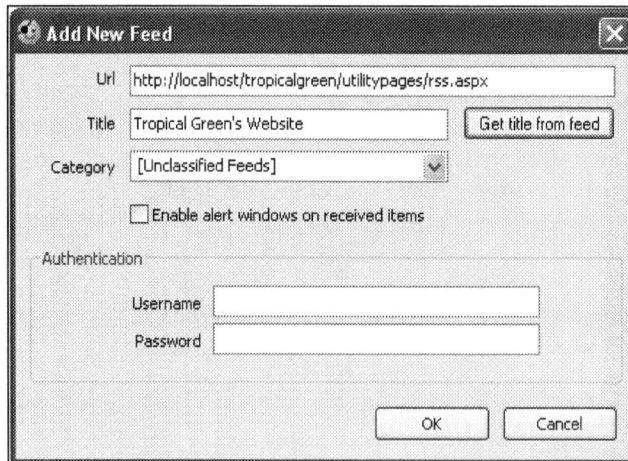

The feed we are generating is an RSS 2.0-compatible feed. If you want to transform the feed into another type, for instance a Podcast compatible feed, you can leverage FeedBurner (www.feedburner.com), which provides this sort of conversion functionality.

Aggregating an RSS Feed into MCMS

For the next example, we will create a placeholder control that will allow users to enter the URL of an RSS feed and aggregate the contents into a posting.

Creating the Placeholder Control

To create the RSS aggregation placeholder control, we will create a new placeholder in the TropicalGreenControlLib project.

1. Load the Tropical Green solution in Visual Studio .NET.
2. Right-click on the TropicalGreenControlLib project and select Add | Add Class.
3. Name the new class RssReaderPlaceholderControl.cs and click OK.
4. Import the following namespaces:

```
using System;
using System.Net;
using System.Text;
using System.Xml;
using System.Web;
using System.Web.UI;
using System.Web.UI.WebControls;
using Microsoft.ContentManagement.Publishing;
using Microsoft.ContentManagement.Publishing.Extensions.Placeholders;
using Microsoft.ContentManagement.WebControls.Design;
using Microsoft.ContentManagement.WebControls;
```

5. As the placeholder can be added to a template via the Visual Studio .NET Toolbox and will be bound to an `XmlPlaceholder`, we need to add some attributes to the class. We also need to inherit the `BasePlaceholderControl` class:

```
[
ToolboxData("<{0}:RssReaderPlaceholderControl runat=server>
</{0}:RssReaderPlaceholderControl>"),
SupportedPlaceholderDefinitionType(typeof(XmlPlaceholderDefinition))
]
public class RssReaderPlaceholderControl : BasePlaceholderControl
{
. . . code continues . . .
```

6. Now we have to declare the enumerators, variables, and controls that will be used by the placeholder control. Add the following declarations after the `RssReaderPlaceholderControl()` constructor:

```
#region Declarations - Variables

enum enmState { none, Channel, Item };
private string RssUrl = "";
private int ItemsToDisplay = int.MaxValue;
private bool ShowOpenArticleLink = true;
private bool ShowDescription = true;
private bool ShowDate = true;
private bool ShowAuthor = true;

#endregion

#region Declarations - Controls

private LiteralControl basePresentationControl;
private System.Web.UI.WebControls.PlaceHolder baseAuthoringContainer;
private TextBox txtRSSUrl;
private DropDownList ddlItemsToDisplay;
private CheckBox chkShowOpenArticleLink;
private CheckBox chkShowDescription;
private CheckBox chkShowDate;
private CheckBox chkShowAuthor;

#endregion
```

7. As a convenience in development, we will create the `BoundXmlPlaceholder` property on the class. This property casts the inherited `BoundPlaceholder` property to an `XmlPlaceholder`:

```
#region Properties

/// <summary>
/// Returns the Strongly Typed
/// Bound XmlPlaceholder
/// </summary>
private XmlPlaceholder BoundXmlPlaceholder
{
  get
  {
    return (this.BoundPlaceholder as XmlPlaceholder);
  }
}

#endregion
```

8. To manage the storage and retrieval of the data for this placeholder, we will create the two methods `LoadSettingsFromXml()` and `GetSettingsAsXml()`:

```
#region Load/Set Settings

/// <summary>
/// Load the settings of the placeholder from an XmlString
/// </summary>
/// <param name="strXml"></param>
public void LoadSettingsFromXml(string strXml)
{
    // Create a new xml Document
    XmlDocument _doc = new XmlDocument();

    // Load the xml into the xml document
    _doc.LoadXml(strXml);

    // Set the variables from the XML
    this.RssUrl = _doc.SelectSingleNode("/Content/RssUrl").InnerText;
    this.ItemsToDisplay = System.Convert.ToInt32(
            _doc.SelectSingleNode("/Content/ItemsToDisplay").InnerText);
    this.ShowOpenArticleLink = Boolean.Parse(
        _doc.SelectSingleNode("/Content/ShowOpenArticleLink").InnerText);
    this.ShowDescription = Boolean.Parse(
            _doc.SelectSingleNode("/Content/ShowDescription").InnerText);
    this.ShowDate = Boolean.Parse(
            _doc.SelectSingleNode("/Content/ShowDate").InnerText);
    this.ShowAuthor = Boolean.Parse(
            _doc.SelectSingleNode("/Content/ShowAuthor").InnerText);
}
```

9. To create the XML string in the `GetSettingsAsXml()` method, we will use a `StringBuilder` class to build the XML string. We could equally use an `XmlTextWriter` object.

```
/// <summary>
///  Get the current set of settings as an Xml string
/// </summary>
/// <returns></returns>
public string GetSettingsAsXml()
{
    // Create a new string builder
    StringBuilder sb = new StringBuilder();

    // Create the Content XML string and populate elements
    sb.Append("<Content>");
    sb.Append("  <RssUrl>" + HttpUtility.HtmlEncode(this.txtRSSUrl.Text)
            + "</RssUrl>");
    sb.Append("  <ItemsToDisplay>"
        + this.ddlItemsToDisplay.Items[ddlItemsToDisplay.SelectedIndex].Value
            + "</ItemsToDisplay>");
    sb.Append("  <ShowOpenArticleLink>"
            + this.chkShowOpenArticleLink.Checked.ToString()
            + "</ShowOpenArticleLink>");
    sb.Append("  <ShowDescription>"
            + this.chkShowDescription.Checked.ToString()
            + "</ShowDescription>");
    sb.Append("  <ShowDate>" + this.chkShowDate.Checked.ToString()
            + "</ShowDate>");
    sb.Append("  <ShowAuthor>" + this.chkShowAuthor.Checked.ToString()
            + "</ShowAuthor>");
    sb.Append("</Content>");
```

```
        // return the string
        return(sb.ToString());
    }

    #endregion
```

Setting up the Authoring Interface

For users to enter the URL of the RSS feed and configure other properties, we will create an authoring interface for this placeholder control. This will also populate the child controls by overriding the CreateAuthoringChildControls(), LoadPlaceholderContentForAuthoring(), and SavePlaceholderContent() methods.

In CreateAuthoringChildControls(), we will create a table containing a TextBox for entering the URL of the RSS feed followed by other controls for modifying the layout of the placeholder in presentation mode:

RSS-Feed Url	
Number of Articles	unlimited ⌄
Render "Open Article" link	☑
Render Description	☑
Render Date	☑
Render Author	☑

```
#region Edit Mode

/// <summary>
/// Create all the controls for the authoring interface
/// </summary>
/// <param name="authorContainer"></param>
protected override void CreateAuthoringChildControls(BaseModeContainer
                                    authorContainer)
{
```

First, we add code to define the outer table to contain the properties:

```
// Set up the Outer Table
Table OuterTable = new Table();
TableRow tableRow = new TableRow();
TableCell tableCell = new TableCell();
OuterTable.Rows.Add(tableRow);
OuterTable.CellPadding = 3;
OuterTable.CellSpacing = 0;
OuterTable.BorderColor = System.Drawing.Color.Green;
OuterTable.BorderWidth = 3;
tableRow.Cells.Add(tableCell);

// Set up the table holding the controls
Table TableHoldingTheControls = new Table();
tableCell.Controls.Add(TableHoldingTheControls);
TableHoldingTheControls.Width = Unit.Percentage(100);
TableHoldingTheControls.CssClass = "RssAuthoringTable";
TableHoldingTheControls.CellPadding = 0;
TableHoldingTheControls.CellSpacing = 0;
TableHoldingTheControls.BackColor = System.Drawing.Color.White;

tableRow = new TableRow();
TableHoldingTheControls.Rows.Add(tableRow);
```

Next, we define each row and create two table cells. We add the label and the textbox web control to the table cells. This process is repeated for each setting the user can specify:

```
// ROW: Text
tableCell = new TableCell();
tableCell.Width = 130;
tableRow.Cells.Add(tableCell);
LiteralControl ltCn = new LiteralControl();
ltCn.Text = "RSS-Feed Url";
tableCell.Controls.Add(ltCn);

tableCell = new TableCell();
tableCell.Width = 10;
tableRow.Cells.Add(tableCell);

// ROW: Url Input Box
tableCell = new TableCell();
tableRow.Cells.Add(tableCell);
txtRSSUrl = new TextBox();
txtRSSUrl.ID = "RssUrl";
txtRSSUrl.Width = 300;
txtRSSUrl.TextMode = System.Web.UI.WebControls.TextBoxMode.SingleLine;
tableCell.Controls.Add(txtRSSUrl);

// New Row
tableRow = new TableRow();
TableHoldingTheControls.Rows.Add(tableRow);

// ROW: Number of Articles
tableCell = new TableCell();
tableRow.Cells.Add(tableCell);
ltCn = new LiteralControl();
ltCn.Text = "Number of Articles";
tableCell.Controls.Add(ltCn);

tableCell = new TableCell();
tableCell.Width = 10;
tableRow.Cells.Add(tableCell);

// Count Input Box
tableCell = new TableCell();
tableRow.Cells.Add(tableCell);
ddlItemsToDisplay = new DropDownList();
ddlItemsToDisplay.EnableViewState = false;
ddlItemsToDisplay.ID = "Count";
ddlItemsToDisplay.Items.Add("5");
ddlItemsToDisplay.Items.Add("10");
ddlItemsToDisplay.Items.Add("15");
ddlItemsToDisplay.Items.Add("20");
ddlItemsToDisplay.Items.Add(new ListItem("unlimited",
                                          int.MaxValue.ToString()));
ddlItemsToDisplay.SelectedIndex = 4;
tableCell.Controls.Add(ddlItemsToDisplay);

// New Row
tableRow = new TableRow();
TableHoldingTheControls.Rows.Add(tableRow);

// Text
tableCell = new TableCell();
tableRow.Cells.Add(tableCell);
ltCn = new LiteralControl();
ltCn.Text = "Render \"Open Article\" link";
```

```
tableCell.Controls.Add(ltCn);

tableCell = new TableCell();
tableCell.Width = 10;
tableRow.Cells.Add(tableCell);

// 'Open Articles' Link
tableCell = new TableCell();
tableRow.Cells.Add(tableCell);
chkShowOpenArticleLink = new CheckBox();
chkShowOpenArticleLink.EnableViewState = false;
chkShowOpenArticleLink.ID = "RenderOpenArticle";
chkShowOpenArticleLink.Checked = true;
tableCell.Controls.Add(chkShowOpenArticleLink);

// New Row
tableRow = new TableRow();
TableHoldingTheControls.Rows.Add(tableRow);

// Text
tableCell = new TableCell();
tableRow.Cells.Add(tableCell);
ltCn = new LiteralControl();
ltCn.Text = "Render Description";
tableCell.Controls.Add(ltCn);

tableCell = new TableCell();
tableCell.Width = 10;
tableRow.Cells.Add(tableCell);

// Description
tableCell = new TableCell();
tableRow.Cells.Add(tableCell);
chkShowDescription = new CheckBox();
chkShowDescription.EnableViewState = false;
chkShowDescription.ID = "RenderDescription";
chkShowDescription.Checked = true;
tableCell.Controls.Add(chkShowDescription);

// New Row
tableRow = new TableRow();
TableHoldingTheControls.Rows.Add(tableRow);

// Text
tableCell = new TableCell();
tableRow.Cells.Add(tableCell);
ltCn = new LiteralControl();
ltCn.Text = "Render Date";
tableCell.Controls.Add(ltCn);

tableCell = new TableCell();
tableCell.Width = 10;
tableRow.Cells.Add(tableCell);

// Date and Author
tableCell = new TableCell();
tableRow.Cells.Add(tableCell);
chkShowDate = new CheckBox();
chkShowDate.EnableViewState = false;
chkShowDate.ID = "RenderDate";
chkShowDate.Checked = true;
tableCell.Controls.Add(chkShowDate);

// New Row
tableRow = new TableRow();
TableHoldingTheControls.Rows.Add(tableRow);
```

400

```
// Text
tableCell = new TableCell();
tableRow.Cells.Add(tableCell);
ltCn = new LiteralControl();
ltCn.Text = "Render Author";
tableCell.Controls.Add(ltCn);

tableCell = new TableCell();
tableCell.Width = 10;
tableRow.Cells.Add(tableCell);

// Date and Author
tableCell = new TableCell();
tableRow.Cells.Add(tableCell);
chkShowAuthor = new CheckBox();
chkShowAuthor.EnableViewState = false;
chkShowAuthor.ID = "RenderAuthor";
chkShowAuthor.Checked = true;
tableCell.Controls.Add(chkShowAuthor);
```

Then we add a placeholder called baseAuthoringContainer, and add the outer table to it. The baseAuthoringContainer is then added to the controls collection of the authoring container:

```
// Finally the Authoring Container
this.baseAuthoringContainer = new System.Web.UI.WebControls.PlaceHolder();
baseAuthoringContainer.Controls.Add(OuterTable);
baseAuthoringContainer.ID = "RssPhAuthoringControl";
authorContainer.Controls.Add(this.baseAuthoringContainer);
}
```

To load the value from the XmlPlaceholder string, we'll create a method called LoadSettingsFromXml(). The contents of the XmlPlaceholder will be loaded into an XmlDocument and then the variables we previously defined will be populated.

```
/// <summary>
/// Load the contents of the placeholder for
/// authoring mode
/// </summary>
/// <param name="e"></param>
protected override void
LoadPlaceholderContentForAuthoring(PlaceholderControlEventArgs e)
{
  try
  {
    // check the child controls were created successfully
    EnsureChildControls();

    // Load the settings for the placeholder control
    this.LoadSettingsFromXml(this.BoundXmlPlaceholder.XmlAsString);

    // Set the values of the web controls
    this.txtRSSUrl.Text = this.RssUrl;
    this.ddlItemsToDisplay.SelectedItem.Value =
                        this.ItemsToDisplay.ToString();
    this.chkShowOpenArticleLink.Checked = this.ShowOpenArticleLink;
    this.chkShowDescription.Checked = this.ShowDescription;
    this.chkShowDate.Checked = this.ShowDate;
    this.chkShowAuthor.Checked = this.ShowAuthor;
  }
  catch(Exception ex)
  {
    // Handle any exceptions
  }
}
```

We will now save the placeholder content back to MCMS by overriding the
SavePlaceholderContent() method. We will retrieve the current settings using the
GetSettingsAsXml() method and set it to the XmlAsString property of the XmlPlaceholder:

```
/// <summary>
/// Save the placeholder content back to MCMS
/// </summary>
/// <param name="e"></param>
protected override void SavePlaceholderContent(PlaceholderControlSaveEventArgs e)
{
    // check the child controls were created successfully
    EnsureChildControls();

    // Set the Xml Placeholder
    this.BoundXmlPlaceholder.XmlAsString = GetSettingsAsXml();
}
#endregion
```

Retrieving and Parsing the RSS Feed

Let's now create the LoadAndRenderRssFeed() method, which will retrieve an RSS feed via an
HTTP request and parse it. It will also output the items in the RSS feed depending on the settings
that have been saved into the XmlPlaceholder.

> For the purposes of this example, we are not coding for proxy server interaction but if
> you have a proxy server you should store the address (and credentials if required) in the
> web.config.

```
#region Retrieving and Parsing the RSS Feed

/// <summary>
/// Load the RSS feed by a WebRequest
/// and then parse the input returning a string
/// </summary>
public string LoadAndRenderRssFeed()
{
```

First, we will load the setting from the XML Placeholder:

```
    // Load the settings from the Xml
    this.LoadSettingsFromXml(this.BoundXmlPlaceholder.XmlAsString);

    enmState CurrentState = enmState.none;
    string Title = "";
    string Link = "";
    string Author = "";
    string PubDate = "";
    string Descript = "";

    // Declare and instantiate the string builder
    // that the HTML will be written to.
    StringBuilder sb = new StringBuilder();
```

Next, we make a web request using the WebRequest class. If you need to specify a proxy,
uncomment the proxy code and replace proxyserver with your proxy name.

```
    // Create a new WebRequest to the URL specified
    // in the <RssUrl> element stored in the XmlPlaceholder
```

```
HttpWebRequest request = (HttpWebRequest)WebRequest.Create(RssUrl);

// uncomment if you have a proxy
// WebProxy proxy = null;
// proxy = new WebProxy("http://proxyserver:port");
// request.Proxy = proxy;

// Get the Response from the web request
HttpWebResponse response = (HttpWebResponse)request.GetResponse();
```

The response is then loaded into an XmlTextReader. We read the contents of the XmlTextReader and generate the HTML for the different articles in the feed, such as the author's name for instance:

```
// load the stream into an XmlTextReader
XmlTextReader rsReader = new XmlTextReader(response.GetResponseStream());

int actItem = 0;

// Loop through the reader
while (!rsReader.EOF)
{
```

A feed can serve many articles. We need to add a check to ensure that only the configured number of articles is displayed:

```
// How many items are we going to display?
if (actItem >= this.ItemsToDisplay)
  break;
```

Now let's iterate through all XML tags of the current feed item and collect all the data for the current item. As different feeds use different standards (like RSS 1.0, 2.0, or Atom), the content we are looking for may be encoded in different tags:

```
// What is the current element of the RSS Feed
switch (rsReader.Name.ToLower())
{
```

The feed or channel element encloses the information about the current RSS feed:

```
case "feed":
case "channel":
{
  CurrentState = enmState.Channel;
  rsReader.Read();
  break;
}
case "title":
{
  if (rsReader.NodeType == XmlNodeType.Element)
    Title = HttpUtility.HtmlDecode(rsReader.ReadInnerXml());
  else
    rsReader.Read();
  break;
}
case "link":
{
  if (rsReader.NodeType == XmlNodeType.Element)
  {
    string Link1 = rsReader.GetAttribute("href");
    string Link2 = rsReader.ReadInnerXml();
    if (Link1 != null)
      Link = Link1;
    else
      Link = Link2;
  }
```

```
            else
              rsReader.Read();
            break;
        }
        case "content":
        {
            bool esc = false;
            string att = rsReader.GetAttribute("mode");
            if (att != null)
              esc = (att.ToLower() == "escaped");
            if (rsReader.NodeType == XmlNodeType.Element)
            {
              Descript = rsReader.ReadInnerXml();
              if (esc)
                Descript = HttpUtility.HtmlDecode(Descript);
            }
            break;
        }
        case "description":
        {
            if (rsReader.NodeType == XmlNodeType.Element)
              Descript = HttpUtility.HtmlDecode(rsReader.ReadInnerXml());
            break;
        }
```

The publishing date can be encoded using pubdate, created, or dc:date elements depending on the type of feed the aggregator is consuming:

```
        case "pubdate":
        case "created":
        case "dc:date":
        {
            if (this.ShowDate)
            {
              if (rsReader.NodeType == XmlNodeType.Element)
                PubDate = DateTime.Parse(rsReader.ReadInnerXml()).ToString();
            }
            else
              rsReader.Read();
            break;
        }
```

The name of the author can be encoded as dc:creator, name, or author elements:

```
        case "dc:creator":
        case "name":
        case "author":
        {
            if (this.ShowAuthor)
            {
              if (rsReader.NodeType == XmlNodeType.Element)
                Author = rsReader.ReadInnerXml();
            }
            else
              rsReader.Read();
            break;
        }
```

We will now process the item or entry elements:

```
        case "item":
        case "entry":
        {
```

The item or entry element encloses the information for a specific article in the feed. When the start tag of the item or entry element shows up in the middle of information about the feed, we know that no more information on the feed will arrive and that we can now render the title, link and description of the feed:

```
if (rsReader.NodeType == XmlNodeType.Element)
{
  if (CurrentState == enmState.Channel)
  {
    sb.Append("<div>\n");
    sb.Append(" <div><a href=\"" + Link + "\">" + Title +
                                            "</a></div>\n");
    sb.Append(" <div>" + Descript + "</div>\n");
    sb.Append("</div>\n\n");
  }
  CurrentState = enmState.Item;
}
```

And here we will handle the end tag of the item or entry element. When this end tag arrives all information of the current article has been consumed and we can now render the article. Specific information will be rendered or not, according to the ShowDate, ShowAuthor, ShowDescription, and ShowOpenArticle flags:

```
if (rsReader.NodeType == XmlNodeType.EndElement)
{

  actItem += 1;

  // Set the seperator to ":" if the author and
  // pubdate aren't empty.
  string sep = ((Author != "") & (PubDate != ""))? " - ":"";

  sb.Append("<div>\n");
  sb.Append("  <div>" +Title+ "</div>\n");

  if (this.ShowDescription)
  {
    sb.Append("  <div>" + Descript + "</div>\n");
  }

  // Are we showing author or date?
  if (this.ShowDate || this.ShowAuthor)
  {

    sb.Append("  <div>");

    // Are we showing both?
    if (this.ShowDate && this.ShowAuthor)
    {
      // Yes, output them and add the separator
      sb.Append(Author + sep + PubDate);
    }
    else
    {
      // No, which ones are we showing

      // Author?
      if (this.ShowAuthor)
      {
        // Append the author
        sb.Append(Author);
      }
```

```
            // Date?
            if (this.ShowDate)
            {
                // Append the Date
                sb.Append(PubDate);
            }
        }

        sb.Append("</div>\n");
    }

    // Are we showing the Open Article Link?
    if (this.ShowOpenArticleLink)
    {
        sb.Append("  <div>");
        sb.Append("<a target=\"_blank\" href=\"" + Link
                + "\">[Open Article]</a>");
        sb.Append("</div>\n");
    }

    sb.Append("</div>\n");
            }
            rsReader.Read();
            break;
        }
        default:
        {
            rsReader.Read();
            break;
        }
    }
}
}

// return the string builder contents
return(sb.ToString());
}

#endregion
```

Rendering the RSS Feed in Presentation Mode

We will now create the interface for presenting the RSS feed. In unpublished mode, the RssReader placeholder control will show Feed will be shown in published mode, and when the placeholder is viewed in published mode, LoadAndRenderRssFeed() will be executed to retrieve the feed and its output will be bound to the basePresentationControl.

First we override CreatePresentationChildControls() to create the presentation child controls:

```
#region Presentation

/// <summary>
/// Create the Presentation Controls
/// </summary>
/// <param name="presentationContainer"></param>
protected override void CreatePresentationChildControls(
                                    BaseModeContainer presentationContainer)
{
    // Instantiate a literal control and
    // set the base presentation control
    this.basePresentationControl = new LiteralControl();

    // Set the ID of the base presentation control
```

```
    this.basePresentationControl.ID = "PresentationControl";

    // Add the base presentation contorl to
    // the presentation container
    presentationContainer.Controls.Add(this.basePresentationControl);
}
```

To load the RSS feed and output the items using the placeholder control, we will override the
`LoadPlaceholderContentForPresentation()` method. The feed will not be rendered in
"Presentation Unpublished" mode for authoring efficiency.

To minimize the hit to the feed provider, we will implement content caching for our placeholder
control. This means even if several users request the posting containing the
`RssReaderPlaceholderControl` within the configured timeframe, only one web request will hit
the feed site. This minimizes traffic and processing overhead for the feed site and as well the
website holding this placeholder control.

The cache duration is currently hardcoded to five minutes. If you need this to be more
flexible, you can either store the cache duration in the `web.config` or add a textbox to the
authoring mode that captures the cache duration and saves it as additional configuration
value for the `XmlPlaceholder`.

```
/// <summary>
/// Load and parse the RSS feed. Output the feed
/// items to the basePresentationControl
/// </summary>
/// <param name="e"></param>
protected override void
LoadPlaceholderContentForPresentation(PlaceholderControlEventArgs e)
{
    // Verify the child controls have been created
    EnsureChildControls();

    try
    {
        // Check the current mode
        if (WebAuthorContext.Current.Mode ==
            WebAuthorContextMode.PresentationUnpublished)
        {
            this.basePresentationControl.Text =
                            "Feed will be shown in published mode";
        }
        else
        {
            // Load the settings from the XML
            this.LoadSettingsFromXml(this.BoundXmlPlaceholder.XmlAsString);

            // Get the current Cache object from HttpContext
            System.Web.Caching.Cache cache = HttpContext.Current.Cache;

            // we will vary the cache entry by the content of the
            // current placeholder object. This will ensure that different
            // feeds can be served from the same website
            string CacheKey = this.BoundXmlPlaceholder.XmlAsString;

            // check if content is already in Cache
            string cacheXml = cache["RssReader." + CacheKey] as string;
            if (cacheXml == null)
            {
```

```
                // Content is not in Cache - request it from the feed
                cacheXml = LoadAndRenderRssFeed();

                // we will now add the content to the cache
                cache.Insert("RssReader."+ CacheKey, cacheXml, null,
                          DateTime.Now.AddMinutes(5), TimeSpan.Zero);
            }
            this.basePresentationControl.Text = cacheXml;
        }
    }
    catch (Exception exp)
    {
        // show the error as placeholder content
        this.basePresentationControl.Text = "Error: " + exp.Message;
    }
}

#endregion
```

Now rebuild the solution.

Adding the Control to a Template

To see this placeholder control working, we will add it to the Column template. We will need to:

- Add an XmlPlaceholder definition on the Column template.
- Add the RssReaderPlaceholderControl to column.aspx.

Creating the Placeholder Definition in the Template

The RssReaderPlacheholderControl will store its data in an XmlPlaceholder. To add the XmlPlaceholder to the Column template, follow these steps:

1. Launch Visual Studio .NET and open the TropicalGreen solution.
2. Switch to the MCMS Template Explorer, and expand the Templates template gallery.
3. Expand the TropicalGreen template gallery, and the Columns template gallery.
4. Right-click on the Column template and select Check Out.
5. Right-click on the Column template again, and select Properties.
6. Click the ellipsis (...) next to the PlaceholderDefinitions property.
7. Click the small down arrow next to the Add button.
8. Select XmlPlaceholderDefinition.
9. On the right-hand side, enter the name RssReader and click OK.
10. Browse back to the MCMS Template Explorer, right-click on the Column template and select Check In.

Adding the RSS Reader Placeholder to the Template

To add the RssReader placeholder control to the template, we will register the control in the template using the @Register directive and add an instance of the control to the center column. Here are the steps:

1. From the MCMS Template Explorer, right-click on the Column template and select Open Template File.

2. Click the HTML tab at the bottom of columns.aspx.

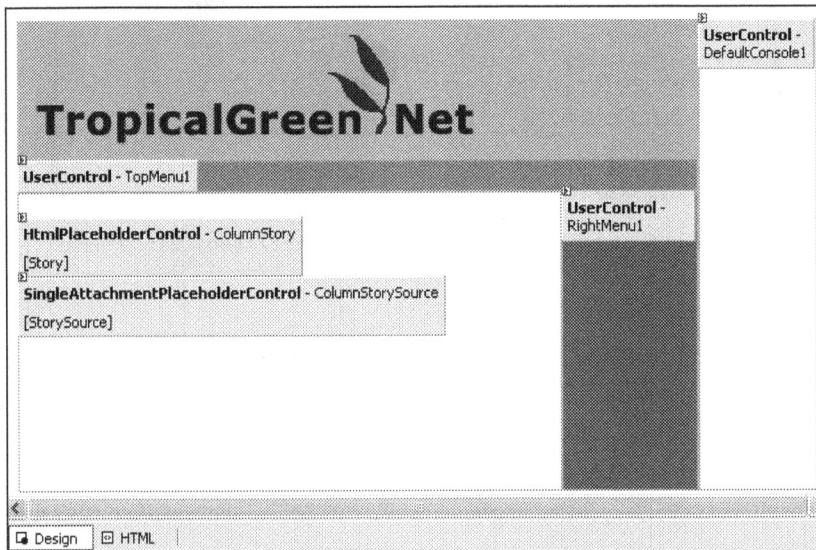

3. At the top of the file, add the following @Register directive:

```
<%@ Register TagPrefix="TropicalGreenControls"
             Namespace="TropicalGreenControlLib"
             Assembly="TropicalGreenControlLib" %>
```

4. Below the SingleAttachmentPlaceholderControl, add the following code to create an instance of the RssReaderPlaceholderControl:

```
<TropicalGreenControls:RssReaderPlaceholderControl runat="server"
 id="RssReader1" />
<br>
```

5. Switch back to Design mode by clicking the Design button at the bottom of the page.

6. Right-click on the RssReader1 control and select Properties.

7. Select the PlaceholderToBind drop-down list, and select the RssReader placeholder.

8. Finally, save columns.aspx.

Testing the Template

To test the RssReader placeholder control, we will modify an existing posting that uses the Column template and aggregate the feed that we built earlier (rss.aspx).

1. Start Internet Explorer and browse to www.tropicalgreen.net.

2. Browse to A Walk Through Jenny's Garden.
   (http://www.tropicalgreen.net/Columns/AWalkThroughJennysGarden.htm)

3. Select Switch to Edit Mode from the Web Author Console.

4. Select Edit from the Web Author Console. You will now see the page in Author Re-edit mode:

RSS-Feed Url	
Number of Articles	unlimited
Render "Open Article" link	☑
Render Description	☑
Render Date	☑
Render Author	☑

5. Enter the feed URL: `http://www.tropicalgreen.net/TropicalGreen/ UtilityPages/Rss.aspx`.

6. Save the posting by clicking Save and Exit.

The posting will now display Feed will be shown in published mode. To see the aggregated feed follow these steps:

1. Publish the posting by clicking Approve in the Web Author Console.

2. Click Switch to Live Site.

3. You will now see the posting aggregating the contents of the specified RSS feed.

Tropical Green's Website
The latest changes from the Tropical Green website.
Coconut Tree

WinNT://DEVELOPERXP/Developer - 17/03/2005 11:07:31 PM
[Open Article]
The Herb Garden (Public View)
This is a story about my beautiful herb garden which started from a single seed.
WinNT://DEVELOPERXP/Developer - 17/03/2005 11:07:31 PM
[Open Article]
Banana Tree

WinNT://DEVELOPERXP/Developer - 17/03/2005 11:07:31 PM
[Open Article]
Ixora

WinNT://DEVELOPERXP/Developer - 17/03/2005 11:07:31 PM
[Open Article]
Man Eating Plant

WinNT://DEVELOPERXP/Developer - 17/03/2005 11:07:31 PM
[Open Article]
Bougainvillea

WinNT://DEVELOPERXP/Developer - 17/03/2005 11:07:31 PM
[Open Article]
Hibiscus

Possible Enhancements

There are several enhancements that could be made to the samples in this chapter.

Enhancements to the RSS Feed Generator

- Author name—The solution could be enhanced by integration with Active Directory to retrieve the author's full name.

- Channel-based feed generation—set up channel properties as configuration parameters for the feed and generate it from a posting or channel rendering script.

- Storing history—Organizations may have a requirement to keep a copy of all historical content that has been on their website. The RSS feed currently potentially changes every 5 minutes (when the cache expires). To make the RSS feed act as content that appears in the page revision history, the request to the feed could be made on save and the generated HTML could be saved into an `HtmlPlaceholder`. An autoupdater tool could then be written to update the aggregated feed at a scheduled time, say every 60 minutes.

Enhancements to the RSS Aggregator Placeholder Control

- Design—The RSS aggregation control only has a rudimentary look and feel that could easily be enhanced by adding `class` attributes to the `div` elements to apply styles defined in the page's CSS stylesheet.

Summary

We have now given the Tropical Green website the ability to syndicate and aggregate content via RSS. Content authors will have the ability to specify RSS feeds to aggregate and display on specific postings. End users will now have the chance to subscribe to an RSS feed on our MCMS website so they can be automatically notified when content changes happen without having to browse to the website. In addition, an MCMS website can now aggregate content from RSS feeds coming from other servers on the Internet and display some of that website's own content.

13

Essential How-Tos, Tips, and Tricks

This chapter covers nine essential tips and tricks that developers can use within their MCMS applications:

- **How to revert a posting to a previous version.** While MCMS allows you to compare and view a posting's revision history, it does not provide an immediate solution to roll back changes. This example shows how to program your own dialog allowing authors to select a previously published version of the page to revert to.

- **How to change a posting's template.** Once a posting has been created, there's no obvious way to change its template. The typical answer given to authors is to manually salvage information from the postings based on the "wrong" templates and create new postings based on the "correct" template. In this how-to, we will show you how to automate this copying process, saving authors hours of valuable time.

- **How to build a recycle bin.** Postings deleted from Web Author are not recoverable, except perhaps from a previous backup of the database (if one exists!). To safeguard authors from accidental deletes, this how-to discusses how a recycle bin can be built to store deleted items and restore them later, should the need arise.

- **How to deal with links to deleted resources.** With different people taking on the tasks of managing resources and authoring postings, there will come a time when someone will inevitably delete a resource that is currently in use by a posting. When that happens, problems follow. In this how-to, we discuss how links to deleted resources can be automatically detected and removed when a posting is saved.

- **How to update a posting's properties directly from a template file.** To update a posting an author has to go to two separate places: first, he or she has to edit the posting. Second, he or she has to click on the Page Properties dialog to update property values. In this how-to, we show you how an author can edit both types of content on the same screen by creating a web user control that updates property values when the posting is saved.

- **How to re-write unfriendly URLs to friendly URLs.** We will use a custom `HttpModule` to re-write all unfriendly URLs whenever they occur so that visitors only see friendly URLs in their browser's address bar.

- **How to export resource gallery items using the Site Deployment API (SDAPI).**
  The SDAPI was built to perform incremental deployments of channels and postings.
  It only includes resource gallery items if they are used within postings. In this
  how-to, we discuss a workaround to trick the SDAPI into exporting resource gallery
  items that we need to include in our export packages.

- **How to configure the position and size of the Web Author Console dialogs.** Did you
  notice that when opening the Resource Manager, Approval Assistant, or Production
  Manager dialogs, part of the window gets truncated, especially when working in
  full-screen mode? This how-to shows how the position and size of these dialogs can be
  adjusted to fit screen boundaries.

- **How to get Frames and IFrames to work correctly in a template file.** When using
  frames and IFrames within a template file, authors will get JavaScript errors when
  using the Web Author Console. In this how-to, we show you a simple way around
  this problem.

Tip #1: How to Revert a Posting to a Previous Version

MCMS provides at least two ways to view and compare the historical revisions of a posting. You
could view the posting as it appeared on a specific date by selecting the View Revisions by Date
option. Or you could choose to view or compare previously published versions from the Revision
History dialog.

Unfortunately, an option to revert to a previously published version of the posting does not exist.
When authors need to roll back a posting's contents to an older version, they typically do so by
copying and pasting content manually from archived versions of the posting.

In this section, we will fill this gap by automating the task of rolling a page back to a previous
version. We will provide authors with a dialog from which to select a previously published version
of the posting. The dialog lists all available revisions with a button next to each entry. When the
button is clicked, all placeholder content and custom property values from the older version are
automatically copied to the current version, effectively rolling back the changes.

The script is broken down into a series of smaller tasks:

- Building the dialog that lists all available revisions
- Programming the button that triggers the page reversion process
- Performing the reversion by copying content from the old revision to the
  current posting
- Adding a new action to the Web Author Console that calls the dialog

The Revert Page to Previous Version Dialog

Let's begin by building the dialog that lists all previously published versions of the page.
Essentially, there are two areas to work on. The first is a table that provides a hyperlink to the
working version of the posting. The second is a DataGrid that lists all available posting revisions.

The grid also holds a **Revert** button for each revision. Authors will also be given a choice of whether to roll back just the placeholder content or to include custom property values as well. Here's the dialog when completed:

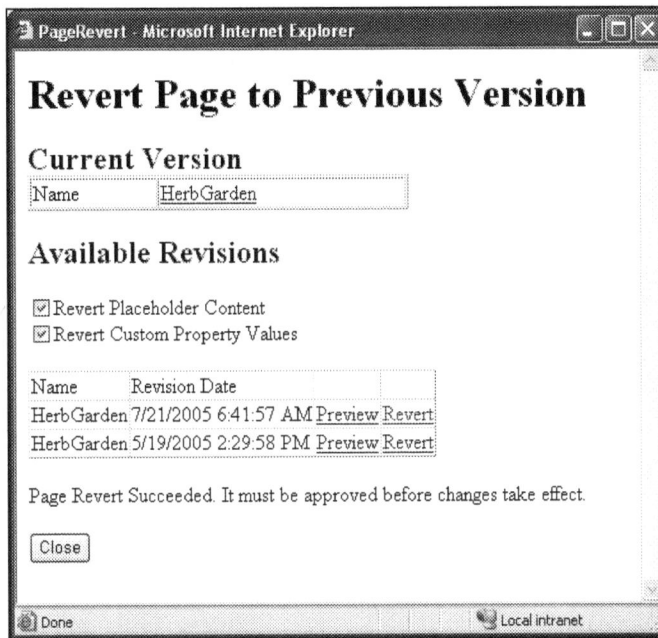

Can I roll back a posting's property values?

Only properties that are versioned by MCMS can be rolled back. Besides the custom properties only two properties are versioned: the posting's name and its description. The other properties are shared between all versions of the posting, including the live version.

To begin, add a web form named `PageRevert.aspx` to the MCMS web application (if you are working with the Tropical Green project, add it to the `Dialogs` folder) and set the form's **Page Layout** to `FlowLayout`.

With `PageRevert.aspx` open in HTML view, add a level-1 header for the form's title between the `<form>` tags, a couple of level-2 headers for the sub-titles, and a button that closes the window.

```
<form id="PageRevert" method="post" runat="server">
  <h1>Revert Page to Previous Version</h1>
  <h2>Current Version</h2>
  <h2>Available Revisions</h2>
  <input type="button" value="Close" onclick="window.close();">
</form>
```

Below the Current Version header, we will add the table that contains the hyperlink to the working version of the posting. Toggle to Design view. Select Table | Insert | Table... from the menu bar and insert a table with one row and two columns. In the table cells on the left-hand column, add the word Name. Drag and drop a HyperLink control (from the Web Forms section of the Toolbox) into the cell on the right-hand side. Give the HyperLink the ID aName (note that we have prefixed it with the letter 'a'), and set its Text property to be an empty string.

Next, drag a DataGrid and drop it below the Available Revisions header. The DataGrid will list all revisions of the posting. Set the ID of the DataGrid to dgPageRevisionsList and the AutoGenerateColumns property to false. Switch to HTML view and add four columns to the grid. The first column displays the name of the posting for that particular version, the second shows the revision date, the third is a hyperlink that links to a preview page, and the fourth is a button that triggers the page reversion process.

```
<asp:DataGrid ID="dgPageRevisionsList" Runat="server"
AutoGenerateColumns="False">
<Columns>
  <asp:BoundColumn DataField="Name" HeaderText="Name"></asp:BoundColumn>

  <asp:BoundColumn DataField="RevisionDate" HeaderText="Revision Date">
  </asp:BoundColumn>

  <asp:HyperLinkColumn Text="Preview" Target="CMSPageRevertPreviewWindow"
    DataNavigateUrlField="Url">
  </asp:HyperLinkColumn>

  <asp:ButtonColumn Text="Revert" CommandName="RevertTo">
  </asp:ButtonColumn>
</Columns>
</asp:DataGrid>
```

Toggle to Design view. Drag two CheckBox controls and drop them above the DataGrid. Set the ID of the first CheckBox to chkRevertContent and its Text property to Revert Placeholder Content. Give the second CheckBox an ID of chkRevertCustomProperties and a Text value of Revert Custom Property Values. Set the Checked property of both CheckBoxes to true.

Drag a Label control and drop it below the DataGrid. Set the Label's ID to lblMessage and its Text property to an empty string. We will display messages (such as errors) from the application here.

Here's what you should see:

Revert Page to Previous Version

Current Version

Name	[aName]

Available Revisions

☐ Revert Placeholder Content
☐ Revert Custom Property Values

Name	Revision Date		
Databound	Databound	Preview	Revert
Databound	Databound	Preview	Revert
Databound	Databound	Preview	Revert
Databound	Databound	Preview	Revert
Databound	Databound	Preview	Revert

[lblMessage]

[Close]

Double-click anywhere on the form to get to its code-behind file. Add the required namespaces above the class's namespace declaration.

```
. . . code continues . . .
using Microsoft.ContentManagement.Publishing;
using Microsoft.ContentManagement.WebControls;
using Microsoft.ContentManagement.Publishing.Extensions.Placeholders;

namespace TropicalGreen.Dialogs
{
    . . . code continues . . .
}
```

Within the Page_Load() event handler, we will do the following:

- Get a reference to the current CmsHttpContext, from which we can obtain a lot of useful information.

- Get an instance of the current posting—the one that needs to be rolled back.

- Check to see if we are in update mode as required for the page reversion process. If we are not, we will perform a redirect to get the dialog to open in the correct mode.

- Set the aName HyperLink to show the current posting's name and to point to the URL.

- Call GetListOfRevisions() (defined later) to populate the DataGrid with the list of available revisions.

Here's the code that does the work. Add the two private variables above the `Page_Load()` event handler and within it add the code shown below:

```
private Posting currentPostingVersion;
private CmsHttpContext cmsContext;

private void Page_Load(object sender, System.EventArgs e)
{
    // Get the current CmsHttpContext
    cmsContext = Microsoft.ContentManagement.Publishing.CmsHttpContext.Current;

    if (cmsContext != null)
    {
        // Get the current posting
        currentPostingVersion = cmsContext.Posting;
        if (currentPostingVersion != null)
        {
            // Are we in update mode?
            if (cmsContext.Mode != PublishingMode.Update)
            {
                // We are not in update mode. Switch to update mode
                Response.Redirect(Request.ServerVariables["URL"] + "?"
                            + currentPostingVersion.QueryStringModeUpdate);
            }

            // Get the list only on the first time the page is loaded
            if (!Page.IsPostBack)
            {
                // Display the properties of the current posting
                aName.Text = currentPostingVersion.Name;
                aName.NavigateUrl = currentPostingVersion.Url;
                aName.Target = "_blank";

                // Get a list of all revisions of the current posting
                GetListOfRevisions();
            }
        }
    }
    else
    {
        lblMessage.Text = "Unable to obtain current CmsHttpContext.";
    }
}
```

How to Get and Sort a List of Page Revisions

To get a list of historical revisions, we use the MCMS PAPI's `Posting.Revisions()` method, which returns a collection of posting revisions and accepts two optional parameters:

- `doIncludePostingRevisions`. A Boolean that when set to `true` (the default value) gets `Posting.Revisions()` to return all revisions that have been created every time a posting was approved and published.

- `doIncludePageResourceRevisions`. A Boolean that when set to `true` (the default value) gets `Posting.Revisions()` to return all revisions that have been created each time a shared resource used by the posting changed (for instance, when replacing a resource in a resource gallery).

Once we have retrieved a collection of all revisions, we sort them by revision dates using the `PostingCollection.SortByRevisionDate()` method. The method accepts a single Boolean that when set to `true` (the default), returns the collection of postings sorted in ascending order of their revision dates. We want to display the list in descending order with latest revision first, so we set the Boolean to `false`.

Once we have retrieved and sorted the collection of revisions, we bind it to the DataGrid, `dgPageRevisionsList`. This is all done in the `GetListOfRevisions()` method, which we add directly below the `Page_Load()` event handler.

```
public void GetListOfRevisions()
{
    // Get a list of all revisions of the current posting
    PostingCollection pc = currentPostingVersion.Revisions(true, false);

    // Sort the revisions by descending order of the revision date
    pc.SortByRevisionDate(false);

    // Bind the collection to the datagrid
    dgPageRevisionsList.DataSource = pc;
    dgPageRevisionsList.DataBind();
}
```

> Unless the revision history is cleared periodically, we could potentially have a large number of revisions for each posting. To clear the revision history, select the Tools | Clear Revision History... option in Site Manager.

Programming the Button that Triggers the Page Reversion Process

The Revert button on the DataGrid triggers the page reversion process. There is one Revert button for each revision listed on the grid. Authors will click on the button of the version they wish to roll the posting back to. Here's how the reversion process works:

- First, the author clicks on the Revert button next to the selected revision.
- When the Revert button is clicked, the `dgPageRevisionsList_ItemCommand()` event handler is called. Within the event handler, we will retrieve the selected revision from the revisions collection and call several key procedures:
  - A `CopyPostingContent()` method, which copies all placeholder content from the selected revision to the working version
  - A `CopyCustomProperties()` method, which copies all custom property values from the selected revision to the working version
- Finally, we refresh the parent window to show the posting with its recently reverted content.

Accessing the ItemCommand() Event Handler of the DataGrid

Let's start by working with the standard ASP.NET behavior of the DataGrid by editing the `ItemCommand()` event handler.

When the Revert button is clicked, the `ItemCommand()` event handler of the `dgPageRevisionsList` DataGrid is fired. This is where we will add the code that carries out the page reversion process. To access this event handler, open `PageRevert.aspx` in Design view. Within the properties window of the `dgPageRevisionsList` DataGrid object, click the Events button (it's the button with the yellow lightning symbol ⚡). Double-click on the ItemCommand field to get to the dgPageRevisionsList_ItemCommand() event handler.

Within the event handler, we first check to see if the command was triggered by the Revert button by checking to see if the command name is RevertTo (we specified the button's command name when designing the grid).

```
private void dgPageRevisionsList_ItemCommand(object source,
        System.Web.UI.WebControls.DataGridCommandEventArgs e)
{
  if (e.CommandName == "RevertTo")
  {
  }
}
```

> Consider adding a confirmation box after the user clicks the Revert button. Page reversion overwrites the posting's content and having a confirmation box will prevent any accidents from happening. However, we will not do so in this example for the sake of simplicity.

Retrieving the Selected Revision

To get the chosen revision, we first get the index of the selected row. This will correspond to the index of the revision in the Posting.Revisions() collection as we have fixed the sort order of the revisions (in descending order of the revision date) and no provision has been made for authors to change this sort order.

```
private void dgPageRevisionsList_ItemCommand(object source,
System.Web.UI.WebControls.DataGridCommandEventArgs e)
{
  if (e.CommandName == "RevertTo")
  {
    // Get the selected revision
    int revisionIndex = (int) e.Item.ItemIndex;
    PostingCollection pc = currentPostingVersion.Revisions(true,false);
    pc.SortByRevisionDate(false);
    Posting revertToPosting = pc[revisionIndex];
  }
}
```

Triggering the Page Reversion Process

Once we have an instance of the selected revision, we are ready to start the page reversion process which is done in two methods that we will define later:

- The CopyPostingContent() method, if the author has chosen to revert placeholder content
- The CopyCustomProperties() method, if custom property values are to be reverted as well

After the page has been reverted, we commit the changes to the content repository. We could add an additional step to approve the posting automatically and make it available on the live site. In this example, we will not do this and the posting will need to be reviewed before it goes live.

We will also inform the user that the page has been successfully reverted and that it must be approved before the changes take effect.

```
private void dgPageRevisionsList_ItemCommand(object source,
        System.Web.UI.WebControls.DataGridCommandEventArgs e)
{
  if (e.CommandName == "RevertTo")
  {
    // Get the selected revision
    int revisionIndex = (int) e.Item.ItemIndex;
    PostingCollection pc = currentPostingVersion.Revisions(true,false);
    pc.SortByRevisionDate(false);
    Posting revertToPosting = pc[revisionIndex];

    if (chkRevertContent.Checked)
    {
      CopyPostingContent(revertToPosting, currentPostingVersion);
    }

    if(chkRevertCustomProperties.Checked)
    {
      CopyPostingCustomProperties(revertToPosting, currentPostingVersion);
    }

    // Commit the posting.
    cmsContext.CommitAll();

    // Display success message
    lblMessage.Text = "Page Revert Succeeded. It must be approved before "
                    + "changes take effect.";
  }
}
```

Rolling Back When the Reversion Process is Unsuccessful

We will trap any errors that occur during the process within a try-catch block. Should the page
reversion process be unsuccessful for any reason, we will roll back the entire transaction and
display the error message.

```
private void dgPageRevisionsList_ItemCommand(object source,
System.Web.UI.WebControls.DataGridCommandEventArgs e)
{
  if (e.CommandName == "RevertTo")
  {
    // Get the selected revision
    int revisionIndex = (int) e.Item.ItemIndex;
    PostingCollection pc = currentPostingVersion.Revisions(true,false);
    pc.SortByRevisionDate(false);
    Posting revertToPosting = pc[revisionIndex];

    try
    {
      if(chkRevertContent.Checked)
      {
        CopyPostingContent(revertToPosting, currentPostingVersion);
      }

      if (chkRevertCustomProperties.Checked)
      {
        CopyPostingCustomProperties(revertToPosting, currentPostingVersion);
      }

      // Commit the posting.
      cmsContext.CommitAll();

      // Display success message
```

```
            lblMessage.Text = "Page Revert Succeeded. It must be approved before "
                            + "changes take effect.";
        }
        catch(Exception ex)
        {
            // Roll back all transactions
            cmsContext.RollbackAll();

            // write the error message to the screen
            lblMessage.Text = "Page Revert Failed.<br>" + ex.Message;
        }
    }
}
```

Refreshing the Parent Window

Finally, we will register a JavaScript function that refreshes the posting in the parent window so that the author gets to see the latest reverted contents without clicking on the browser's Refresh button. We will borrow the WBC_refreshOpenerWindow() JavaScript routine used by Web Author to refresh the parent window. The method sends a POST request, retrieving the latest content directly from the server and bypassing the browser's cache.

```
private void dgPageRevisionsList_ItemCommand(object source,
System.Web.UI.WebControls.DataGridCommandEventArgs e)
{
    if (e.CommandName == "RevertTo")
    {
        . . . code continues . . .

        // Refresh the original screen so that the user gets to see the posting
        // with the reverted contents
        string script = "<script language=\"javascript\">\n";
        script += "<!--\n";
        script += "         window.opener.WBC_refreshOpenerWindow();\n";
        script += "// -->\n";
        script += "</script>";
        if( !Page.IsClientScriptBlockRegistered("RefreshParent") )
        {
            Page.RegisterClientScriptBlock("RefreshParent",script);
        }
    }
}
```

> We have made the assumption that revision history hasn't been purged between the time the dialog was opened and the time the button was clicked, and that the revision we wish to revert to still exists.
>
> During this time, an administrator could in theory clear the revision history by clicking on the Tools | Clear Revision History... option in Site Manager. If that happens, the user will inevitably encounter an error when attempting to revert the posting.

Copying Content from One Placeholder to Another

To revert the posting, we will copy the contents of placeholders in the historical revision. We will keep the process simple and only roll back placeholder content and custom property values. We won't be reverting modifications to template files and posting property values, as most of them aren't versioned by MCMS.

The CopyPostingContent() method copies content from the old version of the posting to the current working version. Information is transferred from once placeholder to another, matching them by their names. We are guaranteed of finding a pair of matching placeholders because placeholder definitions are not versioned. This means that the collection of placeholders will be identical in both the working copy and the revision. For example, if a placeholder definition has been renamed, the current working version and all previous revisions will share the renamed placeholder definition.

One of our template designers has accidentally deleted a placeholder definition. All our content is lost! What can we do?

Because placeholder definitions are not versioned, should a template designer delete a placeholder definition, content will be lost from both the current posting and its revisions.

You can recover the content by re-creating a placeholder definition of the same name and type. Nevertheless, it is always better to be on the safe side and be cautious about deleting anything.

Once we find a match, we copy the placeholder content from the previous version to the current version. In this code sample, we will use Placeholder.DataSource.RawContent to copy the content. This bypasses internal processing of the placeholder object and is usually not recommended for retrieving placeholder content. In this situation, where we are not interested in the content itself but only wish copy it to another placeholder without inspection, Placeholder.DataSource.RawContent can be safely used.

Add the CopyPostingContent() method directly below the dgPageRevisionsList_ItemCommand() event handler within the PageRevert.aspx.cs file.

```
public void CopyPostingContent(Posting source, Posting destination)
{
    // Copy all placeholder contents from the source to the destination
    foreach (Placeholder sourcePH in  source.Placeholders)
    {
        Placeholder destinationPH = destination.Placeholders[sourcePH.Name];

        // We don't worry about how the placeholder internally modifies content
        // before it gets displayed. Even if it is encrypted or whatever - we just
        // copy the content as is from the previous version without modification.
        destinationPH.Datasource.RawContent = sourcePH.Datasource.RawContent;
    }
}
```

Copying Custom Property Values

Next, we deal with custom property values. Custom properties, like placeholder content, are versioned by MCMS. This means that to revert their values, all we need to do is to copy the value stored in the old version over to the working version.

The CopyPostingCutomProperties() method loops through each custom property in the source and sets its value in the corresponding custom property of the destination posting. Add CopyCustomProperties() directly below the CopyPostingContent() method.

```
public void CopyPostingCustomProperties(Posting source, Posting destination)
{
  string errorMessage = "";

  // Copy all custom property values from the source to the destination.
  foreach(CustomProperty customProp in source.CustomProperties)
  {
    if(destination.CustomProperties[customProp.Name]!=null)
    {
      try
      {
        destination.CustomProperties[customProp.Name].Value =
                    customProp.Value;
      }
      catch
      {
        errorMessage += "Failed to copy custom property value for Custom"
                + "Property:" + customProp.Name + "<br>";
      }
    }
  }

  // Throw a summary of all failed items
  if (errorMessage != "")
  {
    throw(new Exception(errorMessage));
  }
 }
}
```

A try-catch block surrounds the statement that sets the custom property value. This traps any exceptions that may occur during the copying process. There's a possibility of exceptions occurring as custom property definitions are not versioned. For example, a template designer could have added a new value to a selection type custom property definition. Trying to save a value that is not part of the current list will generate an exception.

The Page Revert dialog is now complete.

Adding the New Action to the Web Author Console

Let's put a button on the Web Author Console for authors to access the Page Revert dialog that we have just built. When the user clicks on the button, the dialog opens as a new window.

Add a class file named PageRevertButton.cs to the project. If you are working with the downloaded Tropical Green project from the book's companion website, add the file to the ConsoleButtons folder. Otherwise, just add it to an appropriate location in your project.

Add the following namespaces:

```
using System;
using Microsoft.ContentManagement.Publishing;
using Microsoft.ContentManagement.WebControls.ConsoleControls;

namespace TropicalGreen.ConsoleButtons
{
    . . . code continues . . .
}
```

For the author's convenience, the Page Revert dialog will open as a new window. Therefore, our console action will inherit from the BaseNewWindowAction class.

> To learn more about this subject, *Building Websites with Microsoft Content Management Server* (Packt Publishing, January 2005, ISBN 1-904811-16-7) provides a step-by-step tutorial on how you can create custom actions for the Web Author Console.

Within the constructor, we set the button's Text property. The chosen label for the button is Revert Posting (of course, you can give it any meaningful text of your choice).

```
public class PageRevertButton : BaseNewWindowAction
{
  public PageRevertButton()
  {
    // Set the text of the button
    this.Text = "Revert Posting";
  }
}
```

The window that it opens is that of the Page Revert dialog. You may have to adjust the return value here, depending on the path of PageRevert.aspx on your website. The query string for the current posting is appended to the URL. This will ensure that the dialog will be able to access information about the current posting in update mode. Append the overridden UrlNewWindow property to the code.

```
public override string UrlNewWindow
{
  // Set the URL of the new window
  get
  {
    return Page.Request.ApplicationPath + "/Dialogs/PageRevert.aspx?"
        + CmsHttpContext.Current.Posting.QueryStringModeUpdate;
  }
  set
  {
    base.UrlNewWindow = value;
  }
}
```

The button will only be available on the console when the posting has historical revisions and if it is indeed the current working copy. Add the overridden Available property below the constructor.

```
public override bool Available
{
  get
  {
    Posting currentPosting = CmsHttpContext.Current.Posting;
    if ((CmsHttpContext.Current.Mode != PublishingMode.Published)
      && (currentPosting != null))
    {
      // This option is only available
      // if the current posting is the working revision and
      // if it has previous versions
      return ( currentPosting.Revisions(true,false).Count > 0
          && currentPosting.IsWorkingRevision);
    }
    else
    {
      return false;
    }
  }
}
```

Finally, we inject the JavaScript that opens the dialog in a new window by overriding the `ActionJavascript` property of the base class. We will use the built-in `WBC_openWindowOnFocus()` method found in the `windows.js` file that ships with MCMS. The method accepts three parameters: the URL of the page, the name of the window and the size of the window. We get the default size used by other windows (such as the Resource Manager and Approval Assistant) using the `WBC_DefaultSizing()` method. Add the overridden `ActionJavacript` property below the `Available` property.

```
public override string ActionJavascript
{
  get
  {
    if (this.Available)
    {
      return "WBC_openWindowOnFocus('" + this.UrlNewWindow + "', "
          + "'WBC_winPageRevert', "
          + "WBC_UseDefaultSizing(window.top))";
    }
    else
    {
      return "";
    }
  }
}
```

The code is complete. Save and compile the solution.

To add the button to the Web Author Console, we will modify the `DefaultConsole.ascx` file (remember to make a backup of it if you have not already done so). Open `DefaultConsole.ascx`. Ensure that at the top of the page, there is the directive to register the library of the project file (in our example that will be the Tropical Green project). Otherwise, insert the following line of code, replacing the `Namespace` and `Assembly` attributes with the namespace and assembly name of your project:

```
<%@ Register TagPrefix="TropicalGreenConsole"
    Namespace="TropicalGreen.ConsoleButtons" Assembly="tropicalgreen" %>
```

Let's place the Page Revert button below the View Revision By Date button. After the `</CmsConsole:ViewRevisionByDateAction>` closing tag (Hint: locate it by pressing *Ctrl* + *F* and searching for the string `ViewRevisionByDateAction`), add the following block of code:

```
<TropicalGreenConsole:PageRevertButton id="PageRevertAction1" runat="server">
  <A id=PageRevertAnchor
     onclick="<%# Container.ActionJavascript %>;return false" href="#"
     target=_self>
  <%# Container.Text %>
  </A>
  <BR>
</TropicalGreenConsole:PageRevertButton>
```

Save `DefaultConsole.ascx`.

Now navigate to `http://localhost/channels`. Switch to Edit Site view and navigate to any posting within the site. If the posting has historical revisions, the Revert Posting button appears on the Web Author Console.

```
Page Properties
Revision History
View Revisions by Date
Revert Posting
```

Click on the Revert Posting link and the Page Revert dialog that we have created opens. Select the Revert button on any revision to revert the posting. If all goes well, the following message appears on the screen: Page Revert Succeeded. It must be approved before changes take effect and the posting in the parent window refreshes to display the latest updates. Close the dialog. Go ahead and approve the posting to publish the changes.

> Instead of automatically reverting all placeholder content, you could enhance the dialog to provide authors with the option of selecting which placeholders they would like to roll back.

Tip #2: How to Change a Posting's Template

The way to go about creating postings with MCMS out of the box is to first select the template, fill in the placeholder content of the posting and publish it. What happens should the author mistakenly select the wrong template? Some templates may look deceptively similar and the author, not knowing that the template wasn't the right one to begin with, may well publish it anyway.

Or perhaps requirements have changed. To minimize disruption to the current site, a new template co-existing with the current template was built. The time has come to re-launch the site and a sizable number of postings need to switch to the new template. How could the job be accomplished with minimal effort on the part of authors or developers?

According to the documentation, you would have found that the Template property of the posting object is a read-only field. Once a posting has been created, the link between the template and the posting is immutable; there is no simple way to get the posting to use another template.

To get around this constraint, we can choose to:

- Continue using the current template but overwrite the existing placeholder definitions, custom property definitions, or template file values.

  Amending the existing template is the simplest solution and should be considered whenever possible. However, in the case of the author choosing the wrong template, you really need to get the posting to point to another template. It also means that any changes to the template will be seen immediately on the server—not a good scenario if you are updating the template on a production machine. In such cases, amending the existing template is probably not the best idea.

- Create a new posting based on the new template; copying placeholder content and custom property values from the existing posting. This is the approach we will adopt in this how-to.

  Behind the scenes, we will not really perform a switch as what we are really doing is creating a duplicate posting based on the new template. As a consequence, the posting's GUID will change, and it won't continue the revision history that was built in the original posting. In addition, all links to the posting will have to be adjusted after the switch. However, in some cases, like those of authors using the wrong template, this method achieves the best results.

This tip discusses techniques for changing the base template used by a posting. I don't need to change a posting's template, but I need to switch its template file. How can this be done?

Changes to a template file do not involve changes made to a posting's content. To switch a posting's template file, simply set the TemplateFile property of its template (not the posting) to point to the new template file. If you need to change both the template and the template file, then the techniques used in this tip will come into play as well.

In the earlier book, *Building Websites with Microsoft Content Management Server* (Packt Publishing, January 2005, ISBN 1904811167), we discussed a third alternative called Template Switching. This technique plays around with the URL of the template file and the posting's GUID. We can achieve the effect of switching templates by taking the URL of the template file we wish to switch to and appending the posting's GUID as a query string. The problem with this approach is that at the end of the day, the underlying template object is still the one that was used to create the posting. In addition this method only allows switching between connected templates.

In this exercise, we will:

- Provide a dialog for authors to specify the template to switch to.
- Create a copy of the posting based on the new template. Copy the content across from the original posting to the new and commit the changes. Once that is done, we delete the old posting.
- Add a button, named Change Template, to the Web Author Console.

The Change Template Dialog

Let's start by creating the Change Template dialog. Here's a quick list of things that we need the user interface to do:

- The author has to specify the template they wish to switch to.
- A button will be needed to trigger the switching process.
- It must show a list of placeholder definitions found in the source template.

- A set of drop-down lists should be provided to select the matching placeholder definition in the destination template.
- A label will be needed for displaying any success/error messages.

We will take the short cut and request authors to fill in the template's path in a TextBox. If you are feeling adventurous, you could provide a friendlier user interface that allows authors to pick and choose the template from a list or a tree.

Once a template is specified, authors will click on the Switch button to start the process of swapping the posting's templates. The completed dialog looks like this:

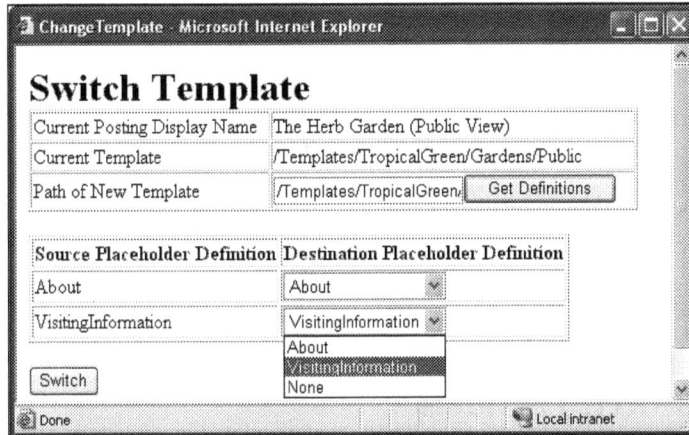

Add a new web form to the project and name it ChangeTemplate.aspx. If you are working with the Tropical Green project download, add the form to the Dialogs folder. Set the Page Layout to FlowLayout.

With the web form open in HTML view, insert a level-1 header that describes what the form does as well as a button that closes the dialog.

```
<form id="ChangeTemplate" method="post" runat="server">
    <h1>Switch Template</h1>
    <input type="button" value="Close" onclick="window.close();">
</form>
```

Toggle to Design view. Select Table | Insert | Table... from the menu bar and insert a table with three rows, two columns, and a width of 550px. Add the words Current Posting Display Name, Current Template, and New Template to the cells in the left-hand column as shown below:

While in Design view, drag and drop the following controls onto the form and arrange them as shown in the diagram below.

Control	Property	Property Value
Label	ID	lblPostingDisplayName
	Text	(empty string)
Label	ID	lblTemplatePath
	Text	(empty string)
TextBox	ID	txtTemplatePath
Button	ID	btnGetPlaceholderDefinitions
	Text	Get Placeholders
Button	ID	btnSwitch
	Text	Switch
	Visible	false
Placeholder	ID	phPlaceholderDefinitions
Label	ID	lblMessage
	Text	(empty string)

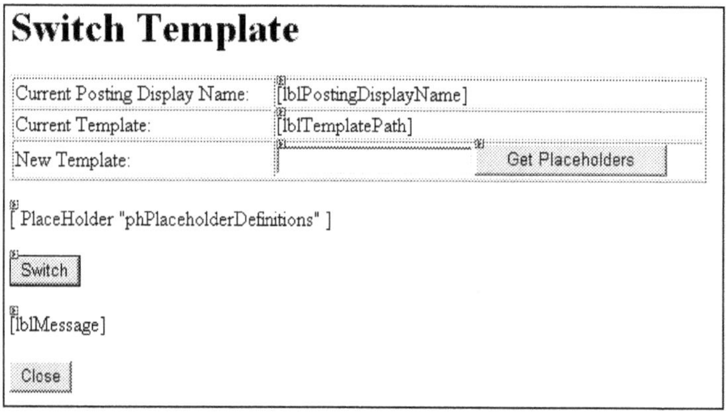

Switch Template

Current Posting Display Name:	[lblPostingDisplayName]
Current Template:	[lblTemplatePath]
New Template:	[ ] Get Placeholders

[PlaceHolder "phPlaceholderDefinitions"]

Switch

[lblMessage]

Close

Double-click anywhere on the form to get to its code-behind file. Add the three namespaces required by the solution above the class's namespace declaration.

```
. . . code continues . . .

using Microsoft.ContentManagement.WebControls;
using Microsoft.ContentManagement.Publishing;
using Microsoft.ContentManagement.Publishing.Extensions.Placeholders;

namespace TropicalGreen.Dialogs
{
    . . . code continues . . .
}
```

The `Page_Load()` event handler will be used to display some basic information:

- The display name of the current posting
- The path of the template it is based on

In addition, we check to see if we are in update mode, which is required as we will be creating and deleting postings. We should already be in the correct mode, as the dialog will be triggered from a custom button (which we will build later) on the Web Author Console that will pass the necessary information to it. If we aren't in update mode, however, we will toggle to it.

```
private CmsHttpContext cmsContext;
private Posting currentPosting;

private void Page_Load(object sender, System.EventArgs e)
{
    // Get the current CmsHttpContext
    cmsContext = CmsHttpContext.Current;

    // Get the current posting
    currentPosting = cmsContext.Posting;

    // Display the current posting's display name
    lblPostingDisplayName.Text = currentPosting.DisplayName;
    // Display the path of the current template
    lblTemplatePath.Text = currentPosting.Template.Path;

    // Check to see if we are in update mode. If we are not, switch.
    if(cmsContext.Mode!=PublishingMode.Update)
    {
        Response.Redirect(Request.ServerVariables["URL"] + "?"
                          + currentPosting.QueryStringModeUpdate);
    }

    // Initialize the controls
    lblMessage.Text = "";
    btnSwitch.Visible = false;
}
```

After the author has specified the template to switch to, he or she clicks on the Get Placeholders button. First, we get the template that has been specified. If the template exists and is visible to the author, we get a list of definitions from both the source and destination template by calling the `DisplayListOfPHDefinitions()` method (defined later). Once we have obtained both the target template and the list of placeholder definitions, we display the Switch button. Any errors that occur during the swapping process are trapped and the error messages displayed on the screen. Toggle to Design view and double-click on the Get Placeholders button to create the `btnGetPlaceholderDefinitions_Click()` event handler.

```
private void btnGetPlaceholderDefinitions_Click(object sender,
System.EventArgs e)
{
    try
    {
        // Get the template specified by the Author
        Template newTemplate =
            cmsContext.Searches.GetByPath(txtTemplatePath.Text.Trim())
                                                        as Template;

        // Get a list of placeholder defintions
        DisplayListOfPHDefinitions(currentPosting.Template, newTemplate);
```

```
        // Display the Switch Button
        btnSwitch.Visible = true;
    }
    catch(Exception ex)
    {
        // Uh-oh. We've hit an error.
        lblMessage.Text = "Failed to get placeholder definitions. " + ex.Message;
    }
}
```

The `DisplayListOfPHDefinitions()` method lists placeholder definitions of both the source and destination templates in a table. Placeholder definitions from the source template are listed on the right-hand side. On the left-hand side, we have a drop-down list containing all the placeholder definitions from the destination template. From the drop-down list, authors can select the destination placeholder definition that maps to the source placeholder definition. Should the author decide not to copy that particular piece of content, he or she can choose the last option, None. Once it's filled up, the table is added to the `phPlaceholderDefinitions` control. Here is an example of what the table may look like when generated:

Source	Destination
About	About
VisitingInformation	VisitingInformation
	About
	VisitingInformation
	None

Let's start by generating the table header, which will consist of two cells—one representing the "Source" column and another for the "Destination" column. Add the `DisplayListOfPHDefinitions()` method directly below the `btnGetPlaceholderDefinitions_Click()` event handler.

```
private void DisplayListOfPHDefinitions(Template source, Template destination)
{
    Table table = new Table();
    table.Attributes.Add("border","1");

    // Add the table headers
    TableRow header = new TableRow();
    table.Rows.Add(header);

    // Define the header
    TableHeaderCell th1 = new TableHeaderCell();
    th1.Text = "Source";
    header.Cells.Add(th1);

    TableHeaderCell th2 = new TableHeaderCell();
    th2.Text = "Destination";
    header.Cells.Add(th2);
}
```

Next, we will loop through all the placeholder definitions on the source template and create a table row for each one.

```
private void DisplayListOfPHDefinitions(Template source, Template destination)
{
    . . . code continues . . .

    // Iterate through all placeholder definitions on the source template
    foreach(PlaceholderDefinition sourceDef in source.PlaceholderDefinitions)
```

```
        {
            // Add a new row
            TableRow tr = new TableRow();
            table.Rows.Add(tr);
        }
    }
```

Each table row will consist of two columns. In the first, we will display the name of the source placeholder.

```
    private void DisplayListOfPHDefinitions(Template source, Template destination)
    {
        . . . code continues . . .

        // Iterate through all placeholder definitions on the source template
        foreach(PlaceholderDefinition sourceDef in source.PlaceholderDefinitions)
        {
            . . . code continues . . .

            // Display the name of the source placeholder definition
            TableCell td1 = new TableCell();
            td1.Text = sourceDef.Name;
            tr.Cells.Add(td1);
        }
    }
```

In the second column of each row, we will provide a dropdown. Authors will choose the destination placeholder from the items in this list.

```
    private void DisplayListOfPHDefinitions(Template source, Template destination)
    {
        . . . code continues . . .

        // Iterate through all placeholder definitions on the source template
        foreach(PlaceholderDefinition sourceDef in source.PlaceholderDefinitions)
        {
            . . . code continues . . .

            // Generate a DropDownList of destination placeholder definitions
            DropDownList ddl = new DropDownList();
            ddl.ID = "ddl" + sourceDef.Name;

            // Add the dropdownlist to a table cell
            TableCell td2 = new TableCell();
            td2.Controls.Add(ddl);
            tr.Cells.Add(td2);
        }
    }
```

The dropdown will list the names of all placeholders in the new template. In addition, it will only show the placeholder if the placeholder definition is identical to that of the source template definition. Moving content between incompatible placeholder types (say from an HtmlPlaceholder to an ImagePlaceholder) does not make sense.

We will also add an option with a value of "None" to the dropdown. Authors can decide not to move content from selected source placeholders by selecting this option from the list.

```
    private void DisplayListOfPHDefinitions(Template source, Template destination)
    {
        . . . code continues . . .

        // Iterate through all placeholder definitions on the source template
        foreach(PlaceholderDefinition sourceDef in source.PlaceholderDefinitions)
```

```
    {
        . . . code continues . . .

    // Generate a DropDownList of destination placeholder definitions
    DropDownList ddl = new DropDownList();
    ddl.ID = "ddl" + sourceDef.Name;

    foreach (PlaceholderDefinition destDef in destination.PlaceholderDefinitions)
    {
        // Only show the placeholder if placeholder definition is of identical type
        if (destDef.GetType() == sourceDef.GetType())
        {
            ListItem li = new ListItem();
            li.Text = destDef.Name;

            // We have a match!
            if (li.Text == sourceDef.Name)
            {
                li.Selected = true;
            }
            ddl.Items.Add(li);
        }
    }

    // Add an option "None"
    ListItem liNone = new ListItem();
    liNone.Text = "None";
    liNone.Value = "";
    ddl.Items.Add(liNone);

    // Add the dropdownlist to a table cell
    TableCell td2 = new TableCell();
    td2.Controls.Add(ddl);
    tr.Cells.Add(td2);
    }
}
```

Finally, we add the generated table to the dialog.

```
private void DisplayListOfPHDefinitions(Template source, Template destination)
{
    . . . code continues . . .

    // Add the table to the dialog
    phPlaceholderDefinitions.Controls.Add(table);
}
```

The swapping of templates occurs when the author clicks on the Switch button. Toggle to Design view and double-click on the Switch button to get the btnSwitch_Click() event handler. The switching of the posting's template is done by calling the SwitchTemplate() method, which we define later.

```
private void btnSwitch_Click(object sender, System.EventArgs e)
{
    try
    {
        // Get the template specified by the Author
        Template newTemplate = cmsContext.Searches.GetByPath(txtTemplatePath.Text)
                                        as Template;

        // We've got the Template object, now let's perform the switch!
        if(newTemplate!=null)
        {
            SwitchTemplate(currentPosting, newTemplate);
        }
    }
```

```
    catch(Exception ex)
    {
        // Uh-oh. We've hit an error. Write the error message back to the screen
        lblMessage.Text = "Switch failed. " + ex.Message;
    }
}
```

Creating a Copy of the Posting Based on the New Template

Since we can't change the posting's template, we will create a new posting with the new template. The `SwitchTemplate()` method starts by getting the channel in which the new posting will be created. As we are going to replace the original posting with the new posting, they will share the same channel.

The new posting will have the same:

- **Property values.** All properties that are writable will be copied across. Read-only properties like the `CreatedDate`, `LastModifiedDate`, etc. will not be preserved. Note that in the code below, we assign the name of the posting last to prevent any complications that may arise from having two postings of the same name in the channel (no matter how short the duration).

- **Custom property values.** Only custom property values of the same name and type will be copied from the original posting to the new. If the new template does not contain the definition for a custom property, the content will be lost after the switch. Custom Property values are copied using the `CopyPostingCustomProperties()` method that we wrote in the earlier tip.

- **Placeholder values.** Based on the mapping of source to destination placeholder definitions made by the author, placeholder values are copied using the `CopyPostingContent()` method.

> You could enhance the solution to provide authors with a set of `DropDownList` controls, similar to the ones we have generated for placeholder definitions for custom property definitions. In this way, authors can map the source custom properties to match the destination custom properties and not be at the mercy of losing content should the template chosen not have the same set of custom property definitions.

Once the new posting has been successfully created, we can delete the original posting. If it's not deleted, there will be two postings of the same name in the same channel. Leaving it there will create complications when attempting to access either posting using their friendly URLs or when calling the `Searches.GetByPath()` or `Searches.GetByUrl()` methods. You may get one of the postings, but not the other and in some instances even null values. Should you not wish to delete the original posting, consider moving it to another channel for retrieval later (see *Tip #3: How to Build a Recycle Bin* for more details).

The final part of the `SwitchTemplate()` method injects JavaScript to refresh the parent window with a view of the newly created posting and closes the dialog.

```
private void SwitchTemplate(Posting p, Template t)
{
    // Get the channel the posting will be created in
```

```
    // It's the same as that of the existing posting
    Channel currentChannel = p.Parent;

    // Create a new posting based on the new template
    if(currentChannel.CanCreatePostings)
    {
      Posting newPosting = currentChannel.CreatePosting(t);

      // Get the name of the posting
      string postingName = p.Name;

      // Copy all properties that can be set, except for the name
      newPosting.DisplayName = p.DisplayName;
      newPosting.Description = p.Description;
      newPosting.ExpiryDate = p.ExpiryDate;
      newPosting.StartDate = p.StartDate;
      newPosting.IsHiddenModePublished = p.IsHiddenModePublished;
      newPosting.IsImportant = p.IsImportant;
      newPosting.IsRobotFollowable = p.IsRobotFollowable;
      newPosting.IsRobotIndexable = p.IsRobotIndexable;
      newPosting.SortOrdinal = p.SortOrdinal;

      // Copy all custom property values.
      CopyPostingCustomProperties(p, newPosting);

      // Copy all placeholder values
      CopyPostingContent(p, newPosting);

      // Commit all changes
      cmsContext.CommitAll();

      // Delete the existing posting
      if(p.CanDelete)
      {
        p.Delete();
        cmsContext.CommitAll();
      }

      // Set the posting's name
      newPosting.Name = postingName;
      cmsContext.CommitAll();

      // Display the posting that we have just created on the parent window
      // Close the dialog
      string script = "";
      string url = "";
      url = WebAuthorContext.Current.GetUrlForMode(newPosting,
                          WebAuthorContextMode.PresentationUnpublished);
      script += "<script language=\"javascript\">";
      script += "window.opener.location.href='" + url + "';";
      script += "window.close();";
      script += "</script>";

      if (!Page.IsClientScriptBlockRegistered("RedirectToNewPosting"))
      {
        Page.RegisterClientScriptBlock("RedirectToNewPosting",script);
      }
    }
  }
}
```

In a real-world implementation, authors would appreciate an extra check by the script to compare the placeholder and custom property definitions of the new and current templates. If the new template is missing some definitions, authors should be warned before the switch is performed. In addition, logic on the new template may require some custom properties to be mandatory and not left blank. Otherwise, you will get calls from irate authors wondering why the application has erased precious content or why the posting ceased to display correctly after the switch.

In *Tip #1: How to Revert a Posting to a Previous Version*, we wrote a `CopyPostingContent()` method that copies the contents from a source posting to a destination posting. In this case, our source is the original posting whose template we want to change; the destination is the new posting based on the new template. The code is roughly the same, except this time the destination placeholder is the one picked out by the author from the drop-down lists. Add the `CopyPostingContent()` method directly below the `SwitchTemplate()` method.

```
public void CopyPostingContent(Posting source, Posting destination)
{
    // Copy all placeholder content from the old version and create a new
    // version with that content
    foreach (Placeholder sourcePH in source.Placeholders)
    {
        // Look for the value in the corresponding DropDownList in the dialog
        string destinationPHName = Request.Form["ddl" + sourcePH.Name];

        // do not copy placeholder if the user chose "None"
        if (destinationPHName != "" )
        {
            Placeholder destinationPH = destination.Placeholders[destinationPHName];

            // we do not bother about how the placeholder internally modifies the
            // content before it gets displayed. Even if it is encrypted or
            // whatever - we just copy the content from the previous version as is
            if(destinationPH !=null)
            {
                destinationPH.Datasource.RawContent = sourcePH.Datasource.RawContent;
            }
        }
    }
}
```

The `CopyPostingCustomProperties()` method is exactly the same as the one we wrote earlier in *Tip #1: How to Revert a Posting to a Previous Version*. Add it directly below the `CopyPostingContent()` method.

```
public void CopyPostingCustomProperties(Posting source, Posting destination)
{
    // Copy all custom property values from the source to the destination.
    foreach (CustomProperty customProp in source.CustomProperties)
    {
        if(destination.CustomProperties[customProp.Name]!=null)
        {
            try
            {
                destination.CustomProperties[customProp.Name].Value =
                                                customProp.Value;
            }
            catch
            {
```

```
                throw (new Exception("Failed to copy custom property value for "
                        + "Custom Property: " + customProp.Name));
            }
        }
    }
}
```

The dialog is finished. Next, we will add a Change Template button to the Web Author Console that will open this dialog in a new window.

Adding the Change Template Button to the Web Author Console

The addition of a new button to the Web Author Console has been covered in detail in *Tip #1: How to Revert a Posting to a Previous Version*. Let's create a similar button for changing a posting's template.

Add a class file named SwitchTemplateButton.cs to your web project (if you are working with the Tropical Green project, add it to the ConsoleButtons folder).

Above the namespace declaration, add the required namespaces.

```
using System;

using Microsoft.ContentManagement.Publishing;
using Microsoft.ContentManagement.WebControls.ConsoleControls;

namespace TropicalGreen.ConsoleButtons
{
    . . . code continues . . .
}
```

As the dialog opens as a new window, the button will inherit from the BaseNewWindowAction class.

```
public class SwitchTemplateButton : BaseNewWindowAction
{
}
```

In the SwitchTemplateButton() constructor, set the label of the button to Switch Template.

```
public SwitchTemplateButton()
{
    // Set the text of the button
    this.Text = "Switch Template";
}
```

Next, we will set the URL of the Switch Template dialog in the overridden UrlNewWindow property. In our example, the dialog has the URL /Dialogs/ChangeTemplate.aspx. You will have to adjust this value according to the location of the ChangeTemplate.aspx file in your website. Append the UrlNewWindow property to the code.

```
public override string UrlNewWindow
{
    get
    {
        // Set the URL of the new window
        return  Page.Request.ApplicationPath + "/Dialogs/ChangeTemplate.aspx?"
            + CmsHttpContext.Current.Posting.QueryStringModeUpdate;
    }
}
```

The button should only be available if the author has rights to create a new posting in the current channel and if the posting is not connected. Add the overridden Available property directly below the UrlNewWindow property.

```
public override bool Available
{
  get
  {
    Channel currentChannel = CmsHttpContext.Current.Channel;
    Posting currentPosting = CmsHttpContext.Current.Posting;

    if (currentPosting != null)
    {
      return (currentChannel.CanCreatePostings && currentPosting.CanDelete
          && !currentPosting.IsConnected);
    }
    else
    {
      return false;
    }
  }
}
```

> In this example, we have assumed that the posting isn't switched between connected templates. Switching templates between connected templates is a straightforward task: simply create a new connected posting based on the connected template you wish to switch to and delete the original posting.

Finally, we will override the ActionJavascript property to provide the client-side script that performs the job of opening the dialog in a new window. Add the ActionJavascript property below the Available property.

```
public override string ActionJavascript
{
  get
  {
    if (this.Available)
    {
      return "WBC_openWindowOnFocus('" + this.UrlNewWindow + "', "
          + "'WBC_winChangePosting', "
          + " WBC_UseDefaultSizing(window.top))";
    }
    else
    {
      return "";
    }
  }
}
```

The console button is complete. Save and compile the project.

Before we can add the button to the Console, we need to ensure that the directive to register the project file library (in our case, it will be tropicalgreen) exists at the top of the page. Otherwise, add it in:

```
<%@ Register TagPrefix="TropicalGreenConsole"
    Namespace="TropicalGreen.ConsoleButtons" Assembly="tropicalgreen" %>
```

An appropriate place to list the button would be below the Move button of the Web Author Console. Let's add it in by inserting the following code snippet after closing the </CmsConsole:MoveAction> tag:

```
<TropicalGreenConsole:SwitchTemplateButton id="ChangeTemplate1"
runat="server">
<a id=ChangeTemplateAnchor
      onclick="<%# Container.ActionJavascript %>;return false" href="#"
      target=_self>
  <%# Container.Text %>
</a>
<br>
</TropicalGreenConsole:SwitchTemplateButton>
```

Let's test our work! Navigate to any posting in Edit Site mode. As long as you have rights to create and delete postings in the channel, the Switch Template button appears on the Web Author Console. Click on the button and the Switch Template dialog opens. Enter the path of a valid alternative template in the New Template textbox and click the Switch Template button.

I have hundreds of postings that need their templates switched. How can I do so without asking my authors to amend them one by one?

The techniques presented in this tip can be translated into a console application. Instead of creating a Web Author Console action button, you could write a loop that calls the SwitchTemplate() method for each posting that you need to process.

Tip #3: How to Build a Recycle Bin

Postings deleted from Site Manager are automatically thrown into the Deleted Items bin. Authors can restore these deleted postings any time by moving them back to the channels they came from.

> Postings in Site Manager can be permanently deleted by pressing the Shift + Delete keys at the same time.

Unfortunately, the same feature isn't available for postings deleted using Web Author or the Publishing API. Once a posting has been deleted from the web interface, it is removed from the content repository and the only way to recover it is from a previous backup. Not exactly the kind of answer that an author who has accidentally deleted an important post would like to hear.

In this section, we attempt to address this problem by building a recycle (or deleted items) bin for postings deleted from the Web Author. As you can guess, the solution won't work if we physically delete the posting and purge it from the repository. What we need to do is a "false" delete, and by that we mean that we will:

- Move the posting to be deleted to a channel marked as the recycle bin.
- Store the posting's original expiry date and channel parent's GUID in its description so that we can recover it later.
- Expire the posting to prevent people from stumbling upon it accidentally.

Of course, once the posting has been deleted, we would like to have the option to restore it painlessly. Restoring a posting is basically the reverse of the delete:

- Reset the posting's expiry date to what it was before the delete.
- Delete any extra information that was written to the posting's description.
- Move it back to the original folder.

Once the posting has been restored, it has to be approved before it becomes live again.

Creating a Recycle Bin Channel

The recycle bin is a common channel for storing postings deleted by authors. Let's create our recycle bin under the root channel, Channels, in Site Manager. You can, of course, create it in any part of the channel hierarchy that's appropriate. We will give the new channel the name RecycleBin and set the Display Name to Recycle Bin. To prevent navigation controls from displaying the bin, make the channel hidden by checking the Hide when Published checkbox.

For our solution to work, we will make the assumption that all users with the ability to delete postings will have at least author access to the recycle bin. As a consequence, everyone with authoring rights gets to see what has been deleted. Naturally, for websites hosting confidential information, showing the contents of deleted postings to people who should not have access may raise a few eyebrows. If this is a concern, consider splitting the recycle bin into multiple channels—one for each user group working on the site. The ultimate split would of course be to have a recycle bin for each sub-channel on the site. In this example, we will keep the problem simple and use a single channel to serve as the recycle bin for the entire site.

> Bear in mind that the optimum number of postings for a channel is approximately 300. Go beyond that and the overall performance of the site may suffer.
>
> To keep the number of items in the recycle bin small, have an MCMS administrator use Site Manager to purge deleted items periodically or write a batch job to clear all items older than a certain number of days. In this example, we will also program a button that clears all items from the recycle bin.

Deleting the Posting

As we can't use the Delete action button that ships with the solution (as it would remove our posting permanently), we will have to build our own custom version of it. As mentioned previously, we won't be actually deleting a posting. We will expire it and move it to a channel designated as the recycle bin.

Add a class file named `DeleteWithRecycle.cs` to the MCMS project. If you are working with the downloaded Tropical Green project, add the file to the `ConsoleButtons` folder.

The class requires the use of the objects in the following namespaces:

```
using System;
using System.Web;
using Microsoft.ContentManagement.Publishing;
using Microsoft.ContentManagement.WebControls.ConsoleControls;

namespace TropicalGreen.Console.Buttons
{
    . . . code continues . . .
}
```

We will make use of some of the features available from the default Delete action, such as the Confirm Delete dialog. To save the effort of recreating these features, our class will inherit from the `DeleteAction` class:

```
public class DeleteWithRecycle : DeleteAction
{
    . . . code continues . . .
}
```

Within the `DeleteWithRecycle()` constructor, we first get the current `CmsHttpContext`. We will use this same context throughout the class. Next, we get an instance of the channel that acts as the recycle bin. In our example, the recycle bin is located directly below the root channel. You may have to adjust the path according to where you have decided to place the channel.

We perform one last task within the constructor—and that is to set the `Text` property of the action button. To differentiate it from the regular Delete action, we add the word (Recycle) next to it.

```
Channel recycleBin;
CmsHttpContext cmsContext;

public DeleteWithRecycle()
{
    // Get the current CmsHttpContext
    cmsContext = CmsHttpContext.Current;

    // Get a reference to the recycle bin
    recycleBin = cmsContext.Searches.GetByPath("/Channels/RecycleBin/")
                           as Channel;

    // Set the Text property of the action button to be "Delete (Recycle)".
    this.Text = "Delete (Recycle)";
}
```

The action button will be made available to the user only if he or she has rights to delete the current posting. We also check to see if he or she is able to view and add content to the recycle bin. Otherwise, the Delete (Recycle) button is hidden.

```
public override bool Available
{
    get
    {
        bool isAvailable = false;

        // Button is available only if:
        // 1. The user has the rights to delete the posting
        // 2. The user has the rights to move the posting to the Recycle bin
        Posting currentPosting = cmsContext.Posting;
```

```
      if (currentPosting != null && recycleBin != null)
      {
        if (currentPosting.CanDelete && recycleBin.CanCreatePostings)
        {
          isAvailable = true;
        }
      }

      return isAvailable;
    }
  }
```

Most of the action takes place in the overridden PerformActionBehavior() method. When the user clicks on the Delete (Recycle) button, he or she gets a prompt: "Deleting this Page will remove it permanently from the system. Continue?" The answer given by the user is stored in a hidden form field named __CMS_ConfirmedDelete (it starts with a double underscore) found on the posting. Selecting OK will set __CMS_ConfirmedDelete to true and Cancel sets it to false (the default value). To determine whether or not the user has decided to proceed, we check the value of this hidden form field.

```
protected override void PerformActionBehavior()
{
  string confirmDelete =
              Page.Request.Form["__CMS_ConfirmedDelete"].ToString();
  if (confirmDelete == "true")
  {
    // User has confirmed the delete
  }
}
```

Once the user has confirmed the delete, we proceed to get an instance of the posting to be deleted. From there, we obtain the URL of its parent channel and redirect the user to this URL after the posting has been deleted.

```
protected override void PerformActionBehavior()
{
  string confirmDelete =
              Page.Request.Form["__CMS_ConfirmedDelete"].ToString();
  if(confirmDelete=="true")
  {
    // User has confirmed the delete

    // Get the current posting
    Posting p = cmsContext.Posting;

    // Get the URL of the posting's parent
    string returnURL = p.Parent.Url;

    // TODO: Enter code for performing the delete operation

    // Redirect the user to the Channel's URL
    HttpContext.Current.Response.Redirect(returnURL);
  }
}
```

"Deleting" the posting is a four-step process. Rather than delete it, we:

1. Store the posting's original expiry date and parent channel's GUID as part of an XML string within its description.
2. Expire the posting.

3. Move it to the RecycleBin channel.

4. Commit the changes.

The posting's expiry date and parent channel's GUID will be stored as part of an XML string within its description. We will use the channel's GUID instead of its path so that the posting can be restored even if the parent channel has moved. This information will come in useful later should we decide to restore the deleted posting. The format of the XML string is:

```
<DeletedItem>
    <ExpiryDate>1 Jan 3000 12:00:00 AM</ExpiryDate>
    <ChannelGuid>{7AF93078-5FF8-4963-A9F9-B1A0977258A7}</ChannelGuid>
</DeletedItem>
```

It doesn't matter if the description holds other values. We simply append the entire XML at the back of the description. The description field can hold up to 500 characters. We will make the assumption that this limit is never reached.

> If hitting the 500 character limit of the Description property is a concern, consider storing the extra information in a posting's custom property (which requires each template to have the custom property defined but has a higher character limit) or in an external database. Alternatively, you could store the content in an XMLPlaceholder and use the PAPI to add the definition to the template if it does not yet exist.

We wrap the entire operation in a `try-catch` block. Should any error occur while "deleting" the posting, we roll back all changes and the error message would be automatically shown on the Error Console.

```
protected override void PerformActionBehavior()
{
    string confirmDelete =
                Page.Request.Form["__CMS_ConfirmedDelete"].ToString();
    if(confirmDelete=="true")
    {
        // User has confirmed the delete

        // Get the current posting
        Posting p = CmsContext.Posting;

        // Get the URL of the posting's parent
        string returnURL = p.Parent.Url;

        try
        {
            // 1. Copy the expiry date and posting's path to its description
            // in the following format:
            // <DeletedItem>
            // <ExpiryDate></ExpiryDate>
            // <ChannelGuid></ChannelGuid>
            // </DeletedItem>
            string deletedInfo = "<DeletedItem>";
            deletedInfo += "<ExpiryDate>";
            deletedInfo += p.ExpiryDate.ToString("dd MMM yyyy hh:mm:ss tt");
            deletedInfo += "</ExpiryDate>";
            deletedInfo += "<ChannelGuid>";
            deletedInfo += p.Parent.Guid;
            deletedInfo += "</ChannelGuid>";
            deletedInfo += "</DeletedItem>";
```

```
            p.Description += deletedInfo;

            // 2. Expire the posting
            p.ExpiryDate = DateTime.Now;

            // 3. Move the posting to the Recycle Bin
            p.MoveTo(recycleBin);
            // 4. Commit the changes
            cmsContext.CommitAll();
        }
        catch
        {
            // Roll back all actions
            cmsContext.RollbackAll();

            // The error's message will be automatically
            // written to the Error Console
        }

        // Redirect the user to the Channel's URL
        HttpContext.Current.Response.Redirect(returnURL);
    }
}
```

And that completes the Delete (Recycle) action button. Let's add it to the Default Console. Follow the steps outlined in *Tip #1: Adding the Button to the Web Author Console*.

Ensure that the directive to register the library of the project file (in our case, that will be tropicalgreen) exists at the top of the page. Otherwise, add it in:

```
<%@ Register TagPrefix="TropicalGreenConsole"
Namespace="TropicalGreen.ConsoleButtons" Assembly="tropicalgreen" %>
```

A suitable place to display the Delete (Recycle) button would be below the existing Delete action button. Just add the following code snippet below the closing </CmsConsole:DeleteAction> tag:

```
<TropicalGreenConsole:DeleteWithRecycle id="DeleteWithRecycle1"
runat="server">
  <a id=DeleteWithRecycleAnchor
     onclick="<%# Container.ActionJavascript %>;return false"
     href="#"
     target=_self>
  <%# Container.Text %>
  </a>
  <br>
</TropicalGreenConsole:DeleteWithRecycle>
```

You may also want to consider removing the original Delete action button altogether to prevent confusion. For our testing purposes, we will just leave it as it is.

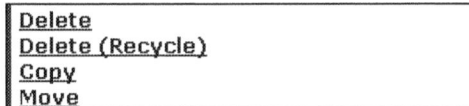

```
Delete
Delete (Recycle)
Copy
Move
```

Navigate to a posting and switch to Edit Site view. Click on the Delete (Recycle) button. When you are prompted to confirm the delete, click OK. Sending a posting to the recycle bin is very similar to deleting it. The posting disappears from the current channel.

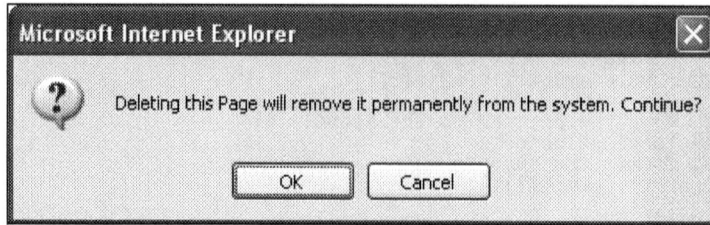

> **The Confirmation dialog still says that "Deleting this Page will remove it permanently from the system". Can we remove the word "permanently" to prevent authors from getting confused?**
>
> The message displayed in the dialog is hard-coded in the `JavaScriptUIStrings.js` file found in the `<install directory>\Microsoft Content Management Server\Server\IIS_CMS\WebAuthor\Client\` folder. To change this message, look for the section labeled `Delete (purge) confirm UI dialogs`, and change the value of the `L_DeleteConfirm_Message` variable to anything you like. Bear in mind that this is a global change and will affect the entire MCMS website. Also, the `JavaScriptUIStrings.js` file may be replaced when hot fixes or service packs are applied. So do back it up should you choose to modify it.

Well, it's really a false delete. You can still see the posting from within Site Manager, but it won't be possible for subscribers to stumble upon the posting as it does not have a live version.

> In this how-to, we show how the delete action is modified by creating a custom button for the Web Author Console. You could do the same thing within the `CmsPosting_Deleting()` event handler. Before the posting gets deleted, you override the delete action and move it to the recycle bin. The advantage of placing the code in an event handler is that you ensure that nothing ever gets deleted from the website.

Restoring the Posting

Now that we have "deleted" the posting and sent it to the recycle bin, let's see how we can go about restoring it. Here's what we will do:

- We will first build a dialog that shows the items stored in the recycle bin.
- Next to each item will be a button labeled Restore. When this button is clicked, the posting is moved back to the channel that it came from with its expiry date and description reset to original values.
- A button named Empty Bin will permanently delete all items found in the recycle bin.
- To conclude, we will create another custom button, labeled Recycle Bin, which opens the dialog.

The Recycle Bin Dialog

The Recycle Bin dialog lists all the postings that have been deleted. It's a relatively simple form, consisting of a DataGrid and a few Label controls.

Add a new web form named `RestorePosting.aspx` to the project (if you are working on the Tropical Green project, add it to the Dialogs folder). Set the Page Layout to `FlowLayout`.

Open the form in HTML view and add a level-1 header that says Recycle Bin and a button that closes the dialog.

```
<form id="RestorePosting" method="post" runat="server">
  <h1>Recycle Bin</h1>
  <input type="button" value="Close" onclick="window.close();">
</form>
```

Toggle to Design view. Drag and drop the following controls onto the form and arrange them as shown in the following diagram.

Control	Property	Property Value
DataGrid	ID	dgDeletedItems
	AutoGenerateColumns	False
Label	ID	lblMessage
	Text	(empty string)
Button	ID	btnEmpty
	Text	Empty Bin

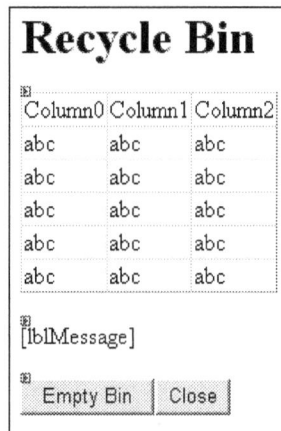

Recycle Bin

Column0	Column1	Column2
abc	abc	abc
abc	abc	abc
abc	abc	abc
abc	abc	abc
abc	abc	abc

[lblMessage]

Empty Bin | Close

Switch back to HTML view and add three columns to the DataGrid. The first column contains the GUID of the deleted posting. The second column displays its name and hyperlinks it to its URL. The last column provides the Restore button to reinstate the posting.

```
<form id="RestorePosting" method="post" runat="server">
  <h1>Recycle Bin</h1>
  <asp:datagrid id="dgDeletedItems" Runat="server"
                AutoGenerateColumns="False">
```

```
      <Columns>
        <asp:BoundColumn DataField="Guid" Visible="False"></asp:BoundColumn>
        <asp:HyperLinkColumn DataNavigateUrlField="Url"
                                      DataTextField="Name"
                                          Target="_blank"
                                      HeaderText="Name">
        </asp:HyperLinkColumn>
        <asp:ButtonColumn Text="Restore " CommandName="Restore">
        </asp:ButtonColumn>
      </Columns>
    </asp:datagrid>
    <br>
    <p><asp:Label Runat="server" ID="lblMessage"></asp:Label></p>
    <p><asp:Button id="btnEmpty" runat="server" Text="Empty
Bin"></asp:Button></p>
  </form>
```

Listing All Deleted Items in the Recycle Bin

To display a list of deleted items, we simply show what is stored in the recycle bin. We have discussed a quick way of doing this in Chapter 1 when we bound a collection of postings directly to a DataGrid. Let's do it again here.

To begin, double-click anywhere on RestorePosting.aspx in Design view to get to its code-behind file. We will add the Microsoft.ContentManagement.Publishing namespace to the list of namespaces that we will be using.

```
. . . code continues . . .

using Microsoft.ContentManagement.Publishing;

namespace TropicalGreen.Dialogs
{
    . . . code continues . . .
}
```

Within the Page_Load() event handler, we first get an instance of the current CmsHttpContext and the channel that is acting as our bin. The bin is actually the current channel because the Web Author Console opens the web form with information about the bin appended to the querystring. The list of sorted postings in the bin is bound directly to the DataGrid.

```
private Channel bin;
private CmsHttpContext cmsContext;

private void Page_Load(object sender, System.EventArgs e)
{
    // Get the current CmsHttpContext
    cmsContext = CmsHttpContext.Current;

    // Get the Recycle Bin
    bin = cmsContext.Channel;

    // Get a list of all Postings in the Recycle Bin
    PostingCollection pc = bin.Postings;

    // Sort the postings by ascending order of their names
    pc.SortByName(true);

    // Bind the table to the datagrid
    dgDeletedItems.DataSource = pc;
    dgDeletedItems.DataBind();
}
```

Restoring a Deleted Item

When a user clicks the Restore button on the grid, several things happen.

1. We get the description of the posting. The description contains information about the posting's original path and expiry dates (our deletion script stored it there).

2. We extract the expiry date and use it to reset the posting's end date. Following which, we get the GUID of the original parent and retrieve the channel that it references. And when we don't have any more use for it, we clean up the description by removing these extra bits of information.

3. We move the posting back to the channel where it came from. All that is done in the `dgDeletedItems_ItemCommand()` event handler.

Any errors that occur during the process are caught using a `try-catch` block. The transaction is rolled back and the error message is displayed on the screen.

With the form opened in Design view, right-click on the DataGrid and view its Events window (open its Properties window and choose the Events button). Double-click on the ItemCommand field to get to the `dgDeletedItems_ItemCommand()` event handler in the code-behind file and enter the following code:

```
private void dgDeletedItems_ItemCommand(object source,
System.Web.UI.WebControls.DataGridCommandEventArgs e)
{
  if (e.CommandName == "Restore")
  {
    try
    {
      // Get the selected revision
      int selectedIndex = (int) e.Item.ItemIndex;
      string guid = e.Item.Cells[0].Text;
      Posting p = cmsContext.Searches.GetByGuid(guid) as Posting;

      // 1. Get the posting's description
      string description = p.Description;

      // 2. Set the posting's expiry date
      //    and original channel
      p.ExpiryDate = GetExpiryDate(description);
      Channel originalChannel = GetOriginalChannel(description);

      // Delete the extra information that was stored in the
      // posting's description
      p.Description = CleanUpDescription(description);

      // 3. Move the posting back to its original location
      p.MoveTo(originalChannel);

      // Commit the change
      cmsContext.CommitAll();

      lblMessage.Text = "Item restored successfully. It must be "
                        + "approved before changes take effect.";
    }
    catch(Exception ex)
    {
      // Roll back all changes
      cmsContext.RollbackAll();
```

```
        // Display the error message
        lblMessage.Text = ex.Message;
      }
    }
  }
```

You probably noticed that the code above makes use of three helper functions: GetExpiryDate(), GetOriginalChannel(), and CleanUpDescription(). Each function grabs the information required from the XML that we stored in the description of the posting.

GetExpiryDate() looks for the start and end <ExpiryDate></ExpiryDate> tags and gets the date that's stored between. That is the original expiry date of the posting. We preserved it right before expiring the posting to fake the delete.

```
private DateTime GetExpiryDate(string description)
{
    // Look for the <ExpiryDate></ExpiryDate> tags
    int startIndex = description.IndexOf("<ExpiryDate>") + 12;
    int endIndex = description.IndexOf("</ExpiryDate>");

    string expiryDate = description.Substring(startIndex, endIndex-startIndex);

    return DateTime.Parse(expiryDate);
}
```

GetOriginalChannel() searches for the opening and closing <ChannelGuid></ChannelGuid> tags. Between the tags lies the GUID of the channel from which the posting came. We will move the posting back to this location when we restore it. The return value for the GetOriginalChannel() is the original channel itself.

```
private Channel GetOriginalChannel(string description)
{
    // Look for the <ChannelGuid></ChannelGuid> tags
    int startIndex = description.IndexOf("<ChannelGuid>") + 13;
    int endIndex = description.IndexOf("</ChannelGuid>");

    string channelGuid = description.Substring(startIndex, endIndex-startIndex);
    Channel originalChannel =
            CmsHttpContext.Current.Searches.GetByGuid(channelGuid)
            as Channel;

    return originalChannel;
}
```

CleanUpDescription() removes the information that was embedded in the posting's description when we performed the delete. It deletes the <DeletedItem></DeletedItem> tags and everything between, restoring the description to its pre-delete value.

```
private string CleanUpDescription(string description)
{
    // Look for the <DeletedItem></DeletedItem> tags
    int startIndex = description.IndexOf("<DeletedItem>");
    int endIndex = description.IndexOf("</DeletedItem>") + 14;

    description = description.Remove(startIndex, endIndex-startIndex);

    return description;
}
```

Permanently Deleting Items from the Bin

Understandably, as time goes by, the number of items that are sent to the recycle bin will increase. Some websites may even experience having thousands of postings sent to the bin in a single week. With a huge collection of deleted items, displaying the list may become painfully slow to the extent that the page can't be rendered within a reasonable time frame. Before that happens, let's program the Empty Bin button to purge all items in the recycle bin.

Toggle to Design view and double-click on the Empty Bin button to get to the `btnEmpty_Click()` event handler. We will get all postings in the bin and delete them one by one.

```
private void btnEmpty_Click(object sender, System.EventArgs e)
{
  // Empty the items in the bin permanently
  foreach(Posting deletedItem in bin.Postings)
  {
    deletedItem.Delete();
    cmsContext.CommitAll();
  }
  dgDeletedItems.DataSource = bin.Postings;
  dgDeletedItems.DataBind();
}
```

The dialog is complete!

Adding the Recycle Bin Button to the Web Author Console

We have built the dialog that displays the contents of the recycle bin. Let's add a Recycle Bin button to the Web Author Console that opens it.

Add a new class file named `RecycleBin.cs` to the project (add it to the `ConsoleButtons` folder if you are working with the Tropical Green project).

The dialog opens up in a new window, so the `RecycleBin` class will inherit from the `BaseNewWindow` class. Basically, it's very much the same as the console action for the earlier tips (Tips #1 and #2). The following code shows the complete implementation. The differences are:

- It carries the label Recycle Bin.
- It opens the Recycle Bin dialog, which in this example is located in `/Dialogs/RestorePosting.aspx`. You may have to adjust this value according to the location of the web form in your site.
- It is available only when the user has access to the Recycle Bin channel.

Here's the completed code:

```
using System;

using Microsoft.ContentManagement.Publishing;
using Microsoft.ContentManagement.WebControls.ConsoleControls;

namespace TropicalGreen.ConsoleButtons
{
  public class RecycleBin: BaseNewWindowAction
  {
    private Channel bin;

    public RecycleBin()
```

```
        {
          // Get the bin
          bin = CmsHttpContext.Current.Searches.GetByPath("/Channels/RecycleBin/")
                                  as Channel;

          // Set the text of the button
          this.Text = "Recycle Bin";
        }

        protected override void PerformActionBehavior()
        {
          base.GenerateStartupScriptActionJavascript();
        }

        public override bool Available
        {
          get
          {
            if (bin != null )
            {
              return true;
            }
            else
            {
              return false;
            }
          }
        }

        public override string ActionJavascript
        {
          get
          {
            if (this.Available)
            {
              return "WBC_openWindowOnFocus('" + this.UrlNewWindow + "', "
                  + "'WBC_winRecycleBin', "
                  + "WBC_UseDefaultSizing(window.top))";
            }
            else
            {
              return "";
            }
          }
        }

        protected override void OnInit(System.EventArgs e)
        {
          base.OnInit(e);

          this.UrlNewWindow = Page.Request.ApplicationPath
                          + "/Dialogs/RestorePosting.aspx?"
                          + bin.QueryStringModeUpdate;
        }
      }
    }
```

> Store the path (or its GUID—amend the code to use Searches.GetByGuid() instead to retrieve it if you do so) to the recycling bin as a key within the <appSettings> tag of the project's web.config file. In this way, you can change its path easily without having to recompile the code.

Add the button to the console as we did in *Adding the Button to the Web Author Console* for Tip #1.

Ensure that the directive to register the project file library (in our case, `tropicalgreen`) is at the top of the page. Otherwise, add it in:

```
<%@ Register TagPrefix="TropicalGreenConsole"
    Namespace="TropicalGreen.ConsoleButtons" Assembly="tropicalgreen" %>
```

An appropriate place for the button is below the Approval Assistant button. So just after the closing `</CmsConsole:ResourceManagerAction>` tags, add the following code:

```
<TropicalGreenConsole:RecycleBin id="RecycleBin1" runat="server">
  <a id=RecycleBinAnchor
      onclick="<%# Container.ActionJavascript %>;return false" href="#"
      target=_self>
  <%# Container.Text %>
  </a>
  <br>
</TropicalGreenConsole:RecycleBin>
```

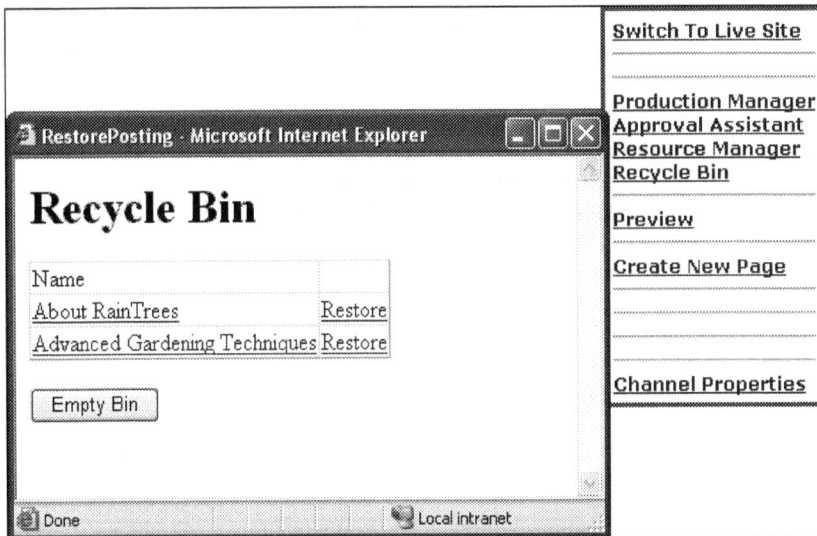

When you have added the Recycle Bin button, click on it. It shows the list of all postings stored in the bin, including the items we deleted earlier. Click on the Restore button for any of the postings and watch them being moved to the channels that they came from. If you check the properties of a restored posting, you will find that it is no longer expired and the description has been cleaned up and does not contain the `<DeletedItem></DeletedItem>` tags.

Tip #4: How to Deal with Links to Deleted Resources

In a typical organization, different teams work on different aspects of the same website. You could have a group of people whose responsibility lies in posting articles and stories (authors, editors, and moderators), and a different group in charge of graphics, pictures, and the overall design (resource managers and template designers). Inevitably, somewhere along the way, someone is going to delete a resource from a resource gallery. Should that resource be used by a posting on a production site, many problems occur.

Earlier, we built a recycle bin to store deleted postings that can be recovered later. Why not build a similar solution for resources? Like postings and channels, resources deleted from the Resource Manager dialog on Web Author are permanently removed from the system. However, unlike postings, there is no immediate way to prevent anyone from deleting resources. There isn't an event handler that you can capture. The PAPI does not provide any way to move resources between galleries. As a result, it is not possible to build a recycle bin for resources. The most you can do to prevent accidental deletes is to remove the Delete Resource button from the dialog altogether; a drastic action to correct the problem.

One of our resource managers has accidentally deleted a resource. We know that the resource is still somewhere in the system, as our Administrator can view it from the posting. We can't upload the resource again as that would mean creating a new resource with a new GUID and URL. Retrieving the content from backup is not possible. What can we do to recover it?

Once deleted, a resource is typically not recoverable. Microsoft now provides a feasible option: if you need to recover deleted resources that have not been purged out of the system by the background process, you can open a support case (reference number: SOX040517700117) to obtain a stored procedure. The stored procedure will restore these deleted resources back to the Deleted Items bin in Site Manager. Administrators can then move them back to the appropriate resource galleries.

What Happens When Resources Used by Postings Get Deleted

For starters, images will show up as broken. Links to attachments will lead to HTTP 404 Page Not Found or HTTP 401 Authentication Required errors. That's not all! Authors will not be able to save pages with links to deleted resources. When they try to do so, they will get the following error:

```
Save Placeholder Failed
-------------------------------------------------------------
Error Details:
The current user does not have rights to edit the requested item. If you are seeing this
exception when a MCMS template is executing, it means that you have removed the
CmsAuthorizationModule from the HttpModules section of your web.config. You can only
remove this module if: 1. All requests for every MCMS template in the web application will only
```

be accessed by anonymous users 2. Guest access is enabled in MCMS (via the SCA) 3. The MCMS guest user has access to all postings based on templates in the web application If any of these requirements are not met, you MUST register the CmsAuthorizationModule in your web.config.

It's a message that indicates that the page contains a link to an item that the author does not have the rights to view. It's the same error message that is displayed when the author has subscriber-only rights to any of the linked resources. In this case, that will be the deleted resource. Internally, MCMS deals with deleted resources by storing them in an internal folder named Archive Folder. You don't get to see this folder in Site Manager or even in Web Author. It's hidden and known only to the system. When the background process determines that no pages on the site use the resource, it purges the item from the archive folder. Until then, the resource is still in the repository, but not accessible by anyone except an administrator and even so, only through the PAPI.

These are definitely strong reasons why resources should never be deleted. However, in organizations where multiple authors work on the same website, resources will inevitably be deleted either accidentally or intentionally for housekeeping and other purposes.

There are many ways to deal with this problem. One of them would be to mandate that no one is allowed to delete resources once they have been uploaded. With a small team of writers, you may just be able to pull that off.

You could also run a dependency report (See *Tip #5: How to Generate a Resource Dependency Report*) that lets resource managers know which resources are being used and by which pages.

Or perhaps, whenever an author faces the problem, he or she can go trough the tedious process of clicking on each link to test to see if any of them lead to a "Page Cannot be displayed" error or a prompt to enter a user name and password. Once all broken links are discovered and removed, the posting can be saved. Alternatively, the author could get an MCMS administrator to save the posting as they are the only ones with access to these deleted resources.

Another possible solution to this would be to automate the process. Links to deleted resources can be programmatically removed when a page is saved. Removing the links to deleted resources kills two birds with one stone—it prevents both the ambiguous error message and dead links.

In the solution presented here, we will remove links to deleted resources. In a nutshell, we will:

- Detect when placeholder content has changed.
- Find a way to detect links that point to resources that have been deleted.
- Scan through links from ImagePlaceholders and AttachmentPlaceholders, removing any dead links that we find.
- Finally—and probably the most challenging of all—we will scan content in HtmlPlaceholders for dead links and remove any that we find.

Detecting When Placeholder Content has Changed

We know when placeholder content has changed when the author clicks on either the Save or the Save and Exit button. To detect when a save occurs, we can choose to:

- Register the method that cleans up links to deleted resources on every template file with the `WebAuthorContext.SavePostingEvent()` event. However, doing so would mean repeating code on all template files in the solution.

- Add the logic required to clean up the dead links within the `CmsPosting_PlaceholderPropertyChanging()` event handler in the `global.asax` file.

While both options are workable, let's choose to place the clean-up code in the `CmsPosting_PlaceholderPropertyChanging()` event handler in the `global.asax` file. This will ensure that any time placeholder content is changed, the clean-up processes are triggered. You are guaranteed that there will be no links to deleted resources for pages that are saved after the resource has been removed.

To begin, let's register the `CmsPosting_PlaceholderPropertyChanging()` event handler.

1. Open the code-behind file of the `global.asax` file (`global.asax.cs`).

2. Add the following namespaces:
```
using Microsoft.ContentManagement.Publishing;
using Microsoft.ContentManagement.Publishing.Events;
using Microsoft.ContentManagement.Publishing.Extensions.Placeholders;
```

3. Below the `Global()` constructor, add the `CmsPosting_PlaceholderPropertyChanging()` event handler:
```
protected void CmsPosting_PlaceholderPropertyChanging( Object sender,
    PropertyChangingEventArgs e )
{
}
```

Resources are typically linked to in three possible locations. They could be used within:

- An `ImagePlaceholder` as an image. Links to resources are at stored in the `Src` property value.

- An `AttachmentPlaceholder` as an attachment. Links to resources are stored in the `Url` property value.

- An `HtmlPlaceholder` as either images or attachments. They are mixed within the content retrieved from the `Html` property value.

> Links to resources can also be found within XmlPlaceholders. Based on your specific XML schema, do consider them in your solution as well.

The following code handles each of these cases in turn. Add the code within the `CmsPosting_PlaceholderPropertyChanging()` event handler in the `global.asax.cs` file.
```
public void CmsPosting_PlaceholderPropertyChanging( Object sender,
PropertyChangingEventArgs e )
{
  string propName = e.PropertyName;
  string propValue = e.PropertyValue as string;
  switch (propName)
  {
    case "Src" : // handle ImagePlaceholder
    case "Url" : // handle AttachmentPlaceholder
    {
```

```
      propValue = HandleImgAndAttPlaceholderTypes(propValue);
      break;
    }
    case "Html" : // handle HtmlPlaceholder
    {
      propValue = HandleImageTags(propValue);
      propValue = HandleAnchorTags(propValue);
      break;
    }
  }
  e.PropertyValue = propValue;
}
```

Identifying Links to Deleted Resources

Links to deleted resources have the following characteristics:

- Only MCMS administrators have the rights to view the linked deleted resource. All other users will be prompted for a user name and password or be redirected to HTTP 404 Page Not Found screens.

Deleted resources exhibit different behaviors depending on whether or not they were deleted using Web Author or through Site Manager.

- For a resource deleted from Web Author, only MCMS administrators are able to retrieve the deleted resource from the PAPI. The `Resource.Path` property will reveal that the deleted resource belongs to the `Archive Folder`.
- When the resource has been deleted using Site Manager, attempts to retrieve the resource using PAPI methods such as `Searches.GetByGuid()` method will return null values for all users (including Administrators).

To identify whether or not a link points to a deleted resource, we use the `IsResourceDeleted()` method. The `IsResourceDeleted()` method accepts a URL as an input string. It uses the techniques above to see if the URL points to a deleted resource and returns a Boolean true if it is deleted and false otherwise.

The resource's GUID can be extracted from its URL, which looks like this:

```
<a href="/NR/rdonlyres/8C78AC41-591D-4626-AFC8-19AC8375914E/0/myresource.gif">
```

Based on the GUID, use the `Searches.GetByGuid()` method to get an instance of the resource object. As only MCMS administrators will have access to the deleted resource, we need an administrator account to retrieve it. If `Searches.GetByGuid()` returns null, then the resource no longer exists and has been deleted.

It gets a little tricky for resources deleted via Web Author, as for such items `Searches.GetbyGuid()` returns an instance of the resource. Once the resource has been retrieved, we check its path. Deleted resources will always return the path `/Archive Folder/resourceName`. Checking the resource's path to see if it is in `Archive Folder` is a sure way of determining whether or not the resource has been deleted.

Add `IsResourceDeleted()` directly below the `CmsPosting_PlaceholderPropertyChanging()` event handler in the `global.asax.cs` file. Remember to change the credentials of the user in the code below to match that of an administrator in your environment in the format `WinNT://servername/userid`.

```
private bool IsResourceDeleted(string link)
{
    // Extract Resource GUID from URL
    string[] splt = link.Split('/');
    string GUID = splt[3];

    // Create new context with admin rights to be able to see deleted items
    CmsApplicationContext appContext = new CmsApplicationContext();
    appContext.AuthenticateAsUser("WinNT://servername/cmsAdmin",
                                  "cmsAdminPassword",
                                  PublishingMode.Unpublished);

    Resource r = appContext.Searches.GetByGuid("{"+GUID+"}") as Resource;

    // Check to see if it belongs to the Archive Folder
    bool isDeleted= false;
    if (r != null)
    {
        // Resource has been deleted
        isDeleted = r.Path.StartsWith("/Archive Folder");
    }
    else
    {
        // Unable to retrieve resource.
        // Possibly because the resource was deleted using Site Manager
        isDeleted = true;
    }

    // Dispose admin context
    appContext.Dispose();
    appContext = null;

    // Return result
    return isDeleted;
}
```

Now that we know how to identify links to deleted resources, we can remove them! Let's start with links within ImagePlaceholders and AttachmentPlaceholders.

> In the example above, we have hard-coded the administrator's user ID and password into the code for simplicity. It's probably a better idea to store it within a web.config file and have the password encrypted. Alternatively, store the user ID and password in a file in another folder and protect it using Windows security measures.

Removing Links from ImagePlaceholders and AttachmentPlaceholders

Removing links from ImagePlaceholders and AttachmentPlaceholders is fairly simple. We first check the values of the ImagePlaceholder.Src and AttachmentPlaceholder.Url properties to see if they contain links to a deleted resource by running their values through the IsResourceDeleted() method. If the link does indeed point to a deleted resource, we set the ImagePlaceholder.Src and AttachmentPlaceholder.Url values to empty strings.

The HandleImgAndAttPlaceholderTypes() method below shows how it is done. Links to internal resources always begin with /nr/rdonlyres/ so we only need to consider links that start with it. Add the following code directly below the IsResourceDeleted() method.

```
private string HandleImgAndAttPlaceholderTypes(string propValue)
{
  if (propValue.ToLower().StartsWith("/nr/rdonlyres"))
  {
    if (IsResourceDeleted(propValue))
    {
      propValue = "";
    }
  }
  return propValue;
}
```

Removing Links from HtmlPlaceholders

As HtmlPlaceholders contain attachments and images mixed up in a mass of HTML tags, removing dead links from them is slightly more complex.

Handling Images

Let's start by dealing with images. Images are linked to an HTML file using the image tag, <img>. An image tag typically contains several attributes, like src, border, etc. Here's an example of an <img> tag:

```
<img src="/NR/rdonlyres/8C78AC41-591D-4626-AFC8-19AC8375914E/0/myresource.gif">
```

A good way to grab the entire tag is to search for the starting <img string and the closing angle bracket >. We check to see if it links to an MCMS resource. If it does, we run it through the IsResourceDeleted() method that we defined earlier. Images that show deleted resource gallery items are deleted by removing the entire <img> tag.

The HandleImageTags() method does the work. Add HandleImageTags() directly below the HandleImgAndAttPlaceholderTypes() method.

```
private string HandleImageTags(string propValue)
{
  // Look for <img> tags within the content
  int start = propValue.ToLower().IndexOf("<img ");

  // Found an <img> tag.
  while (start >= 0)
  {
    // Get the closing angle bracket of the tag
    int end = propValue.IndexOf(">",start);
    if (end > start)
    {
      // Get the entire <img> tag
      string tag = propValue.Substring(start,end-start+1);

      // Get the link to the resource gallery item
      int linkStart = tag.ToLower().IndexOf("\"/nr/rdonlyres");
      if (linkStart >= 0)
      {
        int linkEnd = tag.IndexOf("\"", linkStart+1);
        if (linkEnd > linkStart)
        {
          string linkStr = tag.Substring(linkStart, linkEnd-linkStart+1);

          // Check to see if the link points to the deleted resource
          if (IsResourceDeleted(linkStr))
          {
            // Resource has been deleted. Remove the tag entirely
            propValue = propValue.Replace(tag,"");
            tag = "";
```

```
                }
            }
        }
        // Look for more <img> tags
        start = propValue.ToLower().IndexOf("<img ", start+tag.Length);
    }
}
return propValue;
}
```

Handling Attachments

Handling attachments to deleted resources is similar to handling images with one major difference. With attachments, we work with not just one but a pair of anchor tags: <a> and </a>. Here's an example of how anchor tags appear within HTML:

```
<a href="/NR/rdonlyres/8C78AC41-591D-4626-AFC8-19AC8375914E/0/myresource.gif">
  My Resource
</a>
```

To add to the complication, anchor tags could be nested.

We will start as we did before, by looking for the starting <a> and ending </a> tags. Once we get the entire anchor element, we check to see if it contains links to MCMS resources. If it does, we use the `IsResourceDeleted()` method to determine whether or not the resource has been deleted.

The code that does this is the `HandleAnchorTags()` method. Add it directly below the `HandleImageTags()` method. Should the attachment point to a resource that has been deleted, we remove the pair of tags <a></a> but leave everything between them intact using the `RemoveTagPair()` method described later.

```
private string HandleAnchorTags(string propValue)
{
  // Get the index of the starting <a tag
  int start = propValue.ToLower().IndexOf("<a ");
  while (start >= 0)
  {
    // Get the closing angle bracket of the opening <a> tag
    int end = propValue.IndexOf(">",start);
    if (end > start)
    {
      string tag = propValue.Substring(start, end-start+1);
      int linkStart = tag.ToLower().IndexOf("\/nr/rdonlyres");
      if (linkStart >= 0)
      {
        int linkEnd = tag.IndexOf("\"", linkStart+1);
        if (linkEnd > linkStart)
        {
          string linkStr = tag.Substring(linkStart, linkEnd-linkStart+1);
          if (IsResourceDeleted(linkStr))
          {
            propValue = RemoveTagPair(propValue, tag, "</a>", "<a");
            tag = "";
          }
        }
      }
    }
    start = propValue.ToLower().IndexOf("<a ", start+tag.Length);
  }
}
return propValue;
}
```

The `RemoveTagPair()` method removes the <a></a> tags but leaves the text between them. For example, if the link is: <a href="/NR/rdonlyres/8C78AC41-591D-4626-AFC8-19AC8375914E/0/myresource.gif"> My Resource </a>, then running the text through the `RemoveTagPair()` method would leave only the string, My Resource.

```
private static string RemoveTagPair(string text, string tag, string endtag,
                                    string recursecompare)
{
  // Get the first occurrence of the <a tag within the content
  int start = text.ToLower().IndexOf(tag.ToLower());

  // Initialize the end point to -1
  int end = -1;

  while (start >= 0)
  {
    // Find the end point
    end = FindTag(text, endtag, start, recursecompare);

    // Got the end point. Remove the end tag, </a>
    if (end > start)
    {
      text = text.Remove(end, endtag.Length);
    }

    // Remove the start tag <a>
    text = text.Remove(start, tag.Length);

    // Continue the search for <a></a> tags
    start = text.ToLower().IndexOf(tag.ToLower());
  }
  return text;
}
```

The `FindTag()` method handles nested anchor tags. We may have a situation where one anchor tag is nested within another like this:

```
<a href="/NR/rdonlyres/8C78AC41-591D-4626-AFC8-19AC8375914E/0/myresource.gif">
My Resources @ <a href="http://www.mywebsite.com">MyWebSite</a>. Check it out
now!
</a>
```

While nesting anchor tags does not reflect good programming, it is still a possible scenario, especially when authors use the built-in WYSIWYG editors and don't get a chance to see how the code looks in HTML.

`FindTag()` handles nested tags by checking to see if there are multiple <a></a> tag pairs. If there are, it continues its search until it finds the final ending tag, </a>, that matches the first. Add `FindTag()` directly below the `RemoveTagPair()` method.

```
private static int FindTag(string text, string tag, int start, string
recursecompare)
{
  // Get the position of the next </a> tag
  int pos = text.ToLower().IndexOf(tag.ToLower(), start);

  // Check to see if there are nested hyperlinks
  int check = text.ToLower().IndexOf(recursecompare.ToLower(), start+1);

  // Found a nested <a></a> tag
  if ((check >= 0) & (check < pos))
  {
```

```
       // Keep searching until we find the </a> tag that matches
       // the first <a> tag
       check = FindTag(text, tag, check, recursecompare);
       pos = text.ToLower().IndexOf(tag.ToLower(), check+1);
    }
    return pos;
}
```

The code is complete. Save and compile the solution. The next time you attempt to save a page that contains a link to a deleted resource; the link is immediately removed. Try it!

The screenshots below show an author's view of a page before and after saving a page that contains links to a resource that has been deleted. In this example, the resource that has been deleted is the picture of the Banana Tree, BananaTree.jpg. Both the hyperlink and the image are using it.

Before saving the page, the deleted resource item is still shown on screen:

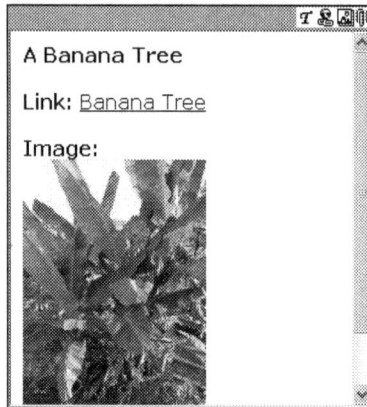

After saving the page, the hyperlink is removed, leaving only the text behind. The image is also deleted:

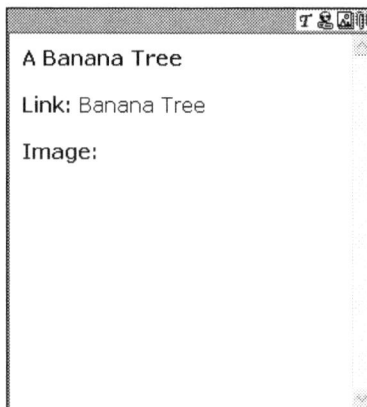

Cleaning up the links to deleted resources works well when postings get saved with Web Author. What about cases where the resource is deleted and the posting is not saved via Web Author (for example, when changes are made through the PAPI)?

The code above could be easily transformed to a console application that walks through all postings recursively and scans all placeholder values and cleans up any links to deleted resources.

Tip #5: How to Generate a Resource Dependency Report

One neat feature of MCMS is the ability to replace resources. Once replaced, all postings that point to the resource immediately reference the most recent version of the file. It's a total self-help module where resource managers have total ownership over their files. They no longer have to ask developers about getting documents updated.

Or do they? Resource managers still call but are now asking different questions. Before replacing a resource, they want to know the pages on the site that are linked to it. Is the resource being used? If not, can it be deleted? Otherwise, where will it be seen? Will anything bad happen if they replace or delete the file? These are valid questions. In the previous section, we have seen the possible issues caused by deleted resources.

Earlier, we tackled the problem by removing links to deleted resources when the page is saved. Some authors may wince at the idea of having the application "correct" their work. An alternative solution is to prepare a dependency report for Resource Managers to consult before deleting a resource.

In this section, we write a script that scans through the entire site for a list of resources that are linked from placeholder content. It uses simple recursion to look for resources used by postings.

Once a resource is found, it writes the following details to a CSV file:

- The path of the resource
- The path of the posting
- The name of the placeholder that contains a link to the resource

You can, of course, use a database to store the data. Using a database is probably a better solution as it makes querying records much easier. However, let's stick to a text file in this example to keep the code simple.

The FindResources Project

To begin, we will create a new C# Console Application project. Name the project `FindResources`. Right-click on the References folder in Solution Explorer and click Add Reference... Add the following references (both library files can be found in the `<install directory>\Microsoft Content Management Server\Server\bin\` directory):

- `Microsoft.ContentManagement.Publishing`
- `Microsoft.ContentManagement.Publishing.Extensions.Placeholders`

Rename `Class1.cs` to `WhereAreMyResources.cs`. Add the following namespaces required by the solution.

```
using System;
using System.IO;
using System.Data;
using System.Collections;
using System.Text.RegularExpressions;
using Microsoft.ContentManagement.Publishing;
using Microsoft.ContentManagement.Publishing.Extensions.Placeholders;

namespace FindResources
{
  class WhereAreMyResources
  {
        . . . code continues . . .
  }
}
```

Within the `Main()` method, we first define the path and name of the dependency report and store it in the variable `filePath`. The name of the generated file contains the current date and time. For example, a report that was generated at 4.00 pm on February 11 will have the name, `Resources11Feb2005160000.csv`. In this way, you can run the script as many times as you like and you won't overwrite previously generated reports.

Next, we create a `CmsApplicationContext` object using the credentials of the Windows account that's running the script. The user that's running the script has to have the following privileges:

- At least subscriber access to all resources and resource galleries
- At least subscriber access to the root channel and all channels and postings that are being scanned

The iterative scanning process starts from the root channel. The method `walkTree()` (defined next) walks through the entire tree, and scans all postings.

For large sites, we need to ensure that the iteration process does not take up too much memory. The problem is, as long as the `CmsApplicationContext` object is not destroyed, allocated server resources like memory are not released. As a result, virtual memory consumption increases significantly. For really large sites, the application may hit an Out-of-Memory exception and terminate prematurely. To avoid such memory problems, we need to:

- Ensure that the lifetime of each item does not extend beyond the time it takes for the batch process to end. To tackle this issue, we will use the `using` statement to create the `CmsApplicationContext`. The `using` statement makes an implicit call to the `CmsApplicationContext.Dispose()` method.
- Make an explicit call to the garbage collector to clear away the disposed `CmsApplicationContext`.

With the `CmsApplicationContext` properly disposed, all resources taken up by it are also released. Add the following code above and within the `Main()` method:

```
private static Stack StackItems = new Stack();
[STAThread]
static void Main(string[] args)
{
```

```
    // The path of the dependancy report
    string filePath = "Resources" + DateTime.Now.ToString("ddMMMyyyyhhmmss")
                                                              + ".csv";
    WriteToLog("Resource Path, Posting Path, Placeholder Name", filePath);
    using (CmsApplicationContext cmsContext = new CmsApplicationContext())
    {
        cmsContext.AuthenticateAsCurrentUser(PublishingMode.Unpublished);

        // Start the iteration from the root channel
        StackItems.Push(cmsContext.RootChannel.Guid);

    }
    // Iteration begins - walk through the entire tree
    WalkTree(filePath);

    // explicitly call garbage collection to free up space release from
    // CmsApplicatonContext to avoid high memory usage
    System.GC.Collect();
}
```

Walking the Tree

We are going to scan all the postings visible to the user running the script. The method named
walkTree() performs the iteration by pushing the GUID of all sub-channels into a stack. The stack
continues to be pushed and popped until all channels in the tree have been processed. It scans each
posting for resources by calling the ScanPlacehholders() method (defined later). Add
walkTree() directly below Main().

```
private static void WalkTree(string filePath)
{
    while (StackItems.Count > 0)
    {
        using (CmsApplicationContext cmsContext = new CmsApplicationContext())
        {
            cmsContext.AuthenticateAsCurrentUser(PublishingMode.Unpublished);
            string channelGuid = (string)StackItems.Pop();

            Channel c = cmsContext.Searches.GetByGuid(channelGuid) as Channel;
            Console.WriteLine(c.Path);

            foreach(ChannelItem ci in c.AllChildren)
            {
                if (ci is Posting)
                {
                    Posting p = ci as Posting;
                    ScanPlaceholders(p, filePath, cmsContext);
                }
                else if (ci is Channel)
                {
                    Channel cc = ci as Channel;
                    StackItems.Push(cc.Guid);
                }
            }
        }
    }
}
```

Scanning Placeholder Content for Resources

To look for resources used within a posting, we search each of the four placeholder types that ship
with MCMS. We check the contents of:

- The Html property of the HtmlPlaceholder
- The Src property of the ImagePlaceholder
- The Url property of the AttachmentPlaceholder
- The XmlAsString property of the XmlPlaceholder

> If you have built your own custom placeholder definition pairs, you will need to search inside those as well.

Once we have retrieved the content of each placeholder, we match it against a regular expression to search for the string /NR/rdonlyres/. If a match is found, it means that the placeholder contains a link to either a resource from the resource gallery or a local attachment.

To differentiate between the two, we use the Searches.GetByGuid() method to retrieve the object referenced by the GUID stored in the URL. If it's not an item in the resource gallery, it will return a null value. Otherwise, we get the resource that the link points to and record its path in the log file. Add ScanPlaceholders() directly below the WalkTree() method.

```
private static void ScanPlaceholders(Posting p, string filePath,
                                     CmsApplicationContext cmsContext)
{
  foreach(Placeholder ph in p.Placeholders)
  {
    string html = "";
    if (ph is HtmlPlaceholder)
    {
      html = ((HtmlPlaceholder)ph).Html;
    }
    else if (ph is ImagePlaceholder)
    {
      html = ((ImagePlaceholder)ph).Src;
    }
    else if (ph is AttachmentPlaceholder)
    {
      html = ((AttachmentPlaceholder)ph).Url;
    }
    else if (ph is XmlPlaceholder)
    {
      html = ((XmlPlaceholder)ph).XmlAsString;
    }

    // Find links to resources
    string pattern = @"/NR/rdonlyres/\S+";
    MatchCollection matches;
    matches = Regex.Matches(html,pattern,RegexOptions.IgnoreCase);

    if (matches.Count > 0)
    {
      foreach(Match match in matches)
      {
        //file is either a resource or a local attachment
        string[] arrUrl = match.Value.Split('/');
        string guid = "";
        Resource r;
        if(arrUrl.Length >= 3)
        {
          guid = "{" + arrUrl[3] + "}";
          if (IsGuid(guid))
          {
```

```
            r = cmsContext.Searches.GetByGuid(guid) as Resource;
            if (r!=null)
            {
                WriteToLog(r.Path + "," + p.Path + "," + ph.Name, filePath);
            }
        }
    }
  }
 }
 }
}
```

We use the helper function IsGuid() to test the string retrieved from the URL to see if it is a valid GUID. Add IsGuid() directly below the ScanPlaceholders() method.

```
private static bool IsGuid(string guid)
{
  try
  {
    string guidRegEx = "[a-fA-F0-9]{8}-[a-fA-F0-9]{4}-[a-fA-F0-9]{4}-["
                     + "a-fA-F0-9]{4}-[a-fA-F0-9]{12}";
    Regex regex = new Regex(guidRegEx);
    Match m = regex.Match(guid);
    if (m.Success)
    {
      return(true);
    }
    else
    {
      return(false);
    }
  }
  catch
  {
    return (false);
  }
}
```

Finally, the helper function WriteToLog() appends a line of text containing information about the resource to the log file. Add it directly below the IsGuid() method.

```
private static void WriteToLog(string message, string filePath)
{
  FileStream fs = File.Open(filePath, FileMode.Append);
  StreamWriter sw = new StreamWriter(fs);
  sw.WriteLine(message);

  sw.Flush();
  sw.Close();
  fs.Close();
}
```

The code is complete. Compile the solution.

This solution looks out for resources. You could write a similar script that records all links to channels and postings, an example of which can be found at:

```
http://www.gotdotnet.com/Community/UserSamples/Details.aspx?SampleGuid=980
4F9C9-54D3-4735-9967-41CF1FD88740
```

The same questions asked by resource managers are usually repeated by authors and editors when considering channels and postings to delete or move.

Generating the Report

Let's run the script to see what a generated report looks like. Press *F5* on Visual Studio .NET's tool bar to run the script. The file will be created in the same folder as the `/bin/Debug` folder of the `FindResources` project. As it is a comma separated variable file (`*.csv`), double-clicking it launches Microsoft Excel.

To get the postings that use a particular resource, simply sort the spreadsheet by resource paths by clicking on the Resource Path column and selecting Data | Sort from the menu bar. Once the data has been sorted, search for the resource you are looking for by pressing *F5*.

You could also find the list of resources used in a particular posting by sorting on the posting's path instead.

Of course, searching within a spreadsheet isn't as easy as querying a database. Instead of writing to a log file, you could have written the data to a database table or to an XML file. You could even write code within event handlers to update the list of resources each time a posting is published. In this way, you could provide a simple query interface for resource managers to find out the answers to their questions in real time.

Check out a ready-to-use tool that does a similar job of generating a list of resources used within postings at:

```
http://www.gotdotnet.com/Community/UserSamples/Details.aspx?SampleGuid=70b
4c5bc-ac3f-4885-8af2-bf283edb9159
```

Tip #6: How to Update Posting Properties Directly from a Template File

MCMS provides separate avenues for updating a posting's placeholder and property values. Placeholder content is updated from a template file. Property and custom property values are updated by accessing the Page Properties dialog. When working on a posting, an author typically needs to update both placeholder and property values. Having to go to two different pages creates the possibility of authors forgetting to update one or the other.

A sure way to ensure that authors don't leave out any important information would be to have a single page that updates everything—all placeholder, property, and custom property values. Ideally that should be the template. When the author clicks on the Edit button, all fields that require editing are displayed. When he or she clicks Save and Exit, the posting can be submitted for publishing straight away. No more messy reminders to get authors to click on the Page Properties button to update custom property and property values!

This is what we will do in this tip:

- We will build a web user control that contains a single textbox for updating the posting's title.
- The textbox is visible only in update mode and is hidden in published mode.
- When the Save or Save and Exit button is clicked, we trap the save() event handler for the posting and write the contents of the textbox to the Posting.DisplayName property.

Although the code sample described here is fairly simple with only a single textbox for the posting's display name, you can extend the technique to include controls for updating just about any number of property or custom property values.

Here's how the Web User Control looks in edit mode.

Display Name: Aloe Vera

Designing the Web User Control

Let's start by adding a Web User Control file named DisplayNameControl.ascx to our MCMS project. With the control open in Design view, drag and drop the following controls from the Web Forms section of the Toolbox onto the Web User Control and set them up as shown.

Control	Property	Property Value
Label	ID	Label1
	Text	Display Name:
TextBox	ID	txtDisplayName

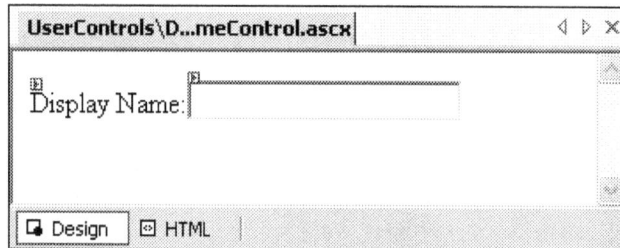

```
UserControls\D...meControl.ascx              ◁ ▷ ✕

 ⊞
 Display Name: ┌──────────────────────────┐
               │                          │
               └──────────────────────────┘


 ▣ Design   ⊡ HTML
```

Double-click anywhere on the form to get to its code-behind file. We will add a couple of namespaces as required by some of the objects used within the control:

```
namespace TropicalGreen.WebUserControls
{
  using System;
  using System.Data;
  using System.Drawing;
  using System.Web;
  using System.Web.UI.WebControls;
  using System.Web.UI.HtmlControls;
  using Microsoft.ContentManagement.Publishing;
  using Microsoft.ContentManagement.WebControls;

  public abstract class DisplayNameControl : System.Web.UI.UserControl
  {
    . . . code continues . . .
  }
}
```

Getting the Posting's Display Name

Within the control's Page_Load() event handler, we will load the posting's display name into the txtDisplayName TextBox. To do so, we simply get an instance of the posting that is being edited and get the value of the Posting.DisplayName property. Add the following code within the Page_Load() event handler.

```
. . . code continues . . .
private void Page_Load(object sender, System.EventArgs e)
{
  // Load the TextBox with the previously saved DisplayName only
  // on the first load
  if (!Page.IsPostBack)
  {
    txtDisplayName.Text = CmsHttpContext.Current.Posting.DisplayName;
  }
}
```

Hiding the Web User Control in Published Mode

We want the control to be visible only in authoring mode. We first check the current Web Author Context mode to see if it is either AuthoringNew or AuthoringReedit. If it is, we show and enable the control, otherwise we hide it. Within the Page_Load() event handler, add the code shown below.

```
private void Page_Load(object sender, System.EventArgs e)
{
    . . . code continues . . .
    // Get the current Web Author Context mode
    WebAuthorContextMode webauthorMode = WebAuthorContext.Current.Mode;

    // Set the control to be visible only in authoring modes
    bool displayControl = false;
    if (webauthorMode == WebAuthorContextMode.AuthoringNew
    || webauthorMode == WebAuthorContextMode.AuthoringReedit)
    {
        displayControl = true;
    }

    this.Visible = displayControl;
}
```

Capturing the Posting's Save Event

When the posting is saved, we want the contents of the TextBox to be written to the DisplayName property of the posting. The tricky part is capturing the save event. The good news is, you can make use of the SavePostingEvent() event handler of the WebAuthorContext class. All we need to do is to write our own event (named saveDisplayName(), which we will define later) of type WebAuthorPostingEventHandler and register it with the SavePostingEvent() handler. The following code shows how this is done within the OnInit() event handler. Add the highlighted portion to OnInit(). You may have to expand the region, Web Form Designer generated code, to see it.

```
override protected void OnInit(EventArgs e)
{
    InitializeComponent();
    base.OnInit(e);

    // Register new event being called during save
    WebAuthorContext.Current.SavePostingEvent += new

WebAuthorPostingEventHandler(saveDisplayName);

}
```

Finally, we write the saveDisplayName() method that saves the display name of the posting. We simply set the posting's DisplayName property with the contents of the TextBox.

Being an event of type WebAuthorPostingEventHandler, the saveDisplayName() method accepts two arguments:

- object sender contains the object that triggered the save. In this case, the sender is either the Save, Save and Exit, or Save New Page button, depending on which was clicked by the author.
- WebAuthorPostingEventArgs e contains the data about the event. The most significant piece of information provided is the posting that is currently being saved.

Add saveDisplayName() directly below the OnInit() event handler.

```
// The event handler that saves the contents of the TextBox to the posting's
// DisplayName property
private void saveDisplayName(object sender, WebAuthorPostingEventArgs e)
{
    e.Posting.DisplayName = txtDisplayName.Text.Trim();
}
```

The control is complete. To use the control, simply drag and drop it onto any template file that requires it. In this example, we have chosen to save only the display name of the posting. You could easily extend the control to work with all other properties and custom properties of the posting.

> If you need to re-use the code across projects, it is more efficient to use a server control instead of a web user control. Here's an example of such a control:
>
> ```
> http://www.gotdotnet.com/Community/UserSamples/Details.aspx?SampleGuid=2A8
> 5D442-286F-4AD6-8A03-82436BF956A5
> ```

Tip #7: How to Re-write Unfriendly URLs as Friendly URLs

MCMS, as you probably know, uses an internal system of "unfriendly URLs" in order to retrieve both the template file and the posting. Visitors to the site typically don't see these unfriendly URLs, except:

- When toggling between Edit Site and Live Site views.
- After performing a postback to the server. For example, the template file could have a button that refreshes certain labels on the page. When the button is clicked, a postback occurs and the URL on the address bar changes from a friendly URL to the unfriendly version.
- When the site has been configured to use unique ID-based URLs.
- When displaying a page within a frameset.

Unfriendly URLs are a composition of the URL of the template file and information about the posting appended in its querystring:

```
http://localhost/TropicalGreen/Templates/Plant.aspx?NRMODE=Published&NRORIGINA
LURL=%2fNR%2fexeres%2f0E0047A0-1560-4BA8-859F-C012826391F0%2cframeless%2ehtm%3
fNRMODE%3dPublished&FRAMELESS=true&NRNODEGUID=%7b0E0047A0-1560-4BA8-859F-C0128
26391F0%7d&NRCACHEHINT=ModifyLoggedIn
```

Sometimes, it could appear in a slightly simpler form:

```
http://localhost/NR/exeres/0E0047A0-1560-4BA8-859F-C012826391F0,
frameless.htm?NRMODE=Published
```

But behind the scenes, MCMS still sees the complex version.

Both URLs really point to the same page, say
http://localhost/tropicalgreen/plantcatalog/coconut.htm, but you can't tell just by looking at them.

Although showing the full URL does not affect the functionality of the site, you may want to hide it to prevent regular users of the site from seeing the location of template files, because it's unfriendly, or for the most compelling reason of all: to give visitors an address that they can remember.

In this section, we explore how the unfriendly URL can be suppressed by building an `HttpModule` class. Before implementing the `HttpModule`, we occasionally get unfriendly URLs:

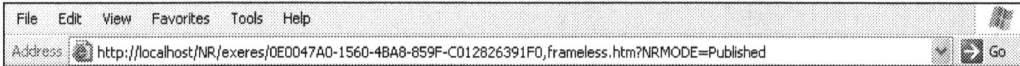

File	Edit	View	Favorites	Tools	Help		
Address	http://localhost/NR/exeres/0E0047A0-1560-4BA8-859F-C012826391F0,frameless.htm?NRMODE=Published						Go

After implementing the `HttpModule`, we get friendly URLs in published mode—always!

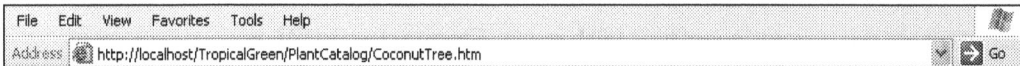

File	Edit	View	Favorites	Tools	Help		
Address	http://localhost/TropicalGreen/PlantCatalog/CoconutTree.htm						Go

An HttpModule to Intercept All Requests

`HttpModules` are ASP.NET's answer for developers wishing to perform pre- and post-processing on all HTTP requests. On a typical MCMS website, they are used for security, output caching, event handling, and other activities. We could probably achieve the same results by using ISAPI filters; however, writing `HttpModules` is much simpler. Implementing an `HttpModule` is a nice solution as it means that you do not have to reproduce this code in each and every template file and channel rendering script built for the site.

To begin, let's create a new Visual C# Class Library project named `CmsHttpModule`. Rename the generated `Class1.cs` file to `NiceUrl.cs`. Add the following references to the project:

- `System.Web`
- `Microsoft.ContentManagement.Publishing` (located in the `<install directory>/Microsoft Content Management Server/Server/bin` directory)

Make the class inherit from `IHttpModule`. For the code to compile we will need to implement the `Dispose()` method of the `IHttpModule` class, but we don't need to do anything within it.

```
using System;
using System.Web;
using System.Web.UI;
using System.Web.UI.HtmlControls;
using Microsoft.ContentManagement.Publishing;

namespace CmsHttpModule
{
  public class NiceUrl : IHttpModule
  {
    public void Dispose()
    {
      // Nothing to do
    }
  }

}
```

A good place to check for unfriendly URLs is within the `PreRequestHandlerExecute()` event handler. This will ensure that the code-block is executed before the page gets executed. As a first step we need to register our event handler in the `Init()` event of the `HttpModule`. Add the following code directly below the `Dispose()` method.

```
public void Init(HttpApplication httpApp)
{
  httpApp.PreRequestHandlerExecute += new
          EventHandler(this.OnPreRequestHandlerExecute);
}

public void OnPreRequestHandlerExecute(object o, EventArgs e)
{
}
```

Converting Unfriendly URLs to Friendly URLs

Here's a sample of an unfriendly URL:

```
http://localhost/TropicalGreen/Templates/Plant.aspx?
NRMODE=Published&
NRORIGINALURL=%2fNR%2fexeres%2f0E0047A0-1560-4BA8-859F-
C012826391F0%2cframeless%2ehtm%3fNRMODE%3dPublished&
FRAMELESS=true&
NRNODEGUID=%7b0E0047A0-1560-4BA8-859F-C012826391F0%7d&
NRCACHEHINT=ModifyLoggedIn
```

Notice that it contains a querystring parameter named `NRORIGINALURL`, which stores a value that starts with `/NR/exeres/` (the slashes have been encoded as `%2f` in the URL). This is what we will look for in a URL to identify whether or not it's unfriendly.

> If your site makes use of custom querystring parameters, the `NRORIGINALURL` parameter may not include them unless you have requested and installed hotfix 836895 from Microsoft.

To correct an unfriendly URL, we simply call for a redirect to the address generated by the `Posting.Url` property. `Posting.Url` will always return a friendly version of the URL, unless more than one postings within the same channel share the same name or the SCA was configured to use unique ID-based URLs. In such a case, the URL will always be the unfriendly URL (with each posting identified by its GUID) and there isn't anything we can do about it.

```
public void OnPreRequestHandlerExecute(object o, EventArgs e)
{
  HttpContext ctx = ((HttpApplication)o).Context;
  IHttpHandler handler = ctx.Handler;

  try
  {
    Posting thisPosting = CmsHttpContext.Current.Posting;
    PublishingMode currentMode = CmsHttpContext.Current.Mode;

    // Only test for unfriendly URLs in published mode
    if (thisPosting != null && currentMode == PublishingMode.Published)
    {
      // Check to see if this is an unfriendly URL
      if ( ctx.Request.QueryString["NRORIGINALURL"] != null)
      {
        if (ctx.Request.QueryString["NRORIGINALURL"].StartsWith("/NR/exeres"))
```

```
    {
        // For postings that share the same name within a channel
        // their URLs will always be unfriendly. There isn't anything
        // we can do about them since calling a redirect
        // will cause an infinite loop
        if (!thisPosting.Url.StartsWith("/NR/exeres") )
        {
            // Redirect to a friendly URL
            ctx.Response.Redirect (thisPosting.Url);
        }
    }
        }
    }
}
catch
{
    // Unable to get a valid CmsHttpContext
}
}
```

Notice that the code is wrapped in a `try-catch` block. This is to prevent errors created when the code is not able to get a valid `CmsHttpContext`. For pages that use forms authentication, calling `CmsHttpContext.Current()` will generate a `CmsAccessDeniedException` when the ticket expires. In such cases, we don't need worry about unfriendly URLs so leaving the `catch` block empty is fine.

Handling Unfriendly URLs Caused by Postbacks

Next, we tackle unfriendly URLs that are generated by postbacks within the template file. You will see these happening in template files that contain links that call the page itself such as buttons, internal bookmarks, etc.

Unfriendly URLs from postbacks are caused by JavaScript generated by the Web Author Console when it is assembled. Here's how it looks in one of our postings (you can see this for yourself by viewing the source of the posting in the browser):

```
<script language="javascript" type="text/javascript">
<!--
    var __CMS_PostbackForm = document.Plant;
    var __CMS_CurrentUrl =
"/tropicalgreen/Templates/Plant.aspx?NRMODE=Published
&NRORIGINALURL=%2fPlantCatalog%2fCoconut%2ehtm&NRNODEGUID=%7b935F294C-A430-
4318-8C59-BB480BB7110F%7d&NRCACHEHINT=NoModifyGuest";
    __CMS_PostbackForm.action = __CMS_CurrentUrl;
// -->
</script>
```

The script sets the `action` attribute of the form to point to the value of the `__CMS_CurrentUrl` variable, which unfortunately stores the unfriendly URL. To overcome this, we need to register our own version of this JavaScript to have the `action` attribute of the form set to a friendly URL instead. The script needs to be written before the Console code is executed and tries to register the original version of the script if we are to ensure that our version of the script will be the active one. To do this, we first register the `OnInit()` event handler of the `HttpModule` to the `Init()` event of the `Page` object. In this way, whenever the page loads, the `OnInit()` event hander of the `HttpModule` is executed. Register the event by adding the highlighted code to the `OnPreRequestHandlerExcute()` event handler.

```
public void OnPreRequestHandlerExecute(object o, EventArgs e)
{
  HttpContext ctx = ((HttpApplication)o).Context;
  IHttpHandler handler = ctx.Handler;

  try
  {
    Posting thisPosting = CmsHttpContext.Current.Posting;
    PublishingMode currentMode = CmsHttpContext.Current.Mode;

    // Only test for unfriendly URLs in published mode
    if (thisPosting != null && currentMode == PublishingMode.Published)
    {
      // Check to see if this is an unfriendly URL
      if ( ctx.Request.QueryString["NRORIGINALURL"] != null)
      {
        if(ctx.Request.QueryString["NRORIGINALURL"].StartsWith("/NR/exeres"))
        {
          // For postings that share the same name within a channel
          // their URLs will always be unfriendly. There isn't anything
          // we can do about them since calling a redirect
          // will cause an infinite loop
          if (!thisPosting.Url.StartsWith("/NR/exeres") )
          {
            //Redirect to a friendly URL
            ctx.Response.Redirect (thisPosting.Url);
          }
        }
      }
    }

    ((System.Web.UI.Page)handler).Init += new EventHandler( this.OnInit );
  }
  }
  catch
  {}
}
```

Next, we implement the OnInit() event handler. The code first checks to see if we are requesting a posting or a page generated by a channel rendering script and that the request is made in Published mode. Then it looks for the HtmlForm object on the page. It uses the form object and the URL of the ChannelItem to generate the same JavaScript as shown above except that the __CMS_CurrentUrl variable holds a friendly URL instead. Add the OnInit() event handler below the OnPreRequestHandlerExcute() event handler.

```
public void OnInit(object sender, EventArgs eventArgs)
{
  System.Web.UI.Page x = sender as System.Web.UI.Page;

  if (CmsHttpContext.Current != null)
  {
    // Works for both postings and channel rendering scripts
    if (CmsHttpContext.Current.Channel != null)
    {
      // Do this only in published mode
      if (CmsHttpContext.Current.Mode == PublishingMode.Published)
      {
        // Find the form tag and get the ID
        foreach (Control c in x.Controls)
        {
          if (c is HtmlForm)
          {
            // Now lets register our script with the nice URL
            x.RegisterClientScriptBlock("__CMS_Page",
              "<script language=\"javascript\" type=\"text/javascript\">\n"
```

```
        + "<!--\n"
        + " var __CMS_PostbackForm = document."+c.ID+";\n"
        + " var __CMS_CurrentUrl = \""
        + CmsHttpContext.Current.ChannelItem.Url+"\";\n"
        + " __CMS_PostbackForm.action = __CMS_CurrentUrl;\n"
        + "// -->\n"
        + "</script>\n");

      // We have found the form, get out of the loop
      break;
      }
     }
    }
   }
  }
 }
}
```

Activating the HttpModule

Finally, the last step is to add CmsHttpModule.NiceUrl to the existing list of HttpModules in the web.config file for the MCMS site. Insert the following line of code between the <httpModules> tags:

```
<httpModules>
   . . . code continues . . .
   <add type="CmsHttpModule.NiceUrl, CmsHttpModule"
                            name="CmsNiceUrlHttpModule" />
</httpModules>
```

Also, either add CmsHttpModule.dll as a reference in the MCMS project or copy it to its bin directory.

Save and build the solution. Now, whenever you toggle between Edit Site mode and Live Site mode, or carry out postbacks, you will always see the friendly URL in Live mode!

Here's an example:

1. Navigate to any posting on the website and click the Switch To Edit Site link.
2. Toggle back to the live site by clicking on the Switch To Live Site link. Notice that instead of getting the unfriendly URL, you see the friendly URL in the browser's address bar.

A more complex version that also works with Internet Explorer on Mac platforms is available on Stefan Goßner's personal blog:

http://blogs.technet.com/stefan_gossner/archive/2004/04/29/122527.aspx

---

Tip #8: How to Export Resource Gallery Items using the Site Deployment API

To automate the process of transporting objects from one server to another, we use the Site Deployment API (SDAPI), which creates export packages containing channels and postings that have been modified since the last deployment.

While exporting channels and postings satisfies the requirements of most websites, many sites make use of resources without postings. Common examples include sites that provide a listing of resources from a channel rendering script, such as a list of documents within a resource gallery. Or perhaps there are links to specific resources from parts of the site, like the company's logo or a site-wide help file. Such links are often found in user controls or web forms. In either case, you will require resources not linked to postings to be exported.

One constraint the SDAPI has is that it does not export resources directly. Only resources that are used by postings modified between the last deployment times will be exported. The only way for site administrators to export specific resources is to manually create the package using the Site Deployment Manager. Not only does this place additional work on the administrator, he or she will also have to keep track of when resources get updated. Should the administrator fail to keep up, the production site won't get the latest information on time.

In this section, we present a solution that exports resources using the SDAPI, regardless of whether or not they have been used within a posting. Here's the plan:

- We know that resources will never be exported unless they are used by a posting that has been modified after the last deployment. Working along these lines, we programmatically create a service posting and create hyperlinks to all resources we wish to export in one of its placeholders.

- Since the resources are now used within a posting that has been just created (and therefore modified since the last deployment), the export SDAPI script will create a package containing both the service posting and all resources linked to it.

- Once the export package has been created, the service posting is deleted.

The SDAPIResourceExport Project

To create the export package with resources and run the export process, let's create a Visual C# Console Application project. Name the project SDAPIResourceExport and store it in a suitable location on your disk (such as c:\). Rename the generated class1.cs file to ResourceExport.cs.

We will assume that the export process will be executed on the source MCMS server itself. Add a reference to the COM MSCMS Site Deployment (Server-side) library (note the 'S' in 'MSCMS'). You can of course choose to run the script on the destination server. If you wish to do so, choose the MCMS Site Deployment (Client-side) library instead.

In addition, add references to the following .NET libraries (found in the <install directory>/ Microsoft Content Management Server/Server/bin/ directory):

- Microsoft.ContentManagement.Common
- Microsoft.ContentManagement.Publishing
- Microsoft.ContentManagement.Publishing.Extensions.Placeholders

Next, add the namespaces that are required for the solution as highlighted below:

```
using System;
using System.Diagnostics;
using Microsoft.ContentManagement.Publishing;
using Microsoft.ContentManagement.Publishing.Extensions.Placeholders;
using SITEDEPLOYSERVERLib;
```

```
namespace SDAPIResourceExport
{
  class ResourceExport
  {
    . . . code continues . . .
  }
}
```

Setting Export Parameters

There are a few parameters that we need to set before running the script. They are:

- The name of the template gallery that will contain the template that will be used for creating the service posting

- The channel that will contain the service posting once it's created

- The name of the placeholder that will be used to store the links to all the resources we plan to export

- The name of the service posting

As these parameter values will be used throughout the class file, we will create class-wide variables to store them. Add them above the Main() routine and set the values accordingly.

```
static string AdminTemplateGallery  = "_Admin";
static string AdminChannel          = "_Admin";
static string AdminTemplateName     = "_ResourceCollectionTpl";
static string AdminPostingName      = "_ResourceCollection";
static string AdminPhName           = "ResourceContainer";

[STAThread]
static void Main(string[] args)
{
  . . . code continues . . .
}
```

As a console application, the Main() routine is the entry point. Here, we'll set the path of the resource gallery containing the items we wish to export as well as a Boolean to indicate whether or not to include all child galleries and their items.

Since part of the process involves creating a service posting and template, we will run the script with the CmsApplicationContext in Update mode. We have chosen to use the credentials of the user executing the job. The user should be at least a channel manager (or preferably, an MCMS administrator) with rights to:

- Create a posting in the channel that stores the service posting

- Create a template in the specified template gallery

- Run the export process

```
[STAThread]
static void Main(string[] args)
{
  // Set the name of the resource gallery
  //that contains the items that we wish to export
  string StartResourceGallery = "/Resources/";

  // Set the boolean to indicate whether Child Galleries and
  //their contents should be exported
```

```
    bool RecursiveExport = true;

    // Create new AppContext in update mode
    CmsApplicationContext appContext = new CmsApplicationContext();
    appContext.AuthenticateAsCurrentUser(PublishingMode.Update);
}
```

Collecting Resources

Next, we get an instance of the resource gallery that contains the resources we wish to export. We write a helper method named `CollectResources()` that returns the HTML consisting of hyperlinks to the resources in the gallery. Later on, we will store this HTML in the service posting.

```
static void Main(string[] args)
{
    . . . code continues . . .

    // Get an instance of the resource gallery
    ResourceGallery rsg = appContext.Searches.GetByPath(StartResourceGallery)
                          as ResourceGallery;

    // Start the iteration process
    Console.Write("Collecting resources.....");
    string imageString = CollectResources(rsg, RecursiveExport);
    Console.WriteLine("Done.");
}
```

The `CollectResources()` method accepts two input parameters. The first is the resource gallery itself and the second is a Boolean indicating whether or not the method should recursively search for resources in sub-galleries. Each resource found is added as a hyperlink to the HTML. When the method finishes, we will have a complete listing of hyperlinks to all resources that we would like to export.

```
static string CollectResources(ResourceGallery gallery, bool recurse)
{
    // The string containing a list of hyperlinks to each resource
    string resString = "";

    // Call this function recursively for each child gallery
    // if the boolean is true
    if (recurse)
    {
        foreach (ResourceGallery rsg in gallery.ResourceGalleries)
        {
            resString += CollectResources(rsg, recurse);
        }
    }

    foreach (Resource item in gallery.Resources)
    {
        resString += "<a href=\""+item.Url+"\">" + item.Path + "</a><br>";
    }
    return resString;
}
```

Creating the Service Posting

Now that we have an HTML string that contains the list of resources for export, we need to store it in a service posting. The helper method that does this is the `CreatePosting()` method. It accepts the `CmsApplicationContext` object and the HTML string value as input parameters. It returns an instance of the service posting that has been found or created.

```
static void Main(string[] args)
{
    . . . code continues. . .
    // Check and return the resource posting if it exists otherwise create it
    Posting p = CreatePosting(appContext, imageString);
}
```

The CreatePosting() method starts off by looking for the channel that stores the service posting. We have a good chance of getting the channel because if we can't find it, we will create it within the CheckChannel() method (described later).

Once we have an instance of the channel, we look for the service posting. If none can be found, we will create one using the template returned from the CheckAdminTemplate() method (described later). The service posting is a hidden posting with a single HtmlPlaceholder for storing the HTML string listing the resources. After the posting has been created, we submit and approve it to make it available for export.

Only postings that are either published or approved get included in export packages created by the SDAPI.

Add CreatePosting() directly below the CollectResources() method.

```
static Posting CreatePosting(CmsContext context, string phContent)
{
    Channel c = CheckChannel(context);

    Console.Write("Check Posting.....");
    Posting p = c.Postings[AdminPostingName];
    if (p == null)
    {
        if (c.CanCreatePostings == false)
        {
            Exception myException = new Exception("Insufficient rights to "
                                + " create AdminPosting
                                + c.Path + "/" + AdminPostingName);
            throw myException;
        }
        Template t = CheckAdminTemplate(context);

        p = c.CreatePosting(t);
        p.Name = AdminPostingName;
        p.IsHiddenModePublished = true;
        Console.WriteLine("Created.");
    }
    else
    {
        Console.WriteLine("Found.");
    }

    HtmlPlaceholder htmlPh = p.Placeholders[AdminPhName] as HtmlPlaceholder;

    if (htmlPh == null)
    {
        Exception myException = new Exception("Placeholder "+AdminPhName
                            + " missing in Posting "+p.Path);
        throw myException;
    }

    htmlPh.Html = phContent;
```

```
      // Submit and Approve the posting
      p.Submit();
      context.CommitAll();
      Console.WriteLine("Posting submitted.");
      while (p.CanApprove)  // handle Editor and Moderator Approvals
      {
        p.Approve();
        context.CommitAll();
        Console.WriteLine("Posting Approved.");
      }
    }
```

The service posting will be stored in the channel directly beneath the root channel, Channels, and given the name specified in the AdminChannel class variable. In our case, the channel's path would be /Channels/_Admin/.

It doesn't matter if the channel hasn't been created yet. The CheckChannel() method will search for it. In the event that the channel can't be found, the method creates it as a hidden channel to ensure that it does not get included in dynamic navigation controls. Of course, if you are expecting the script to create the channel, the user running the script should have sufficient rights on the root channel to create sub-channels otherwise an exception will be thrown.

Once the channel has been found or created, the CheckChannel() routine passes it back to the calling function.

```
static Channel CheckChannel(CmsContext context)
{
  Channel root = context.RootChannel;
  Channel c = root.Channels[AdminChannel];
  Console.Write("Check Channel.....");
  if (c == null)
  {
    if (!root.CanCreateChannels)
    {
      Exception myException = new Exception("Insufficient rights to "
                + "create AdminChannel: "+root.Path+AdminChannel);
      throw myException;
    }
    c = root.CreateChannel();
    if (c == null)
    {
      Exception myException = new Exception("Failed to create "
                + "AdminChannel: "+root.Path+AdminChannel);
      throw myException;
    }
    c.Name = AdminChannel;
    c.IsHiddenModePublished = true;
    context.CommitAll();
    Console.WriteLine("Created.");
  }
  else
  {
    Console.WriteLine("Found.");
  }
  return c;
}
```

In order for the service posting to be created, it needs a template, and before a template can be created, it needs a template gallery. The template that we are looking for is stored directly below the root template gallery and has the name specified in the AdminTemplateGallery class variable. In this example, that will be a gallery with the path /Templates/_Admin/.

If the template gallery can't be found, the CheckAdminTemplate() method attempts to create it. If the user does not have the rights to do so, an exception is thrown. Should there be strong reasons not to give rights to channel managers running the script to create template galleries under the root template gallery, you could either create the template gallery beforehand or create the gallery somewhere else apart from the root.

Once the template gallery is found, we look for the template. The template is the one with the name specified in the AdminTemplateName class variable. Again, if the script can't find the template, it attempts to create it. The template contains a single HtmlPlaceholderDefinition with the name specified in the AdminPhName class variable. Before the template can be used, it has to be submitted. If for some reason, the template can't be submitted, an exception is thrown.

Add CheckAdminTemplate() directly below the CheckChannel() method.

```
static Template CheckAdminTemplate(CmsContext context)
{
  Template t = null;
  TemplateGallery AdminGal = context.RootTemplateGallery
                   .TemplateGalleries[AdminTemplateGallery];

  // Get an instance of the admin template
  if (AdminGal != null)
  {
    t = AdminGal.Templates[AdminTemplateName];
  }

  Console.Write("Check Template.....");

  // Admin template not found. Create it.
  if (t == null)
  {
    // Get instance of template gallery.
    if (AdminGal == null)
    {
      if (context.RootTemplateGallery.CanCreateTemplateGalleries == false)
      {
        Exception myException = new Exception("Insufficient rights to create "
               + "AdminTemplateGallery: /Templates/"
               + AdminTemplateGallery);
        throw myException;
      }
      AdminGal = context.RootTemplateGallery.CreateTemplateGallery();
      if (AdminGal == null)
      {
        Exception myException = new Exception("Failed to create "
              + "AdminTemplateGallery: /Templates/"+AdminTemplateGallery);
        throw myException;
      }
      AdminGal.Name = AdminTemplateGallery;
      context.CommitAll();
      Console.Write("TemplateGallery created.....");
    }

    // Look for admin template within template gallery.
    t = AdminGal.Templates[AdminTemplateName];
```

```
    if (t == null)
    {
        // Check to see if user has rights to create template.
        if (!AdminGal.CanCreateTemplates)
        {
            Exception myException = new Exception("Insufficient rights to create "
                        + "AdminTemplate: "+AdminGal.Path+AdminTemplateName);
            throw myException;
        }

        // Create admin template.
        t = AdminGal.CreateTemplate();
        if (t == null)
        {
            Exception myException = new Exception("Failed to create "
                    + "AdminTemplate: "+AdminGal.Path+AdminTemplateName);
            throw myException;
        }

        // Set the name of the admin template.
        t.Name = AdminTemplateName;

        // Create new HtmlPlaceholder Definition in the Template
        HtmlPlaceholderDefinition phDef = t.CreatePlaceholderDefinition
                ( new HtmlPlaceholderDefinition() ) as HtmlPlaceholderDefinition;
        phDef.Name = AdminPhName;
        phDef.AllowImages = true;
        phDef.Formatting =
                HtmlPlaceholderDefinition.SourceFormatting.NoFormatting;

        // Submit the newly created template
        if (!t.CanSubmit)
        {
            Exception myException = new Exception("Failed to save "
                    + "AdminTemplate: "+AdminGal.Path+AdminTemplateName);
            throw myException;
        }
        t.Submit();
        context.CommitAll();
        Console.Write("Template created.");
    }
}
else
{
    Console.Write("Found.");
}
return t;
}
```

Starting the Export Process

We now have the service posting created and the hyperlinked list of resources tucked safely in one of its placeholders. When we run the export process created from the SDAPI, it will attach all these resources together with the service posting into one package.

More details on coding site deployment scripts can be found in the book *Building Websites with Microsoft Content Management Server* (Packt Publishing, January 2005, ISBN 1-904811-16-7). The snippet below shows the additional lines of code appended to the Main() routine. It sets the starting channel to the service posting's parent, runs the export process based on the credentials of the currently logged on user and creates the package. In our example, the package is named C#Export.sdo and is created in the c:\ directory.

Just after the export process completes, the service posting is deleted. This is an optional step. It is probably worthwhile to note that the service posting is already included in the export package. When you import the package on the destination server, it will be re-created there.

Add the highlighted code to the Main() method.

```
static void Main(string[] args)
{
    . . . code continues . . .
    string ChannelGuid = p.Parent.Guid;

    Console.Write("Creating SDO package.....");
    CmsDeployExport cmsDeployExport = new CmsDeployExportClass();
    cmsDeployExport.AuthenticateAsCurrentUser();

    String strPackageName;
    strPackageName = "c:\\C#Export.sdo";

    String strReportUrl = cmsDeployExport.Export(strPackageName, 1,
                                                 ChannelGuid);
    Console.WriteLine("Done.");

    // Optional: delete Posting after Export
    Console.Write("Deleting Resource Posting.....");
    p.Delete();
    appContext.CommitAll();
    Console.WriteLine("Done.");

    Process.Start("iexplore.exe", "http://localhost"+ strReportUrl);
}
```

The script is complete! To run it, simply press the *F5* key in Visual Studio .NET or run the SDAPIresourceExport.exe file in the /debug/bin/ folder of the project file. The export report will show that the service posting, the service posting's channel, template, and template gallery are included in the package. More importantly, the resources and their resource galleries are exported as well.

Exported Containers and Items

User Selected items are shown in bold. Unbolded items have been included in the export through their connectivity to a *user selected* item.

Channels and Pages

Exported Object	Approved On/ Last Modified
⊟ 🌐 Channel and Page	
📄 /Channels/_Admin/_ResourceCollection	3/4/2005 4:42:17 PM

Template Galleries and Templates

Exported Object	Approved On/ Last Modified
⊟ 🌐 Template Gallery and Template	
⊟ 📁 /Templates	3/4/2005 2:07:42 PM
⊟ 📁 /Templates/_Admin	3/4/2005 4:42:13 PM
📄 /Templates/_Admin/_ResourceCollectionTpl	3/4/2005 4:42:17 PM

Resource Galleries and Resources

Exported Object	Approved On/ Last Modified
⊟ 🌐 Resource Gallery and Resource	
⊟ 📁 /Resources	3/4/2005 2:07:40 PM
⊟ 📁 /Resources/TropicalGreen	3/4/2005 2:07:44 PM
⊟ 📁 /Resources/TropicalGreen/PlantCatalog	3/4/2005 2:07:44 PM
🌀 /Resources/TropicalGreen/PlantCatalog/Bougainvillea.JPG	3/1/2005 2:26:08 PM
🌀 /Resources/TropicalGreen/PlantCatalog/AloeVera.JPG	3/1/2005 2:26:08 PM
🌀 /Resources/TropicalGreen/PlantCatalog/CoconutTree.JPG	3/1/2005 2:26:08 PM

Tip #9: How to Configure the Position and Size of the Web Author Console Dialogs

With regards to screen space, more is always better and bigger is always good. Some authors like to maximize the editing screen space or set their browsers to open in Full Screen mode. Switching between normal and Full Screen mode is as simple as hitting the *F11* key. It removes the title bar and provides a much bigger editing space that occupies the entire screen. Maximizing the window is done by clicking on the Maximize button at the top right hand corner of the window 🔲.

The trouble with authoring postings in maximized or Full Screen mode is that some of the windows (like the Create New Page, Resource Manager, and Production Assistant windows) that open from the Web Author Console don't stay within the screen. Their top and lower right edges are off the screen, hiding essential buttons such as the close button. You will have to drag the window to the left each time you wish to center it.

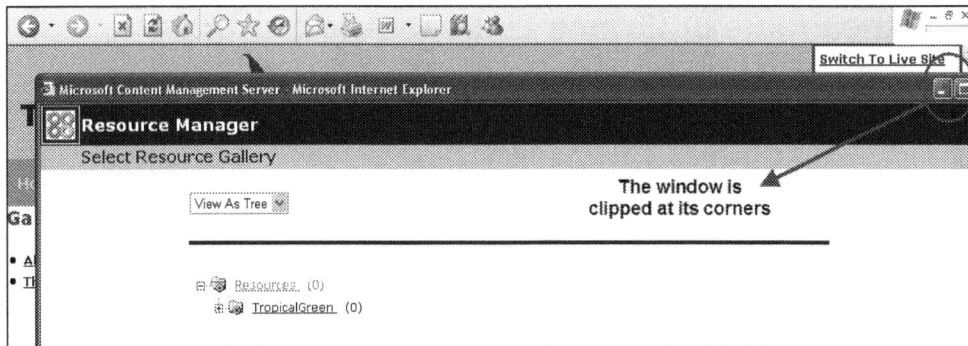

This happens because Web Author is trying to offset the dialogs by a few pixels to let the author know that it's a new window that sits on top of the parent.

A solution to get around this problem is to change the JavaScript that sizes the window. For ASP.NET-based solutions, the file to modify is the windows.js file located in the <install directory>\Microsoft Content Management Server\Server\IIS_CMS\WebAuthor\Client\ directory (gentle reminder: make a backup of the file before you modify it).

Modify the WBC_UseDefaultSizing() function by reducing the height and width of the window to ensure that the new window will reside within the window of the parent.

```
function WBC_UseDefaultSizing(pWindow)
{
  var lWidth = WBC_getWindowWidth(pWindow) - 2 * IDS_WIDTH_OFFSET;
  var lHeight = WBC_getWindowHeight(pWindow) - 2 * IDS_HEIGHT_OFFSET;
  . . . code continues . . .
}
```

The next time you click on a button that opens a new window from the Web Author Console in maximized or Full Screen mode, the window sits perfectly within the screen.

Tip #10: How to Get Frames and IFrames to Work Correctly in a Template File

Frames provide a convenient way to keep portions of the site static as users jump from one page to another. IFrames are often used as mini-windows within a page to display content from other sites. While providing convenient solutions for sticky navigation issues, the added level of complexity that frames bring to any web design often proves to be a bane for many developers.

The same is true for MCMS websites. Frames and IFrames do not work perfectly on template files. JavaScript errors occur when toggling between Live and Edit Site views when:

- The Frame or IFrame embedded within the template file links to another site.
- An MCMS page that the author is working on is located within a Frame or IFrame of another website.

The good news is that both issues can be fixed.

When the Frame or IFrame Links to Another Site

When a Frame or IFrame embedded within a template file contains a page from another site—unless you have already followed this tip—you will get JavaScript errors when toggling between Edit and Live Site views.

Try it: add an <iframe> tag to any template file that you have in your collection right now. Set its source to point to your favorite website, say www.microsoft.com. So somewhere between the <form> tags of your template file, you will have an IFrame tag that looks like this:

```
<form>
    . . . code continues . . .
  <iframe src= "http://www.microsoft.com">
    . . . code continues . . .
</form>
```

Now, save the template file and navigate to any posting that uses it. Try to toggle from Live Site view to Edit Site view and vice versa. Did you get a JavaScript error that says "Permission denied"? You may have to double-click on a little yellow triangle at the bottom left-hand corner of the browser to call up the dialog that shows the details.

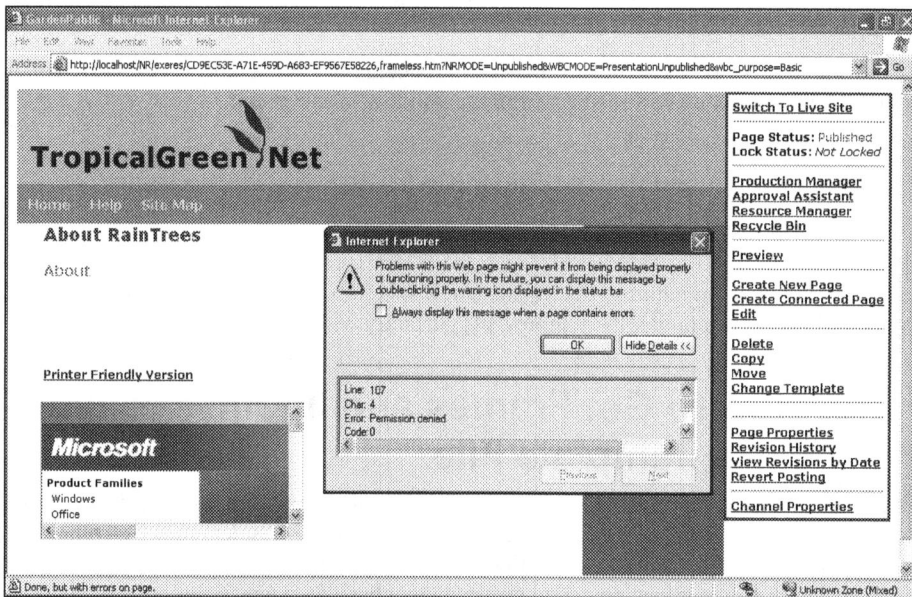

The page appears fine to subscribers when viewed from the live site, so it's not a big issue. But it is a cause for concern for authors working on postings that require frames.

The reason for this strange behavior lies in the Console.js file (located in the <install directory>\Microsoft Content Management Server\Server\IIS_CMS\WebAuthor\Client folder) used by Web Author. It is trying to get all windows in the site to toggle between Live and Edit Site views. Because the site that has been framed (in our example, it's Microsoft's site) isn't the same as the MCMS site, the browser generates a Permission Denied error.

The browser is trying to prevent cross-site scripting (sometimes known as XSS). If it allows client-side script to work across all sites, hackers can easily embed malicious code within a frame to hijack information from your site.

Well, we aren't actually going to do anything bad to the other site, we just want to display its pages. To get around this issue, we need to wrap all calls that toggle between Live and Edit Site views within a `try-catch` block.

Make a backup of `Console.js` before modifying it. Look for the two methods named `UpdateSiblingFramesInPublishedMode()` and `UpdateSiblingFramesInUnpublishedMode()`. Add `try-catch` blocks around the code that attempts to toggle the modes of all frames within the site.

```
/// <summary>
/// Javascript function to update all sibling frames to Unpublished
/// mode after "Switch To Live Site" has been clicked. This is done
/// in case the action is in a framed site.
/// </summary>
function UpdateSiblingFramesInPublishedMode()
{
  for (i=0; i < window.top.frames.length; i++)
  {
    if (window.top.frames[i] != window)
    {
      try
      {
        // refresh it with Published mode URL
        window.top.frames[i].location.href = GetUrlModePublished(
                              window.top.frames[i].location.href );
      }
      catch(e)
      {}
    }
  }
}

/// <summary>
/// Javascript function to update all sibling frames to Unpublished
/// mode after "Switch To Edit Site" has been clicked. This is done
/// in case the action is in a framed site.
/// </summary>
function UpdateSiblingFramesInUnpublishedMode()
{
  for (i=0; i < window.top.frames.length; i++)
  {
    if (window.top.frames[i] != window)
    {
      try
      {
        // refresh it with Unpublished mode URL
        window.top.frames[i].location.href = GetUrlModeUnpublished(
                              window.top.frames[i].location.href );
      }
      catch(e)
      {}
    }
  }
}
```

The next time you attempt to switch between Live and Edit Site views of a page that contains a Frame or IFrame that points to another site, the page will transit between modes without a hitch.

When the MCMS Page is Embedded Within a Frame or IFrame of Another Website

Here's another problem when using Frames and IFrames. You could have an external site that links to an MCMS website (such as a SharePoint Portal site). Everything looks fine in published view. However, when an author decides to switch to Edit Site view from within that frame or if you are using one of the console actions such as the Production Manager, you will get "Access is denied" JavaScript errors.

Let's attempt to recreate the problem. Add a new HTML page named testiframes.htm to, say, the c:\inetpub\wwwroot\ directory of your computer (or a directory of a site that is *not* the MCMS site the frame links to). Insert the following code to the new file. It basically constructs a page consisting of an IFrame that links to the MCMS website.

```
<html>
<body>
  <iframe src="http://www.tropicalgreen.net" width="100%" height="300">
</body>
</html>
```

Save testiframes.htm. Navigate to http://localhost/testiframes.htm and toggle to Edit Site mode and click the Production Manager link. You will hit an "Access is denied" client-side script error as shown below.

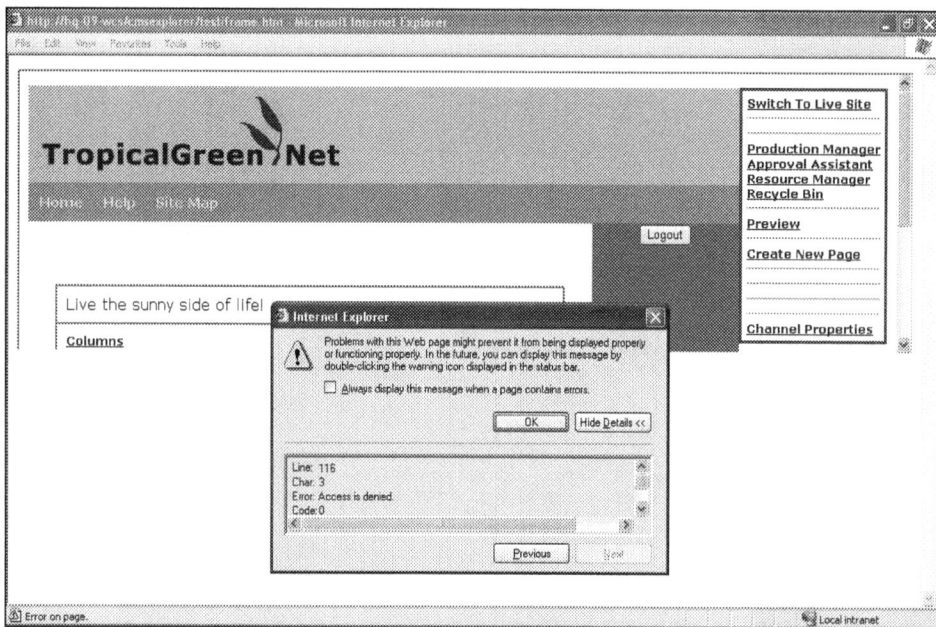

In this case, the problem lies with the code in two files: Console.js and Windows.js. Both are located in the <install directory>\Microsoft Content Management Server\Server\IIS_CMS\webAuthor\Client folder and both are attempting to access information of objects in the top-most frame, which belongs to a different website. Executing client-side scripts across websites is not allowed; hence we get the "Access is denied" JavaScript error.

We need to prevent Web Author from attempting to access the objects of the parent window. Let's start by looking at the code in the `window.js` file that is causing this behavior.

The function attempting to retrieve information from the parent window is the `WBC_openWindowOnFocus()` method shown below. The variable `pWindow` refers to `window.top`, or the parent window that contains the frames. The routine is attempting to create a new browser window from the parent window.

```
// ---- [Public] Open a new window and focus it
function WBC_openWindowOnFocus(strURL, strWinTarget, strWinFeatures)
{
  var pWindow = window.top.open(strURL, strWinTarget, strWinFeatures);
  if (pWindow)
    pWindow.focus();
}
```

The site appears the same regardless of whether or not the new window opens as a child of the top-most window or the current MCMS frame. To prevent cross-site scripting issues, we simply change the code to return the window of the MCMS site and not the parent window by changing the call from `window.top.open()` to just `window.open()`. Modify the code as follows:

```
// ---- [Public] Open a new window and focus it
function WBC_openWindowOnFocus(strURL, strWinTarget, strWinFeatures)
{
  var pWindow = window.open(strURL, strWinTarget, strWinFeatures);
  if (pWindow)
    pWindow.focus();
}
```

The problematic code in the `Console.js` file now tries to determine the new size of the child window to be opened. The original code in the `WBC_UseDefaultSizing()` method retrieves the size of the top-most window using `window.top`, which is not allowed. As a workaround, we will use the size of the current window instead of the size of the parent window to calculate the child window size. To do so, press *Ctrl+H* and replace all instances of:

```
WBC_UseDefaultSizing(window.top)
```

with:

```
WBC_UseDefaultSizing(window)
```

Save both `windows.js` and `Console.js`. Now, try accessing the framed MCMS site again—you will find that the JavaScript errors no longer appear!

Summary

In this chapter we presented nine essential how-tos for every MCMS website:

- How to revert a posting to a previous version
- How to change a posting's template
- How to build a recycle bin
- How to deal with links to deleted resources
- How to generate a resource dependency report
- How to update a posting's properties directly from a template file
- How to rewrite unfriendly URLs to friendly URLs
- How to export resource gallery items using the site deployment API
- How to configure the position and size of the Web Author Console dialogs
- How to get frames and IFrames to work correctly in a template file

Be aware that applying hotfixes or service packs could replace the code files used internally by MCMS and break some of the tips. So if a tip calls for the alteration of any of these files, do keep a copy of the modified files and have them considered as part of your upgrade procedures.

These tips provide solutions to the most requested features by developers from the community. If you have a solution of your own, do share it with everyone by uploading it to the MCMS community workspace at http://www.gotdotnet.com.

A

Setting up MCMS and SPS on the Same Virtual Server

Microsoft Windows SharePoint Services (WSS), SharePoint Portal Server (SPS), and Content Management Server (MCMS) utilize managed URLs for processing client requests. Because these applications utilize managed URLs (where ISAPI filters determine what any request is looking for), some special configurations need to be made in order for SharePoint and MCMS to work together on the same virtual server.

This appendix will explain how the managed URLs of the two products work, and walk through the configuration steps for each product that allow them to work side by side on the same virtual server. Here's a quick synopsis of what we will be doing:

- We will first create a new virtual server in Internet Information Services (IIS) and create a SharePoint portal using our new virtual server.
- We will then configure MCMS to use the same virtual server as an MCMS Web Entry Point.
- Finally, we will configure the SharePoint extended virtual server to allow MCMS requests to be handled by MCMS and ignored by the SharePoint ISAPI filters.

SharePoint and MCMS-Managed URLs

Microsoft's SharePoint is implemented by inserting ISAPI filters into IIS virtual servers. These ISAPI filters intercept all inbound requests as all URLs are managed unlike a typical website where the folder structure is somewhat mirrored in the URL. SharePoint's managed URLs tell it which portal or WSS site and list, document library, or Web Part the user is interacting with.

Microsoft Content Management Server (MCMS) also utilizes ISAPI filters that are configured as global filters for all incoming requests. One of these ISAPI filters checks each HTTP request against the MCMS database to determine if it is an MCMS request or not. If the MCMS ISAPI filter determines the URL is not an MCMS request, it passes it on to IIS or lower priority ISAPI filters for further processing.

On its own, each product works perfectly. However, when they are used together on the same server, there may be conflicts. For example, if the SharePoint ISAPI filters determine a URL is not consistent with a SharePoint request, it returns an HTTP status code of 404 – File Not Found, as SharePoint assumes all requests are to be consumed by its ISAPI filter, unless explicitly excluded. We'll go into excluded paths later in this appendix.

The order of steps in configuring a virtual server for hosting a SharePoint site (WSS/SPS) and MCMS is very important. The following assumes Windows SharePoint Services (including SP1), SharePoint Portal Server (including SP1), and Content Management Server (including SP1a) are all installed as well as all requirements for these installations being met.

In this appendix, we will create a SharePoint portal in a virtual server. We're creating a portal because it provides necessary features, such as customizable search, that we use in Chapter 5, *Searching MCMS with SharePoint*. Note that all the limitations and steps outlined here apply to WSS as well because SharePoint Portal Server (SPS) relies on the WSS engine to process all URLs.

Creating a New Virtual Server

Let's start by creating a new, empty virtual server to host our SharePoint portal and act as our MCMS Web Entry Point.

1. Open IIS, right-click the Web Sites folder and select New | Web Site.

2. Name the new virtual server portal.tropicalgreen.net.

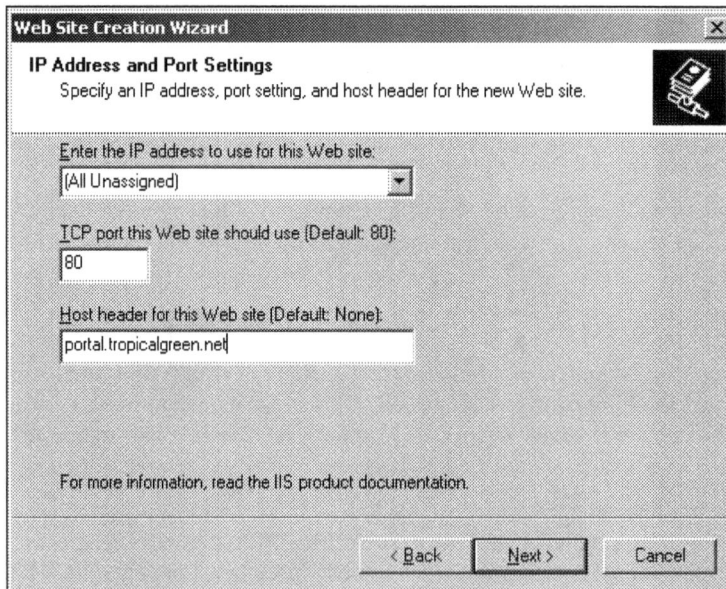

3. Specify a root folder for the virtual server. In this case, we chose `C:\Inetpub\wwwroot_portal.tropicalgreen.net`, but you can put the web root anywhere else on your server. Uncheck the Allow anonymous access to this Web site.

4. On the Web Site Access Permissions dialog, select the Read and Run scripts options, leaving the rest unchecked.

We now have an empty virtual server ready for a new SharePoint portal.

Creating a New SharePoint Portal

We will now create a new SharePoint portal in the virtual server we just set up.

1. Start SharePoint Central Administration by pointing to Start | All Programs | SharePoint Portal Server | SharePoint Central Administration.

2. Under the section Portal Site and Virtual Server Configuration, click the Create a portal site link.

3. On the Create Portal Site for [machine name] page, enter the following information:

   • Portal Creation Options: Create a portal

   • Site Name: Tropical Green Portal

   • Site URL:

       o Virtual Server: portal.tropicalgreen.net

       o URL: http://portal.tropicalgreen.net

   • Owner:

       o Account name: MCMSBOOK\Administrator

       o E-mail address: administrator@foo.com

4. On the final confirmation page, click OK to create your portal.

Creating a New MCMS Web Entry Point

We now have a SharePoint portal created in our virtual server. Now we need to configure MCMS to use our virtual server as an MCMS Web Entry Point.

1. Start the Server Configuration Application by pointing to Start | All Programs | Microsoft Content Management Server | Server Configuration Application.

2. Click the Web tab to view all virtual servers and manage their MCMS configuration.

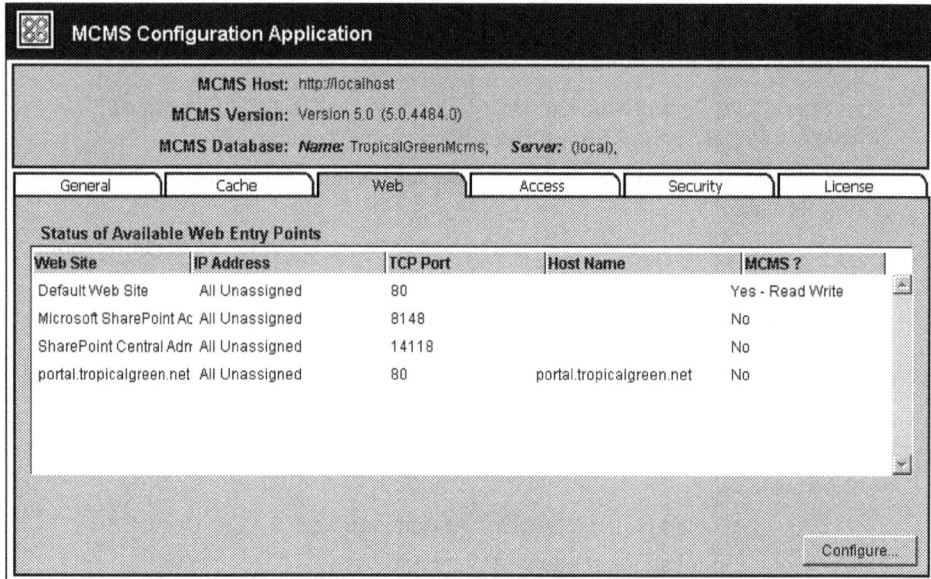

MCMS Configuration Application				

MCMS Host: http://localhost

MCMS Version: Version 5.0 (5.0.4484.0)

MCMS Database: *Name:* TropicalGreenMcms, *Server:* (local),

General	Cache	Web	Access	Security	License

Status of Available Web Entry Points

Web Site	IP Address	TCP Port	Host Name	MCMS ?
Default Web Site	All Unassigned	80		Yes - Read Write
Microsoft SharePoint Ac	All Unassigned	8148		No
SharePoint Central Adm	All Unassigned	14118		No
portal.tropicalgreen.net	All Unassigned	80	portal.tropicalgreen.net	No

Configure...

3. You can see that our new virtual server, `portal.tropicalgreen.net`, is not configured for MCMS. Click the Configure button to edit the virtual servers listed.

4. Set the dropdown for our virtual server in the MCMS ? column to Yes – Read Write. Click OK through the dialog and the configure page.

We now have a SharePoint portal and have configured our new virtual server to be an MCMS Web Entry Point. However MCMS will not currently receive any requests because SharePoint will consume all URLs destined for our virtual server.

Configuring SharePoint to Allow MCMS Requests

As outlined above, the MCMS requests will not be processed correctly at this point because the SharePoint ISAPI filter consumes all requests coming into our virtual server. If a request can't be processed by the SharePoint ISAPI filter, it will simply return an HTTP 404 – File Not Found response to the requestor.

As an example of this, try navigating to a path that does not exist, such as `http://portal.tropicalgreen.net/fakepath`. As this response is sent directly by the

SharePoint ISAPI filter without allowing IIS to continue to process the request, the 404 error page looks different to other 404 errors displayed by IIS or web sites not managed by the SharePoint ISAPI filter:

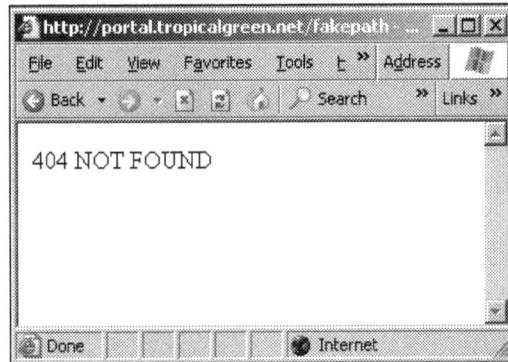

In order to get the MCMS requests working, we now need to tell SharePoint to ignore or exclude MCMS paths from being consumed by the SharePoint ISAPI filter. There are two ways we can accomplish this:

- Using the command-line utility Microsoft added to the MCMS Connector for SharePoint Technologies to automatically exclude all the MCMS channel paths.
- Manually exclude the paths.

Let's first take a look at the utility provided in the MCMS Connector. The `excludeCMS.exe` tool automatically adds the MCMS-relevant URLs (i.e. `NR`, `MCMS`, `NRConfig`, and top-level channels) to the SharePoint ISAPI filter's exclude list. You'll find this tool in the `<install drive>\Program Files\MCMS 2002 Connector for SharePoint Technologies\WSS\bin\` directory after installing the MCMS Connector. Be aware that this tool will always exclude the top-level channels. If you have the Map Channel Names to Host Header Names feature of MCMS enabled, then the tool will not exclude the correct URLs. In this situation you should exclude the URLs manually using the steps outlined below.

The `excludeCMS.exe` utility will not add your MCMS template web application project to the exclude list. This is something you'll need to do after running the tool.

> If you name your MCMS web applications the same as the corresponding top-level channels in MCMS, you won't have to exclude the web application's virtual directory. However be aware that this can cause degradation in performance as the MCMS ISAPI filter will need to analyze more than one level of a URL requesting a resource file such as an image on the file system, a CSS file, or a JavaScript file.

The other method is to manually exclude the paths using the SharePoint administration site. Follow the instructions overleaf to exclude paths from the WSS ISAPI filters in a SharePoint extended virtual server:

1. Start the SharePoint Central Administration application at Start | All Programs | SharePoint Portal Server | SharePoint Central Administration.

2. Under the section Portal Site and Virtual Server Configuration, click the Configure virtual server settings from the Virtual Server List page link.

3. On the Virtual Server List page, select our virtual server by clicking the portal.tropicalgreen.net link.

4. On the Virtual Server Settings page, under the section Virtual Server Management click the Define managed paths link.

The Define Managed Paths page displays all included and excluded URL paths handled and ignored by the SharePoint ISAPI filter. Follow the steps below for each path you need to exclude from SharePoint's ISAPI filter:

1. Enter the path in the Add a New Path textbox and select Excluded path as the type of path.

2. Repeat this for each of the following MCMS paths:

- MCMS

- NR

- webctrl_client

- www.tropicalgreen.net (this is our top-level channel)

- tropicalgreen (this is our template web application)

Excluded Paths

This list specifies which paths within the URL namespace are not managed by Windows SharePoint Services. Excluded paths take precedence over included paths.

✗ Remove selected paths

	Path
☐	uddi
☐	uddipublic
☐	mcms
☐	webctrl_client
☐	www.tropicalgreen.net
☐	tropicalgreen

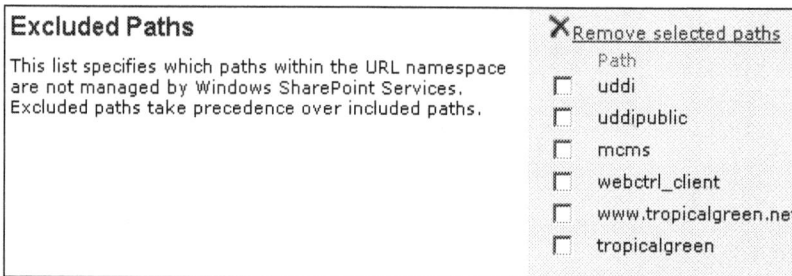

The SharePoint ISAPI filters will handle all requests except those that are listed as excluded paths for the virtual server that has been extended by SharePoint. SharePoint only allows paths to be excluded at the folder level, not the file level. Therefore resources within the root of a virtual server that has been extended by SharePoint as well as configured as an MCMS Web Entry Point will always be processed by SharePoint and not MCMS.

For example, if you had a virtual server that both contains a SharePoint portal and is configured as an MCMS web entry point, SharePoint will process all requests. However, if you add SomeTopLevelChannel as an excluded path, MCMS will be able to process a URL such as http://portal.tropicalgreen.net/SomeTopLevelChannel/foo.htm provided SomeTopLevelChannel is a top-level channel within the MCMS repository.

> The MCMS option of Map Channel Names to Host Header Names presents the MCMS administrator the ability to set the root of a virtual server to consume MCMS-managed resources. Because a SharePoint portal will always be the root of a virtual server, the Map Channel Names to Host Header Names option is not supported when configuring the virtual server to consume MCMS requests in the root of the site (See Microsoft Knowledge Base article #831796: `http://support.microsoft.com/?id=831796`).

All requests to destinations with any of the above first-level subdirectories in the URL (or subdirectories under them) will now be ignored by the SharePoint ISAPI filter and handed down to lower priority ISAPI filters. In this case, the MCMS ISAPI filters will receive such requests, and determine if the page or resource is managed by MCMS, and if not standard processing will take place.

Trust Settings for MCMS Web Applications

MCMS and SharePoint (WSS/SPS) are configured to run under different security trust models. SharePoint can run under Minimal, Medium, or a custom trust level, while MCMS has to run under full trust. Since SharePoint takes the primary host role in a virtual server, its `web.config` file is located in the root of the website, so any web application below the root will inherit the security trust of SharePoint. To resolve this, you will need to modify the MCMS web application's `web.config` file to grant it `Full` trust, overriding the trust level settings of the SharePoint `web.config` file in the root.

Open the `web.config` file of your MCMS web application and add the following code to grant it full trust:

```
<configuration>
  <system.web>
    <pages smartNavigation="false" validateRequest="false" />
    <customErrors mode="RemoteOnly" />
    <authentication mode="Windows" />
    <trust level="Full" originUrl="" />
  </system.web>
</configuration>
```

Verifying that SharePoint and MCMS are Functioning Correctly

Now that we've created a virtual server, created a portal inside, and configured it to present MCMS content, let's test both applications to make sure we've covered all bases.

Open a new browser and navigate to the portal root at `http://portal.tropicalgreen.net/`. If you see the portal homepage, then SharePoint is working. If it's not working, go back and retrace your steps.

Next, navigate to:

`http://portal.tropicalgreen.net/www.tropicalgreen.net/PlantCatalog/`

If you see our Tropical Green plant catalog page, MCMS is working. If you don't see our plant catalog homepage, there's likely an issue with the excluded managed paths. Verify the last step.

You'll notice the last URL we tested looks quite strange as it contains two domains. The code from the first book *Building Websites with Microsoft Content Management Server* (Packt Publishing, January 2005, ISBN 1-904811-16-7), which we'll assume you're using, contains two top level channels: `international.tropicalgreen.net` and `www.tropicalgreen.net`. The first book implemented the MCMS Map Channel Names to Host Header Names option, which is why these channels have domains for their names. Unfortunately the Map Channel Names to Host Header Names feature is not supported when MCMS and SharePoint are running on the same virtual server. Therefore we have to disable this option and then the name of the top level channel we need to test (`www.tropicalgreen.net`) needs to be included in the URL. Usually you would change the channel structure in such a situation so that the domain name is not included in the URL.

If you continue to have problems, refer to Microsoft Knowledge Base article #835248: `http://support.microsoft.com/?id=835248`.

Summary

In this appendix, we have explained how to successfully create a SharePoint portal and an MCMS Web Entry Point on the same virtual server. After configuring the virtual server, we showed how to modify the managed path exclusions in the SharePoint virtual server settings to ensure that the SharePoint ISAPI filter ignores HTTP requests that are to be handled by MCMS.

MCMS Connector for SharePoint Technologies

In February 2004 Microsoft released a free suite to allow site developers to share content between Microsoft Content Management Server 2002 (MCMS) and SharePoint products and technologies. The MCMS Connector for SharePoint Technologies (hereafter referred to as the "Connector") provides three core features:

- Leveraging of SharePoint Portal Server Search within an MCMS site
- Display of pages waiting for approval, pages in production, and page listings within SharePoint web parts
- Publishing of documents from WSS or SPS document libraries on an MCMS site

The three integration methods above are accomplished with server controls (in the case of the search and document library publishing) and web parts (for publishing MCMS content to SharePoint web part pages). Microsoft also included a few command line utilities to assist in the management and configuration of SharePoint.

In this appendix, we will first look at the installation of the Connector and then examine the server controls and web parts included. We will discuss the additional tools that come with the Connector, which can help with integration tasks, and look at what is installed by the Connector and where it's located on the system.

Installation

Installation of the Connector is very simple and straightforward. Simply download the installer that ships as a self-extracting ZIP file containing a single MSI installer. Launch the installer by double-clicking the file and accepting the license agreement:

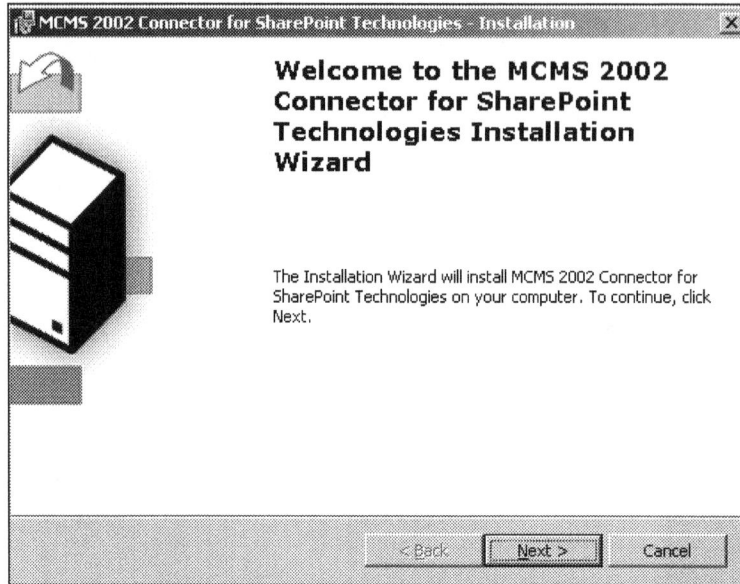

You can download the MCMS Connector for SharePoint Technologies here:
http://www.microsoft.com/downloads/details.aspx?FamilyID=6E9925C4-91DA-404A-86DD-78D51BCF0A51&displaylang=en

The only question you are prompted to answer during installation (other than the license agreement and user information—the registration key is already provided) is whether to install the sample data, which includes a demo project and an SDO file. The SDO file will automatically be imported into your MCMS installation when the sample data is installed. The SDO file contains the necessary templates, channels, and postings used by the sample package to demonstrate the features of the Connector.

Leveraging SharePoint Portal Search within an MCMS Site

The Connector includes three controls that enhance your MCMS templates. Two of these controls are used to collect search query information and to display the results of the query after it has been submitted to the SPS:

- **SearchInputControl**: The SearchInputControl displays an input form where a user can enter keywords to search for.

- **SearchResultControl**: The SearchResultControl is responsible for taking the keywords and advanced properties submitted in the SearchInputControl, constructing the query, and calling the SPS Search service. The control then takes the response from the Search Service web service and displays the search results.

The third search control included in the Connector is:

- **SearchMetaTagGenerator**: This control generates HTML META tag information for MCMS posting properties and custom properties. It is used in combination with an XML mapping file and a command-line utility to configure the SharePoint indexer. This allows users to implement a basic taxonomy for the search function.

The standard and custom properties for which META tags are generated are managed using an XML file called `SearchPropertyCollection.xml` and a console application called `SearchPropertiesSetup.exe`, which configures SharePoint Portal Server search using the advanced properties defined by the XML file.

> The `SearchPropertyCollection.xml` file can be found in the following directory: `C:\Program Files\Microsoft Content Management Server\Server\IIS_CMS\WssIntegration`.
>
> The SearchPropertiesSetup.exe utility program can be found in the following directory: `C:\Program Files\MCMS Connector for SharePoint Technologies\WSS\Bin`.

If SharePoint Portal Server and MCMS reside on separate physical servers, the `SearchPropertyCollection.xml` file needs to exist on both servers. The `SearchInputControl` uses this XML file on the MCMS server and the `SearchPropertiesSetup.exe` utility uses the file on the SharePoint Portal Server.

Some configuration is necessary in order to use SPS as a search engine for your MCMS site. This involves creating a new content source, source group, and source scope within SPS. Fortunately Microsoft included another command-line utility program called `SearchSetup.exe`, which creates the new content source and site path rules within SPS for all top-level channels in your MCMS site.

The `SearchSetup.exe` utility program can be found in the following directory: `C:\Program Files\MCMS Connector for SharePoint Technologies\WSS\Bin`.

Refer to Chapter 5, *Searching MCMS with SharePoint*, for more information regarding MCMS and SharePoint Portal Server search integration.

Integrating MCMS Content into a Portal site

By utilizing a single web part included in the Connector, you can display a list of postings in your SharePoint portal. The Page Listing Web Part displays the postings within a specified channel in one of six different list formats. The following three formats are hard coded in the web part:

- **Page Summary List View**: This view shows all postings with a short title (or display name), description, last modified timestamp, and a summary image. This is the default view for the web part. Each item is linked to the posting's published URL.
- **Basic List View**: The Basic List View displays the postings as a list, each with an importance icon and its short title (or display name).

- **Detailed List View**: Very similar to the Page Summary List View, this view does not display a summary image but it does add the posting owner, the user who last modified the posting, and the status of the posting (if it's published or not).

The web part provides entries for three additional views, which are not shipped with the Connector. These views can be added by a site developer and completely tailored to his or her needs. Refer to Chapter 6, *Publishing Content Between MCMS and SharePoint*, for more information on creating a custom view for the Page Listing Web Part.

Publishing SharePoint Document Library Documents within an MCMS Site

The last integration point Connector for SharePoint Technologies covers is publishing documents of a SharePoint (WSS or SPS) document library within an MCMS posting. The connector ships with a new placeholder definition and a new placeholder control: the `SharePointDocumentPlaceholder` definition and the `SharePointDocumentPlaceholderControl`. A developer can add a `SharePointDocumentPlaceholder` definition to a template definition and a `SharePointDocumentPlaceholderControl` to the template file to display files from a SharePoint document library.

The placeholder displays the documents in a list of the document names, linked to the actual document. If the file type is registered within Microsoft Windows Server, the Connector will generate the icon. Otherwise a default icon for the file type is generated by the Connector. You can also override the icon used for the file type by specifying a value in a stylesheet.

Presentation of the list is entirely customizable via XSLT stylesheets, which are used to transform the properties and contents of the documents in the SharePoint document libraries to HTML.

Refer to Chapter 6, *Publishing Content Between MCMS and SharePoint*, for more information on the `SharePointDocumentPlaceholder` and `SharePointDocumentPlaceholderControl`.

Additional Utilities Included

In addition to the SharePoint web parts, server controls, and MCMS placeholders provided by Connector for SharePoint Technologies to allow content integration, Microsoft included additional SharePoint web parts and command-line utilities to assist you with configuring SharePoint and managing your MCMS website.

The following two administrative SharePoint web parts are included in the Connector to assist MCMS site Authors, Editors, and Moderators with maintaining their MCMS site:

- **Pages in Production Web Part**: This web part displays all postings the current user is currently working on, but has not yet published, which is comparable to the "Production Manager" dialog in MCMS.

- **Pages Waiting for Approval Web Part**: This web part displays all postings that are pending approval on the MCMS site, which is comparable to the "Approval Assistant" dialog in MCMS.

> The Pages in Production Web Part, Pages Waiting for Approval Web Part, and Page Listing Web Part are included in the `CmsWebParts.CAB` web part deployment file, which can be found in the following directory: `C:\Program Files\MCMS Connector for SharePoint Technologies\WSS\Bin`

Previously we mentioned the two command-line utilities:

- `SearchPropertiesSetup.exe`: This utility is used to add the advanced HTML META tags to the SPS Search Service.
- `SetupSearch.exe`: This is used to automatically create SharePoint content sources and search groups for all top-level channels within an MCMS site.

A third command-line utility, `excludeCMS.exe`, will add SharePoint managed path exclusion rules for all MCMS URL paths in a virtual server. It is necessary for all MCMS paths to be excluded from SharePoint's ISAPI filters when SharePoint and MCMS are configured on the same virtual server within Internet Information Services (IIS) or MCMS will not operate correctly.

> All command-line utilities included in the MCMS Connector can be found in the following directory: `C:\Program Files\MCMS Connector for SharePoint Technologies\WSS\Bin`.

MCMS Connector Sample Data, Project, and Documentation

If you choose to install the sample data when you install the Connector, the installation procedure will automatically import all data from an SDO file into your MCMS site.

In addition, the **CmsSharePointConnector** sample project will be installed, which contains the MCMS templates and other controls necessary for the templates and postings in the sample data imported from the SDO.

> If you need to import the sample MCMS data later, you can find the SDO file in the same directory as the sample project: `C:\Program Files\Microsoft Content Management Server\Sample Data\CmsSharePointConnector`.

Finally, a compiled help file containing technical details and documentation on the MCMS Connector will be installed in the following directory: `C:\Program Files\MCMS Connector for SharePoint Technologies\Docs`.

Summary

This short appendix has covered the installation and use of Connector for SharePoint Technologies. We've looked at the tools and settings relevant to websites that wish to combine content from SharePoint and MCMS.

C

Installing the Tropical Green Website

Tropical Green is the fictitious gardening society upon which the book's sample website is based. In the earlier book, *Building Websites with Microsoft Content Management Server* (Packt Publishing, January 2005, ISBN 1-904811-16-7), we built the Tropical Green website from scratch. In this appendix, we provide a quick start guide for setting up the Tropical Green website. In a nutshell, here's what we will do:

- Download the sample code from the Packt website.
- Create the TropicalGreen Web Application.
- Import the objects in the Site Deployment Object file.
- Create an account for the Guest user.
- Ensure that the server settings in Server Configuration Application are correct.
- Set www.tropicalgreen.net to execute locally.
- Configure the browser to bypass the proxy server.

You should already have Microsoft Content Management Server 2002 installed with the latest service packs applied. We will also assume that you are working with Internet Information Services 5.x. If you are running Windows Server 2003 and therefore have IIS 6.0 installed, the steps are similar although some aspects will be different. Have a look at Appendix A if you'd like to see an example of a similar process using IIS 6.

Downloading the Sample Code

First, let's download the sample code from the website.

1. Navigate to Packt Publishing's support site at http://www.packtpub.com/support.
2. Select the book title Building Websites with Microsoft Content Management Server. Choose to download Code.
3. Save and extract the compressed zip file (1167_Code.zip) in an appropriate location on your hard drive, such as C:\1167_FinalCode\.

Creating the TropicalGreen Web Application

Next, let's create and configure a web application for the Tropical Green website.

1. Open Internet Services Manager (point to Start | Administrative Tools | Internet Information Services).
2. Expand the nodes COMPUTERNAME (local computer) | Web Sites.
3. Right-click on Default Web Site and select New Virtual Directory....
4. When the Virtual Directory Creation Wizard opens, click Next.
5. For the Virtual Directory alias, enter TropicalGreen and click Next.
6. On the next page, click Browse and navigate to the location of the `TropicalGreen` directory extracted earlier, something like `c:\1167_FinalCode\TropicalGreen\`. Click Next.
7. Next, choose to allow the following permissions:
    *   Read
    *   Run scripts (such as ASP)
8. Click Next.
9. Click Finish.
10. Right-click on the newly created TropicalGreen virtual directory and click Properties.
11. Select the Directory Security tab, and in the Anonymous access and authentication control section, click Edit....
12. Ensure that the Anonymous access option is checked.
13. Close all open dialogs.

The TropicalGreen virtual directory has been successfully created. However, in order for the site to work correctly, we need to add the CMS virtual directory.

Adding the CMS Virtual Directory

The CMS virtual directory contains the MCMS files that are required by Web Author. It is normally added by the MCMS web project creation wizard when creating a project with Visual Studio. However, since we have downloaded the project and created the virtual directory manually, we need to add the CMS virtual directory ourselves.

1. With Internet Services Manager open, right-click on the newly created TropicalGreen virtual directory and select New | Virtual Directory....
2. This time, enter an alias of CMS, and for the website content directory, choose `Microsoft Content Management Server\Server\IIS_CMS\`.
3. In the Access Permissions dialog, check Read and Run scripts (such as ASP). Click Next, and then Finish.
4. Now we need to configure the CMS virtual directory to use Tropical Green's application domain. Right-click on the new CMS virtual directory, and select Properties.

5. In the Virtual Directory tab, look for the Application Settings section, and click Remove.
6. Click OK to close the Properties dialog.

Importing the Site Deployment Object File

Now that we have created the required virtual directories, let's import the database objects using the Site Deployment Manager.

1. Open Site Manager and log in with an MCMS administrator account.
2. From the menu, select File | Package | Import....
3. In the Site Deployment Import dialog, click the Browse... button. Navigate to the TropicalGreen_Final.sdo file located in the directory containing the extracted files.
4. In the Container Rules tab, set the following:

Property	Value
When Adding Containers	Use package container rights
When Replacing Containers	Keep destination container rights

5. In the Rights Group tab set the following:

Property	Value
Select how Rights Groups are imported	Import User Rights Groups

6. Click Import.
7. The Import Confirmation dialog appears. Click Continue.

Creating the Guest Account

The Tropical Green website allows anonymous guest to view content and uses forms authentication to authenticate content contributors. We need to assign a single Windows account as the guest account. For convenience, we will create a local computer account to act as guest.

1. Open Computer Management (select Start | Administrative Tools | Computer Management, or right-click My Computer and choose Manage).
2. Expand down to the Computer Management (local) | System Tools | Local Users and Groups node.
3. Right-click on the Users node and select New User....
4. Create a new user with the name MCMSGuest and give the account an appropriate password.
5. Click Create and close all open dialogs.
6. Close Computer Management.

Now the guest account has been created, let's assign it to an appropriate MCMS subscriber rights group.

1. Open Site Manager and log in using an MCMS administrator account.
2. Click the User Roles icon on the left panel.
3. In the User Roles panel, click Subscribers.
4. A subscriber rights group named Guests was imported as part of the import process earlier. Right-click on the Guests rights group and select Properties.
5. Click on the Group Members tab and choose Modify....
6. Add the new MCMSGuest account to the Guests rights group.
7. Close all open dialogs, and close Site Manager.

Checking the Server Configuration

Ensure that the SCA (Server Configuration Application) is configured as follows:

General	
URL Format	Hierarchical
Map Channel Names to Host Header Names	Yes
Security	
Allow Guests on Site	Yes
Guest Login Account	ComputerName\MCMSGuest

Setting www.tropicalgreen.net to Execute Locally

The URL of Tropical Green's website is www.tropicalgreen.net. We need this address to work when running the MCMS web application from the local computer. To do so, we need to add the address to the computer's hosts file.

1. Use Notepad to open the hosts file in c:\windows\system32\drivers\etc\.
2. In the hosts file, enter www.tropicalgreen.net below localhost. Give it an IP address of 127.0.0.1. Doing so automatically loops www.tropicalgreen.net back to your computer.

   ```
   127.0.0.1        localhost
   127.0.0.1        www.tropicalgreen.net
   ```

3. Save and close the hosts file.

Configuring the Browser to Bypass the Proxy

If you are connected to the Internet through a proxy server, remember to add `www.tropicalgreen.net` to the exclude list. Otherwise all requests to the site will be sent to the Internet instead of being served from the local machine. To do so:

1. Select Tools | Internet Options in Internet Explorer.
2. Click on the Connections tab.
3. Click LAN Settings.
4. Click Advanced.
5. In the field labeled Do not use proxy server for addresses beginning with, ensure that `www.tropicalgreen.net` is in the list.

Testing the Tropical Green Website

The installation is complete. Open your browser and navigate to `www.tropicalgreen.net`. You should see the cover page as shown below:

Index

indexing, 115
proxy bypassing, 511
quickstart, 507
search options, 113
search page, 129
SharePoint Portal Server, 121
site deployment object file, 509
SPS, 121
testing, 511
web application, creating, 508

U

unfriendly URLs, rewriting, 472
url parameter, Download() method, 333

V

ValidateMCMSObjectName() method, custom method, 43
validation. *See* **content validation,** *See also* **validation controls**
validation controls.
   action, Save and Exit with validation, 299
   action, Save New Page with validation, 299
   action, Save with validation, 300
   ASP.NET validation controls, limitations, 285

custom validation controls, 285, 286
HtmlPlaceholderControl, validation, 287
server-side validation, 302
SingleAttachmentPlaceholderControl, validation, 312
SingleImagePlaceholderControl, validation, 309
validator, adding to template, 297
See also custom validation controls
virtual server
   creating, 494
   MCMS requests, allowing, 496
   MCMS web application, trust settings, 499
   MCMS Web Entry Point, creating, 496
   SharePoint portal, creating, 495
   trust settings, 499

W

Web Entry Point, 496
Web Part. *See* **MCMS connector Web Parts,** *See also* **SharePoint Web Parts**

X

XmlTextWriter, 390

www.ingramcontent.com/pod-product-compliance
Lightning Source LLC
Chambersburg PA
CBHW060952210326
41598CB00031B/4803